APPLICATIONS
PROGRAMMING
IN C++

APPLICATIONS PROGRAMMING IN C++

Richard Johnsonbaugh

Martin Kalin

An Alan R. Apt Book

Prentice Hall
Upper Saddle River, NJ 07458

Library of Congress Cataloging-in-Publication Data

Johnsonbaugh, Richard,
    Applications programming in C++ / by Richard Johnsonbaugh and
Martin Kalin.
        p.   cm.
    Includes bibliographical references and index.
    ISBN 0-13-748963-3
        1. C++ (Computer programming language).   2. Application software–Development
    I. Kalin, Martin   II. Title.
QA76.73.C153J64   1999   98–28583
005.13'3–dc21   CIP

Publisher: *Alan Apt*
Acquisitions Editor: *Laura Steele*
Managing Editor: *Eileen Clark*
Editor in Chief: *Marcia Horton*
Production Editor: *Ann Marie Kalajian*
Editorial Assistant: *Kate Kaibni*
Copy Editor: *Patricia Johnsonbaugh*
Director of Creative Services: *Paula Maylahn*
Associate Creative Director: *Amy Rosen*
Art Director: *Heather Scott*
Assistant to Art Director: *John Christiana*
Designer: *Judith A. Matz-Coniglio*
Illustrators: *PreTEX, Inc.*
Cover Designer: *Jerry Votta*
Manufacturing Buyer: *Donna Sullivan*
Composition: *PreTEX, Inc.*

© 1999 by Prentice Hall, Inc.
Simon & Schuster/ A Viacom Company
Upper Saddle River, New Jersey 07458

Printed in the United States of America

10 9 8 7 6 5 4 3 2 1

ISBN   0-13-748963-3

Prentice-Hall International (UK) Limited, *London*
Prentice-Hall of Australia Pty. Limited, *Sydney*
Prentice-Hall Canada Inc., *Toronto*
Prentice-Hall Hispanoamericana, S.A., *Mexico*
Prentice-Hall of India Private Limited, *New Delhi*
Prentice-Hall of Japan, Inc., *Tokyo*
Simon & Schuster Asia Pte. Ltd., *Singapore*
Editora Prentice-Hall do Brasil, Ltda., *Rio de Janeiro*

TRADEMARK INFORMATION

IBM is a registered trademark of International Business Machines Corporation

Unix is a trademark of Bell Laboratories

Borland C++ is a registered trademark of Borland International, Inc.

SUN refers to Sun Microsystems, a registered trademark of SUN Microsystems, Inc.

Microsoft, MS DOS, and Windows are either registered trademarks or trademarks of Microsoft, Inc.

CodeWarrior is a trademark of Metrowerks

To Warren M. Krueger, our friend
and colleague, for his support,
inspiration, humor, and tutorials on
determining which chilies are hottest.

Preface

Applications Programming in C++ is based on C++ courses given by the authors at DePaul University over the last several years. We assume no prior knowledge of C++, but we do assume programming experience in some high-level language. We provide Chapter 0 as background for those with modest programming experience. More advanced users can begin with Chapter 1. The book can be used for a one-term course in applications programming in C++ or for self-study.

The book and its supplements—an *Instructor's Guide* and a World Wide Web site— provide a comprehensive support system to help the reader master C++. The book includes numerous examples, exercises, sample applications, programming exercises, lists of common programming errors, and illustrations.

Overview

During the 1980s and early 1990s, C became the language of choice for many applications and systems programmers. Most major software available for personal computers was written in C: spreadsheets, word processors, databases, communications packages, statistical software, graphics packages, and so on. Virtually all software written for the UNIX environment was likewise written in C, and many mainframe systems meant to be ported from one platform to another were also coded in C. In the early 1980s, Bjarne Stroustrup of AT&T Bell Labs developed C++ as an extension of C that supports object-oriented programming, a type of programming that is well suited to the large, complex software systems now written for all platforms, from the cheapest personal computers to the most expensive mainframes. C++ also corrects some shortcomings in C, which C++ includes as a subset, and it supports abstract data types and generic functions through templates.

C++ is a highly complex language. Fortunately, most C++ programmers can benefit from its power without mastering each and every one of its features. Because this is an introductory book, we focus on the most useful aspects of the language; but we place some of the more esoteric and specialized parts of the language in end-of-chapter sections labeled *C++ Postscript*. We focus on *using* C++ to write practical programs based on sound design techniques, rather than on tricks and surprises in C++.

This book includes the following features:

- Examples and exercises that cover a wide range of applications.

- Motivating real-world applications.

- A broad variety of programming exercises. The book contains over 160 programming exercises.

- Sections on common programming errors.

- Discussion of standard C++ functions and methods.

- Exercises at the ends of sections so that readers can check their mastery of the sections. The book contains nearly 600 such exercises. Answers to the odd-numbered section exercises are given in the back of the book, and answers to the even-numbered section exercises are given in the *Instructor's Guide*.
- Illustrations to facilitate the learning process.
- The latest changes to the C++ language including new-style headers, new-style casts, type **bool**, namespaces, and the namespace **std**.
- A discussion of algorithms (Section 0.1).
- Coverage of computer systems (Section 0.2).
- An overview of programming languages (Section 0.4).
- A discussion of program development including program specification, algorithm design, coding, and testing (Section 0.5).
- Problem-solving strategies (Section 0.5).
- Early coverage of files (Section 2.5).
- A thorough discussion of recursion (Section 3.8).
- Coverage of STL (the Standard Template Library) (Chapter 10).
- A number of appendices.
- Topics grouped according to their use and their relationships to one another. This organization enables readers to write simple but useful programs immediately and to skip or postpone some of the less often used and more esoteric parts of the language.
- Understandable code. We have opted for clarity rather than subterfuges based on obscure C++ features.

C++: A Hybrid Language

C++ is essentially C with extensions to support object-oriented programming. Because C supports traditional, procedural programming, C++ is a hybrid language; it supports both procedural and object-oriented programming. It is a challenge to teach both procedural and object-oriented programming in the same course and to develop pedagogical strategies to address both programming paradigms. This book reflects our belief, based on our experience teaching C++, that some procedural programming is necessary before moving on to the object-oriented parts of C++. Thus we first cover basic control structures (e.g., loops, **if** statements), data types, operators, arrays, and functions. Once the basics of C++ as a procedural language have been covered, we introduce classes, inheritance, and polymorphism—the key concepts in object-oriented programming. We then turn to operator overloading, storage, templates, and other C++ features. This approach is justified because:

- It is pedagogically sound to begin with less abstract topics (e.g., basic control structures) before moving up to more abstract topics (e.g., classes and inheritance).
- All but the most trivial classes need basic control structures, data types, operators, arrays, and functions. Even if the programming paradigm is "object-oriented," implementation of classes requires basic control structures, data types, operators, arrays, and functions.

Organization of the Book

Chapter 0 serves as an introduction to computer systems and program development. (This chapter can be skipped if this material is already known.) We begin in Section 0.1 by discussing algorithms. Section 0.2 presents an overview of computer systems including hardware (main memory, CPU, etc.) and software (text editors, compilers, etc.). Internal representations of integers, floating-point numbers, characters, and instructions are discussed in Section 0.3. Section 0.4 continues with a discussion of programming languages (assembly languages and high-level languages). Section 0.5 summarizes the phases of program development: program specification, algorithm design, coding, and testing. In addition, several problem-solving strategies are given in Section 0.5. A discussion of the C++ language (Section 0.6) concludes Chapter 0.

Chapters 1 through 4 are devoted to the basics of C++ as a procedural language. In Chapter 1 we discuss integer and floating-point data types; identifiers; and arithmetic, relational, and logical operators. After Chapter 1, readers can immediately begin writing simple, but useful, programs.

In Chapter 2, we discuss the **if-else** statement; **while**, **do while**, and **for** loops; files; the assignment, increment, and decrement operators; the **break**, **continue**, and **switch** statements; promotions and casts; and basic formatting. Because C++ programs compiled under Windows are best used with disk input and output files, we treat files early.

Functions and program structure are discussed in Chapter 3. Parameters and call by value are covered in Sections 3.1 through 3.3. Call by reference is the topic of Section 3.5. Function overloading is introduced in Section 3.7. Recursion is the topic of Section 3.8. Sections 3.4 and 3.6 are devoted to sample applications.

Chapter 4 is devoted to arrays. Pointers and character strings are introduced to underscore their connection with arrays.

After covering the basics of C++ as a procedural language, we introduce the object-oriented features: classes, inheritance, and polymorphism. We cover class basics in Chapter 5: classes and objects, data members and methods, constructors and the destructor, defining classes and using them in programs, and using existing class libraries.

Chapter 6 introduces inheritance, including **protected** members, and constructors and the destructor under inheritance.

Polymorphism (run-time binding) is the topic of Chapter 7. Also, in this chapter, we discuss the difference between run-time binding and features that resemble it. This chapter also explains how an abstract base class can be used to specify an interface and emphasizes the importance of interfaces in the object-oriented model.

Chapter 8 considers operator overloading for classes, including overloading operators as either methods or top-level functions. This chapter abounds with examples to show how operators may be overloaded to advantage.

Storage is the topic of Chapter 9. Compile-time and run-time storage are discussed in detail, as are the main C++ storage classes: **auto**, **static**, and **extern**.

Chapter 10 shows how C++ supports generic functions through templates. This chapter also introduces STL (Standard Template Library) and offers short programs to illustrate STL containers, iterators, algorithms, and function objects.

Chapter Structure

The basic chapter organization is as follows:

> Contents
>
> Overview
>
> Section
>
> Section Exercises
>
> Section
>
> Section Exercises
>
> $\vdots$
>
> C++ Postscript
>
> Common Programming Errors
>
> Programming Exercises

In each of Chapters 1–10, several sections are devoted to sample applications. Each of these sections contains a statement of a problem, sample input and output, a solution to the problem, and a well-documented implementation of the problem in C++. Most of these sections conclude with an extended discussion. In some of the examples, these sections include a line-by-line discussion of the C++ program.

The sample applications include the following:

- Statistics (Section 2.9).
- Simulation (the Monty Hall problem) (Section 3.4).
- Counting votes (Section 4.4).
- A task class (Section 5.6).
- Tracking films (Sections 6.3 and 7.2).
- An associative array class (Section 8.7).
- Sorting and searching (Section 9.4).
- A template stack class (Section 10.2).
- Stock performance reports using STL (Section 10.5).

The *C++ Postscript* sections discuss less-used parts of the language and give additional technical details about certain parts of the language.

The *Common Programming Errors* sections highlight those aspects of the language that are easily misunderstood.

The book contains over 160 programming exercises drawn from a wide variety of applications.

Examples

The book contains over 350 numbered examples, which clarify particular facets of C++ for the reader and show the purpose of various C++ features. A box ■ marks the end of each example.

Exercises

The book contains nearly 600 section review exercises, the answers to which are true or false, short answers, code segments, and, in a few cases, entire programs. These exercises are suitable as homework problems or as self-tests. The answers to the odd-numbered exercises are given in the back of the book, and the answers to the even-numbered exercises are given in the *Instructor's Guide*. Class testing this book has convinced us of the importance of these exercises.

The applications covered in the programming exercises at the ends of the chapters include the following:

- Vote fraud (Programming Exercise 2.12)
- Weight lifting (Programming Exercise 2.13)
- Chaos (Programming Exercise 2.14)
- Simulation (Programming Exercises 3.15 and 5.14)
- Game of *Life* (Programming Exercise 4.18)
- Digital images (Programming Exercise 4.20)
- Data structures (Programming Exercises 5.8, 5.9, and 9.2 through 9.7)
- Databases (Programming Exercise 5.15)
- Scheduling (Programming Exercises 5.18 and 10.14)
- Windows environments (Programming Exercise 7.8)
- Dating services (Programming Exercise 7.10)
- Software engineering (Programming Exercise 9.1)
- World Wide Web (Programming Exercise 10.12)

Not every reader will be interested in all of these applications; however, we think that it is important to show the variety of problems that C++ can address.

Appendices

Five appendices are provided for reference. Appendix A contains the ASCII table. Appendix B explains the C++ preprocessor. Appendix C contains a list of some of the most useful C++ functions and class methods. We describe the parameters and return values for each, the header file to include, and what the function or method does. Appendix D covers run-time type identification (RTTI), and Appendix E covers exception handling.

Recent Language Changes

We have incorporated the latest changes to the C++ language including

- The logical type **bool**.
- New-style headers.
- New-style casts.
- STL (Standard Template Library).
- Exception handling.
- Run-time type identification.
- Namespaces and the namespace **std**.
- The operator **new[ ]**.

We use these new features throughout the book, but for those readers using older compilers, we also explain how to convert to the old-style C++.

Before the logical type **bool** was introduced, integer types were used for false (zero) and true (nonzero).

New-style headers drop the *.h* extension and prefix *c* to the header files acquired from C. For example, the old C++ header file *iostream.h* becomes *iostream*, and the C header file *stdlib.h* becomes *cstdlib*. Standard features furnished by these header files are now grouped under the name **std** (**st**and**ard**). The technical term for a region in which such features are grouped is *namespace*. In order to use these standard features as shown in this book, we add the line

```
using namespace std;
```

after our **#include**s. For example, the old-style **#include**

```
#include <iostream.h>
```

is replaced by

```
#include <iostream>
using namespace std;
```

The old-style cast

```
( int ) x
```

and type conversion

```
int( x )
```

have been replaced by four casts

```
const_cast    dynamic_cast    reinterpret_cast    static_cast
```

Which is used depends on the kind of cast being performed.

The operators **new** and **new[ ]** are now distinct.

World Wide Web Site

The World Wide Web site

```
http://condor.depaul.edu/~mkalin
```

contains the source code, header files, and data files for all of the book's sample applications; the source code for some of the longer examples; sample syllabi; transparencies; and an errata list.

Acknowledgments

We thank the following reviewers: Ed Angel, University of New Mexico; Karen Bernstein, DePaul University; Ralph Ewton, University of Texas at El Paso; Mike Gearen, Punahou High School; Jeanine Ingber, University of New Mexico; and Bina Ramamurthy, SUNY at Buffalo.

We are grateful to our friendly copy editor, Patricia Johnsonbaugh, for smoothing our prose and for deleting words and statements we drafted but should not have.

Our student, Wen Tao Liu, helped us check most of the major code segments.

We are indebted to the School of Computer Science, Telecommunications and Information Systems at DePaul University and its dean, Helmut Epp, for providing time and encouragement for the development of this book.

We received consistent support from the people at Prentice Hall. Special thanks go to Alan R. Apt, publisher, and Laura Steele, acquisitions editor.

R.J.
M.K.

A Brief Table of Contents

Contents

2   CONTROL FLOW   70

CHAPTER 0

COMPUTER SYSTEMS AND PROGRAM DEVELOPMENT

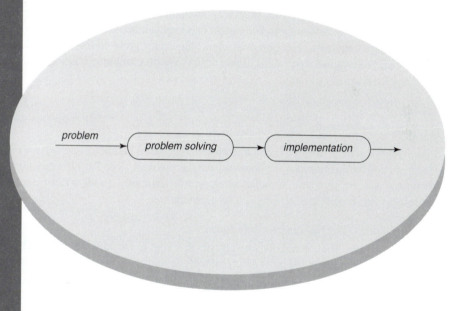

problem → problem solving → implementation

$\mathbf{A}$n algorithm is a step-by-step method for solving a problem. Adlai Stevenson's recipe for cooking carp furnishes an example of an algorithm:

1. Take a 1- to 2-pound carp and allow it to swim in clear water for 24 hours.
2. Scale and fillet the carp.
3. Rub fillets with butter and season with salt and pepper.
4. Place fillets on board and bake in moderate oven for 20 minutes.
5. Throw away carp and eat board.

Examples of algorithms can be found throughout history, starting with ancient Babylonia. Indeed, the word "algorithm" derives from the name of the ninth-century Persian mathematician al-Khowārizmī. Algorithms play a central role in science and engineering. Computers provide the means to automate the execution of algorithms; algorithms are written as computer programs, which are then executed by computers.

After introducing algorithms, we discuss computer systems. We continue by explaining how data are represented within a computer. This explanation is followed by an overview of programming languages. Next we present techniques for problem solving and developing programs. We conclude with a discussion of the C++ programming language.

0.1 ALGORITHMS

Computers are used to solve problems; however, before a computer can solve a problem, it must be given instructions for how to solve the problem. The list of instructions, apart from any specific computer, is called an algorithm. Formally, an **algorithm** is a finite set of instructions having the following characteristics:

- *Precision.* The steps are precisely stated.
- *Uniqueness.* The intermediate results of each step of execution are uniquely defined and depend only on the input and results of the preceding steps.
- *Finiteness.* The algorithm stops after finitely many instructions have been executed.
- *Input.* The algorithm receives input.
- *Output.* The algorithm produces output.
- *Generality.* The algorithm applies to a set of inputs.

EXAMPLE 0.1.1. Consider the following algorithm

Input: n
Output: $\frac{1}{1} + \frac{1}{2} + \cdots + \frac{1}{n}$

1. $sum = 0$
2. $i = 0$
3. $i = i + 1$
4. $sum = sum + 1/i$
5. Repeat lines 3 and 4 until $i == n$.

This algorithm computes the sum of the first n terms of the series $\sum_{i=1}^{n} \frac{1}{i}$.

This algorithm receives n as input and produces as output, *sum*, the sum of the first n terms of the series.

At line 1, the statement *sum* $= 0$ means: "Copy the value 0 into sum." More generally, the statement

$$variable \ = \ expression$$

means: "Copy the value of *expression* into *variable*," or, equivalently, "Replace the current value of *variable* by the value of *expression*." For example, when the statement

$$x \ = \ y$$

is executed, the value of y is copied into x and the value of y is unchanged. The notation $=$ is interpreted as "is assigned." We call $=$ the **assignment operator**.

In line 4, the expression $i == n$ is true if i and n have the same values and false if i and n have different values. The notation $==$ is interpreted as "equals." We call $==$ the **equality operator**. Despite the similar look of the operators $=$ and $==$, their meanings are completely different.

Next we show how the algorithm executes if the input, n, is equal to 3. Simulating the execution of an algorithm for a specific input is called a **trace**. At lines 1 and 2, the algorithm sets *sum* to 0 and i to 0. At line 3, it assigns the value $i + 1$, which is 1 since i is 0, to i. The effect is to add 1 to i. At line 4, it adds $1/i$ (i.e., $1/1$) to *sum*, so that *sum* now has value 1. At line 5, the algorithm tests whether i equals n. Because i equals 1 and n equals 3, the algorithm repeats lines 3 and 4.

At line 3, the algorithm updates i to 2. It then adds $1/i$ (i.e., $1/2$) to *sum*. At this point, the value of *sum* is $1 + 1/2$. Since i now equals 2 and therefore is not equal to n, the algorithm repeats lines 3 and 4.

At line 3, the algorithm updates i to 3. It then adds $1/i$ (i.e., $1/3$) to *sum*. At this point, the value of *sum* is $1 + 1/2 + 1/3$. Since i equals 3, i is now equal to n. Therefore, the algorithm terminates. The value, stored in *sum*, is the sum of the first three terms of the series. ∎

The steps of an algorithm must be stated precisely. The steps of the algorithm in Example 0.1.1 are stated precisely enough so that the algorithm could be mechanically and unambiguously executed by a person or a machine. A person or a machine that executes these instructions for a given value of n will obtain a unique value for *sum*, namely, the sum of the first n terms of the series.

Given values of the input, each intermediate step of an algorithm produces a unique result. For example, given the values

$$sum \ = \ 1 + 1/2, \quad i \ = \ 3$$

at line 4 of the algorithm in Example 0.1.1, *sum* will be set to $1 + 1/2 + 1/3$, regardless of what person or machine executes the algorithm.

After finitely many steps, an algorithm stops with a solution to the given problem. For example, the algorithm in Example 0.1.1 stops after n repetitions and correctly computes the sum of the first n terms of the series.

An algorithm receives input and produces output. The algorithm in Example 0.1.1 receives, as input, a value of n and produces, as output, the value *sum*.

An algorithm must be general. The algorithm in Example 0.1.1 can find the sum of the first n terms of the series *for any* n.

Modern computers relieve people of the tedium of executing algorithms by hand. Algorithms such as those for producing tables used by navigators, scientists, engineers, and accountants, which were once, of necessity, rendered by hand, are now routinely produced by computers. Besides improving time and accuracy, computers have made it possible to execute complex, sophisticated algorithms that would be practically impossible to execute in any other way.

†EXERCISES

1. Write an algorithm that computes the sum of the first n terms of the series $\sum_{i=1}^{\infty} \frac{1}{(1+i)^2}$.

2. Write an algorithm that finds the smallest element among a, b, and c.

3. Write an algorithm that finds the smallest element in the sequence $s_1, s_2, \ldots, s_n$ of n distinct numbers. The input is the sequence, s, and the index, n, of the last term of the sequence. The output is the index of the smallest element in the sequence.

4. How might the algorithm of Example 0.1.1 be made even more general?

5. Consult a telephone book for the instructions for making a long-distance call. Which of the properties of an algorithm—precision, uniqueness, finiteness, input, output, generality—are present? Which properties are lacking?

0.2 COMPUTER SYSTEMS

The term **computer system** refers to all of the components that constitute what we typically call a "computer." These components can be divided into **hardware**—the physical devices that execute instructions, store data, print data, and so on—and **software**—computer programs, which implement algorithms that can be executed by the hardware.

Computers can be roughly divided into the following categories according to size:

• **Mainframes** and **minicomputers**—Large computers designed to be used simultaneously by several people (see Figure 0.2.1). Mainframes are larger than minicomputers, but in recent years the distinction has blurred. Among the prominent manufacturers of mainframes and minicomputers are DEC (Digital Equipment Corporation) and IBM (International Business Machines). Examples are the IBM 3090 and DEC VAX systems.

• **Workstations**—Powerful, single-user, desktop systems. Among the prominent manufacturers of workstations are Sun Microsystems and Hewlett-Packard.

• **Personal computers**—Single-user systems that are similar to workstations, but cheaper and less powerful. The IBM PC and the Apple Macintosh are examples of personal computers.

---

† Solutions to odd-numbered problems are given in the back of the book.

FIGURE 0.2.1 An IBM 3090 mainframe computer. *(Courtesy of International Business Machines Corporation.)*

At the heart of the hardware are **main memory** and the **central processing unit** (**CPU**) (see Figures 0.2.2 and 0.2.3). Main memory stores machine instructions and data, both of which are used by the CPU. The CPU is itself a system with components. The CPU's three main components are the **control unit** (**CU**), the **arithmetic-logic unit** (**ALU**), and the **register bank**.

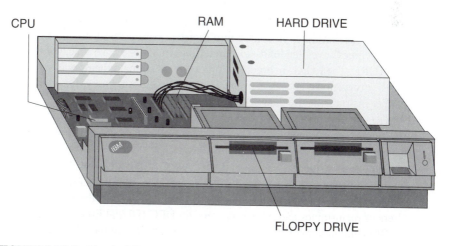

FLOPPY DRIVE

FIGURE 0.2.2 Inside of a PC.

The register bank consists of local scratchpad storage cells called **registers**. Registers are local storage in that they are located on the same integrated circuit as the CPU; they are scratchpad storage in that the CU and the ALU use them to store intermediate results in the course of performing computations. The number of registers in a bank typically ranges from tens to low hundreds. For example, one machine may have 12 CPU registers, whereas another has 128 CPU registers. By contrast, a modern computer typically has millions of storage cells in its main memory. On many modern systems, most instructions require that

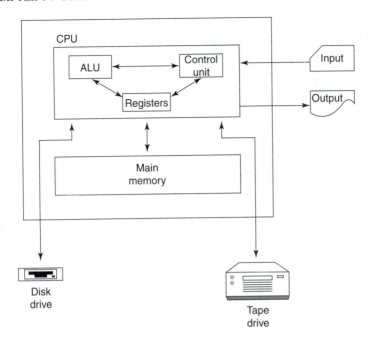

FIGURE 0.2.3 Components of a computer system.

their data be stored in registers. If the data for these instructions reside in main memory, then the data first must be copied into registers before the instructions can be executed. Such machines are called **load-store machines** in honor of two special instructions, LOAD and STORE. The LOAD instruction copies data from main memory into a register, and the STORE instruction copies data from a register into main memory. On a load-store machine, all other instructions use data in CPU registers.

The ALU's operation is what we commonly understand as computing. It executes instructions for arithmetic (e.g., add, subtract), logic (e.g., and, not), comparison (e.g., equals, is greater than), and other operations. The CU provides overall control of the computer's operations. In particular, the CU is responsible for fetching, decoding, and executing instructions. In a modern computer, instructions typically are fetched from main memory into special CPU registers, where they are then decoded. To decode an instruction is to identify it and the data on which it works. For example, to decode an ADD instruction is to identify it as an instruction for addition rather than multiplication or some other operation and to specify the numbers to be added. To execute an instruction is to perform some operation or series of operations that accomplishes the task at hand. For example, to execute an ADD instruction is to perform addition on the specified numbers (typically in CPU registers) and to place their sum in a designated location (typically a CPU register).

Devices external to the CPU and main memory are called **peripheral devices** and include **secondary storage devices**, such as magnetic tape drives, magnetic disk drives, and optical disk drives, and **input/output devices**, such as keyboards, video displays, and printers. Main memory and secondary storage differ in three principal ways. First, just as the CPU has faster access to registers than to main memory, so it has faster access to main memory than to secondary storage. Second, just as CPU registers furnish less storage than main memory (tens or hundreds versus millions of storage cells), so main memory furnishes less storage than secondary storage (low millions versus high millions or even billions of storage cells). Third, main memory is typically volatile, whereas secondary storage typically is not. A storage area is **volatile** if its contents are lost when power is lost. When we turn off a PC, for example, the contents of main memory are lost; but, we hope, the contents of the hard disk or tape drive are not lost. Figure 0.2.4 illustrates the differences among registers, main memory, and secondary storage.

Relatively Fast
Access Time

Relatively Small
Storage Capacity

Relatively Expensive
Devices

Storage Type	Storage Capacity	Storage Location	Volatile?
CPU registers	10s to low 100s of cells	On same integrated circuit (IC) as CPU	Yes
Main memory	1,000s to 1,000,000s of cells	On different ICs than CPU	Yes
Secondary storage	1,000,000s to 1,000,000,000s of cells	On distinct devices such as hard disks or tape drives	No

Relatively Slow
Access Time

Relatively Large
Storage Capacity

Relatively Cheap
Devices

FIGURE 0.2.4 A computer's storage hierarchy.

Magnetic tape for secondary storage is similar to ordinary audio tape. Data are encoded as magnetized patterns.

The surface of a magnetic disk is coated with material that can be magnetized to represent data. **Floppy disks**, made of plastic, can be inserted and removed from a floppy disk drive. On the other hand, a **hard disk**, made of metal, is permanently installed in the hard disk drive. An advantage of floppy disks over hard disks is their portability; a disadvantage is that floppy disks can store significantly less data than can a hard disk.

Optical disks use a technology similar to that used for audio compact disks. (Optical disks for personal computers, called CD-ROMs, are similar to audio compact disks.) Data are represented on an optical disk by patterns that determine how light reflects from its surface. Such disks are read by shining a laser light on the disk and decoding the patterns.

Data on disks or tapes are organized into **files**; thus, we refer to input files (files to be read by programs), output files (files generated by programs), source files (files containing computer programs), executable files (files containing machine instructions that can be loaded into main memory and directly executed), and so on.

Disks are **random access devices**; that is, it is possible to go directly to the desired location by skipping data between the current position and the desired position, much as one can locate a specific page in a book by skipping over intermediate pages. Tapes, by contrast, are **sequential access devices**; locating a desired position on tape requires that all the tape between the current position and the desired position pass through the machine, much as one fast forwards audio or video tape to locate a specific selection.

Software refers to computer programs written by the programmer as well as those provided by the system. System software includes text editors, compilers, and the operating system. As the name suggests, **text editors** are used to generate text. As examples, text editors are used to write programs and to prepare electronic mail messages. A **compiler** is used to translate programs in a language such as C++ or FORTRAN into instructions that can be executed by the CPU.

The **operating system** is a set of programs that manages and allocates the resources of the computer. For example, if a program contains a command to print data, the operating system services this request by allocating the printer and channeling the data to be output to it. On multiuser systems (e.g., mainframes and minicomputers), the operating system allocates resources among the many users competing for the various resources. Examples of operating systems are MS-DOS and Windows for IBM personal computers, VMS for DEC computers, OS/MVS for IBM mainframes, and UNIX, which is used on a wide variety of systems.

EXERCISES

1. Explain the difference between hardware and software.

2. Give examples of peripheral devices different from those mentioned in this section.

3. What advantages do tapes have over disks?

4. Explain the purpose of an operating system.

5. Give examples of activities an operating system might perform on a multiuser mainframe.

0.3 INTERNAL REPRESENTATIONS

A **bit** is a *b*inary dig*it*, that is, a zero or a one. In a digital computer, data and instructions are encoded as bits. (The term "digital" refers to the use of the digits zero and one.) Technology determines how the bits are physically represented within a computer system. Today's hardware relies on the state of an electronic circuit to represent a bit. The circuit must be capable of being in two states—one representing 1, the other 0.

Bits are organized into larger units called **bytes**. Typically, a byte consists of eight bits. Main memory consists of a sequence of consecutive bytes. Common memory sizes of personal computers are 16M to 128M bytes (1M = 1024K, 1K = 1024). Each byte of main memory has an **address**; the first byte has address zero, the second byte has address one, and so on (see Figure 0.3.1). Thus a byte is the smallest addressable unit in main memory. The CPU reads or writes a specific location by specifying its address. Bytes may be further organized into larger units called **words**. For example, a 32-bit word comprises four bytes.

Address

0

1

2

3

FIGURE 0.3.1 Main memory.

Integers

Ordinary integers are written in the **decimal** or **base-10 number system**, in which the symbols 0,1,2,3,4,5,6,7,8,9 are used and the position of a symbol indicates the power of 10 by which it is to be multiplied.

EXAMPLE 0.3.1. The base-10 integer 7036 is interpreted as

$$7036 = 7 \cdot 10^3 + 0 \cdot 10^2 + 3 \cdot 10^1 + 6 \cdot 10^0$$ ∎

Because a computer system uses bits, it is more convenient to represent integers in computer hardware in the **binary** or **base-2 number system**, in which bits (0,1) are used and the position of a bit indicates the power of 2 by which it is to be multiplied. We call a nonnegative integer represented in the binary number system an **unsigned binary integer**, to distinguish it from a two's complement integer, to be described later. In the two's complement system, we can represent both negative and nonnegative integers.

EXAMPLE 0.3.2. The unsigned binary integer 100110 is interpreted as

$$100110_2 = 1 \cdot 2^5 + 0 \cdot 2^4 + 0 \cdot 2^3 + 1 \cdot 2^2 + 1 \cdot 2^1 + 0 \cdot 2^0$$
$$= 32 + 0 + 0 + 4 + 2 = 38_{10}$$

(As shown, we use subscripts to indicate the base.) Figure 0.3.2 shows how the binary integer 100110 could be stored in one byte. ∎

00100110

FIGURE 0.3.2 Storing a one-byte integer.

Since even small integers require several bits to represent them, it is often convenient to use the **hexadecimal** (sometimes shortened to **hex**) or **base-16 number system**, in which the symbols

$$0,1,2,3,4,5,6,7,8,9,A,B,C,D,E,F$$

are used and the position of a symbol indicates the power of 16 by which it is to be multiplied. The symbol A is interpreted as 10 (base 10); B is 11; C is 12; D is 13; E is 14; and F is 15.

EXAMPLE 0.3.3. The hexadecimal integer 30A1 is interpreted as

$$30A1 = 3 \cdot 16^3 + 0 \cdot 16^2 + 10 \cdot 16^1 + 1 \cdot 16^0$$
$$= 12288 + 160 + 1 = 12449_{10}$$ ∎

Hexadecimal notation can be considered as a compact form of binary notation. As Figure 0.3.3 shows, a single, hexadecimal symbol represents a four-bit sequence.

Hex Symbol	Binary Sequence	Hex Symbol	Binary Sequence
0	0000	8	1000
1	0001	9	1001
2	0010	A	1010
3	0011	B	1011
4	0100	C	1100
5	0101	D	1101
6	0110	E	1110
7	0111	F	1111

FIGURE 0.3.3 Hex and binary equivalents.

EXAMPLE 0.3.4. The hexadecimal equivalent of the binary integer 00101110 is 2E. As Figure 0.3.3 shows, the first four bits 0010 correspond to 2, and the last four bits 1110 correspond to E. ∎

The largest one-byte unsigned binary integer is

$$11111111 = FF_{16} = 255_{10}$$

The largest two-byte unsigned binary integer is

$$1111111111111111 = FFFF_{16} = 65,535_{10}$$

The largest four-byte unsigned binary integer is

$$11111111111111111111111111111111 = \text{FFFFFFFF}_{16} = 4{,}294{,}967{,}295_{10}$$

To distinguish positive and negative integers, **two's complement form** is frequently used. In the two's complement system, if the leftmost bit is 0, the integer is zero or positive and the value is that previously described. If the leftmost bit is 1, the integer is negative. In this case the absolute value of the integer is the two's complement of the original expression, which is obtained as follows:

1. Change each 0 to 1 and each 1 to 0 in the bit string. (This is called *one's complement*.)
2. Add 1 to the number. Throw away the final carry bit.

If the absolute value of the integer is *abv*, the original bit string represents the negative integer −*abv*.

EXAMPLE 0.3.5. We convert the 8-bit, two's complement integer

$$10101100$$

to decimal. We first find the absolute value of the integer. We begin by changing each 0 to 1 and each 1 to 0 to obtain

$$01010011$$

We then add 1 to this number to obtain

$$01010100$$

Because

$$01010100 = 64 + 16 + 4 = 84_{10}$$

the original bit string 10101100 represents the decimal number −84. ∎

To write a negative decimal integer as an n-bit two's complement integer, we compute the two's complement of the n-bit unsigned representation of the absolute value of the integer.

EXAMPLE 0.3.6. To write the decimal integer −94 as an 8-bit, two's complement integer, we first write the absolute value 94 as an 8-bit binary integer:

$$94 = 64 + 16 + 8 + 4 + 2 = 2^6 + 2^4 + 2^3 + 2^2 + 2^1 = 01011110$$

Now −94 is represented as the two's complement of 01011110. To compute the two's complement, we first change each 0 to 1 and each 1 to 0:

$$10100001$$

We then add 1 to obtain the 8-bit, two's complement representation of −94:

$$-94 = 10100010$$ ∎

The largest one-byte signed integer is

$$01111111 = 7F_{16} = 127_{10}$$

The smallest one-byte signed integer is

$$10000000 = 80_{16} = -128_{10}$$

The largest two-byte signed binary integer is

$$0111111111111111 = 7FFF_{16} = 32,767_{10}$$

The smallest two-byte signed binary integer is

$$1000000000000000 = 8000_{16} = -32,768_{10}$$

The largest four-byte signed binary integer is

$$01111111111111111111111111111111 = 7FFFFFFF_{16} = 2,147,483,647_{10}$$

The smallest four-byte signed binary integer is

$$10000000000000000000000000000000 = 80000000_{16} = -2,147,483,648_{10}$$

Two's complement representation simplifies basic arithmetic operations, which explains its popularity. For example, to add two two's complement integers, we simply perform ordinary binary addition without worrying about the sign. Any carry bit is discarded.

EXAMPLE 0.3.7. To add the 8-bit, two's complement integers 11011100 and 11000001, we compute

$$
\begin{array}{r}
11011100 \\
+\ \underline{11000001} \\
10011101
\end{array}
$$

The carry bit 1 is discarded. The same computation in decimal is

$$
\begin{array}{r}
-36 \\
+\ \underline{-63} \\
-99
\end{array}
$$

■

EXAMPLE 0.3.8. To subtract the 8-bit, two's complement integer 11011100 from 11000001, we negate 11011100 (by taking two's complement) and add. The two's complement of 11011100 is 00100100. Thus

$$11000001 - 11011100 = 11000001 + 00100100 = 11100101$$

The same computation in decimal is

$$-63 - -36 = -63 + 36 = -27$$

■

Floating-Point Numbers

A **floating-point number** is a number with a decimal point, such as 8.3194, -90.3314, 37.0, and 6.34×10^{20}. The latter number is said to be expressed in **scientific notation**. Scientific notation consists of

- **Mantissa** (6.34 in our example).
- **Base** (10 in our example).
- **Exponent** (20 in our example).

Although the specific details may differ from one machine to another, floating-point numbers are represented in computers in scientific notation. Not surprisingly, the base used is 2. We describe one standard way to represent floating-point numbers known as the **IEEE** (Institute of Electrical and Electronic Engineers) **single-precision standard**. There are also double-precision and quadruple-precision IEEE standards, which provide for larger mantissas and exponents.

The IEEE single-precision standard represents a floating-point number in one 32-bit word (see Figure 0.3.4). The first bit s is the sign bit, with 0 signaling positive and 1 signaling negative. The following eight bits are interpreted as an unsigned integer e'. If $e' \neq 0$, the exponent is defined as $e' - 127$. If $e' = 0$, the exponent is defined as -126. The remaining 23 bits

$$b_1 b_2 \ldots b_{23}$$

are interpreted as the value $m' = 0.b_1 b_2 \ldots b_{23}$ in base 2; that is,

$$m' = 0.b_1 b_2 \ldots b_{23} = b_1 2^{-1} + b_2 2^{-2} + \cdots + b_{23} 2^{-23}$$

If $e' \neq 0$, the mantissa is $1 + m'$. If $e' = 0$, the mantissa is m'. To summarize, if $e' \neq 0$, the number represented is

$$(-1)^s \times (1 + m') \times 2^{e'-127}$$

If $e' = 0$, the number represented is

$$(-1)^s \times m' \times 2^{-126}$$

01010110010010100000000000000000

FIGURE 0.3.4 Storing a 32-bit floating-point number.

EXAMPLE 0.3.9. Suppose that the 32-bit word

$$0 \; 10101100 \; 10010100000000000000000$$

represents a floating-point number using the IEEE single-precision standard. (Spaces separate the sign bit, the exponent bits, and the mantissa bits for clarity. The spaces would *not* be present in the internal representation.)

Since the sign bit is zero, the floating-point number is positive. The exponent bits 10101100 represent the unsigned integer 172 in base 10; thus, the exponent is $172 - 127 = 45$ in base 10. The mantissa bits

$$10010100000000000000000$$

represent the value

$$2^{-1} + 2^{-4} + 2^{-6} = 0.578125$$

in base 10. Since the mantissa is one plus this value, the floating-point number is

$$1.578125 \times 2^{45}$$

∎

EXAMPLE 0.3.10. Suppose that the 32-bit word

$$1\ 00000000\ 01010000000000000000000$$

represents a floating-point number using the IEEE single-precision standard. Since the sign bit is one, the floating-point number is negative. The exponent bits represent zero; thus, the exponent is -126 in base 10. The mantissa bits

$$01010000000000000000000$$

represent the value

$$2^{-2} + 2^{-4} = 0.3125$$

in base 10. Since the exponent bits represent zero, we do *not* add 1 to obtain the mantissa. Thus the floating-point number is

$$-0.3125 \times 2^{-126}$$

∎

EXAMPLE 0.3.11. We give an example to show how positive integers are represented as floating-point numbers using the IEEE single-precision standard.

The binary representation of 300 is 100101100. Shifting the decimal point in a base-10 number one place to the left is equivalent to dividing by 10; similarly, shifting the binary point one place to the left is equivalent to dividing by 2. Therefore, we may write

$$300_{10} = 100101100_2 = 1.00101100_2 \times 2^8$$

The exponent bits equal 135 $(127 + 8)$. Since $135 = 10000111_2$, 300 in the IEEE single-precision standard is

$$0\ 10000111\ 00101100000000000000000$$

∎

Care must be taken when using floating-point numbers since usually the internal representation of a floating-point number is only an approximation of the actual value. For example, the fraction $\frac{1}{3}$ cannot be represented exactly as a terminating decimal or as a terminating binary number. Furthermore, it may not be possible to represent exactly the result of an arithmetic computation, even if the numbers involved are represented exactly. As an example, on our (the authors') system the expression

$$(1.0/3.0) \times 2.5 \ == \ 5.0/6.0$$

is false. A detailed discussion of floating-point arithmetic is beyond the scope of this book; however, we caution against testing whether two floating-point numbers are equal. Rather, we suggest testing whether one floating-point number is less than or equal to another, one is less than another, and so on.

Characters

Characters (letters and symbols such as A, g, $, +) are represented internally as integers, using a table that has been created to give a correspondence between integers and characters. The most common method of representing characters is known as **ASCII** (American Standard Code for Information Interchange). ASCII uses a 7-bit code (integers 0 through 127) to represent characters. Some characters and their internal representations using ASCII are given in Figure 0.3.5. The complete ASCII table is given in Appendix A.

Character	ASCII Code
A	$01000001 = 65_{10}$
g	$01100111 = 103_{10}$
$	$00100100 = 36_{10}$
+	$00101011 = 43_{10}$

FIGURE 0.3.5 Characters and codes.

Machine Instructions

Bit strings may be interpreted as instructions. Each particular processor has its own instruction set and its own mapping of bit strings to instructions. Instructions may be one or more bytes in length. Instructions typically consist of an **operation code** (usually contracted to **opcode**), which signals the type of instruction, and **operands**, which specify the data on which the operation is to be performed.

EXAMPLE 0.3.12.   A sample one-byte instruction for one processor is

$$01xxxyyy$$

The opcode 01 identifies a LOAD instruction, which copies the contents of a main memory storage cell into a CPU register. The bit pattern yyy specifies the source (i.e., the main memory cell) of the copy, and the bit pattern *xxx* specifies the destination (i.e., the CPU register). For example, in the instruction

01111100

xxx is 111 and *yyy* is 100. The instruction thus means: "Load the contents of main memory cell 100 into CPU register 111." ∎

Bit Strings in Memory

A single bit string in memory may have several possible interpretations, including an integer, a floating-point number, a character, and an instruction. The context, defined by the program, determines the correct meaning. Major errors result when misinterpretations occur.

EXAMPLE 0.3.13. The bit string

01100111

has many possible interpretations. If the bit string represents an instruction for the processor of Example 0.3.12, the interpretation is an instruction to copy the value from main memory cell 111 into CPU register 100. If the bit string represents an integer, it is interpreted as the decimal value 103. If the bit string represents a character, it is interpreted as the character *g*, assuming ASCII representation of characters. ∎

EXERCISES

1. Write the unsigned binary integer 11010010 in decimal and in hexadecimal.
2. Write the unsigned binary integer 100101010 in decimal and in hexadecimal.
3. Write the unsigned hexadecimal integer A3 as an 8-bit binary integer and in decimal.
4. Write the unsigned hexadecimal integer A3F2 as a 16-bit binary integer and in decimal.
5. Write the decimal integer 10376 as a 16-bit unsigned binary integer and in hexadecimal.
6. Write the decimal integer 32000 as a 16-bit unsigned binary integer and in hexadecimal.
7. Write the two's complement of 01001000.
8. Write the two's complement of 1001111101000000.
9. Write the signed binary integer 11010010 in decimal.
10. Write the signed binary integer 10010101 in decimal.
11. Write the signed hexadecimal integer A3F2 in decimal.
12. Write the signed hexadecimal integer 737DA3F2 in decimal.
13. Write the decimal integer −1127 as a 16-bit signed binary integer.
14. Write the decimal integer −31677 as a 16-bit signed binary integer.
15. Add the 8-bit, two's complement integers 10011000 and 01110110. Your answer should be an 8-bit, two's complement integer.

16. Subtract 00011000 from 01110110. Assume that both are two's complement integers. Your answer should be an 8-bit, two's complement integer.

17. Write the 32-bit word

$$1\ 11100011\ 11001000000000000000000$$

which represents a floating-point number in the IEEE single-precision standard in the form $\pm x.x \times 2^{\pm y}$ and in the form $\pm x.x \times 10^{\pm y}$.

18. Write the 32-bit word

$$0\ 00000000\ 01000000000000000000000$$

which represents a floating-point number in the IEEE single-precision standard in the form $\pm x.x \times 2^{\pm y}$ and in the form $\pm x.x \times 10^{\pm y}$.

19. What is the value in decimal of the bit string of Exercise 17 if it represents a signed integer?

20. What is the value in decimal of the bit string of Exercise 18 if it represents an integer?

21. Which two characters are represented by the first 16 bits of the bit string of Exercise 18? Assume ASCII encoding of characters.

22. Write the decimal number -1.75×2^{40} as a 32-bit floating-point number in the IEEE single-precision standard.

23. Write the decimal number 1.5×2^{-10} as a 32-bit floating-point number in the IEEE single-precision standard.

24. Write the integer 3000 as a 32-bit floating-point number in the IEEE single-precision standard.

25. Suppose that we list the *consecutive* positive integers $1, 2, \ldots$ that can be represented exactly as 32-bit floating-point numbers in the IEEE single-precision standard. What is the last number in this list?

26. Write the fraction $\frac{1}{3}$ as a 32-bit floating-point number in the IEEE single-precision standard. *Hint*: Begin by dividing 1 by 11_2 in binary.

27. A sample one-byte instruction for a particular processor is

$$11xxxyyy$$

The opcode 11 means ADD. When the instruction executes, the contents of CPU register *xxx* are added to the contents of CPU register *yyy* and the sum is then copied back into register *xxx*. Suppose that register 000 contains hex 42 and that register 111 contains hex 10. Show the contents of these registers after the following instruction executes

$$11000111$$

0.4 PROGRAMMING LANGUAGES

A program that can be directly executed by a computer is a sequence of instructions called **machine instructions**, encoded as bit strings (see Figure 0.4.1). (The examples of machine and symbolic instructions are for purposes of illustration and should not be taken as instructions for an actual CPU.) Execution of the program proceeds as the CPU executes these instructions. Machine instructions are typically quite primitive; examples include copying data from one storage location to another, adding a value stored at one location to the value stored at another location, comparing two values, and so on. In the earliest days of digital computers, programs were written directly in binary—an exceedingly tedious and error-prone process.

```
010100110111101011
101000001010000000
111111010100010110
000101000101011000
111100111111101111
001000010000000110
011110110000001110
111100000010100110
```

FIGURE 0.4.1 A portion of a machine program.

Assembly language replaces bit-string instructions by symbolic instructions using ordinary text. For example, the load instruction

```
01111010
```

that moves the contents of register **R4** into register **R1** is replaced by the symbolic instruction

```
MV      R1,R4
```

where **MV** means "move."

Assembly languages also provide **assembler directives**, which are commands to the assembler to perform some particular task but are not translated into machine instructions. Assembler directives allow the programmer to use symbolic names rather than addresses. For example, a directive such as

```
VIDEO      EQU      3A00H
```

allows the programmer subsequently to use the name **VIDEO** rather than the hexadecimal address **3A00**. For example, the instruction

```
MV      R1,VIDEO
```

moves the address **3A00** into register **R1**.

An assembly language program consists of a sequence of symbolic instructions and assembler directives (see Figure 0.4.2). An **assembler** is a program that receives as input an assembly language program, translates the symbolic instructions into machine instructions, interprets the assembler directives, and produces as output a program of machine instructions. Assembly languages, which are still used today, represent a giant advance over direct coding in machine instructions.

```
LOAD    R3,R5
SUB     R5,R1
LOAD    (VIDEO),R5
DECR    R5
LOAD    (VIDEO),R5
```

FIGURE 0.4.2 A portion of an assembly language program.

High-level computer languages, such as C++, FORTRAN, COBOL, Pascal, and Lisp, represent a major improvement over assembly language. Like assembly language, high-level languages use symbolic instructions and symbolic names rather than addresses. The principal difference between a high-level language and an assembly language is that high-level languages allow the programmer to use much more complex instructions. As a result, one high-level language instruction may translate into many machine instructions.

EXAMPLE 0.4.1.   The C++ statement

```
a = b + c;
```

is an instruction to add **b** and **c** and copy the result into **a** (= is the assignment operator in C++). As in assembly language, **a, b,** and **c** are symbolic names; so the C++ statement means to add the values referenced by **b** and **c** and store the result at the location referenced by **a**. The translation of the C++ statement might be

```
LOAD    R1,(B)
LOAD    R2,(C)
ADD     R1,R2
STORE   (A),R1
```

Here **R1** and **R2** are registers. The value of **A** is the address of the storage referenced by **a** in the C++ program, the value of **B** is the address of the storage referenced by **b**, and the value of **c** is the address of the storage referenced by **c**. The parentheses mean: "Reference the value stored at the address, not the address itself." Thus the first instruction

```
LOAD    R1,(B)
```

copies the value stored at address **B** into register **R1**. The instruction

```
LOAD    R1,B
```

would copy the *value* of **B** (that is, the *address*) into register **R1**. Similarly, the second instruction

    LOAD   R2,(C)

copies the value stored at address **C** into **R2**. The third instruction

    ADD   R1,R2

adds the value in **R2** to **R1** and stores the result in **R1**. The last instruction

    STORE   (A),R1

stores the value in **R1** at address **A**. Indeed, the values in **b** and **c** in the C++ program, which are located at addresses **B** and **C**, respectively, are added; the result is stored in **a**, which is located at address **A**. Notice how the single C++ instruction expanded to four machine instructions. ■

A high-level program consists of a sequence of instructions in a high-level language. A **compiler** is a program that receives as input a high-level program, translates the program into machine instructions, and produces as output a program of machine instructions (see Figure 0.4.3).

FIGURE 0.4.3 The compiler.

It is now common for a compiler to translate a high-level language such as C++ or FORTRAN into assembly language, which the assembler then can translate into machine code. There may be other intermediate translations as well. The important point is that the compiler takes a program written in a high-level language as its input and produces machine instructions as its ultimate output.

A high-level program consists of one or more files of instructions written in the high-level language. These files, called **source files**, are created using an editor in which the programmer enters the code. C++ programs typically have names that end with *.cpp* (on personal computers) or *.C*, *.cc*, or *.cxx* on UNIX systems. The *.cpp*, *.C*, *.cc*, and *.cxx* are called **file extensions**. For example, a C++ program might consist of a single file named *newton.cxx*. A C++ compiler takes as input the file *newton.cxx* and produces as output a file of machine instructions. The name of the output file, for example *newton.o*, is derived from the source file and is called an **object file**. The object file must be further processed by the **linker** before it can be executed. The linker takes as input object files and any needed library routines (e.g., routines for doing input and output) and links them into a single file called the **executable file** (see Figure 0.4.4). For example, after the linker receives *newton.o* and the required library routines, it produces as output an executable file, for example *newton*. This file can be directly executed by the computer. Some compilers automatically invoke the linker, so that it appears that the executable file is produced directly from the source file. We give a simple example to show how the compilation process proceeds for the UNIX GNU C++ compiler.

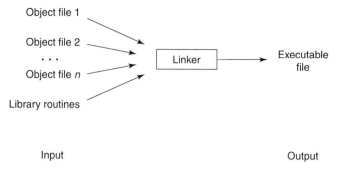

FIGURE 0.4.4 The linker.

EXAMPLE 0.4.2. The UNIX GNU C++ compiler is invoked by typing **g++**. To compile the C++ program that resides in the file *newton.cxx*, we would type

```
% g++ newton.cxx -o newton
```

(We assume that the prompt is **%**.) If there are no errors, the executable file *newton*, whose name is entered after **-o**, is created. The linker was implicitly called, and the object file *newton.o* was created. After the executable file *newton* was created, the object file *newton.o* was automatically deleted. To run the program, we then type

```
% newton
```
∎

EXERCISES

1. Why are assembler directives useful?

2. List features that distinguish high-level languages from assembly languages.

3. C++ can be run on many different computers, but IBM assembler runs only on IBM or IBM-compatible computers. Explain.

4. Explain why compilers produce an intermediate (object) file before the executable file is produced.

5. Why do you think there are so many high-level languages?

0.5 PROBLEM SOLVING AND PROGRAM DEVELOPMENT

To help structure program development, the programming process can be divided into two general parts, problem solving and implementation, each of which is further subdivided (see Figure 0.5.1). The problem-solving stage, which does not involve the computer at all, begins with the problem specification.

Problem solving

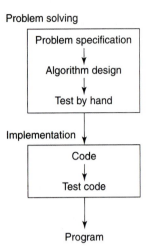

Implementation

Program

FIGURE 0.5.1 Steps in program development.

Problem Specification

The problem to be solved must be carefully stated and the programmer must fully understand it before proceeding. In particular, the input and output must be characterized.

> **EXAMPLE 0.5.1.** Suppose that the problem is to sum the first n terms of the series
>
> $$\sum_{i=1}^{\infty} \frac{1}{i}$$
>
> Here the input is the terminating index n, and the output is the sum of the first n terms of the series. ∎

> **EXAMPLE 0.5.2.** Suppose that the problem is to read references of the form
>
> ```
> Hamilton, W., Tours, IEEE Tr on SE, 35 (1990), 131-155.
> ```
>
> one per line from the file *ref.dat*, sort them alphabetically by author, and write the sorted references to the file *ref.srt*. Here the input is the file *ref.dat*, and the output is the file *ref.srt*. ∎

Real problems that require large programs to solve have highly complex specifications and often require considerable effort to understand. The problems in an introductory book such as this are on a reduced scale and so have simpler specifications.

Algorithm Design and Problem-Solving Strategies

After obtaining the problem specification, an algorithm must be developed to solve the problem.

EXAMPLE 0.5.3.   The following algorithm sums n terms of the series of Example 0.5.1:

Input: n
Output: $\frac{1}{1} + \frac{1}{2} + \cdots + \frac{1}{n}$
  1. $sum = 0$
  2. $i = 0$
  3. $i = i + 1$
  4. $sum = sum + 1/i$
  5. Repeat lines 3 and 4 until $i == n$.   ■

Creating an algorithm involves cleverness and ingenuity, but some general problem-solving strategies can be outlined that aid in constructing algorithms. **Divide-and-conquer** is often a useful approach. In divide-and-conquer, the original problem is *divided* into subproblems, each of which is then solved (*conquered*).

EXAMPLE 0.5.4.   In the reference sorting problem of Example 0.5.2, we were to read references, sort them, and then print them in sorted order. Using the divide-and-conquer approach, we could begin a solution to the problem by listing the steps

1. Read in references.

2. Sort references.

3. Print references.

Of course, each of these steps would require its own algorithmic solution.   ■

Dividing a given problem into subproblems, further subdividing the subproblems, and so on (as in Example 0.5.4), is called **top-down design** or the method of **stepwise refinement**.

Another technique, which is often useful in the initial algorithm design, begins with the question, "How would I solve this problem by hand?" In answering this question, start by taking the simplest possible approach. In particular, simplify the input, perhaps by assuming that the input consists of just a few items. Later, alternative strategies, questions of efficiency, and other algorithms can be considered.

EXAMPLE 0.5.5.   We develop an algorithm to solve subproblem 2 of Example 0.5.4—sorting the references.

We begin by making a simplifying assumption about the input. We assume that it consists of only four items

```
Hamilton, W., Tours, IEEE Tr on SE, 35 (1990), 131-155.
Bohr, N., Atomic particles, Physics Today, 24 (1935), 2-9.
Kalin, M., Philosophy of physics, Philos, 33 (1984), 50-132.
Epp, H., Chemical networks, Network, 4 (1998), 178-179.
```

How could we sort this list by hand? Taking a very simple view of the problem, we observe that the smallest entry (in the sense of alphabetical order with "a" smallest and "z" largest) goes first. Thus we would look for the smallest entry, "Bohr," and put it first. Our partially sorted list is

```
Bohr, N., Atomic particles, Physics Today, 24 (1935), 2-9.
```

We could then repeat this process by looking at the remaining entries

```
Hamilton, W., Tours, IEEE Tr on SE, 35 (1990), 131-155.
Kalin, M., Philosophy of physics, Philos, 33 (1984), 50-132.
Epp, H., Chemical networks, Network, 4 (1998), 178-179.
```

picking the smallest

```
Epp, H., Chemical networks, Network, 4 (1998), 178-179.
```

and putting it second. Our partially sorted list is

```
Bohr, N., Atomic particles, Physics Today, 24 (1935), 2-9.
Epp, H., Chemical networks, Network, 4 (1998), 178-179.
```

Next we could look at the remaining entries

```
Hamilton, W., Tours, IEEE Tr on SE, 35 (1990), 131-155.
Kalin, M., Philosophy of physics, Philos, 33 (1984), 50-132.
```

pick the smallest

```
Hamilton, W., Tours, IEEE Tr on SE, 35 (1990), 131-155.
```

and put it third. Our partially sorted list is

```
Bohr, N., Atomic particles, Physics Today, 24 (1935), 2-9.
Epp, H., Chemical networks, Network, 4 (1998), 178-179.
Hamilton, W., Tours, IEEE Tr on SE, 35 (1990), 131-155.
```

Finally, the single remaining entry

```
Kalin, M., Philosophy of physics, Philos, 33 (1984), 50-132.
```

goes last. Our sorted list is

```
Bohr, N., Atomic particles, Physics Today, 24 (1935), 2-9.
Epp, H., Chemical networks, Network, 4 (1998), 178-179.
Hamilton, W., Tours, IEEE Tr on SE, 35 (1990), 131-155.
Kalin, M., Philosophy of physics, Philos, 33 (1984), 50-132.
```

■

The overall solution to the problem of reading, sorting, and printing references (Example 0.5.2) would be completed by providing algorithms to read the references and print them. These algorithms, combined with the sorting algorithm developed in Example 0.5.5, solve the problem of Example 0.5.2.

Additional Problem-Solving Strategies

We need not create an algorithm at all if one already exists. For example, C++ provides a function named **qsort** that can sort arbitrary data; thus, a simple way to solve a sorting problem is to use **qsort**. Because of the considerable cost of producing software, reuse of code is of major concern.

If an algorithm does not already exist to solve a problem, perhaps an algorithm exists that *almost* solves the given problem. In some cases, the existing algorithm can be modified to solve the given problem.

> **EXAMPLE 0.5.6.**   If a problem calls for data to be sorted in decreasing order and an algorithm is already available that sorts data in increasing order, it will be easy to modify the existing algorithm so that it sorts in decreasing order. All that need be done is to interchange $<$ and $>$ in the comparisons. ∎

> **EXAMPLE 0.5.7.**   Suppose that we want to solve the problem of determining whether a data set contains duplicates. For example, a mail-order house may want to eliminate duplicate names so that duplicate mailings can be avoided. If we observe that in a sorted list duplicates are adjacent, we can first sort the data using an already existing sorting algorithm. If we then scan the data and compare neighbors, we can easily identify all of the duplicates. ∎

Testing by Hand

After an algorithm has been developed, it should be thoroughly checked by hand before it is coded in a high-level language. The importance of checking an algorithm before proceeding cannot be overemphasized. After creating an algorithm, especially one that the programmer is particularly proud of, it is tempting to rush to a computer, code the algorithm, and try it out; but such bustle usually results in a considerable amount of wasted time. Easily revealed using paper and pencil, many errors are more difficult to uncover after coding because of complications introduced by the computer language.

To check an algorithm by hand, we construct sample input for the algorithm and execute it by hand. We should try to make the sample input as difficult and potentially troublesome for the algorithm as possible. Now is the time to try to discover errors in the algorithm and fix them. Especially important input values are **boundary values**, minimum and maximum values. For example, if x is an input value and x is constrained by the problem specification to lie between 0 and 1, the algorithm should be checked for x equal to 0 and for x equal to 1. Also important are input data for which the solution should be trivial. For example, a sorting algorithm should be tested with input that is already sorted.

EXAMPLE 0.5.8. To test the algorithm of Example 0.5.3, we should check it by hand for several values of n. Here the minimum value of n is 1; n has no maximum since n can be equal to any positive integer.

If n is 1, at lines 1 and 2, *sum* and i are set to 0. At line 3, i is incremented to 1. At line 4, *sum* is set to 1. The algorithm terminates at line 5 since i is equal to n; both are equal to 1. The algorithm correctly computes the value 1.

Similarly, we would check some other small values of n, for example $n = 2, 3, 4$, to convince ourselves that the algorithm is correct for small values of n.

Checking the algorithm for small values of n does not *prove* that the algorithm is correct. (It *proves* only that the algorithm is correct for the values that were tested!) However, checking the algorithm for small values of n does give us confidence that the algorithm is correct. To prove that the algorithm is correct, a mathematical technique such as mathematical induction could be used. Such correctness proofs are beyond the scope of this book. ∎

EXAMPLE 0.5.9. To test the algorithm of Example 0.5.5, we should check it by hand for a minimum size input (one item), for several values of n, and for sorted input. ∎

Coding and Testing

After an algorithm has been constructed that solves the original problem and after it has been thoroughly tested by hand, the solution can be coded for execution by a computer. If the algorithm has been given in sufficient detail, much of the coding will be routine. However, every programming language has its own peculiarities, so additional issues will have to be dealt with.

After the solution has been coded, testing proceeds similarly to testing an algorithm by hand. The difference, of course, is that the code will now be executed by the computer several times for different input. Again we should try to make the input as difficult and potentially troublesome for the computer as possible. Boundary values and input for which the solution should be trivial should again be considered. Large input sizes, infeasible to test by hand, must now be tested.

EXERCISES

1. Give examples of the kinds of difficulties that might be experienced if the problem specification is ambiguous.

2. Give an algorithm for subproblem 1 of Example 0.5.4.

3. Give an algorithm for subproblem 3 of Example 0.5.4.

4. Give a complete algorithm that solves the reading, sorting, and printing problem of Example 0.5.2.

5. Give an example of the use of divide-and-conquer in an everyday activity.

6. Write an algorithm to compute the two's complement of an n-bit binary integer. Describe input that would be useful to test your algorithm.

7. In the card game cribbage, for scoring purposes a hand consists of five cards. Face cards count 10, an ace counts one, and the value of each other card is equal to its denomination. Each *distinct* combination of cards in a hand that sums to 15 counts two points. Each combination must be distinct, but cards are allowed to belong to distinct combinations. For example, the hand

$$10\diamond \; J\heartsuit \; 2\diamond \; 3\spadesuit \; 3\diamond$$

has four combinations that total 15: $10\diamond \; 2\diamond \; 3\spadesuit$, $10\diamond \; 2\diamond \; 3\diamond$, $J\heartsuit \; 2\diamond \; 3\spadesuit$, $J\heartsuit \; 2\diamond \; 3\diamond$. Consider the problem of finding the number of combinations in a cribbage hand that sum to 15. What is the input and output to this problem? Write an algorithm to solve this problem. What strategies did you use to obtain your algorithm? Describe input that would be useful to test your algorithm.

0.6 WHY C++?

Over the past two decades, C, the predecessor of C++, became the language of choice for new applications written for diverse computer platforms. Applications ranging from word processors for PCs to transaction database systems for mainframes were written in C. Indeed, most familiar PC programs were written in C, including spreadsheets, databases, statistics packages, word processors, communication systems, graphics packages, compilers, educational software, games, planning and simulation systems, and so on. C has long been the applications language of choice in the UNIX world. The UNIX operating system itself, which is still popular as a desktop and server operating system, is written largely in C. Windows NT, a platform-independent and flagship operating system that Microsoft markets in competition with UNIX, is written mostly in C. The other Windows operating systems such as Windows 98 are also written mostly in C. Now that C++ is widely available on many different platforms, new applications and updates of older applications are migrating to C++ in both the UNIX and Windows worlds. Also, C++ is fast emerging as the language of choice for industrial-strength applications. In this section, we sketch the reasons for the unrivaled popularity of C++ and its C subset, and we indicate what C++ has to offer to applications programmers.

Procedural and Object-Oriented Programming

C++ supports traditional, procedural programming through its C subset. It also supports object-oriented programming by allowing the user to create classes, to define objects, and to use inheritance and polymorphism. A *class* is a user-defined data type that combines data and functions, called *methods*, that operate on that data. An *object* is an instance of a class. One class can be *inherited* from another; that is, a new class can be constructed by inheriting another existing class's data and methods but adding additional data and methods of its own. *Polymorphism* in C++ allows the programmer to create methods in an inheritance hierarchy that have exactly the same declaration so that the system, at run time, can determine which of these to invoke. *Object-oriented programming* is characterized by the use of classes, objects, inheritance, and polymorphism.

Efficiency

C++ has few built-in data types—integer, floating-point, and pointer (address) data types—and these are fundamental to all hardware. Whatever the target computer, a C++ compiler is typically able to generate an efficient executable program from a C++ source file. The executable program is efficient in space and time: the executable program generated by a C++ compiler tends to be small in its storage requirements and fast in its processing speed. C++ compilers, like C compilers before them, have strong optimizing capabilities.

By supporting both procedural and object-oriented programming, C++ allows the programmer to tailor the code to the particular application, taking into account efficiency and other concerns.

Expressive Power

C++ supplies built-in integer and floating-point data types together with standard operations on them. In addition, C++ supports user-defined data types through two mechanisms that can be combined in very powerful ways. First, the user can aggregate elements of the same type into arrays of one or more dimensions. The aggregated elements may be of either built-in or user-defined types. Second, the user can aggregate elements of different types, including functions, into classes.

Arithmetic Types

C++ has integer data types in various sizes, all of which may be signed or unsigned. C++ also has single- and multiple-precision floating-point types. The programmer has broad control over the formatting of all numeric types.

Generic Programming

C++ supports generic programming through *templates*, which allow the programmer to use symbolic data types rather than specific data types. By using templates, the programmer need only write code one time if the underlying algorithm is the same for all data types. For example, in Example 0.5.5 a sorting algorithm was developed to sort lines of text. The same algorithm could be used to sort integers, floating-point numbers, and many other data types. By using templates, the programmer can write the code to implement the algorithm once, using a symbolic name for the type of data to be sorted. To sort a particular data type, C++ provides a mechanism for automatically generating code from the generic code to sort the desired data type. The emerging C++ standard specifies the *Standard Template Library* (STL), which provides a library of standard data structures and common algorithms (e.g., for copying, sorting, and searching) using generic programming. STL also has high-level control constructs to minimize programmer use of error-prone constructs such as loops. We discuss STL in Chapter 10.

Modularity

C++'s modules are files, functions, and classes. A typical C++ program consists of files, each of which can be compiled and tested separately to ensure that it works as required; functions; and classes. C++'s modularity encourages a team approach to large, complex systems. Different team members can write and test different modules, combining them in the end into a single C++ program.

When used as an object-oriented language, the dominant C++ module is the class. C++ classes support *encapsulation*, which is the combining of data and methods (functions) within a class. A class thus contains within it the very methods to process the data distinctive to it. Classes encourage modular programming because the class author typically provides both the variables to store data and the methods to process the data. C++ likewise supports *information hiding* within classes and class hierarchies. Through the prudent use of information hiding, the programmer is able to hide a class's low-level implementation details so that use of the class requires knowledge only of its *public interface*, which typically consists of class methods. C++ allows programmers to create pure *interfaces*, or collections of methods that may be shared among many classes. Common functions such as *Open*, *Close*, and *Copy* available in standard software products such as databases and editors illustrate an interface.

Run-Time Libraries

C++ specifies various run-time class and function libraries, which support string handling, input and output operations, time and date processing, mathematical and scientific computing, simulation, sorting and searching, and more. In addition, the world-wide community of C++ programmers continues to create additional libraries, often providing the source code at little or no expense. C++ support for **namespaces** means that various libraries, even from competitors, may be combined in a single application.

C++ uses libraries to provide a programming environment appropriate to the problem being attacked. For example, major vendors such as Microsoft and Borland support environments for developing complex Windows applications. The C++ systems from such vendors are in fact **application frameworks** that generate much of the boilerplate code that programmers find so tedious to write and so hard to debug. Application frameworks allow the knowledgeable programmer to write very powerful and attractive applications without writing tremendous amounts of code. C++ has proven itself as an extensible language that remains highly efficient through the extensions.

Programming Support

Platforms from PCs through workstations up to mainframes and supercomputers typically provide an assortment of powerful tools to assist in writing, testing, and debugging C++ programs. Most modern editors understand C++ syntax and, therefore, can provide automatic indentation, parenthesis matching, and related conveniences. Many editors allow the programmer to compile within the editor so that, if an error is detected, the editor can immediately highlight the offending code. C++ implementations generally include symbolic debuggers that allow the user to set break points, inspect variables or other expressions, trace function calls, and even assign new values to variables. In the PC environment, there is considerable competition in C++ programming systems, with the resulting benefits of low prices and excellent products.

C++ as the Premier Applications Language

The past decade has seen marked competition among languages for applications programming. Visual Basic, Delphi, Java, Smalltalk, C, and C++ itself come immediately to mind as apparent competitors. On inspection, however, it is clear that when an application requires industrial-strength efficiency, flexibility, reliability, and maintainability, the only real choices are C or C++. Three factors favor C++ over C. First, C++ supports the object-oriented model and its obvious benefits of information hiding, encapsulation, inheritance, and polymorphism. Second, C++ supports generic functions through a high-level construct, the template, and C++ provides a powerful yet efficient template library in STL. C supports generic functions mainly through use of functions that take **void*** or **union** arguments, low-level constructs that challenge the patience and discipline of even the most experienced C programmer. Third, even when used as a straight procedural language, C++ is friendlier than C because C++ relaxes C's rules about where variables may be defined, provides high-level alternatives to C's input and output functions, supports function overloading and default arguments, and so on. C++ is becoming the premier language for applications programming.

CHAPTER 1

INTRODUCTION TO DATA TYPES AND OPERATORS

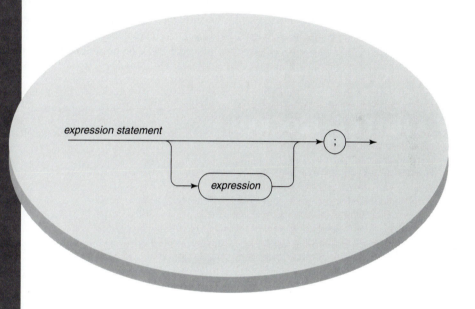

The C++ programming language is an extension of the C programming language that improves certain parts of C and supports object-oriented programming. As such, C++ is a *hybrid* language; the C subset supports traditional programming practices and design, whereas the extensions support the object-oriented paradigm. We begin with basics and then migrate to the object-oriented aspects of the language.

The lineage of C++ can be traced to BCPL (Basic Combined Programming Language). BCPL, invented in 1967 by Martin Richards, was a typeless language that dealt directly with machine words and addresses. Inspired by BCPL, Ken Thompson in 1970 invented the typeless systems programming language B. B and assembly language were used to develop the first versions of the UNIX operating system. In 1972, Dennis Ritchie designed a new language. Since he considered it to be a successor of B, he called it C. C incorporates many of the ideas of BCPL and B but features typing (integers, floating-point numbers, etc.). Bjarne Stroustrup developed C++ in the early 1980s. The first commercial version from Bell Labs appeared in 1985. Because the "++" is C's increment operator (see Section 2.8), the name "C++" suggests that C++ is an incremental extension of C.

In this chapter, we show a simple C++ program and then present basic data types and operators.

1.1 A FIRST C++ PROGRAM

The program in Figure 1.1.1 outputs

```
C++: one small step for the program,
one giant leap for the programmer
```

to the video display.

```cpp
// This program outputs the message
//
//     C++: one small step for the program,
//     one giant leap for the programmer
//
// to the video display
#include <iostream>
using namespace std;
int main() {
   cout << "C++: one small step for the program," << endl
        << "one giant leap for the programmer" << endl;
   return 0;
}
```

FIGURE 1.1.1 A first C++ program.

In C++, a comment, which is ignored by the compiler, starts with `//` and continues to the end of the line. A second type of comment, which can be continued over several lines, begins with `/*` and ends with `*/`.

The line

```
#include <iostream>
```

is a **preprocessor directive** and requests some action before the program is actually translated into machine code. (The preprocessor is discussed in detail in Appendix B.) The `#include` preprocessor directive causes the contents of the named file, *iostream* in this case, to be inserted precisely where the `#include` line appears. Such a file is commonly called a **header file**. Among other things, the file *iostream* provides the proper interface for input and output.

C++ supplies many standard libraries that contain useful features—`cout`, which is used for output, is one example. These standard features are grouped under the name `std` (standard). The technical term for a region in which such features are grouped is **namespace**. (Namespaces are discussed in detail in Section 10.3.) In order to use these standard features as shown, we must add the statement

```
using namespace std;
```

All of our programs will `#include` one or more system files. These `#include`s will then be followed by the statement

```
using namespace std;
```

A C++ program consists of **functions**. In the absence of special functions called *methods* (see Chapter 5), execution of a C++ program begins with the function named `main`. Any function consists of statements enclosed in braces: `{ }`. In this example the program consists of the single function `main`, made up of the statements

```
cout << "C++: one small step for the program," << endl
     << "one giant leap for the programmer" << endl;
return 0;
```

Such statements are executed **sequentially**—the first statement, then the second, and so on.

Single statements are terminated by semicolons (`;`). The first statement

```
cout << "C++: one small step for the program," << endl
     << "one giant leap for the programmer" << endl;
```

shows that a single statement may be written on more than one line. Like most modern, high-level compilers, the C++ compiler does not require the statements of a program to appear in any particular format. We format our programs, especially by using indentation, to help document them.

The occurrence of `cout` signals that expressions are to be written to the standard output, in our case, to the video display. Expressions following `cout <<` and subsequent `<<`'s are interpreted appropriately and sent to the video display. An expression delimited by double quotation marks such as

```
"C++: one small step for the program,"
```

is called a **string**. A string is interpreted as representing the characters between the double quotation marks, so when a string is sent to the video display, these characters (but not the quotation marks themselves) are simply copied to the video display. The expression **endl** is interpreted as a request to generate an end-of-line. The effect is that subsequent output will begin flush left on the next line. Thus when

```
cout << "C++: one small step for the program," << endl
     << "one giant leap for the programmer" << endl;
```

is executed,

```
C++: one small step for the program,
```

is written on one line, an end-of-line is generated, and the next output

```
one giant leap for the programmer
```

is written on the next line. The final **endl** will cause subsequent output (e.g., a system prompt or message) to begin flush left on the next line. In C++, end-of-lines are *not* automatically generated at ends of statements.

When the last line

```
return 0;
```

is executed, **main** signals the system that the program terminated successfully by returning the value 0. The **int** in the line

```
int main() {
```

tells the compiler that **main** returns an **int**eger—in this case, the integer zero.

The namespace **std** has been added recently. To run the program of this section on a compiler that does not support **namespace std**, replace the lines

```
#include <iostream>
using namespace std;
```

by the single line

```
#include <iostream.h>
```

The C++ Postscript at the end of this chapter contains a list of old and new system header names.

EXERCISES

1. Run the program in this section on your system.

2. Run modifications of the program in this section. Experiment by leaving out parts of the program. For example, omit the lines

```
#include <iostream>
using namespace std;
```

Omit a brace. Change one **<<** to **>>**. What errors, if any, result? Can you explain the errors?

3. Find all the errors in the following program:

```
#include <iostream>
main() {
   cout << "There you go again" endl;
   return 0
}
```

1.2 THE int DATA TYPE

The **definition**

```
int n; // define an int variable named n
```

creates a storage cell named **n** that can hold a signed integer:

n

In C++, every variable must be defined. The keyword **int** signifies a C++ integer **data type**. We say that **n** is a **variable** of type **int** or that **n** is an **int**. A data type such as **int** determines

- What sort of information the data type represents.
- How big a storage cell is required to hold a value of the data type.
- Which built-in operations are legal on the data type.

For example, an **int** represents a *signed integer* rather than an unsigned integer or a floating-point number. An **int** cell is four bytes on most modern computers, although it could be bigger or smaller on a particular system.

Several variables, all of the same data type, can be defined in a single statement. The variables are separated by commas.

EXAMPLE 1.2.1.   The statement

```
int i, j;
```

defines two variables named **i** and **j**, each of type **int**.   ∎

Variables defined within a function, such as **main**, do *not* have any particular initial value. We say that such variables contain **garbage**. To simultaneously define and give a variable a value, we can write

```
int i = 1;
```

This statement creates a storage cell named **i** that can hold a signed integer and gives it the initial value 1:

```
┌─────┐
│  1  │
└─────┘
   i
```

After defining an **int** cell, say **n**, we can use the **assignment operator** = to store a value in **n** or to change **n**'s value. For example, to store the value 10 in **n**, we could write

```
n = 10;
```

When the assignment statement is executed, the previous value of **n** is overwritten. The general form of the assignment operator is

var = *expression*;

When this statement is executed, *expression* is evaluated and its value is stored in *var*. The previous value of *var* is overwritten.

> **EXAMPLE 1.2.2.** Suppose that **i** and **j** are variables of type **int**, **i**'s value is 14, and **j**'s value is 78. When the assignment statement
>
> ```
> i = j;
> ```
>
> executes, **j**'s value, 78, is copied into **i**; **i**'s previous value is overwritten; and **j**'s value is unchanged. So after the assignment statement executes, 78 is stored in both **i** and **j**. ∎

Although = is used to specify an initial value in a definition

```
int j = 8;
```

and to denote the assignment operator

```
i = j;
```

the operations are *not* the same. An initial value always appears in a definition. The assignment operator is used *after* variables have been defined.

Another way to store a value in a variable is to use **cin**, which is the input counterpart of **cout**. When the statement

```
cin >> i;
```

executes, the value typed in by the user is stored in **i**. The previous value of **i** is overwritten. Notice that >> is used for input, and << is used for output.

> **EXAMPLE 1.2.3.** Suppose that **i** is a variable of type **int**, and **i**'s value is 77. If the user types in −25, when the statement
>
> ```
> cin >> i;
> ```
>
> executes, **i**'s value becomes −25. The previous value of **i** is overwritten. ∎

Only one value can be read after **>>** in a **cin** statement. For example, the correct way to read a value into the variable **x** and then the next value into the variable **y** is

```
cin >> x >> y;
```

not

```
cin >> x, y; // ***** ERROR *****
```

or

```
cin >> x y; // ***** ERROR *****
```

To output the value of a variable **i**, we use the statement

```
cout << i;
```

EXAMPLE 1.2.4. The output of the code segment

```
int x = 8;
cout << x << endl;
```

is

```
8
```

■

Only one expression can be output after **<<** in a **cout** statement. For example, the correct way to output the value of the variable **x** followed by the value of the variable **y** is

```
cout << x << y;
```

not

```
cout << x, y; // ***** ERROR *****
```

or

```
cout << x y; // ***** ERROR *****
```

Operations

Various arithmetic operations are legal on a numeric data type such as **int**, including addition (**+**), subtraction (**-**), multiplication (*****), and division (**/**). So if **x** and **y** are **int** variables, the expression

```
x + y
```

is legal because addition is legal on **int**s.

EXAMPLE 1.2.5. Suppose that **i**, **j**, and **k** are variables of type **int**, **i**'s value is 7, and **j**'s value is 13. When the assignment statement

```
k = i + j;
```

executes, the value, 20, of the expression **i + j** is copied into **k**. The values of **i** and **j** are unchanged. So after the assignment statement executes, 20 is stored in **k**, 7 is stored in **i**, and 13 is stored in **j**. ■

The expression

```
sizeof( int )
```

gives the size in bytes of an **int** cell on a particular system. The built-in operator **sizeof** gives the size in bytes of any expression. The code segment

```
cout << "An int cell is " << sizeof( int )
     << " bytes on my system." << endl;
```

shows how a **sizeof** expression might be used.

Assume that an **int** is four bytes and that a byte is eight bits. Because an **int** represents a *signed* integer, we have

- 1 bit to represent the integer's sign.
- 31 bits to represent the integer's magnitude.

The range of a 32-bit **int** would then be $-2{,}147{,}483{,}648$ to $2{,}147{,}483{,}647$ (see Section 0.3). An integer data type such as **int** thus determines the *range* of integer values that the data type can represent.

The compiler uses data types to determine how much storage should be allocated for cells and to ensure that only legal operations are performed on a particular data type. The compiler issues warnings or errors when questionable or illegal operations are performed on a data type.

EXERCISES

1. What does the definition

   ```
   int x;
   ```

   tell us about the variable **x**?

2. Suppose that **s** and **t** are variables of type **int**, **s**'s value is 4, and **t**'s value is 8. After the assignment statement

   ```
   s = t;
   ```

   executes, what is **s**'s value? What is **t**'s value?

3. Suppose that **a**, **b**, and **c** are variables of type **int**, **a**'s value is -7, and **b**'s value is 28. After the assignment statement

   ```
   c = a - b;
   ```

   executes, what is **a**'s value? What is **b**'s value? What is **c**'s value?

4. Suppose that **sizeof(int)** is 2 bytes on a system. What is the range of values that an **int** can then represent?

5. Use the **sizeof** operator to determine the number of bytes an **int** occupies on your system. What is the value of the largest **int** on your system? What is the value of the smallest **int** on your system?

1.3 IDENTIFIERS

When we write a program, we must select names for variables, functions, and so on. **Identifier** is the official word for *name* in a high-level language. An identifier in C++ must satisfy the following requirements:

- It must start with a letter (**A** through **Z** or **a** through **z**) or the underscore character (_).
- It must consist only of letters (**A** through **Z** or **a** through **z**), digits (**0** through **9**), and the underscore character (_).
- It must not be a keyword. A **keyword** is a word such as **int** or **return** that has a special meaning. The C++ keywords are listed in the C++ Postscript section at the end of this chapter.

EXAMPLE 1.3.1. The following are legal identifiers:

```
total   total_cars   _sum   column3   TOTAL
```

Uppercase characters are distinguished from lowercase characters. Thus **total** and **TOTAL** are distinct identifiers. ∎

EXAMPLE 1.3.2. The following are *not* legal identifiers:

total$	Illegal character **$**
2nd_sum	Begins with a digit
using	Keyword
second sum	Cannot use blank as a character
TOTAL-CARS	Illegal character –

∎

EXERCISES

1. Are the identifiers **name** and **NAME** different? Explain.
2. What advantages are there in allowing identifiers with long names?

State whether each name in Exercise 3 through 10 is a legal identifier. If the name is not a legal identifier, explain why it is not.

3. **sum_of_credits**
4. **_type_of_car**
5. **namespace**
6. **SECTION_6**
7. **bingo-square**
8. **3_4_99**
9. **initial tree**
10. **final_#**

1.4 SAMPLE APPLICATION: CONVERSION OF LENGTHS

Problem

Prompt the user to enter a length in feet from the keyboard. Then convert the length to inches, and output the original and converted lengths to the video display.

Sample Input/Output

```
Enter length: 3
3 ft
36 in
```

Solution

We need to define an **int** variable to store the value that the user enters. We can define another **int** variable to store the converted value. After writing the original and converted lengths to the video display, the program ends.

C++ Implementation

```
//   This program reads a length in feet from
//   the keyboard, converts the length to inches,
//   and outputs the converted length to the
//   video display. It is assumed that the length
//   is a nonnegative integer.
#include <iostream>
using namespace std;
int main() {
    int foot, inch;
    cout << "Enter length: ";
    cin >> foot;
    inch = 12 * foot;
    cout << foot << " ft" << endl
         << inch << " in" << endl;
    return 0;
}
```

Discussion

The program begins by defining the variables **foot** and **inch**:

```
    int foot, inch;
```

Because these variables are defined to be of type **int**, each can hold one signed integer. To write output to the video display, in this case to prompt the user to enter a length, the program uses **cout**

```
    cout << "Enter length: ";
```

When this statement is executed,

```
    Enter length:
```

is written to the video display.

Next the program uses **cin**

```
cin >> foot;
```

to read from the standard input. When this statement is executed, the next value supplied from the keyboard by the user is read and stored in the variable **foot**.

The **cin** statement is followed by a statement that converts feet to inches:

```
inch = 12 * foot;
```

When this statement is executed, the product of 12 and the value of **foot** is stored in the variable **inch**.

When the next statement

```
cout << foot << " ft" << endl
     << inch << " in" << endl;
```

is executed, the value of the variable **foot** is written, a blank followed by **ft** is written, and an end-of-line is generated. For example, if the value of **foot** is 3,

```
3 ft
```

is written and the next output will begin flush left on the next line. Next, the value of the variable **inch** is written, a blank and **in** are written, and an end-of-line is generated.

After the converted values are output, the program ends with the statement

```
return 0;
```

1.5 OTHER INTEGER DATA TYPES

Besides **int**, C++ has nine other integer data types, which represent signed and unsigned types with varying ranges, and the truth values **true** and **false**. Assume that one byte is eight bits and two's complement representation is used (see Section 0.3). Figure 1.5.1 summarizes the integer data types.

Data Type	Range Includes	Typical Range
unsigned long	unsigned int	0 to 4,294,967,295
signed long	signed int	−2,147,483,648 to 2,147,483,647
unsigned int	unsigned short	0 to 4,294,967,295
signed int	signed short	−2,147,483,648 to 2,147,483,647
unsigned short	unsigned char	0 to 65,535
signed short	signed char	−32,768 to 32,767
unsigned char	—	0 to 255
signed char	—	−128 to 127
char	—	0 to 255 or −128 to 127
bool	—	**true** (nonzero), **false** (zero)

FIGURE 1.5.1 Integer data types and ranges.

Some data types can be abbreviated:

Data Type	Abbreviation
signed long	long
signed int	int
unsigned int	unsigned
signed short	short

The data type **char** is implemented as either **signed char** or **unsigned char**, but exactly which is system-dependent. So the **char** type should be used only when it does not matter whether the implementation is **signed** or **unsigned**. The typical use of **char** is to represent characters in ASCII or some other encoding. In ASCII encoding, characters are represented by integers ranging from 0 through 127 (see Section 0.3). For example,

Character	ASCII Encoding (Decimal)
!	33
%	37
4	52
A	65
a	97
z	122

With an 8-bit byte, a **char** can represent integers in the ASCII range of 0 through 127 regardless of whether a **char** is implemented as a **signed char** or an **unsigned char** on a particular system. (Appendix A gives the entire ASCII table.)

EXAMPLE 1.5.1.   Assuming ASCII encoding, the code segment

```
char c1 = 'A';  // initialize c1 to 65
```

stores the integer 65 in the cell

```
 65
```
c1

because 65 is the ASCII code for the character **A**. By the way, **sizeof(c1)** is 1 because a **char** cell is one byte on every system.   ∎

EXAMPLE 1.5.2.   The code segment

```
char c1 = 'A';     // 65 stored in c1
char c2 = c1 + 2;  // 67 stored in c2
cout << c1      // prints A
     << c2      // prints C
     << endl;
```

prints **A** and **C** to the standard output, given any reasonable character encoding. The integer representing **A** (e.g., 65 in ASCII encoding) is stored in **c1**. Assuming ASCII encoding, the expression

```
c1 + 2
```

evaluates to 67, the ASCII code for **c**.   ∎

It is critical to distinguish between *numbers* and the *characters* (called *numerals*) that are used to represent them.

EXAMPLE 1.5.3.   Assuming ASCII encoding, the code segment

```
char c1 = '3'; // numeral '3' is 51 in ASCII
```

allocates a **char** cell and stores 51 in it:

```
 51
 c1
```

By contrast, the code segment

```
char c2 = 3;
```

allocates a **char** cell and stores 3 in it:

```
 3
 c2
```

So the *character* **'3'** is altogether different from the *number* 3. In ASCII, the *number* 51 represents the *character* **'3'**.   ∎

Special Characters

C++ has symbols for special characters that impact output to a device such as a printer or video display. Here is a summary, with **c** of type **char**:

Value of **c**	Action from **cout << c**
'\a'	Bell rings.
'\b'	Move left 1 column (**b**ack).
'\f'	Move to line 1 and column 1 of next page (**f**orm feed).
'\n'	Move to column 1 of next line (**n**ewline).
'\t'	Move to next tab position (**t**ab).
'\0'	Output nothing (null character).
'\\'	Output a backslash \.
'\''	Output a single quote '.

`sizeof` Integer Data Types

In C++, we must talk about the *typical* range of an integer data type. There are two reasons. First, although the **sizeof** any **char** type must be 1 byte, the size of a byte is not standardized. Although a byte is 8 bits on most systems, it could be more or less than 8 bits. With the typical 8-bit byte, an **unsigned char** can represent values from 0 through 255. With a 16-bit byte, an **unsigned char** can represent values from 0 through 65,535. Second, the **short**, **int**, and **long** data types are defined *in relation to* the **char** types and to one another. So these types are not defined in absolute terms. For example, a **signed int** must include the range of a **signed short**. In most implementations, the range of a **signed int** *exceeds* the range of a **signed short**. Similarly, the range of an **unsigned long** must include the range of an **unsigned int**. On most desktop systems, however, an **unsigned long** and an **unsigned int** have the *same* range.

Bases for Integer Constants

C++ lets the programmer write integer constants in different bases (see Section 0.3). Here is a summary of how to write constants in different bases:

Base	Digits	Leftmost Symbol(s)
10 (decimal)	0–9	Must *not* be **0**.
8 (octal)	0–7	*Must* be **0**.
16 (hexadecimal)	0–**f**	*Must* be **0x** or **0X**.

Here are some examples:

Constant	Value in Decimal
27	27
033	27
0x1B	27

The hexadecimal digits

a,b,c,d,e,f

may be written in uppercase

A,B,C,D,E,F

The term *hexadecimal* is often abbreviated as *hex*.

The header file *climits* defines integer constants for the programmer's convenience (see Figure 1.5.2).

Constant	Interpretation
SCHAR_MIN	Smallest value of **signed char**
SCHAR_MAX	Largest value of **signed char**
UCHAR_MAX	Largest value of **unsigned char**
CHAR_MIN	Smallest value of **char**
CHAR_MAX	Largest value of **char**
SHRT_MIN	Smallest value of **signed short**
SHRT_MAX	Largest value of **signed short**
USHRT_MAX	Largest value of **unsigned short**
INT_MIN	Smallest value of **signed int**
INT_MAX	Largest value of **signed int**
UINT_MAX	Largest value of **unsigned int**
LONG_MIN	Smallest value of **signed long**
LONG_MAX	Largest value of **signed long**
ULONG_MAX	Largest value of **unsigned long**

FIGURE 1.5.2 Integer constants defined in *climits*.

Types of Integer Constants

C++ supports integer constants of different data types, signed or unsigned. An integer constant terminated by **l** or **L** is the first of the types

long, unsigned long

that can represent its value. Integer constants such as **561** (decimal) and **056L** (octal) illustrate the syntax.

An integer constant terminated by **u** or **U** is unsigned. For example, **56U** (decimal) and **0x56u** (hexadecimal) are unsigned integer constants. An unsigned integer constant's type is the first of

unsigned int, unsigned long

that can represent its value. Integer constants such as **56UL** or **65LU** are **unsigned long**.

If a *decimal* integer constant is *not* terminated by **u**, **U**, **l**, or **L**, the constant is the first of the types

int, long, unsigned long

that can represent its value. The integer constants **45612** and **-89** illustrate. If an *octal* or *hexadecimal* integer constant is *not* terminated by **u**, **U**, **l**, or **L**, the constant is the first of the types

int, unsigned int, long, unsigned long

that can represent its value. The integer constants **071** and **0x9876** illustrate.

The Data Type `bool`

The integer type `bool` represents the **bool**ean values `true` and `false`, which are also keywords. The `bool` value `false` has an integer value of 0, and the `bool` value `true` has an integer value of 1. For example, the output of the code segment

```
bool flag;
flag = ( 3 < 5 );
cout << flag << endl;
```

is 1. Since the expression `3 < 5` is true, `flag` is assigned the value `true`. By default, to signal `true` C++ outputs the integer value, 1. The `bool` type is particularly useful with the relational and logical operators that we will meet later in this chapter (Section 1.9).

Some compilers may not yet support the `bool` data type. In this case, it can still be used by adding the following three lines at the top of any file that uses `bool`, `true`, and `false`:

```
typedef unsigned bool; // see C++ Postscript for typedef
const bool true = 1;    // default value for true
const bool false = 0;   // false == zero
```

The C++ Postscript explains `typedef`.

EXERCISES

1. Write a definition for **unsigned char** variables `c1`, `c2`, and `c3`. Initialize `c1` to 66, `c2` to `'\n'`, and `c3` to 87.

2. Write a `cout` statement that outputs the three variables defined and initialized in Exercise 1. Assuming ASCII representation of characters, what is the output?

3. What are the main differences between the data types `int` and `char`?

4. Is the data type `char` always shorthand for **unsigned char**? Explain.

5. Is the data type `long` always shorthand for `signed long`?

6. Write a program that outputs the `sizeof` all the integer data types.

7. Assuming ASCII representation of characters, what is the output?

```
#include <iostream>
using namespace std;
int main() {
    char x = 90;
    cout << x << endl;
    return 0;
}
```

8. Assuming ASCII representation of characters, what is the output?

```
#include <iostream>
using namespace std;
int main() {
    int x = 90;
    cout << x << endl;
    return 0;
}
```

9. Assuming ASCII representation of characters, what is the output?

```
#include <iostream>
using namespace std;
int main() {
    char x = 122;
    cout << x << endl;
    return 0;
}
```

10. Assuming ASCII representation of characters, what is the output?

```
#include <iostream>
using namespace std;
int main() {
    int x = '7', y = 7;
    cout << x << ' '
        << y << endl;
    return 0;
}
```

11. Assuming ASCII representation of characters, what is the output?

```
#include <iostream>
using namespace std;
int main() {
    char x = '7', y = 7;
    cout << x << ' '
        << y << endl;
    return 0;
}
```

12. Write a definition for the **int** variable **x** and initialize **x** to 876 (decimal) as a hexadecimal constant.

13. Write a definition for the **int** variable **x** and initialize **x** to 876 (decimal) as an octal constant.

14. Could the range of an **int** *exceed* the range of a **long**?

15. Could the range of an **int** be the same as the range of a **long**?

16. What is the default integer value for **true**?

1.6 FLOATING-POINT DATA TYPES

C++ has three floating-point data types. Here are typical ranges and precisions:

Type	Typical Range (Absolute Value)	Typical Precision
float	0.0 and 10^{-38} to 10^{38}	6 digits
double	0.0 and 10^{-308} to 10^{308}	15 digits
long double	0.0 and 10^{-4932} to 10^{4932}	19 digits

Most implementations try to meet the IEEE floating-point standards (see Section 0.3). Nonetheless, the ranges and precisions given are *typical* and may differ from one system to another. C++ ensures only that **long double** includes all the values of **double**, which in turn includes all the values of **float**.

Floating-Point Constants

Floating-point constants are distinguished by a decimal point or by **scientific (exponential) notation**.

EXAMPLE 1.6.1. The code segment

```
float        f1 = 3.14,          // double constant
             f2 = -3.14F,        // float constant
             f3 = 3.14f;         // float constant
double       d1 = 3.14,          // double constant
             d2 = -3.14E-4,      // -0.000314 (double cons)
             d3 = -3.14e-4;      // ditto
long double ld1 = 887766.321L,   // long double constant
            ld2 = 8.8776321e+5L, // long double constant
            ld3 = -8.8776321E+5l; // long double constant
```

illustrates various representations of floating-point constants. Constants containing **e** or **E** are written in scientific (exponential) notation. (The meaning is the same whether **e** or **E** is used.) The integer following **e** or **E** gives the exponent for 10. For example, **736.901e15** represents 736.901×10^{15}, and **88.268842E-12** represents $88.268842 \times 10^{-12}$.

A floating-point constant defaults to a **double** unless **F**, **f**, **L**, or **l** occurs at the end. Accordingly, the compiler may issue a warning about the initialization

```
float f1 = 3.14;  // f1 is a float, 3.14 a double
```

because a **float** may not be able to represent all the values of a **double**. The compiler converts the **double** value to a **float**, which is then stored in the variable **f1**. In any reasonable implementation, the **double 3.14** converts without problem to the **float 3.14F**. Finally, the example shows that the floating-point types are signed. ■

The header file *cfloat* defines the constants shown in Figure 1.6.1. These constants specify ranges for the floating-point types on a particular system and, in this way, encourage portable C++ code.

Constant	Interpretation
FLT_DIG	Number of digits of precision for **float**
DBL_DIG	Number of digits of precision for **double**
LDBL_DIG	Number of digits of precision for **long double**
FLT_EPSILON	Smallest positive **float** x such that $1.0 + x \neq 1.0$
DBL_EPSILON	Smallest positive **double** x such that $1.0 + x \neq 1.0$
LDBL_EPSILON	Smallest positive **long double** x such that $1.0 + x \neq 1.0$
FLT_MAX	Largest value of **float**
DBL_MAX	Largest value of **double**
LDBL_MAX	Largest value of **long double**
FLT_MAX_10_EXP	Largest base 10 exponent allowed for **float**
DBL_MAX_10_EXP	Largest base 10 exponent allowed for **double**
LDBL_MAX_10_EXP	Largest base 10 exponent allowed for **longdouble**

FIGURE 1.6.1 Floating-point constants defined in *cfloat*.

EXERCISES

1. What is the data type of the constant **3.14**?

2. What is the data type of the constant **3.14L**?

3. Write 3.14 as a constant of type **float**.

4. Explain why the compiler might complain about this code segment:

```
float f = 999.99;
```

5. What is the relationship between **float** and **double** with respect to range and precision?

1.7 ARITHMETIC OPERATORS

C++ has the standard arithmetic operators:

Operation	Symbol	Syntax
Addition	+	x + y
Subtraction	–	x - y
Multiplication	*	x * y
Division	/	x / y
Modulus	%	x % y
Plus	+	+x
Minus	–	-x

The operations are legal on the integer and floating-point types, except for the modulus operation, which is legal on integers only. The modulus operator is used to compute the *remainder* of an integer division.

EXAMPLE 1.7.1. The code segment

```
cout << 8 % 3   // outputs 2
     << 8 % 4   // outputs 0
     << 8 % 5   // outputs 3
     << endl;
```

illustrates the modulus operator. The expression **8 % 3** evaluates to **2** because when 8 is divided by 3, the remainder is 2. The expression **8 % 4** evaluates to **0** because when 8 is divided by 4, the remainder is 0. The expression **8 % 5** evaluates to **3** because when 8 is divided by 5, the remainder is 3. ∎

Division of *positive* integers truncates the fractional part. For example, $15/4 = 3.75$, and when the fractional part is dropped, the result is 3. Thus the value of

```
15 / 4
```

is 3. Similarly, $3/5 = 0.60$, and when the fractional part is dropped, the result is 0. Thus the value of

```
3 / 5
```

is 0.

Division by zero is illegal. Accordingly, the code segment

```
int num1 = 7,
    num2 = 0;
cout << num1 / num2 << endl; //***** ERROR: division by zero
```

contains an error.

The result of dividing integers, one of which is negative, depends on the particular C++ implementation. Therefore, the value of an expression such as

```
-6 / 4
```

is system-dependent.

C++ does *not* have an exponential operator. The library function **pow** may be used for this operation. (Use of **pow** requires that the header file *cmath* be **#include**d.) The value of **pow(x, y)** is x^y.

EXAMPLE 1.7.2.   The code segment

```
cout << pow( 2, 3 )    // outputs 8
     << pow( 3, 2 )    // outputs 9
     << pow( 4, 10 )   // outputs 1048576
     << endl;
```

shows the values for three invocations of **pow**.   ∎

The addition operator and the plus operator use the same symbol in C++, namely, **+**. The subtraction operator and the minus operator also use the same symbol in C++, namely, **-**. To distinguish the two uses of **+** and **-**, we refer to the addition and subtraction operators as **binary operators**; and we refer to the plus and minus operators as **unary operators**. A binary operator has *two* operands, whereas a unary operator has *one* operand.

EXAMPLE 1.7.3.   The code segment

```
int x = 7,
    y = 2;
cout << x - y << endl   // binary -, 5 is output
     << -x     << endl   // unary -, -7 is output
     << endl;
```

illustrates the difference between the binary and the unary **-**.   ∎

Each arithmetic operator has a **precedence** that determines its order of evaluation in an unparenthesized expression. Figure 1.7.1 shows the precedence of C++ operators and the order in which operators with the same precedence are evaluated. Many of these operators are explained in later chapters.

EXAMPLE 1.7.4.   The value of the expression

```
2 * 3 + 4
```

is 10. The value of

```
4 + 3 * 2
```

Description	Operator	Associates from the	Precedence
Scope resolution	`::`	left	High
Function call	`()`	left	(Evaluated first)
Array subscript	`[ ]`	left	
Class indirection	`->`	left	
Class member	`.`	left	
Size in bytes	`sizeof`	right	
Incr/decr	`++ --`	right	
One's complement	`~`	right	
Unary not	`!`	right	
Address	`&`	right	
Dereference	`*`	right	
Unary plus	`+`	right	
Unary minus	`-`	right	
Storage allocation (single cell)	`new`	right	
Storage allocation (array)	`new[ ]`	right	
Free storage (single cell)	`delete`	right	
Free storage (array)	`delete[ ]`	right	
Member object selector	`.*`	left	
Member pointer selector	`->*`	left	
Multiplication	`*`	left	
Division	`/`	left	
Modulus	`%`	left	
Addition	`+`	left	
Subtraction	`-`	left	
Left shift	`<<`	left	
Right shift	`>>`	left	
Less than	`<`	left	
Less than or equal to	`<=`	left	
Greater than	`>`	left	
Greater than or equal to	`>=`	left	
Equal	`==`	left	
Not equal	`!=`	left	
Bitwise and	`&`	left	
Bitwise exclusive or	`^`	left	
Bitwise inclusive or	`|`	left	
Logical and	`&&`	left	
Logical or	`||`	left	
Conditional	`? :`	right	
Assignment	`= %= += -=`	right	
	`*= /= >>= <<=`		
	`&= ^= !=`		(Evaluated last)
Comma	`,`	left	Low

FIGURE 1.7.1 Precedence of C++ operators (operators between horizontal lines have the same precedence).

is also 10. The multiplication operator * has *higher precedence* than the addition operator +; therefore, 2 and 3 are multiplied *before* 4 is added. By contrast, the value of

```
2 * ( 3 + 4 )
```

or

```
( 4 + 3 ) * 2
```

is 14, because parentheses are used to ensure that the addition occurs before the multiplication.

The value of

```
6 / 3 * 2
```

is 4. Because the division operator / and the multiplication operator * have the *same* precedence, and because these operators associate left to right (see Figure 1.7.1), the division is done before the multiplication. By contrast, the value of

```
6 / ( 3 * 2 )
```

is 1, because parentheses are used to ensure that multiplication is done before the division. Similarly, the value of

```
2 - 3 + 4
```

is 3, whereas the value of

```
2 - ( 3 + 4 )
```

is −5.   ■

EXERCISES

In Exercises 1 through 4, express each number in exponential notation as used in C++.

1. 399481.772

2. −9987768791.19002

3. .00000000022815

4. −.00000005983

5. Is this code segment legal? If so, what is the output?

```
float f = 5678.987;
cout << f % 3 << endl;
```

1.8 SAMPLE APPLICATION: A MATH PUZZLE

Problem

Which is larger: e^{π} or π^{e}? The number e is the base of the natural logarithm and its value correct to 15 places is 2.718281828459045. The value of π correct to 15 places is 3.141592653589793. Notice that the answer to the puzzle is not immediately evident. Going from e^{π} to π^{e}, the base increases (from about 2.718 to about 3.141), which tends to make π^{e} larger, but the exponent decreases (from about 3.141 to 2.718), which tends to make π^{e} smaller. The puzzle is to figure out whether increasing the base or decreasing the exponent has the greater effect.

Sample Input/Output

```
Enter pi: 3.141592653589793
Enter e: 2.718281828459045
e to the pi = 23.140693
pi to the e = 22.459158
```

The output shows that e^{π} is larger than π^{e}.

Solution

We prompt the user to enter the values of π and e. We then compute e^{π} and π^{e} using the function **pow**. Recall (see Section 1.7) that C++ has no exponential operator, but that $\mathbf{x^y}$ can be computed using the function **pow**. The value of **pow(x,y)** is $\mathbf{x^y}$. To use the function **pow** we must include *cmath*.

C++ Implementation

```cpp
// This program prompts the user to enter
// the values of pi (= 3.1415...) and
// e (= 2.71828...). It then computes
// e to the pi and pi to the e so that
// the user can determine which is larger.
#include <iostream>
#include <cmath>
using namespace std;
main() {
    double pi, e;
    cout << "Enter pi: ";
    cin >> pi;
    cout << "Enter e: ";
    cin >> e;
    cout << "e to the pi = " << pow( e, pi ) << endl;
    cout << "pi to the e = " << pow( pi, e ) << endl;
    return 0;
}
```

Discussion

We use type **double** to improve the accuracy of the computations. Recall (see Section 1.6) that on most systems, **double** is accurate to about 15 places. By default, C++ systems display only six digits of precision. Thus we enter the values with 15 digits of precision and internally the computations are carried out using 15 digits of precision. Only six digits of precision are displayed on output, but this is enough to show that e^π is larger than π^e. Before computers and calculators, it was a challenging problem to determine which expression was larger.

Figure 1.8.1 lists some other useful mathematics functions. Complete descriptions of these functions may be found in Appendix C.

Function	Meaning	Function	Meaning
abs	Absolute value	floor	Floor
acos	Arccosine	log	$\log_e x$
asin	Arcsine	log10	$\log_{10} x$
atan	Arctangent	pow	x^y
atof	Convert string to **double**	rand	Generate a random number
atoi	Convert string to **int**	sin	Sine
atol	Convert string to **long**	sinh	Hyperbolic sine
ceil	Ceiling	sqrt	Square root
cos	Cosine	srand	Seed random number generator
cosh	Hyperbolic cosine	tan	Tangent
exp	e^x	tanh	Hyperbolic tangent

FIGURE 1.8.1 Some standard mathematics functions.

1.9 RELATIONAL AND LOGICAL OPERATORS

Relational and logical operators are used to construct relational and logical expressions that evaluate to either **true** or **false**. We look first at the relational operators and then at the logical operators.

Relational Operators

Relational operators can be used to compare integer and floating-point expressions. The six relational operators are described in Figure 1.9.1.

> **EXAMPLE 1.9.1.** Given
>
> ```
> int x = 3, y = 8;
> ```
>
> Figure 1.9.2 shows the values of various expressions involving **x** and **y**. ∎

Operator	Example	true if
==	x == y	x and y are equal
!=	x != y	x and y are not equal
>	x > y	x is greater than y
>=	x >= y	x is greater than or equal to y
<	x < y	x is less than y
<=	x <= y	x is less than or equal to y

FIGURE 1.9.1 The relational operators.

Expression	Value
x == y	false
x != y	true
x > y	false
x >= y	false
x < y	true
x <= y	true

FIGURE 1.9.2 Some relational expressions and their values.

EXAMPLE 1.9.2.   Care must be taken when using the equality operator on floating-point expressions (see Section 0.3). For example, given

```
double e1 = ( 1.0 / 3.0 ) * 2.5,  // roughly 0.833333
       e2 = 5.0 / 6.0;            // roughly 0.833333
```

on our system, the value of the expression

```
e1 == e2
```

is **false**!

A better check for equality would be

```
// is the difference within a threshold?
abs( e1 - e2 ) <= DBL_EPSILON
```

The function **abs** gives the absolute value of its argument (see Figure 1.8.1), and the constant **DBL_EPSILON** is defined in the header file *cfloat* (see Figure 1.6.1). On the same system, the value of the latter expression is **true**. ∎

In expressions involving a mix of relational and arithmetic operations, the *arithmetic* operations are performed *first*; that is, the arithmetic operators have higher precedence than the relational operators (see Figure 1.7.1).

Expression	Value
x < y + z	true
y == 2 * x + 3	false
z <= x + y	false
z > x	true
x != y	true

FIGURE 1.9.3 Values of expressions involving arithmetic and relational operators.

EXAMPLE 1.9.3.   Given

```
int x = 1, y = 4, z = 14;
```

Figure 1.9.3 shows some expressions and their values.

We examine the expression

```
y == 2 * x + 3
```

in detail. The arithmetic operations occur *before* the relational operation. So we first evaluate

```
2 * x + 3
```

Because ***** has a higher precedence than **+**, we evaluate **2 * x** first. Its value is 2 because **x**'s value is 1. We then do the addition, which gives us

```
y == 5
```

Because **y**'s value is 4, the equality expression evaluates to **false**. ∎

Character expressions can occur in relational expressions, with intuitive results.

EXAMPLE 1.9.4.   Assume ASCII encoding and the assignments

```
char c1 = 'f',   // 102 in ASCII
     c2 = 'z',   // 122 in ASCII
     c3 = 'B',   //  66 in ASCII
     c4 = 'Q';   //  81 in ASCII
```

Because **f** comes before **z** in ASCII encoding, the expression

```
c1 < c2 // lowercase comparison
```

evaluates to **true**. Similarly, the expressions

```
c4 > c3 // uppercase comparison
```

and

```
c4 < c1 // uppercase and lowercase comparison
```

are both **true**. ∎

Logical Operators

The three logical operators are

Operator	Name	Example	true *if*
&&	Conjunction	x && y	x and y are both **true**
||	Disjunction	x || y	x or y (or both) is **true**
!	Negation	!x	x is **false**

The following **truth table** illustrates how the logical operators *and* (**&&**), *or* (**||**), and *not* (**!**) may be used in expressions:

x	y	x && y	x || y	!x
true	true	true	true	false
true	false	false	true	false
false	true	false	true	true
false	false	false	false	true

Logical expressions built with the *not* operator **!** are **negations**, those built with the *and* operator **&&** are **conjunctions**, and those built with the *or* operator **||** are **disjunctions**. A **conjunct** is part of a conjunction, and a **disjunct** is part of a disjunction.

In expressions that contain a mix of logical and relational expressions, the rules are (see Figure 1.7.1)

- Logical *not* has higher precedence than the relational operators and the other logical operators.
- The relational operators have higher precedence than the binary logical operators, logical *and* (**&&**) and logical *or* (**||**).
- Logical *and* (**&&**) has higher precedence than logical *or* (**||**).

EXAMPLE 1.9.5.   Given the definitions and initializations

```
bool a = true,
     b = false,
     c = false;
```

here are some expressions and their values:

Expression	Value
a && !b	true
!a && b	false
a || b && c	true
a && b || c	false

Logical *not* has higher precedence than the binary logical operators; hence, logical *not* is evaluated first. Because **b** is **false**, **!b** is **true**. Therefore the expression **a && !b** becomes

```
true && true
```

and so, **a && !b** evaluates to **true**. Similarly, **!a && b** evaluates to **false**.

Logical *and* is evaluated before logical *or*, so the expression **a || b && c** is equivalent to

```
a || ( b && c )
```

Since **a** is **true**, the expression is **true** regardless of the value of **b && c** (which happens to be **false**).

The expression **a && b || c** is equivalent to

```
( a && b ) || c
```

Since **a** is **true** and **b** is **false**, the expression **a && b** is **false**. Thus the expression

```
( a && b ) || c
```

becomes

```
false || c
```

Since **c** is false, the expression becomes

```
false || false
```

which evaluates to **false**.   ■

C++ is efficient in evaluating conjunctions and disjunctions; that is, C++ evaluates a logical expression left to right and stops evaluating subexpressions as soon as the truth value of the expression is known. For example, in the expression

```
2 > 3 && 27 < 99
```

only the first conjunct

```
2 > 3
```

is evaluated. For a conjunction to be **true**, *all* conjuncts must be **true**. Because the first conjunct is **false**, the entire conjunction is **false** regardless of whether the second conjunct is **true** or **false**. Therefore, C++ does not evaluate the second conjunct. Similarly, in the expression

```
2 > 1 || 99 < 10
```

C++ evaluates only the first disjunct. A disjunction is **true** if *any* of its disjuncts is **true**. Because

```
2 > 1
```

is **true**, there is no need to evaluate the second disjunct.

EXAMPLE 1.9.6. The operators `>>` and `<<` are the bitwise shift operators (see the C++ Postscript section at the end of this chapter). Through *overloading*, which allows multiple uses of the same operator, C++ also uses these operators for input and output. Overloading will be dealt with in detail in Section 3.7 and Chapter 8. For now, we emphasize that an operator's precedence as given in Figure 1.7.1 cannot be changed, even if the operator is overloaded. For this reason, the statement

```
int x = 7, y = 10;
// ***** ERROR: << evaluated before <
cout << x < y << endl;
```

is in error because `<<` is evaluated before `<`. The error can be corrected by inserting parentheses:

```
int x = 7, y = 10;
cout << ( x < y ) << endl; // correct
```

The output is **1** (`true`). ∎

Numeric values may be converted to the `bool` values `true` and `false`—nonzero converts to `true`, and zero converts to `false`.

EXAMPLE 1.9.7. Given the definitions and initializations

```
int x = 123,   // true
    y = 0,     // false
    z = 999;   // true
```

here are some expressions and their values:

Expression	Value
`!y > x`	`false`
`z && x <= x`	`true`
`!x || !y == x && z`	`false`
`!y && x > y || !y`	`true`

Let us look closely at the evaluation of

```
!y && x > y || !y
```

Logical *not* has higher precedence than the relational operators and the binary logical operators; hence, logical *not* is evaluated first. Because `y` is 0 or `false`, `!y` is 1 or `true`. The expression therefore becomes

```
true && x > y || true
```

The relational operator `>` has a higher precedence than the binary logical operators, so

```
x > y
```

is evaluated next. Because **x** is 123 and **y** is 0, the expression evaluates to **true** and we have

```
true && true || true
```

Logical *and* is evaluated before logical *or*, so next we evaluate **true && true**. A conjunction is true if all of its conjuncts are true; hence, the expression is **true**. This gives us

```
true || true
```

A disjunction is **true** if any of its disjuncts is **true**; hence, the expression is **true**. ■

EXERCISES

1. What is the output of this code segment?

```
int x = 7, y = -999;
cout << ( x && y )     << endl
     << ( !x || y )    << endl
     << !( x || y )    << endl
     << !( !x && !y )  << endl
     << ( !y || y )    << endl;
```

2. What is the output of this code segment?

```
int x = 11, y = 4;
cout << ( x > y && !y )    << endl
     << ( x + y || y > x ) << endl
     << x * !y + y         << endl
     << !( x * y )         << endl
     << !y * y + 2         << endl;
```

3. What is the value of the expression

```
'z' >= 'f' >= 'a'
```

4. How many conjuncts need to be **true** for the conjunction to be **true**?

5. How many conjuncts need to be **false** for the conjunction to be **false**?

6. How many disjuncts need to be **true** for the disjunction to be **true**?

7. How many disjuncts need to be **false** for the disjunction to be **false**?

8. Explain the error.

```
int x = 7, y = 1;
cout << x && y << endl;
```

C++ POSTSCRIPT

Keywords

The C++ keywords are

and	continue	goto	public	try
and_eq	default	if	register	typedef
asm	delete	inline	reinterpret_cast	
auto	do	int	return	typeid
bitand	double	long	short	typename
bitor	dynamic_cast	mutable	signed	union
bool	else	namespace	sizeof	unsigned
break	enum	new	static	using
case	explicit	not	static_cast	virtual
catch	export	not_eq	struct	void
char	extern	operator	switch	volatile
class	false	or	template	wchar_t
compl	float	or_eq	this	while
const	for	private	throw	xor
const_cast	friend	protected	true	xor_eq

Old and New Header Files

The following table lists the old and new names of many common system header files. The old header files are used *without* the statement

```
using namespace std;
```

New	Old	New	Old
cassert	assert.h	cstddef	stddef.h
cctype	ctype.h	cstdlib	stdlib.h
cerrno	errno.h	cstring	string.h
cfloat	float.h	ctime	time.h
climits	limits.h	fstream	fstream.h
clocale	locale.h	iomanip	iomanip.h
cmath	math.h	iostream	iostream.h
csetjmp	setjmp.h	new	new.h
csignal	signal.h	typeinfo	typeinfo.h
cstdarg	stdarg.h		

The STL header files (see Chapter 10) *algorithm, deque, function, iterator, list, map, numeric, set, stack,* and *vector* must be **#include**d without *.h* and used with namespace **std**; for example,

```
#include <vector>
using namespace std;
```

typedef

The **typedef** statement can be used to **def**ine a data **typ**e.

> **EXAMPLE.** The code segment
>
> ```
> typedef unsigned flagType; // flagType an alias for unsigned
> flagType statusFlag;       // define a variable
> ```
>
> illustrates its use. This **typedef** makes **flagType** synonymous with **unsigned**. After the **typedef**, we refer to **flagType** as an **alias** for **unsigned**.
>
> The general form of a **typedef** is
>
> **typedef** *<data type>* *<alias>* **;**
>
> In our example, **unsigned** is the *data type* and **flagType** is the *alias*. ■

Bitwise Operations

C++ supports bitwise logical and shift operations on integer data types. There are four bitwise logical operators. Assume that **x** and **y** are of type **int**. The following table gives the names and illustrates the syntax of the bitwise operators:

Operator	Name	Syntax
~	Bitwise complement	~x
&	Bitwise and	x & y
|	Bitwise inclusive or	x | y
^	Bitwise exclusive or	x ^ y

We explain the operators with brief examples.

> **EXAMPLE.** Assuming that an **int** is 16 bits, the code segment
>
> ```
> int x = 6;
> ```
>
> initializes **x** to 6, which in binary is
>
> ```
> 0000000000000110
> ```
>
> The *bitwise* or *one's complement* of **x** is ~**x**, which in binary is
>
> ```
> 1111111111111001
> ```
>
> Assuming two's complement representation, the decimal value of ~**x** is −7, *not* −6. By contrast, the expression -**x** does evaluate to −6 in decimal. The operator ~ merely *complements* or *inverts* each bit in its operand. So the bitwise operator ~ is altogether different from the minus operator -. ■

C++ supports three logical operators for bits: the **bitwise and** operator **&**, the **bitwise or** operator **|**, and the **bitwise exclusive-or** operator **^**.

EXAMPLE. Given b_1 and b_2 as two bits, the following table defines the bitwise logical operators:

b_1	b_2	b_1 & b_2	b_1 | b_2	b_1 ^ b_2
1	1	1	1	0
1	0	0	1	1
0	1	0	1	1
0	0	0	0	0

The bitwise *and* of two bits is 1, if *both* are 1, and 0, if *either* is 0. The bitwise *or* of two bits is 1, if *either* is 1, and 0, if *both* are 0. The bitwise *exclusive-or* of two bits is 1, if the two *differ*, and 0, if the two are the same. ■

EXAMPLE. Assuming two's complement representation and 16-bit **int**s, here is a summary of the bitwise complement and the bitwise logical operations

```
int bitstr1 = 12,
    bitstr2 = -35;
```

Expression	Binary Value	Decimal Value
`bitstr1`	0000000000001100	12
`bitstr2`	1111111111011101	−35
`~bitstr1`	1111111111110011	−13
`~bitstr2`	0000000000100010	34
`bitstr1 & bitstr2`	0000000000001100	12
`~bitstr1 & bitstr2`	1111111111010001	−47
`~bitstr1 & ~bitstr2`	0000000000100010	34
`~( bitstr1 & bitstr2 )`	1111111111110011	−13
`bitstr1 | bitstr2`	1111111111011101	−35
`~( bitstr1 | bitstr2 )`	0000000000100010	34
`bitstr1 ^ bitstr2 )`	1111111111010001	−47
`~( bitstr1 ^ bitstr2 )`	0000000000101110	46

■

C++ also supports bitwise shift operations on integers. Assume that **x** is an **int**. Here are the shift operator names and the syntax for each.

Operator	Name	Syntax	Meaning
<<	Bitwise left shift	x << 4	Shift **x**'s bits 4 places left
>>	Bitwise right shift	x >> 4	Shift **x**'s bits 4 places right

Assuming a 16-bit **int** and the definition

```
int x = 'A';   // 65 in decimal
```

here is a summary of how the shift operations work.

Variable	Value	Shift	Value
x	0000000001000001	x << 3	0000001000001000
x	0000000001000001	x << 4	0000010000010000
x	0000000001000001	x >> 2	0000000000010000
x	0000000001000001	x >> 6	0000000000000001

In a *left* shift operation, C++ guarantees that the vacated positions in the bit string will be filled with 0s. So if we shift **x** three positions left, its rightmost three bits are guaranteed to be 0s. In a *right* shift operation, if the leftmost bit is 0, C++ guarantees that the vacated positions in the bit string will be filled with 0s. However, in a *right* shift operation, if the leftmost bit is 1, C++ does *not* guarantee the bit that will fill the vacated positions in the bit string. The leftmost bit of **x** is 0; therefore, if we shift **x** three positions right, its leftmost three bits will be 0s.

EXAMPLE.   Suppose that

```
int s = 0x7A4E; // 31,310 in decimal
```

Assume an 8-bit byte and a 16-bit **int** so that **s** requires two bytes of storage: one byte to hold the eight high-order bits **7A** and one byte to hold the eight low-order bits **4E**.
The following figures

```
7A4E          4E7A
```

depict two different ways in which **s**'s two bytes can be stored. In the left figure, the high-order bits come first. In the right figure, the low-order bits come first. Computers that store the high-order bits first are **big-endian** machines, and those that store the low-order bits first are **little-endian** machines. Most UNIX systems are big-endian, whereas most Windows systems are little-endian. (The terms come from Jonathan Swift's novel *Gulliver's Travels* in which a war breaks out over whether hard-boiled eggs should be opened at the big or the little end.)
Suppose that we need to import binary data from, say, a big-endian to a little-endian machine. We need to reverse the order of the high-order and the low-order bits. Bitwise shift operators can be used for this purpose. The code segment

```
int s = 0x7A4E,    // 31,310
    z,
    mask = 0x00FF; // 0000000011111111 in binary
z = ( ( s >> 8 ) & mask ) | ( s << 8 );
```

copies **s** into **z** but with the bytes swapped. The expression

```
s >> 8
```

shifts **s**'s bits eight positions (i.e., one byte) right. Applying bitwise *and* to the shifted **s** and **0x00FF**

```
( s >> 8 ) & mask // mask is 0000000011111111
```

ensures that zeros occupy **s**'s left byte. For example, if **s** is 7A4E, then the value of the preceding expression is 007A. Similarly, the expression

```
s << 8
```

shifts **s**'s bits eight positions left. C++ guarantees that zeros are used for padding in left shifts. So if **s** is 7A4E, then the left shift evaluates to 4E00. The two values are then bitwise **or**ed

```
007A | 4E00
```

to produce the value 4E7A that is assigned to **z**.   ■

enum

The keyword **enum** is used to created **enumerated types**, which can be tagged or untagged (anonymous).

> **EXAMPLE.**   The code segment
>
> ```
> typedef unsigned successFlag;
> enum { Failed, Succeeded };
> successFlag fileOpened = Failed;
> ```

illustrates an *untagged* or *anonymous* enumerated type. In this type, **Failed** is a symbolic constant with 0 as its value, and **Succeeded** is a symbolic constant with 1 as its value. Had **Succeeded** been the first value

```
enum { Succeeded = 1, Failed = 0 };
```

we would have initialized it to 1 and **Failed** to 0 because the first value defaults to 0, the second to 1, and so on.   ■

> **EXAMPLE.**   The code segment
>
> ```
> enum MaritalStatus { Single, Married, Divorced };
> MaritalStatus myStatus = Married,
>                 fergieStatus = Divorced;
> if ( myStatus == fergieStatus )
>   cout << "Our stars are crossed!" << endl;
> ```

illustrates a tagged enumerated type. In this example, **Single** defaults to 0, **Married** to 1, and **Divorced** to 2.   ■

COMMON PROGRAMMING ERRORS

1. To provide a proper interface to the keyboard and video display commands, the line

   ```
   #include <iostream>
   ```

   must appear before any keyboard input and video display output commands are used. Typically, such **#include** statements are placed at the top of the file.

2. In order to use standard features as shown in this chapter, the line

   ```
   using namespace std;
   ```

   must follow the **#include**d system files. Thus a program might begin

   ```
   #include <iostream>
   using namespace std;
   ```

3. It is an error to use an old-style, "dot h," header file with **using namespace std;**:

   ```
   // ***** ERROR: wrong header file for namespace std
   #include <iostream.h>
   using namespace std;
   ```

   The error is corrected by omitting **.h**

   ```
   #include <iostream>
   using namespace std; // Correct
   ```

   or, if an old-style header is to be used, by omitting **using namespace std;**

   ```
   #include <iostream.h> // Correct
   ```

4. The **main** function should contain a **return** statement. The statement

   ```
   return 0;
   ```

   in **main** indicates that the program terminates normally.

5. The operator **>>** is used with **cin**, *not* **<<**:

   ```
   cin << val;  // ***** ERROR *****
   cin >> val;  // CORRECT
   ```

6. Only one value can be read after **>>** in a **cin** statement. For example, the correct way to read a value into the variable **x** and then the next value into the variable **y** is

   ```
   cin >> x >> y;
   ```

   not

   ```
   cin >> x, y; // ***** ERROR *****
   ```

   or

   ```
   cin >> x y; // ***** ERROR *****
   ```

7. The operator `<<` is used with `cout`, *not* `>>`:

```
cout >> val;   // ***** ERROR *****
cout << val;   // CORRECT
```

8. Only one expression can be output after `<<` in a `cout` statement. For example, the correct way to output the value of the variable **x** followed by the value of the variable **y** is

```
cout << x << y;
```

not

```
cout << x, y; // ***** ERROR *****
```

or

```
cout << x y; // ***** ERROR *****
```

9. To assign the *character* zero to the variable **c**, we write

```
c = '0'; // character code for '0', 48 in ASCII
```

and not

```
c = 0; // number zero
```

10. Except for specially denoted characters such as `'\n'` and `'\a'`, which nonetheless represent just *one* character, only one symbol occurs between single quotation marks. A sequence such as `'lynn'` is an error.

11. The modulus operator `%` may be used only with *integers* as opposed to floating-point numbers.

12. Division of positive integers truncates the fractional part. For example, the value of `20 / 7` is 2, so if we write

```
float x = 20 / 7;
```

the value of **x** is 2.000000, not 2.857143.

13. The operator `<<` is evaluated before the relational, equality, logical, and assignment operators. For this reason, the statement

```
int n = 3, m = 2;
// ***** ERROR: << evaluated before <
cout << n < m << endl;
```

contains an error. The error can be corrected by inserting parentheses:

```
int n = 3, m = 2;
cout << ( n < m ) << endl; // correct
```

14. The logical *and* operator is **&&**, whereas the bitwise *and* operator is **&**. Both are *binary* operators that expect two operands. The *unary* operator **&** is the *address* operator (see Section 4.3).

15. The logical *or* operator is **| |**, whereas the bitwise *or* operator is **|**.

16. If a variable is defined *inside a function*, it is *not* initialized by the compiler. It is therefore an error to assume that such a variable contains some special value such as 0. For example, the program

```
#include <iostream>
using namespace std;
int main() {
  int x; // uninitialized
  cout << x << endl; // arbitrary value printed
  return 0;
}
```

prints an arbitrary value because **x** has not been initialized in its definition or later assigned a value.

PROGRAMMING EXERCISES

1.1. Write a program that prints

    The future's not what it used to be.

to the video display.

1.2. Write a program that prompts the user for a length in yards, converts the length to feet and inches, and outputs the original and converted lengths.

1.3. Write a program that prompts the user for two integers and outputs their sum.

1.4. Write a program that prompts the user for positive integers m and n and outputs m^n.

1.5. Write a program that prompts the user for a dry measure in bushels, converts it to quarts and pecks, and outputs the original and converted measures.

1.6. Write a program that outputs the values on your system of the constants given in Figure 1.5.2.

1.7. Write a program that determines which is larger: $\pi^{(\pi^e)}$ or $e^{(e^\pi)}$.

1.8. The mathematics function **sqrt(x)** gives the square root of **x**. Write a program that uses **sqrt** to output the square root of 2.

1.9. The mathematics function **exp(x)** gives the value of e^x. Write a program that uses **exp** to output the value of e.

1.10. The mathematics function **atan(x)** gives the value of the arctangent of **x** in radians. In particular, the value of **atan(1)** is $\frac{\pi}{4}$. Write a program that uses **atan** to output the value of π.

1.11. Write a program that outputs the values on your system of the constants given in Figure 1.6.1.

CHAPTER

2

CONTROL FLOW

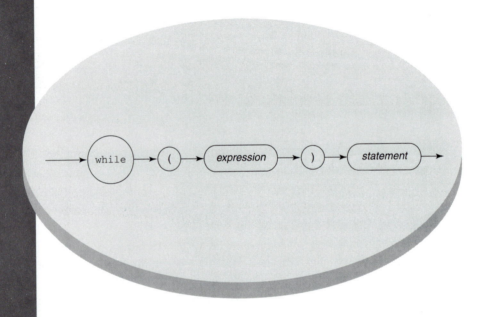

Sometimes the solution to a problem dictates that the program decide *while running* which statements to execute or to skip. For example, if a program is to check a test score and print a message as to whether the test-taker passed, a decision will have to be made while the program is running whether to print **Pass** or **Fail**. By using the relational and logical operators (see Section 1.9) and the **if-else** statement, such conditional decisions can be made.

The programs in Chapter 1 that execute each of their statements once are of limited usefulness. For example, the program of Section 1.4 that converts a single length from feet to inches would be more useful if the user could *repeatedly* enter lengths and have the program convert each to inches. We can use a *loop* to repeatedly execute a section of code.

In this chapter we introduce the **if-else** statement and loops (**while, do while,** and **for** loops). Such constructs are called **control structures** and are essential to writing useful programs. Control structures control the flow (i.e., the order of execution) of the statements.

In addition to control structures, we also discuss input from and output to disk files, the assignment operator in more detail, the increment and decrement operators, promotions and casts (used to convert one data type to another), and formatting (used to determine how input is interpreted and to control the appearance of output).

2.1 THE if-else STATEMENT

The **if-else** statement is used to execute a segment of code conditionally. One form of the **if-else** statement is

```
if ( expression )
    action1
else
    action2
```

When an **if-else** statement is executed (see Figure 2.1.1), *expression* is evaluated. If *expression* is true, *action1* is executed after which the statement immediately following *action2* is executed. In this case, *action2* is *not* executed. But if *expression* is false, *action1* is *not* executed; instead, *action2* is executed after which the statement immediately following it is executed. Each of *action1* and *action2* consists of one statement without braces or one or more statements enclosed in braces.

EXAMPLE 2.1.1. When the code segment

```
int code = 2;
if ( code != 2 ) {
    cout << "The water was too warm" << endl
        << "The waters were all fished out" << endl;
}
```

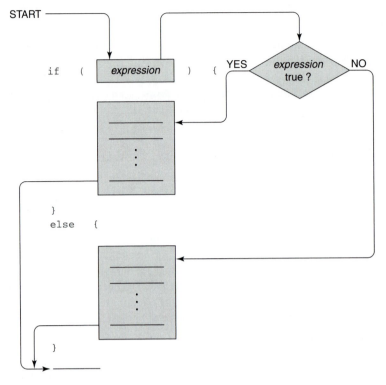

FIGURE 2.1.1 The `if-else` statement.

```
else {
    cout << "It was too late in the season" << endl
         << "The bait was wrong" << endl;
}
cout << "*** End of fishing excuses ***" << endl;
```

executes, the output is

```
It was too late in the season
The bait was wrong
*** End of fishing excuses ***
```

Since the expression `code != 2` is false, the statements enclosed in braces following `else` are executed. ∎

The `else` part of the `if-else` statement is optional. When

```
if ( expression )
    action
```

is executed, *expression* is evaluated. If *expression* is true, *action* is executed after which the statement immediately following it is executed. But if *expression* is false, *action* is *not* executed; instead, the statement immediately following it is executed.

EXAMPLE 2.1.2.   When the code segment

```
int code = 2;
if ( code != 2 ) {
   cout << "The water was too warm" << endl
        << "The waters were all fished out" << endl;
}
cout << "*** End of fishing excuses ***" << endl;
```

executes, the output is

```
*** End of fishing excuses ***
```
∎

Because **if-else** is itself a statement, one **if-else** statement can be the action of another **if-else** statement.

EXAMPLE 2.1.3.   The code segment

```
if ( no_fish == 1 )
   if ( code < 2 )
      cout << "The water was too warm" << endl;
   else
      cout << "The waters were all fished out" << endl;
```

is interpreted as one "outer" **if** statement with one action statement that happens to be an **if-else** statement. That is, this code segment is of the form

```
if ( no_fish == 1 )
   action
```

where *action* is the *single* statement

```
if ( code < 2 )
   cout << "The water was too warm" << endl;
else
   cout << "The waters were all fished out" << endl;
```

(An **if-else** statement is considered to be a single statement.)
When the code segment

```
int no_fish = 1, code = 2;
if ( no_fish == 1 )
   if ( code < 2 )
      cout << "The water was too warm" << endl;
   else
      cout << "The waters were all fished out" << endl;
cout << "*** End of fish story ***" << endl;
```

is executed, the output is

```
The waters were all fished out
*** End of fish story ***
```

Because **no_fish == 1** is true, the action part

```
if ( code < 2 )
   cout << "The water was too warm" << endl;
else
   cout << "The waters were all fished out" << endl;
```

of the first **if** statement is executed. Because the expression **code < 2** is false, the statement

```
cout << "The waters were all fished out" << endl;
```

following the **else** is executed. Finally, the statement

```
cout << "*** End of fish story ***" << endl;
```

is executed.   ■

EXAMPLE 2.1.4. The compiler is insensitive to indentation. Thus if we rewrite the code segment of Example 2.1.3 as

```
int no_fish = 1, code = 2;
if ( no_fish == 1 )
   if ( code < 2 )
      cout << "The water was too warm" << endl;
else
   cout << "The waters were all fished out" << endl;
cout << "*** End of fish story ***" << endl;
```

the output is still

```
The waters were all fished out
*** End of fish story ***
```

The indentation of the revised code segment implies that the programmer intended that if **no_fish == 1** is true,

```
if ( code < 2 )
   cout << "The water was too warm" << endl;
```

is to be executed; but if **no_fish == 1** is false,

```
cout << "The waters were all fished out" << endl;
```

is to be executed. To achieve this result, we must use braces and write

```
int no_fish = 1, code = 2;
if ( no_fish == 1 ) {
   if ( code < 2 )
      cout << "The water was too warm" << endl;
}
else
   cout << "The waters were all fished out" << endl;
cout << "*** End of fish story ***" << endl;
```

The output of this code segment is

```
*** End of fish story ***
```
                                                                                        ■

EXAMPLE 2.1.5.   When the code segment

```
int no_fish = 1;
if ( no_fish == 1 )
    cout << "The water was too warm" << endl;
else ;
    cout << "The waters were all fished out" << endl;
```

executes, the output is

```
The water was too warm
The waters were all fished out
```

The semicolon after **else** is probably a logical error. In any case, the **else** action statement consists of the semicolon all by itself:

```
;
```

The statement consisting of a single semicolon is called the **null statement**. When the null statement executes, nothing happens. Thus when the preceding code segment executes, since the condition **no_fish == 1** is true, the statement

```
cout << "The water was too warm" << endl;
```

between **if** and **else** executes. The action statement for the **else**, namely the null statement, is then skipped. The code segment concludes when

```
cout << "The waters were all fished out" << endl;
```

executes.   ■

By nesting **if-else** statements, we obtain a particularly useful multiway decision structure. Nested **if-else** statements are typically written

```
if ( expression_1 )
    action_1
else if ( expression_2 )
    action_2
else if ( expression_3 )
    action_3
...
else if ( expression_n )
    action_n
else
    default_action
```

When this construct is executed (see Figure 2.1.2), the various expressions are evaluated in order—first *expression_1*, then *expression_2*, and so on—until the first expression, if any, that evaluates to true is found. If *expression_i* is the first true expression, *action_i* is executed, after which the statement following *default_action* is executed. Only *action_i* is executed; all other *action*s are skipped. After the first true expression is found, none of the expressions that follow are evaluated. If no expression is true, *default_action* is executed, after which the statement following it is executed. In this case, only *default_action* is executed; all other *action*s are skipped.

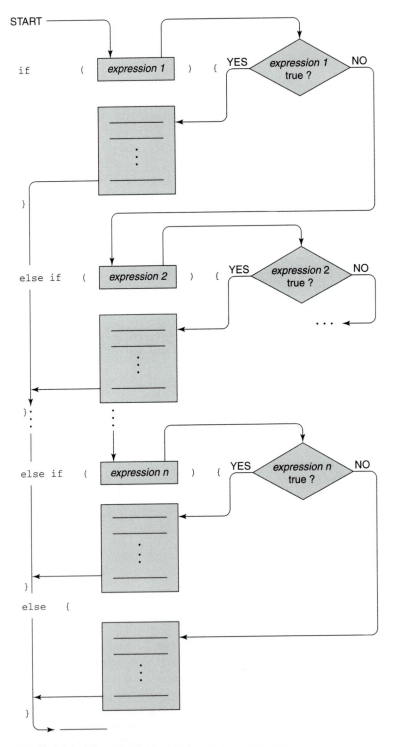

FIGURE 2.1.2 The **if else-if**... **else-if else** statement.

EXAMPLE 2.1.6.   When the code segment

```
int code = 2;
if ( code <= 1 )
   cout << "The bait was wrong" << endl;
else if ( code <= 2 )
   cout << "The water was too warm" << endl;
else if ( code <= 3 )
   cout << "The waters were all fished out" << endl;
else
   cout << "It was too late in the season" << endl;
cout << "*** End of fishing excuses ***" << endl;
```

is executed, the output is

```
The water was too warm
*** End of fishing excuses ***
```

because the first true expression is **code <= 2**. The statement

```
cout << "The waters were all fished out" << endl;
```

is *not* executed even though the expression **code <= 3** is also true. In fact, the expression **code <= 3** is not even evaluated. Only the action that follows the *first* true expression is executed. The code segment concludes when the statement

```
cout << "*** End of fishing excuses ***" << endl;
```

that follows the **if else-if** construct is executed.

If the statement

```
int code = 2;
```

is changed to

```
int code = 10;
```

the output is

```
It was too late in the season
*** End of fishing excuses ***
```                                                              ■

The

```
else
     default_action
```

part of the **if else-if** construct is optional. If

```
else
     default_action
```

is omitted and no expression is true, execution simply resumes with execution of the statement following *action_n*.

EXAMPLE 2.1.7.   When the code segment

```
int code = 10;
if ( code <= 1 )
    cout << "The bait was wrong" << endl;
else if ( code <= 2 )
    cout << "The water was too warm" << endl;
else if ( code <= 3 )
    cout << "The waters were all fished out" << endl;
cout << "*** End of fishing excuses ***" << endl;
```

is executed, the output is

*** End of fishing excuses ***   ■

By including a default action in an **if else-if** construct, we guarantee that *some* action is always executed. This fact is often useful in debugging programs and making programs crash resistant. Suppose that a programmer omits the default action because he or she is convinced that some expression following one of the **if**'s will always be true. When something goes wrong and no expression is true, no action is executed. It is easier to discover the problem if a default action is included that reports the problem.

EXERCISES

1. What is the output?

```
int x = 3, y = 5;
if ( x < 2 )
    cout << x << endl;
else
    cout << y << endl;
```

2. What is the output?

```
int x = 3, y = 5;
if ( x > 2 )
    cout << x << endl;
else
    cout << y << endl;
```

3. What is the output?

```
int x = 3, y = 5;
if ( x == 3 )
    cout << x << endl;
else ;
    cout << y << endl;
```

4. Where is the syntax error?

```
if x > 2
    cout << x << endl;
```

5. What is the output?

```
int code = 2;
if ( code == 1 ) {
   cout << "Mathematician" << endl;
   if ( code == 2 )
      cout << "Artist" << endl;
   else
      cout << "Computer Scientist" << endl;
}
else
   cout << "Public Relations Representative" << endl;
```

6. What is the output?

```
int code = 1;
if ( code == 1 ) {
   cout << "Mathematician" << endl;
   if ( code == 2 )
      cout << "Artist" << endl;
   else
      cout << "Computer Scientist" << endl;
}
else
   cout << "Public Relations Representative" << endl;
```

7. What is the output?

```
int x = 3;
if ( x < 2 )
   cout << x << endl;
else if ( x < 4 )
   cout << 2 * x << endl;
else if ( x < 6 )
   cout << 3 * x << endl;
else
   cout << 4 * x << endl;
```

8. What is the output?

```
int x = 6;
if ( x < 2 )
   cout << x << endl;
else if ( x < 4 )
   cout << 2 * x << endl;
else if ( x < 6 )
   cout << 3 * x << endl;
else
   cout << 4 * x << endl;
```

9. What is the output?

```
int i = 1;
if ( i == 1 )
    cout << "Code red" << endl;
else if ( i == 2 )
    cout << "Code yellow" << endl;
else if ( i == 3 )
    cout << "Code blue" << endl;
```

10. What is the output?

```
int i = 1;
if ( i == 1 )
    cout << "Code red" << endl;
if ( i == 2 )
    cout << "Code yellow" << endl;
if ( i == 3 )
    cout << "Code blue" << endl;
```

11. What is the output?

```
int i = 1;
if ( i == 1 )
    cout << "Code red" << endl;
else if ( i == 2 )
    cout << "Code yellow" << endl;
else if ( i == 3 )
    cout << "Code blue" << endl;
else
    cout << "Code undefined" << endl;
```

12. What is the output?

```
int i = 1;
if ( i == 1 )
    cout << "Code red" << endl;
if ( i == 2 )
    cout << "Code yellow" << endl;
if ( i == 3 )
    cout << "Code blue" << endl;
else
    cout << "Code undefined" << endl;
```

13. What is the output?

```
int i = 4;
if ( i == 1 )
    cout << "Code red" << endl;
else if ( i == 2 )
    cout << "Code yellow" << endl;
else if ( i == 3 )
    cout << "Code blue" << endl;
else
    cout << "Code undefined" << endl;
```

14. What is the output?

```
int i = 4;
if ( i == 1 )
    cout << "Code red" << endl;
if ( i == 2 )
    cout << "Code yellow" << endl;
if ( i == 3 )
    cout << "Code blue" << endl;
else
    cout << "Code undefined" << endl;
```

15. What is the output?

```
int i = 1;
if ( i <= 1 )
    cout << "Code red" << endl;
else if ( i <= 2 )
    cout << "Code yellow" << endl;
else
    cout << "Code undefined" << endl;
```

16. What is the output?

```
int i = 1;
if ( i <= 1 )
    cout << "Code red" << endl;
if ( i <= 2 )
    cout << "Code yellow" << endl;
else
    cout << "Code undefined" << endl;
```

17. What is the output?

```
int i = 4;
if ( i <= 1 )
    cout << "Code red" << endl;
else if ( i <= 2 )
    cout << "Code yellow" << endl;
else
    cout << "Code undefined" << endl;
```

18. What is the output?

```
int i = 4;
if ( i <= 1 )
    cout << "Code red" << endl;
if ( i <= 2 )
    cout << "Code yellow" << endl;
else
    cout << "Code undefined" << endl;
```

2.2 SAMPLE APPLICATION: COMPUTING TAXES

Problem

New Fredonia has a particularly simple system of taxation. Income under 6000 greenbacks (the basic unit of currency in New Fredonia) is taxed at 30 percent, and income greater than or equal to 6000 greenbacks is taxed at 60 percent. Write a program that reads an income as an integer and outputs the income and the tax due. Output the tax as an integer.

Sample Input/Output

We show two sample runs.

```
Income? 2904
Income = 2904 greenbacks
Tax = 871 greenbacks

Income? 32067
Income = 32067 greenbacks
Tax = 19240 greenbacks
```

Solution

After reading the income, we use an **if-else** statement to test whether the income is less than 6000. If the income is less than 6000, the tax is 30 percent of the income; but, if the income is greater than or equal to 6000, the tax is 60 percent of the income. We compute the income and then print the income and the tax.

C++ Implementation

```
// This program reads an income. Income under
// 6000 greenbacks is taxed at 30 percent, and
// income greater than or equal to 6000 greenbacks
// is taxed at 60 percent. After reading the
// income, the program prints the income and tax.
#include <iostream>
using namespace std;
const int cutoff = 6000;
const float rate1 = 0.3;
const float rate2 = 0.6;
int main() {
   int income, tax;
   cout << "Income? ";
   cin >> income;
   if ( income < cutoff )
      tax = rate1 * income;
   else
      tax = rate2 * income;
   cout << "Income = " << income
        << " greenbacks" << endl
        << "Tax = " << tax
        << " greenbacks" << endl;
   return 0;
}
```

Discussion

Instead of using the cutoff value (6000) and the tax rates (0.3 and 0.6) directly in the code, we define them as constants:

```
const int cutoff = 6000;
const float rate1 = 0.3;
const float rate2 = 0.6;
```

We could have written the expression in the **if-else** statement as

```
income < 6000
```

but it is better to avoid embedding numeric constants in programs. Instead, we define **cutoff** as the constant 6000

```
const int cutoff = 6000;
```

The keyword **const** means that after **cutoff** is initialized to 6000, it is not to be reassigned a value (even the value 6000 again) or to have its value changed. Then **cutoff** can be used anywhere instead of 6000. Similarly, **rate1** can be used anywhere instead of 0.3, and **rate2** can be used anywhere instead of 0.6.

There are several advantages to using constants. By using a well-chosen identifier, statements such as

```
income < cutoff
```

become self-documenting. Also, if the values of the constants are changed, all we need to do is change the value of the variables `cutoff`, `rate1`, and `rate2` in their definitions and recompile the program. We are spared the tedium of having to locate all the 6000s, 0.3s, and 0.6s in the program and change them to the new values. (Admittedly, in this program there is only one occurrence of each constant; but in large programs, constant values may occur many times.) If we use a numeric constant throughout a program and the value is changed, we would have to analyze the program's logic to decide at each occurrence of the numeric value whether to change it or not. (The same numeric value could have several different meanings.)

We define variables `income` and `tax` to store the income read and the computed tax

```
int income, tax;
```

After reading the income, we use an `if-else` statement to compute the tax

```
if ( income < cutoff )
    tax = rate1 * income;
else
    tax = rate2 * income;
```

If the condition

```
income < cutoff
```

is true, we execute the statement

```
tax = rate1 * income;
```

But if the condition

```
income < cutoff
```

is false, we execute the statement

```
tax = rate2 * income;
```

In either case, we correctly compute the tax.

In each of the statements

```
tax = rate1 * income;
```

and

```
tax = rate2 * income;
```

the result of the multiplication is a decimal number. However, because the result is assigned to the variable `tax`, which is of type `int`, the fractional part is truncated.

Variables such as `income` and `tax` are visible only within the function in which they are defined. When we discuss functions in detail in Chapter 3, we will see why, in general, it is a good idea to restrict the scope of variables to functions. On the other hand, constants usually need to be visible throughout the entire source file. Placing the definitions of constants outside of all functions at the top of the file (as is the case for `cutoff`, `rate1`, and `rate2`) makes them visible throughout the entire source file. We call such constants **global constants**.

2.3 THE while STATEMENT

The **while** statement has the form

> **while (** *expression* **)**
>   *action*

To execute a **while** statement (see Figure 2.3.1), we first determine whether *expression* is true or false. C++ requires that *expression* be enclosed in parentheses. If *expression* is true, we execute *action* and return to the top of the loop. We again test *expression*, and if *expression* is true, we execute *action* and return to the top of the loop. We repeat this process. But if at any time we are at the top of the loop and *expression* is false, we skip to the statement immediately following *action*. The part of the **while** loop that we have designated *action* consists of one statement without braces or one or more statements enclosed in braces.

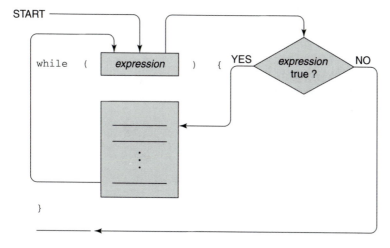

FIGURE 2.3.1 The **while** statement.

EXAMPLE 2.3.1.   When the code segment

```
int x = 0;
while ( x != 2 )
    x = x + 1;
cout << "x = " << x << endl;
```

is executed, the output is

```
x = 2
```

The statement

```
int x = 0;
```

defines and initializes **x** to 0. Since **!=** is the relational operator "not equal to," the expression **x != 2** evaluates to true; thus, we execute the statement

```
x = x + 1;
```

which adds 1 to **x**. We then return to the top of the loop. At this point, **x** is 1. The expression **x != 2** is true; thus, we again add 1 to **x** and return to the top of the loop. At this point, **x** is 2. The expression **x != 2** is now false; thus, we terminate the loop. We then execute the statement

```
cout << "x = " << x << endl;
```

which outputs

```
x = 2
```
■

EXERCISES

1. What is the output?

```
int x = 7;
while ( x >= 0 ) {
   cout << x << endl;
   x = x - 2;
}
```

2. What is the output?

```
int x = 7;
while ( x >= 0 ) {
   x = x - 2;
   cout << x << endl;
}
```

3. What is the output?

```
int x = 7;
while ( x >= 0 )
   x = x - 2;
cout << x << endl;
```

4. What is the output?

```
int x = 1;
while ( x == 1 ) {
   x = x - 1;
   cout << x << endl;
}
```

5. What is the output?

```
int x = 1;
while ( x == 1 )
    x = x - 1;
    cout << x << endl;
```

6. Where is the syntax error?

```
while x > 1 {
    x = x - 1;
    cout << x << endl;
}
```

2.4 SAMPLE APPLICATION: COMPUTING TAXES REVISITED

Problem

Revise the Sample Application of Section 2.2 so that the user can repeatedly enter an income. After each income is entered, the program outputs the income and the tax due. Assume that the user signals the end of input by entering a negative number.

Sample Input/Output

```
Income? 2904
Income = 2904 greenbacks
Tax = 871 greenbacks
Income? 32067
Income = 32067 greenbacks
Tax = 19240 greenbacks
Income? -1
```

Solution

To *repeatedly* input an income, we must use a *loop*—a **while** loop fills the bill. The key is to move the code from Section 2.2 that computes the tax, outputs the income and tax, and reads another income into the body of the **while** loop. The condition in the **while** loop is whether the income is greater than or equal to zero. In order to begin the process, we must ask the user to enter an income before entering the **while** loop.

C++ Implementation

```
// This program repeatedly reads an income. A
// negative number signals the end of input. Income
// under 6000 greenbacks is taxed at 30 percent, and
// income greater than or equal to 6000 greenbacks
// is taxed at 60 percent. After reading each
```

```
// income, the program prints the income and tax.
#include <iostream>
using namespace std;
const int cutoff = 6000;
const float rate1 = 0.3;
const float rate2 = 0.6;
int main() {
    int income, tax;
    cout << "Income? ";
    cin >> income;
    while ( income >= 0 ) {
        if ( income < cutoff )
            tax = rate1 * income;
        else
            tax = rate2 * income;
        cout << "Income = " << income
             << " greenbacks" << endl
             << "Tax = " << tax
             << " greenbacks" << endl
             << "Income? ";
        cin >> income;
    }
    return 0;
}
```

Discussion

After prompting the user for the first income and reading it

```
cout << "Income? ";
cin >> income;
```

we enter the **while** loop

```
while ( income >= 0 ) {
```

If the income is greater than or equal to zero, we execute the body of the loop where we use an **if-else** statement to check whether the income is above or below **cutoff** and compute the tax

```
if ( income < cutoff )
    tax = rate1 * income;
else
    tax = rate2 * income;
```

After outputting the income and tax, we prompt the user for another income, read it, and return to the top of the **while** loop where we check whether the income is greater than or equal to zero. Any time that the income is greater than or equal to zero, we again execute the body of the **while** loop. Any time that the income is negative, we skip to the statement after the body of the **while** loop

```
return 0;
```

that terminates the program.

2.5 FILES

So far, all of our programs have read from the keyboard and written to the video display. It is also possible to read from and write to (disk) files. The technique is to replace **cin** by a variable associated with an input file and to replace **cout** by a variable associated with an output file. We include *fstream* to use files.

EXAMPLE 2.5.1. The program in Figure 2.5.1 modifies the program of Section 2.4 so that it reads from the file *income.in* and writes to the file *tax.out*. Since the program reads from a file, the prompts are removed. Specifically, the program reads incomes from the file *income.in* and outputs the income and tax to the file *tax.out*. The program terminates when a negative integer is encountered.

Because the program in Figure 2.5.1 reads from and writes to files, the line

```
#include <fstream>
```

replaces the line

```
#include <iostream>
```

in the program of Section 2.4, which read from the keyboard and wrote to the video display. We do not need *iostream* because we do not write to the standard output or read from the standard input.

We must define a variable of type **ifstream** to read from a file, and we must declare a variable of type **ofstream** to write to a file:

```
ifstream infile;
ofstream outfile;
```

```
// This program repeatedly reads an income from
// the file income.in until a negative number
// is encountered. Income under 6000 greenbacks
// is taxed at 30 percent, and income greater
// than or equal to 6000 greenbacks is taxed
// at 60 percent. After reading each income,
// the program prints the income and tax.
#include <fstream>
using namespace std;
const int cutoff = 6000;
const float rate1 = 0.3;
const float rate2 = 0.6;
int main() {
   ifstream infile;
   ofstream outfile;
   infile.open( "income.in" );
   outfile.open( "tax.out" );
   int income, tax;
   infile >> income;
   while ( income >= 0 ) {
      if ( income < cutoff )
         tax = rate1 * income;
      else
         tax = rate2 * income;
      outfile << "Income = " << income
              << " greenbacks" << endl
              << "Tax = " << tax
              << " greenbacks" << endl;
      infile >> income;
   }
   infile.close();
   outfile.close();
   return 0;
}
```

FIGURE 2.5.1 A modification of the program of Section 2.4. This version reads from and writes to files.

After defining these variables, we open the files and associate each variable with the actual file to be read or written:

```
infile.open( "income.in" );
outfile.open( "tax.out" );
```

Thereafter in the program, the files are referenced by using the variables **infile** and **outfile**.

Except for the absence of prompts, the next section of code

```
infile >> income;
while ( income >= 0 ) {
   if ( income < cutoff )
      tax = rate1 * income;
   else
      tax = rate2 * income;
   outfile << "Income = " << income
           << " greenbacks" << endl
           << "Tax = " << tax
           << " greenbacks" << endl;
   infile >> income;
}
```

is essentially the same as that of Section 2.4; the output is formatted a bit differently, `cout` is replaced by `outfile`, and `cin` is replaced by `infile`.

Notice that the variables `income` and `tax` are defined after the statements

```
infile.open( "income.in" );
outfile.open( "tax.out" );
```

In C++, variables may be defined anywhere as long as they are defined before they are used. Some programmers prefer to define variables near the point at which they are first used in the program.

After the `while` loop, we close the files:

```
infile.close();
outfile.close();
```

If the variables `infile` and `outfile` go out of existence normally, as happens when the program terminates normally, the files will automatically be closed. However, it is good programming practice to close files when they are no longer used.

The program terminates with the usual

```
return 0;
```

statement.

The values in the file *income.in* may be entered in any desired format. All that is required is for at least one white space (blank, newline, tab) to separate consecutive values. By default, `<<` assumes that white space delimits the data. For example, *income.in* might be

```
2214 10500 31010 -1
```

In this case, after the program terminates, the file *tax.out* is

```
Income = 2214 greenbacks
Tax = 664 greenbacks
Income = 10500 greenbacks
Tax = 6299 greenbacks
Income = 31010 greenbacks
Tax = 18605 greenbacks
```

∎

Testing Whether Files Are Open

After opening a file, it is a good idea to check whether the file was successfully opened. If a file cannot be opened, a message to that effect should be output. In some situations, the only action possible after printing the message is to terminate the program.

After

```
ifstream infile;
infile.open( "scores.dat" );
```

if the file *scores.dat* has been successfully opened, the condition in the **if** statement

```
if ( infile )
   ...
```

is true. If the file cannot be opened, the condition is false. Similarly, if the file *scores.dat* has been successfully opened, the condition in the **if** statement

```
if ( !infile )
   ...
```

is false. If the file cannot be opened, the condition is true.

A program can be terminated anywhere by using the statement

```
exit( 0 );
```

Use of **exit** requires the header file *cstdlib*.

> **EXAMPLE 2.5.2.**   The following code segment attempts to open the input file *scores.dat*. If the file is not successfully opened, an informative message is output and the program is terminated.
>
> ```
> ifstream infile;
> infile.open( "scores.dat" );
> if ( !infile ) {
>    cout << "Unable to open scores.dat" << endl;
>    exit( 0 );
> }
> ```
> ■

Reading Until End-of-File

Suppose that the code segment

```
ifstream infile;
infile.open( "scores.dat" );
```

successfully opens the file *scores.dat*. Suppose further that **val** is a variable of type **int** and that we attempt to read an integer from *scores.dat*

```
infile >> val;
```

If a value is read into **val**, in an **if**-statement or in a loop condition, the expression

```
infile >> val
```

evaluates to **true**. If a value is not read into **val**, as might happen if all of the integers in **scores.dat** have been read, the expression evaluates to **false**. Thus the expression

```
infile >> val
```

can be used in an **if** statement or loop to test for end-of-file.

> **EXAMPLE 2.5.3.**   The code segment
>
> ```
> ifstream infile;
> ofstream outfile;
> infile.open( "scores.dat" );
> outfile.open( "scores.out" );
> int val;
> while ( infile >> val )
>   outfile << val << endl;
> ```
>
> writes the scores in *scores.dat* to *scores.out*, one per line, assuming that *scores.dat* and *scores.out* are successfully opened. ∎

> **EXAMPLE 2.5.4.**   The program in Figure 2.5.2 modifies the program of Figure 2.5.1 so that it reads from the file *incomes.in* until end-of-file. It also checks whether the input and output files are successfully opened. If either file cannot be opened, the program is terminated. ∎

Signaling End-of-File from the Keyboard

End-of-file can be signaled from the keyboard by typing a control character (control-Z on a PC or control-D in UNIX). The control character is typed by simultaneously holding down the control key (typically marked *Ctrl*) and some other key.

> **EXAMPLE 2.5.5.**   The program
>
> ```
> #include <iostream>
> #include <fstream>
> using namespace std;
> int main() {
>    int val;
>    ostream out;
>    out.open( "ints.out" );
>    while ( cin >> val )
>       out << val << endl;
>    return 0;
> }
> ```

```
// This program repeatedly reads an income from
// the file income.in until end-of-file.
// Income under 6000 greenbacks is taxed at 30
// percent, and income greater than or equal to
// 6000 greenbacks is taxed at 60 percent.
// After reading each income, the program
// outputs the income and tax to the file tax.out.
#include <iostream>
#include <fstream>
#include <cstdlib>
using namespace std;
const int cutoff = 6000;
const float rate1 = 0.3;
const float rate2 = 0.6;
int main() {
   ifstream infile;
   ofstream outfile;
   infile.open( "income.in" );
   outfile.open( "tax.out" );
   if ( !infile ) {
      cout << "Unable to open income.in" << endl;
      exit( 0 );
   }
   if ( !outfile ) {
      cout << "Unable to open tax.out" << endl;
      exit( 0 );
   }
   int income, tax;
   while ( infile >> income ) {
      if ( income < cutoff )
         tax = rate1 * income;
      else
         tax = rate2 * income;
      outfile << "Income = " << income
              << " greenbacks" << endl
              << "Tax = " << tax
              << " greenbacks" << endl;
   }
   infile.close();
   outfile.close();
   return 0;
}
```

FIGURE 2.5.2 A modification of the program of Figure 2.5.1. This version tests whether the files are successfully opened and reads input until end-of-file.

copies integers entered from the keyboard to the file *ints.out*, one per line. When the user signals end-of-file by typing a control character, the program ends. For example, if the user types

```
14 -50 13^Z
```

the file *ints.out* becomes

```
14
-50
13
```

After the user types the last number, 13, a control character is typed. On a PC, the control character is control-Z. When the user types this control character, the system displays ^Z to confirm that the control character was typed. ∎

EXERCISES

1. Write a program that reads lengths (assumed to be in yards) from the file *yard.in*, converts the lengths to feet and inches, and outputs the original and converted lengths to the file *length.out*. It is assumed that the lengths are nonnegative integers. The program terminates when it reads a negative integer.

2. Write a program that reads integers from the file *data.in* until it reads a negative integer. Assume that at least one nonnegative integer is in the file. The program outputs the sum of all the nonnegative integers to the file *nonneg.out*.

3. Redo Exercises 1 and 2, only read until end-of-file. Also, check whether the files were successfully opened.

2.6 THE do while STATEMENT

The **do while** statement is similar to the **while** statement; the main difference is that the expression controlling the loop is tested at the bottom of the loop. For this reason, the body of the loop is always executed at least once. The form of the **do while** statement is

```
do
    action
while ( expression );
```

To execute a **do while** statement (see Figure 2.6.1), we first execute *action*. We then determine whether *expression* is true or false. If *expression* is true, we return to the top of the loop and repeat this process. That is, we execute *action* and then determine whether *expression* is true or false. If *expression* is true, we return to the top of the loop. Any time we are at the bottom of the loop and *expression* is false, we skip to the statement immediately following **while (*expression*);**. The part of the **do while** loop that we have designated *action* consists of one statement without braces or one or more statements enclosed in braces.

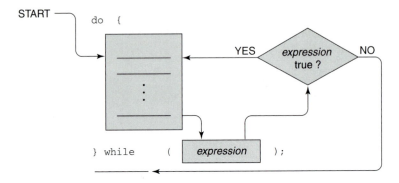

FIGURE 2.6.1 The `do while` statement.

EXAMPLE 2.6.1. The `do while` loop is useful whenever the test naturally occurs at the bottom of the loop, for example, verifying user input. In this situation, the user enters a value and *then* the input is checked. The following code segment asks the user for a positive integer and then checks for valid input. If the input is invalid, the user is prompted again to enter a value:

```
int response;
do {
    cout << "Enter a positive integer: ";
    cin >> response;
} while ( response <= 0 );
```

∎

EXERCISES

1. What is the output?

```
int x = 4;
do {
    x = x - 2;
    cout << "x = " << x << endl;
} while ( x >= 1 );
```

2. Rewrite the code segment of Example 2.6.1 using a `while` loop instead of a `do while` loop.

2.7 THE `for` STATEMENT

The `for` statement, like the `while` and `do while` statements, is used for looping, that is, for executing a code segment repeatedly. The `for` statement is particularly useful for a **counted loop**, that is, a loop that executes a predetermined number of times. The form of the `for` statement is

```
for ( expr1; expr2; expr3 )
    action
```

where typically

- *expr1* is used to initialize loop variables.
- *expr2* is used to test whether to execute *action*.
- *expr3* is used to update a loop counter.
- *action* is the loop body, that is, the statements executed in each loop iteration.

Figure 2.7.1 illustrates.

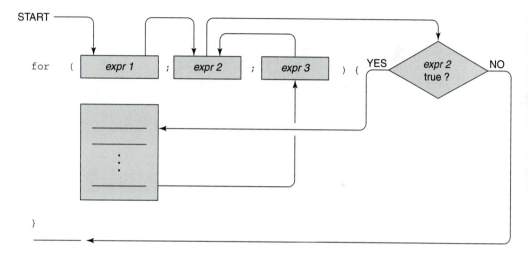

FIGURE 2.7.1 The **for** loop.

Assuming **i** has been defined as an **int** variable, a simple example of a **for** loop is

```
// output 0,1,2,...,7,8,9
for ( i = 0; i < 10; i = i + 1 )
   cout << i << endl;
```

In this case,

- *expr1* is **i = 0**.
- *expr2* is **i < 10**.
- *expr3* is **i = i + 1**.
- *action* is **cout << i << endl**.

When a **for** statement executes, *expr1* is evaluated once—at the beginning of the loop. If *expr1* is **i = 0**, then this assignment occurs just once and right before the looping begins. Next *expr2* is evaluated. If *expr2* is **true**, *action* executes. If *expr2* is **false**, the **for** loop terminates and execution resumes at the first statement after *action*. Assuming *expr2* is **i < 10**, *action* executes if **i**'s value is less than 10. Note that *expr2* is the loop's *test*; that is, the loop's *action* executes if and only if *expr2* evaluates to **true**. In effect, *expr2* tests whether any (more) looping should occur. If *expr2* is **true**, *action* executes. In our example, *action* is **cout << i << endl**, which outputs **i**'s value. After *action* executes, *expr3* evaluates. If *expr3* is **i = i + 1**, then *expr3* updates the loop counter. After *expr3* evaluates, *expr2* evaluates again. The loop cycle now becomes *expr2-action-expr3-expr2*.... This cycle can be described as a *test-action-update* process. The process continues until the test (*expr2*) is **false**, in which case execution resumes at the first statement after *action*.

As noted earlier, a loop's *action* is also called its **body**. A **for** loop's body consists of a *single* statement without braces or one or more statements enclosed in braces. It is always correct to enclose *any* loop's body, including a **for** loop's body, in braces, even if the body consists of just one statement.

It is common in a **for** loop to increment the controlling variable by one. Experienced C++ programmers would write **i++** to increment **i** rather than **i = i + 1**, although each has the same effect—**i**'s value is increased by one. We discuss the increment operator **++** in detail in the next section.

EXAMPLE 2.7.1.   The code segment

```
int i, sum = 0;
for ( i = 0; i < 100; i++ )  {
   sum = sum + i;
   cout << i << endl;
}
cout << "Sum == " << sum << endl;
```

illustrates a loop whose body consists of two statements, which therefore must be enclosed in braces. When the loop test **i < 100** evaluates to **false**, execution resumes at the second **cout** statement, which outputs the sum of the integers 0, 1, ..., 99. We use the expression **i++** to increment **i**.   ∎

EXAMPLE 2.7.2.   A **for** loop such as

```
for ( int i = 0; i < 100; i++ ) // i defined here
   cout << i + 1 << endl; // 1,2,...,99,100
```

may be simulated by a **while** loop such as

```
int i = 0;  // loop counter initialization
while ( i < 100 ) {  // loop test
   cout << i + 1 << endl; // for loop's body
   i++;                    // loop counter update
}
```

By the way, the loop counter **i** may be *defined* in the first expression of the **for** loop, as the example shows.   ∎

EXAMPLE 2.7.3. The code segment

```
for ( int i = 0, int j = 100; i < 100; i++ ) {
   cout << i + j << endl;
   j = j - 10;
}
```

illustrates that a **for** loop's initialization may contain multiple items

```
int i = 0, int j = 100
```

separated by commas. So *expr1* may consist of multiple C++ expressions as long as they are separated by commas. Each C++ expression in *expr1* is executed exactly once in left to right order and before the looping begins with the evaluation of the test expression *expr2*.   ∎

In a **for** loop

for (*expr1*; *expr2*; *expr3*)
   action

any of *expr1*, *expr2*, and *expr3* may be omitted, although the two semicolons *must* be present. For example, the code segment

```
for ( int i = 0; i < 7; ) { // expr3 missing
  cout << i << endl;
  i++;
}
```

omits *expr3*, the update expression. If the test expression *expr2* is missing, it is regarded as **true**. For example, the code segment

```
for ( ; ; ) // infinite loop
   ;
```

is an *infinite* loop because its test always evaluates to **true**. Note that this loop's body consists of the null statement, which does nothing; so, this infinite loop does no useful work whatever.

EXERCISES

1. What is the output?

```
for ( int i = 1; i <= 5; cout << i << endl )
   i++;
```

2. What is the output?

```
for ( int i = 0; i < 20; i++ ) {
   cout << i << endl;
   i = i + 2;
}
```

3. What is the output?

```
for ( int i = 0; i < 5; i++ );
    cout << i << endl;
```

4. What is the syntax error?

```
for ( int i = 0, i < 5, i++ )
    cout << i << endl;
```

2.8 ASSIGNMENT, INCREMENT, AND DECREMENT OPERATORS

C++ has various assignment operators. The basic assignment operator is **=**.

EXAMPLE 2.8.1. The code segment

```
int x;
x = 3;
x = 9;
```

uses the assignment operator twice. In the first assignment, 3 is stored in **x**

x

In the second assignment, 9 is stored in **x**

x

Note that an assignment operation *overwrites* the cell; that is, an assignment *replaces* a cell's *current* value (e.g., 3) with the assigned value (e.g., 9). ∎

C++ has special operators that combine assignment with arithmetic operations.

EXAMPLE 2.8.2. The code segment

```
int x = 1;
x = x + 3;
```

initializes **x** to 1 and then assigns to **x** its current value incremented by 3. After the two operations, **x** has 4 as its value:

x

There is a shortcut to this kind of operation. The code segment

```
int x = 1;
x += 3; // increment x by 3
```

illustrates. The expression **x += 3** assigns to **x** its *current value* (i.e., 1) incremented by 3. ∎

In general, if *op* is either a binary arithmetic operator or a bitwise operator, the expression

   x *op=* **y**

is equivalent to

   x = x *op* **(y)**

Other than the bitwise operators, the special operators that combine assignment with arithmetic operations are

   +=, -=, *=, /=, %=

The operators *op=* have the same precedence as the assignment operator **=** (see Figure 1.7.1).

EXAMPLE 2.8.3. Given the definitions and initializations

   int x = 2, y = 3, z = 4;

the statement

   x *= y + z;

is equivalent to

   x = x * (y + z);

The result, using either version, is the assignment of 14 to **x**. We can think of

   x *= y + z;

as saying "multiply the current value of **x** by **y + z**." ∎

EXAMPLE 2.8.4. Assuming that **x** is an **int** variable, the following table illustrates assignment operations:

x*'s Value Before*	*Expression*	**x***'s Value After*
6	**x = 3**	3
6	**x += 3**	9
6	**x -= 3**	3
6	**x *= 3**	18
6	**x /= 3**	2
6	**x %= 3**	0

Except for **%=**, these assignment operations are also legal on floating-point types. ∎

Assignment Expressions

In C++, the assignment operator = assigns a value to a variable. For example, the code segment

```
int x, y = 6;
x = y; // assignment
```

assigns the value of **y**, which is 6, to **x**. However, in C++, the *expression* **x = y** also has a value—namely, the value assigned (see Figure 2.8.1). The value of the expression **x = y** is therefore 6, the value assigned.

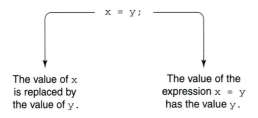

The value of x   The value of the
is replaced by   expression x = y
the value of y.   has the value y.

FIGURE 2.8.1 An assignment expression.

EXAMPLE 2.8.5. In the code segment

```
int x, y, z = 10;
x = ( y = z ); // cascaded assignment
```

the parentheses make it clear that we first evaluate the expression

```
y = z
```

Thus we first assign 10, the value of **z**, to **y**. Because the expression **y = z** has the value 10, the right-hand side of the assignment expression

```
x = ...
```

is 10. Therefore, **x** is also assigned the value 10.   ■

The parentheses in Example 2.8.5 are unnecessary. The statement

```
x = ( y = z );
```

is the same as

```
x = y = z;
```

because the assignment operator associates from the right (see Figure 1.7.1). The effect of

```
x1 = x2 = x3 = ... = xn;
```

is to assign the value of **xn** to **x1** and **x2** and **x3** ....

EXAMPLE 2.8.6.   In the code segment

```
int x = 2;
cout << ( x *= 7 ) << endl;
```

the output is 14, the value of the assignment expression

```
x *= 7
```

After the statement executes, **x**'s value is 14.   ■

It is easy in C++ to use the assignment operator = by mistake when the equality operator == is intended.

EXAMPLE 2.8.7.   The code segment

```
int x = 99, y = 33;
if ( x = y ) //*** meant to say x == y
   cout << x << " equals " << y << endl;
```

illustrates the problem. The assignment expression

```
x = y
```

assigns **y**'s value of 33 to **x**. Because 33 is nonzero, the **if** condition is **true** and the output is

```
33 equals 33
```

Indeed, the assignment ensures that **x** has the same value as **y**. Of course, we meant to write

```
if ( x == y )
```
■

The Assignment Operator = and the Equality Operator ==

The programmer can use the C++ compiler as an ally in trying to prevent inadvertent use of = when == is intended. Consider the comparison of a variable and a constant:

```
if ( x == 0 ) // constant is right-hand side
```

If = is mistakenly used instead

```
if ( x = 0 ) // legal, but unintended
```

no compiler error results because the code is syntactically legal. However, in the equality expression

```
if ( 0 == x )   // constant is left-hand side
```

the constant now occurs on the *left*. If = is mistakenly used instead of ==

```
if ( 0 = x )   //**** ERROR
```

104 CHAPTER 2 / CONTROL FLOW

the compiler issues an error because a constant is not a legal **lvalue**. An lvalue is the target of an assignment, increment, or decrement operation. (The next subsection explains increment and decrement operations). For example, in the code segment

```
int x;
x = 26;
```

variable **x** is the target of an assignment statement and is therefore an lvalue. The *l* in *lvalue* stands for *left* because, in an assignment expression, the target occurs on the left-hand side. An **rvalue** is the *source* of an assignment expression. In the code segment above, 26 is the rvalue. For safety, comparisons involving a constant should have the constant on the left side precisely because a constant is not a legal lvalue.

Increment and Decrement Operators

C++ has four operators used for incrementing and decrementing a variable's value. The **preincrement** and **postincrement** operators increment a variable's value, and the **predecrement** and **postdecrement** operators decrement a variable's value. We clarify with a series of examples.

EXAMPLE 2.8.8. The code segment

```
int x = 3;
cout << ++x << endl; // outputs 4
```

illustrates the preincrement operator. The expression **++x**

- Increments **x** by 1.

- Evaluates to the *incremented* **x**, that is, to 4.

Figure 2.8.2 illustrates. Because **++x** evaluates to the *incremented* **x**, the output is 4. ∎

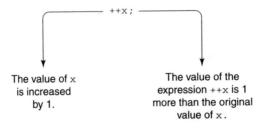

The value of x is increased by 1.　　　The value of the expression ++x is 1 more than the original value of x.

FIGURE 2.8.2 The preincrement operator.

EXAMPLE 2.8.9.   The code segment

```
int x = 3;
cout << x++ << endl; // outputs 3
cout << x << endl;   // outputs 4
```

illustrates the postincrement operator. The expression **x++**

- Increments **x** by 1.

- Evaluates to the *original* **x**, that is, to 3.

Figure 2.8.3 illustrates. Because **x++** evaluates to the *original* **x**, the first output is 3. The second output is 4 because **x++** in the first **cout** statement does increment **x**.   ∎

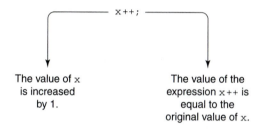

The value of x
is increased
by 1.

The value of the
expression x++ is
equal to the
original value of x.

FIGURE 2.8.3 The postincrement operator.

The expressions **++x** and **x++** both increment **x**. They differ only in their *evaluation*. The expression **++x** evaluates to the incremented **x**, whereas the expression **x++** evaluates to the original **x**.

The decrement operator **--** works similarly to the increment operator **++**, except that it decrements (i.e., subtracts 1 from) the variable. The decrement operator also comes in two forms: the predecrement operator and the postdecrement operator.

EXAMPLE 2.8.10.   The code segment

```
int x = 3;
cout << x-- << endl; // outputs 3
cout << x << endl;   // outputs 2
x = 3;
cout << --x << endl; // outputs 2
cout << x << endl;   // outputs 2
```

illustrates the postdecrement and predecrement operators.   ∎

The increment and decrement operators typically are used to manipulate loop counters and array indexes (see Chapter 4).

EXAMPLE 2.8.11. The code segment

```
unsigned i = 0;
while ( ++i <= 100 )
   cout << i << endl; // 1,2,...,99,100
```

illustrates the use of the preincrement operator to update the loop counter **i**. ■

EXERCISES

1. What is the output?

```
int x = 9;
cout << ( x = 9 ) << endl
     << ( x += 13 ) << endl
     << x << endl;
```

2. What is the output?

```
int x = 9, y = 14;
if ( x = y )
   cout << "x == y" << endl;
else
   cout << "x != y" << endl;
```

3. What is the output?

```
int z = -45;
cout << z + 1 << endl;
cout << ( z *= 2 ) < endl;
cout << z << endl;
```

4. Does this code segment contain an error?

```
int x = 7;
if ( 0 = x )
   ...
```

5. What is the output?

```
int x = 4;
cout << x++ << endl
     << x << endl
     << ++x << endl
     << --x << endl
     << x-- << endl
     << x << endl;
```

2.9 SAMPLE APPLICATION: STATISTICAL MEASURES

Problem

Read floating-point numbers from the standard input until end-of-file, and print a statistical report that includes the largest and smallest values read, the sum of all values, their mean, population variance, and standard deviation. The population variance measures the spread of the values and is given by the formula

$$\frac{\sum_{i=1}^{n} x_i^2}{n} - \bar{x}^2$$

where $\bar{x}$ is the mean of the n values $x_1, x_2, \ldots, x_n$ read. The standard deviation is the square root of the variance.

Sample Input/Output

If the input is

```
3.1 77.6 19.2 54.9 18.6^Z
```

the output is

```
Statistical summary:
    5 numbers read.
    Maximum:  77.6
    Minimum:  3.1
    Sum:      173.4
    Mean:     34.68
    Variance: 749.293
    StdDev:   27.3732
```

After the last value, 18.6, is input, end-of-file is signaled from the standard input on a PC by typing control-Z, which causes ^Z to be output.

Solution

After reading a value from the standard input, the program

1. Counts it.
2. If it is larger than any value so far, records it as the new maximum.
3. If it is smaller than any value so far, records it as the new minimum.
4. Updates the sum of all values read.
5. Updates the sum of squares of all values read.

Once all values have been read, the program computes the mean, variance, and standard deviation. The program outputs a report before exiting.

C++ Implementation

```
#include <iostream>
#include <cmath>
#include <cfloat>
using namespace std;
/** The program reads floating-point numbers from the
    standard input and prints a statistical summary that
    includes the largest value input, the smallest value
    input, the sum of all values input, the mean,
    population variance, and standard deviation. **/
int main() {
    float next,    // next value from standard input
          min,     // minimum value
          max,     // maximum value
          mean,    // average of all values
          sum,     // sum of all values
          sumSqr,  // sum of squares of all values,
          var;     // variance of all values
    unsigned count = 0;
    min = FLT_MAX;
    max = FLT_MIN;
    sum = sumSqr = 0.0F;
    // loop until standard input is empty
    while ( cin >> next ) {
        if ( next > max ) // new maximum?
          max = next;
        if ( next < min ) // new minimum?
          min = next;
        sum += next;              // running sum
        sumSqr += next * next; // sum of squares
        count++;
    }
    mean = sum / count;
    var = sumSqr / count - mean * mean;
    // output results
    cout << "Statistical summary:" << endl;
    cout << '\t' << count << " numbers read." << endl;
    cout << '\t' << "  Maximum:  " << max << endl;
    cout << '\t' << "  Minimum:  " << min << endl;
    cout << '\t' << "  Sum:      " << sum << endl;
    cout << '\t' << "  Mean:     " << mean << endl;
    cout << '\t' << "  Variance: " << var << endl;
    cout << '\t' << "  StdDev:   " << sqrt( var ) << endl;
    return 0;
}
```

Discussion

The variables **min** and **max** are to hold the smallest and largest values, respectively, read from the standard input. We initialize **min** to the constant **FLT_MAX** to ensure that no larger value is read. Of course, it is likely that smaller values will be read. Each time a value is read, we check whether it is smaller than **min** and, if so, we reset **min**. A similar tactic is used for **max**. The constants **FLT_MIN** and **FLT_MAX** are defined in the header file *cfloat* (see Figure 1.6.1).

The **while** loop reads numbers until end-of-file. After each number is read, it updates the maximum, minimum, sum, sum of squares, and count.

The statistical summary uses the library function **sqrt** to compute the standard deviation, which is the square root of the variance. To use this function, we must **#include** the header file *cmath*.

EXERCISES

1. Can we replace the code segment

```
if ( next > max )
  max = next;
if ( next < min )
  min = next;
```

by the code segment

```
if ( next > max )
  max = next;
else
  min = next;
```

2.10 THE **break, continue,** AND **switch** STATEMENTS

The **break** and **continue** statements alter the normal flow of control in loop or **switch** statements. The **switch** statement is an alternative to the **if else-if**... statement when the code to be executed is determined by an integer value. We begin with the **break** and **continue** statements and conclude with the **switch** statement.

The **break** Statement

The **break** statement causes an immediate exit from a loop or a **switch** statement.

EXAMPLE 2.10.1. The code segment

```cpp
unsigned next;
while ( true ) {  // loop indefinitely perhaps
  cin >> next; // read next integer
  if ( 0 == next ) // a zero?
    break;          // if so, exit loop
  cout << next << endl; // otherwise, output integer
}
cout << "0 broke us out of the loop!" << endl;
```

illustrates the syntax and a typical use of a **break**. Were it not for the **break**, the loop would be infinite because the loop condition is always **true**. However, if 0 is read from the standard input, then

```cpp
0 == next
```

is **true** and the **break** is executed. Executing the **break** transfers control to the first statement beyond the loop's body, that is, to

```cpp
cout << "0 broke us out of the loop!" << endl;
```
                                                                              ∎

The `continue` Statement

In a **while** or **do while** loop, the **continue** statement causes an immediate jump to the loop test. In a **for** loop, the **continue** statement causes an immediate jump to the update expression *expr3*.

EXAMPLE 2.10.2.   The code segment

```cpp
unsigned next;
while ( true ) {  // loop indefinitely perhaps
  cin >> next; // read next integer
  if ( next < 0 ) // negative?
    break;          // if so, exit loop
  if ( next % 2 )  // odd number?
    continue;       // if so, jump to loop test
  cout << next << endl; // otherwise, output even integer
}
cout << "negative broke us out of the loop!" << endl;
```

again uses a **break** to exit a potentially infinite loop (see Example 2.10.1). It also uses a **continue** statement to ignore odd numbers. The **if** condition

```cpp
if ( next % 2 )
```

evaluates to **false**, if **next** is even, and to **true**, if **next** is odd. If **next** is odd, the **continue** statement is therefore executed, which causes control to jump immediately to the loop test

```cpp
while ( true )
```

So the loop outputs only nonnegative, even integers.   ∎

The **switch** Statement

The **switch** statement provides an alternative to a construct such as

```
if ( ... )
  ...
else if ( ... )
  ...
else
  ...
```

EXAMPLE 2.10.3. Assume that **filing_code** is a **char** variable. The code segment

```
if ( 'S' == filing_code ) // Single?
  cout << "Single taxpayer" << endl;
else if ( 'M' == filing_code ) // Married?
  cout << "Married taxpayer" << endl;
else if ( 'H' == filing_code ) // Head of household?
  cout << "Head-of-household taxpayer" << endl;
else
  cout << filing_code << " must be S, M, or H." << endl;
```

tests whether **filing_code** is **S**, **M**, **H**, or none of these. The equivalent **switch** statement is

```
switch ( filing_code ) {
case 'S':
  cout << "Single taxpayer" << endl;
  break;
case 'M':
  cout << "Married taxpayer" << endl;
  break;
case 'H':
  cout << "Head-of-household taxpayer" << endl;
  break;
default:
  cout << filing_code << " must be S, M, or H." << endl;
  break;
}
```

The **switch** condition

```
switch ( filing_code ) {
```

evaluates an integer expression such as **filing_code**. Control then jumps to the corresponding **case**, if any. For example, if **filing_code** evaluates to **'M'**, then control jumps to **case 'M':** and the output is

```
Married taxpayer
```

If no **case** matches the **switch** expression, then control jumps to the **default**. If there is no **default**, control simply exits the **switch** construct. Figure 2.10.1 illustrates the **switch** statement.

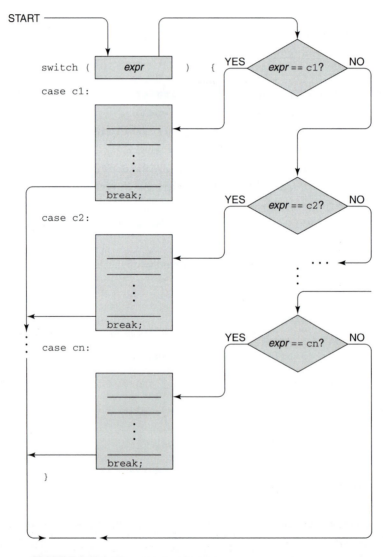

FIGURE 2.10.1 The **switch** statement.

The **case**s in a **switch** statement typically end with a **break**. Suppose that, in our example, **case 'S'** did *not* have a **break**

```
switch ( filing_code ) {
case 'S':
  cout << "Single taxpayer" << endl;
case 'M':
  cout << "Married taxpayer" << endl;
  break;
...
```

and that **filing_code** evaluated to **'S'**. The output then would be

```
Single taxpayer
Married taxpayer
```

Once control enters a **case**, it continues until a **break** is encountered or the **switch** is exited at its closing brace. ∎

EXAMPLE 2.10.4. The code segment

```
char letter;
cin >> letter; // read from standard input
switch ( letter ) {
case 'a':
case 'A':
  cout << "You entered a, either uppercase or lowercase."
       << endl;
  break;
case 'z':
case 'Z':
  cout << "You entered z, either uppercase or lowercase."
  break;
default:
  cout << "We care only about As and Zs, in any case."
       << endl;
}
```

illustrates a situation in which a **case** deliberately omits a **break**. By positioning two **case**s such as

```
case 'z':
case 'Z':
```

we say, in effect: execute this case if **letter** is a lowercase or uppercase Z. There is a **break** after each pair of **case**s so that, for example, execution of the code for **a** or **A** does not continue into the code for **z** or **Z**. ∎

The **case** expressions must be integer constants or **const** variables rather than non**const** variables. For example, the code segment

```
int two = 2;
...
switch ( number ) { // number can be a variable
case 1:  // OK
...
break;
case two: //**** ERROR--two is a variable, not a constant
...
break;
...
```

contains such an error in the second **case**.

EXERCISES

1. What is the output?

```
for ( i = 1; i <= 6; i++ ) {
   if ( i % 2 )
      continue;
   else
      cout << i << endl;
   cout << "bottom of loop" << endl;
}
```

2. What is the output?

```
for ( i = 1; i <= 6; i++ ) {
   if ( i % 2 )
      cout << i << endl;
   else
      break;
   cout << "bottom of loop" << endl;
}
```

3. What is the output?

```
ball_club = 1;
switch ( ball_club ) {
case 0:
   cout << "Devil Rays" << endl;
   break;
case 1:
   cout << "Diamondbacks" << endl;
   break;
```

```
case 2:
    cout << "Rockies" << endl;
    break;
}
cout << "*** End of baseball team listing" << endl;
```

4. What is the output?

```
ball_club = 1;
switch ( ball_club ) {
case 0:
    cout << "Devil Rays" << endl;
case 1:
    cout << "Diamondbacks" << endl;
case 2:
    cout << "Rockies" << endl;
}
cout << "*** End of baseball team listing" << endl;
```

5. What is the output?

```
for ( ball_club = 0; ball_club < 7; ball_club += 2 )
    if ( ball_club < 5 ) {
        switch ( ball_club ) {
        case 0:
            cout << "Devil Rays" << endl;
            break;
        case 1:
            cout << "Diamondbacks" << endl;
            break;
        case 2:
            cout << "Rockies" << endl;
            break;
        default:
            cout << "No team" << endl;
            break;
        }
        cout << "*** End of baseball team listing" << endl;
    }
    else
        cout << "Strike 3" << endl;
```

2.11 SAMPLE APPLICATION: GENERATING PRIME NUMBERS

Problem

Write a program that outputs all positive prime integers less than or equal to *n*, a user-supplied value. A positive integer *i* is **prime** if $i > 1$ and its only divisors are 1 and itself.

Sample Input/Output

```
Limit? (> 0, please) 12
Primes <= 12
2
3
5
7
11
```

Solution

We first prompt the user for **n**, using a **do while** loop to ensure that the user enters a nonzero value. Once **n** has been read from the standard input, a **for** loop steps through the integers 2 through **n**. To test whether the candidate **posPrime** is indeed prime, we use a nested **for** loop to determine whether any of the integers 2 through **posPrime - 1** divides **posPrime**. (This is *not* a very efficient approach. See Exercises 1 and 2 for better methods.) If **posPrime** does have such a divisor, it is not prime and, therefore, we use a **break** to exit the inner loop. If we do not find a divisor, we output **posPrime** as a prime.

C++ Implementation

```cpp
#include <iostream>
using namespace std;
/*** Print positive primes <= a user-supplied value ***/
/*** Selected lines are numbered for later reference. ***/
int main() {
        unsigned posPrime, // possible prime
                 posDiv,   // possible divisor
                 n;        // user supplied limit
        // get nonzero limit
        do {
          cout << "Limit? (> 0, please) ";
          cin >> n;
        } while ( n <= 0 );
        cout << "Primes <= " << n << endl;
/* 1 */ for ( posPrime = 2; posPrime <= n; posPrime++ ) {
            // look for a divisor of a possible prime
```

```
/* 2 */     for ( posDiv = 2; posDiv < posPrime; posDiv++ )
                // if the divisor divides the candidate with
                // zero remainder, the candidate is not prime
/* 3 */         if ( 0 == posPrime % posDiv )
                    break; // stop looking -- not a prime
                // no divisors, hence we have a prime
/* 4 */         if ( posDiv == posPrime )
                    cout << posPrime << endl;
            }
            return 0;
        }
```

Discussion

We trace the program when **n** is 4. Before any looping occurs, **posPrime** is initialized to 2 in the outer **for** loop at line 1. The loop condition

    posPrime <= n // 2 <= 4?

is thus **true** and so the outer loop's body executes. This body begins with a nested **for** loop at line 2. *Each time* the inner loop executes, the initialization at line 2

    posDiv = 2

occurs, thus setting **posDiv**'s value to 2. At this point, the nested loop's condition

    posDiv < posPrime // 2 < 2?

is **false** so the nested loop's body does *not* execute. Instead, control jumps to the first statement beyond the inner loop, which is the **if** statement at line 4. The **if** test at line 4

    if (posDiv == posPrime) // 2 == 2?

is **true**; therefore, 2 is output as a prime. The **if** statement is the last statement in the outer loop's body so control returns to the outer loop's increment expression

    posPrime++ // increments posPrime to 3

Because $3 \leq 4$, the outer loop's test evaluates to **true** and the nested **for** loop again executes. Once again **posDiv** is initialized to 2. The inner loop's test

    posDiv < posPrime // 2 < 3?

is now **true** so the inner loop's body executes at line 3. The **if** test

    if (0 == posPrime % posDiv)

evaluates to

    if (0 == 3 % 2) // 0 == 1?

which is **false**. The inner loop's update at line 2

    posDiv++

increments **posDiv** to 3, which in turn makes the inner loop test

```
posDiv < posPrime // 3 < 3
```

false. Control thus goes again to line 4 and, once again, the **if** condition

```
if ( posDiv == posPrime ) // 3 == 3?
```

evaluates to **true**. Accordingly, 3 is output as a prime. Because the outer loop's body has now completed execution, control returns to the outer loop's update section at line 1 and

```
posPrime++
```

executes. This increments **posPrime** to 4.

    The outer loop condition

```
posPrime <= n // 4 <= 4
```

is still **true**. At line 2, **posDiv** once again is initialized to 2. Now, however, the inner loop condition

```
0 == posPrime % posDiv // 0 == 4 % 2
```

is **true** because 2 divides 4 with a remainder of 0. Therefore, the **break** executes. The **break** terminates execution of the *inner* loop only. Execution thus proceeds to line 4, where the **if** condition

```
if ( posDiv == posPrime ) // 2 == 4?
```

is **false**. Therefore, 4 is *not* output as a prime. Control again returns to the outer loop's update at line 1, which increments **posPrime** to 5.

    The outer loop's condition

```
posPrime <= n // 5 <= 4
```

is now **false** so the outer loop terminates. Control proceeds to

```
return 0;
```

beyond the inner loop, which ends the program.

EXERCISES

1. Show that the integer $i \geq 2$ is prime if and only if no integer k, $2 \leq k \leq \sqrt{i}$, divides i.

2. Use the result of Exercise 1 to speed up the prime number program of this section.

3. Can you suggest additional methods to speed up the prime number program in this section?

2.12 PROMOTIONS AND CASTS

Either the compiler or the programmer may change an expression's data type. The compiler **promotes** an expression of one type (e.g., **short**) to another type (e.g., **int**) under conditions to be explained shortly. The programmer **casts** an expression of one type (e.g., **unsigned int**) to another type (e.g., **int**) for reasons to be explained shortly. C++ has a *new style* and an *old style* for casting. We first introduce the new style and then devote a subsection to the old style.

Promotions

The C++ compiler does not allow binary operations to occur on *mixed* data types such as **float** and **double**, **unsigned long** and **long**, **short** and **float**, and so on. If the types in a binary operation are mixed *in the source code*, the compiler **promotes** one or both of the values so that they have the *same* type.

In binary operations involving mixed integer types, an operand of type **char**, **signed char**, **unsigned char**, **short**, or **unsigned short** is first promoted to **int**, if **int** can represent all values of the original type; otherwise, the operand is promoted to **unsigned int**. Next, the first of the following rules that is applicable is invoked:

- If either operand is **unsigned long**, the other is promoted to **unsigned long**.
- If one operand is **long** and the other is **unsigned int** and **long** can represent all values of **unsigned int**, the **unsigned int** is promoted to **long**; otherwise, both operands are promoted to **unsigned long**.
- If either operand is **long**, the other is promoted to **long**.
- If either operand is **unsigned int**, the other is promoted to **unsigned int**.

EXAMPLE 2.12.1.   In the code segment

```
short s = 7;
int   r = 4;
cout << s + r << endl;
```

s is a **short** but **r** is an **int**. We thus have a binary operation with mixed types in our source code. The compiler eliminates the mix by promoting **s**'s value to **int** so that like data types are added.   ∎

EXAMPLE 2.12.2.   In the code segment

```
unsigned long ulng = 3400000;
long lng = 1280000;
cout << ulng - lng << endl;
```

there is a binary operation with mixed types in the source code. The compiler eliminates the mix by promoting **lng**'s value of type **signed long** to **unsigned long** so that like types are subtracted.   ∎

EXAMPLE 2.12.3.   In the code segment

```
signed char   c = 19;
signed short  s = 8;
int           x = 4;
unsigned      y = 3;
unsigned long z = 7;
cout << c + s << endl  // c's and s's values to signed int
     << c - x << endl  // c's value to signed int
     << z % y << endl; // y's value to unsigned long
```

the promotions ensure that the arithmetic operations occur on like types. ■

In binary operations in which at least one operand is a floating-point type, the first of the following rules that is applicable is invoked:

- If either operand is **long double**, the other is promoted to **long double**.
- If either operand is **double**, the other is promoted to **double**.
- If either operand is **float**, the other is promoted to **float**.

EXAMPLE 2.12.4.   In the code segment

```
float  f1 = 987.123F;
double f2 = 88888.76;
cout << f2 - f1 << endl; // f1's value promoted to double
```

f1's value is promoted to **double** so that the subtraction occurs between like types.
   The code segment

```
cout << 2 / 3.0 << endl;   // 0.666667: 2 promoted to 2.0
cout << 2.0 / 3 << endl;   // 0.666667: 3 promoted to 3.0
```

shows what happens when integer and floating-point data types are mixed in arithmetic operations. In these examples, the **int** constants are promoted to **double**s so that the operations again occur on like types. Recall that the floating-point constant **3.0** is a **double**, whereas **3.0F** or **3.0f** is a **float** and **3.0L** or **3.0l** is a **long double**. ■

Casts

We explain casts through short examples.

EXAMPLE 2.12.5.   Suppose that we use two **int** variables to record for a golfer, such as Tiger Woods, birdie putt opportunities and birdie putts made for a given round. We initialize each to an integer constant:

```
int tried = 11,  // for 18 holes
    made = 7;    // ditto
```

We then try to compute the fraction of birdie putts made. The code segment

```
cout << "Tiger made "
     << made / tried    // outputs 0
     << " of his birdie putts." << endl;
```

outputs 0. Because the two variables are **int**s, *integer* division (see Section 1.7) is performed on their values. Accordingly, **made / tried** becomes **7 / 11** or **0**. We could solve the problem by defining **tried** and **made** as **float**s, of course, but there is a more flexible way. Recall that, in C++, a variable evaluates to its contents. So **made** and **tried** evaluate to the **int**s 7 and 11, respectively. We can *cast* these **int** values to **float** values using this syntax:

```
cout << "Tiger made "
     << static_cast<float>(made) / static_cast<float>(tried)
     << " of his birdie putts." << endl;
```

The output is now **0.636364** because of the casting. The two casts each begin with the keyword **static_cast** followed by the cast type, in this case **float**, enclosed in angle brackets. An expression to be cast, **made** in one cast and **tried** in the other, is enclosed in parentheses. White space inside the angle brackets and parentheses is optional. The two casts in this example change the values of **made** and **tried** from **int** to **float** so that *floating-point* division occurs. The value of the floating-point division is **0.636364**. The example thus shows how an expression of one type such as **int** can be cast on the fly to another type such as **float**. ■

A cast *cannot* change the data type of a variable; rather, a cast can change the data type of a variable's *value*. In Example 2.12.5, for instance, the variables **made** and **tried** are defined as **int**s and remain **int**s throughout the casting. The values of these variables, 7 for **made** and 11 for **tried**, are cast to the floating-point values 7.0 and 11.0 (which reside in temporary storage obtained by the compiler) in order to ensure floating-point division.

Casts To Avoid Promotions

Compiler promotions keep C++ programming from becoming tedious. For instance, the programmer need not worry that **x** and **y** in the code segment

```
int x = 7;
unsigned long y = 11;
cout << x + y << endl;
```

are of different types. The compiler, through promotion, ensures that the addition **x + y** will involve like types. However, promotions can have unforeseen effects.

EXAMPLE 2.12.6. The code segment

```
signed int neg = -1;    // signed int data type
unsigned int pos = 32;  // unsigned int data type
if ( neg > pos )
  cout << "-1 > 32!!!" << endl;
else
  cout << "32 > -1" << endl;
```

prints

```
-1 > 32!!!
```

on any system that uses the two's complement representation for integers (see Section 0.3).

A good compiler warns that

```
if ( neg > pos )
```

is risky because it has mixed data types in the comparison. The compiler eliminates the mixed types by promoting **neg**'s value from **signed int** to **unsigned int**. In the two's complement representation of a **signed** integer, the most significant bit is the sign bit; but in an **unsigned** integer, the most significant bit is one of the *magnitude* bits. Assume that both **sizeof(signed int)** and **sizeof(unsigned int)** are 16 bits. The two's complement representations of **neg**'s value and **pos**'s value, with the leftmost bit as the most significant bit, are

Variable	Value in Binary	Unsigned Value in Decimal
neg	1111111111111111	64,555
pos	0000000000100000	32

Once promoted to an **unsigned int**, **neg**'s value is 64,555 and so is greater than **pos**'s value of 32. The programmer thus should heed the adage about not comparing apples such as **signed int**s and oranges such as **unsigned int**s. ∎

EXAMPLE 2.12.7. The code segment

```
signed int neg = -1;    // signed int data type
unsigned int pos = 32;  // unsigned int data type
if ( neg > static_cast<signed int>(pos) )
  cout << "-1 > 32!!!" << endl;
else
  cout << "32 > -1" << endl;
```

outputs

```
32 > -1
```

The comparison now includes the cast

```
static_cast<signed int>(pos)
```

to convert **pos**'s value from **unsigned int** to **signed int**. As a result, the test compares two *signed* expressions. By the way, because **int** is shorthand for **signed int**, the cast could be simplified to

```
static_cast<int>(pos)
```

∎

Old-Style Casts and Type Conversions

The keyword **static_cast** is relatively new in C++ and some compilers may not yet support it. Also, much C++ code already written uses old-style casts or type conversions, which we explain in this section.

EXAMPLE 2.12.8.   We amend Example 2.12.5

```
int made = 7, tried = 11;
cout << "Tiger made "
     << (float) made / (float) tried
     << " of his birdie putts." << endl;
```

to illustrate old-style casting. The cast data type, in this case **float**, is enclosed in parentheses and placed immediately to the left of the expression to be cast, the variable **made** in one cast and the variable **tried** in the other. White space inside the parentheses is optional. The output is **0.636364** because of the casting. ■

EXAMPLE 2.12.9.   We amend Example 2.12.5

```
int made = 7, tried = 11;
cout << "Tiger made "
     << float( made ) / float( tried )
     << " of his birdie putts." << endl;
```

to illustrate old-style type conversions. The type conversion data type, in this case **float**, occurs immediately to the left of the expression to be converted, which is enclosed in parentheses. White space inside the parentheses is optional. In our example, the expressions to be converted are the variables **made** and **tried**. The output is **0.636364** because of the type conversions. ■

The objection against old-style casts and type conversions is that they can be used for many different purposes, but their syntax does not make clear what the purpose is. The new style is meant to bring clarity and discipline to casting. In the new style, the *basic* cast is the **static_cast**. There are three other new-style casts, which are designed for special situations: casting away **const**ness in expressions, casting across or within inheritance hierarchies (see Appendix D), and implementation-dependent casting. Here we give the names and a brief description. Many compilers support both new-style and old-style casting.

Cast	Typically Used For
const_cast	Casting away **const**ness
dynamic_cast	Casting pointers or references in inheritance hierarchies
reinterpret_cast	Implementation-dependent casting

EXERCISES

1. Assuming ASCII representation of characters, what is the output?

```
char x = 90;
cout << static_cast<int>( x ) << endl;
```

2. What promotions if any occur in this code segment?

```
int x = 9;
long y = 23;
cout << x + y << endl;
```

3. What promotions if any occur in this code segment?

```
float x = 9.0;
long y = 23;
cout << x * y << endl;
```

4. What is the output?

```
cout << 3 / 4.0 << endl;
```

5. What is the output?

```
cout << 2 * 9.6 + 11 << endl;
```

6. What is the output?

```
cout << 4 * ( 8 / 3 ) << endl;
```

7. What is the output?

```
cout << 8 / 42 << endl;
```

8. What is the output?

```
cout << static_cast<float>(8) / static_cast<float>(42)
        << endl;
```

9. Suppose that c's type is **signed char**, and that s's type is **unsigned short**. Explain why the promotion in the expression c + s is machine dependent.

2.13 FORMATTING

To **format** output is to control how information is written to the screen or how it is printed. For example, we may want to output a positive integer in a field 10 columns wide, or we may want to output a floating-point number in scientific (i.e., exponential) notation. Input can be similarly formatted. For example, sometimes we may want to skip white space prior to reading data; at other times, we may want to read the white space. So far we have let the system decide how input and output should be formatted. In this section we show how the programmer can format output and input.

Input and output can be formatted using **manipulators** (see Figure 2.13.1). We have already used the manipulator **endl**, which causes subsequent output to begin in column 1 of the next line. Except for the manipulator **setw**, after a manipulator is used, *all* subsequent input or output is formatted accordingly. The manipulator **setw** applies only to the next item to be output. To use manipulators without arguments (e.g., **endl**), the header file *iostream* must be included. Manipulators with arguments (e.g., **setfill**, **setw**) require the header file *iomanip*.

Manipulator	Effect
endl	Write newline
fixed	Use fixed notation for floating-point numbers: **d.ddd**
left	Left-justify
right	Right-justify
scientific	Use scientific notation for floating-point numbers: **d.dddEdd**
setfill(c)	Make **c** the fill character
setprecision(n)	Set floating-point precision to **n**
setw(n)	Set field width to **n**
showpoint	Always print decimal point and trailing zeros
noshowpoint	Don't print trailing zeros. Drop decimal point, if possible.
showpos	Use + with nonnegative numbers
noshowpos	Don't use + with nonnegative numbers
skipws	Skip white space before input
noskipws	Don't skip white space before input

FIGURE 2.13.1 Some C++ manipulators.

The *field width* is the number of columns into which a data item is to be written. The field width may be set by using the manipulator **setw**. In C++, if the field width is less than the number of columns required to write the item, the item is written anyway. For example, to write the integer 3572, four columns are needed. If the field width is less than 4, the integer is written anyway (in four columns). If the field width is greater than 4, the item is right-justified with blanks added at the left to fill out the specified number of columns. As we shall see, the programmer can specify left justification and can change the fill character. The default value for the field width is zero. Thus, by default, C++ writes each data item in the minimum number of columns. After an item is written, the field width reverts to zero. So if several items are to be written with a particular field width, the field width must be set before each item is written.

The following examples show *typical* behavior of C++ manipulators, but there are differences among systems.

EXAMPLE 2.13.1. The following code segment prints the numbers 1, 10, 100, and 1000 right-justified in a field of width 6:

```
for ( i = 1; i <= 1000; i *= 10 )
   cout << setw( 6 ) << i << endl;
```

The output is

```
     1
    10
   100
  1000
```

The manipulator **setw** must be used as shown. For example, the output of the code segment

```
cout << setw( 6 );
for ( i = 1; i <= 1000; i *= 10 )
   cout << i << endl;
```

is

```
     1
10
100
1000
```

After the field width is set to 6 and **1** is output, the field width reverts to its default value of zero. Thus only the first line is output in a field of size 6. ■

The manipulator **setfill** is used to specify a particular fill character, which is then used to fill the extra space when the field width is larger than the item to be output.

EXAMPLE 2.13.2. The following code segment prints the values 1, 10, 100, and 1000 right-justified in a field of width 6. The asterisk is used to fill the extra columns:

```
cout << setfill( '*' );
for ( i = 1; i <= 1000; i *= 10 )
   cout << setw( 6 ) << i << endl;
```

The output is

```
*****1
****10
***100
**1000
```

Notice that once the fill character is set, it remains in effect until it is changed (e.g., by another call of **setfill**). ∎

The manipulator **setprecision** is used to specify the number of digits of precision of floating-point numbers. The default precision is 6.

EXAMPLE 2.13.3.   The code segment

```
float a = 1.05, b = 10.15, c = 200.87;
cout << setfill( '*' ) << setprecision( 2 );
cout << setw( 10 ) << a << endl;
cout << setw( 10 ) << b << endl;
cout << setw( 10 ) << c << endl;
```

prints the values, 1.05, 10.15, and 200.87, right-justified in a field of width 10. The asterisk is used to fill the extra columns. The output is

```
******1.05
*****10.15
****200.87
```
∎

The manipulators **left** and **right** may be used to left- or right-justify output in its field.

EXAMPLE 2.13.4.   The following code segment prints names, left-justified in a field of width 10, and numbers, right-justified in a field of width 6:

```
int a = 5, b = 43, c = 104;
cout << left << setw( 10 ) << "Karen"
     << right << setw( 6 ) << a << endl;
cout << left << setw( 10 ) << "Ben"
     << right << setw( 6 ) << b << endl;
cout << left << setw( 10 ) << "Patricia"
     << right << setw( 6 ) << c << endl;
```

The output is

```
Karen          5
Ben           43
Patricia     104
```
∎

The **showpoint** manipulator forces a decimal point to be output as well as all trailing zeros. By default, floating-point numbers are printed in either fixed or scientific (i.e., exponential) notation, whichever takes the least number of columns. Scientific notation can be specified using the **scientific** manipulator, and fixed notation can be specified using the **fixed** manipulator.

EXAMPLE 2.13.5. The code segment

```
float a = 5, b = 43.3, c = 10304.31;
cout << showpoint << fixed << setprecision( 2 );
cout << setw( 8 ) << a << endl;
cout << setw( 8 ) << b << endl;
cout << setw( 8 ) << c << endl;
```

prints three floating-point numbers in a field of width 8. The precision is set to 2. The decimal point and trailing zeros are printed because of the **showpoint** manipulator. The **fixed** manipulator forces the output to appear in fixed notation. The output is

```
    5.00
   43.30
10304.31
```

If the **showpoint** and **fixed** manipulators are not used

```
float a = 5, b = 43.3, c = 10304.31;
cout << setprecision( 2 );
cout << setw( 8 ) << a << endl;
cout << setw( 8 ) << b << endl;
cout << setw( 8 ) << c << endl;
```

the output is

```
       5
    43.3
1.03e+04
```

because, by default, floating-point numbers are output in the minimum amount of space. This means dropping trailing zeros, dropping trailing zeros and the decimal point for numbers of the form $x.000000$, and using either fixed or scientific notation, whichever is shortest. ∎

After using the **showpoint** manipulator, its effect can be canceled by using the **noshowpoint** manipulator. Similarly, forcing a plus sign to be printed can be canceled by using the **noshowpos** manipulator, and skipping white space before input can be disabled by using the **noskipws** manipulator.

EXAMPLE 2.13.6.   The following program copies the standard input to the standard output, a character at a time. *All* characters are copied, including white space.

```
#include <iostream>
using namespace std;
int main() {
   char c;
   cin >> noskipws;
   while ( cin >> c )
      cout << c;
   return 0;
}                                                                    ■
```

EXERCISES

1. Write a statement to set the field width on **cout** to 12.

2. Write a statement to set the fill character on **cout** to zero.

3. Write a statement to set the precision on **cout** to zero.

4. Write a statement to set left-justification on **cout**.

5. Write a statement to set right-justification and use + with nonnegative numbers on **cout**.

6. Write a statement to disable printing the decimal point and trailing zeros on **cout**.

7. What is the output of the program of Example 2.13.6 if the input is the program itself?

8. Suppose that we modify the program of Example 2.13.6 by deleting the line

```
cin >> noskipws;
```

What is the output of the revised program if the input is the revised program itself?

9. Write a code segment that first outputs the line

```
Sun  Mon  Tue  Wed  Thu  Fri  Sat
```

(there are two spaces between the days) and then prints the dates, right-aligned under the days. Assume that the variable **day** specifies the starting day: 0 is Sunday, 1 is Monday, and so on. Assume that the variable **stop** specifies the last date. For example, if **day** is 2 and **stop** is 31, the output is

```
Sun  Mon  Tue  Wed  Thu  Fri  Sat
                1    2    3    4    5
  6    7    8    9   10   11   12
 13   14   15   16   17   18   19
 20   21   22   23   24   25   26
 27   28   29   30   31
```

Macros

The **#define** preprocessor directive tells the preprocessor to replace subsequent occurrences of an expression by some value. For example, the directive

```
#define   EOF   -1
```

directs the preprocessor to replace subsequent occurrences of **EOF** with −1. The technical name for the **#define** directive is **macro**.

The preprocessor replaces **EOF** by its value *before* the C++ compiler goes to work. As a result, **EOF** typically cannot be referenced by name in a debugger, which works from the same source code that the compiler sees. Furthermore, macros are untyped and so the compiler is unable to do any type checking. By contrast, **const** variables *are* seen by the compiler and, therefore, can be referenced by name in a debugger. Furthermore, **const** variables are typed. For these and other reasons, **const** variables are preferred to macros when defining constants. Nevertheless, for historical reasons, macros are still common in C++ code.

Macros, including **parameterized macros** (macros that take arguments), are discussed in detail in Appendix B.

The Conditional Operator

The conditional operator **?:** is a convenient alternative to a simple **if-else** construct.

EXAMPLE.   The code segment

```
int x = 8, y = 4, z;
// simple if-else
if ( x > y )
   z = x;
else
   z = y;
// conditional operator
// initialize z to maximum of x and y
z = ( x > y ) ? x : y;
```

illustrates. The conditional operator has a *test expression* to the left of the **?**, in this example **x > y**. If the test expression evaluates to **true**, the operation evaluates to the expression immediately following **?**, in this example **x**. Otherwise, the operation evaluates to the expression immediately following **:**, in this example **y**. If the programmer does not supply the **:** clause, **false** becomes the conditional expression's value if the condition is **false**. ∎

Because **?:** is a built-in *operator*, it may be used to initialize a variable in its definition. An **if-else** *statement* could not be used that way.

EXAMPLE.   The code segment

```
int x = 1,
    y = 2,
    z = ( x < y ) ? x : y; // legal
```

illustrates.   The conditional operator is used to initialize **z** to the minimum of **x** and **y**.   ∎

The goto Statement and Labels

The **goto** statement transfers control to a **label**.

EXAMPLE.   The code segment

```
while ( i < n ) {
  while ( j < k ) {
    if ( j > 2 * i )
      goto loopExit;  // loopExit a label
    ...
  }
  ...
}
loopExit:  // label as target for goto
cout << "Exited both loops" << endl;
```

illustrates the **goto** statement.   If the **goto** statement executes, control resumes at the first executable statement after the label **loopExit**—in this example, the **cout** statement. The **goto** is easily abused and is considered bad form.   ∎

COMMON PROGRAMMING ERRORS

1. The condition in an **if** statement must be enclosed in parentheses. For this reason, it is an error to write

```
if condition   // ***** ERROR *****
   action
```

2. The **if** statement does not include the word **then**. For this reason, it is an error to write

```
if ( condition ) then   // ***** ERROR *****
   action
```

3. In the `if` statement, no semicolon follows the word `else`. For this reason, it is a logical error to write

```
if ( condition )
    action1
else ;        // ***** PROBABLE ERROR *****
    action2
```

4. The condition in a `while` statement must be enclosed in parentheses. For this reason, it is an error to write

```
while condition    // ***** ERROR *****
    action
```

5. The `while` statement does not include the word `do`. For this reason, it is a logical error to write

```
while ( condition ) do  // ***** PROBABLE ERROR *****
    action
```

6. The `while` and `if` statements should not be confused. The `while` statement is used to *repeatedly* execute a segment of code. Thus the statement

```
while ( condition )
    action
```

repeatedly executes *action* as long as *condition* is true. By contrast, the *action* of an `if` statement

```
if ( condition )
    action
```

is executed one time (if *condition* is true) or not at all (if *condition* is false).

7. Any loop or `if` body that contains more than one statement must be enclosed in braces. For example, the loop

```
int i = 0, n = 10;
while ( i < n )
    cout << i << endl;   // in loop body
    i = i + 1;           // ***** CAUTION: not in loop body
```

is infinite, because the statement `i = i + 1;` occurs *outside* the loop's body, indentation notwithstanding. The correction is

```
int i = 0, n = 10;
while ( i < n ) {
    cout << i << endl;   // in loop body
    i = i + 1;           // in loop body
}
```

8. It is an error to modify or assign a value to a `const` variable. For example, after

```
const int cutoff = 70;
```

it is illegal to modify or assign a value to `cutoff`:

```
cutoff = 80;      // ***** ERROR *****
```

Even the assignment

```
cutoff = 70;    // ***** ERROR *****
```

is illegal.

9. The three clauses in a **for** statement are separated by semicolons, not commas:

```
for ( int i = 0, i < n, i++ ) //**** ERROR
```

10. In C++, a semicolon typically does *not* come right after the condition in a loop or an **if** construct, although this is legal:

```
for ( int i = 0; i < 10; i++ ); //**** CAUTION
   cout << i + 1 << endl;
```

The code segment outputs 11. The semicolon by itself, the *null statement*, is the loop's body. So the code executes the null statement 10 times and then the **cout** statement once.

11. Using a single equals sign = when a double equals sign == is intended is a logical error. It is syntactically correct to write

```
if ( x = 1 )    // ***** PROBABLE ERROR *****
   ...
```

but the way that the system interprets this command is usually not what the user intended.

12. The **break** and **continue** statements affect only their containing loop, that is, the *innermost* loop. For example, this **break**

```
while (...) { // outer loop
   while (...) { // inner loop
      ...
      break;
      ...
   }
}
```

causes an exit from the *inner loop* but not from the *outer loop*.

13. In a **switch** construct, the integer expression must be enclosed in parentheses. The erroneous

```
switch i { //***** ERROR
```

is correctly written as

```
switch ( i ) { // ok
```

14. In a **switch** construct, the **case** expressions must be *constants* rather than *variables*.

15. Within a **switch** construct, each **case** normally ends with a **break**. If **break** is omitted, execution continues through other **case** clauses or the **default** clause until a **break** is encountered or the **switch** itself is exited.

16. Caution should be used when comparing expressions of different types with relational operators because the compiler performs promotions so that the comparison occurs between like types. The results may be unexpected. For instance, in the code segment

```
int minus_one = -1; // signed int
unsigned plus_oneThousand = 1000; // unsigned int
if ( minus_one > plus_oneThousand ) //**** caution
   cout << "You're kidding!" << endl;
```

the compiler promotes the **signed int** to **unsigned int**. In a system using two's complement integer representation, the **if** condition is **true**. A cast should be used to ensure that comparisons occur between the same types:

```
int minus_one = -1; // signed int
unsigned plus_oneThousand = 1000; // unsigned int
if ( minus_one > static_cast<signed>(plus_oneThousand) )
   cout << "You're kidding!" << endl;
```

17. In a new-style cast, the cast data type is enclosed in angle brackets rather than parentheses:

```
static_cast(int)(26) //***** ERROR
static_cast<int>(26) // Correct
```

18. In a new-style cast, the cast expression is enclosed in parentheses rather than angle brackets:

```
static_cast<int><26> //***** ERROR
static_cast<int>(26) // Correct
```

PROGRAMMING EXERCISES

In Exercises 2.1 through 2.3, the input is read from the keyboard, and the output is written to the video display.

2.1. Write a program that reads nonnegative integers and then outputs the largest and smallest values. Assume that a negative integer marks the end of the input.

2.2. Write a program that reads nonnegative integers and then outputs the largest and second largest values. Assume that a negative integer marks the end of the input.

2.3. Write a program that reads nonnegative integers and then outputs **Yes** if the numbers do not decrease and **No** otherwise. (The numbers *do not decrease* if, for every pair n_1, n_2 in succession, we have $n_1 \leq n_2$.) *Examples*: If the input is

```
0 14 14 27 78
```

the output is

```
Yes
```

If the input is

```
0  3  1  7  29
```

the output is

```
No
```

Assume that a negative integer marks the end of the input.

2.4. Rewrite the programs of Exercises 2.1 through 2.3. Read from and write to files. Remove the prompts and read data until end-of-file.

2.5. Write a program that reads integers from a file until end-of-file and then outputs the maximum sum of consecutive values to a file. *Example*: If the input is

```
27  6  -50  21  -3  14  16  -8  42  33  -21  9
```

the output is

```
115
```

the sum of

```
21  -3  14  16  -8  42  33
```

If all of the numbers in the input are negative, the maximum sum of consecutive values is defined to be 0.

2.6. The standard input (or, if you like, a disk file) contains the opening balance of a checking account followed by a list of transactions. Write a program that outputs the opening balance followed by the closing balance. For example, if the input is

```
324.56  420.32  -3.54  -87.56
```

the output is

```
Opening Balance:  $324.56
Closing Balance:  $653.78
```

A negative number represents a withdrawal.

2.7. The cost of one type of phone service is $18.50 per month plus 5 cents for each unit used. Write a program that reads a list of units used and outputs a billing cost for each customer. The input looks like

```
18897        46
31556        18
     . . .
```

where the first number is the customer identification number and the second is the number of units used. The output looks like

```
18897      $20.80
31556      $19.40
   . . .
```

2.8. The cost of one type of phone service is $18.50 per month plus 5 cents for each unit over 65 used per month. Write a program that reads a list of units used and outputs a billing cost for each customer as in Programming Exercise 2.7.

2.9. Write a program that reads a list of numeric test scores from the standard input or a disk file and outputs a letter grade according to the harsh scale

Test Score	Grade
95—100	A
90—94	B
85—89	C
80—84	D
0—79	F

2.10. Write a program to graph the function

$$y = \frac{x}{1 + x^2}$$

on the interval 0 to 2 in increments of 0.1. Output a bar graph using a character such as * in which the number of stars is proportional to y for the requested values of x. Here is some sample output:

```
0
0.1 *****
0.2 **********
0.3 **************
0.4 *****************
0.5 ******************
   . . .
```

2.11. Write a program to graph the function $y = \sin x$ on the interval 0 to π in increments of $\frac{\pi}{20}$. The function $\sin x$ is available in the math library. As in Programming Exercise 2.10, use a bar graph to represent the function.

2.12. Opponents of the late Chicago Mayor Harold Washington presented petitions containing 196,000 signatures seeking a referendum on a nonpartisan mayoral election. (Mayor Washington's opponents felt that they had a better chance to unseat him were the election nonpartisan.) To the charge by Mayor Washington's supporters that many of the signatures were invalid, opposition leader Rep. William Lipinski replied: "Normally, petitions are 10 to 15 percent forged. Maybe this, since it is so large, will go 20 percent."

Assume that for each increase of 50,000 signatures, the percentage of forged signatures increases by 5 percent. Write a program that lists the number of signatures and the percentage forged. Begin with 50,000 signatures with 5 percent forged and end when 100 percent of the signatures are forged. The output should be in increments of 50,000.

2.13. A handicapping system is used to determine the winner in power-lifting competitions. A coefficient C is determined by the following table:

Bodyweight (B)	Coefficient (C)
$125.1 \leq B < 135.0$	$0.5208 - 0.0012(B - 125.0)$
$135.0 \leq B < 145.0$	$0.5088 - 0.0011(B - 135.0)$
$145.0 \leq B < 155.0$	$0.4978 - 0.0010(B - 145.0)$
$155.0 \leq B < 165.0$	$0.4878 - 0.0009(B - 155.0)$

Each lifter is then assigned the value

$$C(S + BP + D)$$

where S is the weight lifted in the *squat* position, BP is the weight *bench pressed*, and D is the weight *deadlifted*. The winner is the person with the largest value. Write a program that reads a body weight, squat weight, weight bench pressed, and weight deadlifted for a lifter and outputs the score.

2.14. This exercise comes originally from Mitchell Feigenbaum and was adapted by John Allen Paulos in *Beyond Numeracy* (New York: Alfred A. Knopf, 1990). Consider the deceptively simply formula

$$NextYr = Rate \cdot CurrentYr \cdot \left(1 - \frac{CurrentYr}{1,000,000}\right)$$

which calculates next year's population of, say, egrets on the basis of the current population and the growth rate. The variable *Rate* controls the growth rate and takes on values between 0 and 4. The variable *CurrentYr* gives the current value of the egret population and is assumed to have a value between 0 and 1,000,000. The variable *NextYr* gives the value of the egret population one year later. The formula guarantees that *NextYr* also will have a value between 0 and 1,000,000. For example, if *CurrentYr* is 100,000 and *Rate* is 2.6, *NextYr* is 234,000.

Now suppose that we initialize *CurrentYr* to 100,000 and *Rate* to 2.6 and then compute the egret population 25 years hence by solving for *NextYr*, setting *CurrentYr* to *NextYr*, solving again for *NextYr*, and so on for 25 iterations. The egret population turns out to be roughly 615,365. We get the *same* result if we initialize *CurrentYr* to, say, 900,000 but leave *Rate* set to 2.6. In fact, the population stabilizes at roughly 615,385 for *any* positive value of *CurrentYr* so long as *Rate* is 2.6. For some values of *Rate*, however, the population oscillates. For example, if *Rate* is 3.14, then after about 40 years the egret population takes on this pattern from one year to the next: 538,007 to 780,464 to 538,007 to 780,464 and so on indefinitely. For *Rate* equal to approximately 3.57, however, the population does not stabilize or oscillate but rather varies randomly from one year to the next.

Write a program that prompts the user for *Rate*, an initial *CurrentYr*, and a number of iterations. On each iteration, output the year and the current egret population.

2.15. Amend Programming Exercise 2.14 so that it prompts the user for a number of iterations, an initial *Rate*, an initial *CurrentYr*, a *Rate* increase, and a *Rate* limit. For example, if the user enters 25 for the number of iterations, 100,000 for *CurrentYr*, 3.5 for *Rate*, 0.1 for *Rate* increase, and 3.9 for *Rate* limit, then the program iterates 25 times with *Rate* set to 3.5; 25 times for *Rate* set to 3.6; and so on until *Rate* is set to 3.9. On each iteration, output the year, the *Rate*, and the current egret population.

2.16. Twin primes are two primes that differ by 2 (e.g., 3 and 5, 101 and 103). Write a program that outputs all twin primes less than 10,000. An unsolved problem is whether there are infinitely many twin primes.

2.17. Write a program that replaces two or more consecutive blanks by a single blank. For example, given the input

```
Let's     go      to      the    movies.
```

the output is

```
Let's go to the movies.
```

2.18. The income tax for single taxpayers earning up to $15,610 is given in this table:

Over	Amount But Not Over	Tax
$0	$2,390	$0
$2,390	$3,540	11% of amount over $2,390
$3,540	$4,580	$126.50 + 12% of amount over $3,540
$4,580	$6,760	$251.30 + 14% of amount over $4,580
$6,760	$8,850	$556.50 + 15% of amount over $6,760
$8,850	$11,240	$870.00 + 16% of amount over $8,850
$11,240	$13,430	$1,242.40 + 18% of amount over $11,240
$13,430	$15,610	$1,646.60 + 20% of amount over $13,430

Write a program that reads the taxable incomes of single taxpayers earning less than or equal to $15,610 and lists the taxes for each income.

2.19. Using the 15-year property-accelerated method of depreciation, property bought in January is depreciated 12 percent in the first year, then 10 percent, 9 percent, 8 percent, 7 percent, then 6 percent for four years, and then 5 percent for the remaining six years. For example, property worth $400,000 would be depreciated according to this schedule:

Year	Amount
1	$48,000 (= 12% of $400,000)
2	$40,000 (= 10% of $400,000)
3	$36,000 (= 9% of $400,000)
4	$32,000 (= 8% of $400,000)
5	$28,000 (= 7% of $400,000)
6	$24,000 (= 6% of $400,000)
7	$24,000 (= 6% of $400,000)
8	$24,000 (= 6% of $400,000)
9	$24,000 (= 6% of $400,000)
10	$20,000 (= 5% of $400,000)
11	$20,000 (= 5% of $400,000)
12	$20,000 (= 5% of $400,000)
13	$20,000 (= 5% of $400,000)
14	$20,000 (= 5% of $400,000)
15	$20,000 (= 5% of $400,000)

Write a program that reads a sequence of property values and, for each, outputs a table similar to the preceding table.

CHAPTER
3

FUNCTIONS

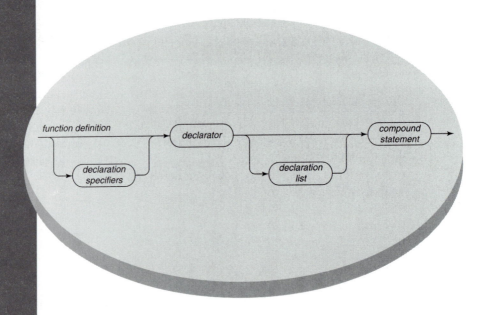

A C++ **function** is a unit of code that can receive values, perform computations, and return a value. C++ functions can be either **top-level functions**, such as **main**, or **methods**, which are functions contained in classes. In this chapter, we consider top-level functions, and in Chapter 5, we deal with classes and their methods.

3.1 INTRODUCTION

A C++ program consists of functions, one of which must be named **main**. Execution begins with **main**, and the program as a whole terminates when **main** does.[†]

EXAMPLE 3.1.1. The program in Figure 3.1.1 reads a midterm grade, a final grade, and a weight; computes a weighted average; and assigns the course grade **P** (for pass), if the weighted average is greater than 7.0, or **F** (for fail), if the weighted average is less than or equal to 7.0. The exam scores, **exam1** and **exam2**, are integers between 0 and 10, inclusive, and **exam1_weight** is a floating-point number between 0.0 and 1.0. The weighted average is computed using the formula

```
exam1_weight * exam1 + ( 1.0 - exam1_weight ) * exam2
```

For example, if **exam1** is equal to 8, **exam2** is equal to 6, and **exam1_weight** is equal to 0.76, the weighted average is

$$0.76 \times 8 + 0.24 \times 6 = 7.52$$

and the course grade is **P**.

The function **grade** computes the weighted average and determines the course grade. When the function **grade** is invoked in **main**

```
letter_grade = grade( mid_term, final, weight );
```

- The value of **mid_term** (in **main**) is assigned to **exam1** (in **grade**).
- The value of **final** (in **main**) is assigned to **exam2** (in **grade**).
- The value of **weight** (in **main**) is assigned to **exam1_weight** (in **grade**).

After these values are assigned, the statements in **grade** begin executing. When a **return** statement executes in **grade**, a value (either **'P'** or **'F'**) is sent back to **main**. The execution of **main**'s statements resumes at the line where it was suspended:

```
letter_grade = grade( mid_term, final, weight );
```

The assignment statement is completed by assigning the returned value from **grade** to the variable **letter_grade**, after which the statement

```
cout << "Grade is: " << letter_grade << endl;
```

executes. ∎

[†] Some implementations may allow a program with no **main** function, but we do not discuss such programs in this book. Also, it is possible to invoke certain library functions such as **exit** to terminate a program anywhere (see Section 3.6). In the absence of such functions, the program terminates when **main** does.

```
#include <iostream>
using namespace std;
const float cutoff = 7.0;
char grade( int exam1, int exam2, float exam_weight );
int main() {
    int mid_term, final;
    float weight;
    char ans, letter_grade;
    do {
        cout << "\n\nCompute another grade (Y)es, (N)o? ";
        cin >> ans;
        if ( ans == 'Y' ) {
            cout << "Enter mid term, final, weight: ";
            cin >> mid_term >> final >> weight;
            letter_grade = grade( mid_term, final, weight );
            cout << "Grade is: " << letter_grade << endl;
        }
    } while ( ans == 'Y');
    return 0;
}
char grade( int exam1, int exam2, float exam1_weight ) {
    float average;
    average = exam1_weight * exam1 + ( 1.0 - exam1_weight ) * exam2;
    if ( average > cutoff )
        return 'P';
    else
        return 'F';
}
```

FIGURE 3.1.1 A program with two functions.

Function Terminology

There are a number of important terms that refer to functions. Any C++ function, except **main**, can be **invoked** or **called** by another. For example, in Figure 3.1.1, **main** invokes **grade**. The invoking function may **pass** information to the invoked function, and the invoked function may **return** information to its invoker. By passing and returning information, functions communicate with one another.

An invoking function passes information by passing **arguments**. In C++, any expression can be an argument. In the invoking function, arguments are evaluated, and the values are passed to the invoked function. In Figure 3.1.1, the arguments to **grade** are **mid_term**, **final**, and **weight**. The arguments are passed when **grade** is invoked in **main**:

```
letter_grade = grade( mid_term, final, weight );
```

An invoked function has **parameters** that catch the information passed to it.[†] In Figure 3.1.1, the parameters in `grade` are `exam1`, `exam2`, and `exam1_weight`. We see that arguments and parameters need not have the same names.

Every function has a **header** and a **body**. In C++ we **define** a function by giving its header and body. A function's header consists of

- The data type returned or the keyword `void` if the function does not return a value. Either `void` or the data type returned *must* be specified.

- The function's name.

- In parentheses, a list of parameters and their types separated by commas, or an empty list if the function has no parameters. (The keyword `void` may also be used in place of an empty parameter list.)

The right parenthesis that terminates the parameter list is *not* followed by a semicolon.

The header is followed by the body. A function's body consists of a sequence of statements enclosed in a pair of braces. The left brace indicates where the body starts, and the right brace indicates where the body ends.

EXAMPLE 3.1.2. The header of the function `grade` of Figure 3.1.1 is

```
char grade( int exam1, int exam2, float exam1_weight )
```

The keyword `char` indicates that `grade` returns to its invoker a value of type `char`. The parameter list

```
int exam1, int exam2, float exam1_weight
```

shows that `grade` has three parameters: `exam1` of type `int`, `exam2` also of type `int`, and `exam1_weight` of type `float`.

The body of `grade` is

```
{
    float average;
    average = exam1_weight * exam1
            + ( 1.0 - exam1_weight ) * exam2;
    if ( average > cutoff )
        return 'P';
    else
        return 'F';
}
```

■

[†] There are functions that expect an arbitrary number of arguments. Such functions catch some of the information differently than described here, and their headers are written differently; see R. Johnsonbaugh and M. Kalin, *Applications Programming in ANSI C*, 3rd ed., Upper Saddle River, N.J.: Prentice Hall, 1996: Section 4.10.

EXAMPLE 3.1.3.   The function `echo_line` has no parameters and returns a value of type `int`:

```
int echo_line() {
   ...
}
```
■

EXAMPLE 3.1.4.   The function `print_stars` has one parameter `size` of type `int` and returns no value:

```
void print_stars( int size ) {
   ...
}
```
■

EXAMPLE 3.1.5.   The function `print_prompt` has no parameters and returns no value:

```
void print_prompt() {
   ...
}
```
■

EXAMPLE 3.1.6.   The function `main`, in the form that we have been using it,

```
int main() {
   ...
}
```

has no parameters and returns a value of type `int`.
■

The `return` Statement

A function returns to its invoker. When a function is invoked, the statements in its body begin executing and continue until either a `return` statement or the last statement in its body is executed, after which the statements in the invoking function resume execution in their regular sequence.

The `return` statement is optional in a function that does not return a value; but, if used, it is written

```
return;
```

If a function that does not return a value contains no `return` statement, the function returns to its invoker after the last statement in the function's body is executed.

A function that returns a value must have at least one `return` statement, which is written

```
return exprn;
```

or

```
return ( exprn );
```

where *exprn* is any legal C++ expression. The two forms have exactly the same meaning. When either is executed, the function returns the value *exprn* to its invoker. A function can return at most *one* value per invocation. For example, when

```
return 45 * 6 + add1( x );
```

is executed, the function returns the value of the expression

```
45 * 6 + add1( x )
```

to its invoker. The expression

```
45 * 6 + add1( x )
```

is complex, involving even a call to the function **add1**. The expression's complexity does not violate the rule that the function may return just a single value, for even the most complicated expression evaluates to just one value.

EXAMPLE 3.1.7.   Since the **main** function

```
int main() {
   ...
}
```

returns an **int**, in our programs we have always included the **return** statement

```
return 0;
```

If **main** has no **return** statement, the system executes the equivalent of

```
return 0;
```

when **main** terminates.   ∎

A function may contain any number of **return** statements. Of course, only one **return** statement is executed per invocation, because the **return** statement returns control, and perhaps a value, to the invoking function. In Figure 3.1.1, the function **grade** has two **return** statements. Using multiple **return** statements in **if-else** or **switch** constructs is common. As a rule of thumb, we suggest keeping the number of **return** statements small; otherwise, functions become hard to understand, hard to debug, and hard to alter.

Invoking Functions

A function is invoked with zero or more arguments. The values of the arguments, which represent information passed from the invoking to the invoked function, are obtained from expressions. If a function has no arguments, it is invoked with an empty argument list.

Functions can be invoked in two different ways. If a function returns a value, the function invocation could appear anywhere a simple variable might appear. For example, in Figure 3.1.1, **grade** appears in the expression

```
letter_grade = grade( mid_term, final, weight );
```

The value returned replaces the function invocation after which the evaluation of the expression continues.

If a function does not return a value, it is invoked with a statement consisting just of its name, arguments in parentheses, and the usual terminating semicolon.

EXAMPLE 3.1.8.   The function **print_stars** of Example 3.1.4 could be invoked as

```
print_stars( 10 );
```
    ∎

EXAMPLE 3.1.9. The function `print_prompt` of Example 3.1.5 could be invoked as

```
print_prompt();
```
■

Function Declarations

A function's declaration is different from its definition. To *define* a function is to create it by giving its header and its body. To *declare* a function is to give the data type of the value that the function returns (or **void** if the function does not return a value), its name, and in parentheses the data types of its parameters separated by commas. C++ requires that every function, except **main**, be declared. Unlike a function definition, a function declaration is terminated by a semicolon. This way of writing function definitions and declarations in which the data types are included within parentheses is called **function prototype form**.

The declaration of a function **f** occurs outside all functions and before the first function that invokes **f** or inside each function that invokes **f**. A function declaration outside all functions serves as a declaration for all functions that follow it in the same file. A function declaration inside a function **g** serves as a declaration only for **g**.

EXAMPLE 3.1.10. In Figure 3.1.1, the declaration for **grade**

```
char grade( int exam1, int exam2, float exam_weight );
```

occurs before **main** because **main** invokes **grade**. We could also have declared **grade** in **main**:

```
#include <iostream>
using namespace std;
const float cutoff = 7.0;
int main() {
    char grade( int exam1, int exam2, float exam_weight );
    int mid_term, final;
    ...
}
```
■

EXAMPLE 3.1.11. To declare the functions of Examples 3.1.3 through 3.1.5, we could write

```
int echo_line();
void print_stars( int size );
void print_prompt();
```
■

In a declaration, the names that follow the data types of the parameters are optional and are ignored by the compiler. (In a *definition*, the parameters should always be named.) Names are typically included in a declaration to help document the function. These names need not be the same as the names of the parameters.

EXAMPLE 3.1.12.   In Figure 3.1.1, either

```
char grade( int, int, float );
```

or

```
char grade( int mid, int fin, float wt );
```

could serve as a declaration of **grade**.   ∎

Arguments and Parameters

In any invocation of a function, the arguments passed must be compatible with the parameters as specified in the function's declaration. The compiler can use a function declaration to check for matches between the declaration and invocation, and between the declaration and definition, and issue appropriate warnings and error messages if it detects problems. For example, if a function has two parameters, it must be invoked with two arguments. If the parameters are of type **int** and **char**, respectively, the first argument should be of type **int** and the second of type **char**. When a function is invoked and the data type of an argument is different from the data type declared for the parameter, the system converts the data type of the argument to the data type declared, if possible, and may issue a warning. If the system is unable to convert the data type, it issues an error message.

EXAMPLE 3.1.13.   If in Figure 3.1.1, we replace the header

```
char grade( int exam1, int exam2, float exam1_weight )
```

by

```
char grade( int exam1, int exam2, int exam1_weight )
```

our system generates the message

```
Can't find function grade( int, int, float )
```
                                                                             ∎

EXAMPLE 3.1.14.   If in Figure 3.1.1, we replace the statement

```
letter_grade = grade( mid_term, final, weight );
```

by

```
letter_grade = grade( mid_term, final );
```

our system generates the message

```
Too few parameters in call to 'grade' in function main
```
                                                                             ∎

When a function is invoked, all of the function's arguments are evaluated before control is passed to the invoked function; however, C++ does *not* guarantee the *order* of evaluation of the arguments.

EXAMPLE 3.1.15.   Consider a function **fun** that expects, as arguments, two **int**s. Suppose that we invoke it, dangerously, as follows:

```
int num = 5;
fun( ++num, ++num ); // ***** CAUTION
```

The values passed to **fun** need *not* be

```
fun( 6, 7 );
```

because C++ does *not* guarantee any particular order of argument evaluation. Indeed, different systems evaluate the arguments in different orders. C++ guarantees only that all the arguments passed to a function will be evaluated before control passes to the function.   ■

Default Arguments

Default arguments may be supplied in a function's declaration.

EXAMPLE 3.1.16.   The declaration of the function **print_char** in Figure 3.1.2 has a default argument for the second parameter **how_many**. If the function is invoked and a value is not supplied for **how_many**, the default value, 60, is assigned to **how_many**. In **main**, when **print_char** is invoked the first time

```
print_char( '*', 30 );
```

the value 30 is supplied for the second parameter, so **how_many** is assigned the value 30; the output is

```
******************************
```

The second time that **print_char** is invoked

```
print_char( '$' );
```

no value for the second parameter is supplied, so **how_many** is assigned the default value 60; the output is

```
$$$$$$$$$$$$$$$$$$$$$$$$$$$$$$$$$$$$$$$$$$$$$$$$$$$$$$$$$$$$$$
```

Notice that default arguments are supplied in the function's *declaration*, *not* in the function's definition.   ■

```
#include <iostream>
using namespace std;
void print_char( char c, int how_many = 60 );
int main() {
    print_char( '*', 30 );
    print_char( '$' );
    return 0;
}
void print_char( char c, int how_many ) {
    int i;
    for ( i = 0; i < how_many; i++ )
        cout << c;
    cout << endl;
}
```

FIGURE 3.1.2 A function with a default argument.

If a default argument is supplied for a parameter, *all* following parameters must also have default arguments.

EXAMPLE 3.1.17.   The following declaration is *illegal* because **flag** has a default value, but the following parameter, **numb**, does not

```
// ***** ERROR: flag has a default value,
// but numb does not
void play_games( int strat, int flag = 1, int numb );
```

The error may be corrected by supplying a default value for **numb**

```
// correct
void play_games( int strat, int flag = 1, int numb = 25 );   ∎
```

Functions in Source Files

Although it is possible to divide the functions that make up a program among several files, the entire definition of each function must reside in one file. For example, we cannot put a function's header in one file and its body in a different file. Also, one function's definition cannot occur in another function's body.

EXAMPLE 3.1.18.   The following is illegal in C++ because **fun2**'s definition is in **fun1**'s body:

```
void fun1( int size ) {
    ...
    int fun2( char c ) {   // ***** ILLEGAL *****
        ...
    }
}
```
∎

EXERCISES

1. (True/False) An invoking function must pass arguments to the invoked function.
2. (True/False) An argument and its corresponding parameter must have the same name.
3. (True/False) Every function returns a value to its invoker.
4. (True/False) Parameters are declared in the function's header.
5. (True/False) Default parameter values are supplied in a function's definition.
6. (True/False) A function's header and body must be defined within the same file.
7. (True/False) A function may contain more than one **return** statement.
8. (True/False) A **return** statement may include an expression that invokes a function.
9. What information is given by the following function declaration?

   ```
   int type( float x );
   ```

10. What is the error in the following function definition?

    ```
    void fun1( int parm1, float parm2 ); {
       ...
    }
    ```

11. What is the error in the following function definition?

    ```
    void fun1( int a, float b ) {
       ...
       return 3.14;
    }
    ```

12. What is the syntax error in the following function declaration?

    ```
    int status( code char, time float );
    ```

13. Write the header of a function **power** with two parameters, **base** of type **double** and **exponent** of type **int**, which returns a value of type **double**. How would **power** be declared?

14. Write a function **echo_chars** with no parameters that copies the standard input to the standard output and returns the number of characters copied.

15. Write a function **main** that invokes the function **echo_chars** of the previous exercise once. Be sure to declare **echo_chars**. After invoking **echo_chars**, **main** prints a message that tells the number of characters copied.

16. Write a function **echo_some_chars**, with one parameter **max_echo**, which copies at most **max_echo char**s from the standard input to the standard output and returns the number of characters copied. The function may copy fewer than **max_echo** characters if end-of-file is encountered.

17. Write a function **main** that repeatedly invokes the function **echo_some_chars** of the previous exercise until end-of-file. First, invoke **echo_some_chars** with the argument equal to 2, then 4, then 8, and so on. After each invocation, have **main** print a message that tells the number of characters copied.

18. If the function **h** is invoked as

    ```
    h( ( a, b, c ) );
    ```

    how many arguments are passed to **h**?

19. Is the following syntactically correct? Explain.

```
return val1, val2;
```

20. Invoke the function

```
void fun( int i, int j ) {
   cout << "i = " << i << ", j = " << j << endl;
}
```

on your system by writing

```
int num = 5;
fun( ++num, ++num );
```

to see how your system evaluates the arguments.

21. Modify **print_char**'s declaration in Figure 3.1.2 so that **c** has a default value of `'*'`.

22. What is the output when the function of Exercise 21 is invoked as

```
print_char();
```

23. What is the error in the following function declaration?

```
void f( int val,
        float s = 12.6,
        char t = '\n',
        int errflag );
```

24. The following function attempts to return **true**, if **c** is a letter (uppercase or lowercase), and **false**, otherwise. Explain why it fails.

```
bool is_letter( char c ) {
   if ( c >= 'a' && c <= 'Z' )
      return true;
   return false;
}
```

25. What is the error in the following function definition?

```
fun( int n ) {
   ...
}
```

3.2 SCOPE

A **block** is a section of code bounded by braces **{ }**. For example, the body of a function is a block. If the definition of a variable is contained in a block, the smallest block that contains its definition is called its **containing block**.

EXAMPLE 3.2.1. In the function **f**

```
/* 1 */  void f() {
/* 2 */     int i;
/* 3 */     for ( i = 0; i < 5; i++ ) {
/* 4 */        int j;
/* 5 */        j = 2 * i;
/* 6 */        cout << j << endl;
/* 7 */     }
/* 8 */ }
```

i's containing block is the opening brace on line 1 through line 8, and **j**'s containing block is the brace at the end of line 3 through line 7. ∎

Every variable has a **scope**—the region of the program in which it is **visible**. A variable is visible in a region if it can be referenced in that region. The visibility of a variable that is defined within a block is restricted to the point at which it is defined to the end of its containing block.

EXAMPLE 3.2.2. In Example 3.2.1, **i** is visible throughout the function **f** but nowhere else. The variable **j** is visible in lines 4 through 7 but nowhere else. In particular, **j** could *not* be referenced after line 7, and neither **i** nor **j** could be referenced in any other function:

```
void f() {
   int i;
   for ( i = 0; i < 5; i++ ) {
      int j;
      j = 2 * i;
      cout << j << endl;
   }
   // ***** ERROR: j not visible here *****
   cout << j << endl;
}
void g() {
   // ***** ERROR: i not visible here *****
   cout << i << endl;
   // ***** ERROR: j not visible here *****
   cout << j << endl;
}
```
∎

Variables such as **i** and **j** in Example 3.2.1 are said to be **local** to the containing blocks in which they reside. For this reason, it is possible for functions to have identically named variables that refer to distinct storage.

EXAMPLE 3.2.3.   In the code

```
void move_left() {
   // This i and j are local to move_left
   int i, j;
   ...
}
void move_right() {
   // This i and j are local to move_right
   int i, j;
   ...
}
```

the variables **i** and **j** in **move_left** are local to **move_left**, and the variables **i** and **j** in **move_right** are local to **move_right**. We have *four* distinct variables, although two happen to be named **i** and the other two **j**. If one programmer writes **move_left** and another writes **move_right**, neither has to worry about what the other uses as names for local variables; hence, each programmer can use variables named **i** and **j**. The compiler ensures that the variables named **i** and **j** in one function are distinct from the variables named **i** and **j** in the other.   ∎

In general, any legal identifier may be used for a function's local variables. However, it is illegal to define two variables that have the same scope and the same name. Also, it is illegal to define a variable within a function with the same name as one of its parameters.

A variable whose definition is not contained in a block is visible from the point of its definition to the end of the file. We call such variables **global variables**.

EXAMPLE 3.2.4.   In the program

```
#include <iostream>
using namespace std;
const int MaxSize = 100;
void f();
int main() {
   ...
}
void f() {
   ...
}
```

the definition of the variable **MaxSize**

```
const int MaxSize = 100;
```

is not contained in a block; thus, **MaxSize** is visible from the point of its definition to the end of the file. In particular, **MaxSize** is visible in both **main** and **f**.   ∎

The scope of parameters is always exactly the body of the function to which they belong.

EXAMPLE 3.2.5. The parameters `size` and `symbol` in the function `print`

```
void print( int size, char symbol ) {
    ...
}
```

are visible throughout the function `print`. They are *not* visible in any other function. ■

EXERCISES

1. What is the scope of each variable and parameter?

```
const int stop = 4;
int f( int k );
int main() {
    int i;
    for ( i = 0; i < stop; i++ ) {
        int j = 3;
        cout << j << ": " << j * f( i ) << endl;
    }
    return 0;
}
int f( int k ) {
    return k * k;
}
```

2. Find all errors in the following function

```
int f( int numb ) {
    int i;
    int numb;
    if ( numb < 0 )
        numb *= -1;
    int i = 0;
    while ( numb > 0 ) {
        i++;
        numb /= 2;
    }
    return i;
}
```

3.3 CALL BY VALUE

Every argument to a function is an expression, which has a value. Unless specifically designated otherwise (see Section 3.5), C++ passes an argument to an invoked function by making a copy of the expression's value, storing it in a temporary cell, and making the corresponding parameter this cell's identifier. This method of passing arguments is known as **call by value**.

EXAMPLE 3.3.1. The function **square** in the program of Figure 3.3.1 computes the square of one plus the value passed to it. When **square** is invoked in **main**

```
square( val );
```

a temporary cell named **numb** is created, and the value, 3, of the argument, **val**, is copied into **numb**. Also, storage is allocated for the local variable **sq** (see Figure 3.3.2).

After **numb** is incremented

```
numb++;
```

its value is 4 (see Figure 3.3.3). Notice that the variable **val** in **main** is still 3 because **square** is working on a *copy* of **val**, not on **val** itself. When **numb** is squared and its value is copied into **sq**

```
sq = numb * numb;
```

the value of **sq** is 16 (see Figure 3.3.4). The statement

```
cout << "sq = " << sq << endl;
```

prints

```
sq = 16
```

When **square** returns, storage for its parameter **numb** and local variable **sq** is released (see Figure 3.3.5). The statement

```
cout << "val = " << val << endl;
```

then prints

```
val = 3
```

Had **square** been invoked a second time, storage for its parameter and local variable would have been reallocated. ∎

```
#include <iostream>
using namespace std;
void square( int numb );
int main() {
    int val = 3;
    square( val );
    cout << "val = " << val << endl;
    return 0;
}
void square( int numb ) {
    int sq;
    numb++;
    sq = numb * numb;
    cout << "sq = " << sq << endl;
}
```

FIGURE 3.3.1 Call by value.

FIGURE 3.3.2 Invoking **square**.

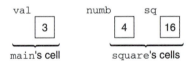

FIGURE 3.3.3 Incrementing **numb**.

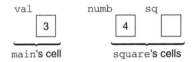

FIGURE 3.3.4 Squaring **numb**.

FIGURE 3.3.5 After **square** returns.

EXAMPLE 3.3.2.   We could modify the program of Figure 3.3.1 (see Figure 3.3.6) by adding a **return** statement to the function **square** so that the square of one plus the value passed by **main** is communicated to **main**. Of course, **val** still retains its original value of 3, but the square, 16, of one plus **val**, which is computed by **square**, is returned by **square** and copied into **sq_val**. The output of the program of Figure 3.3.6 is

```
sq = 16
val = 3
sq_val = 16
```
■

```cpp
#include <iostream>
using namespace std;
int square( int numb );
int main() {
    int val = 3;
    int sq_val;
    sq_val = square( val );
    cout << "val = " << val << endl;
    cout << "sq_val = " << sq_val << endl;
    return 0;
}
int square( int numb ) {
    int sq;
    numb++;
    sq = numb * numb;
    cout << "sq = " << sq << endl;
    return sq;
}
```

FIGURE 3.3.6 Call by value with a return value.

A benefit of call by value is that it protects the values of the arguments in the invoking function from being changed by the invoked function. As shown in Example 3.3.2, one way for the invoking function to obtain a value computed by an invoked function is for the invoked function to use a **return** statement to return the computed value. An alternative is for the invoked function to work directly on the arguments passed and not on copies of them. This method of passing arguments, which is the subject of Section 3.5, is known as *call by reference*.

EXERCISES

1. What is the output?

```cpp
#include <iostream>
using namespace std;
void swap( int a, int b );
int main() {
    int c = 8, d = -2;
    swap( c, d );
    cout << "c = " << c << endl
         << "d = " << d << endl;
    return 0;
}
void swap( int a, int b ) {
    int t;
    t = a;
    a = b;
    b = t;
}
```

2. In the program

```cpp
#include <iostream>
using namespace std;
int square( int numb );
int main() {
    int val = 3;
    int sq_val;
    sq_val = square( val );
    cout << "sq_val = " << sq_val << endl;
    sq_val = square( 8 );
    cout << "sq_val = " << sq_val << endl;
    return 0;
}
int square( int numb ) {
    int sq;
    numb++;
    sq = numb * numb;
    cout << "sq = " << sq << endl;
    return sq;
}
```

how many times is storage allocated for **val**? for **numb**? for **sq**?

3.4 SAMPLE APPLICATION: THE MONTY HALL PROBLEM

Problem

Simulate the Monty Hall problem, which is named for the host of the television game show *Let's Make a Deal*. The problem involves a game played as follows. A contestant picks one of three doors; behind one of the doors is a car, and behind the other two are goats. After the contestant picks a door, the host opens an unpicked door that hides a goat. (Because there are two goats, the host can open a door that hides a goat no matter which door the contestant first picks.) The host then gives the contestant the option of abandoning the picked door in favor of the still closed and unpicked door. The problem is to simulate three different strategies for playing the game:

- Always stay with the door initially picked.
- Randomly stay or switch (e.g., by flipping a coin to decide).
- Always switch to the unpicked and unopened door.

(We assume that the contestant decides the strategy in advance.) The user should be prompted as to which strategy he or she wishes to follow, whether the results of each game should be displayed, and how many times the game should be played. Use the random number generator **rand** to place the car at the start and to simulate the contestant's initial pick. If the contestant follows the second strategy, use the random number generator to determine whether the contestant stays or switches. The program should print the number of games played and the percentage of games won. (A game is won if the contestant gets the car.)

Sample Input/Output

We provide two sample runs.

```
1--never switch
2--always switch
3--randomly switch
Your choice? 3
Play how many games? 10
Display results of each game [Y]es, [N]o? Y

Beginning a new game
Person picks door 1
Car is behind door 1
Host opens door 2
Win

Beginning a new game
Person picks door 1
Car is behind door 1
Host opens door 0
Switch to door 2
Loss
```

```
Beginning a new game
Person picks door 1
Car is behind door 1
Host opens door 2
Win

Beginning a new game
Person picks door 1
Car is behind door 1
Host opens door 2
Win

Beginning a new game
Person picks door 0
Car is behind door 0
Host opens door 2
Switch to door 1
Loss

Beginning a new game
Person picks door 2
Car is behind door 1
Host opens door 0
Loss

Beginning a new game
Person picks door 2
Car is behind door 2
Host opens door 1
Win

Beginning a new game
Person picks door 0
Car is behind door 1
Host opens door 2
Loss

Beginning a new game
Person picks door 0
Car is behind door 1
Host opens door 2
Switch to door 1
Win

Beginning a new game
Person picks door 1
Car is behind door 2
Host opens door 0
Loss
Games played = 10
```

```
Games won = 5
Percent won = 50

1--never switch
2--always switch
3--randomly switch
Your choice? 2
Play how many games? 1000
Display results of each game [Y]es, [N]o? N
Games played = 1000
Games won = 685
Percent won = 68.5
```

Solution

Big problems may require big programs—too big to be written all at one time or to be written, or even understood, by a single programmer. Top-down design (see Section 0.5) decomposes the original problem into smaller problems, then those problems into smaller problems, and so on. Finally each problem is solved by writing a function. After the functions are combined into a program, the original problem is solved. By decomposing a problem into functions, the work can be divided among several programmers. It is then even possible for the programmers to write the functions at different times. There are other advantages as well. One function can be tested separately from the rest. With careful design, one function can be changed without disturbing the rest of the program. The program can be made more readable and more easily understood by delegating intricate or otherwise specialized tasks to appropriate functions. We use top-down design to write the program that simulates the Monty Hall game.

At the top level in **main**, we must

1. Get the strategy.
2. Get the number of games to play.
3. Ask the user whether the results of each game should be displayed.
4. Play the games.
5. Report the number of games played, the number of games won, and the percentage of games won.

We will write separate functions to

- Get the strategy.
- Get the number of games to play.
- Ask the user whether the results of each game should be displayed.
- Play the games.

We could also write a function to report the number of games played, the number of games won, and the percentage of games won, but we elect to just write three **cout** statements instead.

The function to get the strategy should display the strategy menu

```
1--never switch
2--always switch
3--randomly switch
Your choice?
```

read the user's choice, and check whether the response is 1, 2, or 3. If the response is invalid, the user should be prompted again to enter a strategy. If the response is valid, the function should return the response. This function will have no parameters and return an **int**.

The function to get the number of games to play should prompt the user

```
Play how many games?
```

and then read and return the user's response. Here we elect not to check for valid input. (Exercise 4 asks for an enhancement that checks for valid input.) Whatever value the user enters, the program will try, perhaps unsuccessfully, to play that number of games. This function, too, will have no parameters and return an **int**.

Similarly, the function that determines whether to display the results of each game should prompt the user

```
Display results of each game [Y]es, [N]o?
```

and then read and return the user's response. We again elect not to check for valid input. (Exercise 5 asks for an enhancement that checks for valid input.) If the user enters **Y**, we will display the results of each game. If the user enters any other response, we will not display the results of each game. This function will have no parameters and return a **char**.

The function that plays the games is the most complicated. Since it will need to know which strategy to play, how many games to play, and whether to display the results of each game, it will have three parameters.

The code that simulates the game will sit inside a loop that simulates one game. To simulate a game we must

1. Randomly pick the person's door.
2. Randomly place the car.
3. Pick a door for the host to open. (If the person has picked the car, the host will make a random choice between the two available doors.)
4. Determine whether the user should switch doors. (If strategy 1 was chosen, the user will not switch doors. If strategy 2 was chosen, the user will switch doors. If strategy 3 was chosen, the user will randomly decide whether to switch.)
5. Switch doors, if the user is switching.
6. Check whether the user won the game.
7. Return the number of games won when the loop terminates.

In addition, we must display the results of each game if the user has so requested.

We use the library random number generator **rand**, which is declared in the header file *cstdlib*, to simulate a random choice. The function **rand** returns a random integer in the range 0 to **RAND_MAX**, which is a large integer defined in *cstdlib*. We can use the expression

```
rand() % value
```

to obtain a random integer in the range 0 to *value* − 1. (The remainder when we divide any integer by *value* is one of 0, 1, 2, ..., *value* − 1.) For example, if we label the doors 0, 1, and 2, the statement

```
car = rand() % 3;
```

randomly sets the variable **car** to one of 0, 1, or 2, which we can interpret as randomly placing the car behind one of the doors.

C++ Implementation

```cpp
#include <iostream>
#include <cstdlib>
using namespace std;
int get_strat();
int get_no_games();
char get_each_game_flag();
int play_games( int strat, int no_games, char each_game_flag );

int main() {
   int strat, no_games, won;
   char each_game_flag;
   strat = get_strat();
   no_games = get_no_games();
   each_game_flag = get_each_game_flag();
   won = play_games( strat, no_games, each_game_flag );
   cout << "Games played = " << no_games << endl;
   cout << "Games won = " << won << endl;
   cout << "Percent won = " <<
           100.0 * won / no_games << endl;
   return 0;
}

int get_strat() {
   int strat;
   do {
      cout << "1--never switch" << endl
           << "2--always switch" << endl
           << "3--randomly switch" << endl
           << "Your choice? ";
      cin >> strat;
   } while ( strat < 1 && strat > 3 );
   return strat;
}
```

```
int get_no_games() {
   int no_games;
   cout << "Play how many games? ";
   cin >> no_games;
   return no_games;
}
char get_each_game_flag() {
   char each_game_flag;
   cout << "Display results of each game [Y]es, [N]o? ";
   cin >> each_game_flag;
   return each_game_flag;
}
int play_games( int strat, int no_games, char each_game_flag ) {
   int i, car, host, sw_flag, person, win;
   for ( win = 0, i = 0; i < no_games; i++ ) {
      if ( each_game_flag == 'Y' )
         cout << "\n\nBeginning a new game\n";
      // pick person's door
      person = rand() % 3;
      if ( each_game_flag == 'Y')
         cout << "Person picks door " << person << endl;
      // place car behind a door
      car = rand() % 3;
      if ( each_game_flag == 'Y' )
         cout << "Car is behind door " << car << endl;
      // if person has picked the car, the host
      // has a random choice of doors to open
      if ( person == car )
         host = ( 1 + person + rand() % 2 ) % 3;
      // otherwise the host's door is the door
      // other than the person's that does not
      // contain the car
      else {
         host = ( person + 1 ) % 3;
         if ( host == car )
            host = ( host + 1 ) % 3;
      }
      if ( each_game_flag == 'Y' )
         cout << "Host opens door " << host << endl;
      switch ( strat ) {
      case 1: // never switch
         sw_flag = 0;
         break;
      case 2: // always switch
         sw_flag = 1;
         break;
```

```
      case 3: // randomly switch
         sw_flag = rand() % 2;
         break;
   }
   if ( sw_flag ) {
      // the person switches to the door
      // the host did not open
      person = ( person + 1 ) % 3;
      if ( person == host )
         person = ( person + 1 ) % 3;
      if ( each_game_flag == 'Y' )
         cout << "Switch to door " << person << endl;
   }
   if ( car == person ) {
      if ( each_game_flag == 'Y' )
         cout << "Win" << endl;
      win++;
   }
   else if ( each_game_flag == 'Y' )
      cout << "Loss" << endl;
   }
   return win;
}
```

Discussion

The function **main** defines variables **strat**, **no_games**, **each_game_flag**, and **won**. The value of **strat** is 1 (never switch), 2 (always switch), or 3 (randomly switch). The value of **no_games** is the number of games to play. The value of **each_game_flag** is **Y** (display the results of each game) or **N** (do not display the results of each game). The value of **won** is the number of games won.

The value of **strat** is obtained from the function **get_strat**

```
strat = get_strat();
```

Similarly, the value of **no_games** is obtained from **get_no_games**

```
no_games = get_no_games();
```

and the value of **each_game_flag** is obtained from **get_each_game_flag**

```
each_game_flag = get_each_game_flag();
```

The values of **strat**, **no_games**, and **each_game_flag** are used as arguments to **play_games**. The value of **won** is obtained from **play_games** (which also plays the games)

```
won = play_games( strat, no_games, each_game_flag );
```

After invoking the functions to get the user's input and to play the games, **main** reports the results

```
cout << "Games played = " << no_games << endl;
cout << "Games won = " << won << endl;
cout << "Percent won = " <<
        100.0 * won / no_games << endl;
```

The function **get_strat** uses a **do while** loop to display a menu and obtain the user's choice

```
do {
   cout << "1--never switch" << endl
        << "2--always switch" << endl
        << "3--randomly switch" << endl
        << "Your choice? ";
   cin >> strat;
} while ( strat < 1 && strat > 3 );
```

After receiving a valid response (one of 1, 2, or 3), **get_strat** returns it

```
return strat;
```

The functions **get_no_games** and **get_each_game_flag** work in a similar way, except that they do not check for valid input.

The parameters of the function **play_games**, whose header is

```
int play_games( int strat, int no_games, char each_game_flag )
```

are used to determine the strategy, the number of games to play, and whether to display the results of each game. After all the games have been simulated, **play_games** returns the number of games won.

A **for** loop is used to repeatedly play the games

```
for ( win = 0, i = 0; i < no_games; i++ ) {
   ...
}
```

At appropriate points within this **for** loop, if **each_game_flag** is equal to `'Y'`, information about the current game is printed. For example, at the top of the **for** loop, we have

```
if ( each_game_flag == 'Y' )
   cout << "\n\nBeginning a new game\n";
```

Within the loop, we begin by randomly picking the person's door and randomly placing the car behind a door

```
person = rand() % 3;
car = rand() % 3;
```

Next the host opens an unpicked door that hides a goat. If the person has picked the car, the host has a random choice of doors to open

```
host = ( 1 + person + rand() % 2 ) % 3;
```

person	Value of **host** if rand % 2 equals 0	Value of **host** if rand % 2 equals 1
0	1	2
1	2	0
2	0	1

FIGURE 3.4.1 The host's door to open when the person has picked the car.

Figure 3.4.1 shows that whatever the value of **person**, the host has an even chance of opening either of the other two doors.

If the person has picked a goat, the host's choice is determined

```
host = ( person + 1 ) % 3;
if ( host == car )
   host = ( host + 1 ) % 3;
```

Here the code initially moves the host one door past the person's door (assuming that door 0 follows door 2); if that door has a car behind it, the code moves the host one additional door past the person's door. In the latter case, the resulting door must have a goat behind it.

Next the local variable **sw_flag** is set to 1 (switch) or 0 (do not switch)

```
switch ( strat ) {
case 1: // never switch
   sw_flag = 0;
   break;
case 2: // always switch
   sw_flag = 1;
   break;
case 3: // randomly switch
   sw_flag = rand() % 2;
   break;
}
```

Next if **sw_flag** is equal to 1, the person switches to the unopened door

```
person = ( person + 1 ) % 3;
if ( person == host )
   person = ( person + 1 ) % 3;
```

Here the code initially moves the person one door past the person's original door (again assuming that door 0 follows door 2); if that door was picked by the host, the code moves the person one additional door past the person's original door.

Finally, the code checks whether the person won, and if so, updates **win**

```
if ( car == person ) {
   ...
   win++;
}
```

It is an interesting exercise to determine the expected percentage of wins for the various strategies (see Exercises 1, 2, and 3). These percentages can be determined by reasoning about the abstract problem or by looking closely at the code. The analysis of the situation is more complicated if the user does not commit to a strategy before playing the game. For a technical discussion of the various aspects of this puzzle, see L. Gillman, "The car and the goats," *Amer. Math. Mo.* 99 (1992): 3–7.

Random number generators such as **rand** are more properly called *pseudorandom number generators* because the numbers generated by such functions are determined by the code and are therefore not truly random. Nonetheless, it is possible to write code in such a way that the numbers appear to be random. [For a discussion of pseudorandom number generators see D. Knuth, *The Art of Computer Programming*, vol. 2, *Seminumerical Algorithms*, 2nd ed. (Reading, Mass.: Addison-Wesley, 1981).]

Simulations, which are routinely used in areas such as computational mathematics and systems design, are useful and indispensable in situations in which it is difficult or time-consuming to obtain an exact solution. The inventor, Stanislaw Ulam, of a particular simulation method known as the *Monte Carlo technique* wrote [in S. M. Ulam, *Adventures of a Mathematician* (New York: Scribner's, 1976): 196–197]:

The idea for what was later called the Monte Carlo method occurred to me when I was playing solitaire during my illness. I noticed that it may be much more practical to get an idea of the probability of the successful outcome of a solitaire game by laying down the cards, or experimenting with the process and merely noticing what proportion comes out successfully, rather than to try to compute all the combinatorial possibilities which are an exponentially increasing number so great that, except in very elementary cases, there is no way to estimate it. This is intellectually surprising, and if not exactly humiliating, it gives one a feeling of modesty about the limit of rational or traditional thinking. In a sufficiently complicated problem, actual sampling is better than an examination of all the chains of possibilities.

Program Development

In writing a complex program, it is *not* a good idea to write the entire program, type it all in, and then try to get it to work. Instead it is better to start by writing one function and getting it to work, then writing another function and getting it to work, and so on, until the whole program is written and working.

In this program, we would first write **main**, since it calls all the other functions, and test it. Until we write the other functions, we will replace them with **stubs**. A stub is just a place-holder and does minimal work. For example, a stub might report that the function was called and return a value, if required. Later the stubs will be replaced with the desired code. Thus initially our program is

```cpp
#include <iostream>
#include <cstdlib>
using namespace std;
int get_strat();
int get_no_games();
char get_each_game_flag();
int play_games( int strat, int no_games, char each_game_flag );

int main() {
    int strat, no_games, won;
    char each_game_flag;
    strat = get_strat();
    no_games = get_no_games();
    each_game_flag = get_each_game_flag();
    won = play_games( strat, no_games, each_game_flag );
    cout << "Games played = " << no_games << endl;
    cout << "Games won = " << won << endl;
    cout << "Percent won = " <<
            100.0 * won / no_games << endl;
    return 0;
}

int get_strat() {
    cout << "get_strat entered" << endl;
    return 1;
}

int get_no_games() {
    cout << "get_no_games entered" << endl;
    return 1;
}

char get_each_game_flag() {
    cout << "get_each_game_flag entered" << endl;
    return 'Y';
}

int play_games( int strat, int no_games, char each_game_flag ) {
    cout << "play_games entered" << endl;
    return 5;
}
```

Here the actual return values are of no consequence; they are supplied to make the program syntactically correct.

Next we write the simplest functions. In this program, we might write **get_strat**. We should test **get_strat** by entering each valid value—1, 2, and 3—for **strat**, as well as some invalid values.

After **get_strat** is written and tested, we can write and test **get_no_games**, and then write and test **get_each_game_flag**.

To complete the program, we write **play_games**. Since this function is somewhat complex, we might initially simplify it by coding only the "never switch" strategy. Since this strategy does not involve the host, we can omit the host. We do want to include the code that reports on the status of the game so we can check whether our code is correct. Without comments the function is

```
int play_games( int strat, int no_games, char each_game_flag ) {
    int i, car, person, win;
    for ( win = 0, i = 0; i < no_games; i++ ) {
        if ( each_game_flag == 'Y' )
            cout << "\n\nBeginning a new game\n";
        person = rand() % 3;
        if ( each_game_flag == 'Y')
            cout << "Person picks door " << person << endl;
        car = rand() % 3;
        if ( each_game_flag == 'Y' )
            cout << "Car is behind door " << car << endl;
        if ( car == person ) {
            if ( each_game_flag == 'Y' )
                cout << "Win" << endl;
            win++;
        }
        else if ( each_game_flag == 'Y' )
            cout << "Loss" << endl;
    }
    return win;
}
```

After writing and testing this abbreviated version of **play_games**, we can extend it to include the host and to play the other two strategies. After testing this final version, the program is complete.

EXERCISES

1. What is the expected percentage of wins if the "never switch" strategy is used?

2. What is the expected percentage of wins if the "always switch" strategy is used?

3. What is the expected percentage of wins if the "random switch" strategy is used?

4. Modify **get_no_games** so that it checks whether the user's response is greater than or equal to 0.

5. Modify **get_each_game_flag** so that it checks whether the user's response is **Y** or **N**.

3.5 CALL BY REFERENCE

We saw in Section 3.3 how C++ uses call by value to pass arguments. In call by value the invoked function receives *copies* of the arguments. It is possible to avoid copying arguments and let the invoked function work directly on the arguments. This method of passing arguments is called **call by reference**. To indicate that an argument is to be passed by reference, we append an ampersand **&** to the data type.

> **EXAMPLE 3.5.1.** In the program in Figure 3.5.1, because of the ampersands following the data types
>
> ```
> void f( int& a, int& b )
> ```
>
> arguments to the function **f** are passed by reference. When **main** invokes **f** with arguments **x** and **y**
>
> ```
> f( x, y );
> ```
>
> **f**'s parameter **a** refers to **x**, *not* a copy of **x** (see Figure 3.5.2). Similarly, **f**'s parameter **b** refers to **y**. Thus when the statements
>
> ```
> a = -3;
> b = 7;
> ```

```
#include <iostream>
using namespace std;
void f( int& a, int& b );

int main() {
    int x, y;
    x = 8;
    y = 10;
    f( x, y );
    cout << "x = " << x << endl;
    cout << "y = " << y << endl;
    return 0;
}

void f( int& a, int& b ) {
    a = -3;
    b = 7;
}
```

FIGURE 3.5.1 Passing arguments by reference.

execute in **f**, the value of **x** is changed to −3, and the value of **y** is changed to 7. The output of the program is

```
x = -3
y = 7
```

■

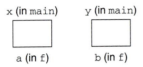

x (in main)   y (in main)

a (in f)   b (in f)

FIGURE 3.5.2 In call by reference, **f**'s parameter **a** in Figure 3.5.1 refers to **x** in **main**, *not* a copy of **x**. Similarly, **f**'s parameter **b** refers to **y** in **main**.

Since call by reference allows the invoked function to change the values of the arguments passed by the invoking function, we use call by reference when we require the invoked function to change the values of the arguments.

EXAMPLE 3.5.2. The function **swap**

```
// call by reference
void swap( int& x, int& y ) {
   int temp;
   temp = x;
   x = y;
   y = temp;
}
```

swaps the values of arguments passed. For example if the value of **a** is 3 and the value of **b** is 18, after

```
swap( a, b );
```

the value of **a** is 18 and the value of **b** is 3 (see Figure 3.5.3). Notice that if the arguments were passed by *value*

```
// call by value
void swap( int x, int y ) {
   int temp;
   temp = x;
   x = y;
   y = temp;
}
```

after

```
swap( a, b );
```

the values of **a** and **b** would be unchanged (see Figure 3.5.4). In call by value, the function works on *copies* of the arguments *not* on the actual arguments. ■

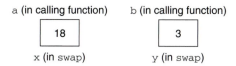

x (in swap)   y (in swap)

FIGURE 3.5.3 Call-by-reference version of **swap**.

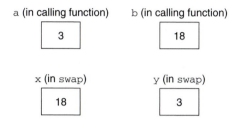

FIGURE 3.5.4 Call-by-value version of **swap**.

EXAMPLE 3.5.3.   The function **print_row**

```
void print_row( ofstream& out, char c, int n ) {
   int i;
   for ( i = 0; i < n; i++ )
       out << c;
   out << endl;
}
```

writes the character **c**, **n** times, followed by a newline to the file associated with the variable **out**. As shown, the variable **out** is passed by reference

```
ofstream& out
```

In fact, the variable **out** must *not* be passed by value. To write to a file, the variable **out** must be changed because it must keep track of details such as formatting information (field width, whether to skip white space, etc.) and where in the buffer to write the next output.   ■

The other major reason to use call by reference is to avoid the overhead of copying a variable—especially when the cell to which the variable refers occupies a large amount of storage. For this reason, *objects*, which we will discuss in detail in Chapter 5, are typically passed by reference.

Return by Reference

By default in C++, when a function returns a value

return *expression*;

expression is evaluated and its value is copied into temporary storage, which the invoking function can then access. We call this method of returning a value **return by value**.

EXAMPLE 3.5.4. When the function

```
int val1() {
    ...
    return i;
}
```

is invoked, the value **i** is copied into temporary storage, which the invoking function can then access.

If the function **val1** is invoked as

```
j = val1();
```

the value **i** is copied into temporary storage and then copied into **j** (see Figure 3.5.5). ∎

i temporary storage j

i		copy to			copy to	

```
i           storage         j
 ___       copy to   ___   copy to   ___
| 8 |   ⟹        | 8 |   ⟹        | 8 |
 ‾‾‾                ‾‾‾                ‾‾‾
```

FIGURE 3.5.5 Return by value.

An alternative to return by value is **return by reference**, in which the value returned is *not* copied into temporary storage. Rather the actual cell in the **return** statement is made available to the invoking function. Return by reference is signaled by appending an ampersand to the return type.

EXAMPLE 3.5.5. Because the return type **int&** in the function

```
int& val2() {
    ...
    return i;
}
```

has an ampersand, it returns its value by reference. When the **return** statement is executed, the cell **i** is made available to the invoking function.

If the function **val2** is invoked as

```
j = val2();
```

the value in **i** is copied into **j** (see Figure 3.5.6). Unlike return by value, this is the only copy that takes place. ∎

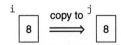

```
i           j
 ___  copy to  ___
| 8 |   ⟹    | 8 |
 ‾‾‾          ‾‾‾
```

FIGURE 3.5.6 Return by reference.

Since a function that uses return by reference returns an actual cell, it is important that the cell remain in existence after the function returns.

EXAMPLE 3.5.6.   The function

```
int& f() {
   int i;
   ...
   // ***** ERROR: i goes out of existence
   return i;
}
```

contains an error. When **f** returns **i**, **i** goes out of existence. Thus the invoking function cannot access the cell **i** that is returned.

There is *no* error if return by value is used:

```
int f() {
   int i;
   ...
   // OK
   return i;
}
```

Here the value of **i** is copied into temporary storage to which the invoking function has access.   ∎

EXERCISES

1. Write a function **upper** with one parameter **c** of type **char**, which is passed by reference. If **c** is a lowercase character, **upper** changes **c** to uppercase. If **c** is not a lowercase character, **upper** does not change **c**. Assume ASCII representation of characters.

2. Write a function **lower** with one parameter **c** of type **char**, which is passed by reference. If **c** is an uppercase character, **lower** changes **c** to lowercase. If **c** is not an uppercase character, **lower** does not change **c**. Assume ASCII representation of characters.

3. Find the error and correct it.

```
void read_data( ifstream in, short a, int n ) {
   in >> a >> n;
}
```

4. Find the error.

```
int& dbl( int i ) {
   int j = 2 * i;
   return j;
}
```

3.6 SAMPLE APPLICATION: PRINTING A CALENDAR

Problem

Write a program that prints a calendar for a year. Prompt the user for the year and print the year and the calendar to the file *calendar.dat*.

January 1 in year x begins on day

$$\left(x + \left\lfloor \frac{x-1}{4} \right\rfloor - \left\lfloor \frac{x-1}{100} \right\rfloor + \left\lfloor \frac{x-1}{400} \right\rfloor \right) \bmod 7$$

where $\lfloor x \rfloor$ denotes the greatest integer less than or equal to x, and $m \bmod n$ denotes the remainder when m is divided by n. Sunday corresponds to 0, Monday to 1, and so on. For example, if $x = 1998$,

$$\left(1998 + \left\lfloor \frac{1998-1}{4} \right\rfloor - \left\lfloor \frac{1998-1}{100} \right\rfloor + \left\lfloor \frac{1998-1}{400} \right\rfloor \right) \bmod 7$$

$$= (1998 + 499 - 19 + 4) \bmod 7 = 2482 \bmod 7 = 4$$

thus, January 1, 1998 begins on Thursday.

Year x is a leap year if

x is divisible by 4 and not by 100

or

x is divisible by 400

For example, 1998 is divisible by neither 4 nor 400, so 1998 is not a leap year. 1996 is a leap year since 1996 is divisible by 4 and not by 100. 2000 is a leap year since 2000 is divisible by 400. 1900 is not a leap year since 1900 is divisible by 4 and by 100, and 1900 is not divisible by 400.

Sample Input/Output

```
Enter the year: 1998
```

The output file *calendar.dat* begins

```
1998

January

Sun   Mon   Tue   Wed   Thu   Fri   Sat
                          1     2     3
  4     5     6     7     8     9    10
 11    12    13    14    15    16    17
 18    19    20    21    22    23    24
 25    26    27    28    29    30    31

February

Sun   Mon   Tue   Wed   Thu   Fri   Sat
  1     2     3     4     5     6     7
  8     9    10    11    12    13    14
 15    16    17    18    19    20    21
 22    23    24    25    26    27    28
```

Solution

The top-level design is

- Open the output file *calendar.dat*.
- Prompt the user for the year and read the response.
- Output the calendar.

We write a function that opens the output file and tests whether the file was opened successfully. If the file was not opened successfully, the program terminates. We also write a function that outputs the calendar. The **main** function invokes the file-opening function and the output function.

The function that outputs the calendar invokes a function that determines the day on which January 1 of the specified year begins and a function that determines whether the specified year is a leap year. These latter two functions use the formulas given in the Problem section.

C++ Implementation

```cpp
// This program prints a calendar for a year.
// The user enters the year, after which
// the year and calendar are printed to the
// file calendar.dat.

#include <iostream>
#include <iomanip>
#include <fstream>
#include <cstdlib>
using namespace std;
void open_or_die( ofstream& out );
void print_calendar( int year, ofstream& out );
int get_day_code( int year );
bool get_leap_code( int year );

int main() {
   ofstream outfile;
   open_or_die( outfile );
   int year;
   cout << "Enter the year: ";
   cin >> year;
   print_calendar( year, outfile );
   return 0;
}

void open_or_die( ofstream& out ) {
   out.open( "calendar.dat" );
   if ( !out ) {
      cerr << "Unable to open calendar.dat" << endl;
      exit( EXIT_FAILURE );
   }
}
```

```
// print_calendar prints the calendar specified
// by parameter year to the output file specified
// by parameter out.
void print_calendar( int year, ofstream& out ) {
   int day_code, month, day, days_in_month;
   bool leap_code;
   out << year;

   // get_day_code returns the day on which January
   // 1 of year begins. The return value is coded
   // as: 0 is Sunday, 1 is Monday, and so on.
   day_code = get_day_code( year );

   // get_leap_code returns true, if year is a
   // leap year; and false, otherwise.
   leap_code = get_leap_code( year );

   // month is coded as 1 for Jan, 2 for Feb,
   // and so on.
   for ( month = 1; month <= 12; month++ ) {
      // print name and set days_in_month
      switch ( month ) {
      case 1:
         out << "\n\nJanuary";
         days_in_month = 31;
         break;
      case 2:
         out << "\n\nFebruary";
         if ( leap_code )
            days_in_month = 29;
         else
            days_in_month = 28;
         break;
      case 3:
         out << "\n\nMarch";
         days_in_month = 31;
         break;
      case 4:
         out << "\n\nApril";
         days_in_month = 30;
         break;
      case 5:
         out << "\n\nMay";
         days_in_month = 31;
         break;
      case 6:
         out << "\n\nJune";
         days_in_month = 30;
         break;
```

```cpp
      case 7:
         out << "\n\nJuly";
         days_in_month = 31;
         break;
      case 8:
         out << "\n\nAugust";
         days_in_month = 31;
         break;
      case 9:
         out << "\n\nSeptember";
         days_in_month = 30;
         break;
      case 10:
         out << "\n\nOctober";
         days_in_month = 31;
         break;
      case 11:
         out << "\n\nNovember";
         days_in_month = 30;
         break;
      case 12:
         out << "\n\nDecember";
         days_in_month = 31;
         break;
   }

   out << "\n\nSun  Mon  Tue  Wed  Thu  Fri  Sat\n";

   // advance to correct position for first day
   for ( day = 1; day <= day_code * 5; day++ )
      out << " ";

   // print the dates for one month
   for ( day = 1; day <= days_in_month; day++ ) {
      // field width is 3 because day names
      // are 3 characters.
      out << setw( 3 ) << day;
      if ( ( day + day_code ) % 7 > 0 ) // before Sat?
         // move 2 spaces to next day in same week.
         // (2 spaces separate the day names.)
         out << "  ";
      else  // skip to next line to start with Sun
         out << endl;
   }
   // set day_code for next month to begin
   day_code = ( day_code + days_in_month ) % 7;
   }
}
```

```
// get_day_code returns the day on which January
// 1 of the specified year begins. The return
// value is coded as: 0 is Sunday, 1 is Monday,
// and so on.
int get_day_code( int year ) {
   return ( year + ( year - 1 ) / 4 - ( year - 1 ) / 100
            + ( year - 1 ) / 400 ) % 7;
}

// get_leap_code returns true, if the specified
// year is a leap year; and false, otherwise.
bool get_leap_code( int year ) {
   return year % 4 == 0 && year % 100 != 0
          || year % 400 == 0;
}
```

Discussion

The **main** function implements the top-level design previously discussed. It invokes **open_or_die**, which tries to open the output file. It then prompts the user for the year and invokes **print_calendar** to output the calendar.

Function **open_or_die** tries to open the output file

```
out.open( "calendar.dat" );
```

The file parameter **out** must *not* be passed by value (see Section 3.5). Next **open_or_die** tests whether the file was opened successfully

```
if ( !out ) {
   cerr << "Unable to open calendar.dat" << endl;
   exit( EXIT_FAILURE );
}
```

If the file was opened successfully, in the **if** statement, **!out** evaluates to **false**, and **open_or_die** simply returns. If, on the other hand, the file was not opened successfully, in the **if** statement, **!out** evaluates to **true**, and **open_or_die** outputs an error message and then invokes the system function **exit**

```
cerr << "Unable to open calendar.dat" << endl;
exit( EXIT_FAILURE );
```

The variable **cerr** is similar to **cout**; its default destination is the user's screen. The reason for using **cerr** is that even if **cout** is rerouted somewhere other than the user's screen, error messages can still be sent to the user's screen. Function **exit** terminates the program and returns the value **EXIT_FAILURE** to the invoking process. Both **exit** and **EXIT_FAILURE** require the header file *cstdlib*. By the way, **exit** can signal successful termination by using the value **EXIT_SUCCESS**.

Function **print_calendar** has two parameters specifying the year and the output file. Again the file parameter must not be passed by value.

Function **print_calendar** invokes **get_day_code**, which signals the day on which January 1 of the year begins

```
day_code = get_day_code( year );
```

The return value is 0 if January 1 begins on Sunday, 1 if January 1 begins on Monday, and so on.

Similarly, **print_calendar** invokes **get_leap_code**, which returns **true** if the year is a leap year, and **false** otherwise

```
leap_code = get_leap_code( year );
```

A **for** loop steps through the 12 months

```
for ( month = 1; month <= 12; month++ ) {
```

A **switch** statement outputs the month and sets the variable **days_in_month**.

Next the days are output

```
out << "\n\nSun  Mon  Tue  Wed  Thu  Fri  Sat\n";
```

Notice that each day's name is three characters long, and the names are separated by two spaces.

The correct position for the first date is set by writing an appropriate number of spaces

```
for ( day = 1; day <= day_code * 5; day++ )
   out << " ";
```

For example, if January 1 begins on Sunday, no spaces should be output. This is what happens since Sunday corresponds to **day_code** having value 0. If January 1 begins on Monday, 5 spaces should be output (3 for the name and 2 for the name separator). This is what happens since Monday corresponds to **day_code** having value 1.

A **for** loop steps through the dates

```
for ( day = 1; day <= days_in_month; day++ ) {
```

The date is printed in a field of width 3, since the names of the days are three characters long

```
out << setw( 3 ) << day;
```

The default action is to right-justify output in its field. We take advantage of this default action to right-align the dates as desired. If the date last printed is not Saturday, we move two spaces to print the next date

```
if ( ( day + day_code ) % 7 > 0 ) // before Sat?
   out << "  ";
```

Otherwise, we skip to the next line to resume with Sunday

```
out << endl;
```

After printing all the dates for the month, we reset **day_code** to be ready to print the next month's dates

```
day_code = ( day_code + days_in_month ) % 7;
```

The functions **get_day_code** and **get_leap_code** are direct translations of the formulas for the day on which January 1 begins and determining whether a year is a leap year.

3.7 OVERLOADING FUNCTIONS

C++ permits identically named functions within the same scope if they can be distinguished by the number and type of parameters. If there are multiple definitions of a function **f**, **f** is said to be **overloaded**. The compiler determines which version of an overloaded function to invoke by choosing from among the identically named functions the one function whose parameters best match the arguments supplied. The precise rules for determining which function is the "best match" are complicated; however, an *exact* match is always the best match.

EXAMPLE 3.7.1. The program shown in Figure 3.7.1 overloads the function **print**. When the statement

```
print( x );
```

is executed, the function

```
void print( int a ) {
   cout << a << endl;
}
```

is invoked because the argument is of type **int**. However, when the statement

```
print( y );
```

is executed, the function

```
void print( double a ) {
   cout << showpoint
        << a << endl;
}
```

is invoked because the argument is of type **double**. ∎

EXAMPLE 3.7.2. The mathematics function **sqrt** is overloaded to support the three floating-point data types:

```
float sqrt( float );
double sqrt( double );
long double sqrt( long double );
```

If a **float** argument is passed, the value of the square root is returned as a **float**. If a **double** argument is passed, the value of the square root is returned as a **double**. If a **long double** argument is passed, the value of the square root is returned as a **long double**. The other mathematics functions (e.g., **sin**) are similarly overloaded. ∎

```
#include <iostream>
#include <iomanip>
using namespace std;
void print( int a );
void print( double a );

int main() {
   int x = 8;
   double y = 8;
   print( x );
   print( y );
   return 0;
}

void print( int a ) {
   cout << a << endl;
}

void print( double a ) {
   cout << showpoint
        << a << endl;
}
```

FIGURE 3.7.1 Overloading the function `print`.

Function Signatures

C++ requires that overloaded functions have distinct **signatures**. A function's signature consists of

- Its name.
- The number, data types, and order of its arguments.

To be distinct, functions must have distinct signatures.

EXAMPLE 3.7.3. The functions

```
void f();
void g();
```

have distinct signatures because they have distinct names. ∎

EXAMPLE 3.7.4. The functions

```
void f();
void f( int );
```

have distinct signatures despite sharing a name. The number of arguments distinguishes the *two* functions named `f`. ∎

EXAMPLE 3.7.5. The functions

```
void p( double );
void p( unsigned );
```

have distinct signatures because the data types of their single arguments differ. ■

EXAMPLE 3.7.6. The functions

```
void m( double, int );
void m( int, double );
```

have distinct signatures because the order of their two arguments differs, even though each function has one **double** and one **int** argument. ■

The return type is *not* part of a function's signature. Therefore, functions cannot be distinguished by return type alone.

EXAMPLE 3.7.7. The functions

```
int s( int );
double s( int ); // ***** ERROR: not distinct from s above
```

are not distinct and the compiler will issue an error message to that effect. ■

Why Overload?

Overloaded functions are used to give a common name to similar behavior on different data types. In Example 3.7.1, "print" is a common name for similar behavior on different data types. From the point of view of the user, there is a single function **print** that prints different data types.

It is also possible to have multiple definitions of operators such as + or -, in which case, we say that the operator is *overloaded*. For example, the operator + is overloaded by the system because + can refer to any numeric type. The compiler determines which version of an overloaded operator to invoke by checking the types of the arguments. For example, if **i** and **j** are **int**s, the system executes instructions appropriate for adding **int**s in evaluating **i + j**. On the other hand, if **x** and **y** are **double**s, the system executes instructions appropriate for adding **double**s in evaluating **x + y**. As additional examples, the right-shift operator >> is overloaded for input, and the left-shift operator << is overloaded for output. In Chapter 8, we will show how the programmer can extend the C++ operators by further overloading them.

EXERCISES

1. Further overload the function **print** of Example 3.7.1 by writing a version that has one **char** parameter **c**. This version prints the ASCII value of **c**.

2. Further overload the function **print** of Example 3.7.1 by writing a version that has a **char** parameter **c** and an **int** parameter **n**. This version prints **n** **c**'s followed by a newline.

†3.8 RECURSION

A **recursive function** is a function that invokes itself. C++ supports recursive functions; any C++ function, except **main**, can invoke itself. Recursion is a powerful, elegant, and natural way to solve a large class of problems. A problem in this class can be solved by decomposing it into subproblems of the same type as the original problem. Each subproblem, in turn, can be decomposed further until the process yields subproblems that can be solved in a straightforward way. Finally, solutions to the subproblems can be combined to obtain a solution to the original problem.

EXAMPLE 3.8.1   Factorial Function.   The **factorial** of n (written $n!$) is defined as

$$n! = \begin{cases} 1, & \text{if } n = 0 \\ n(n-1)(n-2)\cdots 2 \cdot 1, & \text{if } n \geq 1 \end{cases}$$

That is, if $n \geq 1$, $n!$ (read "n factorial") is equal to the product of all the integers between 1 and n inclusive. (For technical reasons, $0!$ is defined to be 1.) As examples,

$$3! = 3 \cdot 2 \cdot 1 = 6$$
$$6! = 6 \cdot 5 \cdot 4 \cdot 3 \cdot 2 \cdot 1 = 720$$

Let us define the **factorial function** as

$$\text{factorial}(n) = n!$$

Notice that the factorial function can be written "in terms of itself" since, if we "peel off" n, the remaining product is simply $(n-1)!$; that is,

$$\begin{aligned} \text{factorial}(n) &= n! \\ &= n(n-1)(n-2)\cdots 2 \cdot 1 \\ &= n(n-1)! \\ &= n \cdot \text{factorial}(n-1) \end{aligned}$$

For example,

$$\begin{aligned} \text{factorial}(5) &= 5! \\ &= 5 \cdot 4 \cdot 3 \cdot 2 \cdot 1 \\ &= 5 \cdot 4! \\ &= 5 \cdot \text{factorial}(4) \end{aligned}$$

The equation

$$\text{factorial}(n) = n \cdot \text{factorial}(n-1)$$

---

† This section can be omitted without loss of continuity.

Problem	Simplified Problem
5!	5 * 4!
4!	4 * 3!
3!	3 * 2!
2!	2 * 1!
1!	None

FIGURE 3.8.1 Decomposing the factorial problem.

shows how to decompose the original problem (compute $n!$) into increasingly simpler subproblems [compute $(n - 1)!$, compute $(n - 2)!, \ldots$] until the process reaches the straightforward problem of computing 1!. The solutions to these subproblems can then be combined, by multiplying, to solve the original problem.

For example, the problem of computing 5! is reduced to computing 4!; the problem of computing 4! is reduced to computing 3!; and so on. Figure 3.8.1 summarizes this process.

Once the problem of computing 5! has been reduced to solving subproblems, the solution to the simplest subproblem can be used to solve the next simplest subproblem, and so on, until the original problem has been solved. Figure 3.8.2 shows how the subproblems are combined to compute 5!.

Problem	Solution
1!	1
2!	$2 * 1! = 2 \times 1 = 2$
3!	$3 * 2! = 3 \times 2 = 6$
4!	$4 * 3! = 4 \times 6 = 24$
5!	$5 * 4! = 5 \times 24 = 120$

FIGURE 3.8.2 Combining subproblems to compute 5!.

In Figure 3.8.3, we write a recursive function that computes factorials. (Exercise 1 is to write a nonrecursive function that computes factorials.) The code is a direct translation of the equation

$$\text{factorial}(n) = n \cdot \text{factorial}(n - 1)$$

Figure 3.8.4 gives a trace of the execution when the user enters the value 5. We label the calls to **fact** "**fact-1st**," "**fact-2nd**," and so on to aid in the clarification.

```
#include <iostream>
using namespace std;
int fact( int num );

int main() {
    int num;
    cout << "Please enter a number: ";
    cin >> num;
    if ( num < 0 )
        cout << "ERROR--number must be >= 0." << endl;
    else
        cout << num << "! = " << fact( num ) << endl;
    return 0;
}

int fact( int num ) {
    if ( num <= 1 )  // base cases
        return 1;
    // recursive call
    return num * fact( num - 1 );
}
```

FIGURE 3.8.3 Factorial function.

Invoking Function	Invoked Function	Argument	Value Returned
`main`	`fact-1st`	5	5 * `fact( 4 )` to `main`
`fact-1st`	`fact-2nd`	4	4 * `fact( 3 )` to `fact-1st`
`fact-2nd`	`fact-3rd`	3	3 * `fact( 2 )` to `fact-2nd`
`fact-3rd`	`fact-4th`	2	2 * `fact( 1 )` to `fact-3rd`
`fact-4th`	`fact-5th`	1	1 to `fact-4th`

FIGURE 3.8.4 Tracing the recursive factorial function.

When **main** calls **fact-1st** with 5 as the argument, the condition

```
num <= 1
```

is false; thus, **fact-1st** invokes **fact-2nd** with 4 as the argument. In this call to **fact-2nd**, the condition

```
num <= 1
```

is again false; thus, **fact-2nd** invokes **fact-3rd** with 3 as the argument. The recursive calls continue until **num** is 1 when the condition

```
num <= 1
```

is true. In this case, `fact-5th` invokes no functions but simply returns 1 [the value of `fact( 1 )`] to its invoker `fact-4th`. Next, `fact-4th` returns 2 [the value of `2 * fact( 1 )`] to its invoker `fact-3rd`. Next, `fact-3rd` returns 6 [the value of `3 * fact( 2 )`] to its invoker `fact-2nd`. Next, `fact-2nd` returns 24 [the value of `4 * fact( 3 )`] to its invoker `fact-1st`. Finally, `fact-1st` returns 120 [the value of `5 * fact( 4 )`] to its invoker `main`. ■

Three points need emphasis. First, there must be some situations in which a recursive function does *not* invoke itself; otherwise, it would invoke itself forever. In the function `fact`, if `n` ≤ 1, `fact` does not invoke itself. We call the values for which a recursive function does not invoke itself the *base cases*. To summarize, every recursive function must have base cases.

Second, in any function invocation, recursive or not, *the function invoked always returns to its invoker*. When `main` invokes `fact`, `fact` returns to `main`. When `fact` invokes itself, the invoked `fact` returns to the invoking `fact`. So when `fact-1st` invokes `fact-2nd` with 4 as the argument, `fact-2nd` returns to `fact-1st` 4 multiplied by the value of 3!. It is thus a bit misleading to say that a recursive function "invokes itself." It would be better to say that a recursive function invokes a *copy* of itself; however, we use the standard terminology and say that a function invokes itself.

The third point is that when a function invokes itself *the values used in testing for the base cases must change*. For example, suppose that we mistakenly wrote the `return` statement in the function `fact` as

```
return num * fact( num ); // ***** TROUBLE!!!
```

Every recursive call to the function `fact` passes the same value as it received; so unless `num` is less than or equal to 1, the condition

```
num <= 1
```

is never true. In this case, the function `fact` will keep invoking itself. We say that "infinite recursion" results. In the correct version, the function `fact` always invokes itself with a different argument from the one it received; `fact` receives `num` and passes `num - 1`. This changes the value in the test for the base cases.

A key challenge in writing recursive functions is to avoid infinite recursion. A recursive function must test for base cases in which no recursive call occurs. In the function `fact`, the base case occurs when the parameter is less than or equal to 1. Since each recursive call decrements the argument it receives before passing it along, the base case eventually is satisfied.

EXAMPLE 3.8.2   Tower of Hanoi. The **Tower of Hanoi** is a puzzle consisting of three pegs mounted on a board and *n* disks of various sizes with holes in their centers (see Figure 3.8.5). If a disk is on a peg, only a disk of smaller diameter can be placed on top of it. Given all the disks properly stacked on one peg as in Figure 3.8.5, the problem is to transfer the disks to another peg by moving one disk at a time.

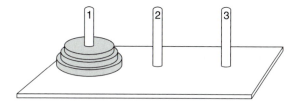

FIGURE 3.8.5 The Tower of Hanoi puzzle.

The Tower of Hanoi puzzle was invented by Édouard Lucas in the late nineteenth century. The following myth was also created to accompany the puzzle (and, one assumes, to help market the puzzle). The puzzle was said to be derived from a mythical gold tower that consisted of 64 disks. The 64 disks were to be transferred by monks according to the rules set forth previously. It was said that before the monks finished moving the tower, the tower would collapse, and the world would end on a clap of thunder. Since at least 18,446,744,073,709,551,615 moves are required to solve the 64-disk Tower of Hanoi puzzle, we can be fairly certain something would happen to the tower before it was completely moved.

For small values of n, the solution is evident; however, if n is 8 or so, the solution is not immediately obvious. Fortunately, if we think recursively, the problem is much less forbidding.

Consider the n-disk problem. Assume that, as in the factorial example (Example 3.8.1), we can reduce the original problem to a subproblem of the same type. Specifically, assume that we can solve the $(n-1)$-disk problem. Now, suppose that we fix the bottom disk. We can then recursively move the $n-1$ top disks from peg 1 to peg 2 (see Figure 3.8.6). Next, we move the remaining disk on peg 1 to peg 3. Finally, we again solve the $(n-1)$-disk problem; we move the $n-1$ disks on peg 2 to peg 3. We have succeeded in moving all n disks from peg 1 to peg 3. The base case is the 1-disk problem. Figure 3.8.7 contains a listing of a program that solves the puzzle. ∎

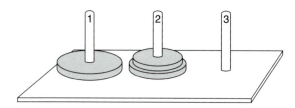

FIGURE 3.8.6 The first moves in a recursive solution to the Tower of Hanoi puzzle.

```
#include <iostream>
using namespace std;
void hanoi( char peg1, char peg2, char peg3, int how_many );

int main() {
    char peg1 = 'A',    // origin
         peg2 = 'B',    // destination
         peg3 = 'C';    // spare
    int how_many;  // number of disks initially on the origin
    // Prompt for and warn about the number of disks to be moved.
    cout << "\nHow many disks initially on peg A?"
         << "\nIf more than 7, the solution may seem to "
         << "take forever! ";
    cin >> how_many;
    cout << endl << endl;
    // Anything to move?
    if ( how_many < 1 )
        cout << "There's nothing to move!" << endl;
    // Otherwise solve with:
    //    -- peg1 as the origin
    //    -- peg2 as the destination
    //    -- peg3 as the spare
    else
        hanoi( peg1, peg2, peg3, how_many );
    return 0;
}
// p1 -- origin
// p2 -- destination
// p3 -- spare
// how_many -- number of disks to move
void hanoi( char p1, char p2, char p3, int how_many ) {
    // If there is only 1 disk on p1, then move it to p2
    // and quit as the problem is solved.
    if ( how_many == 1 ) {
        cout << "Move top disk from peg " << p1
             << " to peg " << p2 << endl;
        return;
    }
    // Otherwise:
    //     (1) Move how_many - 1 disks from p1 to p3:
    //         p1 is the origin, p3 is the destination,
    //         and p2 is the spare.
    //
    //     (2) Move the top disk from p1 to p2.
    //
    //     (3) Move how_many - 1 disks from p3 to p2:
    //         p3 is the origin, p2 is the destination,
    //         and p1 is the spare.
    hanoi( p1, p3, p2, how_many - 1 );
    cout << "Move top disk from peg " << p1
         << " to peg " << p2 << endl;
    hanoi( p3, p2, p1, how_many - 1 );
}
```

FIGURE 3.8.7 Solving the Tower of Hanoi puzzle.

EXAMPLE 3.8.3   Robot Walking and the Fibonacci Sequence. A robot can take steps of 1 meter or 2 meters. Write a function to calculate the number of ways the robot can walk n meters. As examples:

Distance	Sequence of Steps	Number of Ways to Walk
1	1	1
2	1, 1 or 2	2
3	1, 1, 1 or 1, 2 or 2, 1	3
4	1, 1, 1, 1 or 1, 1, 2 or 1, 2, 1 or 2, 1, 1 or 2, 2	5

Let walk(n) denote the number of ways the robot can walk n meters. We have observed that

$$\text{walk}(1) \ = \ 1, \quad \text{walk}(2) \ = \ 2$$

Now suppose that $n > 2$. The robot can begin by taking a step of 1 meter or a step of 2 meters. If the robot begins by taking a 1-meter step, a distance of $n - 1$ meters remains; but, by definition, the remainder of the walk can be completed in walk$(n - 1)$ ways. Similarly, if the robot begins by taking a 2-meter step, a distance of $n - 2$ meters remains and, in this case, the remainder of the walk can be completed in walk$(n - 2)$ ways. Since the walk must begin with either a 1-meter or a 2-meter step, all of the ways to walk n meters are accounted for. We obtain the formula

$$\text{walk}(n) \ = \ \text{walk}(n - 1) + \text{walk}(n - 2)$$

For example,

$$\text{walk}(4) \ = \ \text{walk}(3) + \text{walk}(2) = 3 + 2 = 5$$

We can write a recursive function **walk_recur** (see Figure 3.8.8) to compute walk(n) by translating the equation

$$\text{walk}(n) \ = \ \text{walk}(n - 1) + \text{walk}(n - 2)$$

directly into a program. The base cases are $n = 1$ and $n = 2$.

The body of **walk_recur** contains a conditional statement that tests for the base cases: **dist** equals 1 or **dist** equals 2. The recursion occurs within the **return** statement. If **dist** is greater than 2, **walk_recur** returns the sum of the values obtained by recursive calls with argument **dist - 1** and argument **dist - 2**.

The sequence

$$\text{walk}(1), \text{walk}(2), \text{walk}(3), \ldots$$

whose values begin

$$1, 2, 3, 5, 8, 13, \ldots$$

is called the **Fibonacci sequence** in honor of Leonardo Fibonacci (ca. 1170–1250), an Italian merchant and mathematician. After returning from the Orient in 1202, he wrote his most famous work *Liber Abaci*, which, in addition to containing what we now call the Fibonacci sequence, advocated the use of Hindu-Arabic numerals and was a major factor in Western Europe's adoption of the decimal number system. Fibonacci signed much of his work Leonardo Bigollo. *Bigollo* translates as "traveler" or "blockhead." There is some evidence that Fibonacci enjoyed having his contemporaries consider him a blockhead for advocating the new number system. ∎

```
#include <iostream>
using namespace std;
int walk_recur( int dist );
int main() {
   int distance,      // how far to walk
       count_walks; // how many ways to walk distance meters
   cout << "How far to walk? ";
   cin >> distance;
   if ( distance < 1 ) // distance must be positive
      cout << "ERROR -- distance must be positive." << endl;
   else {
      count_walks = walk_recur( distance );
      cout << "The robot can walk " << distance
           << " meters in " << count_walks
           << " ways." << endl;
   }
   return 0;
}

int walk_recur( int dist ) {
   // base cases: 1 meter -- 1 way, 2 meters -- 2 ways
   if ( dist <= 2 )
      return dist;
   // recursive call -- walk( dist - 1 ) + walk( dist - 2 )
   return walk_recur( dist - 1 ) + walk_recur( dist - 2 );
}
```

FIGURE 3.8.8 Solving the robot walking problem using recursion.

Our examples show that recursive functions provide a natural and elegant way to solve certain problems. In the factorial and robot examples, the C++ code practically copies the mathematical descriptions of the functions. Yet the robot example, in particular, also illustrates a problem that sometimes arises with recursion—inefficiency.

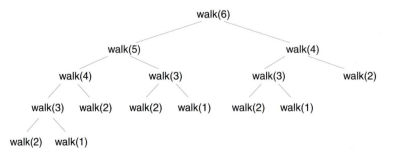

FIGURE 3.8.9 Counting the number of base cases computed during recursion.

Figure 3.8.9 shows how many times **walk_recur** computes walk(2) and walk(1), the two base cases, in the course of computing walk(6). The value walk(2) is computed 5 times, and walk(1) is computed 3 times. Thus, the base cases are computed a total of 8 times. (Other cases, in turn, are repeatedly recomputed.) Notice that walk(5) is also equal to 8. In general, when **walk_recur** is passed the argument $n \geq 2$, it computes the base cases walk($n - 1$) times (see Exercise 6). Since walk(n) grows exponentially with n (see Exercise 7), as n gets large, it becomes infeasible to use **walk_recur** to compute the walk function.

Of course, it is more efficient to compute walk(1) and walk(2) once each. We can write a function that does just this.

EXAMPLE 3.8.4. The function **walk_non_recur** (see Figure 3.8.10) also computes the number of ways a robot can walk n meters by taking steps of 1 meter or 2 meters, but more efficiently than does **walk_recur**. We assume that **walk_non_recur** also is invoked from **main**, which passes only positive integers to it.

```
int walk_non_recur( int dist ) {
   int previous, // walk(n - 1)
       current,  // walk(n)
       temp;
   if ( dist <= 2 )
      return dist;
   previous = 1; // starts as walk(1)
   current = 2;  // starts as walk(2)
   // compute walk(3), then walk(4), ..., until walk(dist)
   --dist;
   while ( --dist ) {
      temp = previous;
      previous = current;
      current += temp;
   }
   return current;
}
```

FIGURE 3.8.10 Solving the robot walking problem without recursion.

During one invocation, **walk_non_recur** computes each member of the sequence walk(1), walk(2), ... one time, for it works "from the bottom up"—walk(1) to walk(2) to walk(3) and so on up to walk(n). If $n > 2$, the function **walk_non_recur** is more efficient than **walk_recur**, which during a single invocation computes the base cases several times. Notice that **walk_recur** works "from the top down"—from walk(n) to walk($n - 1$) to walk($n - 2$) and so on down to walk(2) to walk(1). ∎

A recursive function in which the recursive call occurs in the last statement is said to be *tail recursive*. For example, both the factorial function (Example 3.8.1) and the function to solve the robot walking problem (Figure 3.8.8) are tail recursive. A tail recursive function can always be rewritten as an iterative function (see, e.g., Example 3.8.4). On most systems, a tail recursive function runs more slowly and uses more memory than an equivalent iterative version.

Should we *always* rewrite a recursive function nonrecursively? The answer is an emphatic "No!" On some systems, certain recursive functions run *faster* than versions from which the recursion has been removed. Such systems are designed to optimize the performance of certain kinds of recursive functions. Tail recursive functions are typically *not* optimized.

Finally, recursion is the most natural way to solve some problems. For example, the code for **walk_recur** follows straightforwardly from the formula, whereas the code for **walk_non_recur** does not. Even though we may eventually code a function nonrecursively, we still may begin with a recursive version to be sure that the function is correct.

EXERCISES

1. Write a nonrecursive function that computes factorials.

2. Trace the execution of the Tower of Hanoi program for the case of three disks.

3. Write a recursive function that computes

$$S(n) \,=\, 2 + 4 + 6 + \cdots + 2n$$

[*Hint*: $S(n) = S(n-1) + 2n$.]

4. If the standard input is

   abcd

   what is the output?

```
#include <iostream>
#include <iomanip>
using namespace std;
void mystery();

int main() {
   cin >> noskipws;
   mystery();
   return 0;
}

void mystery() {
   char c;
   if ( cin >> c ) {
      mystery();
      cout << c;
   }
}
```

5. A robot can take steps of 1 meter, 2 meters, or 3 meters. Write a recursive function to calculate the number of ways the robot can walk n meters.

6. [For readers comfortable with mathematical induction.] Prove that the number of times that **walk_recur** computes the base cases, when the argument is $n \geq 1$, is $\text{walk}(n - 1)$. Define $\text{walk}(0) = 1$.

7. [Also for readers comfortable with mathematical induction.] Prove that for $n \geq 5$,

$$\text{walk}(n) > \left(\frac{3}{2}\right)^n$$

COMMON PROGRAMMING ERRORS

1. There are no semicolons in a function's header. For example, the following is an error:

```
// ***** ERROR: no trailing semicolon in header
void print_report( int fcode, int no_recs );
```

2. A function's body is enclosed in braces, but its header is not. Note the difference:

```
// ***** ERROR: header enclosed in braces
{ void print_report( int fcode, int no_recs ) } {
   // print_report's body
}

// correct syntax
void print_report( int fcode, int no_recs ) {
   // print_report's body
}
```

3. Because a function may return at most one value, the following is an error:

```
// ***** ERROR: attempt to return two values
int count_animals( int species1, int species2 ) {
   int count1, count2;
   ...
   return count1 count2;
}
```

However, a returned value may be any legal C++ expression (including a function invocation), and so the following is legal:

```
int count_animals( int species1, int species2 ) {
   int count1, count2;
   ...
   return count1 + count2;
}
```

4. A function whose return type is not **void** must contain at least one statement of the form

   ```
   return expression;
   ```

   For this reason, the following function contains an error:

   ```
   int square( int x ) {
       int sq;
       sq = x * x;
       // ***** ERROR: no return statement
   }
   ```

5. Definitions for a program's functions may be spread across several files; however, the entire definition of a particular function must occur in one file, and so it is an error to put the function's header in one file and its body in another.

6. It is an error to define one function inside another. For example:

   ```
   // ***** ERROR: can't nest one function
   // definition in another function's body
   void fun1( float x, float y ) {
       ...
       void fun2( int p ) {   // ***** ERROR
           ...
       }
   }
   ```

7. Every function must be declared before it is invoked. For this reason, in the following code an error occurs because **f** was not declared prior to use:

   ```
   #include <iostream>
   using namespace std;
   int main() {
       int i = 3;
       // test f
       f( i );
       return 0;
   }

   void f( int k ) {
       k++;
       cout << k << endl;
   }
   ```

   The error is corrected by declaring **f** before **main**

   ```
   #include <iostream>
   using namespace std;
   void f( int k );

   int main() {
       ...
   ```

8. Since it is illegal to invoke an undeclared function, each system function must be declared. Typically, system functions are declared by including system header files such as *cstdlib* and *cmath*, which contain the required function declarations. Thus

```
#include <iostream>
using namespace std;

int main() {
   double x, y, z;
   // ***** ERROR: pow not declared
   x = pow( y, z );
   ...
}
```

is illegal since **pow** is not declared. This error can be corrected by adding the line

```
#include <cmath>
```

before **main**, because *cmath* contains a declaration of **pow**.

9. It is an error to omit the parentheses and data types of the parameters when declaring a function, even if the function has no parameters. For example, the following is an incorrect declaration of the *function* **strength**

```
// ***** ERRONEOUS way to declare the function strength
float strength;
```

The preceding is interpreted as the definition of a *variable* **strength** as distinct from the *function* **strength**. The proper declaration, assuming that **strength** has no parameters, is

```
// correct way to declare strength (no parameters)
float strength();
```

10. When a function is invoked, all of its arguments are evaluated before control passes to it. However, the order in which the arguments are evaluated is not specified. So it is an error to depend on left-to-right, right-to-left, or some other order of evaluation.

11. In any invocation of a function, the arguments passed must be compatible with the parameters specified in the function's declaration. For this reason

```
char compute_grade( int sc );

int main() {
   char c;
   // ***** ERROR: "35" not of type int
   c = compute_grade( "35" );
   ...
}
```

contains an error. The *string*, **"35"**, is not of type **int**, and the system will not convert it to an **int**.

12. All parameters without default values must come first in the parameter list and then be followed by all the parameters with default values. For this reason, the following is an illegal function declaration:

```
// ***** ERROR: illegal order of parameters
// with default values
int f( float x = 1.3, int i, char c = '\n' );
```

The error can be corrected by omitting the default value for **x** or by adding a default value for **i**.

13. If a parameter does not have a default value, an argument must be supplied when the function is invoked. For example, if the declaration of **f** is

```
int f( float x, int i, char c = '\n' );
```

legal invocations of **f** are

```
// Legal
f( 93.6, 0, '\t' );
f( 93.6, 0 );
```

but

```
// ***** ERROR: parameter i has no value
f( 93.6 );
```

is illegal.

14. A variable defined inside a function is visible only in that function. For this reason, the following is an error:

```
#include <iostream>
using namespace std;
void square();
int main() {
   int x = 4;
   square();
   cout << "x = " << x << endl;
   return 0;
}

void square() {
   // ***** ERROR: x not visible here
   x = x * x;
}
```

15. It is illegal to define two variables that have the same scope and the same name or to define a variable within a function with the same name as one of its parameters. For example, the following is an error:

```
int match( int person1, int person2 ) {
   // ***** ERROR: same name as parameter
   int person1;
   ...
}
```

16. In call by value, a function receives *copies* of the arguments. It is an error to assume that the value of a variable that furnishes an argument can be changed by the invoked function. For example, the output of the following program is **y = 5**.

```
#include <iostream>
using namespace std;
// call by value
void square( int x );

int main() {
    int y = 5;
    square( y );
    cout << "y = " << y << endl;
    return 0;
}

void square( int x ) {
    x = x * x;
}
```

By contrast, in call by reference the invoked function *can* change the values of the arguments in the invoking function since the invoked function works directly on the arguments in the invoking function, not on copies. For example, in

```
#include <iostream>
using namespace std;
// call by reference
void square( int& x );

int main() {
    int y = 5;
    square( y );
    cout << "y = " << y << endl;
    return 0;
}
void square( int& x ) {
    x = x * x;
}
```

the output is **y = 25**.

17. Input and output variables must *not* be passed by value, because they must keep track of details such as formatting information and where in the buffer to read or write the next data. For this reason, the following contains an error:

```
// ***** ERROR: out should be passed by reference
void print( ofstream out, char c ) {
   ...
}
```

The error is corrected by passing **out** by reference

```
// Correct
void print( ofstream& out, char c ) {
   ...
}
```

18. Since a function that uses return by reference returns an actual cell, the cell must remain in existence after the function returns. The function

```
int& f() {
   int i;
   ...
   // ***** ERROR: i goes out of existence
   return i;
}
```

contains an error. When **f** returns **i**, **i** goes out of existence. Thus the invoking function cannot access the cell **i** that is returned. There is *no* error if return by value is used:

```
int f() {
   int i;
   ...
   // OK
   return i;
}
```

Here the value of **i** is copied into temporary storage to which the invoking function has access.

19. C++ requires that overloaded functions have distinct signatures. Because the return type is *not* part of a function's signature, functions cannot be distinguished by the return type alone. For this reason, the following is an error:

```
char grade( int );
// ***** ERROR: same signature as preceding function
int grade( int );
```

20. In every recursive function, there must be some base cases in which the function does not invoke itself. For this reason, the following is an error:

```
int fact( int num ) {
   // ***** ERROR: no base cases
   return num * fact( num - 1 );
}
```

PROGRAMMING EXERCISES

3.1. Write a program in which the function **main** prompts the user for one of the six letters **a, b, p, q, x**, or **y**. The function **main** then invokes one of the six functions **print_a**, **print_b, print_p, print_q, print_x**, or **print_y**. Each prints a large uppercase version of the letter made out of the corresponding lowercase letter. (None has any arguments.) For example, if the user enters the letter **p, print_p** prints something like

```
ppppppppp
ppp     ppp
ppp     ppp
ppp     ppp
ppppppppp
ppp
ppp
ppp
ppp
```

3.2. The resistance of a resistor is given by colored bands. The colors correspond to integer codes as given in the following table:

Color	Code	Color	Code
Silver	−2	Yellow	4
Gold	−1	Green	5
Black	0	Blue	6
Brown	1	Violet	7
Red	2	Gray	8
Orange	3	White	9

If the integer codes of the bands are (in order) $c1$, $c2$, and $c3$, the resistance in ohms is $(10 \cdot c1 + c2)10^{c3}$. Write a program that displays a menu of colors, prompts the user to enter three colors (e.g., **B** for black, **N** for brown, **R** for red, etc.), and prints the resistance. Write a function **print_codes** that displays the menu; and a function **decode_char**, with a parameter to receive a color, that converts the color to its corresponding numeric code and returns the code. All other computation is done in **main**.

3.3. Modify Programming Exercise 3.2 to decode a fourth band, if present. If there is no fourth band, the *tolerance* (the percentage by which the rated resistance might vary) is 20 percent. If the fourth band is silver, the tolerance is 10 percent. If the fourth band is gold, the tolerance is 5 percent. The program should print the smallest possible resistance and the largest possible resistance.

3.4. Write a function **color_band** with one parameter that holds a resistance. The function **color_band** prints the color codes that represent the resistance (see Programming Exercise 3.2). Write a **main** function that reads a resistance and passes it to **color_band**. You may write some auxiliary functions if you wish.

3.5. The expression $C(n, r)$ denotes the number of r-element subsets of an n-element set. For example, $C(4, 2)$ is 6 because there are six 2-element subsets of a 4-element set. The value of $C(n, r)$ is given by the formula

$$C(n, r) = \frac{n!}{r!(n - r)!}$$

Write a program that computes $C(n, r)$ using the following component functions, which are invoked by **main**:

- **input**: prompts the user for two numbers, storing them in **n** and **r**, respectively.
- **check**: compares **r** and **n**. If **r > n**, **check** invokes the function **err_msg**, which prints an error message.
- **comb**: computes $C(n, r)$.
- **fact**: computes factorial.

The function **main** prints the result.

3.6. Redo Exercise 3.5. Compute $C(n, r)$ by writing a recursive function based on the formula
$$C(n, r) = C(n - 1, r - 1) + C(n - 1, r)$$

3.7. Write a function **power** that expects two arguments, **x** and **n**, and returns **x** to the power **n**. The argument **x** is of type **double** and **n** is of type **int**.

3.8. Write a function that returns the square root of the argument x passed to it. Use *Newton's method*. Repeatedly replace the approximate square root r with

$$\frac{\frac{x}{r} + r}{2}$$

Begin by setting r to 1. Stop when $|r^2 - x| < 0.0001$.

3.9. Redo Exercise 3.8, stopping when the absolute difference of two successive approximations to the square root differs by at most 0.0001.

3.10. Redo Exercise 3.8. Pass the argument by reference and have the function assign the argument the square root.

3.11. Write a program that computes the net pay for a wage earner. Assume that each wage earner can be identified through a unique five-digit identification code, ranging from 00000 to 99999. Use the following simplified formulas, with lowercase names as variables and uppercase names as **const** variables:

```
gross_pay = REG_HRS * wage + overtime * OT_WAGE
soc_secur_tax = SOC_SECUR_RATE * gross_pay
deductions = DEPENDENT_DEDUCTION * dependents
fed_inc_tax = FIT_RATE * ( gross_pay - deductions )
union_dues = UNION_DUES_RATE * gross_pay
net_pay = gross_pay - soc_secur_tax - fed_income_tax
          - union_dues
```

Choose realistic values for the constants. The function **main** should prompt the user for the required data, including the wage earner's unique numeric identification code, and print the net pay.

3.12. The following table gives the monthly cost of financing $1000 over 30 years for a home loan at various rates of interest:

Rate	Monthly Cost
6.0%	$6.00
7.0%	$6.66
8.0%	$7.34
9.0%	$8.05
10.0%	$8.78
10.5%	$9.15
11.0%	$9.52

Write a program that prompts the user for the price of a home, the current interest rate, and the percentage of the total price made as a down payment. Print the amount of the down payment, the amount to be financed, the monthly payment, and the total amount of interest paid over 30 years. For example, if the input is

```
Price of home: 100000
Interest rate: 9
Percent as down payment: 20
```

the output is

```
Down payment: 20000
Amount financed: 80000
Monthly payment: 644
Total interest: 131840
```

All input/output operations should be done in the function **main** and all calculations in whatever other functions seem appropriate.

3.13. Write a program that computes the sum

$$\sum_{i=1}^{n} \frac{1}{i^2}$$

in two ways: first, in the order

$$1 + \frac{1}{2^2} + \frac{1}{3^2} + \cdots$$

then in the order

$$\frac{1}{n^2} + \frac{1}{(n-1)^2} + \cdots$$

Use two different functions to compute the sums. Write a function **main** that invokes each function for $n = 10, 100, 1000, 10000$.

3.14. For the program of Exercise 3.13, if the two functions give different values, answer the following questions:

- Why are the sums different?
- Which do you think is more accurate, and why?

3.15. Write a program to simulate throwing darts. (See the following figure.)

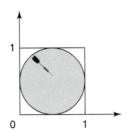

Use a random number generator to obtain 1,000 pairs of floating-point numbers (x, y) satisfying $0 < x < 1, 0 < y < 1$. Print the proportion P of throws that hit the dart board, that is, the proportion of pairs (x, y) that are inside the circle. Also print $4 * P$. Notice that the geometry of the problem leads us to expect P to be about $\frac{\pi}{4}$. Thus $4 * P$ provides an approximation of π.

3.16. The *greatest common divisor* (gcd) of two integers, $M \geq 0$ and $N > 0$, can be computed as follows, where $\mathrm{mod}\,(M, N)$ is the remainder when M is divided by N:

$$\mathrm{gcd}(M, N) = \begin{cases} N, & \text{if } \mathrm{mod}(M, N) = 0 \\ \mathrm{gcd}(N, R), & \text{if } \mathrm{mod}(M, N) = R, R > 0 \end{cases}$$

Write a recursive function that computes the greatest common divisor.

3.17. Suppose that we have a $2 \times n$ rectangular board divided into $2n$ squares. Write a function that computes the number of ways to cover this board exactly by 1×2 dominoes.

3.18. A robot can take steps of 1 meter or 2 meters. Write a function that lists all of the ways that the robot can walk n meters.

3.19. A robot can take steps of 1 meter, 2 meters, or 3 meters. Write a function that lists all of the ways that the robot can walk n meters.

3.20. One version of Ackermann's function *ack* is defined as follows:

$$ack(M, N) = \begin{cases} N + 1, & \text{if } M = 0 \\ ack(M - 1, 1), & \text{if } M \neq 0 \text{ and } N = 0 \\ ack(M - 1, ack(M, N - 1)), & \text{if } M \neq 0 \text{ and } N \neq 0 \end{cases}$$

Write a recursive function that computes Ackermann's function.

3.21. Although the Tower of Hanoi puzzle is most easily solved by using recursion, there is a nonrecursive solution. (See, for example, E. R. Berlekamp, J. H. Conway, and R. K. Guy, *Winning Ways*, vol. 2, New York: Academic Press, 1982: 753–754.) Write a nonrecursive function that solves the Tower of Hanoi puzzle.

3.22. The *four-peg Tower of Hanoi puzzle* consists of four pegs mounted on a board and n disks of differing sizes with holes in their centers; otherwise, the rules are the same as for the three-peg puzzle. An optimal solution to this puzzle and a *proof* that it is optimal have never been found. (The solution to the three-peg puzzle given in Example 3.8.2 is known to be optimal.)

Construct a solution to the four-peg Tower of Hanoi puzzle that uses fewer moves than does the solution to the three-peg puzzle. (*Hint*: Modify the solution to the three-peg puzzle by fixing more than one bottom disk. The best solution known to the four-peg puzzle uses this method and fixes the optimum number of bottom disks. This optimum number varies with the total number of disks.)

CHAPTER

4

ARRAYS

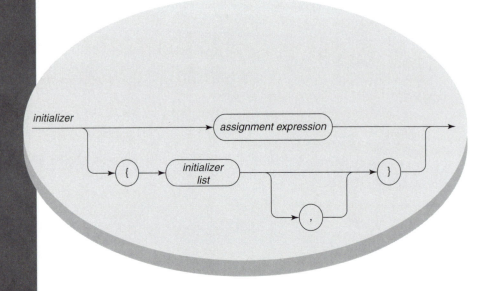

Arrays, pointers, and strings are related topics in C++. This chapter introduces all three topics, with emphasis on array and string basics. We then use arrays and strings throughout the remainder of the book.

4.1 WHY ARRAYS?

An **array** groups distinct variables of the *same type* under a *single* name. For example, suppose that an application tracks temperatures from 100 different sites, storing each in a **float** variable. It is more convenient to have an array of 100 **float**s than 100 individual **float** variables, each with its own name.

> **EXAMPLE 4.1.1.**   The code segment
>
> ```
> float temps[ 100 ]; // 100 float variables
> ```
>
> defines an array named **temps** of 100 **float** variables. This is more convenient than defining 100 individual **float** variables:
>
> ```
> float temp1;
> float temp2;
> ...
> float temp99;
> float temp100;
> ```
> ■

An array is an **aggregate**, that is, a collection of variables. We contrast an array of variables with a **scalar** variable, that is, a variable that does *not* belong to an aggregate.

> **EXAMPLE 4.1.2.**   The code segment
>
> ```
> double income;
> double outgo[ 1000 ];
> ```
>
> defines a scalar variable **income** and an array **outgo** of 1,000 **double** variables.   ■

An array's members are called its **elements**. In Example 4.1.2, **outgo** is an array of 1,000 elements, each a **double** variable. An array's elements are **contiguous**; that is, they lie next to one another.

> **EXAMPLE 4.1.3.**   The code segment
>
> ```
> char a[ 3 ];
> ```
>
> defines an array of three elements, which can be depicted as

Each element is a **char** variable.   ■

EXERCISES

Exercises 1 through 4 assume the definition

```
int studentIds[ 25 ];
```

1. How many elements are in the array?
2. What is the data type of each element?
3. Suppose that 25 is changed to 5000. How many elements are then in the array?
4. Must all variables in an array be of the same type?
5. Give a sample definition of an array.
6. Give a sample definition of a scalar variable.

4.2 THE INDEX OPERATOR

In C++, the square brackets [ ] have two distinct uses with respect to arrays. The brackets are used to specify

- An array's **size** when the array is first defined. An array's size is the number of elements it aggregates under a single name.
- A particular array element through an offset $0, 1, \ldots, n-1$ from the *first* element. The array's first element has an offset of 0, its second an offset of 1, and its last element an offset of $n-1$, where n is the array's size.

In the second use, the square brackets are the **index operator**, that is, the operator that specifies an array element by giving its offset or distance from the first element. If `temps` is an array, then the expression

```
temps[ 2 ]
```

specifies the array's *third* element, that is, the element with an offset of 2 from the first element. We elaborate on this point shortly.

Specifying an Array's Size with the Square Brackets [ ]

An array's size is specified in its *definition* by a *integer constant expression* inside the square brackets [ ].

EXAMPLE 4.2.1. The code segment

```
const unsigned arraySize = 100;
char a1[ 100 ];
char a2[ 90 + 10 ];
char a3[ arraySize ];
char a4[ 10 * 10 ];
```

defines four arrays of **char**, each of size 100. In each definition, an integer expression inside the square brackets is used to specify the size. The index expression may be a **const** variable such as **arraySize**, an integer constant such as 100, or an integer constant expression such as **10 * 10**, **90 + 10**, and the like. ∎

A non**const** variable may *not* be used to specify an array's size.

EXAMPLE 4.2.2.   The code segment

```
const int n = 10;
int k = 4;
char a1[ n ]; // OK -- n is const
char a2[ k ]; //****** ERROR: k is not const
```

contains an error because **k** is *not* **const**. The definition of **a1** is legal because variable **n** is a **const**ant. ∎

Specifying an Array Element with the Index Operator [ ]

The index operator is used to specify an element within an array. The desired element is specified by giving *offset from the first element*, where the offset is an *integer expression* enclosed in the index operator **[ ]**.

EXAMPLE 4.2.3.   The code segment

```
unsigned primes[ 4 ]; // primes defined
primes[ 0 ] = 2;       // 1st variable accessed
primes[ 1 ] = 3;       // 2nd variable accessed
primes[ 2 ] = 5;       // 3rd variable accessed
primes[ 3 ] = 7;       // 4th variable accessed
```

defines an array of four **unsigned** variables under the name **primes**. The array may be depicted as follows, with the index expressions shown under the corresponding elements and the element's position in the array shown above it:

1st	2nd	3rd	4th
2	3	5	7
[0]	[1]	[2]	[3]

A statement such as

```
primes[ 2 ] = 5;       // 3rd variable accessed
```

uses the index operator to specify a particular array element, in this case the array's third element. The expression

```
primes[ 0 ]
```

specifies the array's *first* element, that is, the element that has an offset of *zero* from the first element. The number 0 is called the **index**. Variable `primes[ 0 ]` has 2 as its contents. The expression

```
primes[ 2 ]
```

specifies the array's *third* element, that is, the element that has an offset of *two* from the first element. The index is thus 2. Variable `primes[ 2 ]` has 5 as its contents. In general, the *i*th array element has *i* − 1 as its index.

An array's size is an *illegal* index because, in C++, the legal indexes are 0, 1, . . . , *size* − 1, where *size* is the array's size. ∎

EXAMPLE 4.2.4. The code segment

```
float ar[ 2 ];  // 2 elements
ar[ 0 ] = 3.14; // 1st element
ar[ 1 ] = 4.13; // 2nd and last element
ar[ 2 ] = 1.43; //***** ERROR: array overflow
```

illustrates an illegal index. The array's size is two. Therefore, the legal indexes are 0 (first element) and 1 (second and *last* element). The expression

```
ar[ 2 ]
```

is an error because it tries to access the *third* element in an array that has only *two* elements:

3.14	4.13	
[0]	[1]	[2]

We characterize this error as **array overflow** to underscore that the illegal index, in this case 2, goes *beyond* the right end of the array.

Array underflow occurs when an index expression is negative. The code segment

```
char a[ 10 ];
a[ -6 ] = 1; //***** ERROR: array underflow
```

illustrates array underflow. ∎

Bounds Checking and Access Violations

C++ does *not* do **bounds checking** on arrays; that is, the system does *not* check whether an index expression falls between 0 and *size* − 1, where *size* is the array's size.

EXAMPLE 4.2.5. The array definition

```
int a[ 3 ]; // legal indexes: 0,1,2
a[ 0 ] = 9;  // ok
a[ 1 ] = 8;  // ok
a[ 2 ] = 7;  // ok
a[ 3 ] = 6;  //***** ERROR: array overflow
```

allocates three **int** cells but mistakenly tries to access a fourth cell:

9	8	7	6
[0]	[1]	[2]	!!!!!

The system is *not* required to detect an error on the erroneous expression

```
a[ 3 ]     //***** ERROR: illegal index (array overflow)
```
■

Array underflow and overflow typically result in an **access violation**, a run-time error that usually causes the offending program to stop executing. Different operating systems may issue different messages about access violations, but most penalize the offending program by stopping it at once. So the programmer puts the program in peril by using illegal index expressions. The programmer, not the system, is responsible for ensuring that indexes are legal. In summary, the programmer rather than the system is responsible for ensuring that

- An array has sufficient size to store however many elements are intended for it.

- An index does not overflow or underflow the array.

Initializing Arrays

An array may be initialized in its definition.

EXAMPLE 4.2.6.   The code segment

```
int nums[ 3 ] = { 9, 4, 7 };
```

defines an array **nums** of three elements and initializes them to the integers 9, 4, and 7:

9	4	7
[0]	[1]	[2]

The initializing values occur between matching braces **{ }** and are separated by commas. Had we provided fewer initial values than the array's size

```
int nums[ 3 ] = { 9 }; // only 1 initial value
```

then zero becomes the initial value for all the remaining cells:

9	0	0
[0]	[1]	[2]

■

EXAMPLE 4.2.7.   Suppose that we want to initialize an array to all zeros. We could use a loop

```
short scores[ 1000 ];
for ( int i = 0; i < 1000; i++ )
   scores[ i ] = 0;
```

or provide zero as *one* initial value. The compiler then uses zero as the initial value for all the remaining array elements

```
short scores[ 1000 ] = { 0 }; // all elements to zero
```                                                                   ■

EXAMPLE 4.2.8.   The code segment

```
int nums[ 100 ] = { -1 };
```

initializes **nums**'s first element to −1 and its remaining 99 elements to 0.   ■

It is an error to provide *more* initial values than the array can hold.

EXAMPLE 4.2.9.   The code segment

```
int nums[ 3 ] = { 1, 2, 3, 4 }; //***** ERROR
```

is in error because the array has only *three* elements, but *four* initial values are given.
                                                                                      ■

If an array is initialized in its definition, its size may be omitted.

EXAMPLE 4.2.10.   The code segment

```
int nums[ ] = { 1, 2, 3, 4 }; // size == 4
```

provides four initial values in **nums**'s definition. Therefore, the compiler makes the array's size *four*. If initial values are *not* given, then the array's size *must* be given explicitly. The code segment

```
int nums[ ]; //****** ERROR: size must be given
```

is therefore in error.   ■

If an array is defined *inside a block* and not initialized in its definition, then it contains *garbage*; that is, its elements contain arbitrary values that are of no use to the program. The programmer should make no assumption about the contents of an uninitialized array.

EXAMPLE 4.2.11.   The definition

```
int main() {
   short nums[ 100 ]; // defined inside a block
   ...
}
```

allocates storage for 100 **short** integers but does not initialize the array **nums**. The array therefore contains *garbage*, arbitrary values about which the programmer should make no assumptions.   ■

If an array is defined *outside all blocks*, the compiler initializes to zero all cells for which the programmer does not provide initial values.

EXAMPLE 4.2.12.   Assume that the definition

```
int globalArray[ 100 ];
```

occurs outside all blocks. In this case, the compiler initializes all **globalArray**'s cells to zero. Assume that the definition

```
int nums[ 25 ] = { -1 };
```

also occurs outside all blocks. In this case, **nums**'s first cell contains −1 and its remaining 24 cells contain zero.   ∎

The sizeof Operator and Arrays

The **sizeof** operator (see Section 2.1) may be used to determine an array's size in bytes rather than its size in elements.

EXAMPLE 4.2.13.   The code segment

```
int codes[ 400 ];
cout << "codes has "
     << sizeof( codes )  // sizeof an array
     << " bytes." << endl;
```

illustrates. The array **codes** has 400 elements, each an **int**. If **sizeof(int)** is 4, then **sizeof(codes)** is **400 * sizeof(int)** or **400 * 4**, which equals 1600. Thus the array **codes** occupies 1600 bytes. The expressions **sizeof(codes)** and **400 * sizeof(codes[0])** are equal, because *each* array element is the *same* type and, therefore, the same size in bytes as every other element.   ∎

EXERCISES

1. In the code segment

```
char array[ 4 ];
array[ 2 ] = 'B';
```

which of **array**'s cells now has **B** stored in it: the second or the third?

2. What are the contents of **n**'s cells?

```
short n[ 100 ] = { -999, 4 };
```

3. Explain the error in this code segment.

```
char a[ 10 ];
a[ 10 ] = 'Z';
```

4. What are the legal indexes for the array **n**?

```
double n[ 400 ];
```

5. When does array underflow occur?

6. If **nums** is an array with 100 elements, what is the index of its 18th element?

7. What is bounds checking?

8. In C++, is the programmer, the system, or some combination of the two responsible for bounds checking?

9. What is the error?

```
int nums[ 3 ] = { 9, 8, 7, 6 };
```

10. What is the size of array **nums**?

```
short nums[ ] = { 18, 44, 507, 899 };
```

11. Assume that an **int** cell is four bytes. How many bytes does the array

```
int x[ 10 ];
```

require? How many elements does it have?

12. What is the error?

```
int a[ ];
```

4.3 ARRAYS AND POINTERS

Arrays and pointers (addresses) are closely related in C++. Here we highlight the crucial distinction between a pointer *constant* and a pointer *variable*.

A **pointer** is an expression that evaluates to an *address*. In C++, the ampersand **&** is the **address operator**. For example, the statement

```
int x = 6;
```

defines and initializes an **int** variable **x**. Suppose that **x**'s address in memory happens to be 877, which we write above **x**'s cell:

```
      877
    ┌─────┐
    │  6  │
    └─────┘
      x
```

The value of **x**, or **x**'s *contents*, is 6. The value of **&x**, or **x**'s *address*, is 877.

An array's name evaluates to the address of the first cell in the array.

EXAMPLE 4.3.1.   Suppose that the array

```
short n[ ] = { 9, 8, 7, 6 }; // four elements
```

occupies memory cells with addresses 480, 482, 484, and 486:

```
   480     482     484     486
 +-------+-------+-------+-------+
 |   9   |   8   |   7   |   6   |
 +-------+-------+-------+-------+
  [ 0 ]   [ 1 ]   [ 2 ]   [ 3 ]
```

(We assume a **short** occupies *two* bytes so that the addresses increment by 2: 480 to 482 to 484 to 486.) The array's name **n** has as its value the address of its first element; that is, the value of **n** is 480. In equivalent terms, **n** is a *pointer* to its first element. Notice that the value of **&n[0]** is also 480.   ■

An array's name is a **pointer constant**. Therefore, an array's name cannot have its value changed through, for instance, an assignment expression.

EXAMPLE 4.3.2.   The code segment

```
char ar[ 100 ];
ar = 26;          //***** ERROR: ar is a constant
ar[ 2 ] = 88;     // OK, ar[ 2 ] is a variable
```

contains an error because it tries to assign a value to **ar**, the array's name; and an array's name is *not* a legal lvalue (see Section 2.7) precisely because it is a constant.   ■

Pointer Constants and Pointer Variables

Pointers come in two flavors, constants and variables. The definition of **ptr**

```
int x = -1; // assume &x == 45
int* ptr;
ptr = &x;   // ptr's value is 45, x's address
```

illustrates the syntax for defining a pointer variable. The statement

```
int* ptr;
```

defines **ptr** as a *variable* of type **int***, which is read "pointer to **int**." Accordingly, **ptr** can hold the address of an **int** such as **x**. So the assignment

```
ptr = &x;
```

stores **x**'s address in **ptr** (see Figure 4.3.1).

45 (x's address)

```
45
```
ptr

```

```
x

FIGURE 4.3.1 After **ptr** = **&x;** executes.

The crucial difference between a *pointer variable* such as **ptr** and a *pointer constant* such as an array's name is that **ptr** is a legal lvalue. Therefore, **ptr** may have its value changed through, for example, assignment expressions such as

```
ptr = &x;
```

EXAMPLE 4.3.3. The code segment

```
int n[ 3 ];
int* p = n;    // n assigned to p
n = &n[ 1 ];   //***** ERROR: n is a constant
p = &n[ 1 ];   // OK, p is a variable
p = n + 2;     // p points to n[ 2 ]
p = n + 0;     // p points to n[ 0 ]
p = &n[ 0 ];   // ditto
```

illustrates some pointer syntax. The expression

```
int* p = n;
```

is equivalent to the pair of expressions

```
int* p;
p = n;
```

The result is that **p** and **n** both point to **n[0]** (see Figure 4.3.2).
The attempt to reset **n** so that it points elsewhere

```
n = &n[ 1 ];   //***** ERROR: n is a constant
```

is an error because **n** is a *constant*. By contrast, **p** is a *variable* and so may have its value changed as often as we like through expressions such as

```
p = &n[ 1 ];
```

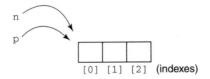

n
p

```
[0]  [1]  [2]   (indexes)
```

FIGURE 4.3.2 **p** and **n** pointing to **n[0]**.

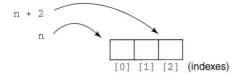

n + 2

n

[0] [1] [2] (indexes)

FIGURE 4.3.3 **n + 2** pointing to **n[2]**.

and

```
p = n + 2;
```

The latter expression may be more intuitive than the former. Because **n** points to **n[0]**, **n + 2** points *two* elements *beyond* **n[0]**, that is, to **n[2]** (see Figure 4.3.3). ■

Two points need emphasis. First, an array's name is indeed a *pointer* (i.e., an *address*), but it is a pointer *constant* whose value cannot be changed. An array's name always points to the array's *first* element. Second, the index operator **[ ]** can be used to generate an offset from the base address provided by an array's name. For example, in the expression

```
n[ 1 ] = -999; // n is an array's name
```

the index operator **[ ]** accesses the array's *second* element, that is, the element with an offset of 1 from the array's base address—the address of its first element. The array's name **n** thus provides a base address from which the index operator **[ ]** generates the appropriate offset.

The index operator may be used to generate an offset from either a pointer constant or a pointer variable.

EXAMPLE 4.3.4. The code segment

```
int nums[ ] = { -2, -1, 0, 1, 2 }; // size == 5
int* p;     // pointer to int
p = nums;  // p points to nums[ 0 ]
for ( int i = 0; i < 5; i++ )
   p[ i ] += 2;
```

increments each element in the array **nums** by 2. After setting pointer variable **p** so that it points to the first element in **nums** (see Figure 4.3.4), we then use the index operator

```
p[ i ] += 2;
```

to generate offsets from **p** as the base address.

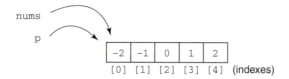

FIGURE 4.3.4 `p` pointing to `nums[ 0 ]`.

Of course, we just as easily could have used pointer constant **nums** in the loop

```
for ( int i = 0; i < 5; i++ )
    nums[ i ] += 2;
```

to provide the base address. ■

EXERCISES

1. Explain the error.

   ```
   char a[ 3 ];
   char b[ ] = { 'P', 'Q', 'R' };
   a = b;
   ```

2. Consider the array **nums**:

   ```
   float nums[ ] = { 3.12F, .0897F };
   ```

   What is the value of the array name **nums**?

3. Suppose that **int** cell **x**

   ```
   int x = 7;
   ```

   is at address 42. What is the value of **x**? What is the value of **&x**?

4. What is the main difference between a pointer constant and a pointer variable?

   The remaining exercises assume the definition

   ```
   char letters[ ] = { 'A', 'B', 'C', 'D' };
   ```

5. To which array element does **letters** point?

6. What is the value of the cell to which **letters + 2** points?

7. Does the expression **&letters[1]** have the same value as the expression **letters + 1**?

8. Is **letters** a pointer?

9. Is **letters** a pointer variable?

10. What is the data type of **letters[2]**?

11. What is the data type of **letters**?

4.4 SAMPLE APPLICATION: TOTALING VOTES

Problem

Write a program to total votes from a Chicago election held to select an official city bird. The election data are in the input file *votes.dat* whose records are formatted

< precinct code >< bird code >< vote count >

A record such as

49   0   340

represents 340 votes from precinct 49 for the bird with code 0, which happens to be a pigeon. A record such as

17   2   1445

represents 1,445 votes from precinct 17 for the bird with code 2, which is a peregrine falcon. (Peregrine falcons were reintroduced into several of Chicago's 50 precincts, in part to help control the pigeon population.) The bird codes are

Code	Bird	Why Nominated?
0	Pigeon	Most common bird in Chicago
1	Dove	A clean pigeon
2	Falcon	Eats pigeons
3	Robin	Raises false hope of an end to a Chicago winter

The input records are in arbitrary order, and we assume that the records are formatted correctly. After totaling the votes, print a report to the standard output that lists

- The bird's name.
- The total votes for the bird regardless of precinct.

Sample Input/Output

For the sample input file

```
20 0 98
1   3 561
18 1 324
20 2 2556
6   2 4571
17 0 124
...
```

the output is

```
Vote totals are:
Pigeon:   37654
Dove:     4591
Falcon:   651097
Robin:    12077
```

Solution

Our program has two sections. First, we read data from the input file *votes.dat*. In each record, we discard the precinct code and use the bird code and the vote count because the application requires only that we list the *total* votes for each bird, regardless of the precinct in which the votes were cast. The totals are stored in the array **counts**, whose elements are **unsigned** integers. The array's size is four because there are four candidate birds: **counts[0]** stores the vote total for the pigeon, the bird with code 0; **counts[1]** stores the vote total for the dove, the bird with code 1; **counts[2]** stores the vote total for the falcon, the bird with code 2; and **counts[3]** stores the vote total for the robin, the bird with code 3. Second, we iterate through the array to print the vote total for each bird.

C++ Implementation

```cpp
#include <iostream>
#include <fstream>
using namespace std;

int main() {
    ifstream infile;        // data file
    const unsigned n = 4; // number of candidate birds
    unsigned counts[ n ] = { 0 }; // ballot totals per bird
    unsigned precinct, bird, votes;
    // Read counts from input file and update totals
    infile.open( "votes.dat" );
    while ( infile >> precinct >> bird >> votes )
      counts[ bird ] += votes; // update vote count
    infile.close();
    // Print vote totals to the standard output
    cout << "Vote totals are:" << endl;
    for ( unsigned i = 0; i < n; i++ ) {
      switch ( i ) {
      case 0: // pigeon
        cout << "Pigeon:   "; break;
      case 1: // mourning dove
        cout << "Dove:     "; break;
      case 2: // falcon
        cout << "Falcon:   "; break;
      case 3: // robin
        cout << "Robin:    "; break;
      }
      cout << counts[ i ] << endl;
    }
    return 0;
}
```

Discussion

After defining the variable **infile** of type **ifstream**, we open the input file

```cpp
infile.open( "votes.dat" );
```

and then use a **while** loop to read the data until end-of-file:

```
while ( infile >> precinct >> bird >> votes )
  counts[ bird ] += votes; // update vote count
```

If we successfully read data, we increment a bird's total votes

```
counts[ bird ] += votes;
```

by using **bird** as an index into the array and incrementing the cell by the integer value **votes**. Recall that **counts** has *four* elements precisely because there are four birds in the running. Further, the integer codes for the birds are 0, 1, 2, and 3—the very integer values that are legal indexes into the array **counts**.

In the definition of **counts**

```
unsigned counts[ n ] = { 0 }; // ballot totals per bird
```

we provide only one initial value, 0, even though **counts** has four cells. If an array's initialization contains fewer values than the array's size, the remaining cells are initialized automatically to zero. So our initialization causes *all* of **counts**'s cells to be initialized to zero. If we did not initialize **counts**, its cells would contain arbitrary values.

We use a **for** loop for our report because we know that exactly **n** iterations are required, one for each candidate bird. The input loop uses a **while** loop because we do not know how many iterations are required: the input loop must iterate until the end of the input file is reached. The report loop uses a **switch** construct to print bird names (e.g., **Falcon**) rather than bird codes (e.g., **2**).

EXERCISES

1. Remove the initialization from the definition of **counts** and run the program.

2. Amend the sample application so that, in the report, it prints the percentage of the total vote that each bird receives.

3. Amend the sample application so that it prints the total votes *per precinct* for each bird.

4.5 CHARACTER STRINGS

C++ has no data type for character strings, called *strings* for short. Instead, a string is an *array* of **char** in which the last element is the null terminator **'\0'**. Recall that **'\0'** designates *one* character.

EXAMPLE 4.5.1.   The string constant

```
"Anchee"
```

is represented as the null-terminated array:

'A'	'n'	'c'	'h'	'e'	'e'	'\0'
[0]	[1]	[2]	[3]	[4]	[5]	[6]

Although the string *Anchee* has six characters, its C++ representation requires seven **char** cells because of the null terminator. ∎

It is critical to distinguish between the *character* **'A'**, which is *one* character

and the C++ representation of the *string* **"A"**, which is an array of *two* characters, the string character **'A'** and the null-terminator character **'\0'**:

'A'	'\0'

EXAMPLE 4.5.2.   The code segment

```
char c1, c2;
c1 = 'A'; // OK, 1 character
c2 = "A"; //***** ERROR: "A" is a string!
```

contains an error because it tries to assign the *string* **"A"** to the **char** variable **c2**. The string **"A"** contains the string character **'A'** and the null terminator **'\0'**. So the string **"A"** requires an array of *two* **char** cells, not a single **char** cell. ∎

Storing Strings in Arrays

There are various ways to store a string in an array of **char**. We illustrate with a series of examples.

EXAMPLE 4.5.3.   The code segment

```
char stooge1[ 4 ];
stooge1[ 0 ] = 'M';
stooge1[ 1 ] = 'o';
stooge1[ 2 ] = 'e';
stooge1[ 3 ] = '\0';
```

stores the string *Moe* in the array `stooge1`—and does it the hard way, character by character. Note that the array size is four even though *Moe* has only three characters. Again, we must leave room for the terminating `'\0'`. The C++ representation is

'M'	'o'	'e'	'\0'
[0]	[1]	[2]	[3]

Once the assignments are done, a statement such as

```
cout << stooge1 << endl;
```

may be used to print *Moe* to the standard output.   ∎

EXAMPLE 4.5.4.   The code segment

```
char stooge1[ 4 ] = { 'M', 'o', 'e', '\0' };
```

also stores the string *Moe* in the array `stooge1` and again does it the hard way by providing the individual characters as initial values. Because initial values are provided, the array's size need not be given explicitly:

```
char stooge1[ ] = { 'M', 'o', 'e', '\0' };
```

In either case, the initial values are enclosed in braces and separated by commas.   ∎

EXAMPLE 4.5.5.   The code segment

```
char stooge1[ 4 ] = "Moe";
```

initializes the array to the string constant `"Moe"`, which contains a null terminator. Because the array is initialized in its definition, the array's size need not be given explicitly:

```
char stooge1[ ] = "Moe";
```

∎

An array may be assigned a string constant *only in its definition*. Otherwise, an error results.

EXAMPLE 4.5.6.   The code segment

```
char stooge1[ 4 ];
stooge1 = "Moe"; //***** ERROR: stooge1 is a constant!
```

defines the array `stooge1` but does *not* initialize it in the definition. When we then try to assign *Moe* to `stooge1`

```
stooge1 = "Moe"; //***** ERROR: stooge1 is a constant!
```

an error results because an array's name is a pointer *constant* (see Section 4.3) and, therefore, it is not a legal lvalue. An array may be initialized to a string *only in its definition*. The code segment

```
char stooge1[ 4 ] = "Moe"; // define and initialize
```

is thus legal.   ∎

Reading and Writing Strings

Strings may be read from disk files or the standard input using the operator `>>`, and strings may be written to disk files or the standard output using the operator `<<`. We illustrate with `cin` and `cout`.

When the operator `>>` is used to read a string into an array of `char`, `>>` ignores white space characters such as blanks, tabs, and newlines. After reading the first non-white space character, `>>` continues reading until it encounters a white space character. After it stops reading, `>>` adds a null terminator to ensure a string.

When used to write an array of `char`, the operator `<<` writes until it encounters the null terminator. Assuming `name` is an array of `char`, the statement

```
cout << name << endl;
```

causes `<<` to start writing at address `name`, that is, at the address of the array's *first* character; and `<<` continues writing characters in the array until it encounters a null terminator. If the array does *not* have a null terminator, the likely outcome is an access violation.

EXAMPLE 4.5.7. The code segment

```
char stooge1[ 50 ]; // lots of room!
cout << "Please enter first stooge's name: ";
cin >> stooge1;
cout << "You have entered " << stooge1
     << " as the first stooge's name." << endl;
```

uses `cin` to read a string into the array `stooge1` from the standard input. For example, suppose that the standard input is

```
    moe     larry
```

There are three blanks to the left of the `m` in `moe`, and four blanks between the `e` in `moe` and the `l` in `larry`. Given the above definition of `stooge1` as an array of `char`, the statement

```
cin >> stooge1;
```

reads `moe` into `stooge1` as a null-terminated sequence of characters. For safety, we give `stooge1` a size of 50 so that the string read from the standard input is not likely to overflow the array. Even if the user enters *larry*, the array still has room for the string characters and the null terminator. In Section 4.7 we discuss ways to *ensure* that no overflow occurs.

The statement

```
cout << "You have entered " << stooge1
     << " as the first stooge's name." << endl;
```

writes

```
You have entered moe as the first stooge's name.
```

to the standard output. ∎

EXAMPLE 4.5.8.   The code segment

```
int main() {
  char a1[ ] = "foo"; // a string
  char a2[ 3 ];        //***** Caution: not a string
  cout << a1    // OK: foo written to standard output
       << endl;
  cout << a2     //***** Caution: access violation likely
       << endl;
  ...
}
```

defines two arrays of **char**. Array **a1** is initialized to the string constant *foo* and, there-fore, contains a null terminator. Array **a2** is not initialized and therefore contains garbage. In particular, we must *not* assume that **a2** miraculously contains a null termi-nator. The likely outcome when we print **a2** is an access violation because **<<** keeps writing until it encounters a null terminator.   ∎

Strings and Bounds Checking

Strings are tricky in C++ because of the null terminator. Care must be taken to ensure that an array meant to hold a string has room for the terminating null. Otherwise, array overflow occurs because there are more characters to store than array elements.

EXAMPLE 4.5.9.   The code segment

```
char stooge1[ 4 ] = "Larry"; //**** ERROR: overflow
```

illustrates array overflow. The definition of **stooge1** allocates four **char** cells

[0]	[1]	[2]	[3]

but then tries to store *six* characters in it

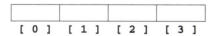

'L'	'a'	'r'	'r'	'y'	'\0'
[0]	[1]	[2]	[3]	*****	*****

The extra two characters, the **'y'** and the **'\0'**, therefore, overflow the array. The penalty may be an access violation (see Section 4.2).   ∎

Differences between Arrays of **char** and Other Types

Arrays of **char** behave different from arrays of other data types with respect to the output operator **<<**. Given the definition and initialization

```
char a1[ ] = { 'm', 'o', 'e', '\0' };
```

the statement

```
cout << a1 << endl; // prints moe
```

prints the string **moe** to the standard output. Because **a1**'s data type is **char***, the output operator **<<** treats **a1** as a *string*, that is, as the address of a null-terminated sequence of **char**s. The output operation therefore prints each **char** in the sequence until a null terminator is encountered. By contrast, given the definition and initialization

```
int a2[ ] = { 1, 2, 3, 4 };
```

the statement

```
cout << a2 << endl; // prints a2 as a address
```

does *not* print each integer in **a2**. Instead, the statement prints **a2**'s value, which is the address of the its first cell. On our system, for example, the output from the statement on a sample run was **0012FF64**, which is the address (in hex) of **a2**'s first cell. To print each cell in **a2**, we could use a loop such as

```
for ( int i = 0; i < 4; i++ )
   cout << a2[ i ] << endl;
```

EXERCISES

1. Does C++ have a data type for strings?

2. How are strings represented in C++?

3. How many string characters are in *Foo*?

4. How many characters are required for the C++ representation of *Foo*?

5. What is the size of array **song**?

```
char song[ ] = "Free to Decide";
```

6. Explain the error.

```
char a1[ ] = "flotsam";
char a2[ 20 ];
a2 = "jetsam";
```

7. Explain the error.

```
char novel[ 10 ] = "War and Peace";
```

8. Explain the error.

```
char s = "A";
```

9. How many **char** cells are required to store the character **'A'**?

10. How many **char** cells are required to store the string **"A"**?

11. Suppose that the standard input contains the string   Anchee . There are three
    blanks to the left of the **A** in **Anchee** and another blank after the last **e**. After the **cin**
    statement, what is the first character in array **name**? Is **name** a string?

```
char name[ 50 ];
cin >> name;
```

12. Assume that the standard input contains the string **Anchee**. What is the error?

```
char name[ 5 ];
cin >> name;
```

13. Explain why an access violation is the likely result of this code segment.

```
char s[ ] = { 'M', 'o', 'e' };
cout << s << endl;
```

14. What is the output?

```
#include <iostream>
using namespace std;
int main() {
   char s[ ] = { 'O', 'k', '\0' };
   int n[ ] = { 9, 8, 7, 6 };
   cout << s << endl << n << endl;
   return 0;
}
```

4.6 ARRAYS AND FUNCTIONS

An array can be passed as an argument to function. Consider, for example, a function **sum**
that computes the sum of the array elements

```
a[ 0 ],a[ 1 ],..., a[ n ]
```

Two parameters are required—an array parameter **a** to catch the array passed and a parameter
n to catch the index of the last item in the array to be summed. Assuming that the array is
an array of **int**s and that the index **n** is of type **int**, the parameters in **sum** can be described
as

```
// sum's header
int sum( int a[ ], int n )
```

```
#include <iostream>
using namespace std;
const int MaxElts = 100;
int sum( int a[ ], int n );
int main() {
   int b[ MaxElts ], x, m;
   m = 0;
   while ( m < MaxElts && cin >> b[ m ] )
      m++;
   // reset m so it is the index of
   // the last item in the array
   m--;
   cout << m + 1 << " items input" << endl;
   x = sum( b, m );
   cout << "sum = " << x << endl;
   return 0;
}

int sum( int a[ ], int n ) {
   int partial_sum, i;
   i = partial_sum = 0;
   while ( i <= n ) {
      partial_sum += a[ i ];
      i++;
   }
   return partial_sum;
}
```

FIGURE 4.6.1 A function to sum an array.

The parameter declaration for the array includes square brackets to indicate that the first parameter refers to an array. Note that the number of cells is *not* enclosed in square brackets. The ordinary **int** parameter **n** is declared in the usual way.

If in some other function we want to invoke the function **sum** to compute

$$b[\ 0\ ] + b[\ 1\ ] + \cdots + b[\ m\ ]$$

and store the result in **x**, we write

```
// invoking a function with an array argument
x = sum( b, m );
```

To pass the array **b**, we simply enter its name as the argument. Figure 4.6.1 gives a complete program in which we initialize an array and invoke the function **sum** to sum its entries.

It is a slight abuse of the language to say that "we pass an array to a function." What we really pass is *the address of the first cell in the array*. Recall (see Section 4.3) that if **b** is an array, the value of the expression **b** is the address of the first element in the array. Thus in Figure 4.6.1, when we pass the array argument **b** to the function **sum**, we are passing the address of the array's first element to **sum**. Within **sum** this address is copied to the parameter **a**. Once the address of the first cell is known, it is possible to access any cell in the array. For example, after **sum** receives the address of the first cell in the array **b**, it uses the index operator **[ ]** to access the various cells within the array. The statement

```
partial_sum += a[ i ];
```

accesses the cell at index **i** in array **b** and adds its value to **partial_sum**.

A function that has an array parameter works on the *actual* cells of the array, *not* on copies of the cells of the array. The function **reverse** in Figure 4.6.2 reverses the array **vals** in **main**. When **main** calls **reverse**, the only copy that occurs is when the address of the first cell in the array **vals** is copied to the array parameter **a**. In call by value (see Section 3.3), C++ passes arguments to an invoked function by copying the arguments' values into temporary cells and making the corresponding parameters the cells' identifiers. In particular, call by value is in effect with respect to array arguments.

```
#include <iostream>
using namespace std;
void reverse( int a[ ], int end );

int main() {
   int vals[ ] = { 1, 5, 8, 32 };
   int i;
   // reverse works on the cells in
   // array vals, not on copies of
   // these cells
   reverse( vals, 3 );
   // output is: 32 8 5 1
   for ( i = 0; i <= 3; i++ )
      cout << vals[ i ] << ' ';
   cout << endl;
   return 0;
}

// reverse a[ 0 ],...,a[ end ]
void reverse( int a[ ], int end ) {
   int start, temp;
   start = 0;
   while( start < end ) {
      // swap a[ start ] and a[ end ]
      temp = a[ start ];
      a[ start ] = a[ end ];
      a[ end ] = temp;
      start++;
      end--;
   }
}
```

FIGURE 4.6.2 Reversing an array. Function **reverse** works on the cells of the array **vals** in **main**, *not* on a copy of the cells in **vals**.

const with Arrays

If a function has an array parameter and the contents of the array will not be changed by the function, the parameter may be marked as **const**. The compiler will then try to uncover illegal attempts to modify the cells. Thus marking an array parameter as **const** achieves the protection of call by value, but with the efficiency of not copying the contents of all of the cells of the array.

EXAMPLE 4.6.1.   Since the function

```
void print_array( const int a[ ], int size ) {
   int i;
   for ( i = 0; i < size; i++ )
      cout << a[ i ] << endl;
}
```

does not modify the array, the parameter **a** is marked as **const**.   ■

EXAMPLE 4.6.2.   The function

```
// copy size ints from array a2 to array a1
// ***** ERROR: a1 should NOT be marked const
void copy( const int a1[ ], const int a2[ ], int size ) {
   int i = 0;
   for ( i = 0; i < size; i++ )
      a1[ i ] = a2[ i ];
}
```

contains an error, because array **a1** is marked **const**, but it is modified by the assignment statement

```
a1[ i ] = a2[ i ];
```

The error is corrected by changing the header to

```
// correct header
void copy( int a1[ ], const int a2[ ], int size )
```

Notice that **a2** is properly marked **const** because the cells of **a2** are *not* modified.   ■

EXAMPLE 4.6.3.   The function **length**

```
int length( const char s[ ] ) {
   for ( int len = 0; s[ len ] != '\0'; len++ )
      ;
   return len;
}
```

computes the *length* of a string, which is defined to be the number of characters (not including the null terminator) in the string. For example, the length of the string *beavis* is 6.

The function steps through the characters, incrementing `len`, until it finds the null terminator that marks the end of the string. At this point, the value of `len` is equal to the length of the string.

The parameter `s` is marked `const` because `length` does not change the contents of the array.

The condition

```
s[ len ] != '\0'
```

could be simplified to

```
s[ len ]
```

because the null terminator is equal to zero (`false`), whereas an actual character's code is nonzero (`true`). ∎

EXERCISES

1. Suppose that we have an array `sample` defined as

```
float sample[ 10 ];
```

Explain the difference between what is passed to the functions `f1` and `f2`.

```
f1( sample );
f2( sample[ 2 ] );
```

2. What is the error?

```
void fun( double bigs );
int main() {
   double bignums[ 20 ];
   // invoke fun with bignums as argument
   fun( bignums );
   ...
}
void fun( double bigs ) {
   ...
}
```

3. What is printed?

```
#include <iostream>
using namespace std;
void f( int x[ ], int y );
int main() {
   int a[ 5 ], b, i;
   for ( i = 0; i < 5; i++ )
      a[ i ] = 2 * i;
   b = 16;
   f( a, b );
   for ( i = 0; i < 5; i++ )
      cout << a[ i ] << endl;
   cout << b << endl;
   return 0;
}

void f ( int x[ ], int y ) {
   int i;
   for ( i = 0; i < 5; i++ )
      x[ i ] += 2;
   y += 2;
}
```

4. (True/False) The following function returns **true** if

```
v[ low ],...,v[ high ]
```

is in ascending order, and **false** otherwise. Explain.

```
bool order( int v[ ], int low, int high ) {
   bool flag = true;
   for ( ; low < high; low++ )
      if ( v[ low ] <= v[ low + 1 ] )
         flag = true;
      else
         flag = false;
   return flag;
}
```

5. Write a function **find** with two parameters: **s** of type array of **char** and **c** of type **char**. Assume that the first argument is a null-terminated array of **char**. The function returns **true**, if **c** is in **s**, and **false**, if **c** is not in **s**.

4.7 STRING-HANDLING FUNCTIONS

Because strings are not a built-in data type in C++, C++ does not have built-in operators for strings. Instead, C++ provides a library of string-handling functions. To use these functions, the programmer must **#include** the header file *cstring*. In this section we focus on how the string-handling functions may be used to advantage.

strlen

The function **strlen** expects a string as its single argument and returns an integer that represents the string's length, which is the number of characters in it *excluding* the null terminator.

EXAMPLE 4.7.1. The code segment

```
#include <cstring> // for string-handling functions
cout << "Groucho Marx as a string has length "
     << strlen( "Groucho Marx" )
     << endl;
```

shows how the library function **strlen** might be used. The expression

```
strlen( "Groucho Marx" )
```

evaluates to 12, the number of string characters in *Groucho Marx*. In particular, **strlen** does *not* count the null terminator. By the way, **strlen**'s argument may be either a string constant

```
cout << strlen( "Karl Marx" ) << endl;
```

or a string stored in an array

```
char theNotSoFunnyMarx[ ] = "Karl Marx";
cout << strlen( theNotSoFunnyMarx ) << endl;
```

EXAMPLE 4.7.2. The code segment

```
char emptyString[ ] = "";      // array's size is 1, for \0
cout << strlen( emptyString ) << endl;  // outputs 0
```

outputs 0, the number of string characters in **emptyString**. Note that **emptyString** is indeed a string, that is, a null-terminated array of **char**.

The prototype for **strlen** may be written

```
size_t strlen( const char s[ ] );
```

where **size_t** is an alias for a built-in integer type such as **unsigned** or **unsigned long**. The argument is **const** because **strlen** does not change the string but rather computes its length.

strcat, strncat

These functions are used for *string concatenation*. To concatenate two strings is to combine them into one string. The function **strcat** expects two strings as arguments. It concatenates the two strings by appending *all* the characters in the second argument, including the null terminator, to the end of the first string. The *end* of the first string is its null terminator. The second argument is unchanged.

EXAMPLE 4.7.3. The definitions

```
char s1[ 8 ] = "M ";
char s2[ ] = "Curie";
```

create the initialized arrays

'M'	' '	'\0'	'\0'	'\0'	'\0'	'\0'	'\0'
[0]	[1]	[2]	[3]	[4]	[5]	[6]	[7]

'C'	'u'	'r'	'i'	'e'	'\0'
[0]	[1]	[2]	[3]	[4]	[5]

After the function call

```
strcat( s1, s2 );
```

s2 is unchanged, but **s1** is changed to

'M'	' '	'C'	'u'	'r'	'i'	'e'	'\0'
[0]	[1]	[2]	[3]	[4]	[5]	[6]	[7]

Array **s1** thus must have enough cells to hold its original string **char**s and *all* of the **char**s in **s2**. So **s1**'s size must be at least

```
strlen( s1 ) + strlen( s2 ) + 1
```

or 8. In the concatenation, **s2**'s characters are copied into **s1** precisely where **s1**'s null terminator occurs, that is, the third cell in **s1** (i.e., **s1[2]**); and the copying of characters from **s2** into **s1** continues until **s2**'s null terminator is encountered. The function **strcat** thus requires that *each* of its arguments be a string, that is, a *null-terminated* array of **char**.

The prototype for **strcat** is

```
char* strcat( char dest[ ], const char src[ ] );
```

The first argument is not **const** because **strcat** *changes* the first array by concatenating characters from the second array. The function returns its first argument **dest**, which is of type **char*** ("pointer to **char**"): **dest** points to an element, usually the first, in a **char** array. This return value supports code segments such as

```
cout << strcat( s1, s2 ) // outputs M Curie
     << endl;
```

■

Library function **strncat** also does string concatenation but has a third argument as its prototype shows:

```
char* strncat( char dest[ ], const char src[ ], size_t n );
```

The third argument specifies how many characters are to be copied from **src** into **dest**. For example, the code segment

```
char s1[ 20 ] = "Leontyne"; // 20 for safety
char s2[ ] = "Price";
cout << strcat( s1, s2 ) << endl;      // LeontynePrice
```

outputs **LeontynePrice**, whereas the code segment

```
char s1[ 20 ] = "Leontyne"; // 20 for safety
char s2[ ] = "Price";
cout << strncat( s1, s2, 2 ) << endl; // LeontynePr
```

outputs **LeontynePr** because only two characters are copied from **s2** into **s1**.

strcmp, strncmp

These functions are used for string comparisons. When comparing two different strings, there are two possibilities:

- The strings have different lengths, and each character in the shorter string is identical to the corresponding character in the longer string. For example, *dog* is shorter than *doghouse* but the two strings match up to three characters.

- The strings have the same or different lengths, and, at some position, the characters in the two strings differ. For example, *tan* and *tin* have the same length but differ in their second characters.

Whenever the first possibility holds, the *shorter* string precedes the *longer*. So *dog* precedes *doghouse*. If the second possibility holds, we locate the leftmost position *p* at which the two strings differ. The order of the strings is then determined by the order of the characters at *p*. So *tan* precedes *tin* because *a* precedes *i*. This method of ordering is known as **lexicographic order**.

The library function **strcmp** expects two string arguments and returns an **int**:

```
int strcmp( const char s1[ ], const char s2[ ] );
```

The two arguments are **const** because **strcmp** only *compares* the strings; it does not change them. The returned **int** is interpreted as follows:

- 0 means the two strings are equal. So

```
strcmp( "a", "a" )
```

returns 0.

- A *negative* integer means that the *first* precedes the second. So

```
strcmp( "tan", "tin" )
```

returns a negative integer.

- A *positive* integer means that the *second* precedes the first. So

```
strcmp( "tempting", "tangential" )
```

returns a positive integer.

The function **strncmp**

```
int strncmp( const char s1[ ], const char s2[ ], size_t n );
```

behaves just like **strcmp** except that it compares only the first **n** characters in each. For example,

```
cout << strcmp( "abc", "abz" ) << endl;
```

outputs a *negative* integer because the *c* in the first string precedes the *z* in the second. However,

```
cout << strncmp( "abc", "abz", 2 ) << endl;
```

outputs 0 because the two strings are identical in their first two characters.

strcpy, strncpy

These functions are used to copy strings. The function **strcpy** copies its second argument into its first argument, leaving its second argument unchanged.

EXAMPLE 4.7.4.   The code segment

```
char s1[ ] = "My One and Only"; // array size is 16
char s2[ ] = "South Pacific";    // array size is 14
cout << s1 << endl; // My One and Only
strcpy( s1, s2 );
cout << s1 << endl; // South Pacific
cout << s2 << endl; // South Pacific
```

illustrates **strcpy**. Its first argument is a string *destination*, that is, an array of **char** big enough to hold all the string characters in its second argument *and* a null terminator. In this example, **s1** is big enough to hold the 13 string characters in **s2** together with a null terminator because **s1**'s size is 16. After the code segment executes, **s1** contains the string *South Pacific*; and **s2** *still* contains the string *South Pacific*. ∎

The prototype for **strcpy** is

```
char* strcpy( char dest[ ], const char src[ ] );
```

The **dest**ination array is not **const** because the copying changes the characters in the array. The source string is **const** because **strcpy** does not change it. The return value is the destination array, which allows code segments such as

```
char dest[ 100 ]; // 100 for safety
cout << strcpy( dest, "The High and the Mighty" )
     << endl;
```

which outputs

```
The High and the Mighty
```

The library function **strncpy**

```
char* strncpy( char dest[ ], const char src[ ], size_t n );
```

copies exactly **n** characters from a source string **src** to **dest**, an array of **char** whose size should be at least **n**. If the length of string **src** is less than **n**, null terminators are used to fill **dest**. However, if the length of **src** is greater than or equal to **n**, the result in **dest** is *not* null terminated. The code segment

```
char s1[ 20 ];
char s2[ ] = "Miles Davis";
strcpy( s1, s2 );
cout << s1 << endl; // Miles Davis
```

copies *all* the characters from **s2** into **s1**. By contrast, the code segment

```
char s1[ 20 ];
char s2[ ] = "Miles Davis";
strncpy( s1, s2, 5 );
s1[ 5 ] = '\0';
cout << s1 << endl; // Miles
```

copies only the first five characters from **s2** into **s1**. Note that we add a null terminator at index 5 to ensure a string, which shows that **strncpy** must be used with caution. The null terminator in **"Miles Davis"** occurs at index 11 because the null terminator is the *last* character in the string. If we **strncpy** only five characters from this string, we do *not* copy the null terminator into the source **s1**. Therefore, we must add the null terminator ourselves to ensure that **s1** is a string.

strstr, strchr, strrchr, strpbrk

These four library functions are alike in that they search a string for a specified component, either another string or a single character. The library function **strstr** is short for *string in string*. The library functions **strchr** and **strrchr** are short for *string has character*. The library function **strpbrk** is short for *string point and break*.

EXAMPLE 4.7.5. The code segment

```
cout << strstr( "photon", "to" ) << endl;
```

outputs **ton**. Function **strstr** searches for the leftmost occurrence of the string *to* in the string *photon*, returning the address of the *t* in *to*. The output thus *begins* with *t* in *photon* and *ends* when a null terminator is encountered. It is critical that both arguments to **strstr** be strings, that is, null-terminated arrays of **char**. ■

There are two versions of **strstr**:

```
const char* strstr( const char s1[ ], const char s2[ ] );
char* strstr( char s1[ ], const char s2[ ] );
```

The first version is perhaps more intuitive. Since **strstr** does not change characters in either string, **s1** and **s2** are both marked **const**. If the search succeeds, **strstr** returns the address of the leftmost occurrence of **s2** in **s1**. Because the address returned is of a character in **s1**, the return type is also marked **const**; string **s1** is not to be changed.

If the search fails, **strstr** returns **NULL**, which is **#define**d as **0** in the header file *cstddef* and, for convenience, in several other header files as well. The key point is that **NULL** is *not* a legal address. When a function such as **strstr** is supposed to return an address or pointer but cannot, it can return **NULL** (**0**).

The second version is provided to support a calling function that uses **strstr** and intends to change **s1**. This version also returns the address of the leftmost occurrence of **s2** in **s1**, or **NULL**, if **s2** is not found in **s1**. In this version, **const** is deleted from parameter **s1** and the return type, allowing string **s1** to be changed.

Function **strchr** searches a string for the *leftmost* occurrence of a character, whereas **strrchr** searches a string for the *rightmost* occurrence of a character. (The second **r** in **strrchr** stands for *rightmost*.)

EXAMPLE 4.7.6. The code segment

```
cout << strchr( "photon", 'o' ) << endl;
```

outputs **oton**. Function **strchr** searches **photon** for the leftmost occurrence of **o**, returning its address if successful. The output begins at this address and ends at the null terminator. By contrast, the code segment

```
cout << strrchr( "photon", 'o' ) << endl;
```

outputs **on** because **strrchr** searches for the *rightmost* occurrence of **o**, returning its address. ■

The prototypes for these character-searching functions are

```
const char* strchr( const char s[ ], int c );
char* strchr( char s[ ], int c );
const char* strrchr( const char s[ ], int c );
char* strrchr( char s[ ], int c );
```

Note that the second argument for each function is an **int** rather than a **char**, which is no problem, because an **int** can hold all the values of a **char**. Both functions return **NULL** if the character **c** is not contained in the string **s**. Again, two versions of each function are supplied to allow a calling function to use a **const** or non**const** string **s**.

Among the character-searching functions, **strpbrk** may be the most flexible. Its prototype is

```
const char* strpbrk( const char s1[ ], const char s2[ ] );
char* strpbrk( char s1[ ], const char s2[ ] );
```

The function **strpbrk** searches **s1** for the *leftmost* occurrence of *any* string character in string **s2**, returning this character's address in **s1** in case of success and **NULL** if no character in **s2** occurs in **s1**. Again, two versions of the function are supplied to allow a calling function to use a **const** or non**const** string **s1**.

> **EXAMPLE 4.7.7.** The code segment
>
> ```
> cout << strpbrk( "photon", "my,oh,my" ) << endl;
> ```
>
> outputs **hoton**. Although the second string contains both an **o** and an **h**, the address of **h** is returned in **photon** because the **h** is the *leftmost* of the search characters in **photon**. If the second argument is changed to
>
> ```
> my,o,my
> ```
>
> then the output is **oton**. ∎

strspn, strcspn

These functions are short for *string span* and *string complement of span*. Their prototypes are

```
size_t strspn( const char s1[ ], const char s2[ ] );
size_t strcspn( const char s1[ ], const char s2[ ] );
```

strspn returns the number of consecutive characters in **s1**, beginning with the first, that occur somewhere in **s2**; and **strcspn** returns the number of consecutive characters in **s1**, beginning with the first, that do *not* occur anywhere in **s2**.

> **EXAMPLE 4.7.8.** The code segment
>
> ```
> cout << strspn( "abcd", "ab" );
> ```
>
> outputs 2. The function searches its first argument **abcd** for characters in its second argument **ab**, halting as soon as it finds any character in the first string that is *not* in the second string. In this example, the search thus ends at **c** because **c** is *not* in the second string. The function then returns, as an integer, the *length* of the initial sequence in **s1** that contains characters from **s2**. So
>
> ```
> strspn( "abcd", "ab" )
> ```

returns 2. By contrast, the code segment

```
cout << strspn( "xabcd", "ab" );
```

outputs 0 because the search stops at the very first character **x**, which is *not* in the second string. By the way, the order of characters in the second string is immaterial. The output for the code segment

```
cout << strspn( "abcd", "ba" );
```

is still 2.   ■

Function **strcspn** is the *complement* or opposite of **strspn**.

EXAMPLE 4.7.9.   The code segment

```
cout << strcspn( "abcd", "cd" ) << endl;
```

outputs 2 because the first argument has an initial sequence of *two* characters, **ab**, that are *not* in the second argument. So **strcspn** stops searching once it finds, in the first string, any character in the second string. The function then returns the number of characters read before stopping.   ■

strtok

The library function **strtok** is short for *string tokenizer*. Its prototype is

```
char* strtok( char s[ ], const char delims[ ] );
```

The first argument is a string to be broken up into **tokens** or parts. The first argument is not **const** because **strtok** changes the string. The second argument is a list of **delimiters**, that is, symbols that separate tokens. The return value is the address of the *next token*. The function returns **NULL** when it encounters the null terminator, which signals that there are no more tokens in the string.

EXAMPLE 4.7.10.   The code segment

```
char s[ ] = "vonneumann@ias.princeton.edu";
char d[ ] = ".@"; // delimiters are . and @
cout << strtok( s, d ) << endl;       // vonneumann
cout << strtok( NULL, d ) << endl; // ias
cout << strtok( NULL, d ) << endl; // princeton
cout << strtok( NULL, d ) << endl; // edu
```

outputs

```
vonneumann
ias
princeton
edu
```

The order of the tokens is irrelevant. The code works the same whether we have

```
char d[ ] = ".@";
```

or

```
char d[ ] = "@.";
```

The first call to **strtok** has two string arguments, the string to be broken up into tokens and the delimiters to be used to separate tokens from one another. A non**NULL** first argument tells **strtok** where to *begin* searching for tokens. It stops searching when it finds a delimiter, substituting a null terminator for the delimiter. So when **strtok** finds the **@** in string **s**, it substitutes **\0** for this delimiter. This explains why the first output is

```
vonneumann
```

In the subsequent calls, we use **NULL** instead of **s** as the first argument in order to signal **strtok** that it should continue from its *current position*—the delimiter just replaced by a null terminator—in its search for tokens. Were the second call

```
cout << strtok( s, d ) << endl;
```

instead of

```
cout << strtok( NULL, d ) << endl;
```

the output would be

```
vonneumann
```

again instead of

```
ias                                                              ■
```

In the typical use of **strtok**, there is *one* call with a string to be tokenized as the first argument and subsequent calls with **NULL** as the first argument. The second argument typically remains unchanged, as we normally use the same delimiters throughout.

Nesting String-Handling Functions

The string-handling functions support *nested calls* whenever these are appropriate.

EXAMPLE 4.7.11. The code segment

```
char dest[ 100 ];          // 100 for safety
char m[ 50 ] = "Madame "; // 50 for safety
char b[ ] = "Butterfly";
cout << strcpy( dest, strcat( m, b ) ) << endl;
cout << m << endl;
cout << b << endl;
```

outputs

```
Madame Butterfly
Madame Butterfly
Butterfly
```

The **strcat** is nested inside **strcpy**. Recall that **strcat** returns its first argument, which is a string. Function **strcpy** expects a string as its second argument, namely, a string to copy into its first argument. Recall, too, that **strcpy** returns a string, namely, its first argument, which now contains a copy of its second argument. ■

EXAMPLE 4.7.12. The code segment

```
char s1[ 100 ] = "One-Eyed "; // 50 for safety
char s2[ ] = "Jacks";
cout << strlen( strcat( s1, s2 ) ) << endl;
```

outputs 14, the number of string characters in the concatenated string

```
One-Eyed Jacks
```
                                                                          ■

EXERCISES

1. In the code segment

```
unsigned n = strlen( "baz" );
```

what value is stored in **n**?

2. Inside **main** write a code segment that computes the length of the string *To the Faithful Departed*.

3. What is the size of array **s**?

```
char s[ ] = "";
```

Is **s** a *string*?

4. What is the output?

```
char s[ ] = "";
cout << s << endl;
```

5. Consider the array of **char**

```
char s[ ] = { 'O', 'h', ' ', 'N', 'o', '!' }
```

which is *not* a string. Invoke the library function **strlen** with **s** as the argument

```
unsigned n = strlen( s );
```

What happens on your system?

6. What is the output?

```
char dest[ 100 ];
char src[ ] = "Six Easy Pieces";
strcpy( dest, src );
cout << dest << endl;
cout << src << endl;
```

7. What is the output?

```
char dest[ 100 ];
char src[ ] = "Six Easy Pieces";
strncpy( dest, src, 3 );
dest[ 3 ] = '\0';
cout << dest << endl;
cout << src << endl;
```

8. What is the output?

```
char dest[ 50 ] = "Mighty ";
char src[ ] = "Mite";
strcat( dest, src );
cout << src << endl;
cout << dest << endl;
```

9. What is the output?

```
char dest[ 50 ] = "Mighty ";
char src[ ] = "Mite";
strncat( dest, src, 2 );
cout << src << endl;
cout << dest << endl;
```

10. What is the output?

```
cout << strcmp( "abc", "abc" ) << endl;
```

11. What is the output?

```
cout << strcmp( "abcdefg", "abc" ) << endl;
```

12. What is the output?

```
cout << strcmp( "xy", "abc" ) << endl;
```

13. Inside **main**, write a code segment that checks whether the character `'A'` is in the string **Destry Rides Again**.

14. Explain in words what the prototype

```
char* strrchr( char s[ ], int c );
```

tells us about the library function **strrchr**.

15. What is the output?

```
char s1[ 20 ] = "foo ";
char s2[ ] = "baz";
char s3[ 20 ];
cout << strcpy( s3, strcat( s1, s2 ) ) << endl;
cout << s3 << endl;
cout << s2 << endl;
cout << s1 << endl;
```

4.8 SAMPLE APPLICATION: MERGING FILES

Problem

Prompt the user for the names of two sorted input files and the name of an output file to hold the **merged** records of the input files. To *merge* sorted files is to combine their records into a sorted output file. A **record** is a sequence of bytes, including embedded white space such as blanks and tabs, terminated by the newline character **\n**. (Assume a maximum record size of 80, including the terminating newline.) One or both of the input files may be empty. The input files may have the same number of records, although typically they have different numbers of records. In any case, the merge must continue until *both* input files have been read to end-of-file.

Sample Input/Output Files

Given that *inputFile1* is

```
Bambi
Jules et Jim
Name of the Rose
South Pacific
```

and *inputFile2* is

```
Dirty Dozen with Dirty Harry
Marvin Gardens
```

the merged output file is

```
Bambi
Dirty Dozen with Dirty Harry
Jules et Jim
Marvin Gardens
Name of the Rose
South Pacific
```

Solution

After prompting the user for the input files and the output file, we read records from the input files using the library function **getline**, which reads records, including embedded white space such as blanks and tabs, and converts the records into *strings* by replacing the newline character with a null terminator. Using strings lets us use the operator **<<** to write to the output file; and by appending a newline character to each string as we write it, we convert the string back into a *record*. We assume that the two input files are sorted in ascending order, which means that the output file is also sorted in ascending order. We use the library function **strcmp** to compare the input records now stored as strings, printing whichever string lexicographically precedes the other. Whenever we output a string from a file, we read another input record from the same file. When we reach end-of-file in one input file, we output the remaining records in the other file. In this way, all records from both input files are merged into the output file.

C++ Implementation

```cpp
#include <iostream>
#include <fstream>
#include <cstring>
using namespace std;
const unsigned MaxRecLen = 80;
const unsigned MaxFileName = 200;
int main() {
    ifstream if1, if2;
    ofstream of;
    char infile1[ MaxFileName + 1 ],
         infile2[ MaxFileName + 1 ],
         outfile[ MaxFileName + 1 ];
    char rec1[ MaxRecLen ],
         rec2[ MaxRecLen ];

    // Prompt for and read file names.
    cout << "Input file 1: ";
    cin >> infile1;
    cout << "Input file 2: ";
    cin >> infile2;
    cout << "Output file: ";
    cin >> outfile;

    // Open the files.
    if1.open( infile1 );
    if2.open( infile2 );
    of.open( outfile );
```

```
// Merge the files until both are empty. An empty record
// is one whose length as a string is zero. We assume
// that records are terminated by a newline character
// and that the input files are sorted.
//*** loop prologue
if1.getline( rec1, MaxRecLen );
if2.getline( rec2, MaxRecLen );
//*** While both input files still contain records,
//     compare the records and output the one
//     that lexicographically precedes the other.
while ( strlen( rec1 ) && strlen( rec2 ) ) {
  // if rec1 < rec2, output rec1 and get another
  if ( strcmp( rec1, rec2 ) < 0 ) {
    of << rec1 << endl;
    if1.getline( rec1, MaxRecLen );
  }
  // rec2 <= rec1, so output rec2 and get another
  else {
    of << rec2 << endl;
    if2.getline( rec2, MaxRecLen );
  }
}

//*** If the first file still contains records but the
//     the second does not, output the remaining records
//     from the first file.
while ( strlen( rec1 ) ) {
    of << rec1 << endl;
    if1.getline( rec1, MaxRecLen );
}

//*** If the second file still contains records but the
//     first does not, output the remaining records from
//     the second file.
while ( strlen( rec2 ) ) {
  of << rec2 << endl;
  if2.getline( rec2, MaxRecLen );
}

// Close the input and output files and exit.
if1.close();
if2.close();
of.close();
return 0;
}
```

Discussion

We use the global constant

```
const unsigned MaxRecLen = 80;
```

for convenience and program robustness. If we decide, for example, to increase the maximum record length from 80 to 1350, we need to make only *one* change in the program:

```
const unsigned MaxRecLen = 1350;
```

The global constant is defined and initialized right above **main**, which makes it visible throughout **main**. We also define **MaxFileName** as a global constant. It represents the maximum length of a file's name. We initialize it to 200 to accommodate long file names.

 After prompting the user for the names of two input files and an output file, we open the three files. (For a review of files, see Section 2.5.) The input files are of type **ifstream** and the output file is of type **ofstream**. Use of these data types requires an **#include** of the header file *fstream*. We also **#include** the header file *iostream* so that we can use **cout** and **cin** for prompting the user and reading user input. The header file *cstring* is **#include**d because we use **strlen** and **strcmp**.

 Our program merges input files regardless of their size. For example, both input files could be empty. In this case, of course, the output file is also empty. If one input file is empty and the other is nonempty, the output file is identical to the nonempty input file. If both input files are nonempty, they contain either the same or a different number of records. In either case, our program merges the two files until one of them runs out of records. The remaining records in the other file are then written to the output file. The program has three **while** loops to handle these possibilities. The first **while** loop executes as long as *both* input files still contain records to be read. This loop terminates when the end of either input file is reached. The second **while** loop executes as long as the first input file still contains records to be read, but end-of-file has been reached in the second input file. The third loop executes as long as the second input file still contains records to be read, but end-of-file has been reached in the first input file.

 Just before executing the first **while** loop, we read a record from each input file into an array of **char**: the array **rec1** is used for the first input file and the array **rec2** is used for the second input file. We use **getline**

```
if1.getline( rec1, MaxRecLen );
if2.getline( rec2, MaxRecLen );
```

for reading records. The variables **if1** and **if2** are of type **ifstream**, and **getline** is a function associated with this type. For now, our concern is the syntax of using **getline**.

 Our version of **getline** expects two arguments, an array into which to read characters and an integer **n** that bounds the number of characters:

```
file.getline( array, n );
```

This version of **getline** reads characters until it

- Reaches end-of-file.
- Encounters a newline character.
- Reads **n** − 1 characters.

whichever happens first. After it stops reading, `getline` adds a null terminator to the array to make a *string*. If `getline` stops reading because it encounters a newline character, `getline` does *not* store the newline character in the array but rather discards it. Note that `getline` never reads more than **n** − 1 characters. If the array's size **MaxRecLen**

```
char rec1[ MaxRecLen ],
     rec2[ MaxRecLen ];
```

is the same as `getline`'s second argument

```
if1.getline( rec1, MaxRecLen );
```

then array overflow cannot occur (see Section 4.2).

If `getline` reaches end-of-file without reading any characters, it puts a null terminator in the array. This explains our prologue and test for the first **while** loop:

```
if1.getline( rec1, MaxRecLen );
if2.getline( rec2, MaxRecLen );
while ( strlen( rec1 ) && strlen( rec2 ) ) {
```

Suppose that both input files are empty. In this case, `getline` reaches end-of-file *before* reading any characters. It still writes a null terminator to each array, **rec1** and **rec2**, so that the null terminator becomes the *first* byte in each array. This means that **rec1** and **rec2** are *empty strings*, that is, strings with a length of zero. Our first loop's test

```
while ( strlen( rec1 ) && strlen( rec2 ) ) {
```

therefore succeeds only if *both* input files are nonempty, in which case **rec1** and **rec2** have a length greater than zero. If either **rec1** or **rec2** has a length of zero, the loop test fails because zero is **false**.

If neither input file is empty, we compare their records

```
// if rec1 < rec2, output rec1 and get another
if ( strcmp( rec1, rec2 ) < 0 ) {
  of << rec1 << endl;
  if1.getline( rec1, MaxRecLen );
}
// rec2 <= rec1, so output rec2 and get another
else {
  of << rec2 << endl;
  if2.getline( rec2, MaxRecLen );
}
```

using `strcmp` to determine which to write. If we write **rec1** to the output file, we immediately read another record from **rec1**'s input file **if1**. The procedure is the same if **rec2** is written.

The second and third **while** loops handle the two cases in which either **if1** or **if2** still has records to be read but the other input file does not. For example, if the first **while** loop exits because end-of-file is reached in **if1** but not in **if2**, then the third **while** loop reads and outputs the remaining records from **if2**.

Sorting Files

The merge of two sorted files is also sorted. For example, suppose that *in1* is the input file

```
Only The Lonely
```

and that *in2* is the input file

```
Born To Run
```

The two input files are *singleton files*, that is, files that contain one record apiece. A singleton file is sorted. Their merge is the output file

```
Born To Run
Only The Lonely
```

which is also sorted. By repeatedly merging sorted input files, we produce ever larger output files that are sorted. The output files can be used as input files for further merges and so on indefinitely.

Testing for End-of-File

An application may have to read data from a file without knowing in advance how much data the file contains. In this case, the application can read data until it reaches the end of the file, provided that the program has some way of detecting the end of the file. Our merge application is such an example. We detect end-of-file by checking whether **getline** places an empty string in its array. A common alternative is to use the function **eof**.

The function **eof** returns **true**, if end-of-file has been reached, and **false**, otherwise. An attempted read beyond the end of the file *must* be made before **eof** returns **true**. For this reason, use of **eof** may differ from some alternative way of detecting end-of-file. We illustrate by comparing **eof** and **getline**.

If **getline** stops reading before end-of-file (e.g., if **getline** encounters a newline), end-of-file is *not* reached, so **eof** returns **false**. For example, if the file *test* is

```
fooBarBaz\n
```

where the last two characters in the file are **z** and newline, Figures 4.8.1 and 4.8.2 both output

```
fooBarBaz\n
```

In Figure 4.8.1, the first call to **getline** stores **fooBarBaz** and the second call to **getline** stores the empty string. In Figure 4.8.2, the first call to **getline** stores **fooBarBaz**, but end-of-file is not reached. Thus the first time the condition in the **while** loop is true. The second call to **getline** reaches end-of-file, so the second time the condition in the **while** loop is false.

Now suppose that the file *test* is changed to

```
fooBarBaz
```

(i.e., the trailing newline is removed.) Figure 4.8.1 still outputs

```
fooBarBaz\n
```

```
#include <iostream>
#include <fstream>
#include <cstring>
using namespace std;
const int MaxBuff = 200;
int main() {
   ifstream if1;
   char buff[ MaxBuff ];
   if1.open( "test" );
   if1.getline( buff, MaxBuff );
   while ( strlen( buff ) ) {
     cout << buff << endl;
     if1.getline( buff, MaxBuff );
   }
   if1.close();
   return 0;
}
```

FIGURE 4.8.1 Detecting end-of-file using `strlen`.


```
#include <iostream>
#include <fstream>
using namespace std;
const int MaxBuff = 200;
int main() {
   ifstream if1;
   char buff[ MaxBuff ];
   if1.open( "test" );
   if1.getline( buff, MaxBuff );
   while ( !if1.eof() ) {
     cout << buff << endl;
     if1.getline( buff, MaxBuff );
   }
   if1.close();
   return 0;
}
```

FIGURE 4.8.2 Detecting end-of-file using `eof`.

The first call to `getline` still stores `fooBarBaz` and the second call to `getline` still stores the empty string. This time Figure 4.8.2 produces no output. The first call to `getline` stores `fooBarBaz` and end-of-file *is* reached. Thus the condition in the `while` loop is false.

Thus, if every line, including the last line, of a file is terminated with a newline, using `eof` or testing `getline`'s array produces the same behavior. Different behavior results if the last line of a file is not terminated with a newline.

EXERCISES

1. What is the time complexity of merge?

2. Give a short example to show that the merged file need not be sorted if the input files are not sorted.

3. If the input file is

   ```
   1 2 3
   ```

   what is the output?

   ```
   int n;
   while ( !cin.eof() ) {
      cin >> n;
      cout << n << endl;
   }
   ```

4.9 MULTIDIMENSIONAL ARRAYS

The square brackets may occur more than once in an array's definition. An array's **dimension** is the number of times the square brackets **[ ]** occur in its definition.

EXAMPLE 4.9.1. The code segment

```
int vector[ 10 ];        // 1-dimensional
int matrix[ 10 ][ 10 ]; // 2-dimensional
```

defines two arrays, a one-dimensional array named **vector** and a two-dimensional array named **matrix**. The square brackets occur *once* in **vector**'s definition and *twice* in **matrix**'s definition. ∎

The number of cells in any array is the product of its dimension sizes. In Example 4.9.1, **vector** has one dimension with a size of 10. Therefore, **vector** has 10 cells. By contrast, **matrix** has two dimensions, each with size 10. Therefore, **matrix** has $10 \times 10 = 100$ cells. The following table defines arrays of various dimensions and sizes:

Definition	Dimensions	Number of Cells
`char ram[ 1000 ];`	1	1,000
`float nums[ 10 ][ 1000 ];`	2	10,000
`short board[ 5 ][ 10 ][ 10 ];`	3	500
`double temps[ 10 ][ 10000 ];`	2	100,000

C++ has no restrictions on how many dimensions an array may have. Arrays with more than one dimension are known generically as **multidimensional arrays**. A two-dimensional array is sometimes called a **matrix**.

Array Size and Number of Elements

In a one-dimensional array, the array's *size* determines

- How many cells it has.
- How many elements it has.

In a one-dimensional array, the number of cells *equals* the number of elements. In a multidimensional array, this is not true. In a multidimensional array

- The product of *all* the dimension sizes determines how many cells it has.
- The size of the *first* dimension determines how many elements it has.

EXAMPLE 4.9.2. The array

```
int n[ 2 ][ 3 ];
```

has *two elements* and *six cells*. Each element is itself an *array*, that is, an array of three **int** elements. The array's first element consists of the first three **int** cells

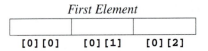

and its second consists of the second three **int** cells

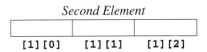

So each of **n**'s two elements is itself an *array* that has **int** cells as elements:

First Element			Second Element		
[0][0]	[0][1]	[0][2]	[1][0]	[1][1]	[1][2]

To identify a particular cell in **n**, we need *two* occurrences of the index operator. The first index expression gives us the array *element*: 0 for **n**'s first element or 1 for **n**'s second element. The second index expression gives us the cell offset within the element: 0 for the first cell, 1 for the second cell, or 2 for the third cell. For example, the first element's second cell has the index

```
[ 0 ][ 1 ] // 1st element, 2nd cell
```

The expression

```
n[ 0 ]  // 1st element
```

designates the array's first element. The second index expression

```
n[ 0 ][ 1 ] // 1st element, 2nd cell
```

then specifies an *offset* of 1 within the first element, giving us the *second* cell in the first element. ∎

EXAMPLE 4.9.3. The code segment

```
int n[ 2 ][ 3 ];
int k = 0;
for ( int i = 0; i < 2; i++ )    // elements
   for ( int j = 0; j < 3; j++ ) // cells
      n[ i ][ j ] = k++;
```

amends Example 4.9.2 by populating the two-dimensional array. The result is

First Element			*Second Element*		
0	1	2	3	4	5
[0][0]	[0][1]	[0][2]	[1][0]	[1][1]	[1][2]

The outer **for** loop iterates through the *elements* and so executes twice. The inner **for** loop iterates through the three cells in each of the two elements and so, on each iteration of the outer loop, executes three times. To access a particular cell, we require an index for both the element and for the cell within the element. Therefore, the assignment statement

```
n[ i ][ j ] = k++;
```

has two occurrences of the index operator, with **i** as the index for the element and **j** the index for the cell within an element. ■

Matrices are probably the most common type of multidimensional array because they are convenient, intuitive, and relatively easy to process. For instance, a matrix may be used to represent a **table**, that is, a collection of *rows*, each of which has the same number of *columns*. Figure 4.9.1 shows a **square matrix**, that is, a matrix that has the same number of rows and columns. The rows and columns are labeled with names of cities and each table entry, a number, represents the estimated road distance in kilometers between the two cities. For instance, the estimated road distance from Warsaw to Prague is 479 kilometers. Game boards are another example. A chess board also can be represented as a square matrix:

```
char chessBoard[ 8 ][ 8 ];
```

We leave as an exercise populating **chessBoard** with characters to represent the chess pieces.

	Amsterdam	*Berlin*	*Budapest*	*Copenhagen*	*Prague*	*Warsaw*
Amsterdam	0	520	916	518	739	865
Berlin	520	0	586	362	219	345
Budapest	916	586	0	948	367	394
Copenhagen	518	362	948	0	581	707
Prague	739	219	367	581	0	479
Warsaw	865	345	394	707	479	0

FIGURE 4.9.1 A table of estimated road distances.

Initializing Multidimensional Arrays

A multidimensional array may be initialized in its definition; however, this can be tedious if the array is large or has many dimensions.

EXAMPLE 4.9.4.   The code segment

```
short nums[ 2 ][ 3 ] = { { 1, 3, 5 },     // 1st element
                         { 7, 9, 11 } }; // 2nd element
```

defines and initializes a matrix. As usual, the initial values are enclosed in braces. Because **nums** has *two* elements, there are *two* nested braced-expressions: **{ 1, 3, 5 }** and **{ 7, 9, 11 }**. The nested expressions contain three integers apiece because each of **nums**'s elements is an array of three **short** integers.   ∎

Strings and Two-Dimensional Arrays of **char**

A one-dimensional array of **char** can be used to represent *one* string. A two-dimensional array of **char** can be used to represent *n* strings, where *n* is the number of array *elements*.

EXAMPLE 4.9.5.   The code segment

```
char stooges[ 3 ][ 6 ]; // 3 elements, each 6 chars
strcpy( stooges[ 0 ], "moe" );    // 1st element
strcpy( stooges[ 1 ], "curly" ); // 2nd element
strcpy( stooges[ 2 ], "larry" ); // 3rd element
for ( int i = 0; i < 3; i++ )
   cout << stooges[ i ] << endl; // print ith string
```

first defines a two-dimensional array of **char** that has *three* elements. Each element is an array of 6 **char**s. The elements have 6 **char** cells apiece because *curly* and *larry* require storage for 5 string characters and the null terminator. Although *moe* requires only 4 **char** cells, the element to represent this string likewise has 6 **char** cells.

The code segment then uses **strcpy** to copy a string into each element: *moe* into the first element, *curly* into the second element, and *larry* into the third element. The first argument in the three calls to **strcpy** deserves a close look. For example, in the call

```
strcpy( stooges[ 0 ], "moe" );
```

the first argument is **stooges[0]**. Each element in **stooges** is itself an *array*, namely, an array of 6 **char**s. So **stooges[0]** points to the *first* of the 6 **char**s that are the first element in **stooges**; that is, **stooges[0]** points to the **char** cell that holds the **m** in **moe** after the **strcpy** finishes. In short, the expression

```
stooges[ 0 ] == &stooges[ 0 ][ 0 ]
```

evaluates to **true**. (Recall that **&** is the C++ address operator; see Section 4.3.) Similarly, **stooges[1]** points to the first of the 6 **char**s that are the second element in **stooges**; that is, **stooges[1]** points to the **char** cell **stooges[1][0]**, which holds the **c** in **curly** after the **strcpy**. Finally, **stooges[2]** points to **stooges[2][0]**, which is the first **char** cell of **stooges**'s third element. Figure 4.9.2 illustrates.

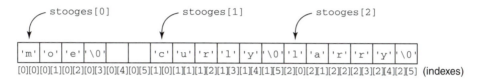

FIGURE 4.9.2 A two-dimensional array of **char**.

After the three **strcpy**s, a **for** loop prints each string. To print a string with the **<<**, recall that we provide the string's *address* (see Section 4.5); that is, we provide the address of the string's *first* character. The expression **stooges[0]** is the address of the *first* string, that is, the address of the **m** in **moe**. In like fashion, **stooges[1]** is the address of the **c** in **curly**, and **stooges[2]** is the address of **l** in **larry**. ■

If a two-dimensional array of **char** is to represent *n* strings, then the array's *first* dimension has size *n*. In Example 4.9.5, **stooges**'s first dimension is thus 3 because there are three stooge names to represent. The *second* dimension's size is the length of the *longest* string plus 1 for the null terminator. In Example 4.9.5, the second dimension's size is thus 6 because the length of *curly* and *larry* is 5; and the null terminator requires an additional **char** cell, which makes 6.

Passing Multidimensional Arrays to Functions

Suppose that we want to pass the array **job_table**, whose definition is

```
int job_table[ 100 ][ 4 ];
```

to the function **print_table**, which prints each entry in the job table. We can pass the two-dimensional array **job_table** just as we pass a one-dimensional array—by giving its name as an argument:

```
print_table( job_table );
```

However, the parameter declaration in **print_table** is more complicated than the declaration for a one-dimensional array. *To declare a parameter for a multidimensional array, we must specify the number of cells, as a constant, in all dimensions beyond the first.* Thus **print_table**'s header is

```
// parameter for a 2-dimensional array
void print_table( int jobs[ ][ 4 ] )
```

If another array, **job_table3**, has three dimensions

```
int job_table3[ 100 ][ 4 ][ 6 ];
```

and we pass it to **print_report**, the parameter declaration in **print_report** looks like

```
// parameter for a 3-dimensional array
void print_report( int jobs[ ][ 4 ][ 6 ] )
```

EXAMPLE 4.9.6. Suppose that we define the array **names** as

```
char names[ 100 ][ 81 ];
```

so that **names** can hold up to 100 strings, each of length 80. (The extra cell is for the null terminator.) Assuming that **size** strings have been stored in **names**, the function

```
void print_names( char n[ ][ 81 ], int size ) {
   int i;
   for ( i = 0; i < size; i++ )
      cout << n[ i ] << endl;
}
```

prints them.   ■

The reason that we must specify the number of cells in all dimensions beyond the first when we pass a multidimensional array to a function is that the function must be able to locate each element in the array. In Example 4.9.6, for the function **print_names** to locate element **i** in the array **n**, that is, the element **n[i]**, it must know that the size of each element is 81 bytes. For example, **n[1]** is 81 bytes from the beginning of the array **n**; **n[2]** is 162 bytes from the beginning of the array **n**; and so on.

The reason that the number of cells in the second dimension must be specified as a *constant* is that C++ requires that every type be stipulated. The parameter declaration

```
char n[ ][ 81 ]
```

in the function **print_names** of Example 4.9.6 says that **n** is an array of elements, each of which is an array of 81 **char**s. If 81 were replaced by a variable, the elements of **n** would not be a valid type. (A variable-sized array is not a legal C++ type.)

EXAMPLE 4.9.7. The following code segment is in error

```
void add( int n,                 // 2nd dimension's size
          float a[ ][ n ],       // *** ERROR: n not a constant
          float b[ ][ n ],       // *** ERROR: n not a constant
          float c[ ][ n ] ) { // *** ERROR: n not a constant
   int i, j;
   for ( i = 0; i < n; i++ )
      for ( j = 0; j < n; j++ )
         c[ i ][ j ] = a[ i ][ j ] + b[ i ][ j ];
}
```

because the size of the second dimension must be given as a constant. The error may be corrected by changing **n** to a constant:

```
// Correct version
void add( float a[ ][ 10 ],
          float b[ ][ 10 ],
          float c[ ][ 10 ] ) {
   int i, j;
   for ( i = 0; i < 10; i++ )
      for ( j = 0; j < 10; j++ )
         c[ i ][ j ] = a[ i ][ j ] + b[ i ][ j ];
}
```

■

EXERCISES

Exercises 1–3 refer to the array

```
char a[ 10 ][ 100 ][ 400 ][ 23 ];
```

1. How many dimensions does the array have?
2. How many cells does the array have?
3. How many elements does the array have?
4. In a one-dimensional array, is the number of the *elements* the same as the number of *cells*?
5. In a multidimensional array, is the number of *elements* the same as the number of *cells*?
6. How do we compute the number of cells in a multidimensional array?
7. Given a two-dimensional array named **nums**

```
short nums[ 2 ][ 6 ];
```

explain the role of each index expression in the assignment statement

```
nums[ 1 ][ 4 ] = -999;
```

8. For the array

```
int a[ 4 ][ 3 ];
```

draw a figure that shows where each of its four elements starts.

9. Assume that the array

```
char months[ 12 ][ 20 ];
... // store January, February,...,December
```

contains 12 strings, each representing a month of the year. Write a **for** loop that prints the months to the standard output.

10. Is the array

```
float a[ 100 ][ 100 ];
```

a square matrix? Explain.

11. Give a short example that initializes a two-dimensional array in its definition.

12. Given the definition

```
char names[ 100 ][ 81 ];
```

write a statement that invokes the function **store**, with the array **names** as the only argument.

13. Write a declaration of the function **store** of Exercise 12.

14. Write a definition of the function **store** of Exercise 12, which reads 100 names into the array **names**.

4.10 SAMPLE APPLICATION: MAINTAINING AN ADDRESS BOOK

Problem

Write a program to maintain an address book. The program should repeatedly ask the user whether to display the names and addresses, to add a name and address, to delete a name and address, or to quit. When the names are displayed, they should be listed in alphabetical order. When the program terminates, the names and addresses should be written to a file. The first time the program is run, the program should create the address book; thereafter, each time the program is run, it should read the file and then present the options to the user.

Sample Input/Output

The following sample input/output results from running the program the first time; that is, the address book is created during this run.

```
[S]how names and addresses
[A]dd a name and address
[D]elete a name and address
[Q]uit
Your choice? A
Name and address to add
Reagon, Wilma  312 7th Ave.  New York, NY

[S]how names and addresses
[A]dd a name and address
[D]elete a name and address
[Q]uit
Your choice? A
Name and address to add
Bently, Susan  9 Lakeview Dr.  Chicago, IL
```

```
[S]how names and addresses
[A]dd a name and address
[D]elete a name and address
[Q]uit
Your choice? A
Name and address to add
Westerfield, Harry  20A Bronco Drive  Cheyenne, WY

[S]how names and addresses
[A]dd a name and address
[D]elete a name and address
[Q]uit
Your choice? S
   0 Bently, Susan  9 Lakeview Dr.  Chicago, IL
   1 Reagon, Wilma  312 7th Ave.  New York, NY
   2 Westerfield, Harry  20A Bronco Drive  Cheyenne, WY

[S]how names and addresses
[A]dd a name and address
[D]elete a name and address
[Q]uit
Your choice? D
Number of name to delete? 0

[S]how names and addresses
[A]dd a name and address
[D]elete a name and address
[Q]uit
Your choice? S
   0 Reagon, Wilma  312 7th Ave.  New York, NY
   1 Westerfield, Harry  20A Bronco Drive  Cheyenne, WY

[S]how names and addresses
[A]dd a name and address
[D]elete a name and address
[Q]uit
Your choice? A
Name and address to add
Mendez, Alberto  77 Sunset Strip  Minneapolis, MN

[S]how names and addresses
[A]dd a name and address
[D]elete a name and address
[Q]uit
Your choice? S
   0 Mendez, Alberto  77 Sunset Strip  Minneapolis, MN
   1 Reagon, Wilma  312 7th Ave.  New York, NY
   2 Westerfield, Harry  20A Bronco Drive  Cheyenne, WY
```

```
[S]how names and addresses
[A]dd a name and address
[D]elete a name and address
[Q]uit
Your choice? Q
```

The next time the program is run, the address book will contain the data

```
Mendez, Alberto   77 Sunset Strip   Minneapolis, MN
Reagon, Wilma   312 7th Ave.   New York, NY
Westerfield, Harry   20A Bronco Drive   Cheyenne, WY
```

Solution

At the top level in **main**, we must

1. Read the names and addresses from the input file, if the file exists (i.e., if this is not the first time the program is run).

2. Display the menu to the user.

3. Get the user's input.

4. Display the names and addresses, if the user chooses **Show**.

5. Prompt the user for the name and address to add, read the name and address, and add the name and address to the address book, if the user chooses **Add**.

6. Prompt the user for the record to delete and delete it, if the user chooses **Delete**.

7. Write the names and addresses to a file and terminate the program, if the user chooses **Quit**.

We delegate the details to functions. The function **init** tries to open the input file. If successful, it reads the names and addresses until the end of the file. The function **show** displays the names and addresses. The function **add** adds the name and address supplied by the user. The function **del** deletes the requested name and address. The function **quit** writes the names and addresses to the file.

We use a two-dimensional **char** array **addr** to store the records (see Figure 4.10.1). We arbitrarily set the size of its first dimension to 30 so that it can store up to 30 names and addresses, and we set the size of its second dimension to 81 so that the maximum length of each record is 80. An extra cell is allocated to hold the string's null terminator.

When we add a record, we must maintain alphabetical order. To do so, we begin at the end of the address book and move each record down one cell until finding the correct position for the added record (see Figure 4.10.2). This method of sorting records is known as **insertion sort**.

To delete the record at index **i**, we move each record following record **i** up one cell (see Figure 4.10.3).

```
          81
addr ┌──────────────┐
┌───┬───┬───┬─────────┐
│   │   │   │  ...    │ ┐
├───┼───┼───┼─────────┤ │
│   │   │   │  ...    │ │
├───┼───┼───┼─────────┤ │
│   │   │   │  ...    │ │
├───┼───┼───┼─────────┤ │
│   │   │   │  ...    │ │
├───┴───┴───┴─────────┤ │ 30
│      ...            │ │
├───┬───┬───┬─────────┤ │
│   │   │   │  ...    │ │
├───┼───┼───┼─────────┤ │
│   │   │   │  ...    │ ┘
└───┴───┴───┴─────────┘
```

FIGURE 4.10.1 The two-dimensional **char** array **addr** that is used to store records.

| Bentley... |
| Reagon... |
| Westerfield... |
| |
| ... |

Before

| Bentley |
| Hu |
| Reagon |
| Westerfield |
| ... |

After

FIGURE 4.10.2 Adding a record.

| Bentley... |
| Hu... |
| Reagon... |
| Westerfield... |
| ... |

Before

| Bentley |
| Hu |
| Westerfield |
| ... |

After

FIGURE 4.10.3 Deleting a record.

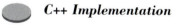

C++ Implementation

```cpp
#include <iostream>
#include <fstream>
#include <iomanip>
#include <cstdlib>
#include <cstring>
using namespace std;
```

```
const int MaxNo = 30; // max numb of names and addresses
const int MaxFld = 81; // max length of one record
const char filename[ ] = "address.dat";
const int RespSize = 30; // max length of user response
void show( char list[ ][ MaxFld ], int no );
bool add( char name[ ], char list[ ][ MaxFld ], int& no );
bool del( int i, char list[ ][ MaxFld ], int& no );
void init( char list[ ][ MaxFld ], int& no );
void quit( char list[ ][ MaxFld ], int no );

int main() {
    char addr[ MaxNo ][ MaxFld ];
    char name[ MaxFld ];
    char resp[ RespSize ];
    int number;
    int index;
    // read in names from a file if it exists
    // and set number to the number of records
    init( addr, number );
    do {
        cout << "\n\n[S]how names and addresses\n"
             << "[A]dd a name and address\n"
             << "[D]elete a name and address\n"
             << "[Q]uit\n"
             << "Your choice? ";
        cin.getline( resp, RespSize );
        switch ( resp[ 0 ] ) {
        case 'S':
        case 's':
           show( addr, number );
           break;
        case 'A':
        case 'a':
           cout << "Name and address to add\n";
           cin.getline( name, MaxFld );
           if ( !add( name, addr, number ) )
              cout << "\a*** Out of room, unable to add: "
                   << name << endl;
           break;
        case 'D':
        case 'd':
           cout << "Number of name to delete? ";
           cin.getline( resp, RespSize );
           index = atoi( resp );
           if ( !del( index, addr, number ) )
              cout << "\a*** Unable to delete number: "
                   << index << endl;
           break;
```

```
               case 'Q':
               case 'q':
                  quit( addr, number );
                  break;
               default:
                  cout << "\a*** Illegal choice; try again\n";
                  break;
            }
      } while ( resp[ 0 ] != 'Q' && resp[ 0 ] != 'q' );
      return 0;
}

// show prints the records and numbers them
// starting with zero. The numbers are printed
// in a field of width 3, which is why
// setw( 3 ) is used.

// show also prints PerScreen (20) records per screen.
void show( char list[ ][ MaxFld ], int no ) {
   int i;
   char resp[ RespSize ];
   const int PerScreen = 20;
   for ( i = 0; i < no; i++ ) {
      cout << setw( 3 ) << i << ' '
           << list[ i ] << endl;
      if ( ( i + 1 ) % PerScreen == 0 ) {
         cout << "Hit RETURN to continue: ";
         cin.getline( resp, RespSize );
      }
   }
}

// add adds a record if possible and
// updates the number of records
bool add( char name[ ], char list[ ][ MaxFld ], int& no ) {
   int i;
   // out of room?
   if ( no >= MaxNo )
      return false;
   // find correct position for name
   for ( i = no - 1;
            i >= 0 && strcmp( name, list[ i ] ) < 0;
            i-- )
      strcpy( list[ i + 1 ], list[ i ] );
   strcpy( list[ i + 1 ], name );
   no++;
   return true;
}
```

```
// del deletes the record at index i
// and updates the number of records
bool del( int i, char list[ ][ MaxFld ], int& no ) {
    int j;
    // is i in bounds?
    if ( i < 0 || i >= no )
        return false;
    // move names down to delete entry i
    for ( j = i; j < no - 1; j++ )
        strcpy( list[ j ], list[ j + 1 ] );
    no--;
    return true;
}

// init reads names from the file address.dat
// and sets no to the number of records read.
// If address.dat does not exist, init simply sets
// no to zero and returns.
void init( char list[ ][ MaxFld ], int& no ) {
    ifstream in;
    in.open( filename );
    no = 0;
    // check if file exists; if not, return.
    if ( !in )
        return;
    // read records until out of room or end-of-file
    while ( no < MaxNo ) {
        in.getline( list[ no ], MaxFld );
        if ( !strlen( list[ no ] ) )
            break;
        no++;
    }
    in.close();
}

// quit writes the records to address.dat
void quit( char list[ ][ MaxFld ], int no ) {
    ofstream out;
    out.open( filename );
    int i;
    // write records to address.dat
    for ( i = 0; i < no; i++ )
        out << list[ i ] << endl;
    out.close();
}
```

Discussion

The various constants are defined as **const** variables

```
const int MaxNo = 30; // max numb of names and addresses
const int MaxFld = 81; // max length of one record
const char filename[ ] = "address.dat";
const int RespSize = 30; // max length of user response
```

The two-dimensional array to hold the data is defined as

```
char addr[ MaxNo ][ MaxFld ];
```

Thus **addr** can hold up to 30 records each of size 81. The file name *address.dat* is stored in the array **filename**. The variable **RespSize** defines a size for an array to hold user responses. For example, in **main** we define the array **resp**

```
char resp[ RespSize ];
```

of size 30 to hold a user response.

The function **main** begins by invoking **init**

```
init( addr, number );
```

which reads in names from the file *address.dat*, if the file exists, and sets **number** to the number of records in the address book. If the file *address.dat* does not exist, **init** sets **number** to zero.

The **do while** loop in **main** then presents the menu to the user

```
cout << "\n\n[S]how names and addresses\n"
     << "[A]dd a name and address\n"
     << "[D]elete a name and address\n"
     << "[Q]uit\n"
     << "Your choice? ";
```

and uses **getline** to read the user's response[†]

```
cin.getline( resp, RespSize );
```

Next a **switch** statement is used to determine the appropriate action for the user's response

```
switch ( resp[ 0 ] ) {
case 'S':
case 's':
   ...
   break;
case 'A':
case 'a':
   ...
   break;
```

[†] In Microsoft Visual C++ 5.0, **getline** does not work properly when reading from the standard input. For this application, the *Enter* key must be hit twice after the first item is input.

```
case 'D':
case 'd':
   ...
   break;
case 'Q':
case 'q':
   quit( addr, number );
   break;
default:
   cout << "\a*** Illegal choice; try again\n";
   break;
}
```

We allow the user to type the response in either uppercase or lowercase. For example, if the user enters either **S** or **s**, the code following **case 's':** executes. We include a **default** condition to trap illegal responses. If the response is illegal, we ring the bell **\a** and print an error message. Whenever the user enters **Q** or **q**, the function **quit** is invoked, the **do while** loop terminates

```
do {
   ...
} while ( resp[ 0 ] != 'Q' && resp[ 0 ] != 'q' );
```

and the program ends.

Since the first argument in **del**, which represents the index of the record to delete, is of type **int**, we must convert the user response, which is a string, to **int**

```
index = atoi( resp );
```

The library function **atoi**, which requires the header file *cstdlib*, takes a string argument and returns the converted value as an **int**.

The function **init** has two parameters

```
void init( char list[ ][ MaxFld ], int& no )
```

list, which receives the two-dimensional array; and **no**, which is set by **init** to the correct number of records. Notice that **no** is passed by *reference*, so that **init** can modify it.

The function **init** defines a variable of type **ifstream**, tries to open the input file **filename** whose value is *address.dat*

```
ifstream in;
in.open( filename );
no = 0;
```

and initializes **no** to zero.

It next checks whether the file was opened:

```
if ( !in )
   return;
```

The condition `!in` is true if the file was not opened. The file will fail to be opened if it does not exist. In this case, `init` simply returns. If the file was opened, `init` reads records and counts them until the capacity of the array is exceeded or end-of-file is reached:

```
while ( no < MaxNo ) {
   in.getline( list[ no ], MaxFld );
   if ( !strlen( list[ no ] ) )
      break;
   no++;
}
```

After closing the file, `init` returns.

The function **show** prints records to the screen, **PerScreen** (20) at a time.

The function **add** has three parameters

```
bool add( char name[ ], char list[ ][ MaxFld ], int& no )
```

name, the record to add; **list**, which receives the two-dimensional array; and **no**, which is updated by **add** if it succeeds in adding the record. As in **init**, **no** is passed by reference, so that **add** can modify it.

The function **add** adds a record after first checking whether there is room:

```
if ( no >= MaxNo )
   return false;
```

If there is room to add the record **name**, **add** compares **name** with the existing records in the address book beginning with the last record (see Figure 4.10.2)

```
for ( i = no - 1;
      i >= 0 && strcmp( name, list[ i ] ) < 0;
      i-- )
```

If **name** is less than the existing record `list[ i ]`, it moves `list[ i ]` down one cell:

```
strcpy( list[ i + 1 ], list[ i ] );
```

When either the first record has been moved down or **name** is greater than or equal to the existing record `list[ i ]`, it copies **name** into the available slot:

```
strcpy( list[ i + 1 ], name );
```

It then increments **no** and returns **true**.

The function **del** has three parameters

```
bool del( int i, char list[ ][ MaxFld ], int& no )
```

i, the index of record to delete; **list**, which receives the two-dimensional array; and **no**, which is updated by **del** if it succeeds in deleting the record. As in **init** and **add**, **no** is passed by reference, so that **del** can modify it.

The function **del** begins by checking whether the index of the record to delete is in bounds:

```
if ( i < 0 || i >= no )
   return false;
```

If it is not in bounds, **del** returns **false**.

Next, **del** moves each record following the one at index **i** up one (see Figure 4.10.3):

```
for ( j = i; j < no - 1; j++ )
    strcpy( list[ j ], list[ j + 1 ] );
```

It then decrements **no** and returns **true**.

The function **quit** has two parameters

```
void quit( char list[ ][ MaxFld ], int no )
```

list, which receives the two-dimensional array; and **no**, the number of records. Since **quit** will *not* modify **no**, **no** is passed by value.

The function **quit** defines a variable of type **ofstream** and opens the file **filename** whose value is *address.dat* for output:

```
ofstream out;
out.open( filename );
```

The file *address.dat* is the same file that **init** tried to open for input. Thus **quit** creates *address.dat*, if *address.dat* did not exist when **init** was invoked, or updates *address.dat* if **init** opened and read it. After **quit** writes the records to *address.dat*, it closes the file.

Program Development

To develop this program, we begin by writing **main** and stubs for the other functions. After **main** has been thoroughly tested, we can write **init** and **show** to be sure that we can read data from the input file and write the records to the screen. Also, these functions are slightly easier to write than **add** and **del**.

To test **init** and **show**, we can create a file, *address.dat*, (by just typing the names into the file). To test whether **show** correctly prints **PerScreen** records per screen, it is easiest to temporarily set **PerScreen** to a small value such as 3.

Next, we write **quit** and test it. We may then write **add**, delete the existing file *address.dat*, and test **init** and **add** on an initially empty input file. The function **add** should be tested by adding a record to the beginning of the list, in the middle of the list, and at the end of the list. An attempt should also be made to add a record after the address book is full. This latter test is simplified by temporarily changing **MaxNo** to a small value such as 3.

We complete the program by writing **del** and testing it. The function **del** should be tested by deleting the first record, a record in the middle of the list, and the last record. An attempt should also be made to delete a record at an illegal index.

It is a good idea to make **RespSize** somewhat larger than the expected size of user input. (In our implementation **RespSize** is 30.) A larger size will accommodate mistakes in user input and will more likely conform to possible modifications of the program. Making a *single* array larger than necessary is marginally wasteful. Making a *multidimensional* array larger than necessary *is* wasteful. For example, if **MaxNo** were 1000 and **MaxFld** were increased by a mere 10 bytes, the *overall* storage required for the multidimensional array **addr** would increase by 10,000 bytes.

The **mem** Library Functions

The header file *cstring* also has prototypes for functions that begin with **mem** such as **memcpy** and **memcmp**. These functions are *not* restricted to string arguments and instead may be used on arbitrary data.

EXAMPLE. The code segment

```
const int n = 1000;
int a1[ n ], a2[ n ];
// populate a1 with random numbers
for ( int i = 0; i < n; i++ )
    a1[ i ] = rand();
// copy a1 into a2
memcpy( a2, a1, sizeof( a1 ) );
```

copies **sizeof(a1)** bytes from array **a1** into array **a2**. The result is that **a2** is byte-per-byte identical to **a1**. Because **a1** is not a string, **strcpy** is not appropriate for this task. ∎

EXAMPLE. The code segment

```
char a1[ ] = { 'A', 'B', 'C' }; // not a string
char a2[ ] = { 'A', 'B', 'Z' }; // ditto
int flag = memcmp( a1, a2, sizeof( a1 ) );
if ( 0 == flag )
  cout << "a1 == a2" << endl;
else if ( flag > 0 )
  cout << "a1 > a2" << endl;
else
  cout << "a1 < a2" << endl;
```

outputs

```
a1 < a2
```

The two arrays are *not* strings and so **strcmp** is not appropriate. Function **memcmp** is like **strncmp** in that the third argument determines how many bytes are used in the comparison. ∎

EXAMPLE. The code segment

```
#include <cstring>
int main() {
   char lotsOfZs[ 500 ];
   memset( lotsOfZs, 'Z', 400 )
   ...
}
```

copies the character Z into the first 400 cells of array **lotsOfZs**. The remaining 100 cells contain garbage, as the array was not initialized. ∎

Appendix C describes the **mem** functions in detail.

COMMON PROGRAMMING ERRORS

1. It is an error to define an array without specifying its size, unless the array is initialized in its *definition*:

   ```
   char ar1[ ]; //***** ERROR: no size given
   char ar2[ ] = { 'A', 'B' }; // OK
   ```

   The compiler sets the size of **ar2** to 2 because two initial values are given in the initialization.

2. It is an error to use an index expression that underflows or overflows an array:

   ```
   char nums[ 10 ];
   nums[ -8 ] = 226; //***** ERROR: index underflow
   nums[ 10 ] = 123; //***** ERROR: index overflow
   ```

   For an array of size n, the legal indexes are $0, 1, \ldots, n - 1$.

3. It is an error to use a non**const** variable to specify an array's size in its *definition*:

   ```
   int n = 100;
   const int c = 500;
   int a[ n ]; //***** ERROR: nonconst variable
   int b[ c ]; //OK--c is const
   ```

   However, a non**const** variable may be used as *index expression*:

   ```
   int a[ 100 ];
   int i;
   for ( i = 0; i < 100; i++ )
     a[ i ] = i + 1; // OK
   ```

4. If an array's size is specified in its definition and the array is initialized in its definition, it is an error to provide more initial values than the array's size:

   ```
   char ar[ 2 ] = { 'P', 'Q', 'R' }; //***** ERROR: overflow
   ```

Array **ar** has *two* cells but *three* initial values are given. The error can be corrected by letting the *compiler* set the size from its count of the initial values:

```
char ar[ ] = { 'P', 'Q', 'R' }; // OK (size is 3)
```

5. It is an error to assume that an uninitialized array defined *inside a block* contains anything except garbage. For example, the code segment

```
int main() {
    int nums[ 100 ]; // uninitialized
    ...
}
```

defines the array **nums** inside **main**'s body and does *not* initialize the array. Therefore, **nums** contains garbage. If even one initial value is provided, then the compiler initializes the *remaining* array cells to zero. For example, the code segment

```
int main() {
    int nums[ 100 ] = { 0 }; // all zeros
    ...
}
```

provides an initial value for **nums[0]**. The compiler then initializes the remaining 99 cells to zero. (This is a standard technique for zeroing out an array defined inside a block. Arrays defined outside all blocks are automatically initialized to zero unless the user provides different initial values.)

6. Because an array's name is a *constant*, an array's name is *not* a legal lvalue:

```
float odds[ 50 ];
odds = .33; //***** ERROR: odds not a legal lvalue
odds++;     //***** ERROR: odds not a legal lvalue
--odds;     //***** ERROR: odds not a legal lvalue
```

An array *element*, by contrast, is a legal lvalue:

```
odds[ 1 ] = .33F; // OK
odds[ 1 ]++;      // OK
```

7. It is an error to treat an array as a string if the array is *not* null terminated:

```
char stooge1[ ] = { 'M', 'o', 'e' };
cout << stooge1 << endl; //***** ERROR: not a string
```

The code segment

```
char stooge1[ ] = { 'M', 'o', 'e', '\0' };
cout << stooge1 << endl; // OK
```

or the code segment

```
char stooge1[ ] = "Moe";
cout << stooge1 << endl; // OK
```

corrects the error by ensuring that **stooge1** is null terminated.

8. It is an error to assign a *string* to a **char** variable:

```
char c = "A";    //***** ERROR: "A" is a string
char d = 'A';    // OK, 'A' is one character
char ar[ 3 ];
ar[ 2 ] = "Z";   //***** ERROR: "Z" is a string
ar[ 2 ] = 'Z';   // OK, 'Z' is one character
```

A string such as **"A"** consists of *two* characters: the character **'A'** and the null terminator **'\0'**.

9. A parameter **a** that receives an array can be declared

> *type* **a[ ]**

If the brackets are omitted, **a** is an ordinary, nonarray parameter of type *type*; for example,

```
void sort( int a, int size );

int main() {
   int b[ 30 ];
   ...
   // ***** ERROR: b not of type int
   sort( b, 30 );
   ...
}
```

Assuming that the first parameter of **sort** is supposed to receive an array of **int**s, the error can be corrected by declaring **a** as

```
void sort( int a[ ], int size );
```

10. To pass an *array* to a function, we place its name in the argument list. To pass a *cell* within the array to a function, we use the array name with the index operator to specify the cell. Note the difference:

```
int main() {
   int b[ 30 ], i;
   ...
   // pass the array b to sort
   sort( b, 30 );

   // pass the ith cell b[ i ] to output
   for ( i = 0; i < 30; i++ )
      output( b[ i ] );
   ...
}
```

11. If an array parameter is marked **const**, none of its cells should be modified:

```
void sort( const int a[ ], int size ) {
    ...
    // ***** ERROR: cells of a can't be modified
    a[ i ] = a[ i + 1 ];
    ...
}
```

12. It is an error to invoke library functions with the wrong number of arguments. For example, the code segment

```
char author[ 50 ];
char ja[ ] = "Jane Austen";
strncpy( author, ja ); //***** ERROR: too few arguments
```

contains an error because **strncpy** expects *three* arguments, not two.

13. It is an error to invoke library functions with the wrong types of arguments. The code segment

```
cout << strlen( 'A' ) << endl; //***** ERROR: wrong type
```

contains an error because **strlen** expects a *string* argument, not a character argument.

14. If a multidimensional array is passed as an argument to a function, the size for all but the array's first dimension must be included in the parameter declaration. Note the difference:

```
int main() {
    // 2-dimensional array
    int numbers[ 10 ][ 10 ];
    ...
    add1( numbers );
    sub1( numbers );
    ...
}

// correct
void add1( int array[ ][ 10 ] ) {
    ...
}

// ***** ERROR: size of 2nd dim missing
void sub1( int array[ ][ ] ) {
    ...
}
```

15. When a multidimensional array is passed as an argument to a function, the sizes for all but the array's first dimension must be specified as constants:

```
const int size = 10;

// correct
void f( float a[ ][ 10 ] )
{
    ...
}

// correct
void g( float a[ ][ size ] )
{
    ...
}
```

It is an error to use a variable as a dimension's size:

```
// ***** ERROR: size of 2nd dim must be a constant
void f( int size, float a[ ][ size ] ) {
    ...
}
```

PROGRAMMING EXERCISES

4.1. Write a program with an array **nums** defined and initialized as

```
int nums[ 100 ] = { 1, 3, 5 };
```

Although **nums** can hold 100 integers, only three of its cells have been initialized. Your program should store integers in the remaining cells according to the formula

```
nums[ i ] = nums[ 0 ] + nums[ 1 ] + ... + nums[ i - 1 ]
```

for $i = 3, \ldots, 99$. For example,

```
nums[ 3 ] = nums[ 0 ] + nums[ 1 ] + nums[ 2 ] = 9
```

After computing the values, print the array.

4.2. Write a program that defines an array of 1,000 **int**s and populates the array with random integers that are odd. The modulus operator **%** can be used to test whether an integer is odd. In the code segment

```
if ( x % 2 ) // nonzero remainder when divided by 2?
```

the **if** condition is **true** if **x** is odd.

4.3. Write a program that prints your name to the terminal in the style

```
TTTTTTT  IIIIIII  N     N     AAA
   T        I     N N   N    A   A
   T        I     N  N  N   A     A
   T        I     N   N N   AAAAAAA
   T        I     N    NN   A     A
   T     IIIIIII  N     N   A     A
```

Use a two-dimensional array to represent each oversized letter. Our example uses four two-dimensional arrays, each with six rows and seven columns. The array elements are a mix of uppercase letters such as **A** and blanks.

4.4. Write a program that prompts the user for a string, which is then read from the standard input into an array of **char**. The string has a maximum length of 80 characters. Write a function that reverses the string. Print the original string and the reversed string to the standard output.

4.5. Write a program that reads words from a file, computes their length, stores the words in a two-dimensional array if the length is not equal to 4 (we want to discourage four-letter words), and then prints the words stored in the array to the standard output. Assume that no word has a length greater than 80.

4.6. Write your own version of **strchr**.

4.7. Write your own version of **strstr**.

4.8. A string that reads the same either backward or forward is called a *palindrome*. Examples are *anna* and *otto*. Write a program that prompts the user for a string, tests whether it is a palindrome, and prints an appropriate message. The test should be done in a separate function.

4.9. Write a function **insert** with three parameters: **str**, **substr**, and **i**. The parameters **str** and **substr** are **char** arrays. The parameter **i** is an **int**. The function **insert** inserts the string **substr** into **str** immediately after index **i**. Assume that **str** is large enough to hold the added characters. *Example*: If

```
str is "He has his ahead of him"
substr is " future"
i is 9
```

after

```
insert( str, substr, i );
```

str is "He has his future ahead of him".

Write a **main** function that invokes **insert** several times to demonstrate that it is working properly.

4.10. Write a program that prompts the user for a string of maximum length 255 and reads the string from the standard input. The program then prompts the user for two characters, and reads them from the standard input. The program then invokes a function that substitutes the second character for all occurrences of the first character in the string. Finally, the program prints the string to the standard output. For example, if the user enters *matter*, *t*, and *d*, the program prints *madder* after substituting *d* for *t*.

4.11. Write a program that prompts the user for a valid e-mail address such as *johnson-baugh@cs.depaul.edu*. For purposes of the program, an e-mail address is valid if it satisfies these conditions:

- The symbol @ must occur exactly once. For example, *baz.cs.dpu.edu* and *bar@cs@dpu* are not valid e-mail addresses.

- There must be a nonblank symbol to the left of the @ sign. For example, *@cs.dpu.edu* is not a valid e-mail address.

- There must be at least one **.** in the e-mail address. For example, *baz@cs* is not a valid e-mail address.

- Every occurrence of the symbol **.** must have a nonblank symbol on either side. For example, *bar@cs.* and *bar@ .depaul* are not valid e-mail addresses.

4.12. An International Standard Book Number (ISBN) is a code of 10 characters separated by dashes such as 0-670-82162-4. An ISBN consists of four parts: a group code, a publisher code, a code that uniquely identifies the book among the publisher's offerings, and a check character. For the ISBN 0-670-82162-4, the group code is 0, which identifies the book as one from an English-speaking country. The publisher code 670 identifies the book as a Viking Press publication. The code 82162 uniquely identifies the book among the Viking Press publications (Homer: *The Odyssey*, translated by Robert Fagles). The check character is computed as follows:

1. Compute the sum of the first digit plus two times the second digit plus three times the third digit... plus nine times the ninth digit.

2. Compute the remainder of this sum divided by 11. If the remainder is 10, the last character is X; otherwise, the last character is the remainder.

For example, the sum for ISBN 0-670-82162-4 is

$$0 + 2 \times 6 + 3 \times 7 + 4 \times 0 + 5 \times 8 + 6 \times 2 + 7 \times 1 + 8 \times 6 + 9 \times 2 = 158$$

The remainder when 158 is divided by 11 is 4, the last character in the ISBN. Write a program that prompts the user for an ISBN, reads the candidate ISBN from the standard input, invokes a function to check whether the candidate is a valid ISBN, and prints an appropriate message to the standard output.

4.13. Write a program that defines the arrays

```
int i1[ 5 ], i2[ 5 ], sum[ 6 ];
```

The program prompts the user to enter five digits with repetitions allowed. Each digit is stored in one of **i1**'s cells. The process is repeated for **i2**. The program treats **i1** and **i2** as if they represented single integers. For example, if we read the digits 2, 3, 0, 3, 5 into **i1**, the program treats **i1** as if represented the integer 23,035. The program then adds the 5-digit integers **i1** and **i2** and stores the sum in **sum**. For example, if we read 45,071 into **i1** and 92,987 into **i2**, these two arrays are

4	5	0	7	1

9	2	9	8	7

and **sum** is

1	3	8	0	5	8

4.14. Modify Programming Exercise 4.13 by adding an extra cell to the arrays **i1**, **i2**, and **sum**. The first (leftmost) cell in each array holds either 1 to indicate a negative integer or 0 to indicate a positive integer.

4.15. Modify Programming Exercise 4.14 to compute the product rather than the sum of two integers. The program should handle positive and negative integers.

4.16. Write a program that reads a string, with a maximum length of 512 characters, from the standard input. The program then changes any uppercase characters in the string to lowercase characters. Next, the program encodes the string using the arrays

```
char plainText[ ]  = "abcdefghijklmnopqrstuvwxyz";
char encodeText[ ] = "jmartyvwbdlqncxgzekipufohs";
```

The encoding works as follows. Suppose that the user enters the string *Marsha*. After converting all uppercase characters to lowercase, our array looks like

'm'	'a'	'r'	's'	'h'	'a'	'\0'

We look up the **m** in **marsha** in **plainText**, finding that its index is 12. Because **encodeText[12]** is **n**, we replace **m** with **n**. After the encoding, our string becomes

'n'	'j'	'e'	'k'	'w'	'j'	'\0'

The program prints the original string and its encoding to the standard output.

4.17. Modify Sample Application 4.8 so that it merges four files at a time instead of two at a time.

4.18. John H. Conway (*Scientific American*, October 1970, p. 120) invented a game called *Life* to model the process of birth, survival, and death. The idea is that organisms require others to survive and procreate but that overcrowding results in death.

We can use a square matrix to implement the game. We start with a 10 × 10 array:

```
const unsigned n = 10;
char life[ n ][ n ];
```

Each cell holds an asterisk * or a blank. The asterisk represents the presence of an organism and the blank its absence. The game starts with an initial generation, which consists of any mix of asterisks and blanks. However, the game becomes interesting only with certain mixes of asterisks and blanks. The game progresses as generations succeed one another.

Three rules govern the transition from one generation to the next:

- *Birth Rule*: An organism is born into an empty cell that has exactly three living neighbors.
- *Survival Rule*: An organism with either two or three living neighbors survives from one generation to the next.
- *Death Rule*: An organism with four or more neighbors dies from overcrowding. An organism with fewer than two neighbors dies from loneliness.

A *neighbor* of cell C is any cell that touches C. For example, the cells labeled **N** are neighbors of **A**:

N	**N**	**N**	
N	**A**	**N**	
N	**N**	**N**	

A cell that does not lie along an edge has exactly eight neighbors. Because of the rules, it is relatively easy for an organism along an edge to die and relatively hard either for an edge organism to survive or a new organism to be born into an edge cell.

Write a program that reads an initial generation into the array `life` and then produces N new generations, $N > 20$. Print each generation to the standard output.

4.19. Write a program that converts Roman numerals into decimal equivalents. The program prompts the user for a Roman numeral, which is entered as a string. After converting the Roman numeral to decimal, the program prints the decimal numeral. The program halts with an error message if the user enters a string that is not a valid Roman numeral. Assume that each Roman numeral has a maximum length of 10. The following table gives the Roman symbols and their decimal equivalents:

Roman	*Decimal*
M	1,000
D	500
C	100
L	50
X	10
V	5
I	1

The algorithm for converting a Roman numeral

$$R_1, R_2, \ldots, R_n$$

to decimal is

1. Set i to 1, where i is the position of the symbol currently being scanned.
2. Set *convert* to 0. At the conclusion of the algorithm, *convert* is the decimal value of the Roman numeral.

3. If $i = n$, add the decimal value of R_n to *convert* and stop.

4. If $R_i \geq R_{i+1}$ in decimal, add the decimal value of R_i to *convert*, set i to $i + 1$, and go to step 3.

5. If $R_i < R_{i+1}$ in decimal, subtract the decimal value of R_i from *convert*, set i to $i + 1$, and go to step 3.

Example: The decimal value of the Roman numeral XIV is 14. Initially, *convert* is 0. Because X's value is greater than I's, we add 10 to *convert* so that *convert* now equals 10. Because I's value is less than V's, we subtract 1 from *convert*, which now equals 9. Because V is the last numeral, we add 5 to *convert* to obtain 14.

4.20. A **binary (digital) picture** is a two-dimensional array, each of whose elements is 0 or 1. The image is interpreted as light (1) on a dark (0) background. For example, here is a binary picture of a football:

```
0  0  0  0  0  0  0
0  0  1  1  1  0  0
0  1  1  1  1  1  0
0  0  1  1  1  0  0
0  0  0  0  0  0  0
```

In analyzing the picture, it is often necessary to identify the edges. A **pixel (picture element)** is an edge pixel if it is 1 and at least one of the pixels immediately above, below, left, or right is 0. We can show the edges by setting each edge pixel to 1 and all other pixels to 0. After identifying the edges in the preceding picture, we obtain

```
0  0  0  0  0  0  0
0  0  1  1  1  0  0
0  1  0  0  0  1  0
0  0  1  1  1  0  0
0  0  0  0  0  0  0
```

Write a program that reads a binary picture and prints the picture showing the edges.

4.21. Redo Programming Exercise 3.5. Compute $C(n, r)$, the number of r-element subsets of an n-element set, using the formula

$$C(n, r) = C(n - 1, r - 1) + C(n - 1, r)$$

to fill in a two-dimensional array `c`, where `c[n][r]` is equal to $C(n, r)$. This method of computing a recursive formula is known as *dynamic programming*.

4.22. Write a program that populates an array of n **int**s with random integers, where $n > 5$. Use the library function **rand** to generate the integers. Next, sort the array using selection sort. The algorithm for selection sort is

1. Repeat steps 2 and 3 for $i = 0, 1, \ldots, n - 2$.

2. Select the smallest element among $a[i], a[i + 1], \ldots, a[n - 1]$.

3. Swap the smallest element with $a[i]$.

After sorting the array, print its elements to the standard output.

4.23. Extend Programming Exercise 4.22 as follows. After sorting the array, the program goes into a loop that prompts the user for an integer to serve as a *search key* or *key* for short, that is, an integer to be searched for in the array; reads the integer from the standard input; searches the array for the key; and prints a message to the standard output about whether the key occurs in the array. The program halts if the user enters a negative integer as a search key. To search the array, use binary search. The algorithm for binary search is

1. Repeat steps 2 through 4 until the search key is found or there is nothing left to search. If there is nothing left to search, stop *with failure*.
2. Find the array's approximate midpoint.
3. Compare the key against the midpoint element. If match, stop *with success* because the key has been found.
4. If key < midpoint element, search the array's left half only. If key > midpoint element, search the array's right half only.

4.24. In comparison-based searching such as binary search, efficiency typically is measured in terms of how many comparisons of a search key with an array element are required. We say that the *average case time* of binary search for n array elements is $\Theta(\log n)$, thereby indicating that, on average, binary search requires about $C \log n$ comparisons to search an array of n elements, for some constant C. Prove that the average case time of binary search is $\Theta(\log n)$.

4.25. Write a program that grades a true/false exam, converts the numeric scores into letter grades, and prints the letter grade for each student. Assume a class of 30 students, each identified by a social security number. The exam has 25 questions, and the correct answers are stored in the array **correct**:

```
char correct[ ] = "FFTFTTFTFFTTTFTTTFTFTFTTT";
```

The social security numbers and test results are read from a file, in which each line contains a social security number and the test results for that student:

```
234567601    FFTFTTFTFFTTTFTTTFTFTFTTT
446367211    FFTFTTTTFFTFTFTFTFTFTTTTT
. . .
```

The instructor, a bit on the strict side, curves the results using these rules:

- The top 10 percent get As.
- The next highest 15 percent get Bs.
- The next highest 50 percent get Cs.
- The next highest 15 percent get Ds.
- The bottom 10 percent get Fs.

Write a function to grade a student's exam. Write another function to print each student's social security number and letter grade.

CHAPTER

5

CLASSES

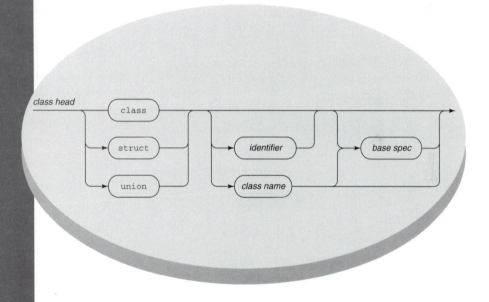

Object-oriented programming in C++ begins with classes, which are user-defined data types. This chapter introduces the basic concepts, advantages, and programming techniques associated with classes. We begin with an overview of how object-oriented programming differs from procedural programming.

5.1 OBJECT-ORIENTED AND PROCEDURAL PROGRAMMING

Programs consist of **modules**, which are parts that can be written and tested separately and then assembled to form a program. C++ is descended from C, which is a **procedural language** because its modules are procedures. In C as in C++, a *function* is a procedure. C++ can be used simply as improved C, that is, as a procedural language in which a program's modules are its functions.

Procedural programming is associated with a design technique known as **top-down design** (see Section 0.5). Recall that, in top-down design, a *problem* is associated with a *procedure*. For example, consider the problem of producing a schedule for a manufacturing task such as building an automobile. We label the problem *MainProblem*. We intend to use a procedural language such as C, Pascal, or even procedural C++ to solve the problem. If we choose procedural C++, we assign *MainProblem* to the C++ procedure **main**. Because *MainProblem* is too complex to solve straightforwardly in **main**, we *decompose* the problem into subproblems such as

- Building the chassis.
- Building the engine.
- Building the drivetrain.
- Assembling the already built components.
- Inspecting the components and their assembly.

We assign each *subproblem* to a *subprocedure*, which is a function that **main** invokes. Just as the problem *MainProblem* decomposes into various subproblems, so the procedure **main** decomposes into various subprocedures to handle the subproblems. The subprograms may be further decomposed, of course, which then is mirrored by a decomposition of the subprocedures (see Figure 5.1.1). This process of **top-down, functional decomposition** continues until a subproblem is straightforward enough that the corresponding subprocedure can solve it.

Top-down design has the appeal of being intuitive and orderly. Many hard problems continue to be solved using this design technique. Yet the technique has drawbacks, especially with respect to what is known euphemistically as **software maintenance**, which deals with the testing, debugging, and upgrading of software systems. Experienced programmers know that the most difficult task is not writing a program in the first place, but rather *changing* it afterwards because the program is flawed ("infected by bugs"), the program's requirements change, the program needs to execute more efficiently, and so on. Suppose that we need to change significantly the program that solves *MainProblem*. The change is so significant that we need to change **main**. In particular, suppose that **main** must now pass an additional argument to *each* of the subprocedures that it invokes, and that each of these must pass this additional argument to their subprocedures, and so on until the change has rippled throughout the entire hierarchy sketched in Figure 5.1.1. This phenomenon is known as **cascading changes**: a change in a procedure such as **main** cascades or ripples down to its subprocedures and to their subprocedures and so on until the change impacts much if not all of the decomposition hierarchy. The threat of cascaded changes can take the fun out of maintenance programming!

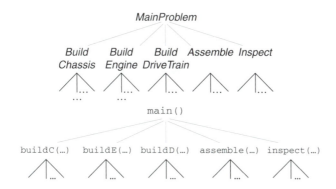

FIGURE 5.1.1 Problem and procedure decomposition.

Object-oriented programming is an alternative to procedural programming. The design technique associated with object-oriented programming is **object-oriented design**. Object-oriented programming and object-oriented design are meant to address major problems associated with procedural programming and top-down design, problems such as cascading changes. In an object-oriented program, the modules are **classes** rather than procedures. A **class** is a collection of **objects**. For example, the class *humans* is a collection of objects, that is, human beings such as you, me, and Mary Leakey. Objects in a class share **properties** or **attributes**. Humans, for instance, share the properties of being *featherless*, *bipedal*, and *risible*. There are also distinctive actions or processes associated with a class. For instance, humans *eat*, *laugh*, *work*, *tango*, and so on. For convenience, we call such actions or processes *operations*. To use C++ as an object-oriented language is thus to use classes. Next we sketch some advantages of the object-oriented approach to programming and design.

Classes and Information Hiding

Consider the challenge that faces modern software products such as word processors, databases, spreadsheets, and the like. These products undergo rapid development cycles in which a new and perhaps significantly different version replaces an older version. How can users survive such changes? For one thing, the products try to maintain a consistent **interface**. Consider your word processor. From one version to the next, it still supports commands that allow you to *Open* a new document, *Save* a document, *Print* a document,

Copy a document, *Format* a document in some special way, and the like. The word processor's *interface* is the functionality made available to the user through commands such as the ones just listed. We say that the interface is **public** to underscore that it is visible to the user. What is typically *not* public in a modern software product is the underlying **implementation**. An experienced programmer might be able to *guess* how the word processor works under the hood, but the vendor deliberately hides these details from the user. For one thing, the product would be too hard to use if the user had to know thousands of technical details. For another, the vendor may be in the process of fixing known bugs and would like to leave them hidden until the fix is implemented as a patch or even a new version. We say that the implementation is **private** to underscore that it is *not* visible to the user. The implementation is *hidden* from the user, whereas the interface is *exposed* to the user. A goal of modern software design is thus to keep a product's public interface as constant as possible so that users remain fluent in the product even as its *private* implementation improves or otherwise changes.

In an object-oriented language, a class is a *module that supports information hiding*. In a C++ class, we can use the keywords `public` and `private` to control access to the class's properties and operations. We can use the keyword `public` to expose the class's interface and the keyword `private` to hide its implementation. The next section goes into details of syntax. Our concern now is the underlying idea.

Encapsulation

In procedural programming, the modules are procedures, and data are manipulated by procedures. We have seen the typical C++ mechanism for this style of data manipulation: passing arguments to and returning a value from a function. In object-oriented programming, the modules are classes. Data and the procedures to manipulate the data can be **encapsulated** or contained within a class. Imagine a *String* class that can be used to create strings, concatenate them, change the characters they contain, check whether a given character occurs in a *String*, and so on. The *String* class would have **data members**—variables—to represent the characters in a *String* and, perhaps, such other information as a *String*'s length. Such variables are encapsulated within the class in the sense that every *String* object has the variables specified in the *String* class. A *String* class also would have **function members** to manipulate its data members. Function members are commonly called **methods**. For example, the *String* class presumably would have a method to create a new *String* object, another method to clone one *String* object from another, another method to check whether a *String* object contains a character, and so on. Methods, like data members, also are encapsulated within the class. A method is thus a function encapsulated in a class. A top-level function, such as a C++ program's `main`, is *not* encapsulated in any class.

Abstract Data Types

The concepts of information hiding and encapsulation relate closely to that of an **abstract data type**. Suppose that our goal is to build a *WordProcessor* class that has the functionality of a modern word processor. To make the class easy to use, we distinguish sharply between a public interface consisting of high-level operations such as *Save* and *Print* and a private implementation consisting of low-level details in support of the public interface. In this case, our class is an **abstract data type**. A data type is *abstract* if it exposes in its public interface only high-level operations and hides all low-level implementation details. C++ supports classes, which enable information hiding; and information hiding—specifically, the hiding of low-level implementation details—is the key to creating abstract data types. Further, an obvious way to deliver the required functionality in an abstract data type is to encapsulate the appropriate functions as class methods.

>**EXAMPLE 5.1.1.**   Suppose that we define a *Stack* class whose public interface consists of methods to
>
>- Insert an object into a *Stack* if the *Stack* is not full. Such an operation is known as a *push*.
>- Remove the most recently inserted object from a *Stack* if the *Stack* is not empty. Such an operation is known as a *pop*.
>- Inspect the most recently inserted object, if any, but without removing it. Such an object occupies the *top* of a *Stack*.
>
>A *Stack* is called a **LIFO** list (**L**ast **I**n, **F**irst **O**ut) because insertions and deletions occur at the same end, known as the *top*. Figure 5.1.2 shows a *Stack* of letters in three states. In the left subfigure, the *Stack* is empty. The middle subfigure shows the *Stack* after the operations *push(A)* and *push(B)* have occurred. Because *B* was inserted last, it is at the top. The right subfigure shows the *Stack* after a *pop* operation, which removes *B*. After *B* has been removed, *A* is at the top.
>
>The *Stack* operations are high-level in that they require no knowledge of the *Stack*'s underlying implementation. Accordingly, the *Stack* as described is an abstract data type.   ∎

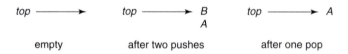

FIGURE 5.1.2 A *Stack* in three states.

Abstract data types spare the programmer the job of learning implementation details. Further, abstract data types can be studied formally to reveal important properties about them. For example, the *Stack* described in our example cannot overflow or underflow because pushes occur only if a *Stack* is not full, and pops occur only if a *Stack* is not empty. At least one successful push therefore precedes the first successful pop. The number of objects on a *Stack* equals the total number of pushes minus the total number of pops. If the total number of pushes always exceeds the total number of pops, then a *Stack* is empty only before the first *push*, but never thereafter.

Abstract data types can be implemented in procedural languages such as C and Pascal, but these languages provide little direct support for abstract data types. By contrast, the class construct of object-oriented languages provides direct support for abstract data types through information hiding and encapsulation. An object-oriented language such as C++ is usually the tool of choice for building abstract data types.

The Client/Server Model

Object-oriented programming is based on a **client/server model** of computing. This model explains the emphasis placed on information hiding in object-oriented programming. Suppose that we build a *String* class with a private implementation that supports a public interface consisting of methods to create and destroy *String*s, concatenate them, search them for characters, and so on. The *String* class is a provider of services for string processing. The *String* class is a server of *String* objects that provide string-processing functionality. An application such as a C++ program that uses the *String* class is a *client*. A client requests services from a *String* object by invoking one of its methods, which is characterized as sending a **message** to the object. For example, the code segment

> *String s1;*
> *s1.set("The Day the Music Died");*
> *n = s1.getLen();*

first creates a *String* object *s1*. The code segment then sends a message to *s1*, the request that *s1* set its value to the string *The Day the Music Died*. Finally, the code segment requests that *s1* return its length, the number of characters in *The Day the Music Died*. This code segment occurs in a program that acts as a *client* of the *String* object *s1*, a server. Note that we pass a message to a server such as *s1* by invoking one of its methods, that is, one of the functions encapsulated in *s1* as a *String* object.

A good server provides services with a minimum of effort on the client's part. In particular, the client should *not* be required to know *how* the server provides the services. The server's implementation details should be hidden from the client. The client should need to know *only* the server's interface, which typically consists of methods that the client can invoke. Such methods send messages to the server, which are requests for services. The server may send data back to the client, perform actions that the client requests, and so on. Good servers practice information hiding so that clients find them easy to use.

Inheritance

Classes can occur in **inheritance hierarchies**, which consist of parent/child relationships among classes. Inheritance supports a form of **code reuse**, which we explain through an example. Suppose that we build a *Window* class to represent windows that appear on a computer's screen. The *Window* class has data members to represent a window's width and height, its *x* and *y* screen coordinates, its background and foreground colors, its border width, its style (e.g., framed), and so forth. We encapsulate appropriate methods to provide functionality for creating and destroying windows, moving them, resizing and reshaping them, changing their properties (e.g., background color), and so on. Once the *Window* class is built, we decide to refine or specialize it by building a *MenuWindow* subclass that inherits *all* the *Window* data members and methods but then adds some of its own. For example, the *MenuWindow* subclass has data members and methods to support lists of menu items, user choices of menu items, and so on. Other subclasses are possible. Figure 5.1.3 illustrates a possible inheritance hierarchy with *Window* as the parent class. The arrows point from the child to the parent.

Inheritance supports code reuse in that a child class has all of the functionality of its parents. How to design and use inheritance hierarchies are central issues in object-oriented design and programming. We pursue these issues in Chapter 6.

FIGURE 5.1.3 An inheritance hierarchy.

Polymorphism

The term *polymorphism* is derived from Greek and means *having many forms*. In an object-oriented language, there can be *many methods with the same signature*. In Figure 5.1.3, an appropriate *Window* method is *display*, which displays the *Window* object on the screen. Yet different types of windows display themselves differently. For example, a *MenuWindow* presumably displays a list of choices when it displays itself, whereas a *MessageWindow* may show only a single message. So there should be various *forms* or versions of the *display* method, presumably a separate one for each class in the *Window* hierarchy. Nonetheless, it is easier on the client (that is, the user of the *Window* hierarchy) to send a *single* display message to any type of *Window*. For example, regardless of whether *w* is a *MenuWindow* or a *MessageWindow*, we should be able to execute

w.display( ); // display yourself

If *w* happens to be a *MenuWindow*, then this class's *display* method should be invoked. If *w* happens to be a *MessageWindow*, then this class's *display* method should be invoked. The system, not the client, should determine *w*'s type and, from the type, determine which version of *display* to invoke. In this example, *display* is thus a *polymorphic* method. Chapter 7 explains how to exploit the power of polymorphism in C++.

In the remainder of the book, we turn to the syntax and semantics of object-oriented programming in C++. The topic is a rich one and so requires several chapters. We begin with basic concepts and syntax.

EXERCISES

1. What are program modules?
2. In a procedural language, what is the basic program module?
3. In an object-oriented language, what is the basic program module?
4. In the context of top-down functional decomposition, what are cascading changes?
5. What is a class?
6. What is a class interface?
7. What is a class implementation?
8. How does a class support information hiding?
9. What is an abstract data type?
10. What does a class encapsulate?
11. Briefly describe how the client/server model relates to object-oriented programming.

12. What is a message?

13. Give an example of inheritance.

14. Briefly describe what polymorphism is and why it is so powerful a programming technique.

5.2 CLASSES AND OBJECTS

Class Declarations and Object Definitions

In C++, a class is a user-defined data type. The user creates the data type through a **class declaration**, which describes the data members and methods encapsulated in the class.

EXAMPLE 5.2.1. The class declaration

```
class Human {
  // data members and methods go here
  ...
};
```

creates the class **Human**. The declaration *describes* the data members and methods that characterize a **Human** but the declaration does not create any **Human** objects.

In the declaration, the term **class** is a C++ keyword. The term **Human** is sometimes called the class **tag**; the tag is the *name* of the data type created by the declaration. Note that a semicolon follows the closing brace in the class declaration; the semicolon is required.

The **object definition**

```
Human maryLeakey; // create an object
```

creates a **Human** object named **maryLeakey**, which has the very properties and operations described in the declaration of **Human**. Just as the statement

```
int x; // built-in type int
```

defines an **int** variable, so

```
Human maryLeakey; // user-defined type Human
```

defines a **Human** variable. In C++, an **object** is a variable of some *class* data type such as **Human**. ∎

A class declaration must come *before* the definition of any class objects. In Example 5.2.1, the declaration of **Human** therefore comes before the definition of **maryLeakey** as a **Human** object.

Once created, a class is a full-fledged data type. Given the declaration of **Human** in Example 5.2.1, we can define either stand-alone **Human** objects such as **maryLeakey** or arrays of **Human** objects.

EXAMPLE 5.2.2. Given the declaration of class **Human** in Example 5.2.1, the code segment

```
Human latvians[ 3600000 ];
```

defines an array **latvians** that has 3,600,000 elements, each a **Human** object. ■

Information Hiding in C++

The C++ keyword **private** can be used to *hide* class data members and methods, and the keyword **public** can be used to *expose* class data members and methods. (C++ also has the keyword **protected** for information hiding; see Chapter 6.) In the spirit of object-oriented design, we can use **private** to hide the class *implementation* and **public** to expose the class *interface*.

EXAMPLE 5.2.3. The class declaration

```
const unsigned MaxString = 600;
class String {
public:
   void       set( const char string[ ] );
   const char* get();
private:
   char s[ MaxString + 1 ]; // +1 for \0
};
```

creates a **String** class whose interface consists of two **public** methods, **set** and **get**, and whose implementation consists of a **char** array **s**. A colon **:** follows the keywords **private** and **public**. The keyword **public** occurs first in our example, although the declaration could have be written as

```
const unsigned MaxString = 600;
class String {
private:
   char s[ MaxString + 1 ]; // +1 for \0
public:
   void       set( const char string[ ] );
   const char* get();
};
```

or even as

```
const unsigned MaxString = 600;
class String {
public:
   void        set( const char string[ ] );
private:
   char s[ MaxString + 1 ]; // +1 for \0
public:
   const char* get();
};
```

The last version is not good style, but it shows that the **private** and **public** class members may be intermixed within the class declaration.

Clients of the **String** class can request services by invoking the **set** and **get** methods, which are **public**; but clients have no access to implementation array **s**, which is **private**. The next example shows how the methods can be invoked.

The *class* declaration contains *method* declarations for **set** and **get** (see Section 3.1 to review function declarations). The method declarations provide the function prototypes for the methods. The two methods need to be *defined*, but we have not yet provided the definitions. We do so shortly.   ■

The Member Operator .

Access to any class member, whether data member or method, is supported by the C++ **member operator**. The period **.** is the member operator.

EXAMPLE 5.2.4.   The code segment

```
const unsigned MaxString = 600;
class String {
public:
   void        set( const char string[ ] );
   const char* get();
private:
   char s[ MaxString + 1 ]; // +1 for \0
};
int main() {
   String s1;              // create a String object
   s1.set( "Turandot" ); // invoke its set method
   ...
}
```

illustrates the member operator. In **main** we first define **s1** as a **String** object and then invoke its **set** method

```
s1.set( "Turandot" );
```

The member operator occurs *between* the class object **s1** and the class member, in this case the method **set**.   ■

EXAMPLE 5.2.5. In Section 4.8, our sample application defines `if1` as an object of type `ifstream`, that is, as an object that can access an `input` file as a stream of bytes. We then invoke

```
if1.getline( rec1, MaxRecLen );
```

to read a record from this stream. Note that the member operator again occurs between the object, `if1`, and the `if1` member, in this case the method `getline`. ■

The member operator is used to access either data members or methods. However, recall that a client has access only to a class's **public** members, whether they be data members or methods.

EXAMPLE 5.2.6. The program

```
#include <iostream>
using namespace std;
const unsigned MaxString = 600;
class String {
public:
    void      set( const char string[ ] );
    const char* get();
private:
    char s[ MaxString + 1 ]; // +1 for \0
};
int main() {
    String s1;              // create a String object
    s1.set( "Turandot" );   // invoke its set method
    cout << s1.s << endl;   //***** ERROR: s is private
    return 0;
}
```

contains an error because **main** tries to access **s**, a **private** data member in the **String** class. Only **String** methods such as **set** and **get** have access to its **private** members. ■

Class Scope

A class's **private** members have **class scope**; that is, **private** members can be accessed *only* by class methods. (To be precise, **private** members can be accessed only by class methods or **friend** functions, which are explained in Chapter 8.)

EXAMPLE 5.2.7. The class declaration

```
class C {
public:
    void m();  // public scope
private:
    char d;    // class scope (private scope)
};
```

gives data member **d** class scope because **d** is **private**. By contrast, method **m** has what we call *public scope* because, as a **public** member, it can be accessed from outside the class.   ■

In C++, class scope is the *default* for members. Members default to **private** if the keywords **public** or **protected** (see Chapter 6) are not used.

EXAMPLE 5.2.8.   The class declaration

```
class Z {
  int x;
};
```

is equivalent to

```
class Z {
private:
  int x;
};
```

In the first case, **x** defaults to **private**. In the second case, **x** occurs in a region of the declaration explicitly labeled **private**.   ■

Our style is to put the **public** members first inside a declaration because this forces us then to use the label **private**, which adds clarity to the declaration. Besides, the **public** members constitute the class's interface and, in this sense, deserve to come first.

The principle of information hiding encourages us to give the class's implementation, particularly its data members, class scope. Restricting data members to class scope is likewise a key step in designing classes as abstract data types.

Defining Class Methods

Some earlier examples use the class declaration

```
const unsigned MaxString = 600;
class String {
public:
  void      set( const char string[ ] );
  const char* get();
private:
  char s[ MaxString + 1 ]; // +1 for \0
};
```

which *declares* but does not *define* the methods **set** and **get**. Class methods may be defined in either one of two ways:

- A method may be *declared inside* the class declaration but *defined outside* the class declaration.
- A method may be *defined inside* the class declaration. Such a definition is said to be **inline**, a C++ keyword. An **inline** definition also serves as a declaration.

We use two examples to clarify the distinction.

EXAMPLE 5.2.9. The code segment

```
#include <cstring>
const unsigned MaxString = 600;
class String {
public:
    void        set( const char string[ ] );
    const char* get();
private:
    char s[ MaxString + 1 ]; // +1 for \0
};

// define String's method set
void String::set( const char string[ ] ) {
    strncpy( s, string, MaxString );
    s[ MaxString ] = '\0'; // ensure a string
}
// define String's method get
const char* String::get() {
    return s;
}
```

declares **string** methods inside the class declaration and then defines the methods outside the class declaration. The definitions use the **scope resolution operator** ::, which is the double colon. This operator is needed because many classes other than **String** might have methods named **set** and **get**. In addition, there might be top-level functions with these names. To the operator's left comes the class name, in this case **String**; to its right comes the method's name together with its parameter list. ∎

Some C++ programmers like to write a top-level function such as **strcpy** in the style

```
::strcpy
```

Because no class name occurs to the left of the scope resolution operator ::, this syntax emphasizes that **strcpy** is *not* a class method but rather a top-level function.

EXAMPLE 5.2.10. The code segment

```
#include <cstring>
const unsigned MaxString = 600;
class String {
public:
    void set( const char string[ ] ) {
        strncpy( s, string, MaxString );
        s[ MaxString ] = '\0'; // ensure a string
    }
    const char* get() { return s; }
private:
    char s[ MaxString + 1 ]; // +1 for \0
};
```

defines **String**'s methods inside the class declaration. The methods are therefore **inline**.

An inline definition *recommends* to the compiler that the method's body be placed wherever the method is invoked so that a function call does not occur in the translated code. For example, if the compiler heeds the recommendation to make **set** inline, then a code segment such as

```
String s1;                      // create a String object
s1.set( "Hi, world!" ); // compiler: please make inline!
```

would be translated so that the code for **set**'s body, which consists of a call to **strncpy**, would be placed where the call to **set** occurs. The compiler is *not* required to follow the recommendation.   ∎

A function may be defined inline even if its definition occurs *outside* the class declaration by using the keyword **inline** in a method declaration.

EXAMPLE 5.2.11.   In the code segment

```
#include <cstring>
const unsigned MaxString = 600;
class String {
public:
    inline void       set( const char string[ ] );
    inline const char* get();
private:
    char s[ MaxString + 1 ]; // +1 for \0
};

// define String's method set
void String::set( const char string[ ] ) {
    strncpy( s, string, MaxString );
    s[ MaxString ] = '\0';
}
// define String's method get
const char* String::get() { return s; }
```

the **String** methods **set** and **get** are still inline, although they are defined *outside* the class declaration. The reason is that the keyword **inline** occurs in the declaration for each method.   ∎

Using Classes in a Program

Classes are created ultimately to be used in programs. Before a class can be used in a program, its declaration must be visible to any functions that are meant to use the class. Figure 5.2.1 shows a complete program that uses the **String** class. For clarity, we include the class declaration, all method definitions, and **main** in the same file. The program is quite simple, consisting only of the top-level function **main**; but it illustrates the key features in

```
#include <iostream>
#include <cstring>
using namespace std;
const unsigned MaxString = 600;
class String {
public:
   void       set( const char string[ ] );
   const char* get();
private:
   char s[ MaxString + 1 ]; // +1 for \0
};
// define String's method set
void String::set( const char string[ ] ) {
   strncpy( s, string, MaxString );
   s[ MaxString ] = '\0';
}
// define String's method get
const char* String::get() { return s; }

// main is the only function in this client program,
// which requests String services from the String class
int main() {
   String s1;               // create a single String
   String stooges[ 3 ]; // create an array of Strings
   s1.set( "Pascal" );   // set s1's contents
   // set the stooges
   stooges[ 0 ].set( "moe" );
   stooges[ 1 ].set( "larry" );
   stooges[ 2 ].set( "curly" );
   // print
   cout << s1.get() << endl;
   for ( int i = 0; i < 3; i++ )
      cout << stooges[ i ].get() << endl;
   return 0;
}
```

FIGURE 5.2.1 A complete program using a class.

any program using a class: the class declaration, the method definitions, and client functions that request class services.

A class declaration can be placed in a header file, which is then **#include**d wherever needed. We could amend the program in Figure 5.2.1 by placing the declaration for the **String** class in the file *stringDec.h*. We place the definitions for **String::set**, **String::get**, and **main** in the file *stringCode.cpp*. Assuming that *stringDec.h* and *stringCode.cpp* occur in the *same* directory, the file *stringCode.cpp* begins as follows:

```
#include <iostream>
#include <cstring>
#include "stringDec.h"
using namespace std;
const unsigned MaxString = 600;
// definitions for String::set, String::get, and main follow
```

There are two styles of **#include** statement in use here. The familiar

```
#include <iostream>
```

places the name of the file to be **#include**d in angle brackets. The angle brackets tell the system to *search in a predefined directory* for the file to be **#include**d, in this case for *iostream*. A system header file such as *iostream* is typically *not* in the same directory as the file in which it is to be **#include**d, in this case *stringCode.cpp*. For this reason, system header files usually occur in angle brackets in **#include** statements.

By contrast, we assume that the header file *stringDec.h* does occur in the same directory as the file, *stringCode.cpp*, in which it is to be **#include**d. Therefore, we enclose *stringDec.h* in double quotes rather than in angle brackets:

```
#include "stringDec.h"
```

The double quotes tell the system to search for the **#include** file in the *same* directory as the file in which it is to be **#include**d. In general, system header files are enclosed in angle brackets, whereas programmer header files are enclosed in double quotes.

EXERCISES

1. Explain the error in this class declaration:

```
class Person {
  // data and function members
}
```

2. Given the class declaration

```
class Airplane {
  // data members and methods
};
```

define an object of type **Airplane** and an array of such objects.

3. In the class

```
class Person {
  unsigned ageInYears;
  // other data members, and methods
};
```

is **ageInYears** a **private** or a **public** data member?

4. In the class

```
class Person {
  unsigned ageInYears;
  unsigned getAge();
  // other data members and methods
};
```

is `getAge` a **private** or a **public** method?

5. In a C++ class declared with the keyword **class**, do members default to **public** or **private**?

6. Given the class declaration

```
class Circus {
public:
  float getHeadCount();
  // other methods, and data members
};
```

create a **Circus** object and invoke its **getHeadCount** method.

7. Can any method be defined inside the class declaration?

8. Can any method be defined outside the class declaration?

9. Explain the error

```
class Circus {
public:
  float getHeadCount();
  // other methods, and data members
};

float getHeadCount() {
   // function body
}
```

in this attempt to define method **getHeadCount** outside the class declaration.

10. If a method is defined inside the class declaration, is it automatically inline even if the keyword **inline** is not used?

11. Give an example of how the keyword **inline** is used to declare as inline a method defined outside the class declaration.

12. Why are class declarations commonly placed in header files?

5.3 SAMPLE APPLICATION: A CLOCK CLASS

Problem

Create a **Clock** class to represent a clock that, once set to some initial value, can keep time by ticking to the next value. A **Clock**'s public interface should consist of methods to **set** it to an integer value, **tick** it to the next integer value, and **print** its current number of ticks. The **Clock**'s implementation should be private.

Sample Output

The test client in Figure 5.3.1 creates two **Clock** objects and then invokes the **tick** method, which increments an internal counter, and the **print** method, which outputs the counter. The output for the test client is

```
Current ticks == 0
Current ticks == 2
Current ticks == 100999
```

The first two lines are for **Clock** object **c1**, and the last line is for **Clock** object **c2**.

Solution

We use an **unsigned long** data member to represent the number of times that a **Clock** has ticked. Because an **unsigned long**'s range is typically 0 to 4,294,967,295, our **Clock** can keep on **tick**ing for a long time if **set** initially to 0. We **print** the number of ticks to the standard output using **cout**. A **Clock** is **tick**ed by invoking its **tick** method.

```
#include "Clock.h" // header file with Clock declaration
#include <iostream>
using namespace std;
int main() {
   Clock c1;
   c1.set();      // defaults to 0
   c1.print();   // 0
   c1.tick();    // ticks++
   c1.tick();    // ticks++
   c1.print();   // 2
   Clock c2;
   c2.set( 999 ); // initialize to 999
   for ( int i = 0; i < 100000; i++ )
      c2.tick(); // ticks++
   c2.print();      // 100999
   return 0;
}
```

FIGURE 5.3.1 A sample client for the **Clock** class.

C++ Implementation

```
class Clock {
public:
   void set( unsigned long t = 0 ) { ticks = t; }
   void tick() { ticks++; }
   void print() { cout << "Current ticks == " << ticks << endl; }
private:
   unsigned long ticks;
};
```

Discussion

We practice *information hiding* by making the **Clock**'s internal representation **private**. The implementation consists of a single data member, the **unsigned long** variable **ticks**. The class's three methods—**set**, **tick**, and **print**—all belong to its **public** interface. As functions contained in a class, the three methods are *encapsulated* within the class together with the data member. Because a **Clock**'s three methods are straightforward and short, we define them inside the **Clock** declaration.

A **Clock** object's interface allows a client application to **set** the **Clock** to some initial value such as 0. At any time the **Clock** can be reset to 0 simply by invoking **set** with no argument; to support this convenience, the **set** method has a default argument of 0. Invoking the **tick** method causes the **Clock**'s internal counter to increment by 1, and invoking the **print** method causes the **Clock**'s current state (that is, the value of its **private ticks** member) to be printed to the standard output.

Program Development

The **Clock** class provides services to client applications. How do we test whether the class provides the services as described in the class and method declarations? We write a **test client**, also called a **test driver** or simply **driver**. Figure 5.3.1 shows a test client that defines two **Clock** objects and invokes their methods in various ways. We assume that **Clock**'s declaration is in the header file *Clock.h*, which is therefore **#include**d in our sample client. We enclose the **#include** file *Clock.h* in double quotes because it resides in the same directory as our test client (see Section 5.2). We comment the code to indicate what is **print**ed for each **Clock** object. Although the **Clock** class and the sample client application are relatively simple, they illustrate the basics of creating classes and using them in applications.

Whenever a class is designed, a test driver should be provided that checks whether the class delivers the advertised functionality. Testing is a critical part of implementing any class.

EXERCISES

1. Add a **get** method to the **Clock** class, which returns the current number of ticks.

2. Offer a reason for defining **Clock**'s methods inside the class declaration.

3. Explain why the **#include** in the test client places the header file *Clock.h* in double quotes rather than angle brackets.

5.4 SAMPLE APPLICATION: A TIME STAMP CLASS

Problem

A **time stamp** is a value that represents an instant in time. A time stamp can be used to record when an event occurs. In a business, for example, we might use one time stamp to record when an invoice is received and another time stamp to record when the corresponding payment is sent.

Create a **TimeStamp** class that can be used to

- Set a time stamp to record when an event occurs.
- Print a time stamp as an integer.
- Print a time stamp as a string.
- Decompose a time stamp into a year, a month, a day, an hour, a minute, and a second so that these can be printed separately.

The class's public interface should include methods to provide these services.

The **TimeStamp** class should be suitable as a *utility class* for other classes. For example, an **Invoice** class might have two data members of type **TimeStamp**: one to record when the **Invoice** was sent and another to record when it was paid:

```
class Invoice {
public:
  ...
private:
  TimeStamp timeSent;
  TimeStamp timeReceived;
  ...
};
```

Sample Output

Figure 5.4.1 shows the output for the test client of Figure 5.4.2, which creates a **TimeStamp** object named **ts** and then tests its methods. Each output section shows the **TimeStamp** as an integer and as a string. The string representation is then divided into substrings, which represent the year, the month, the day of the week, the hour, the minute, and the second.

Solution

Our **TimeStamp** class leverages code from C++'s standard library. In particular, we use two functions whose prototypes are in the header file *ctime*: **time** and **ctime**. The library function **time** returns the current time, typically as an integer that represents the elapsed seconds from a predetermined instant (e.g., midnight on January 1, 1970) to the present instant. We provide methods to set a **TimeStamp** to the current time or to a user-specified time. There is also a method that returns a **TimeStamp** as an integer. The library function **ctime** converts a return value from **time** into a human-readable string (e.g., *Mon Apr 1 11:45:07 1999*). We provide a method that returns such a string, but also we provide methods that break apart the string into substrings. For example, the method **getYear** would select *1999* from our sample string and return it as a string; the method **getHour** would select *11* and return it as a string.

```
Testing methods:
   857330442
   Sun Mar 02 11:20:42 1997
   1997
   Mar
   Sun
   11
   20
   42

Testing methods:
   857530442
   Tue Mar 04 18:54:02 1997
   1997
   Mar
   Tue
   18
   54
   02

Testing methods:
   857030442
   Thu Feb 27 00:00:42 1997
   1997
   Feb
   Thu
   00
   00
   42

Testing methods:
   857330442
   Sun Mar 02 11:20:42 1997
   1997
   Mar
   Sun
   11
   20
   42
```

FIGURE 5.4.1 Output of the test client in Figure 5.4.2.

Our **TimeStamp** class incorporates functionality already provided in a procedural library but does so in an object-oriented style with the benefits of information hiding and encapsulation. Such a class is called a **thin wrapper** to underscore that the class does not provide radically new functionality, but rather packages in an object-oriented style the functionality already provided in a procedural library. Details of our implementation are given in the Discussion section.

```
#include <iostream>
#include <ctime>
#include <cstring>
#include "TimeStamp.h" // declaration for TimeStamp
using namespace std;
// test client for TimeStamp class
void dumpTS( TimeStamp& );
int main() {
   TimeStamp ts;
   time_t now = time( 0 );
   // tests
   ts.set();                    // default arg
   dumpTS( ts );
   ts.set( now + 200000 ); // user-supplied arg 1
   dumpTS( ts );
   ts.set( now - 300000 ); // user-supplied arg 2
   dumpTS( ts );
   ts.set( -999 ); // bogus user-supplied arg, rests to current time
   dumpTS( ts );
   return 0;
}
void dumpTS( TimeStamp& ts ) {
   cout << endl << "Testing methods: " << endl;
   cout << '\t' << ts.get() << endl;
   cout << '\t' << ts.getAsString();
   cout << '\t' << ts.getYear() << endl;
   cout << '\t' << ts.getMonth() << endl;
   cout << '\t' << ts.getDay() << endl;
   cout << '\t' << ts.getHour() << endl;
   cout << '\t' << ts.getMinute() << endl;
   cout << '\t' << ts.getSecond() << endl;
}
```

FIGURE 5.4.2 Test client for the **TimeStamp** class.

C++ Implementation

```
#include <iostream>
#include <ctime>
#include <cstring>
using namespace std;
class TimeStamp {
public:
   void       set( long s = 0 );
   time_t     get();
   const char* getAsString();
   const char* getYear();
```

```
      const char* getMonth();
      const char* getDay();
      const char* getHour();
      const char* getMinute();
      const char* getSecond();
   private:
      const char* extract( int, int );
      time_t stamp;
      char    string[ 30 ]; // holds ctime's return string
   };
   void TimeStamp::set( long s ) {
      if ( s <= 0 )
         stamp = time( 0 );
      else
         stamp = s;
   }
   time_t TimeStamp::get() {
      return stamp;
   }
   const char* TimeStamp::getAsString() {
      return ctime( &stamp );
   }
   const char* TimeStamp::extract( int offset, int count ) {
      char temp[ 30 ];
      strcpy( temp, ctime( &stamp ) );
      strncpy( string, temp + offset, count );
      string[ count ] = '\0';   // ensure a string
      return string;
   }
   const char* TimeStamp::getYear() {
      return extract( 20, 4 );
   }
   const char* TimeStamp::getMonth() {
      return extract( 4, 3 );
   }
   const char* TimeStamp::getDay() {
      return extract( 0, 3 );
   }
   const char* TimeStamp::getHour() {
      return extract( 11, 2 );
   }
   const char* TimeStamp::getMinute() {
      return extract( 14, 2 );
   }
   const char* TimeStamp::getSecond() {
      return extract( 17, 2 );
   }
```

Discussion

We begin with two top-level functions declared in the header file *ctime* because our `TimeStamp` class uses these functions. The prototype for the function `time` is

```
time_t time( time_t* ptr );
```

The data type `time_t` is an alias for a type such as `long` or `unsigned long`. The function returns a value that represents the current time. Many systems return the number of elapsed seconds since midnight on January 1, 1970. In any case, the returned value represents the *current* time. The argument may be either the address of a `time_t` variable or 0 (`NULL`).

The prototype for `ctime` is

```
char* ctime( const time_t* ptr );
```

The function expects the address of a `time_t` variable, typically a variable whose value has been set by a previous call to `time`. Function `ctime` returns the current time as a string. On our system, for example, the code segment

```
time_t now = time( 0 );
cout << now << endl
     << ctime( &now ) << endl;
```

outputs

```
853661241
Sun Jan 19 00:07:21 1997
```

The string returned by `ctime` is actually

```
Sun Jan 19 00:07:21 1997\n
```

so that the last character is a newline `\n`. The string is always formatted as follows:

- The first three characters represent the day, e.g., `Sun`.
- The fourth character is a blank.
- The fifth through seventh characters represent the month, e.g., `Jan`.
- The eighth character is a blank.
- The ninth and tenth characters represent the day of the month, e.g., `19`.
- The 11th character is a blank.
- The 12th and 13th characters represent the hour, going from `00` (midnight) through `23` (11 PM).
- The 14th character is a colon.
- The 15th and 16th characters represent the minute, going from `00` through `59`.
- The 17th character is a colon.
- The 18th and 19th characters represent the second, going from `00` through `59`.
- The 20th character is a blank.
- The 21st through 24th characters represent the year, e.g., `1997`.
- The 25th character is a newline.
- The 26th character is a null terminator.

We use this information to extract parts of the returned string. For example, the method

```
const char* TimeStamp::getYear() {
    return extract( 20, 4 );
}
```

invokes **private** method **extract** with two arguments. The first argument, **20**, is the C++ offset in the array **string** that stores the **ctime** string. The second argument, **4**, is the number of characters in the **ctime** year (e.g., 1997). Method **extract** does the work:

```
const char* TimeStamp::extract( int offset, int count ) {
    char temp[ 30 ];
    strcpy( temp, ctime( &stamp ) );
    strncpy( string, temp + offset, count );
    string[ count ] = '\0';   // ensure a string
    return string;
}
```

This **private** method, meant to be invoked only by the class's **public** methods, first copies **ctime**'s return value, a string, into a **temp**orary array. Then **strncpy** extracts a substring from **temp** by copying **count** characters from **temp**, starting at **offset**, into data member **string**, which is also an array of **char**. Recall from Section 4.3 that an array's name is a *base address*. Therefore, the expression **temp + offset** references the character with an offset of **offset** from this base address (see Figure 5.4.3). So **temp + offset** references the character at which the desired substring begins. The year substring, for example, starts at the 21st character and has four characters; hence, **getYear** invokes extract with **20** and **4** as arguments. Because **strncpy** need not return a string (see Section 4.7), **extract** ensures a string by appending a null-terminator. The method then returns data member **string**, which holds the substring. The methods to extract the month, day of the week, and other substrings invoke **extract** in a similar manner. Method **getMinute**, for instance, invokes **extract** with an offset argument of 14 and a length argument of 2.

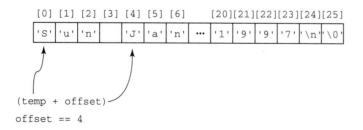

FIGURE 5.4.3 The expression `temp + offset`.

The **TimeStamp** class has two **private** data members: a **time_t** variable named **stamp**, which stores the time stamp; and a **char** array **string**, which is used to hold substrings of the `ctime` string. The data members are hidden so that the user need not know anything about them in using a `TimeStamp`. The `public` method `set` is used to set the `TimeStamp` to an integer. Eight other `public` methods are used to access the `ctime` string or substrings of it. The `private` method represents a functional decomposition of these `public` methods, as it does the low-level work. The user need not know how `extract` works or even that it exists at all.

Once a `TimeStamp` object has been defined in a code segment such as

```
int main() {
    TimeStamp ts; // define a TimeStamp object
    ...
}
```

its `set` method may be invoked with either zero arguments or one argument

```
TimeStamp ts1, ts2;
ts1.set();                          // argument defaults to 0
ts2.set( time( 0 ) + 1000 ); // now + 1,000 ticks
```

because `set`'s prototype has a default value for the parameter

```
class TimeStamp {
public:
    void        set( long s = 0 );
    ...
};
```

Method `set` checks whether the user supplied a parameter

```
void TimeStamp::set( long s ) {
    if ( s <= 0 )
        stamp = time( 0 );
    else
        stamp = s;
}
```

and sets `stamp` to the user-supplied value if the parameter is greater than 0. Otherwise, `set` uses the current time, obtained by a call to the library function `time`. The parameter `s` is of type `signed long` so that we can trap a negative integer passed as an argument

```
TimeStamp ts;
ts.set( -999 );   // bad TimeStamp value
```

In this invocation, `ts`'s `stamp` would be set to the current time rather than to -999, as we do not accept negative values as legal times.

The remaining `public` methods such as `get`, `getAsString`, `getYear`, and the like return the time stamp string or a substring thereof to the invoker. In the code segment

```
TimeStamp ts;
ts.set();                           // set to current time
cout << ts.get() << endl            // output as integer
     << ts.getAsString()            // output as string
     << ts.getMonth() << endl       // output month only
     << ts.getYear() << endl;       // output year only
```

the call to **get** returns the time stamp as an integer. The remaining calls return as a string either the entire time stamp string or a substring of it.

Our implementation gives priority to security over time efficiency. For example, every invocation of **public** method **getAsString**

```
const char* TimeStamp::getAsString() {
   return ctime( &stamp );
}
```

requires an invocation of **ctime**. An alternative would be to call **ctime** just once, in **set**, and to store **ctime**'s returned string in a data member array such as **string**. We then could have **getAsString** return the array's *name* (that is, the array's *address*) instead of calling **ctime**. This would save some time, though on a modern computer the savings would be negligible in all but the most time-critical applications. The downside is that information hiding could be compromised. Although **getAsString** returns a pointer to **const**ant characters, which the user cannot straightforwardly change, there are programming techniques that would allow a user to do mischief given the address of a data member array. Using techniques explained in Chapter 9, the user could *change* the array's contents. Therefore, we recompute the time string each time **getAsString** and related methods such as **getYear** are invoked by invoking **ctime** with the address of **private** data member **stamp** as the argument. The user has *no* access whatever to **stamp**, which bolsters **TimeStamp**'s information hiding.

Program Development

We tested the **TimeStamp** class with several sample runs. On our system, one test run produced the output shown in Figure 5.4.1. The test client makes four calls to **TimeStamp**'s **set** method. The first call tests whether **set** can be called with no arguments. Because the method's declaration has a single argument with a default value of 0, this call should work. The second call invokes **set** with an argument that represents a future time. The third call invokes **set** with an argument that represents a past time. The fourth and last call invokes **set** with an illegal argument, namely, a negative integer. After each call to **set**, we test the other eight methods to see if they return the proper values. From the output we can determine whether the various **get** methods work as they should.

Our **TimeStamp** class is a thin wrapper: our class repackages, in an object-oriented style, functionality already present in a traditional procedural library, in this case the library described in the header file *ctime*. The repackaging is a convenience to clients in that the **TimeStamp** class and its methods are easier to use than the functions and supporting constructs described in *ctime*.

EXERCISES

1. Explain why the **TimeStamp** class is known as a *thin wrapper*.

2. The **TimeStamp** method **extract** includes the statement

   ```
   string[ count ] = '\0';
   ```

   Explain why this statement is needed to make the class robust.

3. Explain how the **TimeStamp** class practices information hiding.

4. What functionality does the **TimeStamp** class encapsulate?

5. The **TimeStamp** class overloads the **public** method **set** so that it may be invoked with no arguments or with a single argument. Summarize how each overloaded function works.

6. Why is the **extract** method made **private** rather than **public**?

7. Write another client to test whether the **TimeStamp** class delivers the advertised functionality.

5.5 CONSTRUCTORS AND THE DESTRUCTOR

Class methods typically are invoked *by name*.

EXAMPLE 5.5.1.   Assume that **Window** is a class defined in the header file *windows.h*. The code segment

```
#include "windows.h" // class Windows, etc.
int main() {
    Window mainWin;    // create a Window object
    mainWin.show();    // invoke show method
    ...
}
```

creates a **Window** object **mainWin** and then invokes its **show** method by name

```
mainWin.show(); // invoke show by name
```                                                                    ■

Some methods need not be invoked explicitly by name, for the compiler invokes them automatically. **Class constructors** and the **class destructor** typically are invoked automatically *by the compiler* rather than by the programmer. We examine the constructors first.

Constructors

A **constructor** is a method whose name is the same as the class. A suitable constructor is invoked automatically whenever a class object is created.

EXAMPLE 5.5.2.   The code segment

```
const unsigned MaxString = 600;
class String {
public:
    String(); // constructor
    String( const char s[ ] ); // constructor
    void set( const char string[ ] );
    const char* get();
```

```
private:
    char s[ MaxString + 1 ]; // +1 for \0
};
```

declares a class **String** that has a **private** data member and four **public** methods. Two of the methods are the constructors

```
String();
String( const char s[ ] );
```

These methods have the same name as the class, **String**, and have *no return value*. A constructor must *not* have a return value. So, for example, the declaration

```
void String(); //***** ERROR: no return type!
```

is an error.   ■

As Example 5.5.2 shows, a class may have more than one constructor. Class constructors thus can be *overloaded*. However, each constructor must have a distinct signature (see Section 3.7). In Example 5.5.2, the two constructors have distinct signatures: the first expects no arguments and the second expects a single **String** argument.

EXAMPLE 5.5.3.   The code segment

```
int main() {
    String s1;                      // default constructor
    String s2( "J. Coltrane" ); // parameterized constructor
    ...
}
```

illustrates how constructors for the class of Example 5.5.2 are invoked. The definition of **s1** causes the **default constructor** to be invoked. The default constructor has no arguments; all other constructors are known generically as **parameterized constructors**. The definition of **s2**

```
String s2( "J. Coltrane" );
```

makes it look as if **s2** were a function that expected a single argument. Instead, **s2** is an *object*. The syntax signals the compiler that, in creating **s2**, its parameterized constructor should be called with **"J. Coltrane"** as the argument.   ■

As the name suggests, a *constructor* is a method called when an object is first being *constructed*, that is, created. The idea behind constructors is to provide a class with special methods that are invoked automatically whenever an object is created. In short, the programmer need not remember to invoke a constructor. Constructors are used to initialize data members and to do any other processing appropriate to an object's creation. Constructors are particularly useful in making classes *robust*.

EXAMPLE 5.5.4.   The code segment

```
const unsigned MaxString = 600;
class String {
public:
   void set( const char string[ ] );
   const char* get();
private:
   char s[ MaxString + 1 ]; // +1 for \0
};

int main() {
   String s1;   //*****Caution: s1's s not initialized
   cout << s1.get() << endl; // access violation likely
   ...
}
```

illustrates the danger of not having at least a default constructor. Object **s1** is created but its array **s** may *not* be a string because **s1**'s **set** is not invoked. The likely outcome is a run-time error, namely, an access violation (see Section 4.2).

By including in the **String** class a default constructor to initialize **s**

```
const unsigned MaxString = 600;
class String {
public:
   String() {
      s[ 0 ] = '\0'; // ensure a string
   }
   void set( const char string[ ] );
   const char* get();
private:
   char s[ MaxString + 1 ]; // +1 for \0
};

int main() {
   String s1;   // default constructor invoked automatically
   cout << s1.get() << endl; // ok, no access violation
   ...
}
```

we can ensure that **String** objects such as **s1** have a string in data member **s**.   ■

EXAMPLE 5.5.5.   By including a parameterized constructor in the **String** class

```
const unsigned MaxString = 600;
class String {
public:
   String() {
      s[ 0 ] = '\0'; // ensure a string
   }
```

```
   String( const char string[ ] ) {
      strncpy( s, string, MaxString );
      s[ MaxString ] = '\0';  // ensure a string
   }
   void set( const char string[ ] );
   const char* get();
private:
   char s[ MaxString + 1 ]; // +1 for \0
};
```

we support code segments such as

```
int main() {
   String s1;               // default constructor
   String s2( "kamiko" ); // parameterized constructor
   cout << s1.get() << endl  // empty string
        << s2.get() << endl; // kamiko
   ...
}
```

The parameterized constructor is robust because it copies at most **MaxString** characters from the parameter into **s** and then null terminates **s** to ensure a string.   ■

Arrays of Class Objects and the Default Constructor

If **C** is a class, we can define an array of **C** objects. If **C** has a default constructor, the default constructor is invoked for each array element, that is, for each **C** object in the array.

EXAMPLE 5.5.6.   The code segment

```
#include <iostream>
using namespace std;
unsigned count = 0;
class C {
public:
   C() { cout << "Creating C" << ++count << endl; }
};

C ar[ 1000 ];
```

produces the output

```
Creating C1
Creating C2
...
Creating C999
Creating C1000
```

The default constructor is invoked automatically for *each* of the 1,000 **C** objects in the array **ar**.   ■

Restricting Object Creation Through Constructors

Suppose that we have an **Emp**loyee class with a data member that represents an employee's unique identification number (e.g., a social security number)

```
class Emp {
private:
   unsigned id; // unique id number
   ...
};
```

and that we want to prevent an **Emp** object from being created without initializing **id**. In short, we want to disallow a definition such as

```
Emp elvis; // undesirable--no id specified
```

If **Emp** has no default constructor or a **public** default constructor, then the code segment is legal. In the code segment

```
class Emp {
public:
   Emp( unsigned ID ) { id = ID; }
private:
   unsigned id; // unique id number
   Emp();        //**** private
   ...
};

int main() {
   Emp elvis; //***** ERROR: Emp() is private
   Emp cher( 111222333 ); // OK, Emp( unsigned ) is public
   ...
}
```

the compiler generates an error at the definition of **elvis**. Creating object **elvis** would require the compiler to invoke **Emp**'s default constructor in **main**, but **Emp**'s default constructor is **private** and so inaccessible in **main**. The creation of **cher** is legal because **Emp**'s parameterized constructor is **public** and, therefore, accessible in **main**.

C++ programmers often make selected constructors **private** and others **public** to ensure that objects are properly initialized when created. A **private** constructor, like any **private** method, has *class scope* and therefore cannot be invoked outside the class.

The Copy Constructor and Convert Constructors

Up to now we have divided constructors into two groups: the *default constructor*, which takes *no* arguments, and the *parameterized constructors*, which take *one or more* arguments. Among the parameterized constructors, however, two types are important enough to have special names: **copy** and **convert constructors**.

The copy constructor *clones* an object by creating a new object that is a copy of the original. The copy constructor's prototype is

```
String( String& ); //***** Note: String reference
```

The argument is a *reference* of the same class. The prototype

```
String( String ); //***** ERROR: illegal constructor
```

is in error because the **String** copy constructor must take a **String** *reference*, not a **String** value, as its single argument.

If the user does not provide a copy constructor, the compiler does. The compiler's version does a byte for byte copy of the original object to the clone; that is, the compiler's version copies the values of the original object's data members to the clone's corresponding data members. The corresponding data members in the two objects have *exactly the same values* after the copy completes. Chapter 9 explains when the programmer should write a copy constructor.

EXAMPLE 5.5.7. The code segment

```
String orig( "Dawn Upshaw" ); // create a String object
String clone( orig );         // clone it
```

illustrates the copy constructor. Assuming that the compiler's copy constructor is used, objects **orig** and **clone**, although distinct, now have data members that are byte for byte identical. ∎

A convert constructor for class **C** is a one-parameter constructor (where the parameter's type is other than **C&**) used to convert integers, strings, and the like into class objects. We have seen a convert constructor already.

EXAMPLE 5.5.8. The class

```
const unsigned MaxString = 600;
class String {
public:
   String() {
      s[ 0 ] = '\0'; // ensure a string
   }
   String( const char string[ ] ) {
      strncpy( s, string, MaxString );
      s[ MaxString ] = '\0';  // ensure a string
   }
   void set( const char string[ ] );
   const char* get();
private:
   char s[ MaxString + 1 ]; // +1 for \0
};
int main() {
   String soprano( "Dawn Upshaw" );
   ...
}
```

has a default constructor, and a convert constructor that converts a string such as **"Dawn Upshaw"** into a **String** object such as **soprano**. ∎

The Convert Constructor and Implicit Type Conversion

A convert constructor can be used as an alternative to function overloading. Suppose that function **f** expects a **String** *object* as an argument

```
void f( String s ); // declaration
```

but that the programmer forgets and invokes it with a string constant such as

```
f( "Turandot" );
```

If the **String** class has this convert constructor

```
String( const char s[ ] ); // convert constructor
```

then the *compiler* invokes the convert constructor on the string constant **"Turandot"** so that a **String** *object* is available as **f**'s expected argument. The **String** convert constructor thereby supports an **implicit type conversion**; that is, the constructor converts a **const char*** to a **String**. The conversion is implicit in that the compiler performs it; the programmer does not need to provide an explicit cast.

The implicit type conversion from a string constant to a **String** is convenient for the programmer. However, an application may need to *disable* implicit type conversions of the sort just illustrated. Implicit type conversions may lead to unforeseen—and very subtle and hard to detect—errors. The keyword **explicit**, which occurs in a convert constructor's declaration, may be used to disable implicit type conversions through a convert constructor.

EXAMPLE 5.5.9. The code segment

```
class String {
public:
   // convert constructor marked as explicit
   explicit String ( const char s [ ] ) {...}
...
};
void f( String s ) {...} //*** note: f expects a String
int main() {
   String s1( "foo" ); // convert constructor used
   f( s1 );    // ok, s1 is a String
   f( "bar" ); //***** ERROR: no implicit type conversion
   return 0;
}
```

illustrates the syntax and use of **explicit**. The first call to **f** is legal because its argument **s1** is a **String**. The second call is illegal because its argument is a **const char***, not a **String**. Because the **String** convert constructor has been marked **explicit**, it cannot be used to convert **"bar"** to a **String** in order to match **f**'s prototype. The result is a fatal compile-time error rather than a run-time error, which might have subtle but serious consequences. ■

Passing and Returning Objects by Reference

Objects, like other variables, may be passed by value or by reference to functions. An object also may be returned by value or by reference.

EXAMPLE 5.5.10.   The code segment in Figure 5.5.1 illustrates passing and returning objects by value and by reference. For instance, **c1** is passed by value to **f** but by reference to **g**. Function **h** returns a **C** object by value, whereas **k** returns a reference to one of its arguments, both of which are passed by reference. The program's output is

```
Creating c1
Creating c2
Creating c3
Creating c4
  **** Oh, no! Object cloned!
c1 clone: To f by value
c2: To g by reference
Creating temp
temp: Returning temp from h by value
  **** Oh, no! Object cloned!
c1: To k by reference (1st arg)
c2: To k by reference (2nd arg)
c1: Returning from k by reference
```

Object **c1** is passed by value to **f**, which causes the copy constructor to be called. Object **temp** is returned by value from **h**, which likewise causes the copy constructor to be called. When the objects are passed or returned by reference, the copy constructor is not involved. ∎

Passing or returning an object by value is inefficient for two reasons. First, an object passed or returned by value is first *copied*, and it is the copy that is passed or returned. The copy, like the original object, has **sizeof(C)** bytes, where **C** is the class. It is thus an inefficient use of storage to copy objects whose size in bytes is large. Second, an object is copied through a call to the copy constructor, which means that passing or returning an object by value involves a method call. If the copy constructor does a large amount of processing, either directly or through calls to other functions, the process may be very time-consuming. The call to the copy constructor is not obvious from the source code, as it is the compiler rather than the programmer that writes the call. Accordingly, it is easy for the programmer to forget the overhead associated with passing or returning by value.

The class designer can disable passing or returning by value for functions outside the class. If the copy constructor is **private**, top-level functions and methods in other classes cannot pass or return class objects by value precisely because this requires a call to the copy constructor. For example, if we amend the program in Figure 5.5.1 by placing the copy constructor's declaration in the **private** region

```
class C {
public:
   ...
private:
  C( C& ); // copy constructor
   ...
};
```

```
#include <iostream>
#include <cstring>
using namespace std;
class C {
public:
   C( const char n[ ] ) {
     setName( n );
     cout << "Creating " << name << endl;
   }
   C( C& c ) { cout << " **** Oh, no! Object cloned!" << endl; }
   void m( const char msg[ ] ) { cout << name << ": " << msg << endl; }
   void setName( const char n[ ] ) { strcpy( name, n ); }
private:
   C(); // must provide a name
   char name[ 100 ];
};
void f( C );      // pass by value
void g( C& );     // pass by reference
C h();            // return by value
C& k( C&, C& );   // return by reference
int main() {
   C c1( "c1" ), c2( "c2" ), c3( "c3" ), c4( "c4" );
   f( c1 );               // pass by value
   g( c2 );               // pass by reference
   c3 = h();              // return by value
   c4 = k( c1, c2 );      // return by reference
   return 0;
}
void f( C c ) {
   c.setName( "c1 clone" );
   c.m( "To f by value" );
}
void g( C& c ) {
   c.m( "To g by reference" );
}
C h() {
   C temp( "temp" );
   temp.m( "Returning temp from h by value" );
   return temp;
}
C& k( C& c1, C& c2 ) {
   c1.m( "To k by reference (1st arg)" );
   c2.m( "To k by reference (2nd arg)" );
   c1.m( "Returning from k by reference" );
   return c1;
}
```

FIGURE 5.5.1 Passing and returning objects by value and reference.

the compiler issues fatal errors on the calls to **f** and **h** in **main** because these calls require the copy constructor.

For the sake of efficiency, objects in general should be passed *by reference* unless there is a compelling reason to pass them by value. We shortly discuss why caution must be used in returning objects by reference.

If an object is passed by reference to a function that does not modify the object, the corresponding parameter should be marked as **const**.

EXAMPLE 5.5.11. The code segment

```
class String {
public:
   String( const char s[ ] ) {...}
   bool equalsIgnoreCase( const String& s ) {...}
   ...
};
int main() {
  String s1( "foo" ), s2( "bar" );
  if ( s1.equalsIgnoreCase( s2 ) )
    ...
}
```

defines the method **equalsIgnoreCase** that expects a **const** reference to a **String** object. The **const**, as usual, signals that the function does not modify any of the object's data members. ∎

An object defined *within a function's body* should *not* be returned by reference. Objects defined inside a block, like other variables defined inside a block, go out of existence once control exits the block. If a function returns a reference to an object defined inside its body, in the calling function this reference is a reference to a nonexistent object.

EXAMPLE 5.5.12. The code segment

```
String& f(); // returns a String reference
int main() {
  String s = f(); //***** Caution: nonexistent reference
  ...
}
String& f() {
   String s; // define object inside block
   ...
   return s;
} //***** DANGER! s goes out of existence
```

illustrates the problem. Function **f** creates the **String** object **s** inside its body and then returns **s** by reference. But **s** goes out of existence once **f** exits. Therefore, **main** receives a reference to an object that no longer exists. The likely result is a run-time error. The error can be corrected by returning **s** by value. ∎

The Constructor Header and const Member Initializations

Consider the class

```
class C {
public:
   C() {
     x = 0; // OK, x not const
     c = 0; //***** ERROR: c not a legal lvalue
   }
private:
   int x;
   const int c; // const data member
};
```

that has a constructor to initialize its two data members. The problem is that data member **c** is **const** and, therefore, cannot be the target of an assignment operation. The solution is to initialize **c** in the constructor's *header*.

EXAMPLE 5.5.13.   The code segment

```
class C {
public:
   C() : c( 0 ) { x = -1; }
private:
   int x;
   const int c; // const data member
};
```

illustrates the syntax for initializing a **const** data member in the constructor's header. The constructor's header initialization section is introduced by a colon **:** followed by members and their initializing values in parentheses. In our example, only **c** is initialized in the header and its value, 0, is enclosed in parentheses after its name. This is the *only* way to initialize a **const** data member such as **c**.   ∎

Header initialization is legal only in constructors. Any data member may be initialized in a constructor's header. Of course, **const** data members cannot be initialized in any other way.

EXAMPLE 5.5.14.   We amend Example 5.5.13

```
class C {
public:
   C() : c( 0 ), x( -1 ) { } // empty body
private:
   int x;
   const int c; // const data member
};
```

by initializing both **const** member **c** and non**const** member **x** in the constructor's header. The initializations could occur in any order and are separated by a comma. Because the header initializations do all the work, the default constructor's body is now empty. This style is quite common among C++ programmers. ∎

The Destructor

A class constructor is automatically invoked whenever an object belonging to the class is created. The **class destructor** is automatically invoked whenever an object belonging to the class is destroyed (e.g., when the object goes out of scope). The destructor, like the constructors, is a class method. For class **C**, the destructor's prototype is

```
~C();
```

White space can occur between ~ and the class name. The destructor takes no arguments so there can be only one destructor per class. The destructor, like the constructors, has no return value. The destructor declaration

```
void ~C();   //***** ERROR: no return value!
```

is therefore in error.

> **EXAMPLE 5.5.15.** The output for the program in Figure 5.5.2 is
>
> ```
> hortense constructing.
> anonymous constructing.
> foo constructing.
>
> foo destructing.
> anonymous destructing.
> hortense destructing.
> ```
>
> At line 1, a **C** object is created
>
> ```
> C c0( "hortense" ); // parameterized constructor
> ```
>
> and the parameterized constructor is invoked automatically. Object **c0** exists from the time of its creation until right before **main** exits at line 5. *Before* **main** exits, **c0**'s destructor is invoked automatically, which outputs a message to that effect.
>
> Lines 2 and 3 create objects **c1** and **c2**. For **c1**, the default constructor is invoked; for **c2**, the parameterized constructor is invoked. Lines 2 and 3 occur *inside* a block. Objects **c1** and **c2** exist only within the block. Therefore, right before the block exits at line 4, **c1**'s destructor and **c2**'s destructor are automatically invoked. ∎

The class destructor typically does whatever clean up operations are appropriate when an object is destroyed, just as the class constructors typically do whatever initialization operations are appropriate when an object is created. We recommend that every class with data members have at least a default constructor to handle initializations. Other constructors and the destructor should be added as needed.

```
#include <iostream>
#include <cstring>
using namespace std;
class C {
  char name[ 25 ];
public:
  C() { // default constructor
     strcpy( name, "anonymous" );
     cout << name << " constructing." << endl;
  }
  C( const char* n ) { // parameterized constructor
     strcpy( name, n );
     cout << name << " constructing" << endl;
  }
  ~C() { cout << name << " destructing." << endl; }
};
int main() {
/* 1 */ C c0( "hortense" ); // parameterized constructor
        {
/* 2 */    C c1; // default constructor
/* 3 */    C c2( "foo" ); // parameterized constructor
           cout << endl;
/* 4 */ } // c1 and c2 destructors called

/* 5 */ return 0; // c0 destructor called
}
```

FIGURE 5.5.2 Constructor and destructor calls.

EXERCISES

1. Explain the error.

```
class C {
public:
   c(); // default constructor
   ...
};
```

2. Explain the error.

```
class Z {
public:
   void Z(); // default constructor
   ...
};
```

3. Can a class's constructors be overloaded?

4. Can a class constructor be `private`?

5. Must a class constructor be defined outside the class declaration?

6. In the class declaration

```
class C {
public:
  C();
  C( int );
  ...
};
```

indicate which constructor is the *default* constructor.

7. Explain the error.

```
class K {
private:
   K();
};
int main() {
   K k1;
   return 0;
}
```

8. In the code segment

```
class C {
public:
   C() {...}
};
C array[ 500 ];
```

how many times is `C`'s default constructor invoked?

9. Explain the error:

```
class R {
public:
  R( R arg ); // copy constructor
};
```

10. What is the purpose of the copy constructor?

11. Write a code segment that illustrates how the copy constructor might be used.

12. If the programmer does not provide a copy constructor, does the compiler automatically provide one?

13. What is a convert constructor?

14. Declare a class `C` with two convert constructors.

15. Does the following program contain any errors?

```
class C {
public:
   C( int x ) {
    // method's body
   }
};
void g( C );
int main() {
   g( 999 );
   return 0;
}
void g( C arg ) {
   // function's body
}
```

16. Explain the error.

```
class Foo {
public:
  explicit Foo( int arg ) {
    // constructor's body
  }
};
void g( Foo f ) {
  // g's body
}
int main() {
   Foo f1;
   g( f1 );
   g( -999 );
   return 0;
}
```

17. Explain the error.

```
class C {
  C( int a ) { c = a; }
private:
  const int c;
};
```

18. For the class

```
class C {
public:
   // public methods
private:
   const int c;
};
```

define a convert constructor that expects an **int** argument and initializes data member **c** to this argument's value.

19. Explain the error.

```
class Z {
public:
   Z( int a ) : c( a ), x( -5 ) { }
   void f( int a ) : c( a ) { }
private:
   const int c;
   int x;
};
```

20. Explain the error.

```
class A {
public:
   void ~A();
};
```

21. What is the output?

```
#include <iostream>
using namespace std;
class Z {
public:
   Z( unsigned a ) : id( a ) {
     cout << id << " created" << endl;
   }
   ~Z() {
     cout << id << " destroyed" << endl;
   }
private:
   unsigned id;
};
int main() {
   Z z1( 1 ), z2( 2 ), z3( 3 );
   return 0;
}
```

5.6 SAMPLE APPLICATION: A TASK CLASS

Problem

Create a **Task** class that represents a task to be scheduled. In addition to a required identifying *name*, a **Task** has a *start time*, *finish time*, and a *duration*. The public interface should provide methods for accessing these **Task** properties. When a **Task** is destroyed, a record describing it should be written to a log file.

```
#include <iostream>
#include <ctime>
#include <cstring>
#include <fstream>
using namespace std;
//*** class declarations and method definitions
//    for TimeStamp and Task are here
int main() {
  time_t now = time( 0 );
  Task t1( "Defrost pizzas" ),
       t2( "Open beer" ),
       t3( "Eat pizzas and drink beer" );
  t1.setST( now );
  t1.setFT( now + 3600 );        // an hour from now
  t2.setST( t1.getFT() );        // when pizzas defrosted
  t2.setFT( t2.getST() + 2 );    // fast work
  t3.setST( t2.getFT() + 1 );    // slight delay
  t3.setFT( t3.getST() + 7200 ); // leisure meal
  return 0;
}
```

FIGURE 5.6.1 Test client for the **Task** class.

Sample Output

The output file for the test client in Figure 5.6.1 is

```
ID: Eat pizzas and drink beer
   ST: Sat Sep 06 11:21:50 1997
   FT: Sat Sep 06 13:21:50 1997
   DU: 7200

ID: Open beer
   ST: Sat Sep 06 11:21:47 1997
   FT: Sat Sep 06 11:21:49 1997
   DU: 2

ID: Defrost pizzas
   ST: Sat Sep 06 10:21:47 1997
   FT: Sat Sep 06 11:21:47 1997
   DU: 3600
```

Each output block begins with a **Task**'s identifying name, for example, **Defrost pizzas**. Next comes the **Task**'s start time and finish time as strings. The last entry is the **Task**'s duration as an integer, which is the start time as an integer subtracted from the finish time as an integer. The **Defrost pizzas** task has a duration of 3,600 time units, whereas the **Open beer** task has a duration of only two time units. The output file reverses the order in which the **Task**s occur. For example, **Defrost pizzas** is listed last but occurs first.

The output file reflects the order in which the **Task** destructors execute. The **Task** named **Defrost pizzas** is created first and *destroyed last* in our sample client, which accounts for its position in the log file. The Discussion section explains how the programmer can control the log file's output.

Solution

We use the **Task** constructors to ensure that a **Task** has an identifying name, represented as a string. To represent a **Task**'s start and finish times, we leverage the **TimeStamp** class (see Section 5.4). In particular, a **Task** has two **private TimeStamp** data members, one to represent a start time and another to represent a finish time. Instead of storing a **Task**'s duration in a data member, we compute the duration as needed by using the library function **difftime**, which returns the difference between two **time_t** values. For logging **Task** data to a file, we use an **ofstream** object opened in **app**end mode.

C++ Implementation

```cpp
#include <iostream>
#include <ctime>
#include <cstring>
#include <fstream>
using namespace std;
class Task {
public:
   // constructors-destructor
   Task( const char id[ ] );
  ~Task();
   // set-get methods
   void          setST( time_t st = 0 );
   time_t        getST();
   const char* getStrST();
   void          setFT( time_t ft = 0 );
   time_t        getFT();
   const char* getStrFT();
   void          setID( const char ID[ ] ) {
      strncpy( id, ID, MaxId );
      id[ MaxId ] = '\0';
   }
   const char* getID() { return id; }
   double        getDU();
   void          logToFile();
private:
   enum { MaxId = 50, MaxLogFile = 20 };
   Task(); // default constructor disallowed
   TimeStamp  st;
   TimeStamp  ft;
   char       id[ MaxId + 1 ];
   char       logFile[ MaxLogFile + 1 ];
};
```

```
Task::Task( const char ID[ ] ) {
    strncpy( id, ID, MaxId );
    id[ MaxId ] = '\0';
    strcpy( logFile, "log.dat" );
    setST();
    ft = st; // so far, no duration
}
Task::~Task() {
    logToFile(); // if client forgets
}
void Task::logToFile() {
    // set finish if duration still 0
    if ( getFT() == getST() )
      setFT();
    // log the Task's vital statistics
    ofstream outfile( logFile, ios::app );
    outfile << endl << "ID: " << id << endl;
    outfile << "  ST: " << getStrST();
    outfile << "  FT: " << getStrFT();
    outfile << "  DU: " << getDU();
    outfile << endl;
    outfile.close();
}
void Task::setST( time_t ST ) {
    st.set( ST );
}
time_t Task::getST() {
    return st.get();
}
const char* Task::getStrST() {
    return st.getAsString();
}
void Task::setFT( time_t FT ) {
    ft.set( FT );
}
time_t Task::getFT() {
    return ft.get();
}
const char* Task::getStrFT() {
    return ft.getAsString();
}
double Task::getDU() {
    return difftime( getFT(), getST() );
}
```

Discussion

The **Task** class has two data members of type **TimeStamp**, which means that the class declaration for **TimeStamp** and the code that implements **TimeStamp** methods *must* be part of any program that uses the **Task** class. To run a test program, we first put the **TimeStamp** class declaration in the file *TimeStamp.h* and then **#include** this file at the top of the test program file. We also place the declaration for the **Task** class in the header file *Task.h* and **#include** this file as well. Our test program file contains

- Definitions for the **TimeStamp** methods.
- Definitions for the **Task** methods.
- A sample client program consisting of **main**.

The **Task** class has three **private** data members: **id**, a string that represents the **Task**'s name; **st**, a **TimeStamp** that represents the **Task**'s start time; and **ft**, a **TimeStamp** that represents the **Task**'s finish time. There are **public** methods to **set** and **get** these data members.

The class declaration for **Task** has two constructors, a default constructor and a constructor that expects a single string argument, which represents a **Task**'s name. To disallow uninitialized definitions of **Task** objects such as

```
Task takeExam; // no name provided!
```

we place the declaration for the default constructor in the **private** section

```
class Task {
public:
   ...
private:
   Task(); // default constructor disallowed
   ...
};
```

We do *not* have to define the default constructor. Declaring it in the **private** section is sufficient to make the compiler issue a fatal error at an attempted definition such as

```
int main() {
   Task takeExam; //***** ERROR: default constructor private!
   ...
}
```

The **public** convert constructor takes a single string argument, which is the **Task**'s identifying name. This combination of a **private** default constructor and a **public** convert constructor means that the user *must* supply a **Task** name when creating a task. The convert constructor initializes all data members:

```
Task::Task( const char ID[ ] ) {
   strncpy( id, ID, MaxId );
   id[ MaxId ] = '\0';
   strcpy( logFile, "log.dat" );
   setST();
   ft = st; // so far, no duration
}
```

To set a **Task**'s **id** to the constructor's parameter, we use **strncpy** to prevent array overflow and we add a null terminator to ensure a string. To set a **Task**'s **logFile** name, we use **strcpy** because we specify the name, in the constructor's body, as the string constant **log.dat**. An anonymous **enum** (see Chapter 1, C++ Postscript) in the **private** section of **Task**'s declaration defines the integer constants **MaxId** and **MaxLogFile**, which specifies the maximum number of characters in the log file's name. The log file's name is stored in the **private** data member **logFile**.

The constructor calls the **Task** method **setST** to initialize the starting time to the *current* time. Method **setST** invokes the **TimeStamp** method **set**, which in turn invokes the library function **time**. After setting the start time to the current time, we set the **Task**'s finish time to its start time so that the two coincide. Because *duration* is the difference between *finish* and *start* times, duration is 0 when a **Task** is first created.

By using **TimeStamp**s to represent a **Task**'s start and finish times, we can leverage the functionality of the **TimeStamp** class. For example, the **Task** class has methods to set and get the start and the finish time:

```
void Task::setFT( time_t FT ) {
    ft.set( FT );
}
time_t Task::getFT() {
    return ft.get();
}
```

Because **ft** is a **TimeStamp**, we delegate the setting and getting to the underlying **TimeStamp** methods **set** and **get**. This is an example of code reuse and wrapping: our **Task** class has methods such as **getFT** that are thin wrappers around **TimeStamp** methods, which do the actual work.

There is **public** method for logging **Task** data to a file. If **t1** is a **Task**, then

```
t1.logToFile()
```

may be invoked whenever desired. The method

```
void Task::logToFile() {
    // set finish if duration still 0
    if ( getFT() == getST() )
      setFT();
    // log the Task's vital statistics
    ofstream outfile( logFile, ios::app );
    outfile << endl << "ID: " << id << endl;
    outfile << "  ST: " << getStrST();
    outfile << "  FT: " << getStrFT();
    outfile << "  DU: " << getDU();
    outfile << endl;
    outfile.close();
}
```

does the work. The **if** checks whether a **Task**'s finish time has ever been set beyond its initialization to its start time. If not, **logToFile** sets the **Task**'s finish time to the current time. Our use of **ofstream** requires the header file *fstream*. In Chapter 2, we invoked **ofstream**'s **open** method to open a file. Here we use the constructor

```
ofstream outfile( logFile, ios::app );
```

instead of a separate call to **open**

```
ofstream outfile;
outfile.open( logFile, ios::app );
```

For **ofstream**s, the constructor and the **open** method are overloaded. Here we use the two-argument constructor. The second argument **ios::app** is the **mode** in which file named **logFile** is opened, in this case *append* mode. When a file is opened in append mode, new records are written at the *end*. Figure 5.6.2 lists the modes and their meanings.

Name	Purpose
in	Open for reading
out	Open for writing
ate	Open and move to end-of-stream
app	Open for appending
trunc	Discard stream if it already exists
binary	Open as a binary stream

FIGURE 5.6.2 Mode flags.

Because the programmer may forget to invoke a **Task**'s **logToFile** method before the **Task** is destroyed, the **Task** class has a destructor that invokes **logToFile**. The destructor thus ensures that the **Task**'s data is logged. In the code segment

```
int main() {
   Task t1( "foo" );
   {
     Task t2( "bar" );
     ...
   } // t2's destructor invoked
   return 0; // t1's destructor invoked
}
```

t2's destructor is invoked when control exits the block and, therefore, **t2** goes out of scope. The destructor for **t1** is invoked when **main** exits with the **return** statement.

1. What change in behavior results if the mode is changed from **ios::app** to **ios::out** in the **logToFile** method?

2. Write a test driver for the **Task** class to test whether its **public** methods work as intended.

5.7 CLASS DATA MEMBERS AND METHODS

So far we have seen data members and methods that belong to individual *objects*. For example, for the **Task** class of Section 5.6, the definitions

```
Task t1( "clean flotsam" );  // create a Task
Task t2( "purge jetsam" );   // create another
```

create two **Task** objects, *each* with its own data members **id**, **st**, and **ft**. C++ also supports members that belong *to the class as a whole* rather than to individual objects in the class. We call these **class members** as opposed to **object members**. The keyword **static** is used to create a *class* member.

EXAMPLE 5.7.1. The declaration

```
class Task {
public:
   ...
private:
   static unsigned n; // count of Task objects
   ...
};
```

shows the syntax. The **Task** class now contains a data member **n** that belongs to the class a whole; that is, there is *one* **unsigned** cell **n** for the entire class, not one **unsigned** cell **n** per **Task** object. Figure 5.7.1 illustrates.

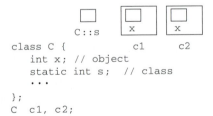

```
class C {
   int x; // object
   static int s;  // class
   ...
};
C  c1, c2;
```

FIGURE 5.7.1 Class versus object data member.

We might use **n** to keep track of how many **Task** objects currently exist. To do so, we could amend the parameterized constructor and the destructor as follows:

```
Task::Task( const char ID[ ] ) {
   strncpy( id, ID, MaxId );
   id[ MaxId ] = '\0';
   setST();
   ft = st; // so far, no duration
   n++;     // increment n, another Task created
}

Task::~Task() {
   logToFile(); // if client forgets
   n--;     // decrement n, another Task destroyed
}
```

Assuming that **static** data member **n** is initialized to zero, **n** would keep a running count of **Task** objects. ∎

A **static** *data member* may be *declared* inside the class declaration, as Example 5.7.1 shows. However, such a **static** data member still must be *defined*.

EXAMPLE 5.7.2. The code segment

```
class Task {
public:
   ...
private:
   static unsigned n; // count of Task objects
   ...
};

unsigned Task::n = 0; // define static data member
```

amends Example 5.7.1 by adding a *definition* for **static** data member **n**. A **static** data member declared inside the class declaration must be *defined outside all blocks*, as we show here. Note that the data member's name is **Task::n** and not **n**. Although we initialize **Task::n** to zero, this is not required. Any variable defined outside all blocks is initialized automatically to zero unless the programmer supplies a different initial value. ∎

A class also may have **static** methods.

EXAMPLE 5.7.3.   The declaration

```
class Task {
public:
   static unsigned getN() { return n; }
   ...
private:
   static unsigned n; // count of Task objects
   ...
};
```

now includes an inline definition for the **static** method **getN**. As Example 5.7.1 shows, an *object* method such as a constructor or the destructor may access a **static** data member such as **n**. As this example shows, a **static** method may access a **static** data member. The difference is that a **static** method may access *only* **static** members. Therefore, the code segment

```
class Task {
public:
   static unsigned getN() {
      setST();         //***** ERROR: not static!
      st = time( 0 );  //***** ERROR: not static!
      return n;        // ok, n is static
   }
   ...
private:
   static unsigned n; // count of Task objects
   ...
};
```

contains two errors. The **static** method **getN** may access only **static** members, whether data members or methods.

By the way, a **static** method need not be defined **inline**. To avoid the error, we could change the example to

```
class Task {
public:
   static unsigned getN(); // declaration
   ...
private:
   static unsigned n; // count of Task objects
   ...
};
unsigned Task::getN() { // definition
   return n;
}
```

Suppose that **c** is a class with a **static** data member **sVar** and a **static** method **sMeth**, both **public**:

```
class C {
public:
   static int  sVar;
   static void sMeth();
   ...
};
```

There are different ways to access the **static** members, through either **c** objects or *directly*.

EXAMPLE 5.7.4.   Given that **sVar** and **sMeth** are **static** and **public** members of **c**, the code segment

```
int main() {
   C c1;
   c1.sMeth(); // through an object
   C::sMeth(); // directly
   unsigned x = c1.sVar; // through an object
   unsigned y = C::sVar; // directly
   ...
}
```

shows the two different ways to access the **static** members. Of course, information hiding recommends against **public** data members. We make **sVar public** only to illustrate the syntax. ∎

Assuming that

- Object **c** belongs to class **c**.
- Method **om** is an object (i.e., non**static**) method in **c**.
- Method **cm** is a class (i.e., **static**) method in **c**.

the following table summarizes the differences:

Method Type	*Has Access To*	*Legal Invocations*
Object	Object and class members	**c.om()**
Class	Class members only	**C::cm()**, **c.cm()**

static Variables Defined Inside Methods

A local variable in a *method* can be **static**. In this case, the method has *one* underlying cell shared by *all* class objects when they invoke the method.

EXAMPLE 5.7.5. The code

```
class C {
public:
  void m();   // object method
private;
  int x;      // object data member
};
void C::m() {
  static int s = 0; //***** Caution: 1 copy for all objects
  cout << ++s << endl;
}
int main() {
  C c1, c2;
  c1.m();     // outputs 1
  c2.m();     // outputs 2
  c1.m();     // outputs 3
  return 0;
}
```

defines a **static** variable **s** inside method **m**'s body. Because **s** is defined inside a block, it has block scope and, therefore, is accessible only inside **m**, which increments **s** each time that it is called. Because **m** is a method, its **static** local variable is shared by *all* class objects. By contrast, each class object has its *own* copy of non**static** data member **x**. Every invocation of **m** accesses the *same* underlying cell for **s**. So, in **main**, the first invocation **c1.m()** increments **s** from 0 to 1. The invocation **c2.m()** increments **s** from 1 to 2. The second invocation **c1.m()** increments **s** from 2 to 3. ∎

EXERCISES

1. What is the difference between an *object data member* and a *class data member*?

2. Declare a class **c** with a **static** data member of type **int**.

3. Explain the error.

```
#include <iostream>
using namespace std;
class C {
public:
    void f() { cout << ++x << endl; }
private:
    static int x;
};
int main() {
  C c1;
  c1.f();
  return 0;
}
```

4. Explain the error.

```
class C {
public:
   static void s() { ++x; }
private:
   int x;
};
```

5. What is the output?

```
class Z {
public:
   void f() {
      static int s = 0;
      cout << ++s << endl;
   }
};
int main() {
   Z z1, z2;
   z1.f();
   z2.f();
   z1.f();
   return 0;
}
```

5.8 USING CLASS LIBRARIES

Object-oriented programmers not only create classes but also use classes already created. Such classes reside in a *class library*, the object-oriented analog of a *function library* such as C++'s math library. Some class libraries are furnished by C++. The input/output library, whose classes are declared in header files such as *iostream*, is an example. Other libraries come from vendors. For example, Microsoft provides the class library MFC (**M**icrosoft **F**oundation **C**lasses), and Borland provides the class library OWL (**O**bject **W**indow **L**ibrary). We call libraries such as MFC and OWL **outside libraries** to underscore that they do not belong officially to C++, although they provide C++ functionality.

The advantage of using a class library is that the programmer can reuse code already written rather than writing the code from scratch. The gain in productivity can be enormous. The disadvantage of using a class library is that the programmer must first learn the classes and their interfaces. This can be time consuming and frustrating, as class libraries tend to become big and complex. Nonetheless, the trend among C++ programmers is to make liberal use of the many outside libraries available. Indeed, the availability of so many outside class libraries makes C++ very attractive as an applications language.

Enabling a program to use an outside C++ class library typically involves two steps:

1. One or more header files must be **#include**d so that the library's class declarations are visible. The header file is also minimum documentation for the class's interface.

2. A binary file known as a *link library* must be linked into the program. The link library contains the implementation of the class's methods and global variables. Library authors provide details about how to link. Linking is generally automatic for a C++ compiler (e.g., Microsoft's Visual C++) associated with a class library (e.g., MFC) and appears to the user as part of the compilation process.

Figure 5.8.1 is a program that uses the utility class **CString** from MFC. The required header file is *afx.h* (*application framework*—the *x* does not stand for anything). The **CString** class handles character strings in an intuitive and robust manner. For example, the **CString** class automatically manages storage requirements for strings. The class also provides a variety of methods to create and manipulate strings. Classes such as **CString** illustrate the advantages of object-oriented programming.

```
#include <afx.h>
#include <iostream>
using namespace std;
int main() {
   // create two CStrings
   CString singer( " Ella   " );
   CString blower( "Miles Davis" );
   // trim white space from singer
   singer.TrimRight(); // " Ella"
   singer.TrimLeft();  // "Ella"
   // append a last name to singer
   singer += " Fitzgerald"; // "Ella Fitzgerald"
   // reverse the string
   singer.MakeReverse();    // "dlaregztiF allE"
   // reverse it back again
   singer.MakeReverse();    // "Ella Fitzgerald"
   // check for characters in a CString
   if ( singer.FindOneOf( "aZ" ) ) // true
     cout << "There's an 'a' or 'Z' in singer." << endl;
   // determine lexicographical order of CStrings
   if ( singer < blower ) // true
     cout << "The singer comes first!" << endl;
   else
     cout << "The blower comes first!" << endl;
   // change case for blower
   blower.MakeLower(); // "miles davis"
   return 0;
}
```

FIGURE 5.8.1 A program that uses the MFC class library.

The program begins by creating two **CString** objects, **singer** and **blower**. In each case, a **CString** convert constructor is used to convert a string constant into a **CString** object. Other constructors are available, including a default constructor. The definition

```
CString sleep( 'Z', 1000 );
```

uses a two-argument constructor to create a **CString** initialized to 1,000 **z**s.

The program invokes the **CString** methods **TrimRight** and **TrimLeft** to trim white space from **singer**, which is initialized to **" Ella "**. The next statement

```
singer += " Fitzgerald";
```

is intuitive, although we have not yet covered the technical details. Recall that **+=** is a C++ *operator*. C++ allows most operators, including **+=**, to be overloaded. Chapter 8 goes into the details. Our interest here is with the functionality. **CString** overloads **+=** to implement string concatenation (see Section 4.7). After the concatenation, **singer** is **Ella Fitzgerald**.

The method **MakeReverse** is used to reverse **singer** once and then back again. The documentation shows what the **CString** looks like in each step. **CString** has various methods for locating and extracting characters, including **FindOneOf**. We use this method to check whether **singer** contains an **a** or a **Z**.

CString overloads relational operators such as **<** so that these can be used intuitively in comparisons. We illustrate by checking whether **singer** lexicographically precedes **blower** (see Section 4.7).

The **CString** methods **MakeUpper** and **MakeLower** can be used to change **CString**s to all uppercase or lowercase characters, respectively. We illustrate with a call to **MakeLower**. **CString** has other useful methods, including many overloaded operators. If we were writing an application that required string handling, we would use a class such as this from an outside library instead of writing our own version. MFC has other utility classes as well (e.g., **CFile** and **CDate**) and many classes for doing Windows graphics programming. Learning to leverage the functionality provided in such libraries is part of becoming proficient in C++.

5.9 POINTERS TO OBJECTS AND THE INDIRECT SELECTION OPERATOR

The member operator **.** is used with an object or an object reference to access an object's members.

EXAMPLE 5.9.1.   The code segment

```
class C {
public:
  void m() { ... }
};
void f( C& ); // pass by reference
```

```
int main() {
   C c1;
   c1.m();    // object
   f( c1 );
   ...
}
void f( C& c ) {
   c.m();     // object reference
}
```

reviews the syntax of the member operator by showing it in use with the object **c1** and the object reference **c**. In both cases, the member operator is used to invoke the object's method **m**.   ■

The member operator may be used *only* with objects and object references. However, C++ also supports access to an object's members through a *pointer* (see Section 4.3) to the object. For pointer access, C++ provides the **indirect selection operator ->**. The indirect selection operator consists of the *minus sign* - followed by the *greater than sign* >.

EXAMPLE 5.9.2.   We amend Example 5.9.1

```
class C {
public:
  void m() { ... }
};
void f( C* ); // pass a pointer
int main() {
   C c1;
   c1.m();    // object
   f( &c1 ); // address of object
   ...
}
void f( C* p ) {
   p->m();   // pointer to C object
}
```

by passing **f** a *pointer* to **c1** rather than a reference to **c1**. We get a pointer to **c1** by applying the address operator **&** to **c1**. In **f**, the indirect selection operator occurs *between* the pointer **p** to the object (in this case, **c1**) and the member being accessed (in this case, method **m**). Because **f** receives a pointer to rather than a reference to **c1**, the member operator cannot be used with the pointer to invoke **m**:

```
void f( C* p ) {
   p.m();   //**** ERROR: p not an object or object reference
   p->m(); // correct: p a pointer to a C object
}
```

White space may not occur between the two symbols that make up the indirect selection operator, although white space can occur on either side of the operator:

```
void f( C* p ) {
    p->m();     // ok
    p -> m();   // ok
    p-> m();    // ok, though peculiar
    p ->m();    // ditto
    p- >m();    //***** ERROR: white space between - and >
}
```
∎

Pointers to objects typically are used in two contexts in C++. First, pointers to objects may be passed as arguments to functions or returned by functions. Example 5.9.2 illustrates this context by passing a pointer to **f**. Second, objects may be created dynamically (see Chapter 7) by using the **new** and **new[ ]** operators, which return a pointer to the dynamically created object or objects. This context is very important for C++ polymorphism and so we defer discussion of it until Chapter 7.

In forthcoming chapters, our examples involve a mix of objects, object references, and pointers to objects. In these examples, we discuss the reasons behind the mix. For now, our concern is limited to the syntax of the indirect selection operator. For accessing an object's members:

- The member operator **.** is used exclusively with *objects* and *object references*.

- The indirect selection operator **->** is used exclusively with *object pointers*.

EXERCISES

1. What is the error?

```
#include <iostream>
using namespace std;
class C {
public:
    void m() { cout << "C::m" << endl; }
};
void g( C* );
int main() {
    C c1;
    g( &c1 );
    ...
}
void g( C* p ) {
    p.m();
}
```

2. What is the error?

```
class C {
public:
  void m() {...}
};
int main() {
  C c1;
  C* p;
  p = &c1;
  p - >m();
  ...
}
```

3. Explain when the member operator **.** is used with objects.

4. Explain when the indirect selection operator **->** is used with objects.

C++ POSTSCRIPT

Two Ways to Create Classes: `class` and `struct`

Classes may be created using either of the keywords **class** or **struct**. If **class** is used, then all members default to **private**. If **struct** is used, then all members default to **public**.

EXAMPLE.   In the declaration

```
class C {
  int x;
  void m();
};
```

data member **x** and method **m** default to **private**. By contrast, in the declaration

```
struct C {
  int x;
  void m();
};
```

both default to **public**. Whichever keyword is used, objects of type **C** may be defined in the usual way:

```
C c1, c2, c_array[ 100 ];
```

EXAMPLE.   The declaration

```
class C {
    int x;  // private by default
public:
    void setX( int X ); // public
};
```

is equivalent to

```
struct C {
    void setX( int X ); // public by default
private:
    int x;
};
```

in that each declaration makes **x** a **private** data member and **m** a **public** method. ■

Our examples typically use **class** to emphasize the object-oriented principle of information hiding: a class's members default to **private** unless they are explicitly selected as part of its **public** interface.

COMMON PROGRAMMING ERRORS

1. It is an error to omit the closing semicolon in a class declaration:

```
class C {
...
}  //***** ERROR: no semicolon
```

The correct syntax is

```
class C {
...
};
```

2. The declaration for class **C** must occur *before* objects of type **C** are defined:

```
C c1, c2; //***** ERROR: class C not yet declared
class C {
...
}; // must go before definitions of c1 and c2
```

For this reason, it is common to put class declarations in header files that can be **#include**d wherever needed:

```
#include "classDecs.h" // including one for class C
C c1, c2; // ok
```

3. It is an error to access a non**public** class member in a function that is neither a method nor a **friend**:

```
class C {
public:
  void m() {...}
private:
  int x;
};
int main() {
   C c1;
   c1.m();    // ok, m is public in C
   c1.x = 3; //***** ERROR: x is private in C
   ...
}
```

4. It is an error to treat a class *method* as if it were a top-level function:

```
class C {
public:
  void m() {...}
...
};
int main() {
   C c1;
   m();     //***** ERROR: m is a method
   c1.m(); // ok
   ...
}
```

5. It is an error to omit the class member operator when accessing an object's members:

```
class C {
public:
  void m() {...}
...
};
int main() {
   C c1;
   c1m();   //***** ERROR: member operator missing
   c1.m(); // ok
   ...
}
```

6. It is an error to use the keyword **inline** outside a class declaration. If an **inline** method is to be *defined* outside the class declaration, then the keyword **inline** is used *only in the declaration*:

```
class C {
public:
  inline void m(); // declaration is ok
  ...
};
// definition of C::m
inline void C::m() { //***** ERROR: inline occurs in
  ...                 //***** declaration, not definition
}
```

7. If a class has no constructors, it is an error to assume that object members are initialized when the object is defined:

```
class C {
public:
  char* getS() { return s; }
private:
  char s[ 10 ];
};
int main() {
  C c1;
  cout << c1.getS() //***** Caution--s not a string!
       << endl;
  ...
}
```

An access violation is likely in this example. A default constructor

```
class C {
public:
  char* getS() { return s; }
  C() { s[ 0 ] = '\0'; } // s is a string
private:
  char s[ 10 ];
};
int main() {
  C c1;
  cout << c1.getS() << endl; // ok
  ...
}
```

could be used to ensure that **c1**'s member **s** is a string.

8. It is an error to show a return value, even **void**, for a constructor in its declaration or definition:

```
class C {
public:
    void C();    //***** ERROR: no return value allowed
    int C( C& ); //***** ERROR: no return value allowed
};
void C::C() { //***** ERROR: no return value allowed
    ...
}
```

The correct syntax is

```
class C {
public:
    C();
    C( C& );
};
C::C() {
    ...
}
```

9. It is an error to show a return value, even **void**, for a destructor in its declaration or definition:

```
class C {
public:
    void ~C();   //***** ERROR: no return value allowed!
};
void C::~C() { //***** ERROR: no return value allowed!
    ...
}
```

The correct syntax is

```
class C {
public:
    ~C();
};
C::~C() {
    ...
}
```

10. It is illegal for a destructor to have an argument:

```
class C {
public:
    ~C( int );   //***** ERROR: no args allowed
};
C::~C( int ) { //***** ERROR: no args allowed
    ...
}
```

The correct syntax is

```
class C {
public:
    ~C();
    ...
};
```

Because a destructor takes no arguments, there can be only one destructor per class. Constructors, by contrast, can be many in number because arguments can be used to give each a distinct signature.

11. It is an error for a class **C** constructor to have a single argument of type **C**:

```
class C {
public:
    C( C );        //***** ERROR: single arg can't be a C
    C( C, int ); // ok, two args
    ...
};
```

The *copy* constructor does take one argument, but it is a *reference*:

```
class C {
public:
    C( C& ); // ok
    ...
};
```

12. It is an error to set a **const** data member's value through an assignment operation, even in a constructor:

```
class C {
public:
    C() { c = 0; } //***** ERROR: c is const!
private:
    const int c; // const data member
};
```

A **const** member must be initialized in a constructor's header:

```
class C {
public:
    C() : c( 0 ) { } // ok
private:
    const int c; // const data member
};
```

13. It is an error to invoke an *object method* as if it were a *class method*, that is, a **static** method:

```
class C {
public:
   void m() {...}         // nonstatic: object method
   static void s() {...} // static: class method
   ...
};
int main() {
   C c1;
   c1.m();   // ok
   c1.s();   // ok
   C::s();   // ok, s is static
   C::m();   //***** ERROR: m is not static
   ...
}
```

14. If a **static** data member is declared inside the class's declaration, it is an error not to define the **static** data member outside all blocks:

```
class C {
   static int x; // declared
   ...
};
int main() {
   int C::x; //***** ERROR: defined inside a block!
   ...
}
```

The correct definition is

```
class C {
public:
   static int x; // declared
   ...
};
int C::x;   // define static data member
int main() {
   ...
}
```

Even if **x** were **private**, it would be defined the same way.

15. It is an error to use the member operator **.** with a *pointer* to an object. The code segment

```
class C {
public:
   void m() {...}
};
```

```
int main() {
  C c1;      // define a C object
  C* p;      // define a pointer to a C object
  p = &c1; // p points to c1
  p.m();     //***** ERROR: member operator illegal!
  c1.m();  // ok, c1 is an object
  ...
}
```

illustrates. The member operator may be used only with an *object* or an *object refer-ence*. The indirect selection operator `->` is used with pointers to objects to access their members. The preceding error can be corrected by writing

```
p->m(); // ok, p a pointer to an object
```

16. It is an error to use the indirect selection operator with a class object or object reference. The code segment

```
class C {
public:
  void m() {...}
};
int main() {
  C c1;
  c1->m(); //***** ERROR: c1 is an object, not a pointer
  ...
}
void f( C& r ) {
  r->m(); //***** ERROR: r is a reference, not a pointer
}
```

illustrates the error with object `c1` and object reference `r`. In both cases, the member operator `.` should be used:

```
class C {
public:
  void m() {...}
};
int main() {
  C c1;
  c1.m(); // ok
  ...
}
void f( C& r ) {
  r.m(); // ok
}
```

17. It is an error to have white space between the two symbols that make up the indirect selection operator:

```
class C {
public:
   void m() {...}
};
int main() {
  C c1;     // define a C object
  C* p;     // define a pointer to a C object
  p = &c1; // p points to c1
  p->m();    // ok
  p -> m();  // ok
  p-> m();   // ok
  p ->m();   // ok
  p- >m();   //***** ERROR: white space between - and >
  ...
}
```

PROGRAMMING EXERCISES

5.1. Implement a `Car` class that includes data members to represent a car's make (e.g., Honda), model (e.g., Civic), production year, and price. The class interface includes methods that provide appropriate access to the data members (e.g., a method to set the car's model or to get its price). In addition, the class should have a method

```
void compare( Car& )
```

that compares a `Car` against another using whatever criteria seem appropriate. The `compare` method prints a short report of its comparison.

5.2. Implement a class to represent an International Standard Book Number, or ISBN for short (see Programming Exercise 4.12). The class should have methods to set and get the `ISBN` as a string and to check whether the `ISBN` is valid.

5.3. Implement a `Book` class that represents pertinent information about a book, including the book's title, author, publisher, city and date of publication, and price. The class should include the data member

```
ISBN isbnNum;
```

where `ISBN` is the class implemented in Programming Exercise 5.2.

5.4. Implement a `Calendar` class. The public interface consists of methods that enable the user to

- Specify a start year such as 1776 or 1900.
- Specify a duration such as 1 year or 100 years.
- Specify generic holidays such as Tuesdays.

- Specify specific holidays such as the third Thursday in November.

- Specify a month-year such as July-1776, which results in a display of the calendar for the specified month-year.

Holidays should be marked so that they can be readily recognized as such whenever the calendar for a month-year is displayed.

5.5. Implement a `CollegeStudent` class with appropriate data members such as `name`, `year`, `expectedGrad`, `major`, `minor`, `GPA`, `coursesAndGrades`, `maritalStatus`, and the like. The class should have at least a half-dozen methods in its public interface. For example, there should be a method to compute `GPA` from `coursesAndGrades` and to determine whether the `GPA` merits honors or probation. There also should be methods to display a `CollegeStudent`'s current course load and to print remaining required courses.

5.6. Implement a `Deck` class that represents a deck of 52 cards. The public interface should include methods to shuffle, deal, display hands, do pairwise comparisons of cards (e.g., a Queen beats a Jack), and the like. To simulate shuffling, you can use a random number generator such as the library function `rand`.

5.7. Implement a `Profession` class with data members such as `name`, `title`, `credentials`, `education`, `avgIncome`, and the like. The public interface should include methods that compare `Profession`s across the data members. The class should have at least a dozen data members and a dozen methods.

5.8. A **queue** is a list of zero or more elements. An element is added to a queue at its **rear**; an element is removed from a queue at its **front**. If a queue is **empty**, a removal operation is illegal. If a queue is **full**, then an add operation is illegal. Implement a `Queue` class for character strings.

5.9. A **deque** is a list of zero or more elements with insertions and deletions at either end, its front or its rear. Implement a `Deque` class whose elements are character strings.

5.10. A **semaphore** is a mechanism widely used in computer systems to enforce synchronization constraints on shared resources. For example, a semaphore might be used to ensure that two processes cannot use a printer at the same time. The semaphore mechanism first grants exclusive access to one process and then to the other so that the printer does not receive a garbled mix from the two processes. Implement a `Semaphore` class that enforces synchronization on files so that a process is ensured exclusive access to a file. The public interface consists of methods that *set* a semaphore for a specified file, that *release* a semaphore protecting a specified file, and that *test* whether a semaphore is currently protecting a specified file.

5.11. Implement an interactive `Calculator` class that accepts as input an arithmetic expression such as

```
25 / 5 + 4
```

and then evaluates the expression, printing the value. In this example, the output would be

9

There should be methods to validate the input expression. For example, if the user inputs

```
25 / 5 +
```

then the output should be an error message such as

```
ERROR: operator-operand imbalance.
```

5.12. Implement a `Set` class, where a **set** is an unordered collection of zero or more elements with no duplicates. For this exercise, the elements should be `int`s. The public interface consists of methods to

- Create a `Set`.
- Add a new element to a `Set`.
- Remove an element from a `Set`.
- Enumerate the elements in the `Set`.
- Compute the **intersection** of two `Set`s `S1` and `S2`, that is, the set of elements that belong both to `S1` and to `S2`.
- Compute the **union** of two `Set`s `S1` and `S2`, that is, the set of elements that belong to `S1` or to `S2` or to both.
- Compute the **difference** of two `Set`s `S1` and `S2`, that is, the set of elements that belong to `S1` but not to `S2`.

5.13. Implement a `Bag` class. A **bag** is like a set except that a bag may have duplicates. For this exercise, the bag's elements should be `int`s. The public interface should support the counterpart operations given in Programming Exercise 5.12.

5.14. Create a `Spaceship` class suitable for simulation. One of the constructors should allow the user to specify the `Spaceship`'s initial position in 3-dimensional space, its trajectory, its velocity, its rate of acceleration, and its target, which is another `Spaceship`. The simulation should track a `Spaceship`'s movement every clock tick (e.g., every second), printing such relevant data as the `Spaceship`'s identity, its trajectory, and so forth. If you have access to a graphics package, add graphics to the simulation.

5.15. Implement a `Database` class where a `Database` is a collection of *tables*, which in turn are made up of *rows* and *columns*. For example, the employee table

Employee ID	Last Name	Department	Boss
111-11-1234	Cruz	ACC	Werdel
213-44-5649	Johnstone	MIS	Michaels
321-88-7895	Elders	FIN	Bierski

has three records, each of which has four fields (Employee ID, Last Name, Department, and Boss). The public interface should allow a user to

- Create a table.

- Change a table's structure by adding or removing fields.

- Delete a table.

- Add records to a table.

- Remove records from a table.

- Retrieve information from one or more tables at a time using a suitable query language.

5.16. Implement a `BankTransaction` class that allows the user to

- Open an account.

- Close an account.

- Add funds to an already open account.

- Remove funds from an already open account.

- Transfer funds from one open account to another.

- Request a report on one or more open accounts.

There should be no upper bound on the number of accounts that a user may open. The class also should contain a method that automatically issues a warning if an account is overdrawn.

5.17. Introduce appropriate classes to simulate the behavior of a **local area network**, hereafter **LAN**. The network consists of **nodes**, which may be devices such as personal computers, workstations, FAX machines, telecommunications switches, and so forth. A LAN's principal job is to support data communications among its nodes. The user of the simulation should, at a minimum, be able to

- Enumerate the nodes currently on the LAN.

- Add a new node to the LAN.

- Remove a node from the LAN.

- Configure a LAN by giving it, for example, a **star** or a **bus** topology.

- Specify packet size, which is the size in bytes of message that goes from one node to another.

- Send a packet from one specified node to another.

- Broadcast a packet from one node to all others.

- Track LAN statistics such as the average time it takes a packet to reach the most distant node on the LAN.

5.18. Implement a **Schedule** class that produces a conflict-free, maximum-size subset of activities given an input set of activities together with the start and finish time for each activity. The conflict-free subset, together with the start and finish times, is a schedule. The schedule is conflict-free because, given any two distinct activities, one finishes before the other starts. For example, given the input set

Activity	Start Time	Finish Time
A1	6	10
A2	1	5
A3	1	6
A4	9	12
A5	5	7
A6	6	14
A7	3	7
A8	10	14
A9	13	16

an optimal **Schedule** would be

Activity	Start Time	Finish Time
A2	1	5
A5	5	7
A4	9	12
A9	13	16

Given the input set, it is impossible to produce a **Schedule** of five or more non-conflicting activities. The public interface should include methods for creating, destroying, revising, and combining **Schedule**s. There also should be a method that explains exactly why the produced **Schedule** cannot be expanded to include any more of the input activities. *Hint*: Iterate through the activities, picking in each iteration the activity with the minimal finish time that does not conflict with any previously selected activity for the **Schedule**.

5.19. Implement a **SymbolTable** class. A **symbol table** lists all identifiers (e.g., function and variable names) in a program's source code together with pertinent information such as the identifier's data type, its role within the program (e.g., whether the identifier is a function name, variable name, or a label), and its position in a source code file (e.g., a line number designating the source code line in which the identifier occurs). The public interface should allow the user to specify one or more source files from which the **SymbolTable** is to be built. There also should be methods for displaying and editing a **SymbolTable**.

5.20. Implement a `RegExp` class to represent **regular expressions**, which are used in pattern matching. A regular expression is a character string that consists of ordinary and special characters. For example, the regular expression

    `aRgT`

matches only other strings with exactly these four characters in this order. Regular expressions are more interesting and useful when they include special characters such as these:

Special Character	What It Matches
`.`	Any character.
`[<list>]`	Any character in `list`. For instance,
	`[aBc]` matches **a**, **B**, or **c**.
`[^<list>]`	Any character not in `list`.
`[<X>-<Y>]`	Any character in range **X** to **Y**. For instance,
	`[a-c]` matches **a**, **b**, or **c**.
`*`	Zero or more occurrences of the preceding `RegExp`.
	For instance, `ab*` matches **ab**, **abb**, **abbb**, etc.

The class's interface should include methods to create and destroy `RegExp`s as well as to match `RegExp`s against other strings.

5.21. Implement a `Date` class to represent a date such as *Friday, December 31, 1999*. The class should have constructors to set a `Date` to the current date or to a user specified `Date`; to move forward n `Date`s, where n is 1, 2, . . . ; to move backward n `Date`s, where n is 1, 2, . . . ; to print a `Date` as a whole or a part (e.g., only the month); and to print all the dates from one `Date` (e.g., *Thursday, December 2, 1999*) to another (e.g., *Friday, December 31, 1999*).

5.22. Implement an `Employee` class. The class should restrict construction to `Employee`s with an identifier such as a social security number. The class should represent `Employee` properties or features such as *last name, first name, marital status, home address, home phone number, salary, office, office phone number, title(s), current projects*, and the like. The class interface should include methods to access and, where appropriate, to change `Employee` properties.

5.23. Implement a `Product` class. The class should allow construction of `Product`s with only a name; with a name and price; and with a name, price, and shelf life in days. A `Product` also has a manufacturer; a description of no more than n words ($n = 1, 2, . . .$); flags to signal whether the `Product` is fragile or edible; and an availability date, which indicates when the `Product` will first be available for consumer purchase. Add at least three other features to the class implementation. The class interface should include methods to access the implementation.

5.24. Implement a `Pair` class for `int`egers:

```
class Pair {
public:
    // appropriate methods
private:
    int first;
    int second;
};
```

The class interface should include methods to create `Pair`s, to set and to get each element in the `Pair`, and to swap the elements so that, after the swap, the first element becomes the second, and the second becomes the first.

CHAPTER

6

INHERITANCE

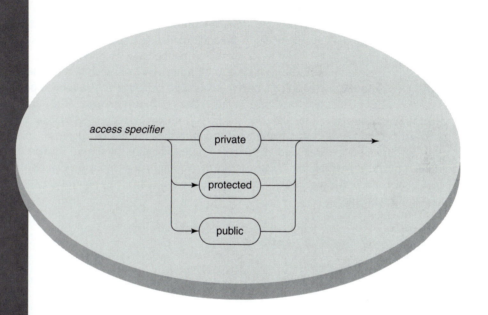

In C++, we can build a new class by deriving the new class from an already existing class. The mechanism for this derivation is **inheritance**, and the derived class is said to be **inherited** from the original class. In this chapter, we introduce inheritance, and in the remainder of the book, we show how inheritance and virtual methods (the topic of Chapter 7) form the heart of object-oriented programming and give it its power and expressiveness.

6.1 INTRODUCTION

Suppose that a class **Student** has already been designed and implemented and that a new application needs a class **GradStudent**. Since a **GradStudent** is a **Student**, rather than build the class **GradStudent** from scratch, we can add to the class **Student** whatever data and methods it needs to become a **GradStudent**. For example, class **GradStudent** might need additional data members to describe particular departmental exams that only graduate students must take and pass, as well as methods to store and retrieve this data. The resulting class **GradStudent** is said to be **inherited** from the class **Student**. The new class **GradStudent** is called a **derived class** or a **subclass** of **Student**. The original class **Student** is called the **base class** or **superclass** of **GradStudent**. The derived class **GradStudent** inherits all the data and methods from the existing class **Student** (except for constructors, the destructor, and an overload of the assignment operator). A derived class thus has all of the data and methods (with the exceptions noted) of its base class, in addition to added data and methods. Such a derivation is depicted as in Figure 6.1.1. As shown, the base class is placed above the derived class, and an arrow points from the derived class to the base class.

FIGURE 6.1.1 Class **GradStudent** is derived from class **Student**.

Inheritance promotes code reuse because the code in the base class is inherited by the subclass and thus need not be rewritten. By reusing code, we reduce the amount of code to be created. Furthermore, if the code inherited from the base class is correct, it will also be correct in the derived class. If the code were rewritten, bugs might inadvertently be introduced. For example, when class **GradStudent** is inherited from class **Student**, the code in **Student** need not be rewritten for the **GradStudent** class. Furthermore, assuming that the code for the **Student** class is correct, the part of **GradStudent** inherited from **Student** will be correct in the **GradStudent** class.

Inheritance also provides a mechanism to express the natural relationships among the components of a program. For example, a **GradStudent** *is a* **Student** and this *is a* relationship is precisely mirrored in the code through the inheritance mechanism.

Inheritance is required for *polymorphism* in which the particular method to invoke depends on the class to which the object belongs, but the class to which the object belongs is not known until the program is executing. This very powerful technique is thoroughly examined in Chapter 7.

Besides the *is a* relationship present in inheritance (e.g., a **GradStudent** *is a* **Student**), we can think of a derived class as a specialized version of the base class. For example, in Figure 6.1.2, the base class **Pen** models a pen that can draw in black ink. The derived class **CPen** models a pen that can draw in several colors, including black. A **CPen** is a **Pen** (both can draw). Furthermore, a **CPen** is a specialized version of **Pen**.

FIGURE 6.1.2 Class **CPen** is derived from class **Pen**.

A derived class can itself serve as a base class for another class. For example, in Figure 6.1.3 class **Car** is derived from class **Vehicle**, and class **Coupe**, in turn, is derived from class **Car**. We call a relationship such as that in Figure 6.1.3 a **class hierarchy**. Notice that a **Coupe** *is a* **Car**, which, in turn, *is a* **Vehicle**. Notice also that as we move from the top (class **Vehicle**) to the bottom (class **Coupe**), each class is a specialized version of its base class.

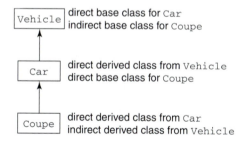

FIGURE 6.1.3 A class hierarchy.

C++ also supports **multiple inheritance**, in which a derived class can have multiple base classes. We defer the discussion to the C++ Postscript.

Classes directly support the creation of abstract data types. Inheritance extends that support by promoting the derivation of new abstract data types from already existing ones. Object-oriented languages thus provide programmers with the tools for programming with abstract data types. Graphics packages, such as *Windows* and *Motif*, illustrate the point. In *Motif*, for example, there is an extended class hierarchy in which each class represents an abstract data type such as windows, fonts, and geometrical drawings. The user knows only the *public interface* to such classes, where such an interface comprises the methods that are used to create, manipulate, and destroy instances of an abstract data type. Implementation details are hidden from the user, who is all the better off by being spared the very details that cause programming tedium and error. In effect, a package such as *Motif* is a library of abstract data types presented as an object-oriented graphics toolkit.

EXERCISES

1. Draw a class hierarchy in which a base class has multiple derived classes.

2. Explain the relationship among the terms *superclass*, *subclass*, *base class*, and *derived class*.

3. Give examples of data members and methods that might be added when a class **Employee** is derived from the class **Person**. (**Person** contains methods for entering and retrieving information such as name, address, city, and state.)

4. Show a class hierarchy that might be used to track customers and accounts at a bank.

6.2 BASIC CONCEPTS AND SYNTAX

To derive class **D** from class **BC**, we write

```
// BC is the base class; D is the derived class
class D : public BC {
   ...
};
```

Except for

```
: public BC
```

the preceding declaration looks like an ordinary class declaration. The keyword **public** indicates that the derivation is public, and **BC** indicates that class **D** is derived from class **BC**. In public inheritance, the **public** members in the base class are **public** in the derived class. (The C++ Postscript section discusses the other types of inheritance, in which the keyword **public** is replaced by either **private** or **protected**.)

EXAMPLE 6.2.1.   The code segment declares a class **Pen**

```
class Pen {
public:
   void set_status( int );
   void set_location( int, int );
private:
   int x;
   int y;
   int status;
};
```

If **p** is an object of type **Pen**, the statement

```
p.set_location( x, y );
```

positions **p** at the location whose coordinates are (**x,y**). The statement

```
p.set_status( 1 );
```

turns the ink in the **Pen** on, and the statement

```
p.set_status( 0 );
```

turns the ink in the **Pen** off.

    Now suppose that our hardware is upgraded so that we have a colored pen. Rather than declare a brand new class to describe the colored pen, we can derive a colored pen class from the pen class:

```
class CPen : public Pen {
public:
    void set_color( int );
private:
    int color;
};
```

The class **CPen** inherits all of the data and methods from the class **Pen** (see Figure 6.2.1). The declaration of class **CPen** adds the data member **color** and the method **set_color**. Colors are coded as integers, so when the method **set_color** is invoked and a value is passed to a **CPen** object, the member **color** is set to this value.

    Because of the keyword **public** in the line

```
class CPen : public Pen {
```

the methods **set_status** and **set_location**, which are **public** in **Pen**, are also **public** in **CPen** and so can be invoked on an object of type **CPen** anywhere in the program. ∎

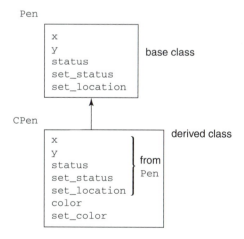

FIGURE 6.2.1 Deriving one class from another.

`private` Members in Inheritance

Each **private** member in a base class is visible only in the base class. In particular, a **private** base class member is *not* visible in a derived class. A **private** base class member *is* inherited by the derived class, but it is not visible in the derived class. In Example 6.2.1, data members **x**, **y**, and **status** are inherited by **CPen** from **Pen** even though they are *not* visible in **CPen**. Whenever an object of type **CPen** is created, storage for **x**, **y**, and **status** is allocated. Although a **private** base class member may not be directly accessed in a derived class, it might be indirectly accessed through a derived method as the following example shows.

EXAMPLE 6.2.2.   Given the class declarations

```
class Point {
public:
   void set_x( int x1 ) { x = x1; }
   void set_y( int y1 ) { y = y1; }
   int get_x() { return x; }
   int get_y() { return y; }
private:
   int x;
   int y;
};

class Intense_point : public Point {
public:
   void set_intensity( int i ) { intensity = i; }
   int get_intensity() { return intensity; }
private:
   int intensity;
};
```

the members of the derived class **Intense_point** are

Member	Access Status in Intense_point	How Obtained
x	Not accessible	From class **Point**
y	Not accessible	From class **Point**
set_x	public	From class **Point**
set_y	public	From class **Point**
get_x	public	From class **Point**
get_y	public	From class **Point**
intensity	private	Added by class **Intense_point**
set_intensity	public	Added by class **Intense_point**
get_intensity	public	Added by class **Intense_point**

Class **Intense_point** inherits data members **x** and **y**, which are visible only in class **Point**. Nevertheless, class **Intense_point** can indirectly access these data members through the methods **set_x**, **set_y**, **get_x**, and **get_y**, which *are* visible in **Intense_point**.   ■

Name Hiding

If a derived class adds a data member with the same name as a data member in the base class, the local data member **hides** the inherited data member.

EXAMPLE 6.2.3.   In the code segment

```
class B { // base class
public:
   int x;   // B::x
};

class D : public B { // derived class
public:
   int x;   // ***** DANGER: hides B::x
};

int main() {
   D d1;
   d1.x = 999;   // D::x, not B::x
   d1.B::x = 4; // ok -- but clumsy!
   ...
}
```

class **D** inherits **x** from **B**. However, **D** also has a local data member named **x**, which means that the local data member hides the inherited data member in the sense that **B::x** is not in class **D**'s scope. The only way to access **B::x** in **D** is by using the scope resolution operator, as in the second assignment statement.   ■

Similarly, if a derived class adds a method with the same name in the base class, the added method hides the base class's method.

EXAMPLE 6.2.4.   In the code segment

```
class B { // base class
public:
   void h( float ); // B::h
};

class D : public B { // derived class
public:
   void h( char [ ] );   // ***** DANGER: hides B::h
};
```

```
int main() {
   D d1;
   d1.h( "Boffo!" ); // D::h, not B::h
   d1.h( 707.7 ); // ***** ERROR: D::h hides B::h
   d1.B::h( 707.7 ); // OK: invokes B::h
   ...
}
```

The error occurs because method **D::h** expects a **char** **[ ]** argument rather than a **float** argument. The inherited **B::h**, which does expect a **char** **[ ]** argument, is hidden in **D** by **D::h** and so must be invoked with the scope resolution operator. ■

Indirect Inheritance

Data members and methods may traverse several inheritance links as they are included from a base to a derived class. For example, suppose that **B** is **D**'s base class and that **D** is **X**'s base class (see Figure 6.2.2). In this case, **X** inherits **D**'s data members and methods—including whatever data members or methods **D** inherits from **B**. Inheritance thus may be either direct (to a derived class from a direct base class) or indirect (to a derived class from an indirect base class).

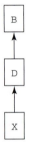

FIGURE 6.2.2 Indirect inheritance.

EXAMPLE 6.2.5.   In the code segment

```
// direct base class for Cat,
// indirect base class for HouseCat
class Animal {
public:
   char   speciesInLatin[ 100 ];
   float lifeExpectancy;
   bool   warmBlooded_P;
};
```

```
// direct derived class from Animal,
// direct base class for HouseCat
class Cat : public Animal {
public:
   char   range[ 100 ][ 100 ];
   float favoritePrey[ 100 ][ 100 ];
};

// indirect derived class from Animal,
// direct derived class from Cat
class HouseCat : public Cat {
public:
   char toys[ 10000 ][ 100 ];
   char catPsychiatrist[ 50 ];
   char catDentist[ 50 ];
   char catDoctor[ 50 ];
   char apparentOwner[ 50 ];
};
```

HouseCat has 10 data members: five are added, two are inherited directly from **Cat**, and three are inherited indirectly from **Animal** by way of **Cat**. The inherited data members remain **public** in **HouseCat**. ∎

EXERCISES

1. In the code segment

```
class A {
   int x;
};
class B : public A {
   int y;
};
B b1;
```

   how many data members does **b1** have?

2. Explain the error.

```
class A {
private:
   int x;
};
class B : public A {
public:
   void f() { y = x; }
private:
   int y;
};
```

3. Draw an inheritance hierarchy in which **P** has a direct inheritance link to base class **Q** and an indirect inheritance link to base class **R**.

4. Draw a class hierarchy that is at least five deep. Label each base class with its direct and indirect derived classes, and label each derived class with its direct and indirect base classes.

6.3 SAMPLE APPLICATION: TRACKING FILMS

Problem

Develop an inheritance hierarchy to track films, including specialized films such as foreign films and directors' cuts (versions updated by the director after the initial release). Since every film has a title, director, time, and quality (0 to 4 stars), first implement a base class **Film** with data members to hold the common information, methods to store information in the data members, and a method to output the data.

Next derive a class **DirectorCut** from **Film**. Add data members to hold the revised time and the changes, methods to store the added information in the data members, and a method to output the data.

Finally derive a class **ForeignFilm** from **Film**. Add a data member to hold the language, a method to store the language in the data member, and a method to output the data.

Sample Output

The output of the **main** function in Figure 6.3.1 is

```
Film--
Title: Rear Window
Director: Alfred Hitchcock
Time: 112 mins
Quality: ****

DirectorCut--
Title: Jail Bait
Director: Ed Wood
Time: 70 mins
Quality: **
Revised time: 72 mins
Changes: Extra footage not in original is included

ForeignFilm--
Title: Jules and Jim
Director: Francois Truffaut
Time: 104 mins
Quality: ****
Language: French
```

```
int main() {
   Film f;
   f.store_title( "Rear Window" );
   f.store_director( "Alfred Hitchcock" );
   f.store_time( 112 );
   f.store_quality( 4 );
   cout << "Film--" << endl;
   f.output();
   cout << endl;

   DirectorCut d;
   d.store_title( "Jail Bait" );
   d.store_director( "Ed Wood" );
   d.store_time( 70 );
   d.store_quality( 2 );
   d.store_rev_time( 72 );
   d.store_changes( "Extra footage not in original is included" );
   cout << "DirectorCut--" << endl;
   d.output();
   cout << endl;

   ForeignFilm ff;
   ff.store_title( "Jules and Jim" );
   ff.store_director( "Francois Truffaut" );
   ff.store_time( 104 );
   ff.store_quality( 4 );
   ff.store_language( "French" );
   cout << "ForeignFilm--" << endl;
   ff.output();

   return 0;
}
```

FIGURE 6.3.1 A test client for the **Film–DirectorCut–ForeignFilm** hierarchy.

Solution

Class **Film** should have four **private** data members:

Data Member	Type	Purpose
title	Array of **char**	Hold a title
director	Array of **char**	Hold a director
time	int	Hold a time in minutes
quality	int	0 stars (bad) to 4 stars (tops)

Class **Film** should have four **public** methods, corresponding to the four data members, to copy data passed into the data members. For example, method **store_title** should have a parameter of type **const** array of **char** that copies the value passed into data member **title**. Class **Film** should also have a method **output** that outputs the values of the four data members.

Since class **DirectorCut** is derived from class **Film**, **DirectorCut** inherits **Film**'s data members and methods. We will add two **private** data members to **DirectorCut** to hold the revised time and changes and add two **public** methods, corresponding to the two data members, to copy data passed into the data members. For example, method **store_rev_time** copies the revised time into data member **rev_time**. Class **Director-Cut** will have its own method **output** that outputs the values of the six data members—four inherited from **Film** and two that were added. **DirectorCut**'s method **output** will hide **Film**'s method **output** because they have the same name.

Similarly, class **ForeignFilm** is derived from class **Film** and so inherits **Film**'s data members and methods. We will add a **private** data member to **ForeignFilm** to hold the film's language and a **public** method to copy data passed into the data member. Class **ForeignFilm** will also have its own method **output** that outputs the values of its data members.

C++ Implementation

```
#include <iostream>
#include <cstring>
using namespace std;
const int asize = 512;

class Film {
public:
    void store_title( const char[ ] );
    void store_director( const char[ ] );
    void store_time( int );
    void store_quality( int );
    void output();
private:
    char title[ asize ];
    char director[ asize ];
    int time; // in minutes
    int quality; // 0 (bad) to 4 (tops)
};

void Film::store_title( const char t[ ] ) {
    strcpy( title, t );
}

void Film::store_director( const char d[ ] ) {
    strcpy( director, d );
}
```

```cpp
void Film::store_time( int t ) {
   time = t;
}

void Film::store_quality( int q ) {
   quality = q;
}

void Film::output() {
   cout << "Title: " << title << endl;
   cout << "Director: " << director << endl;
   cout << "Time: " << time << " mins" << endl;
   cout << "Quality: ";
   for ( int i = 0; i < quality; i++ )
      cout << '*';
   cout << endl;
}

class DirectorCut : public Film {
public:
   void store_rev_time( int );
   void store_changes( const char [ ] );
   void output();
private:
   int rev_time;
   char changes[ asize ];
};

void DirectorCut::store_rev_time( int t ) {
   rev_time = t;
}

void DirectorCut::store_changes( const char s[ ] ) {
   strcpy( changes, s );
}

void DirectorCut::output() {
   Film::output();
   cout << "Revised time: " << rev_time << " mins" << endl;
   cout << "Changes: " << changes << endl;
}

class ForeignFilm : public Film {
public:
   void store_language( const char [ ] );
   void output();
private:
   char language[ asize ];
};
```

```
void ForeignFilm::store_language( const char l[ ] ) {
   strcpy( language, l );
}

void ForeignFilm::output() {
   Film::output();
   cout << "Language: " << language << endl;
}
```

Discussion

The implementation begins by defining the constant used as an array size

```
const int asize = 512;
```

In all classes, **asize** is used as the size of a **char** array.

Class **Film** has four **private** data members and four **public** methods, corresponding to the data members, to copy data passed into the data members. Strings are copied using **strcpy**, for example,

```
void Film::store_title( const char t[ ] ) {
   strcpy( title, t );
}
```

and **int** values are copied using the assignment operator, for example,

```
void Film::store_time( int t ) {
   time = t;
}
```

Method **output** prints the title, director, time, and quality (expressed as a number of asterisks), each suitably annotated

```
void Film::output() {
   cout << "Title: " << title << endl;
   cout << "Director: " << director << endl;
   cout << "Time: " << time << " mins" << endl;
   cout << "Quality: ";
   for ( int i = 0; i < quality; i++ )
      cout << '*';
   cout << endl;
}
```

Class **DirectorCut** is publicly derived from **Film**

```
class DirectorCut : public Film {
   ...
};
```

and so inherits **Film**'s data members and methods. Since the methods **store_title**, **store_director**, **store_time**, and **store_quality** are **public** in **Film**, they are also **public** in **DirectorCut**. **Film**'s **private** members, **title**, **director**, **time**, and **quality** are visible *only* in **Film**; in particular, they are *not* visible in **DirectorCut**. However, these data members can be indirectly accessed through the **public** methods **store_title**, **store_director**, **store_time**, and **store_quality**.

DirectorCut adds two **private** data members, **rev_time** and **changes**, and two **public** methods, corresponding to these data members, to copy data passed into the data members.

Like the base class **Film**, **DirectorCut** has a method named **output**. **Director-Cut**'s **output** thus hides **Film**'s **output**. In **DirectorCut**'s **output**, we first invoke **Film**'s **output**

```
Film::output();
```

to output the title, director, time, and quality. We could *not* write

```
cout << "Title: " << title << endl;
```

because **title** is not visible in **DirectorCut**. Method **output** concludes by writing the revised time and the changes.

We omit a detailed discussion of class **ForeignFilm** because it is implemented similarly to **DirectorCut**.

Program Development

One customary reason to use a class hierarchy is to provide a common interface. In our application, each class has **store**-methods to put data into the objects, and each has a method named **output** to output data. Thus each of our classes does have a common interface.

To develop a class hierarchy, the classes themselves must first be identified and their methods specified. In coding the hierarchy, it is best to first write the code for the base class; then, debug and test it. After the base class is working properly, we would code, debug, and test each derived class. In our example, we would first code, debug, and test class **Film**. Each of **Film**'s methods should be coded and tested one-by-one. After **Film** is coded correctly, we could code, debug, and test derived class **DirectorCut**. Each of the methods added by **DirectorCut** should be coded and tested one-by-one. The methods inherited from **Film** should be tested in **DirectorCut**. After **Film** and **DirectorCut** are coded correctly, we would code, debug, and test derived class **ForeignFilm**. Each of the methods added by **ForeignFilm** should be coded and tested one-by-one, and the methods inherited from **Film** should be tested.

6.4 protected MEMBERS

Besides **private** and **public** members, C++ provides **protected** members. In the absence of inheritance, a **protected** member is just like a **private** member; it is visible only within the class. In public inheritance, a **protected** member differs from a **private** member in that a **protected** member in the base class is **protected** in the derived class. Thus when a derived class inherits a **protected** member from a base class, that **protected** member *is* visible in the derived class.

EXAMPLE 6.4.1. In the declarations

```
class B { // base class
public:
    int x;
protected:
    int w;
private:
    int z;
};

class D : public B {
public:
    int y;
    void set_w( int a ) { w = a; }
};
```

class D is derived from base class B. The members of the derived class D are

Member	Access Status in D	How Obtained
x	public	From class B
w	protected	From class B
z	Not accessible	From class B
y	public	Added by class D
set_w	public	Added by class D

In the code

```
int main() {
    D d1;
    d1.x = 33; // ok -- x is public
    d1.y = 99; // ok -- y is public
    d1.w = 77; // ***** ERROR: w is protected
    d1.z = 88; // ***** ERROR: z is private to B
    ...
}
```

main can access the **public** members x and y of D but not the **protected** member w, which is visible only within the class hierarchy. Within class D, it is legal to access w:

```
void set_w( int a ) { w = a; } // ok
```

It is also an error to try to access z outside of B. In particular, z cannot be accessed even in D:

```
class D : public B {
    ...
    // ***** ERROR: z is accessible only within B
    void set_z( int a ) { z = a; }
    ...
};
```

■

A derived class may access **protected** members that it *inherits* from a base class. A derived class may access these **protected** members precisely because, once inherited, they belong to the derived class and are visible in the derived class. Yet a derived class may *not* access **protected** members of a base class *object*, that is, an object that belongs to the base class but *not* to the derived class.

EXAMPLE 6.4.2.   In the code segment

```
class B { // base class
protected:
    int w;
};
class D : public B { // derived class
public:
    // w belongs to D because it is inherited from B
    void set_w( int a ) { w = a; }
    // ***** ERROR: b.w not visible in D since b.w is
    // a member of B, not D
    void base_w( B b ) { b.w = 0; }
};
```

the reference to **w** in class **D**

```
void set_w( int a ) { w = a; } // OK
```

is legal because this **w** is **D**'s member, which is inherited from **B**. It is visible in **D** because it is **protected** in **B**. The reference to **b.w** in class **D**

```
void base_w( B b ) { b.w = 0; } // ***** ERROR
```

is illegal because this **w** is **B**'s member and it is visible only in **B**. In other words, **b.w** is the data member of a **B** object that is *not* a **D** object.   ■

A **private** member is inherited but *not* visible in a derived class. Except for a **friend** function (see Section 8.4), only methods of a class can access a **private** member of that class. A **protected** member is inherited *and* visible in a derived class. Thus a **protected** member can be visible throughout the class hierarchy. Except for a **friend** function, only methods within the class hierarchy can access a **protected** member. By making a member of a class **public**, we make the member visible wherever the class is visible.

EXAMPLE 6.4.3.   Figure 6.4.1 shows the status of the variables for the declarations

```
class B {
public:
    void m() { x = 0; }
protected:
    int y;
private:
    int x;
};
```

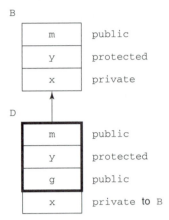

FIGURE 6.4.1 The status of the variables for the declarations of Example 6.4.3.

```
class D : public B {
public:
    void g() { y = 0; m(); }
};
```

EXERCISES

1. Explain the difference between **private** and **protected** with respect to a class's data members and methods.

2. Explain the advantage of **protected** over **private** data members or methods.

3. Explain the advantage of **protected** over **public** data members or methods.

4. In the code segment

```
class B { // base class
protected:
    int num1;
    int num2;
};

class D : public B { // derived class
    int num3;
};
D d1;
```

how many data members does **d1** have?

5. Explain the error.

```
class A {
protected:
    float f1, f2;
private:
    int x;
};

int main() {
    A a1;
    a1.f1 = 3.14;
    ...
}
```

6. Explain the error.

```
class A {
protected:
    int x;
};

class B : public A {
    int y;
    void f( A a ) { y = a.x; }
};
```

7. Write the body of **init**, which initializes **D**'s members.

```
class B { // base class
protected:
    int num1;
    int num2;
};

class D : public B { // derived class
public:
    void init( int, int, int );
private:
    int num3;
};

void D::init( int n1, int n2, int n3 ) {
    ...
}
```

6.5 CONSTRUCTORS AND DESTRUCTORS UNDER INHERITANCE

Constructors Under Inheritance

A derived class is a specialization of a base class. An object in a derived class inherits characteristics from the base class but also has characteristics that are specific to the derived class (see Figure 6.5.1). For this reason, a base class constructor (if any) is invoked when a derived class object is created. The base class constructor handles initialization and other matters for the "from the base class" part of the object. If the derived class has a constructor of its own, this constructor can handle the "added by derived class" part of the object.

obj

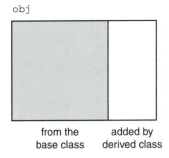

from the   added by
base class   derived class

FIGURE 6.5.1 A derived class as a specialization of a base class.

> **EXAMPLE 6.5.1.**   In the code segment
>
> ```
> class B {  // base class
> public:
>   B() { x = y = -1; } // base constructor
> protected:
>   int x;
>   int y;
> };
>
> class D : public B { // derived class
> public:
>   void write() { cout << x * y << endl; }
> };
>
> int main() {
>    D d1;        // d1.B() invoked
>    d1.write(); // 1 written to standard output
>    ...
> }
> ```

B's default constructor is invoked when **d1** is defined because **D** is derived from **B**. The constructor initializes **d1.x** and **d1.y** to **-1**. Note that **d1** inherits its only data members from **B**. ∎

Base class constructors are often sufficient for the derived class. Sometimes, however, it makes sense for a derived class to have its own constructors. A constructor specific to a derived class may invoke a base class constructor, if one exists.

EXAMPLE 6.5.2. The code segment

```
const int MaxName = 100;

class Animal {
public:
   Animal() { strcpy( species, "Animal" ); }
   Animal( char s[ ] ) { strcpy( species, s ); }
protected:
   char species[ MaxName + 1 ];
};

class Primate: public Animal {
public:
   Primate() : Animal( "Primate" ) { }
   Primate( int n ) : Animal( "Primate" )
      { heart_cham = n; }
private:
   int heart_cham;
};

Animal slug;                // Animal()
Animal tweety( "canary" ); // Animal( char [ ] )

Primate godzilla;           // Primate()
Primate human( 4 );         // Primate( int )
```

has four constructors: two for base class **Animal** and two for derived class **Primate**.

The two **Primate** constructors invoke a base class **Animal** constructor in their headers:

```
Primate() : Animal( "Primate" ) { }
Primate( int n ) : Animal( "Primate" )
   { heart_cham = n; }
```

The syntax indicates that each **Primate** constructor invokes an **Animal** constructor *before* executing its own body. For instance, the default **Primate** constructor invokes the base class constructor **Animal(char [ ])** before executing its own body, which happens to be empty. In the case of the **Primate** constructor with one argument, the body contains an assignment of **n** to **heart_cham**. ∎

In a deep inheritance hierarchy, creation of an object belonging to a derived class may have a domino effect with respect to constructor invocation.

EXAMPLE 6.5.3.   In the code segment

```
const int MaxName = 100;
class Animal {
public:
   Animal() { strcpy( species, "Animal" ); }
   Animal( char s[ ] ) { strcpy( species, s ); }
protected:
   char species[ MaxName + 1 ];
};
class Primate: public Animal {
public:
   Primate() : Animal( "Primate" ) { }
   Primate( int n ) : Animal( "Primate" )
      { heart_cham = n; }
protected:
   int heart_cham;
};
class Human : public Primate {
public:
   Human() : Primate() { }
   Human( int c ) : Primate( c ) { }
};
Human jill();     // Human()
Human fred( 4 ); // Human( int )
```

the inheritance hierarchy is now three deep. **Human** inherits **heart_cham** directly from **Primate** and **species** indirectly from **Animal** by way of **Primate**. Each of the **Human** constructors invokes a direct base class constructor **Primate** before executing an empty body. The **Primate** constructor, in turn, invokes an **Animal** constructor before executing its own body. The effect is that the bodies of the constructors are executed in a top-down order, where **Animal** is at the top, **Primate** in the middle, and **Human** at the bottom of the inheritance hierarchy (see Figure 6.5.2).   ■

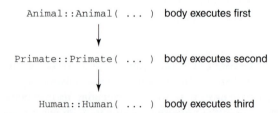

FIGURE 6.5.2 Constructor body execution in the **Animal-Primate-Human** hierarchy.

Derived Class Constructor Rules

If a base class has constructors *but no default constructor*, then a derived class constructor *must* explicitly invoke some base class constructor.

EXAMPLE 6.5.4. The code segment

```
// B has constructors but no
// default constructor
class B { // base class
public:
  B( int a ) { x = a; y = 999; }
  B( int a1, int a2 ) { x = a1; y = a2; }
private:
  int x;
  int y;
};

// D has a constructor (any constructor
// will do for the example)
class D : public B { // derived class
public:
  // ***** ERROR: D( int ) must explicitly
  //         invoke a B constructor
  D( int n ) { z = n; }
private:
  int z;
};
```

is in error because **B** does not have a *default* constructor and **D**'s constructor does *not* explicitly invoke a **B** constructor. We can correct the error in two ways: by having **D**'s constructor explicitly invoke, in its header, one of **B**'s constructors or by giving **B** a default constructor. We amend the code segment to illustrate the two approaches:

```
// approach 1: have D's constructor explicitly
// invoke one of B's constructors
class B { // base class
public:
  B( int a ) { x = a; y = 999; }
  B( int a1, int a2 ) { x = a1; y = a2; }
private:
  int x;
  int y;
};
```

```
// D's constructor explicitly invokes a
// B constructor in its header
class D : public B { // derived class
public:
  // ok: D( int ) explicitly invokes B( int, int )
  D( int n ) : B( n, n + 1 ) { z = n; }
private:
  int z;
};

// approach 2: give B a default constructor
class B { // base class
public:
  B() { x = 1; y = 2; } // default
  B( int a ) { x = a; y = 999; }
  B( int a1, int a2 ) { x = a1; y = a2; }
private:
  int x;
  int y;
};

// D's constructor need not invoke a B
// constructor because B how has a
// default constructor
class D : public B { // derived class
public:
  // ok: B has a default constructor
  D( int n ) { z = n; }
private:
  int z;
};
```

There is rarely a good reason for a base class not to have a default constructor. Giving a base class a default constructor avoids the problem and still allows a derived class constructor to invoke any base class constructor. Accordingly, we recommend that every base class have a default constructor. ∎

Suppose that a base class has a default constructor and that a derived class has constructors, none of which explicitly invokes a base class constructor. In this case, the base class default constructor is invoked automatically whenever a derived class object is created.

EXAMPLE 6.5.5.   The output for the code segment

```
class B { // base class
public:
  B() { cout << "B::B() executes..." << endl; }
private:
  int x;
};
```

```
class D : public B { // derived class
public:
  D() { cout << "D::D() executes..." << endl; }
private:
  int y;
};

int main() {
  D d;
  ...
}
```

is

```
B::B() executes...
D::D() executes...
```

It is legal but unnecessary for **D**'s constructor to invoke **B**'s default constructor explicitly:

```
// legal but unnecessary
D() : B() {...}
```                                                                ■

We now summarize the rules, using **D** as a class derived from **B**.

- If **D** has constructors but **B** has no constructors, then the appropriate **D** constructor executes automatically whenever a **D** object is created.

- If **D** has no constructors but **B** has constructors, then **B** must have a default constructor so that **B**'s default constructor can execute automatically whenever a **D** object is created.

- If **D** has constructors and **B** has a default constructor, then **B**'s default constructor executes automatically whenever a **D** object is created unless the appropriate **D** constructor *explicitly* invokes, in its header, some other **B** constructor.

- If **D** and **B** have constructors but **B** has no default constructor, then each **D** constructor must explicitly invoke, in its header, a **B** constructor, which then executes when a **D** object is created.

It makes sense that the creation of a derived class object should cause some base class constructor, if any, to execute. A derived class constructor may depend upon actions from a base class constructor. For example, the derived class may depend upon the base class constructor to perform some data member initializations. Also, a derived class object is a specialization of a base class object, which means that the body of a base class constructor, if the class has constructors, should execute *first* when a derived class object is created. The body of a more specialized constructor, which is the local derived class constructor, then can handle any special details.

Destructors Under Inheritance

Constructor bodies in an inheritance hierarchy execute in a

- base class to derived class

order. Destructor bodies in an inheritance hierarchy execute in a

- derived class to base class

order. So the destructor bodies execute in the reverse order of the constructor bodies.

> **EXAMPLE 6.5.6.** The output of the code segment
>
> ```
> class A {
> public:
>    A() { cout << "A's constructor" << endl; }
>    ~A() { cout << "A's destructor" << endl; }
> };
> class B : public A {
> public:
>    B() : A() { cout << "B's constructor" << endl; }
>    ~B() { cout << "B's destructor" << endl; }
> };
> int main() {
>    B b;
>    return 0;
> }
> ```
>
> is
>
> ```
> A's constructor
> B's constructor
> B's destructor
> A's destructor
> ```
> ∎

Unlike constructors, a destructor never explicitly invokes another destructor. Since each class has at most one destructor, it is unambiguous which destructor, if any, should execute.

EXERCISES

1. Explain the error.

```
class B {
public:
  B( int a ) { x = a; }
private:
  int x;
};
class D : public B {
public:
  D() {...}
  ...
};
```

2. In Example 6.5.3, the default constructor for **Human** explicitly invokes the default constructor for **Primate** but does not explicitly invoke the default constructor for **Animal**. Why not?

3. What is the output?

```
class B {
public:
   B() { cout << "B constructor" << endl; }
   ~B() { cout << "B destructor" << endl; }
};

class D1 : public B {
public:
   D1() : B() { cout << "D1 constructor" << endl; }
   ~D1() { cout << "D1 destructor" << endl; }
};

class D2 : public D1 {
public:
   D2() : D1() { cout << "D2 constructor" << endl; }
   ~D2() { cout << "D2 destructor" << endl; }
};

int main() {
    B b;
    D1 d1;
    D2 d2;
    return 0;
}
```

4. Is it mandatory that a derived class have a constructor?

5. Is it mandatory that a base class have a constructor?

6. Is it mandatory that a derived class have a destructor?

7. Is it mandatory that a base class have a destructor?

8. Is it possible for a derived class to have a constructor but its base class not to have a constructor?

9. Suppose that base class **B** has two constructors, the default constructor **B::B()** and the constructor **B::B(int)**. **D** is derived from **B** and has a single constructor, **D::D(int)**. Must **D** invoke *both* of **B**'s constructors before executing its own body?

10. C++ requires that when a derived class object is created, a base class constructor, if one exists, be invoked. Explain the reasoning behind this rule.

11. Extend the class hierarchy of Example 6.5.3 at least two more levels, writing constructors for each of the additional classes.

12. Must a derived class destructor invoke a base class destructor if one exists?

6.6 SAMPLE APPLICATION: A SEQUENCE HIERARCHY

 Problem

Develop an inheritance hierarchy to handle sequences of strings and sorted sequences of strings. A **sequence** is a list in which there is a first element, a second element, and so on. For example, in the sequence

    Abby George Ben

Abby is the first member, **George** is the second member, and **Ben** is the third member. This sequence is considered *distinct* from the sequence

    George Ben Abby

because, for example, the first member, **George**, is different from the first member, **Abby**, of the first sequence.

A **sorted sequence** is a sequence in which the elements are in *sorted* (ascending) order. For example, the sequence

    Abby Ben George

is a sorted sequence because the elements are in sorted order. The sequence

    Abby George Ben

is *not* a *sorted* sequence because **Ben** should *precede* **George** in sorted order.

Class **Sequence** has data members

- To hold strings.
- To hold a file name.
- To hold the index of the last string.
- To handle input and output files.

These members are **protected** so that they are visible throughout the class hierarchy.

Class **Sequence** has **public** methods to

- Add a string at a designated position.
- Delete a string at a designated position.
- To output the sequence.

Class **Sequence** also has a default constructor, a one-parameter **char [ ]** constructor, and a destructor.

The default constructor

- Sets the index of the last string to −1 to indicate that no strings are in the sequence.
- Sets the file name to the null string to indicate that no file name has been given.

The one-parameter **char [ ]** constructor

- Sets the index of the last string to −1 to indicate that no strings are in the sequence.
- Copies the file name passed into the data member that holds a file name.
- Attempts to open the file for input. If the file cannot be opened, the constructor simply returns.
- Reads the sequence from the file until end-of-file or until storage is exhausted, whichever occurs first.
- Closes the file.

The destructor

- Returns if the file name is the null string.
- Opens the file for output.
- Writes the sequence to the file.
- Closes the file.

Since a sorted sequence is a sequence, class **SortedSeq** is derived from class **Sequence**. Class **SortedSeq** adds no data members but rather inherits its data members from **Sequence**.

Class **SortedSeq** provides its own method to add an element to the sequence. This method has one parameter—the item to add. It does need a parameter to indicate where to add the item; it is added at the index consistent with the sorted order.

Class **SortedSeq** has a method **sort** to sort a sequence. Since this method is used internally only, it is **protected**.

Class **SortedSeq** has a default constructor and a one-parameter **char [ ]** constructor. **SortedSeq** has no destructor; instead it uses **Sequence**'s destructor.

The default constructor invokes **Sequence**'s default constructor. The one-parameter **char [ ]** constructor invokes **Sequence**'s one-parameter constructor and then sorts the sequence that was input.

Sample Input/Output

The first session shows the class **Sequence** in action using the test client of Figure 6.6.1. The file *test.dat* does not exist; thus the sequence is initially empty. When **main** finishes executing and the **Sequence** object **items** is destroyed, the **Sequence** destructor writes the sequence created to the file *test.dat*.

```
int main() {
    char inbuff[ MaxSize ];
    char where[ MaxSize ];
    int wh, ans;
    Sequence items( "test.dat" );

    while ( true ) {
        cout << endl << "Sequence output: " << endl;
        items.output();
        cout << endl << "1 -- add" << endl
             << "2 -- delete" << endl
             << "3 -- quit" << endl;
        cin.getline( inbuff, MaxSize );
        if ( ( ans = atoi( inbuff ) ) == 3 )
            break;
        switch ( ans ) {
        case 1:
            cout << endl << "item to add: ";
            cin.getline( inbuff, MaxSize );
            cout << "add where? ";
            cin.getline( where, MaxSize );
            wh = atoi( where );
            if ( items.addS( wh, inbuff ) )
                cout << "item added" << endl;
            else
                cout << "item not added" << endl;
            break;
        case 2:
            cout << endl << "where to delete: ";
            cin.getline( where, MaxSize );
            wh = atoi( where );
            if ( items.del( wh ) )
                cout << "item deleted" << endl;
            else
                cout << "item not deleted" << endl;
            break;
        }
    }
    return 0;
}
```

FIGURE 6.6.1 A test client for the Sequence class.

```
Sequence output:

1 -- add
2 -- delete
3 -- quit
1

item to add: George
add where? 0
item added

Sequence output:
0   George

1 -- add
2 -- delete
3 -- quit
1

item to add: Ben
add where? 1
item added

Sequence output:
0   George
1   Ben

1 -- add
2 -- delete
3 -- quit
1

item to add: Abby
add where? 0
item added

Sequence output:
0   Abby
1   George
2   Ben

1 -- add
2 -- delete
3 -- quit
2

where to delete: 1
item deleted

Sequence output:
0   Abby
1   Ben
```

```
1 -- add
2 -- delete
3 -- quit
1

item to add: Pat
add where? 0
item added

Sequence output:
0   Pat
1   Abby
2   Ben

1 -- add
2 -- delete
3 -- quit
3
```

The next session shows the class **SortedSeq** in action using the test client of Figure 6.6.2, where the **SortedSeq** object is created using the constructor whose argument is the name of the file created by the preceding **Sequence** session.

```
SortedSeq output:
0   Abby
1   Ben
2   Pat

1 -- add
2 -- delete
3 -- quit
1

item to add: Doris
item added

SortedSeq output:
0   Abby
1   Ben
2   Doris
3   Pat

1 -- add
2 -- delete
3 -- quit
2

where to delete: 1
item deleted

SortedSeq output:
0   Abby
```

```
1   Doris
2   Pat

1 -- add
2 -- delete
3 -- quit
3
```

```cpp
int main() {
    char inbuff[ MaxSize ];
    char where[ MaxSize ];
    int wh, ans;
    SortedSeq sortitems( "test.dat" );
    while ( true ) {
        cout << endl << "SortedSeq output: " << endl;
        sortitems.output();
        cout << endl << "1 -- add" << endl
             << "2 -- delete" << endl
             << "3 -- quit" << endl;
        cin.getline( inbuff, MaxSize );
        if ( ( ans = atoi( inbuff ) ) == 3 )
            break;
        switch ( ans ) {
        case 1:
            cout << endl << "item to add: ";
            cin.getline( inbuff, MaxSize );
            if ( sortitems.addSS( inbuff ) )
                cout << "item added" << endl;
            else
                cout << "item not added" << endl;
            break;
        case 2:
            cout << endl << "where to delete: ";
            cin.getline( where, MaxSize );
            wh = atoi( where );
            if ( sortitems.del( wh ) )
                cout << "item deleted" << endl;
            else
                cout << "item not deleted" << endl;
            break;
        }
    }
    return 0;
}
```

FIGURE 6.6.2 A test client for the `SortedSeq` class.

Solution

In class **Sequence**, we use a two-dimensional array of **char** to hold the strings in the sequence. We use a one-dimensional array of **char** to hold the file name. An **int** member holds the index of the last element in the sequence. The constructors therefore initialize this member to −1.

The member **addS** attempts to add an element to the sequence at the specified index. If successful, **addS** returns **true**; otherwise, it returns **false**. The method could fail to add an element if the index specified is illegal or if the storage provided is full. Therefore **addS** returns a **bool**.

Similarly, the member **del** attempts to delete an element at the specified index. If successful, **del** returns **true**; otherwise, it returns **false**. The method could fail to delete an element if the index specified is illegal. Therefore **del** also returns a **bool**.

The method **output** steps through the two-dimensional array of **char** and prints each string together with its index.

Class **SortedSeq** is publicly derived from class **Sequence**. Class **SortedSeq** inherits its data members from **Sequence**.

SortedSeq's **addSS** locates the index, defined by the sorted order, at which to add the item. It then invokes **addS** to insert the item.

SortedSeq's **sort** method uses **insertion sort** to sort the sequence. The logic is explained in the Discussion section.

C++ Implementation

```
#include <iostream>
#include <fstream>
#include <cstdlib>
#include <cstring>
using namespace std;
const int MaxStr = 50;
const int MaxSize = 80;

class Sequence {
public:
   bool addS( int, char [ ] );
   bool del( int );
   void output();
   Sequence();
   Sequence( char [ ] );
   ~Sequence();
protected:
   char s[ MaxStr ][ MaxSize ];
   char filename[ MaxSize ];
   int last;
   ifstream in;
   ofstream out;
};
```

```
bool Sequence::addS( int pos, char entry[ ] ) {
   if ( last == MaxStr - 1
        || pos < 0
        || pos > last + 1 )
      return false;
   for ( int i = last; i >= pos; i-- )
      strcpy( s[ i + 1 ], s[ i ] );
   strcpy( s[ pos ], entry );
   last++;
   return true;
}

bool Sequence::del( int pos ) {
   if ( pos < 0 || pos > last )
      return false;
   for ( int i = pos; i < last; i++ )
      strcpy( s[ i ], s[ i + 1 ] );
   last--;
   return true;
}

void Sequence::output() {
   for ( int i = 0; i <= last; i++ )
      cout << i << "  " << s[ i ] << endl;
}

Sequence::Sequence() {
   last = -1;
   filename[ 0 ] = '\0';
}

Sequence::Sequence( char fname[ ] ) {
   last = -1;
   strcpy( filename, fname );
   in.open( filename );
   if ( !in )
      return;
   while ( last < MaxStr - 1 ) {
      in.getline( s[ last + 1 ], MaxSize );
      if ( !strlen( s[ last + 1 ] ) )
         break;
      last++;
   }
   in.close();
}
```

```
Sequence::~Sequence() {
   if ( filename[ 0 ] == '\0' )
      return;
   out.open( filename );
   for ( int i = 0; i <= last; i++ )
      out << s[ i ] << endl;
   out.close();
}

class SortedSeq : public Sequence {
public:
   bool addSS( char [ ] );
   SortedSeq();
   SortedSeq( char [ ] );
protected:
   void sort();
};

void SortedSeq::sort() {
   char temp[ MaxSize ];
   for ( int i = 0; i <= last - 1; i++ ) {
      strcpy( temp, s[ i + 1 ] );
      for ( int j = i; j >= 0; j-- ) {
         if ( strcmp( temp, s[ j ] ) < 0 )
            strcpy( s[ j + 1 ], s[ j ] );
         else
            break;
      }
      strcpy( s[ j + 1 ], temp );
   }
}

bool SortedSeq::addSS( char entry[ ] ) {
   for ( int i = 0; i <= last; i++ )
      if ( strcmp( entry, s[ i ] ) <= 0 )
         break;
   return addS( i, entry );
}

SortedSeq::SortedSeq() : Sequence() { }

SortedSeq::SortedSeq( char fname[ ] ) : Sequence( fname ) {
   sort();
}
```

Discussion

Sequence's data members

```
char s[ MaxStr ][ MaxSize ];
char filename[ MaxSize ];
int last;
ifstream in;
ofstream out;
```

are **protected,** so that they are visible in classes such as **SortedSeq** publicly derived from **Sequence** but *not* outside the class hierarchy.

The two-dimensional array **s** is used to hold the strings that make up the sequence. The value of **s[i]** is the address of the first character in string **i**.

Method **adds** first checks whether the array **s** is full

```
last == MaxStr - 1
```

or whether the requested index is out of bounds

```
pos < 0 || pos > last + 1
```

If either condition is **true**, **adds** returns **false**. Otherwise, **adds** moves strings up, beginning at the end, to make room for the added item

```
for ( int i = last; i >= pos; i-- )
   strcpy( s[ i + 1 ], s[ i ] );
```

stores the item at index **pos**, updates **last**, and returns **true**

```
strcpy( s[ pos ], entry );
last++;
return true;
```

Method **del** checks whether the requested index is out of bounds

```
pos < 0 || pos > last
```

If **pos** is out of bounds, **del** returns **false**. Otherwise, **del** moves each item after **pos** down one

```
for ( int i = pos; i < last; i++ )
   strcpy( s[ i ], s[ i + 1 ] );
```

updates **last**, and returns **true**

```
last--;
return true;
```

The default constructor sets **last** to **-1** to indicate that the sequence is empty and sets **filename** to the null string by putting zero in the first byte

```
Sequence::Sequence() {
   last = -1;
   filename[ 0 ] = '\0';
}
```

The one-parameter constructor receives a file name

```
Sequence::Sequence( char fname[ ] )
```

It then sets **last** to **-1** to indicate that the sequence is empty, copies **fname** to **filename**, and tries to open the file

```
last = -1;
strcpy( filename, fname );
in.open( filename );
```

If the file cannot be opened, the constructor simply returns

```
if ( !in )
    return;
```

Otherwise, it reads the file until end-of-file or until the storage is exhausted and closes the file

```
while ( last < MaxStr - 1 ) {
    in.getline( s[ last + 1 ], MaxSize );
    if ( !strlen( s[ last + 1 ] ) )
        break;
    last++;
}
in.close();
```

The destructor first checks whether **filename** is the null string; if it is the null string, it simply returns

```
if ( filename[ 0 ] == '\0' )
    return;
```

Otherwise, it opens the file for output, writes the strings to the file, and closes the file

```
out.open( filename );
for ( int i = 0; i <= last; i++ )
    out << s[ i ] << endl;
out.close();
```

Class **SortedSeq** is publicly derived from **Sequence**

```
class SortedSeq : public Sequence {
    ...
};
```

SortedSeq also has a method **addSS** to add an item. It first finds the correct place in which to insert the item to be added

```
for ( int i = 0; i <= last; i++ )
   if ( strcmp( entry, s[ i ] ) <= 0 )
      break;
```

and then adds it by invoking **addS**

```
return addS( i, entry );
```

The method **sort** is used internally (by the one-parameter constructor) and so is **protected**. Thus, **sort** is visible throughout the class hierarchy but not outside the hierarchy. The logic of **sort** is that of insertion sort. It assumes that

```
s[ 0 ],s[ 1 ],...,s[ i ]
```

is sorted. It then places **s[i + 1]** in the correct position in this list. To do so, it first copies **s[i + 1]** into **temp**

```
strcpy( temp, s[ i + 1 ] );
```

It then compares **temp** with **s[j]**, for **j = i**. If

```
temp < s[ j ]
```

it moves **s[j]** to the next position

```
if ( strcmp( temp, s[ j ] ) < 0 )
   strcpy( s[ j + 1 ], s[ j ] );
```

and repeats after decrementing **j**. If

```
temp ≥ s[ j ]
```

the correct position for **temp** has been found and **temp** is copied into that position

```
strcpy( s[ j + 1 ], temp );
```

The default constructor simply invokes **Sequence**'s default constructor

```
SortedSeq::SortedSeq() : Sequence() {
}
```

The one-parameter constructor first invokes **Sequence**'s one-parameter constructor, which sets **last** to **-1**, copies **fname** to **filename**, tries to open the file, reads the file until end-of-file if the file was successfully opened, and closes the file. It then sorts the sequence by invoking method **sort**.

C++ POSTSCRIPT

Multiple Inheritance

In multiple inheritance, a derived class has multiple base classes. The derived class typically represents a *combination* of its base classes.

EXAMPLE. In the declarations

```
class B1 {
public:
   void print_x();
   void store_x( int );
protected:
   int x;
};

class B2 {
public:
   void print_y();
   void store_y( int );
protected:
   int y;
};

class D : public B1, public B2 {
public:
   void print_z();
   void store_z( int );
protected:
   int z;
};
```

class D is derived from B1 and B2. Since D inherits all of the members of B1 and B2, D's members are

Member	Status	How Obtained
x	protected	From class B1
print_x()	public	From class B1
store_x()	public	From class B1
y	protected	From class B2
print_y()	public	From class B2
store_y()	public	From class B2
z	protected	Added by class D
print_z()	public	Added by class D
store_z()	public	Added by class D

protected Inheritance

In a **protected** derivation

- Each **public** member in the base class is **protected** in the derived class.

- Each **protected** member in the base class is **protected** in the derived class.

- Each **private** member in the base class is visible only in the base class.

EXAMPLE.   In the code segment

```
class B { // base class
public:
    int x;
protected:
    int w;
private:
    int z;
};

class D : protected B { // protected derived class
public:
    int y;
};
```

class **D** is derived from the base class **B**. The derivation is **protected**. The members of the derived class **D** are

Member	Access Status in D	How Obtained
x	protected	From class B
w	protected	From class B
z	Not accessible	From class B
y	public	Added by class D

private Inheritance

In a **private** derivation

- Each **public** member in the base class is **private** in the derived class.

- Each **protected** member in the base class is **private** in the derived class.

- Each **private** member in the base class is visible only in the base class.

EXAMPLE.   In the code segment

```
class B { // base class
public:
    int x;
protected:
    int w;
private:
    int z;
};

class D : private B { // private derived class
public:
    int y;
};
```

class **D** is derived from the base class **B**. The derivation is **private**. The members of the derived class **D** are

Member	Access Status in **D**	How Obtained
x	private	From class **B**
w	private	From class **B**
z	Not accessible	From class **B**
y	public	Added by class **D**

■

EXAMPLE.   In a derivation, **private** inheritance is the default; thus, the declaration of class **D** in the preceding example is equivalent to

```
class D : B { // private (default) derived class
public:
    int y;
};
```

■

Access Declarations

Access to an inherited member may be adjusted to that of the base class by declaring it **public** or **protected** in the derived class. It is an error to try to use an access declaration to change an inherited member's status to something different from that in the base class.

EXAMPLE.   In the code segment

```
class B { // base class
public:
   int z;
protected:
   int x, y;
};

class D : private B { // private inheritance
public:
   B::z;
   int w;
protected:
   B::x;
};
```

the access declaration

```
   B::x;
```

adjusts **x** in **D** to the same **protected** status that this data member has in base class **B**. The adjustment is done by placing the declaration in the **protected** section of **D**. Without the declaration, **x** would be **private** in **D** because the inheritance from **B** to **D** is **private**. Similarly, the access declaration

```
   B::z;
```

adjusts **z** to its **public** status in the base class **B** by declaring it in the **public** section of the derived class **D**. Inherited member **y** is **private** in **D** because **D** is obtained by **private** inheritance from **B**, and **y**'s status was not adjusted. Added member **w** is **public**. ∎

COMMON PROGRAMMING ERRORS

1. In a derivation, **private** inheritance is the default, so to obtain **public** inheritance, the keyword **public** *must* be specified. For example, in the following code segment

```
class B { // base class
protected:
   int x;
};

// Caution: public not specified so inheritance
// is private
class D : B {
   ...
};
```

the inheritance is `private`; that is, the preceding code segment is equivalent to

```
class B { // base class
protected:
    int x;
};

class D : private B {
    ...
};
```

To obtain `public` inheritance, use the keyword `public`:

```
class B { // base class
protected:
    int x;
};

class D : public B { // public inheritance
    ...
};
```

2. It is an error to access a `protected` member outside its class hierarchy except through a `friend` function. For example,

```
class B { // base class
protected:
    int x;
};

class D : public B { // derived class
public:
    void f() { x = 0; } // OK: x is protected in D
    ...
};

int main() {
    B c1;
    c1.x = 9; // ***** ERROR: x is protected in B
    ...
}
```

contains an error because `x` is accessible only to `B`'s methods and `friend`s and to methods and `friend`s of certain classes, such as `D`, that are derived from `B`.

3. It is an error to access a `private` member outside its class except through a `friend` function. For example

```
class B { // base class
private:
    int x;
};
```

```
class D : public B { // derived class
public:
   // ***** ERROR: x not visible in D
   int f() { return x; }
};
```

contains an error because **x** is accessible only to **B**'s methods and **friend**s. Member **x** is not even accessible in classes derived from **B**.

4. If a base class has constructors but no default constructor, then a derived class constructor *must* explicitly invoke a base class constructor in its header:

```
class B {
public:
   // constructors -- but no default constructor
   B( int a ) { x = a; z = -1; }
   B( int a1, int a2 ) { x = a1; z = a2; }
private:
   int x, z;
};

class D1 : public B {
public:
   // **** ERROR: D1( int ) must explicitly invoke
   // one of B's constructors
   D1( int a ) { y = a; }
private:
   int y;
};

class D2 : public B {
public:
   // ok -- D2 explicitly invokes a B
   // constructor in its header
   D2( int a ) : B( a ) { y = a; }
private:
   int y;
};
```

5. If a derived class has a method with the same name as a base class method, then the derived class's method *hides* the base class method. It is therefore an error to invoke the base class method:

```
class B { // base class
public:
   void f( double );
   ...
};
```

```
class D : public B { // derived class
public:
   void f( char [ ] ); // CAUTION -- hides B::f
   ...
};

int main() {
   D d;
   // ***** ERROR: D::f, which hides B::f,
   // expects a character array, not a double
   d.f( 3.14 );
   ...
}
```

PROGRAMMING EXERCISES

6.1. Derive an additional class **Documentary** from class **Film** of Section 6.3. Add appropriate data members and methods, including a method to output the data. Implement a test client to test the hierarchy.

6.2. Derive a class **RevSortedSeq** from class **Sequence** of Section 6.6. **RevSortedSeq** is just like **SortedSeq** except that the strings are sorted in *reverse* alphabetical order. Implement a test client to test the hierarchy.

6.3. Implement a **Library** hierarchy with at least a dozen classes. For purposes of the exercise, consider a *library* to be a collection of literary or artistic materials that is not for sale. In addition to the constructors and destructors, the classes should include methods that describe the classes much in the way that a human librarian might describe a class or subclass of materials among the library's holdings.

6.4. Implement an integer array hierarchy in which the base class represents a one-dimensional array, and the derived classes represent different multidimensional arrays. The base class uses a one-dimensional array to store the integers

```
class intArray { // base class
public:
// interface
protected:
   int ar[ MaxArray ];
   int n; // element count
   // rest of implementation
};
```

and each derived class uses the inherited array to store its integers. A **Matrix** class could add a data member **rowCount** to store the number of rows and a data member **colCount** to store the number of columns. The data could be stored in **ar** by rows: row 1 first, then row 2, and so on.

Each class defines its own print method. For example, **intArray**'s print method might include the statement

```
// print elements on one line, separated by blanks
for ( int i = 0; i < n; i++ )
   cout << ar[ i ] << ' ';
```

whereas **Matrix**'s print method might include the statements

```
// print elements with each row on one line
for ( int row = 0; row < rowCount; row++ ) {
   for ( int col = 0; col < colCount; col++ )
      cout << ar[ col + row * colCount ] << ' ';
   cout << endl;
}
```

Other classes that might be included in the hierarchy are **Array3D**, which could be directly derived from **intArray**, and **SquareMatrix**, which could be derived from **Matrix**. After creating the classes, write a test client for the hierarchy.

6.5. Implement a **CardGame** class that represents an ordinary 52-card deck with four suits (hearts, clubs, diamonds, and spades) and 13 cards per suit: ace, king, queen, jack, 10, ..., 2. Represent the deck in any convenient way. Derive a **Bridge** class that includes a method **deal** to divide the deck into four 13-card hands. Derive a **Poker** class that includes a method **deal** to divide the deck into a specified number (between 2 and 7, inclusive) of 5-card hands. After creating the classes, write a test client for the hierarchy.

6.6. Implement a **Vehicle** class that includes data members to represent a vehicle's make, model, production year, and price. The class interface includes methods that provide appropriate access to the data members. Derive a **Car** class (see Programming Exercise 5.1) and a **Truck** class from **Vehicle**. Each of these derived classes should add appropriate data members and methods. Also, derive two classes from **Car** that represent particular cars and two classes from **Truck** that represent particular trucks. Implement a test client to test the hierarchy. Propose other classes to derive from **Vehicle**.

6.7. Derive classes **Reference**, **Fiction**, and **Periodical** from class **Book** of Programming Exercise 5.3. Add appropriate data members and methods to each of these classes. Implement a test client to test the hierarchy.

6.8. Implement a **Person** class that includes data members to represent name, address, and identification number. The class interface includes methods that provide appropriate access to the data members. Derive a **CollegeStudent** class (see Programming Exercise 5.5) and a **Professor** class from **Person**. Each of these derived classes should add appropriate data members and methods. Implement a test client to test the hierarchy. Propose classes to derive from **CollegeStudent** and **Professor**. What data members and methods might these derived classes add?

6.9. Derive classes **CEO**, **Actor**, and **Telemarketer** from class **Profession** of Programming Exercise 5.7. Add appropriate data members and methods to each of these classes. Implement a test client to test the hierarchy.

6.10. Implement an `AbsCollection` class that includes an array to represent `int`s, an `int` member `last`, whose value is the index of the last item stored in the array, and a method to enumerate the elements stored in the array. Derive a `Set` class (see Programming Exercise 5.12) and a `Bag` class (see Programming Exercise 5.13) from `AbsCollection`. Each of these derived classes should add appropriate data members and methods. Implement a test client to test the hierarchy. Propose other classes to derive from `AbsCollection`. What data members and methods might these derived classes add?

6.11. Derive classes `Manager`, `HourlyWorker`, and `Consultant` from class `Emp` of Programming Exercise 5.22. Also derive at least one class from each of `Manager`, `HourlyWorker`, and `Consultant`. For example, `Officer` could be a class derived from `Manager`. Each subclass should represent information that distinguishes it. For example, an `HourlyWorker` has an hourly wage and overtime rate, but an `Officer` has neither of these. Add appropriate data members and methods to each of these classes. Implement a test client to test the hierarchy.

6.12. Derive classes `Fruit`, `Dairy`, and `Meat`, appropriate for a grocery chain, from class `Product` of Programming Exercise 5.23. Also, derive classes from each of `Fruit`, `Dairy`, and `Meat`. (For example, `Milk` and `Butter` might be derived from `Dairy`.)

Include any reasonable data members and methods. For example, suppose that the chain changes prices on products monthly, based on supply and demand, and that the percentage change depends on the particular product. For example, in a given month, the price of ice cream might decrease 0.5 percent, whereas the price of beef might increase 6 percent. Assume that every product has `supply` and `demand` data members whose values are one of the qualitative values `low`, `medium`, or `high`. Include a method that computes a product's price change based on its values of `supply` and `demand`. Implement a test client to test the hierarchy.

CHAPTER 7

POLYMORPHISM

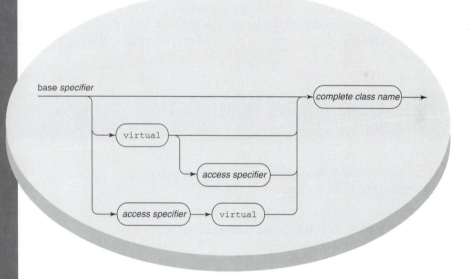

This chapter examines a powerful feature of object-oriented languages known as **polymorphism**. In technical terms, polymorphism is the *run-time binding* of a function's name to the code that implements the function. When a C++ program executes, the code that implements each of its component functions resides someplace in the computer's storage system. The *starting address* at which a function's code resides is the function's **entry point**. For example, a C++ program has a top-level function called **main**. Function **main**'s entry point is the address, in the computer's storage system, at which the executable code for **main** begins. So polymorphism is the run-time binding of a function's name to its entry point.

From the programmer's standpoint, polymorphism is a powerful tool. Imagine a hierarchy with **Window** as its base class and with 20 or so derived classes; and suppose that each class in the hierarchy has a polymorphic **close** method, which not only closes the **Window** on the screen but also does whatever background cleanup operations are appropriate for a particular type of **Window**. Assume, further, that all of the **close** methods have the same signature. The programmer can invoke a **Window**'s **close** method, but without knowing exactly which **Window** type or subtype is involved. The programmer needs to remember only one method signature to invoke 20 or so different methods. Through examples and a sample application, we illustrate the power of polymorphism. We begin with a technical overview.

7.1 RUN-TIME VERSUS COMPILE-TIME BINDING IN C++

A function's name is bound to or associated with an entry point, the starting address of the code that implements the function.

EXAMPLE 7.1.1.   In the code segment

```
#include <iostream>
using namespace std;
void sayHi();
int main() {
    sayHi();
    return 0;
}
void sayHi() {
    cout << "Hello, cruel world!" << endl;
}
```

the function name **sayHi** is associated with a function body that consists of the statement

```
cout << "Hello, cruel world!" << endl;
```

The compiler binds any call to **sayHi**, such as the one in **main**, to the code that implements **sayHi**, in this case a single **cout** statement. We say that **compile-time binding** occurs for **sayHi** because the *compiler* determines what code is to be executed whenever **sayHi** is invoked. In more technical language, the compiler binds any invocation of **sayHi** to **sayHi**'s entry point. ■

Compile-time binding has been in effect throughout our examples so far. The alternative is **run-time binding**, that is, the binding of a function's name to an entry point when the program is *running*, not when the program is being compiled. A function is *polymorphic* if its binding occurs at run time rather than compile time. In *pure* object-oriented languages such as Smalltalk, *all* functions are polymorphic. In a hybrid language such as C++, functions may be either polymorphic (bound at run time) or nonpolymorphic (bound at compile time). In particular, C++ allows only selected *methods* to be polymorphic.

Requirements for C++ Polymorphism

Polymorphism in C++ has three requirements:

- There must be an *inheritance hierarchy*.
- The classes in the hierarchy must have a **virtual** method with the same signature. (**virtual** is a keyword.)
- There must be either a pointer or a reference to a base class. The pointer or reference is used to invoke a **virtual** method.

EXAMPLE 7.1.2. The program in Figure 7.1.1 illustrates polymorphism and its three requirements in C++. First, there is an inheritance hierarchy with **TradesPerson** as the base class for two derived classes, **Tinker** and **Tailor**. Second, there is a **virtual** method named **sayHi**; it is defined three times, once for each class in the hierarchy. Third, there is a pointer **p** to a base class; in this case, **p** is of type **TradesPerson*** ("pointer to **TradesPerson**"). The pointer **p** is used to invoke the **virtual** method **sayHi**.

In **main**, we define three objects: **trade** of type **TradesPerson**, **tink** of type **Tinker**, and **tail** of type **Tailor**. We then prompt the user for an integer 1, 2, or 3. If the user enters 1, we assign the address of **trade** to **p**. If the user enters 2, we assign the address of **tink** to **p**. If the user enters 3, we assign the address of **tail** to **p**. No cast is needed in assigning **p** the address of either **tink** or **tail** because, in C++, a pointer to a *base class* may point to any base class or derived class object. We then use **p** with the indirect selection operator -> (see Section 5.9) to invoke one of the three **virtual** methods:

```
p->sayHi();   //**** run-time binding in effect
```

Because **sayHi** is **virtual**, the system binds its invocation at *run time*. If **p** points to **trade**, the system binds the call to **TradesPerson::sayHi**. If **p** points to **tink**, the system binds the call to **Tinker::sayHi**. If **p** points to **tail**, the system binds the call to **Tailor::sayHi**. In a sample run, we entered 2 and the output therefore was

```
Hi, I tinker.
```

```
#include <iostream>
using namespace std;
class TradesPerson { // base class
public:
   virtual void sayHi() { cout << "Hi from on top." << endl; }
};

class Tinker : public TradesPerson { // derived class 1
public:
   virtual void sayHi() { cout << "Hi, I tinker." << endl; }
};

class Tailor : public TradesPerson { // derived class 2
public:
   virtual void sayHi() { cout << "Hi, I tailor." << endl; }
};

int main() {
   TradesPerson trade; // create a base class object
   Tinker tink;    // create a Tinker object
   Tailor tail;    // create a Tailor object
   TradesPerson* p; // pointer to base class
   int which;
   // prompt user for a number:
   // *** 1 == TradesPerson
   //     2 == Tinker
   //     3 == Tailor
   do {
      cout << "1 == TradesPerson, 2 == Tinker, 3 == Tailor ";
      cin >> which;
   } while ( which < 1 || which > 3 );
   // set pointer p depending on user choice
   switch ( which ) {
   case 1: p = &trade; break;
   case 2: p = &tink; break;
   case 3: p = &tail; break;
   }
   // invoke the sayHi method via the pointer
   p->sayHi();  //**** run-time binding in effect
   return 0;
}
```

FIGURE 7.1.1 Polymorphism (run-time binding) in C++.

In another sample run, we entered 3 and the output therefore was

```
Hi, I tailor.
```
■

The program in Figure 7.1.1 uses the keyword **virtual** in all three versions of **sayHi**. This is good practice but not a requirement. If a *base class* method is declared **virtual**, then any derived class method with the same signature is automatically **virtual**, even if such a method is not explicitly declared **virtual**. For example, we could amend the program in Figure 7.1.1 by not explicitly declaring **Tinker::sayHi** to be **virtual**:

```
class TradesPerson {
public:
   virtual void sayHi() { cout << "Hi from on top." << endl; }
};

class Tinker : public TradesPerson {
public:
   void sayHi() { cout << "Hi, I tinker." << endl; }
};
...
```

Nonetheless, **Tinker::sayHi** is still **virtual** because it has the same signature as **Trades-Person::sayHi**, the base class version that is declared **virtual**.

If a **virtual** method is defined outside the class declaration, then the keyword **virtual** occurs only in the method's *declaration*, not in its definition.

EXAMPLE 7.1.3.   In the code segment

```
class C {
public:
  virtual void m();  // declaration--"virtual" occurs
  ...
};

void C::m() // definition--"virtual" does not occur
{
   ...
}
```

virtual method **m** is defined outside the class declaration. Therefore, the keyword **virtual** occurs only in its declaration.   ■

C++ allows only *methods* to be **virtual**. A top-level function cannot be **virtual**.

EXAMPLE 7.1.4.   The code segment

```
virtual void f(); //****** ERROR: not a method!
int main() {
   ...
}
```

contains an error because it declares **f**, a top-level function rather than a method, to be **virtual**.   ■

Inheriting `virtual` Methods

A `virtual` method, like a regular method, can be inherited by a derived class from a base class.

> **EXAMPLE 7.1.5.** If we amend the program in Figure 7.1.1 by removing the definition of `Tinker::sayHi`
>
> ```
> class TradesPerson {
> public:
>    virtual void sayHi() { cout << "Hi from on top." << endl; }
> };
>
> class Tinker : public TradesPerson {
>    //**** remove Tinker::sayHi
> };
> ...
> ```
>
> and enter 2 for `Tinker` when prompted, the output is
>
> ```
> Hi from on top.
> ```
>
> Because class `Tinker` does not provide its own definition for `sayHi`, it inherits the definition from its base class `TradesPerson`. If we enter 1 for `TradesPerson`, the output is also
>
> ```
> Hi from on top.
> ```
>
> However, if we enter 3 for `Tailor`, the output is still
>
> ```
> Hi, I tailor.
> ```
>
> because `Tailor` does have its own definition of the `virtual` method `sayHi`.
>   We can summarize the amended example by saying that `Tailor` **overrides** the `virtual` method `sayHi` by providing a `Tailor`-specific version. By contrast, `Tinker` does not override this `virtual` method but rather uses the version inherited from its base class `TradesPerson`. ∎

Run-Time Binding and the Vtable

C++ uses a **vtable** (virtual **table**) to implement the run-time binding of `virtual` methods. Although a vtable's implementation is system-dependent, its purpose is to support a run-time lookup that allows the system to bind a function's name to a particular entry point.

EXAMPLE 7.1.6.   Suppose that our application uses the inheritance hierarchy

```
class B { // base class
public:
   virtual void m1() {...} // 1st virtual method
   virtual void m2() {...} // 2nd virtual method
};

class D : public B { // derived class
public:
   virtual void m1() {...} // override of 1st virtual method
};
```

Assuming that **m1** and **m2** are our application's only **virtual** methods, here is a conceptual representation of the vtable, with the sample entry points given in hexadecimal:

virtual *Method*	*Sample Entry Point*
B::m1	0x7723
B::m2	0x23b4
D::m1	0x99a7
D::m2	0x23b4

There is a separate vtable entry for *each* **virtual** method in the application. However, **B::m2** and **D::m2** have the same entry point (0x23b4) because derived class **D** does not override **virtual** method **m2** but rather uses the version inherited from its base class **B**.

When our application executes a code segment such as

```
int main() {
   B  b1;    // base class object
   D  d1;    // derived class object
   B* p;     // pointer to base class
   ...       // p is set to b1's or d1's address
   p->m1(); //*** vtable lookup for run-time binding
   ...
}
```

the system needs to bind the function call

```
   p->m1(); //*** vtable lookup for run-time binding
```

to an entry point. The system first determines where **p** points. If **p** points to the **B** object **b1**, then the system looks in the vtable for **B::m1**'s entry point. If **p** points to the **D** object **d1**, then the system looks in the vtable for **D::m1**'s entry point. Once the vtable lookup is done, the appropriate function body is executed. ■

A program that uses run-time binding incurs a performance penalty. The penalty in space is the amount of storage needed for the vtable. The penalty in time is the amount of time needed for vtable lookups. Pure object-oriented languages incur a relatively heavy performance penalty because *all* functions are bound at run time. In C++, by contrast, the programmer can be selective in using run-time binding (that is, **virtual** methods) and, in this way, enjoy the benefits of run-time binding without incurring a heavy performance penalty.

Dynamic Creation of Class Objects

The program in Figure 7.1.1 wastes storage. The program defines three class objects: **trade** of type **TradesPerson**, **tink** of type **Tinker**, and **tail** of type **Tailor**. The program also defines a pointer **p** of type **TradesPerson***. Depending on user input, **p** is assigned the address of exactly *one* of the three objects. So *two* of the defined objects are never used. We can correct this deficiency by using the **new** operator to create just one object dynamically. To create an object **dynamically** is to create it at *run time*.

EXAMPLE 7.1.7. We revise the program in Figure 7.1.1. In the revised program (see Figure 7.1.2), *no* class objects are defined, although there is still a pointer to the base class **p**, which is of type **TradesPerson***. Again we prompt the user for input, storing the input in the **int** variable **which**. A **switch** statement again uses **which** to determine where **p** points, but this time **p** points to a dynamically created object:

```
switch ( which ) {
case 1: p = new TradesPerson; break;
case 2: p = new Tinker; break;
case 3: p = new Tailor; break;
}
```

For instance, if the user enters 2, we dynamically create a **Tinker** object with the **new** operator:

```
p = new Tinker;
```

In this case, operator **new** requests storage for a **Tinker** object. If the request is granted, **new** returns the object's address, which we store in **p**. (Throughout our examples, we assume that **new** allocates the requested storage. See the C++ Postscript about what happens if **new** fails.) We then use **p** to invoke the object's **sayHi** method:

```
p->sayHi();  //**** run-time binding in effect
```

Run-time binding is again in effect because **p** is a pointer to the base class **Trades-Person**, **sayHi** is **virtual**, and **p** is used to invoke the polymorphic method **sayHi**.

```
#include <iostream>
using namespace std;
class TradesPerson { // base class
public:
   virtual void sayHi() { cout << "Hi from on top." << endl; }
};

class Tinker : public TradesPerson { // derived class 1
public:
   virtual void sayHi() { cout << "Hi, I tinker." << endl; }
};

class Tailor : public TradesPerson { // derived class 2
public:
   virtual void sayHi() { cout << "Hi, I tailor." << endl; }
};

int main() {
   TradesPerson* p; // pointer to base class
   int which;
   // prompt user for a number:
   // *** 1 == TradesPerson
   //     2 == Tinker
   //     3 == Tailor
   do {
      cout << "1 == TradesPerson, 2 == Tinker, 3 == Tailor ";
      cin >> which;
   } while ( which < 1 || which > 3 );
   // set pointer p depending on user choice
   switch ( which ) {
   case 1: p = new TradesPerson; break;
   case 2: p = new Tinker; break;
   case 3: p = new Tailor; break;
   }
   // invoke the sayHi method via the pointer
   p->sayHi();  //**** run-time binding in effect
   delete p;    //**** free the dynamically allocated storage
   return 0;
}
```

FIGURE 7.1.2 Revision of the Figure 7.1.1 program to illustrate dynamic storage allocation.

Before exiting **main**, we release the storage for the dynamically created object by using the **delete** operator:

```
delete p; //*** free the dynamically allocated storage
```

It is good practice to **delete** any dynamically created object once the object is no longer needed. ∎

EXAMPLE 7.1.8.   The program in Figure 7.1.3 defines an array of 10 pointers to the base class **TradesPerson**

```
TradesPerson* ptrs[ 10 ];
```

and then dynamically creates 10 objects:

```
// randomly create TradesPersons, Tinkers, and Tailors
for ( i = 0; i < 10; i++ ) {
  which = 1 + rand() % 3;
  switch ( which ) {
  case 1: ptrs[ i ] = new TradesPerson; break;
  case 2: ptrs[ i ] = new Tinker; break;
  case 3: ptrs[ i ] = new Tailor; break;
  }
}
```

A randomly generated integer determines whether we dynamically create a **Trades-Person**, a **Tinker**, or a **Tailor**. Next we iterate through the array, invoking each object's polymorphic **sayHi** method:

```
// polymorphically invoke the sayHi methods
for ( i = 0; i < 10; i++ ) {
  ptrs[ i ]->sayHi();
  delete ptrs[ i ]; // release the storage
}
```

After invoking an object's **sayHi** method, we release the object's dynamically allocated storage with the **delete** operator.

We seed the random number generator with a call to **srand**

```
srand( time( 0 ) );
```

so that the program does not generate the same random numbers, hence the same output, each time it is run. ∎

```cpp
#include <iostream>
#include <cstdlib>
#include <ctime>
using namespace std;
class TradesPerson { // base class
public:
    virtual void sayHi() { cout << "Hi from on top." << endl; }
};

class Tinker : public TradesPerson { // derived class 1
public:
    virtual void sayHi() { cout << "Hi, I tinker." << endl; }
};

class Tailor : public TradesPerson { // derived class 2
public:
    virtual void sayHi() { cout << "Hi, I tailor." << endl; }
};

int main() {
    srand( time( 0 ) );
    TradesPerson* ptrs[ 10 ]; // pointers to base class
    unsigned which, i;
    // randomly create TradesPersons, Tinkers, and Tailors
    for ( i = 0; i < 10; i++ ) {
      which = 1 + rand() % 3;
      switch ( which ) {
      case 1: ptrs[ i ] = new TradesPerson; break;
      case 2: ptrs[ i ] = new Tinker; break;
      case 3: ptrs[ i ] = new Tailor; break;
      }
    }
    // polymorphically invoke the sayHi methods
    for ( i = 0; i < 10; i++ ) {
      ptrs[ i ]->sayHi();
      delete ptrs[ i ]; // release the storage
    }
    return 0;
}
```

FIGURE 7.1.3 Using an array of pointers to illustrate polymorphism.

If a class has constructors, these execute as expected for dynamically created objects. If a class has a destructor, it executes if a dynamically created object is destroyed.

EXAMPLE 7.1.9. The code segment

```
#include <iostream>
using namespace std;
class C {
public:
  C() { cout << "C::C() executing" << endl; }
  C( const char* s ) { cout << "C::C( string ) executing"
                            << endl; }
  ~C() { cout << "C::~C() executing" << endl; }
};

int main() {
  C *p1, *p2, *p3;      // define three pointers to C
  p1 = new C;           // default constructor
  p2 = new C();         // explicit call to constructor
  p3 = new C( "foo" );  // convert constructor
  // destroy the three objects
  delete p1; delete p2; delete p3;
  return 0;
}
```

dynamically allocates three **C** objects. **C** has a default constructor and a convert constructor. The statement

```
p1 = new C;
```

does not explicitly invoke a **C** constructor; but, because **C** has a default constructor, the default constructor executes when the object is created dynamically. The statement

```
p2 = new C();
```

is a stylistic variant of the first statement; in this case, the default constructor is explicitly invoked. The third statement

```
p3 = new C( "foo" );
```

invokes the convert constructor in dynamically creating a **C** object. Before **main** exits by executing the **return** statement, we destroy the three dynamically created objects by invoking **delete** on each pointer. Because **C** has a destructor, the destructor is called for each object when it is destroyed. The program's output is

```
C::C() executing
C::C() executing
C::C( string ) executing
C::~C() executing
C::~C() executing
C::~C() executing
```

Constructors and the Destructor

A constructor cannot be **virtual**. A destructor can be **virtual**.

EXAMPLE 7.1.10. The code segment

```
class C {
public:
   virtual C();        //***** ERROR: constructor
   virtual C( int ); //***** ERROR: constructor
   virtual ~C();       // ok, destructor
   virtual void m(); // ok, regular method
};
```

contains two errors because it declares the default and convert constructors as **virtual**. However, a destructor may be **virtual** (see Section 9.5). ∎

Object Methods and Class Methods

Only a non**static** method may be **virtual**. In different words, only an *object* as opposed to a *class* method can be **virtual** (see Section 5.7).

EXAMPLE 7.1.11. The code segment

```
class C {
public:
   static virtual void f(); //***** ERROR: static and virtual
   static void g();  // ok, not virtual
   virtual void h(); // ok, not static
};
```

contains an error because it tries to make a method both **static** and **virtual**. ∎

EXERCISES

1. Explain what a function's entry point is.
2. Explain the difference between compile-time and run-time binding.
3. What are three requirements for polymorphism in a C++ program?
4. Is every C++ function automatically polymorphic?
5. Explain the error.

```
#include <iostream>
using namespace std;
virtual void hi();
int main() {
   hi();
   return 0;
}
void hi() {
  cout << "Hello, world!" << endl;
}
```

6. Explain the error.

```
class B {
public:
    void m();
};
virtual void B::m() {...}
```

7. Can a **virtual** method be inherited?

8. What is the output?

```
#include <iostream>
using namespace std;
class B {
public:
    virtual void m() { cout << "B::m()" << endl; }
};
class D : public B {
public:
    void m() { cout << "D::m()" << endl; }
};
int main() {
    D d1;
    B* p = &d1;
    p->m();
    return 0;
}
```

9. What does it mean to *override* a **virtual** method?

10. What is the purpose of the vtable?

11. What are the performance penalties for run-time binding?

12. If class **z** has a default constructor, does it execute in the code segment

```
Z* p = new Z; // dynamically create a Z object
```

13. If class **z** has a destructor and a **z** object is created dynamically, does the destructor execute when the object is destroyed?

14. Suppose that class **c** has a convert constructor that expects an **int** argument. Is the following code segment legal?

```
class C {
public:
    C( int x ) {...}
};
C* p = new C( -999 );
```

15. Explain the error:

```
class A {
public:
   virtual void m() { cout << "A::m" << endl; }
   virtual A() { cout << "A::A" << endl; }
   virtual ~A() { cout << "A::~A" << endl; }
};
```

7.2 SAMPLE APPLICATION:
TRACKING FILMS REVISITED

Problem

Amend the Sample Application of Section 6.3 as follows:

- Provide a polymorphic **input** method that reads records for **Film**s, **DirectorCut**s, and **ForeignFilm**s from an input file. Each set of records in the input file represents an object in the **Film** hierarchy. Assume that the input file is correctly formatted.

- Dynamically create objects in the **Film** hierarchy to represent the corresponding sets of input records.

- Make the **input** method in the **Film** hierarchy polymorphic and use it to read, from an input stream, data for each dynamically created object in the **Film** hierarchy.

- Make the **output** method in the **Film** hierarchy polymorphic and use it to print, to the standard output, data for each dynamically created object in the **Film** hierarchy.

Sample Input/Output

For the sample input file

```
Film
Mean Streets
Martin Scorsese
168
4
Film
The Best Years of Our Lives
William Wyler
172
4
ForeignFilm
Diva
Jean-Jacques Beineix
123
3
```

```
French
DirectorCut
A Passage To India
David Lean
180
3
197
Cave scene twice as long; more local color
Film
Orlando
Sally Potter
97
3
```

our test client (see Figure 7.2.1) produces the output

```
Title: Mean Streets
Director: Martin Scorsese
Time: 168 mins
Quality: ****
Title: The Best Years of Our Lives
Director: William Wyler
Time: 172 mins
Quality: ****
Title: Diva
Director: Jean-Jacques Beineix
Time: 123 mins
Quality: ***
Language: French
Title: A Passage To India
Director: David Lean
Time: 180 mins
Quality: ***
Revised time: 197
Changes: Cave scene twice as long; more local color
Title: Orlando
Director: Sally Potter
Time: 97 mins
Quality: ***
```

Solution

We use the same class hierarchy as the original application, with **Film** as the base class and **ForeignFilm** and **DirectorCut** as the derived classes. For robustness, we add default constructors to all three classes so that all data members are initialized when objects are created.

Our test client (see Figure 7.2.1) is now relatively short because input comes from a disk file. We use the **static** method in the base class, **read_input**, to read records from

```
#include "films.h" // class declarations, etc.
int main() {
   const unsigned n = 5;
   Film* films[ n ];
   // attempt to read input file and create objects
   if ( !Film::read_input( "films.dat", films, n ) ) {
     cerr << "Unable to read file films.dat: exiting." << endl;
     exit( EXIT_FAILURE );
   }
   // output to the standard output
   for ( unsigned i = 0; i < n; i++ )
     films[ i ]->output(); // polymorphic output
   return 0;
}
```

FIGURE 7.2.1 Test client for the `Film` hierarchy.

the input file. (For a review of **static** methods, see Section 5.7.) The records are grouped according to whether they are **Film**s, **ForeignFilm**s, or **DirectorCut**s. An initial record identifies a group. For example, the record

> Film

signals that the following records are for **Film**s. After reading a record-group identifier such as **Film**, we dynamically create the corresponding object (e.g., a **Film** object) and store a pointer to it in the array **films**. We then invoke the object's polymorphic **input** method to read the remaining records. Each class's **input** method is designed specifically to read input records appropriate to that class. Note that **films** is an array of pointers to the base class **Film**, which supports the polymorphic output loop at the end of **main**.

Class method **read_input** returns **true**, if it succeeds in opening the input file, and **false**, if it fails to do so. (We assume that the input file is properly formatted.) If **read_input** returns **false**, we write a message to the standard error by using **cerr**, which is similar to **cout**. (On most systems, the standard error defaults to the video display.) The **exit** function, which requires the header file *cstdlib*, causes the program to exit. We invoke **exit** with the constant **EXIT_FAILURE**, an integer constant defined for each system in *cstdlib*, to signal that the program has terminated under error conditions.

We also handle output polymorphically. In each class, **output** is now a **virtual** method designed specifically to output its *local* data members. For example, **Foreign-Film**'s **output** method handles its **language** data member. **ForeignFilm**'s output method *first* invokes its parent class's (i.e., **Film**'s) **output** method to handle the *inherited* data members. This design allows a derived class **output** to delegate part of the output task to its parent class. The design principle can be applied if the hierarchy grows, thus managing the complexity of hierarchy growth. The polymorphic **input** methods use the same technique. For example, **ForeignFilm**'s **input** method *first* invokes **Film**'s **input** method to handle input of the *inherited* data members; **ForeignFilm**'s own **input** method then handles input of the *local* data member.

C++ Implementation

```cpp
#include <iostream>
#include <fstream>
#include <cstring>
#include <cctype>
using namespace std;

const int asize = 512;
class Film {
public:
    Film();
    void store_title( const char[ ] = "" );
    void store_director( const char[ ] = "" );
    void store_time( int = 0 );
    void store_quality( int = 0 );
    virtual void output();
    virtual void input( ifstream& );
    static bool read_input( const char[ ], Film*[ ], int );
private:
    char title[ asize ];
    char director[ asize ];
    int time;    // in minutes
    int quality; // 0 (bad) to 4 (tops)
};

Film::Film() {
    store_title();
    store_director();
    store_time();
    store_quality();
}

void Film::store_title( const char t[ ] ) {
    strcpy( title, t );
}

void Film::store_director( const char d[ ] ) {
    strcpy( director, d );
}

void Film::store_time( int t ) {
    time = t;
}

void Film::store_quality( int q ) {
    quality = q;
}
```

```cpp
// Reads title, director, time, and quality.
void Film::input( ifstream& fin ) {
   const unsigned n = 200;
   char inbuff[ n ];
   fin.getline( inbuff, n );
   store_title( inbuff );
   fin.getline( inbuff, n );
   store_director( inbuff );
   fin.getline( inbuff, n );
   store_time( atoi( inbuff ) );
   fin.getline( inbuff, n );
   store_quality( atoi( inbuff ) );
}

// Writes title, director, time, and quality.
void Film::output() {
   cout << "Title: " << title << endl;
   cout << "Director: " << director << endl;
   cout << "Time: " << time << " mins" << endl;
   cout << "Quality: ";
   for ( int i = 0; i < quality; i++ )
      cout << '*';
   cout << endl;
}

class DirectorCut : public Film {
public:
   DirectorCut();
   void store_rev_time( int = 0 );
   void store_changes( const char [ ] = "" );
   virtual void output();
   virtual void input( ifstream& );
private:
   int rev_time;
   char changes[ asize ];
};

DirectorCut::DirectorCut() {
   store_rev_time();
   store_changes();
}

void DirectorCut::store_rev_time( int t ) {
   rev_time = t;
}

void DirectorCut::store_changes( const char s[ ] ) {
   strcpy( changes, s );
}
```

```
// Reads revised time and changes.
void DirectorCut::input( ifstream& fin ) {
   Film::input( fin );
   const unsigned n = 200;
   char inbuff[ n ];
   fin.getline( inbuff, n );
   store_rev_time( atoi( inbuff ) );
   fin.getline( inbuff, n );
   store_changes( inbuff );
}

// Writes revised time and changes.
void DirectorCut::output() {
   Film::output();
   cout << "Revised time: " << rev_time << endl;
   cout << "Changes: " << changes << endl;
}

class ForeignFilm : public Film {
public:
   ForeignFilm();
   void store_language( const char[ ] = "" );
   virtual void output();
   virtual void input( ifstream& );
private:
   char language[ asize ];
};

ForeignFilm::ForeignFilm() {
   store_language();
}

void ForeignFilm::store_language( const char l[ ] ) {
   strcpy( language, l );
}

// Reads language.
void ForeignFilm::input( ifstream& fin ) {
   Film::input( fin );
   const unsigned n = 200;
   char inbuff[ n ];
   fin.getline( inbuff, n );
   store_language( inbuff );
}

// Writes language.
void ForeignFilm::output() {
   Film::output();
   cout << "Language: " << language << endl;
}
```

```
// class method: Film::read_input
// Reads data from an input file, dynamically creating the
// appropriate Film object for each record group. For instance,
// a ForeignFilm object is dynamically created if the data
// represent a foreign film rather than a regular film or a
// director's cut. Pointers to dynamically created objects are
// stored in the array films of size n. Returns true to
// signal success and false to signal failure.

bool Film::read_input( const char file[ ], Film* films[ ], int n ) {
   const int buffSize = 200;
   char inbuff[ buffSize ];
   ifstream fin( file );
   if ( !fin )   // opened successfully?
     return false; // if not, return false

   // Read until end-of-file. Records fall into
   // groups. 1st record in each group is a string
   // that represents a Film type:
   //    "Film", "ForeignFilm", "DirectorCut", etc.
   // After reading type record, dynamically create
   // an object of the type (e.g., a ForeignFilm object),
   // place it in the array films, and invoke its
   // input method.

   int next = 0;
   while ( fin.getline( inbuff, buffSize ) && next < n ) {
      if ( strcmp( inbuff, "Film" ) == 0 )
        films[ next ] = new Film();          // regular film
      else if ( strcmp( inbuff, "ForeignFilm" ) == 0 )
        films[ next ] = new ForeignFilm(); // foreign film
      else if ( strcmp( inbuff, "DirectorCut" ) == 0 )
        films[ next ] = new DirectorCut(); // director's cut
      else //**** error condition: unrecognized film type
        continue;
      films[ next++ ]->input( fin ); // polymorphic method
   }
   fin.close();
   return true;
}
```

Discussion

We use the same global constant for array sizes as the original application:

```
const int asize = 512;
```

All data members remain the same and are **private**.

Our first significant change is to add default constructors to handle data member initializations. For example, the default constructor for **Film**

```
Film::Film() {
    store_title();
    store_director();
    store_time();
    store_quality();
}
```

invokes methods to set the **Film**'s title, director, running time, and quality. For robustness, these methods all have default arguments. For example, the default argument for **store_title** is the empty string; the default time for **store_time** is 0. The other default constructors take the same approach towards their local data members.

To initiate input from a disk file, we use the **static** method **read_input**, which is declared in **Film**:

```
class Film {
public:
    ...
    // class methods
    static bool read_input( const char[ ], Film*[ ], int );
private:
    ...
};
```

This method's arguments are the name of the input file, an array of pointers to dynamically created objects in the **Film** hierarchy, and the array's size, respectively. The method returns **false** if it fails to open the input file; otherwise, it returns **true**. This allows a client, such as our **main**, to test for failure:

```
int main() {
    const unsigned n = 5;
    Film* films[ n ];
    // attempt to read input file and create objects
    if ( !Film::read_input( "films.dat", films, n ) ) {
      cerr << "Unable to read file Film.dat. Exiting."
            << endl;
      exit( EXIT_FAILURE );
    }
    ...
```

If **read_input** opens the input file, it uses an **ifstream** object's **getline** method to read records from the file. The loop

```
int next = 0;
while ( fin.getline( inbuff, buffSize ) && next < n ) {
   if ( strcmp( inbuff, "Film" ) == 0 )
     films[ next ] = new Film();          // regular film
   else if ( strcmp( inbuff, "ForeignFilm" ) == 0 )
     films[ next ] = new ForeignFilm(); // foreign film
   else if ( strcmp( inbuff, "DirectorCut" ) == 0 )
      films[ next ] = new DirectorCut(); // director's cut
   else //**** error condition: unrecognized film type
      continue;
   films[ next++ ]->input( fin ); // polymorphic method
}
```

halts if **getline** reaches the end of the input file or if the array of **Film** pointers is filled. The input file's records are divided into groups: the first record of each signals whether the following records are for a **Film**, **ForeignFilm**, or **DirectorCut** object. After reading the record that identifies the group, we use an **if** construct to determine its type. If the record is for, say, a **ForeignFilm** object, then we dynamically create such an object and store its address in array **films**:

```
else if ( strcmp( inbuff, "ForeignFilm" ) == 0 )
  films[ next ] = new ForeignFilm(); // ForeignFilm object
```

We have similar statements for **Film** and **DirectorCut** objects. We then invoke the newly created object's **input** method

```
films[ next++ ]->input( fin ); // polymorphic method
```

We also update **next**, which serves as an index into array **films**. The invocation of **input** is polymorphic. Which **input** method is invoked depends on the type of the newly created object. For example, if we just created a **ForeignFilm** object, then **ForeignFilm::input** is invoked. Note that the system, not the programmer, determines the appropriate method to call. This eases the programming burden by shifting a significant part of the load to the system.

The polymorphic **input** methods are designed to read data into *local* data members. For example, **Film::input** reads data only into **Film** data members. In similar fashion, **DirectorCut::input** reads data only into **DirectorCut** data members. Because **ForeignFilm** and **DirectorCut** are derived classes with **Film** as their base class, **ForeignFilm** and **DirectorCut** inherit **Film**'s data members. Therefore, each derived class's **input** *first* invokes **Film::input** to handle its inherited data members and then reads data into its own local data members. For example, **DirectorCut::input** begins as follows:

```
void DirectorCut::input( ifstream& fin ) {
   Film::input( fin );
   ...
}
```

The polymorphic versions of **input** work very much like their original, non**virtual** counterparts in that each derived class's **input** method invokes its inherited base class method. The big difference has to do with how an **input** method is invoked. In the original application, the *programmer* explicitly invokes either `Film::input`, `Foreign-Film::input`, or `DirectorCut::input`. In the polymorphic revision, the *system* automatically invokes the appropriate `input` method for a dynamically created object. This frees the programmer from the task of determining exactly which `input` method to invoke. As the class hierarchy grows, the benefit to the programmer increases.

The polymorphic versions of `output` are identical, in internal structure, to their non`virtual` counterparts in the original application. Again the big difference has to do with who determines which `output` method to invoke. In the original application, this task falls to the programmer. In the revision, this task falls to the system.

Program Development

Real-world applications are rarely, if ever, finished products. Such applications typically undergo constant change: bugs must be fixed, new functionality must be added to meet new requirements, application performance must be streamlined, and so on. Application design plays a major role in determining how hard it will be to make required changes. We focus here on one example.

Suppose that, over time, the `Film` hierarchy expands by several hundred new classes. Several benefits result from having the `input` and `output` methods be polymorphic and from making each class's `input` and `output` methods responsible for *local* data members only. Consider first the required changes to our application on the input side. The class method `readInput` would be changed, but in a straightforward manner. Each new class would require an `else if` in the style

```
else if ( strcmp( inbuff, "ForeignFilm" ) == 0 )
   films[ next ] = new ForeignFilm(); // ForeignFilm object
```

No other change to `readInput` would be required because the appropriate `input` method is invoked polymorphically:

```
films[ next++ ]->input( fin ); // polymorphic method
```

If each class's `input` method is responsible only for its own local data members, it can first call its base class's `input` method; and if this base class has a base class itself, the process continues straightforwardly. This design mimics the calling sequence of constructors in an inheritance hierarchy (see Section 6.5). Input complexity is manageable because the labor is distributed among different `input` methods, each responsible for only its own local data members. As new classes are added to the hierarchy, their authors need to focus only on a class's local data members in overriding `input`. The inherited data members are handled somewhere up the hierarchy by `input` methods that likewise focus on their own local data members. If an error occurs during `input` and the input file is correctly formatted, then the error can be traced to a specific class's `input` method. The design thus makes the application easier to write and to manage. The overall application also should gain robustness from this modular design.

On the output side, our application's test driver would not need to change at all. The `output` methods are invoked polymorphically from within a `for` loop:

```
// output to the standard output
for ( unsigned i = 0; i < n; i++ )
   films[ i ]->output(); // polymorphic output
```

This loop works the same for any mix of objects dynamically created from the input, and it works the same whether **n** is 3 or 3,000,000.

EXERCISES

1. Remove all occurrences of **virtual** from the sample application, recompile, and run the program using the same input file as before. What happens when the input and output methods are not **virtual**?

2. Our application uses the class method **readInput** to handle such basic input tasks as opening the file and creating objects to hold data in the input file. Why is a class method more appropriate than a top-level function for these tasks?

7.3 NAME OVERLOADING, NAME OVERRIDING, AND NAME HIDING

We describe a function as *polymorphic* only if it is bound at *run time*. In C++, only **virtual** methods are subject to run-time binding; hence, only **virtual** methods are truly polymorphic. C++ has constructs that *resemble* run-time binding but are quite distinct from it. Accordingly, we use this section to distinguish sharply between compile-time and run-time constructs in C++.

Name Overloading

Top-level functions can share a name if they have different signatures. Methods in the same class can share a name if they have different signatures. In either case, this is known as *name overloading*. Name overloading always involves *compile-time* binding, regardless of whether methods or top-level functions are involved.

EXAMPLE 7.3.1. In the code segment

```
class C {
public:
   C() {...}         // default constructor
   C( int x ) {...}  // convert constructor
};

void f( double d ) {...}
void f( char c ) {...}
int main() {
   C c1;         // default constructor called
   C c2( 26 ); // convert constructor called
   f( 3.14 );  // f( double ) called
   f( 'Z' );   // f( char ) called
   ...
}
```

there are two top-level functions named **f** and two constructors named **c**. Invocations of all four functions involve *compile-time* binding. The compiler uses the constructor *signatures* to do the bindings. Because **c1** is created with no initial value, the compiler invokes the default constructor. Because **c2** is created with an initial integer value, the compiler invokes the convert constructor.

In similar fashion, the compiler binds the invocation

```
f( 3.14 );
```

to the function named **f** that expects a single **double** argument. The compiler binds the invocation

```
f( 'Z' );
```

to the function named **f** that expects a single **char** argument. ■

Compile-time binding is always at work in name overloading. In this respect, overloaded functions—whether methods or top-level functions—differ sharply from **virtual** methods, which are bound at run-time.

Name Overriding

Suppose that base class **B** has a method **m** and its derived class **D** also has a method **m** with the *same* signature. If the methods are **virtual**, run-time binding is at work in any invocation of **m** through pointers or references. If the methods are **virtual**, the derived class method **D::m** *overrides* the base class method **B::m**. If the methods are *not* **virtual**, compile-time binding is at work in *any* invocation of **m**.

> **EXAMPLE 7.3.2.** The output for the code segment
>
> ```
> #include <iostream>
> using namespace std;
> class B {   // base class
> public:
>   void m() { cout << "B::m" << endl; }
> };
>
> class D : public B { // derived class
> public:
>   void m() { cout << "D::m" << endl; }
> };
>
> int main() {
>   B* p;        // pointer to base class
>   p = new D; // create a D object
>   p->m();      // invoke m
>   return 0;
> }
> ```
>
> is
>
> ```
> B::m
> ```

Note that **p** points to a **D** object, not to a **B** object. Further, **p** is used to invoke **m**. This *looks* like run-time binding, but it is not because **m** is not **virtual**—and only **virtual** methods are bound at run time in C++. The compiler uses **p**'s data type **B*** ("pointer to **B**") to bind the call to **B::m**. Recall that **D** inherits **m** from **B**. It just so happens that **D** has a *local* method named **m** with the same signature as the *inherited* method **m**. The compiler uses **p**'s data type to bind the call

```
p->m();
```

to the *inherited* **m**. The call is thus shorthand for

```
p->B::m();
```

■

EXAMPLE 7.3.3. We amend the program in Figure 7.1.2 by removing the keyword **virtual** and making no other changes (see Figure 7.3.1).

The user again enters an integer used in a **switch** statement to create a single object: a **TradesPerson** object if the user enters 1, a **Tinker** object if the user enters 2, and a **Tailor** object if the user enters 3. Pointer **p** holds the address of the dynamically created object, and **p** is used to invoke the object's **sayHi** method:

```
p->sayHi();
```

Regardless of whether **p** points to a **TradesPerson** object, a **Tinker** object, or a **Tailor** object, **TradesPerson::sayHi** is always invoked and, therefore, the output is always

```
Hi from on top.
```

Suppose, for example, that the user enters 2 for **Tinker**. In this case, the statement

```
p = new Tinker;
```

results in **p**'s pointing to a dynamically created **Tinker** object. Then the function call

```
p->sayHi();
```

executes. Because **sayHi** is *not* **virtual**, *compile-time* binding is in effect. Because **p**'s data type is **TradesPerson***, the compiler binds the call

```
p->sayHi();
```

to **TradesPerson::sayHi**. Note that **Tinker** has **TradesPerson** as its base class; hence, **Tinker** inherits **TradesPerson::sayHi** so that the **Tinker** object to which **p** points has a **TradesPerson::sayHi** method in addition to its **Tinker::sayHi**. Were **sayHi** a **virtual** method as in Figure 7.1.2, then *run-time* binding would be in effect. At run time, the system would determine *the type of object* to which **p** points and would then invoke that object's **sayHi** method, in our case **Tinker**'s **sayHi** method. In our current example, compile-time binding is at work; so the compiler determines which **sayHi** to invoke by using **p**'s data type **TradesPerson***. As a result, **TradesPerson::sayHi** is invoked even if **p** points to a **Tinker** object. ■

```
#include <iostream>
using namespace std;
class TradesPerson { // base class
public:
   void sayHi() { cout << "Hi from on top." << endl; }
};

class Tinker : public TradesPerson { // derived class 1
public:
   void sayHi() { cout << "Hi, I tinker." << endl; }
};

class Tailor : public TradesPerson { // derived class 2
public:
   void sayHi() { cout << "Hi, I tailor." << endl; }
};

int main() {
   TradesPerson* p; // pointer to base class

   int which;
   // prompt user for a number:
   // *** 1 == TradesPerson
   //     2 == Tinker
   //     3 == Tailor
   do {
      cout << "1 == TradesPerson, 2 == Tinker, 3 == Tailor ";
      cin >> which;
   } while ( which < 1 || which > 3 );
   // set pointer p depending on user choice
   switch ( which ) {
   case 1: p = new TradesPerson; break;
   case 2: p = new Tinker; break;
   case 3: p = new Tailor; break;
   }
   // invoke the sayHi method via the pointer
   p->sayHi();  //**** compile-time binding in effect
   delete p;    //**** free the dynamically allocated storage
   return 0;
}
```

FIGURE 7.3.1 Compile-time binding in the `TradesPerson` hierarchy.

Name Hiding

Suppose that base class **B** has a non**virtual** method **m** and its derived class **D** also has a method **m**. **D**'s local method **D::m** is said to *hide* the inherited method **B::m**. Name hiding is particularly tricky if the derived class's method has a *different signature* than the base class's method of the same name.

EXAMPLE 7.3.4.   The program

```
#include <iostream>
using namespace std;
class B {
public:
   void m( int x ) { cout << x << endl; }
};

class D : public B {
public:
   void m() { cout << "Hi" << endl; }
};

int main() {
   D d1;
   d1.m();     // OK: D::m expects no arguments
   d1.m( 26 ); //***** ERROR: D::m expects no arguments
   return 0;
}
```

generates a fatal compile-time error because it tries to invoke D's method m with a single argument. D's base class B does have a method m that expects a single argument, and D inherits this method. The problem is that D has a method *with the same name*. Therefore, the local D::m *hides* the inherited B::m. To invoke the inherited m with an argument, we must amend the code to

```
d1.B::m( 26 ); // OK: explicitly call B::m
```
■

Name hiding can occur with **virtual** as well as non**virtual** methods. In effect, name hiding occurs with **virtual** methods whenever a derived class **virtual** method fails to override the base class **virtual** method with the same name.

EXAMPLE 7.3.5.   The program

```
#include <iostream>
using namespace std;
class B {
public:
   virtual void m( int x ) { cout << x << endl; }
};

class D : public B {
public:
   virtual void m() { cout << "Hi" << endl; }
};
```

```
int main() {
    D d1;
    d1.m();
    d1.m( 26 ); //***** ERROR: D's m takes no arguments
    return 0;
}
```

generates a fatal compile-time error. **D**'s local method **D::m**, which happens to be **virtual**, expects no arguments. **D** does inherit a **virtual** method **B::m**, and the inherited **B::m** does expect one argument. The problem is that **D**'s local **D::m** hides the inherited **B::m**. That the two methods happen to be **virtual** is irrelevant to the name hiding. One fix is to invoke the inherited **B::m** explicitly

```
d1.B::m( 26 ); // OK: B::m explicitly invoked
```

This solves the problem but represents bad programming practice. For polymorphism to occur, **B::m** and **D::m** must have the *same signature*, not just the same name.

Finally, it should be emphasized that the two **m**'s are *unrelated*, although each happens to be **virtual**. For polymorphism to occur with respect to base class **B** and derived class **D**, there must be a **virtual** method in each *with the same signature*. In this example, the two **m**'s have two different signatures. In more technical terms, **D::m** does *not* override **B::m** because **D::m** has a different signature. Instead, we have two unrelated **virtual** methods named **m**. ∎

Name Sharing in C++ Programming

The examples in this section illustrate some problems that can arise if functions share a name. Nonetheless, it is sometimes desirable for functions to share a name. The obvious cases are

- Top-level functions with overloaded names. This is a convenience to programmers, who then can use one name such as **print** to invoke many different **print** functions, that is, many functions whose *signatures* differ but whose name happens to be **print**. It is quite common to overload operators such as **<<** as top-level functions (see Chapter 8).

- Constructors with overloaded names. A class often has more than one constructor, which requires name overloading for the constructors.

- Nonconstructor methods of the same class with the same name. A class **C**, for example, might have three **print** methods for convenience. The motivation here is the same as in overloading top-level functions.

- Methods, especially **virtual** ones, in a hierarchy. For polymorphism to occur, the **virtual** methods must have the *same signature* and, therefore, the same name. In typical polymorphism, a derived class's local **virtual** method *overrides* a **virtual** method inherited from the base class. For overriding to occur, the methods must be **virtual** and have the *same signature*.

When functions in a hierarchy share a name but *not* a signature, name hiding becomes a danger. So we recommend that this type of name sharing be used with great caution, if at all.

EXERCISES

1. Give an example of name overloading for top-level functions.

2. Given an example of name overloading for class constructors.

3. Is compile-time binding or run-time binding at work in name overloading?

4. Give an example of name hiding for non**virtual** methods.

5. Is compile-time binding or run-time binding at work in name sharing for non**virtual** methods?

6. Give an example of name overriding for **virtual** methods.

7. Is compile-time binding or run-time binding at work in name overriding for **virtual** methods?

8. Give an example of name hiding.

In Exercises 9 through 13, find all the errors, if any, and explain what is wrong. If there are no errors, show what is output.

9.
```cpp
#include <iostream>
using namespace std;
class A {  // base class
public:
  void m() { cout << "A::m" << endl; }
};

class Z : public A { // derived class
public:
  void m() { cout << "Z::m" << endl; }
};

int main() {
  A* p;
  p = new Z;
  p->m();
  return 0;
}
```

10.
```cpp
#include <iostream>
using namespace std;
class A {  // base class
public:
  virtual void m() { cout << "A::m" << endl; }
};

class Z : public A { // derived class
public:
  void m() { cout << "Z::m" << endl; }
};
```

```
    int main() {
      A* p;
      p = new Z;
      p->m();
      return 0;
    }
```

11.
```
    #include <iostream>
    using namespace std;
    class A {
    public:
       virtual void m( double d ) { cout << d << endl; }
    };

    class Z : public A {
    public:
       virtual void m() { cout << "foo" << endl; }
    };

    int main() {
       A a1;
       a1.m();
       a1.m( 3.14 );
       return 0;
    }
```

12.
```
    #include <iostream>
    using namespace std;
    class A {
    public:
       virtual void m( double d ) { cout << d << endl; }
    };

    class Z : public A {
    public:
       virtual void m() { cout << "foo" << endl; }
    };

    int main() {
       A* p = new A;
       p->m();
       p->m( 3.14 );
       return 0;
    }
```

13.
```
    #include <iostream>
    using namespace std;
    class A {
    public:
       virtual void m( int x ) { cout << x << endl; }
    };
```

```
class Z : public A {
public:
   virtual void m() { cout << "baz" << endl; }
};

int main() {
   Z z1;
   z1.m();
   z1.A::m( 26 );
   return 0;
}
```

7.4 ABSTRACT BASE CLASSES

An **abstract base class** is *abstract* in that no objects can instantiate it. Such a class can be used to specify `virtual` methods that any derived class *must* override in order to have objects instantiate the derived class. We begin with technical details and then offer examples of abstract base classes and reasons for using them.

A class must meet one requirement to be an abstract base class:

* The class must have a **pure** `virtual` method.

A pure `virtual` method is one initialized to zero in its declaration.

> **EXAMPLE 7.4.1.** The code segment
>
> ```
> class ABC {  // Abstract Base Class
> public:
>    virtual void open() = 0;
> };
> ```
>
> creates an abstract base class named `ABC` that has a single method, the pure `virtual` method named `open`. By initializing `open` to zero in its declaration, we make it *pure* `virtual`. By making `open` pure `virtual`, we thereby make `ABC` an abstract base class.
>
> The initialization of `open` to zero is a syntactic convention that makes `open` a pure `virtual` method and, therefore, `ABC` an abstract base class. When a *variable* is initialized to zero, a value is actually stored in the variable. By contrast, when a `virtual` method is initialized to zero, the method is simply marked as pure `virtual`, and its containing class thereby becomes abstract. ∎

> **EXAMPLE 7.4.2.** Given the definition for the abstract base class in Example 7.4.1, it is an error to define objects of type `ABC`:
>
> ```
> class ABC {  // Abstract Base Class
> public:
>    virtual void open() = 0;
> };
> ABC obj; //***** ERROR: ABC is an abstract class
> ```
> ∎

Although an abstract base class cannot have objects instantiate it, such a class can have derived classes. A class derived from an abstract base class *must* override all of the base class's *pure* **virtual** methods; otherwise, the derived class itself becomes abstract and no objects can instantiate the derived class.

EXAMPLE 7.4.3. We derive two classes from the abstract base class **ABC** in Example 7.4.1:

```
class ABC { // Abstract Base Class
public:
   virtual void open() = 0;
};
class X : public ABC { // 1st derived class
public:
   virtual void open() {...} // override open()
};
class Y : public ABC { // 2nd derived class
   //*** open is not overridden
};
ABC a1;  //***** ERROR: ABC is abstract
X   x1;  //***** Ok, X overrides open() and is not abstract
Y   y1;  //***** ERROR: Y is abstract--open() not defined
```

Class **X** overrides the pure **virtual** method inherited from the abstract base class **ABC**. Therefore, **X** is nonabstract and may have objects instantiate it. By contrast, **Y** does not override the pure **virtual** method inherited from **ABC**. Therefore, **Y** becomes an abstract base class and cannot have objects instantiate it. ∎

Abstract base classes are useful for specifying, as pure **virtual** methods, functions that any derived class must override in order to have objects instantiate the derived class.

EXAMPLE 7.4.4. In the inheritance hierarchy

```
class BasicFile {  // Abstract Base Class
public:
  // methods that any derived class should override
  virtual void open() = 0;
  virtual void close() = 0;
  virtual void flush() = 0;
};
class InFile : public BasicFile {
public:
  virtual void open() {...}  // definition
  virtual void close() {...} // definition
  virtual void flush() {...} // definition
};
InFile f1; // OK, InFile is not abstract
```

abstract base class **BasicFile** specifies three pure **virtual** methods that any derived class must override if the derived class is not to be abstract. **InFile** is not abstract precisely because **InFile** overrides all of the pure **virtual** methods specified in its abstract base class **BasicFile**. ■

One pure **virtual** method suffices to make a class an abstract base class. An abstract base class may have other methods that are not pure **virtual** or not even **virtual** at all. Further, an abstract base class may have data members. An abstract base class's members may be **private**, **protected**, or **public**.

EXAMPLE 7.4.5. We amend Example 7.4.1

```
class ABC { // Abstract Base Class
public:
   ABC() {...}                   // default constructor
   ABC( int x ) {...}            // convert constructor
  ~ABC() {...}                   // destructor
   virtual void open() = 0;      // pure virtual
   virtual void print() {...}    // virtual, not pure
   int getCount() { return n; }  // nonvirtual
private:
   int n; // data member
};
```

by having a mix of methods in **ABC** and by adding a data member. **ABC** remains abstract, however, because it still has the pure **virtual** method **open**. Therefore, no objects can instantiate **ABC**. Any class derived from **ABC** still must override **open** if the derived class is not to become abstract itself. However, a derived class can simply use the inherited versions of **print** and **getCount**. ■

Restrictions on Pure Functions

Only a **virtual** method can be pure. Neither a non**virtual** nor a top-level function can be initialized to zero in its declaration.

EXAMPLE 7.4.6. The code segment

```
void f() = 0; //***** ERROR: not a virtual method
class C {
public:
   void open() = 0; //***** ERROR: not a virtual method
};
```

contains two errors because **f** is not a method at all and **open** is not a **virtual** method. Therefore, neither **f** nor **open** can be initialized to zero in its declaration. ■

Uses of Abstract Classes

Abstract base classes can be used to specify design requirements. For example, suppose that we are working on a large project involving many programmers, each of whom is responsible for several classes. During the project's design phase, we decide that each class should have two **public** methods: **listFields** lists the class's data members and data types and prints a brief explanation of the data member's role in the class, and **listMethods** lists the class's methods and prints a brief explanation of the functionality that the method provides. To enforce this design decision, we provide an abstract base class

```
class IIntrospect { // introspection interface
public:
  virtual void listFields() = 0;
  virtual void listMethods() = 0;
};
```

and require that *all* classes in the project be derived from **IIntrospect**. Any class derived from **IIntrospect** must override the two pure **virtual** methods in order to have objects instantiate it. In this way, we ensure that objects used in the project will have the methods **listFields** and **listMethods**. We pursue the point with a commercial example. By the way, because an abstract base class often has only **public** methods as members, it is common to use the keyword **struct** to declare an abstract base class.

Microsoft's COM (**C**omponent **O**bject **M**odel) is an infrastructure for building applications out of prebuilt software components. For example, Microsoft itself provides a *Calendar* component that has an intuitive graphical interface for entering dates. This component might be plugged into an application that requires a user to enter, for example, a birth date. The user would enter a date on the calendar and then push a button to complete the operation. Under COM, a component must implement at least one interface, which is a list of functions that the component supports. At the C++ level, a COM interface is an abstract base class with pure **virtual** methods that the component must override. For example, Microsoft's calendar control implements an interface that includes functions such as **GetMonth** and **GetYear**, which can be used to get integer values that represent a date's month and year, respectively. COM requires that every interface be derived from **IUnknown**, a C++ abstract base class with three pure **virtual** methods:

- **QueryInterface**. This function supports navigation among multiple COM interfaces. Suppose that component *C* (e.g., the calendar) has two interfaces, *I1* and *I2*. For application *A* to use *C*, *A* must have access to one of the interfaces. Suppose that *A* has access to *I1*. Because *I1* must be derived from **IUnknown**, and because *C* implements *I1*, *A* can use the implementation of **QueryInterface**, as specified in *I1*, to gain access to *C*'s other interface, in this case *I2*. In general, **QueryInterface** allows a component's client to move among the component's interfaces, if the component supports multiple interfaces. Many COM components do implement multiple interfaces.

- **AddRef**. A key principle of component software is that a component's client (that is, an application using the component) should not be able to halt the component's execution. Instead, the component itself should keep a *count* of its clients and halt its own execution when the count is zero. This approach is known as **reference counting**.

A COM component implements **AddRef** so that a client can increment the component's reference count. If the count ever equals zero, the component itself terminates its execution.

• **Release**. A component's client invokes this method to decrement the component's reference count.

Because COM components must implement at least one interface, and because *every* interface must be derived from **IUnknown**, every COM component must implement the three pure **virtual** methods in **IUnknown**. COM has other standard interfaces as well. To become proficient in COM is to become fluent in COM interfaces, that is, in the pure **virtual** methods specified in COM's abstract base classes.

EXERCISES

1. What condition must a class meet to be an abstract base class?

2. Explain the error:

```
class A {
public:
   virtual void m() = 0;
private:
   int x;
};
A a1;
```

3. Explain the error:

```
class A {
public:
   void m() = 0;
private:
   int x;
};
```

4. Must every method in an abstract base class be pure **virtual**?

5. Explain the error:

```
struct A {
   virtual void m1() = 0;
   virtual void m2() = 0;
};
class Z : public A {
public:
   void m1() { cout << "Hi!" << endl; }
};
Z z1;
```

6. Suppose that **ABC** is an abstract base class and **z** is derived from it. What condition must **z** satisfy to be a nonabstract class, that is, a class that can have objects instantiate it?

7. Can an abstract base class have non**virtual** methods?

8. Can an abstract base class have data members?

C++ POSTSCRIPT

Failed Requests for Dynamic Storage

If operator **new** succeeds in allocating run-time storage, it returns a pointer to the storage. If **new** fails to allocate the requested storage, **new** throws a **bad_alloc** exception by default. The exception is handled by either the system or the programmer. The programmer can intercept a thrown exception such as a **bad_alloc** exception. If the programmer does *not* intercept a thrown exception, the system's default action is to terminate the program. Appendix E explains the details of exception-handling. Here we focus on the basic syntax for catching an exception thrown by a failed attempt to allocate storage. Using a **catch**er is one way to intercept a thrown exception. To catch a **bad_alloc** exception, we place the request for storage in a **try** block and provide a **catch**er for the exception. (**try** and **catch** are C++ keywords.)

EXAMPLE. The following program places the call to **new** in a **try** block, below which is a **catch** block that catches the **bad_alloc** exception thrown by **new** if it fails to allocate the requested storage:

```
#include <iostream>
using namespace std;
class C {
public:
   void m() { cout << "ok" << endl; }
};
int main() {
   C* p; // pointer to a C object
   try {
      p = new C; // request storage
   }
   // provide a catcher for a bad_alloc exception thrown
   // by new if it fails to allocate requested storage
   catch( bad_alloc ) {
      cout << "Unable to allocate a C object. Exiting..."
           << endl;
      exit( EXIT_FAILURE ); // terminate program
   }
   // if new succeeds, invoke the allocated C's m
   p->m();
   delete p;
   return 0;
}
```

The **catch** block resembles a function, except that its name is always **catch** and it has no return data type. The exception's data type, in this case **bad_alloc**, occurs as if it were a parameter data type. Our **catch** block prints a message about the failed memory allocation and then **exit**s the program. In general, a **catch** block may contain any legal C++ statement. A **catch** block typically prints an error message before taking whatever action is deemed appropriate for a particular type of exception. If **new** succeeds, no exception is thrown and execution resumes immediately after the **catch** block. In this example, we use **p** to invoke the **C** object's method **m** if the memory allocation succeeds. ∎

Having **new** throw a **bad_alloc** exception is a relatively new addition to C++. Some compilers may not support it yet. The compilers that do not support **bad_alloc** will likely have **new** return **NULL** (0) if it fails to allocate the requested storage.

Strong and Weak Polymorphism

Some authors distinguish in C++ between *strong* and *weak* polymorphism. In this case, *strong* polymorphism refers to the run-time binding of overridden **virtual** methods. *Weak* polymorphism has two forms: overloading of top-level functions or methods, and name sharing among non**virtual** methods in a hierarchy. We use *polymorphism* to describe only the run-time binding of overridden **virtual** methods. We use *overloading*, *name sharing*, and other terms to describe C++ constructs that may resemble run-time binding but which, in fact, involve only compile-time binding.

COMMON PROGRAMMING ERRORS

1. It is an error to declare a top-level function **virtual**:

   ```
   virtual bool f(); //***** ERROR: f is not a method
   ```

   Only *methods* can be **virtual**.

2. It is an error to declare a **static** method **virtual**:

   ```
   class C {
   public:
      virtual void m();       // ok, object method
      virtual static void s(); //***** ERROR: static method
   };
   ```

3. If a **virtual** method is *defined outside* the class declaration, then the keyword **virtual** occurs in its declaration but not in its definition:

   ```
   class C {
   public:
      virtual void m1() {...} // ok, declaration + definition
      virtual void m2();      // ok, declaration
   };
   ```

```
//***** ERROR: virtual should not occur in a definition
//              outside the class declaration
virtual void C::m2() {
  ...
}
```

4. It is an error to declare any constructor **virtual**, although the destructor may be **virtual**:

```
class C {
public:
   virtual C();       //***** ERROR: constructor
   virtual C( int ); //***** ERROR: constructor
   virtual ~C();      // ok, destructor
};
```

5. It is bad programming practice not to **delete** a dynamically created object *before* the object is inaccessible:

```
class C {
  ...
};
void f() {
   C* p = new C; // dynamically create a C object
   ...           // use it
} //****** ERROR: should delete the object!
```

Once control exits **f**, the object to which **p** points can no longer be accessed. Therefore, storage for this object ought to be freed:

```
void f() {
   C* p = new C; // dynamically create a C object
   ...           // use it
   delete p;     // delete it
}
```

6. If a method hides an inherited method, then it is an error to try to invoke the inherited method without using its full name:

```
class A {
public:
   void m( int ) {...} // takes 1 arg
};
class Z : public A {
public:
   void m() {...}      // takes 0 args, hides A::m
};
```

```
int main() {
  Z z1;
  z1.m( -999 );    //***** ERROR: Z::m hides A::m
  z1.A::m( -999 ); // ok, full name
  z1.m();          // ok, local method
  ...
}
```

The error remains even if **m** is **virtual** because **A::m** and **Z::m** do not have the same signature.

7. It is an error to expect run-time binding of non**virtual** methods. In the code segment

```
class A {
public:
  void m() { cout << "A::m" << endl; }
};
class Z : public A {
public:
  void m() { cout << "Z::m" << endl; }
};
int main() {
  A* p = new Z; // ok, p points to Z object
  p->m();       // prints A::m, not Z::m
  ...
}
```

m is *not* **virtual**. Because compile-time binding is in effect, the call

```
p->m();
```

is to **A::m** since **p**'s data type is **A*** ("pointer to **A**"). It is irrelevant that **p** happens to point to a **Z** object. If we make **m** a **virtual** method

```
class A {
public:
  virtual void m() { cout << "A::m" << endl; }
};
```

then the output is **Z::m** because *run-time* binding is in effect and **p** points to a **Z** object.

8. It is an error to expect a derived class **virtual** method **D::m** to override a base class **virtual** method **B::m** if the two methods have *different* signatures. The code segment

```
class A {
public:
  virtual void m(); // base class virtual method
};
class Z : public A {
public:
  //***** Caution: Z::m hides A::m
  virtual void m( int ); // derived class virtual method
};
```

has two **virtual** methods named **m**, but **Z::m** does *not* override **A::m** because the two methods have different signatures. For useful polymorphism to occur, the **virtual** methods must have the same *signature*, not just the same name. In this example, the two **virtual** methods are completely unrelated. They simply happen to share a name.

9. It is an error to try to define objects that instantiate an abstract base class:

```
class ABC { // abstract base class
public:
   virtual void m() = 0; // pure virtual method
};
ABC a1; //***** ERROR: ABC is abstract
```

10. If a class **C** is derived from an abstract base class **ABC** and **C** does not override *all* of **ABC**'s pure **virtual** methods, then **C** is abstract and cannot have objects instantiate it:

```
class ABC { // abstract base class
public:
   virtual void m1() = 0; // pure virtual method
   virtual void m2() = 0; // pure virtual method
};
class C : public ABC {
public:
   virtual void m1() {...} // override m1
                           // m2 not overridden
};
C c1; //***** ERROR: C is abstract
```

PROGRAMMING EXERCISES

7.1. Derive an additional class **SongAndDance** from class **Film** of Section 7.2. Add appropriate data members and methods, including overrides of the **virtual** methods for input and output. Implement a test client to test the hierarchy and, in particular, the overrides.

7.2. Revise the **intArray** hierarchy of Programming Exercise 6.4 by making the **print** method **virtual**. After revising the classes, write a test client for the hierarchy.

7.3. Implement a hierarchy with **Date** as the base class with a **virtual** method **print**. Derived classes are **ShortE**, **MediumDate**, and **LongDate**. **Date**'s **print** uses the format

    10-1-50

where 10 is the month (October), 1 is the day of the month, and 50 is the year 1950. **ShortE**'s **print** uses the European format

    1-10-50

MediumDate's **print** uses the format

    Oct. 1, 1950

and **LongDate**'s **print** uses the format

```
October 1, 1950
```

Write a test client for the **Date** hierarchy to test the implementations of **print**.

7.4. Revise the **CardGame** hierarchy of Programming Exercise 6.5 by making the **deal** method **virtual**. After revising the classes, write a test client for the hierarchy.

7.5. Implement an index hierarchy with a base class **Entry** to represent entries in a book's index. The base class represents a basic index entry such as

```
quark, 234, 512, 901
```

A basic entry consists of a term such as **quark** followed by the page numbers on which the word occurs. Here are samples of other entry types that should be included in the hierarchy:

```
//*** Sample: proper name followed by pages
Gauss, Carl, 67, 69, 106

//*** Sample: entry with multiple subentries
topology, 46, 78-80
   map-coloring problems, 45-47
   Mordell's conjecture, 107

//*** Sample: entry with descriptive subentry
music, harmony in, 37
```

The hierarchy should have a polymorphic **format** method that correctly formats a particular entry type as the entry is printed. Write a test client that has an array of pointers to the base class **Entry**, with each pointer pointing to a particular type of entry. The output code segment might look like this:

```
// print index entries, correctly formatted
for ( int i = 0; i < n; i++ )
   entries[ i ]->format();
```

7.6. Revise the **Emp**loyee hierarchy of Programming Exercise 6.11 by implementing polymorphic **input** and **output** methods to handle reading data into data members and printing data members to the standard output (see Section 7.2). Implement a test client for the hierarchy.

7.7. Many object-oriented systems support **persistence**, which saves an application's objects in nonvolatile storage (e.g., a disk file) when the application is not running. Persistence is typically implemented through either a database or **serialization**, which saves a binary representation of an object to a sequential file. The name *serialization* underscores that an object's binary representation is written to file in serial fashion, that is, one bit after the other. Serialization saves the object's *type*, which is the class to which it belongs, together with its members' values. Saving an object to a file is serializing *out*, and restoring an object from a file is serializing *in*. Create a class hierarchy with **Object** as an abstract base class and **serialize** as a pure **virtual** method. Classes derived from **Object** override **serialize** so that their objects can be serialized out and in. *Hint*: Provide **Object** with a data member **classID**, which uniquely identifies a class. Each derived class's constructors are then responsible for setting its **classID**, which can be used to identify objects during serialization. In particular, when an object is serialized in, the first *n* bytes are its **classID**. Once the **classID** is known, a call to the **new** operator can be used to create an object of the corresponding type. Data members can be saved and restored as bytes rather than as C++ data types such as **float**, **int**, and so forth.

7.8. Windows systems such as Motif and Windows NT are object-oriented. In such systems, there is a hierarchy of **Window** classes with appropriate methods such as **create**, **show**, **hide**, **move**, and **destroy** to manipulate particular types of **Window** objects. Simulate an object-oriented windows systems by using simple console graphics. For example, the figure

represents a **SimpleWindow**, whereas

```
+============+
|Title       |
+------------+
|Client area |
+------------+
|Status line |
+============+
```

represents a **FramedWindow**. Implement a **Window** hierarchy with at least four derived classes. Classes in the hierarchy should implement an interface that consists of polymorphic methods to create, destroy, show, hide, move, and resize **Window** objects.

7.9. For the **Product** hierarchy of Programming Exercise 6.12, suppose that, once a month, the chain runs an application that contains the loop

```
for ( int i = 0; i < productCount; i++ )
    products[ i ]->adjustPrice();
```

where **products** is an array of pointers to the base class **Product**, which has a **virtual** method **adjustPrice**. The **virtual** method adjusts the price of each **Product** object depending on the corresponding class's **supply** and **demand** members. Derive at least 10 classes from **Product**, overriding the **adjustPrice** in each. Implement a test client that uses sample data to test the hierarchy.

7.10. The No Guarantees Dating Service (hereafter, NGDS) includes, for an extra charge, a breakup service in which NGDS generates a form letter to announce the breakup and handles any subsequent correspondence from the dumpee. The form letter is based on a personality profile that NGDS social scientists put together for each client. The personality categories are

- Normal.
- Slightly Neurotic.
- Passive/Aggressive.
- Comatose.
- Beavis or Butthead.
- Loose Cannon.
- Freddy.

Create an inheritance hierarchy to represent the personality profiles. The base class should have a pure **virtual** method called **dearJohn** that, when invoked, generates a breakup letter appropriate for the personality profile. Write a test client to generate letters for a mix of objects that belong to the different personality classes.

7.11. Implement a shape hierarchy with **Shape** as an abstract base class that has the pure **virtual** methods **draw** and **resize**. Derived classes should include **Point**, **Line**, **Circle**, **Triangle**, and **Rectangle**. Each derived class implements the **draw** method to draw an appropriate representation of an object in the class and the **resize** method to change an object's initial size. If you have access to a graphics package such as Visual C++, use the drawing capabilities provided; otherwise, use basic console graphics. Write a test client for the hierarchy.

7.12. Administrative software for computer networks provides various services that require **hosts**—that is, machines on the network—to be polled. A polled host typically responds with its network address and other pertinent information. Create a hierarchy with **Host** as the abstract base class with a pure **virtual** method **poll** whose declaration is

```
virtual HostInfo& poll() = 0;
```

The returned **HostInfo** reference contains pertinent information about a host such as its network address; its type (e.g., *applications server*, *file server*, *workstation*, *router*, *personal computer*, *print server*, etc.); most recent connect time to network; status (e.g., *active* or *idle*); and the like. Classes derived from **Host** are different types of host such as **Workstation**, **FileServer**, and so forth. Each class derived from **Host** overrides **poll** to return, as a **HostInfo** reference, appropriate information about itself. After creating the necessary hierarchy and auxiliary classes such as **HostInfo**, write a test client that includes a loop such as

```
for ( int i = 0; i < hostCount; i++ )
   printReport( hosts[ i ]->poll() );
```

7.13. For the **Vehicle** hierarchy of Programming Exercise 6.6, provide the **virtual** methods

- **start**, which outputs the steps in a recipe to start the **Vehicle** in question.
- **computeDepr**, which computes a **Vehicle**'s depreciation over **expected-Life**, which is a **Vehicle** data member that gives the expected life in years.
- **diagnose**, which tries to guide the user through a troubleshooting session by asking appropriate questions (e.g., *Does the engine turn over when the ignition is turned on?*).

7.14. Implement an **AbsCollection** abstract base class that specifies common operations on an abstract collection such as *add*, *delete*, *removeAll*, *enumerate*, *getCount*, *append* (from one abstract collection to another), *containsMember*, and *isEqual*. The abstract base class should also include an array of **int**s, which represents the objects in an abstract collection (see Programming Exercise 6.10). Derive classes such as **Set** (see Programming Exercise 5.12) and **Bag** (see Programming Exercise 5.13) from the abstract base class, and override all the inherited pure **virtual** methods in appropriate ways.

7.15. Implement a **PropSheet** abstract base class with the pure **virtual** method whose prototype is

```
virtual void listProps() = 0;
```

A derived class should override **listProps** to describe briefly, in messages to the standard output, what each of the class's data members represents and how these members may be accessed. For example, given the class

```
class Emp : public PropSheet {
public:
    void listProps() { ... }
    void setId( int n ) { id = n; }
    // other public methods
private:
    unsigned id;
    char      dept[ 10 ];
    // other data members
}
```

the override of **listProps** might print to the standard output messages such as

```
id:    Stores unique identification number.
          Must be set in constructor as unsigned.
          Read via getId().
          Not writable after construction.
dept:  Stores home department.
          Optionally set in constructor.
          Read via getDept().
          Written via setDept( const char[ ] ).
```

Write a test client to demonstrate the override of **listProps** for at least three classes.

CHAPTER

8

OPERATOR
OVERLOADING

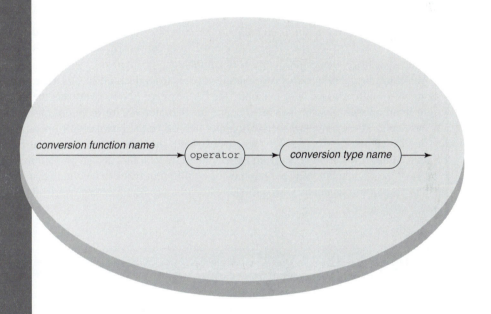

Overloading refers to multiple meanings of the same name or symbol. An *overloaded function* (see Section 3.7) is a function with multiple definitions. In this chapter we discuss **operator overloading**, which refers to multiple definitions of the various C++ operators such as **+**, **++**, and **[ ]**. These operators are overloaded by writing special kinds of functions.

Arithmetic operators such as **+** and **/** are overloaded in the C++ language. For example, the **/** operator may designate either integer division

```
2 / 3     // divide 2 by 3, which gives 0
```

or floating-point division

```
2.0 / 3.0    // divide 2.0 by 3.0, which gives 0.666667
```

Different algorithms are required to compute the two divisions even though **/** designates division in both cases. At the programmer level, it is convenient to have one symbol to designate division—whatever the type of the numbers to be divided.

The convenience of operator overloading extends from the built-in C++ types, such as **int** and **float**, to classes. For example, the C++ system library overloads the operator **>>**, for input of class objects such as **cin**, and the operator **<<**, for output of class objects such as **cout**. These operators were originally defined as the bitwise shift operators (see the C++ Postscript for Chapter 1). Once overloaded, the same symbol, **>>**, can be used for input of many different types from the keyboard, from a file, and so on. Similarly, the same symbol, **<<**, can be used for output of many different types to the video display, to a file, and so on. In this chapter we will show how the programmer can overload the C++ operators for classes.

8.1 BASIC OPERATOR OVERLOADING

C++ allows any operator to be overloaded except for these five:

Operator	Purpose
.	Class member operator
.*	Class member dereference operator
::	Scope resolution operator
? :	Conditional operator
sizeof	Size in bytes operator

Every overloaded operator in a base class, except the assignment operator (**=**), is inherited in a derived class.

If we want to overload the operator **+** for the class **C** so that we can add two **C** objects with the result being another **C** object, we can declare a method named **operator+** in the class **C**

```
class C {
public:
   C operator+( C& );
   ...
};
```

The method is implemented in the usual way

```
C C::operator+( C& c ) {
   ...
}
```

Following the usual syntax for invoking a method, **operator+** can be invoked as

```
C a, b, c;
a = b.operator+( c );
```

where **a**, **b**, and **c** are objects in the class **C**. Notice that since the result of the **+** operation is supposed to be a **C** object, this method properly returns type **C**. Because of the keyword **operator**, this method can, and normally would, be invoked as

```
a = b + c;
```

In the latter case, the meaning is clear; we add the **C** objects **b** and **c** to obtain another **C** object, which is then assigned to the **C** object **a**. Notice that in the declaration in the class **C**

```
C operator+( C& );
```

operator+ has *one* parameter, even though **+** takes *two* arguments. The first argument is the object on which the method is invoked. In the code segment

```
a = b + c;
```

the method is invoked on **b**, which is clear in the alternative syntax

```
a = b.operator+( c );
```

The second argument **c** is passed to the method **operator+**, which accounts for the one parameter of type **C&**. In general, if we use a method to overload a binary operator (i.e., an operator that takes two arguments), the method has one parameter. If we use a method to overload a unary operator (i.e., an operator that takes one argument), the method has no parameters.

EXAMPLE 8.1.1. The code segment

```
class C {
public:
   C operator=( C& );
   C operator!();
   ...
};
```

shows how to declare operator overloads of the binary assignment operator **=** and the unary not operator **!**.   ∎

EXAMPLE 8.1.2. Consider the string class

```
class String {
public:
   ...
private:
   char str[ 100 ];
   int len;
};
```

in which we represent a string by storing the characters of the string in the array **str** and the length of the string in the variable **len**. To overload the operator **==** to test for equality of strings, we write a method

   operator==

Since **==** is a binary operator that compares **String**s, this method has one argument of type **String&**. The other argument of type **String** is the object on which this method is invoked. The result of the comparison is **true** or **false**, so **operator==** returns type **bool**. Thus, **operator==** is declared in class **String** as

```
class String {
public:
   ...
   bool operator==( const String& ) const;
private:
   char str[ 100 ];
   int len;
};
```

The two **const**s indicate that the overload will not change the two **String** objects that are compared. The first **const** indicates that the argument will not be changed, and the second indicates that the object on which **operator==** is invoked will not be changed.

The result of the string comparison is **true** precisely when the strings have the same length and identical characters. Thus the method may be implemented as

```
bool String::operator==( const String& s ) const {
   if ( len != s.len )
      return false;
   for ( int i = 0; i < len; i++ )
      if ( str[ i ] != s.str[ i ] )
         return false;
   return true;
}
```

The overloaded equality operator could be used in a context such as

```
String s1, s2;
...
if ( s1 == s2 ) {
   ...
}
```

The expression **s1 == s2** is interpreted as

```
s1.operator==( s2 )
```

which therefore invokes the code for method **operator==**. If this method returns **true**, the expression **s1 == s2** thus evaluates to **true**, and the body of the **if** statement executes. If, on the other hand, the method returns **false**, the expression **s1 == s2** evaluates to **false**, and the body of the **if** statement does not execute.

The built-in meaning of **==** for integers and floating-point numbers is equality of numbers in the usual sense. By overloading **==** for the **String** class, we have extended this built-in meaning for numbers to strings so that the meaning of **==** for strings is equality of strings in the usual sense. ∎

Operator Precedence and Syntax

Operator precedence and syntax cannot be changed through overloading. For example, the binary operator | | always occurs *between* its two arguments, whether built-in or overloaded; and | | retains its original precedence even when overloaded.

EXAMPLE 8.1.3.   In the code segment

```
int main() {
   Complex c1, c2, c3, ans;
   ...
   ans = c1 + c2 * c3;
   ...
}
```

the expression

```
ans = c1 + c2 * c3;
```

is equivalent to

```
ans = c1 + ( c2 * c3 );
```

There is no way to change the precedence of the built-in operators **+** and ***** so that, for example, **+** has a higher precedence than ***** for the class **Complex**. Also, the *binary* operator **+** always occurs *between* its two arguments. There is no way to overload the binary **+** so that it occurs either before or after its two arguments. In a similar fashion, the unary **+** always occurs *before* its argument, even if the operator is overloaded. ∎

If a built-in operator is unary, then all overloads of it remain unary. If a built-in operator is binary, then all overloads remain binary.

EXAMPLE 8.1.4. The class declaration

```
class C {
public:
   C operator%(); // ***** ERROR: % is binary
   ...
};
```

contains an error. The operator % is *binary*, not *unary*, so when overloaded as a method must have *one* parameter. ∎

EXERCISES

1. Explain the error.

```
class String {
   ...
   bool operator>( const String& ) const;
   ...
};

bool String::>( const String& s ) const {
   ...
}
```

2. Explain the error.

```
class String {
   ...
   bool operator>( const String&, const String& ) const;
   ...
};

bool String::operator>( const String& s1,
                        const String& s2 ) const {
   ...
}
```

3. Explain the error.

```
class String {
   ...
   bool operator>( const String& ) const;
   ...
};

bool String::operator>( const String& s ) {
   ...
}
```

4. Explain the error.

```
class String {
    ...
    int operator.( const String& ) const;
    ...
};

int String::operator.( const String& s ) const {
    ...
}
```

5. Show a declaration of a method in class **String** that overloads the operator **!**.

In Exercises 6 through 11, overload the given operator for the **String** class of Example 8.1.2. Show the declaration and write the definition. (Assume that the array **str** does *not* necessarily store a null terminator.)

6. <

7. <=

8. >

9. >=

10. !=

11. + (for concatenation)

8.2 SAMPLE APPLICATION: A COMPLEX NUMBER CLASS

Problem

A *complex number* is a number of the form $z = a + bi$, where a and b are floating-point numbers. The symbol i represents the square root of -1. The term a is called the *real part* of z, and b is called the *imaginary part* of z. Arithmetic operations on complex numbers are defined as follows:

$$(a + bi) + (c + di) = (a + c) + (b + d)i$$
$$(a + bi) - (c + di) = (a - c) + (b - d)i$$
$$(a + bi) \times (c + di) = (ac - bd) + (ad + bc)i$$
$$(a + bi)/(c + di) = (ac + bd)/(c^2 + d^2) + [(bc - ad)/(c^2 + d^2)]i$$

Implement a class that represents complex numbers and

- Overloads **+**, **-**, *****, and **/** to support complex arithmetic.
- Contains a method **write** to output a complex number to the standard output.
- Provides a default constructor that sets the real and imaginary parts of the complex number to zero.
- Provides a one-parameter constructor that sets the real part of the complex number to the value passed and sets the imaginary part of the complex number to zero.
- Provides a two-parameter constructor that sets the real and imaginary parts of the complex number to the values passed.

Sample Output

If **c1** represents the complex number $7.7 + 5.5i$ and **c2** represents the complex number $4.2 - 8.3i$, when the method **write** is used to print the sum, difference, product, and quotient of **c1** and **c2**, the output, suitably annotated, is

```
c1 + c2 = 11.9 + -2.8i
c1 - c2 = 3.5 + 13.8i
c1 * c2 = 77.99 + -40.81i
c1 / c2 = -0.153819 + 1.005547i
```

Solution

We declare the class **Complex** with two **double** data members to represent the real and imaginary parts of a complex number. We overload the **Complex** operators using methods. Since each operator is a *binary* operator, as a method each has *one* parameter of type **Complex**. Since the result of each operation is of type **Complex**, each method returns type **Complex**. For example, to overload **+**, we declare the method **operator+** as

```
Complex operator+( const Complex& ) const;
```

C++ Implementation

```
class Complex {
public:
    Complex();                  // default
    Complex( double );          // real given
    Complex( double, double );  // both given

    void write() const;
    // operator methods
    Complex operator+( const Complex& ) const;
    Complex operator-( const Complex& ) const;
    Complex operator*( const Complex& ) const;
    Complex operator/( const Complex& ) const;
private:
    double real;
    double imag;
};
```

```cpp
// default constructor
Complex::Complex() {
    real = imag = 0.0;
}

// constructor -- real given but not imag
Complex::Complex( double re ) {
    real = re;
    imag = 0.0;
}

// constructor -- real and imag given
Complex::Complex( double re, double im ) {
    real = re;
    imag = im;
}

void Complex::write() const {
    cout << real << " + " << imag << 'i';
}

// Complex + as binary operator
Complex Complex::operator+( const Complex& u ) const {
    Complex v( real + u.real,
               imag + u.imag );
    return v;
}

// Complex - as binary operator
Complex Complex::operator-( const Complex& u ) const {
    Complex v( real - u.real,
               imag - u.imag );
    return v;
}

// Complex * as binary operator
Complex Complex::operator*( const Complex& u ) const {
    Complex v( real * u.real - imag * u.imag,
               imag * u.real + real * u.imag );
    return v;
}

// Complex / as binary operator
Complex Complex::operator/( const Complex& u ) const {
    double abs_sq = u.real * u.real + u.imag * u.imag;
    Complex v( ( real * u.real + imag * u.imag ) / abs_sq,
               ( imag * u.real - real * u.imag ) / abs_sq );
    return v;
}
```

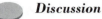

Discussion

We declare two **double** data members: **real**, to represent the real part of a complex number, and **imag**, to represent the imaginary part of a complex number.

The class **Complex** has three constructors. The default constructor initializes the data members **real** and **imag** to 0.0. The one-parameter constructor initializes **real** to the value passed and **imag** to 0.0. The two-parameter constructor initializes **real** and **imag** to the values passed.

The three constructors could be combined into one by keeping only the two-parameter constructor and providing default values for the parameter in the declaration:

```
class Complex {
   ...
   Complex( double = 0.0, double = 0.0 );
   ...
};
```

The method **write** is implemented so that it outputs a **Complex** number in the form

real part + *imaginary part***i**

The implementation of each operator overload follows the same pattern. A **Complex** object is created and initialized using the two-parameter constructor. The values supplied are those given by the formulas for complex arithmetic. Then the object is returned. For example, the overload of **+**

```
Complex Complex::operator+( const Complex& u ) const {
   Complex v( real + u.real,
              imag + u.imag );
   return v;
}
```

defines a **Complex** object **v** and initializes its real part to

```
real + u.real
```

and its imaginary part to

```
imag + u.imag
```

because of the formula

$$(a + bi) + (c + di) = (a + c) + (b + d)i$$

for complex addition. For example, if **x1** and **x2** are **Complex** objects, the expression

```
x1 + x2
```

translates as

```
x1.operator+( x2 )
```

Thus when the code

```
Complex Complex::operator+( const Complex& u ) const {
   Complex v( real + u.real,
              imag + u.imag );
   return v;
}
```

executes, **real** and **imag** refer to **x1**'s real and imaginary parts, and **u.real** and **u.imag** refer to **x2**'s real and imaginary parts. Thus in **v**, we have **v.real** equal to **x1.real** + **x2.real** and **v.imag** equal to **x1.imag** + **x2.imag** as indicated by the definition of complex addition. The overload concludes by returning the object **v**. Incidentally, the overload could be written more simply as

```
Complex Complex::operator+( const Complex& u ) const {
   return Complex( real + u.real, imag + u.imag );
}
```

The function **main** shown in Figure 8.2.1 shows the **Complex** class in action. The output is

```
c1 + c2 = 11.9 + -2.8i
c1 - c2 = 3.5 + 13.8i
c1 * c2 = 77.99 + -40.81i
c1 / c2 = -0.153819 + 1.005547i
```

When a statement such as

```
c3 = c1 / c2;
```

executes, the appropriate overload (**operator/** in this case) is invoked. This overload defines a **Complex** object that represents the result of the operation. The execution of the statement concludes when the assignment operator copies the object returned by the overload into **c3**. When an object is copied by the assignment operator

```
obj1 = obj2;
```

each of **obj2**'s data members is copied to the corresponding data member in **obj1**. (The action of the assignment operator can be changed because the assignment operator can itself be overloaded!) In our case, the values of the data members **real** and **imag** of the object defined by the overload are copied into **c3**'s **real** and **imag** data members. Thus **c3** represents the result of the arithmetic operation.

```
int main() {
    Complex c1( 7.7, 5.5 );
    Complex c2( 4.2, -8.3 );
    Complex c3;

    c3 = c1 + c2;
    cout << "c1 + c2 = ";
    c3.write();
    cout << endl;

    c3 = c1 - c2;
    cout << "c1 - c2 = ";
    c3.write();
    cout << endl;

    c3 = c1 * c2;
    cout << "c1 * c2 = ";
    c3.write();
    cout << endl;

    c3 = c1 / c2;
    cout << "c1 / c2 = ";
    c3.write();
    cout << endl;
    return 0;
}
```

FIGURE 8.2.1 The `Complex` class in action.

EXERCISES

1. Could **operator+** be implemented so that its declaration is

   ```
   Complex operator+( const Complex ) const;
   ```

   Explain.

2. Could **operator+** be implemented so that its declaration is

   ```
   Complex& operator+( const Complex& );
   ```

   Explain.

3. The *conjugate* of the complex number $a + bi$ is $a - bi$. Overload ~ so that it returns the complex conjugate of the **Complex** object.

4. The *absolute value* of the complex number $a + bi$ is $\sqrt{a^2 + b^2}$. Overload ! so that it returns the absolute value of the **Complex** object.

8.3 OPERATOR OVERLOADING USING TOP-LEVEL FUNCTIONS

An overloaded operator is a user-defined function that retains the convenience of operator syntax. In general, an overloaded operator must be either a method, as explained in Sections 8.1 and 8.2, or a top-level function, which is the subject of this section and the next. Except for the memory-management operators, **new**, **new[ ]**, **delete**, and **delete[ ]**, an operator that is overloaded as a top-level function must include a class object among its arguments. The operators **[ ]** (index operator), **=** (assignment operator), **()** (function call operator), and **->** (indirect selection operator) must be implemented as methods.

It makes sense for C++ to require that an operator such as **%** be either overloaded as a method or take at least one class object as an argument. Otherwise, in an expression such as

```
int x = 11, y = 3, z;
z = x % y;
```

the system could not distinguish between the built-in **%** and some user-defined overload of **%**. If **%** is overloaded either as a method or as a top-level operator function that takes a class object as an argument, the system can determine which **%** operator to invoke in a particular context.

To overload the operator **+** using a top-level function so that we can add two **C** objects with the result being another **C** object, we define a top-level function named **operator+**

```
C operator+( C& c1, C& c2 ) {
   ...
}
```

Notice that the class name and the scope resolution operator **::** do *not* appear in a top-level function overload—it is *not* a method. Notice also that both of the objects involved in the overload have names: **c1** and **c2**. When a binary operator is overloaded as a method, only the second object has an explicit name (see Section 8.2). Notice also that since the result of the **+** operation is a **C** object, this function returns type **C**.

Following the usual syntax for invoking a function, the top-level function overload can be invoked as

```
a = operator+( b, c );
```

where **a**, **b**, and **c** are objects in class **C**. Because of the keyword **operator**, this function can, and normally would, be invoked as

```
a = b + c;
```

The *top-level function* **operator+** has *two* parameters—the two **C** objects to add. Recall that when we overload **+** using a *method* in class **C**, the method has *one* parameter (see Section 8.1). If **+** is overloaded as a method, in the code segment

```
a = b + c;
```

the method is invoked on object **b**. The second argument **c** is passed to the method **operator+**. In general, if we use a method to overload a binary operator, the method has one parameter. If we use a top-level function to overload a binary operator, the function has two parameters, which correspond to the two arguments that are passed to the operator. Similarly, if we use a method to overload a unary operator, the method has no parameters. If we use a top-level function to overload a unary operator, the function has one parameter, which corresponds to the single argument that is passed to the operator.

EXAMPLE 8.3.1.   The code segment

```
// ***** ERROR: neither a method nor a
// a function that takes a class argument
void operator%( float f1, float f2 ) {
   ...
}
```

contains an error because an overloaded operator either must be a class method or take a class object as an argument.   ■

EXAMPLE 8.3.2.   The code segment

```
// ***** ERROR: [ ] must be overloaded as a method
void operator[ ]( String& s ) {
   ...
}
```

contains an error because the index operator **[ ]** must be overloaded as a method rather than as a top-level function. The same holds for the function call operator **( )**. If these operators could be overloaded as top-level functions, the system could not determine in a particular context whether to invoke the built-in or some user-defined version.   ■

We have not yet indicated any advantage to overloading an operator as a top-level function rather than as a method. The next examples illustrate one advantage.

EXAMPLE 8.3.3.   Consider a **main** function

```
int main() {
   Complex a, b( 4.3, -8.2);
   // OK: uses convert constructor
   a = b + 54.3;
   // ***** ERROR: first arg not a Complex object
   a = 54.3 + b;
   ...
}
```

that uses the **Complex** class of Section 8.2. The statement

```
a = b + 54.3;
```

is interpreted as

```
a = b.operator+( 54.3 );
```

There is no method **operator+** in class **Complex** that takes a floating-point argument, but there is a convert constructor

```
class Complex {
   ...
   // convert constructor converts double to Complex
   Complex( double );
   ...
};
```

that can convert a floating-point value to a **Complex** object. After the constructor converts **54.3** to a **Complex** object, the method **operator+**, which takes a **Complex** argument, executes. Thus the statement

```
a = b + 54.3;
```

executes properly. (This situation is similar to that in which an **int** and **double** are added, and the system converts the **int** to a **double** before performing the addition.)

The statement

```
a = 54.3 + b;
```

is interpreted as

```
a = 54.3.operator+( b ); // ***** ERROR
```

Here an error results since the member operator cannot be applied to the nonobject **54.3**. Furthermore, the system does *not* convert **54.3** to an object so that the member operator can be applied. ∎

EXAMPLE 8.3.4.   Suppose that + is overloaded as a top-level function for class **Complex**

```
Complex operator+( const Complex& c1, const Complex& c2 ) {
   ...
}
```

In the **main** function

```
int main() {
   Complex a, b( 4.3, -8.2);
   // OK: uses convert constructor
   a = b + 54.3;
   // OK: also uses convert constructor
   a = 54.3 + b;
   ...
}
```

both statements are now legal. When the first statement, which is interpreted as

```
a = operator+( b, 54.3 );
```

executes, the convert constructor converts **54.3** to a **Complex** object, after which the top-level function

```
Complex operator+( const Complex& c1, const Complex& c2 ) {
   ...
}
```

executes. Similarly, when the second statement, which is interpreted as

```
a = operator+( 54.3, b );
```

executes, the convert constructor converts **54.3** to a **Complex** object, after which the top-level overload function again executes. Here no member operator is used, so no error results from applying the member operator to a nonmember. Thus an advantage of using a top-level function rather than a method to overload a binary operator is that the two arguments are treated in the same way by the system; either can be converted, if necessary. When a method is used to overload a binary operator, the first argument *must* be an object from the appropriate class. ∎

Consider overloading **+** for the **Complex** class of Section 8.2 using a top-level function. The code might look like

```
Complex operator+( const Complex& t, const Complex& u ) {
   return Complex( t.real + u.real,
                   t.imag + u.imag );
}
```

However, this will *not* work because **real** and **imag** are **private** in class **Complex**, and **operator+** cannot access them. The problem can be solved in several ways. One possibility is to make **real** and **imag public** in class **Complex**; however, this violates the principle of hiding the implementation. Another possibility, which we implement in the next example, is to add methods to class **Complex** that return the values of **real** and **imag**. A third possibility is to make **operator+** a **friend** of class **Complex**. If a function **f** is a **friend** of class **C**, **f** may access **C**'s **private** and **protected** members. We discuss this last technique in the next section.

EXAMPLE 8.3.5. We add methods to the class **Complex** of Section 8.2 that return the values of **real** and **imag**, and overload the arithmetic operators using top-level functions (see Figure 8.3.1). The implementation of the constructors and method **write** is unchanged. ∎

```
class Complex {
public:
   Complex();                  // default
   Complex( double );          // real given
   Complex( double, double ); // both given

   void write() const;
   // added methods
   double get_real() const { return real; }
   double get_imag() const { return imag; }
private:
   double real;
   double imag;
};


// Complex + as top-level function
Complex operator+( const Complex& t, const Complex& u ) {
   return Complex( t.get_real() + u.get_real(),
                   t.get_imag() + u.get_imag() );
}


// Complex - as top-level function
Complex operator-( const Complex& t, const Complex& u ) {
   return Complex( t.get_real() - u.get_real(),
                   t.get_imag() - u.get_imag() );
}


// Complex * as top-level function
Complex operator*( const Complex& t, const Complex& u ) {
   return Complex( t.get_real() * u.get_real()
                   - t.get_imag() * u.get_imag(),
                   t.get_imag() * u.get_real()
                   + t.get_real() * u.get_imag() );
}


// Complex / as top-level function
Complex operator/( const Complex& t, const Complex& u ) {
   double abs_sq = u.get_real() * u.get_real()
                   + u.get_imag() * u.get_imag();
   return Complex( ( t.get_real() * u.get_real()
                     + t.get_imag() * u.get_imag() ) / abs_sq,
                   ( t.get_imag() * u.get_real()
                     - t.get_real() * u.get_imag() ) / abs_sq );
}
```

FIGURE 8.3.1 Overloading the `Complex` arithmetic operators as top-level functions.

EXERCISES

1. Explain the error.

```
bool operator||( bool b1, bool b2 ) {
   ...
}
```

2. Explain the error.

```
class C {
   ...
};
bool operator&&( C& c ) {
   ...
}
```

3. Explain the error.

```
bool operator()( bool b1, bool b2, bool b3 ) {
   ...
}
```

4. Overload ~ using a top-level function so that it returns the complex conjugate of the **Complex** object.

5. Overload **!** using a top-level function so that it returns the absolute value of the **Complex** object.

8.4 friend FUNCTIONS

A class's **private** members are accessible only to its methods and its **friend** functions. A class's **protected** members are accessible only to methods in its class hierarchy and its **friend** functions. To make a function **f** a **friend** of class **C**, we declare **f** within **C**'s declaration using the keyword **friend**:

```
class C {
   ...
   friend int f(); // friend function
   ...
};
```

Because **f** is *not* a method, the declaration serves only to give **f** access rights to **C**'s **private** and **protected** members; thus, the declaration may be placed within the **private**, **protected**, or **public** part of the declaration of class **C**. Because a **friend** function is not a **C** method, yet has access to **C**'s **private** and **protected** members, a **friend** function violates a strict interpretation of object-oriented principles. Accordingly, **friend** functions are controversial and open to misuse. We recommend using **friend** functions only in operator overloading.

EXAMPLE 8.4.1.   In the previous section, we overloaded the arithmetic operators in the **Complex** class of Section 8.2 using top-level functions. We added methods to access **Complex**'s **private** members so that these top-level functions could obtain the values of the **private** members.

```
class Complex {
public:
    Complex();                  // default
    Complex( double );          // real given
    Complex( double, double ); // both given

    void write() const;
    // friend functions
    friend Complex operator+( const Complex&, const Complex& );
    friend Complex operator-( const Complex&, const Complex& );
    friend Complex operator*( const Complex&, const Complex& );
    friend Complex operator/( const Complex&, const Complex& );
private:
    double real;
    double imag;
};

// Complex + as top-level friend
Complex operator+( const Complex& t, const Complex& u ) {
    return Complex( t.real + u.real,
                    t.imag + u.imag );
}

// Complex - as top-level friend
Complex operator-( const Complex& t, const Complex& u ) {
    return Complex( t.real - u.real,
                    t.imag - u.imag );
}

// Complex * as top-level friend
Complex operator*( const Complex& t, const Complex& u ) {
    return Complex( t.real * u.real - t.imag * u.imag,
                    t.imag * u.real + t.real * u.imag );
}

// Complex / as top-level friend
Complex operator/( const Complex& t, const Complex& u ) {
    double abs_sq = u.real * u.real + u.imag * u.imag;
    return Complex( ( t.real * u.real + t.imag * u.imag ) / abs_sq,
                    ( t.imag * u.real - t.real * u.imag ) / abs_sq );
}
```

FIGURE 8.4.1 The **Complex** class with operators overloaded as top-level **friend** functions.

Another way to overload the arithmetic operators in the `Complex` class as top-level functions is to make the top-level functions **friend**s of `Complex` (see Figure 8.4.1). As **friend**s, the top-level functions have access to `Complex`'s **private** members. The implementations of the constructors and method **write** are not shown because they are unchanged. ∎

An advantage of adding methods to return the values of **private** and **protected** members needed by top-level overload functions rather than using **friend** functions is that **private** members remain visible only within the class and **protected** members remain visible only within the class hierarchy—sound object-oriented principles are not violated. A disadvantage is that the methods added to return the values of **private** or **protected** members may confuse and clutter the interface. Such methods may provide access to the client of mysterious values, particularly if such values are buried deep within the implementation. In such a situation, it is probably better to use **friend** functions and not muddle the interface. Of course, the whole issue of exposing **private** and **protected** members can be avoided if the overloads are implemented using methods. In so doing one gives up the advantage discussed in Example 8.3.4. Further, there are situations in which the overloads *must* be implemented using top-level functions (see Section 8.5).

EXERCISES

1. Explain the error.

```
class C {
public:
   ...
private:
   bool stored;
   ...
};

void operator!( C& c ) {
   c.stored = !c.stored;
}
```

2. Explain the error.

```
class C {
public:
   ...
private:
   bool stored;
   friend void operator!( C& );
   ...
};

void operator!( C& c ) {
   stored = !stored;
}
```

3. Explain the error.

```
class C {
public:
    ...
private:
    bool stored;
    friend void operator!( C& );
    ...
};
void C::operator!( C& c ) {
    c.stored = !c.stored;
}
```

4. Overload ~ using a top-level **friend** function so that it returns the complex conjugate of the **Complex** object.

5. Overload ! using a top-level **friend** function so that it returns the absolute value of the **Complex** object.

In Exercises 6 through 12, overload the given operator for the **String** class of Example 8.1.2 using a top-level **friend** function. Show the **friend** declaration and write the definition. (Assume that the array **str** does *not* necessarily store a null terminator.)

6. <

7. <=

8. >

9. >=

10. ==

11. !=

12. + (for concatenation)

8.5 OVERLOADING THE INPUT AND OUTPUT OPERATORS

The system library overloads the right-shift operator **>>** for formatted input of built-in types as a method in an appropriate system class. For example, if **i** is an **int**,

```
cin >> i
```

is interpreted as

```
cin.operator>>( i )
```

The overload is written so that system code executes that reads and stores a value in **i**.

The operator **>>** can be further overloaded for user-defined types. Notice that it *cannot* be overloaded as a method, because this would require modification of the system class. We should not modify the system class even if we could. Thus **>>** must be overloaded as a top-level function.

EXAMPLE 8.5.1. To overload `>>` to read two floating-point numbers, interpreted as a single complex number, into a `Complex` object (see Section 8.2), we could write a top-level function `operator>>`

```
istream& operator>>( istream& in, Complex& c ) {
   return in >> c.real >> c.imag;
}
```

The system supplies a **typedef** for **istream** so that **istream** can be used to refer to input streams including **cin** and variables of type **ifstream**. The overloaded input operator could be used as

```
Complex c_obj;
cin >> c_obj;
```

The second statement

```
cin >> c_obj;
```

is equivalent to

```
operator>>( cin, c_obj );
```

and, when evaluated, is equivalent to

```
cin >> c_obj.real >> c_obj.imag;
```

Thus the statement does indeed read two floating-point numbers, interpreted as a single complex number, into the `Complex` object `c_obj`.

Both parameters are passed by reference. Input stream objects are always passed by reference because the system needs to update certain information about the stream in order to do input. The `Complex` object is passed by reference because we modify it; its data members are updated to the values read. The stream is returned so that we can chain input

```
Complex c1_obj, c2_obj;
cin >> c1_obj >> c2_obj;
```

just as we can for the built-in types.

As written, `operator>>` requires access to `Complex`'s **private** members. In order to provide this access, we make `operator>>` a **friend** of `Complex`

```
class Complex {
   ...
   friend istream& operator>>( istream&, Complex& );
   ...
};
```

Similarly, the system library overloads the left-shift operator `<<` for formatted output of built-in types as a method in an appropriate system class. The operator `<<` can be further overloaded for user-defined types as a top-level function.

EXAMPLE 8.5.2.   To overload `<<` to output a **Complex** object, we would write a top-level function **operator<<**

```
ostream& operator<<( ostream& out, const Complex& c ) {
   return out << c.real << " + " << c.imag << 'i';
}
```

The system supplies a **typedef** for **ostream** so that **ostream** can be used to refer to output streams including **cout** and variables of type **ofstream**. Since **operator<<** requires access to **Complex**'s **private** members, we would make **operator<<** a **friend** of **Complex**.   ∎

EXERCISES

1. Explain the error.

```
istream& operator>>( istream& in, Complex c ) {
   ...
}
```

2. Explain the error.

```
istream operator>>( istream in, Complex& c ) {
   ...
}
```

3. Show the declaration of the overload in Example 8.5.2 in the **Complex** class.

4. Use a **friend** function to overload `>>` to input a **String** object (see Example 8.1.2).

5. Use a **friend** function to overload `<<` to output a **String** object (see Example 8.1.2).

8.6 OVERLOADING SOME SPECIAL OPERATORS

In this section, we show how to overload some special operators: the index operator, `[ ]`; the function call operator, `( )`; the increment and decrement operators, `++` and `--`; and the type conversion operator.

Overloading the Index Operator

The index operator **[ ]** *must* be overloaded as a method. Its declaration looks like

```
class C {
   ...
   returntype operator[ ]( paramtype );
   ...
};
```

If **c** is a **C** object, the expression

```
c[ i ]
```

is interpreted as

```
c.operator[ ]( i )
```

EXAMPLE 8.6.1. C++ does no checking for out-of-bounds indexes in arrays; however, by overloading the index operator, such checking can be added. The class **intArray** in Figure 8.6.1 implements an **int** array with bounds checking.

The unimplemented default constructor is **private** to force the user to provide an array size to the one-parameter constructor, which sets **size** to the value passed. Only **size** bytes of the array **a** of size 100 are used; thus, from the point-of-view of the user, the object represents an array of size **size**.

The overloaded index operator is declared as

```
int& operator[ ]( int );
```

The programmer uses the **int** parameter as an index into an ordinary array; that is, the programmer writes

```
arr[ i ]
```

where **arr** is an **intArray** object. The system interprets this to mean

```
arr.operator[ ]( i )
```

The overload is written so that, if the index **i** is in bounds, the value **a[i]** is returned

```
int& intArray::operator[ ]( int i ) {
   if ( i < 0 || i >= size ) {
      cerr << "index " << i
           << " out of bounds: ";
      return a[ 0 ];
   }
   return a[ i ];
}
```

If the index is not in bounds, the overload prints a message and returns **a[0]**. (The idea is to flag the error but to let the program continue to execute.)

```
const int MaxSize = 100;
class intArray {
public:
   int& operator[ ]( int );
   intArray( int s );
   int get_size() { return size; }
private:
   int size;
   int a[ MaxSize ];
   intArray();
};
int& intArray::operator[ ]( int i ) {
   if ( i < 0 || i >= size ) {
      cerr << "index " << i
           << " out of bounds: ";
      return a[ 0 ];
   }
   return a[ i ];
}
intArray::intArray( int s ) {
   if ( s <= MaxSize )
      size = s;
   else {
      cerr << "Array size too big\n";
      exit( 0 );
   }
}
```

FIGURE 8.6.1 Bounds checking by overloading the index operator.

The overload returns an **int** reference so that if **arr** is an **intArray** object, **arr[i]** can be used on either side of an assignment expression

```
arr[ i ] = 8;
j = arr[ i ];
```

The output of the following **main** function

```
int main() {
   intArray b( 5 );
   int i;
   for ( i = 0; i < b.get_size(); i++ )
      b[ i ] = 2 * i;
   for ( i = 0; i < 6; i++ )
      cout << b[ i ] << endl;
   return 0;
}
```

is

```
0
2
4
6
8
index 5 out of bounds: 0
```

■

Overloading the Function Call Operator

Like the index operator, the function call operator **()** *must* be overloaded as a method. Its declaration looks like

```
class C {
    ...
    returntype operator()( paramtypes );
    ...
};
```

where *paramtypes* is the list of parameter types separated by commas. Suppose that there are two parameters; the first is of type **float**, and the second is of type **char***. If **c** is a **C** object, **x** is a variable of type **float**, and **name** is an array of **char**, the expression

```
c( x, name )
```

is interpreted as

```
c.operator()( x, name )
```

EXAMPLE 8.6.2. The **intTwoArray** class in Figure 8.6.2 has the functionality of a two-dimensional array of **int** but also incorporates bounds checking. Instead of accessing the cells as **b[i][j]**, we overload the function call operator so that the cells are accessed as **b(i, j)**.

The unimplemented default constructor is **private** to force the user to provide the sizes of the two dimensions to the two-parameter constructor. The first parameter gives the size of the first dimension, and the second parameter gives the size of the second dimension. The constructor sets **size1** to the first value passed and **size2** to the second value passed. The item at location **i,j** (from the user's point of view) is stored at cell **i * size2 + j** in the one-dimensional array **a** (see Figure 8.6.3).

The overloaded function call operator is declared as

```
int& operator()( int, int );
```

The programmer uses the **int** parameters as indexes into the two-dimensional array (from the user's point of view again); that is, the programmer writes

```
arr( i, j )
```

```
const int MaxSize = 100;
class intTwoArray {
public:
    int& operator()( int, int );
    intTwoArray( int, int );
    int get_size1() { return size1; }
    int get_size2() { return size2; }
private:
    int a[ 100 ];
    int size1;
    int size2;
    intTwoArray();
};

int& intTwoArray::operator()( int i, int j ) {
    if ( i < 0 || i >= size1 ) {
        cerr << "first index " << i
             << " out of bounds: ";
        return a[ 0 ];
    }
    if ( j < 0 || j >= size2 ) {
        cerr << "second index " << j
             << " out of bounds: ";
        return a[ 0 ];
    }
    return a[ i * size2 + j ];
}

intTwoArray::intTwoArray( int s1, int s2 ) {
    int size = s1 * s2;
    if ( size <= MaxSize ) {
        size1 = s1;
        size2 = s2;
    }
    else {
        cerr << "Array size too big\n";
        exit( 0 );
    }
}
```

FIGURE 8.6.2 Bounds checking by overloading the function call operator.

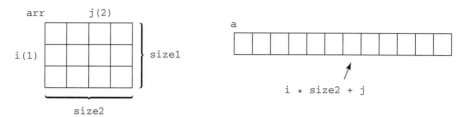

FIGURE 8.6.3 Indexing from the user's point-of-view versus the actual implementation. The value of **size1** is 3, and the value of **size2** is 4. The user references **intTwoArray(1,2)**, which maps to **a[1*4 + 2]**.

where **arr** is an **intTwoArray** object. The system interprets this to mean

```
arr.operator()( i, j )
```

The overload is written so that, if the indexes are in bounds, the value returned is **a[i * size2 + j]**

```
int& intTwoArray::operator()( int i, int j ) {
   if ( i < 0 || i >= size1 ) {
      cerr << "first index " << i
           << " out of bounds: ";
      return a[ 0 ];
   }
   if ( j < 0 || j >= size2 ) {
      cerr << "second index " << j
           << " out of bounds: ";
      return a[ 0 ];
   }
   return a[ i * size2 + j ];
}
```

If the indexes are not in bounds, the overload prints a message and returns **a[0]**.

The overload returns an **int** reference for exactly the same reason that the overloaded index operator returned an **int** reference in Example 8.6.1.

The output of the **main** function of Figure 8.6.4 is

```
0 1 2 3
2 3 4 5
4 5 6 7
first index 4 out of bounds: 0
second index 8 out of bounds: 0
```

```
int main() {
   intTwoArray b( 3, 4 );
   int i, j;
   for ( i = 0; i < b.get_size1(); i++ )
      for ( j = 0; j < b.get_size2(); j++ )
         b( i, j ) = 2 * i + j;
   for ( i = 0; i < b.get_size1(); i++ ) {
      for ( j = 0; j < b.get_size2(); j++ )
         cout << setw( 2 ) << b( i, j );
      cout << endl;
   }
   cout << b( 4, 2 ) << endl;
   cout << b( 2, 8 ) << endl;
   return 0;
}
```

FIGURE 8.6.4 A test driver for the overloaded function call operator of Figure 8.6.2.

Overloading the Increment and Decrement Operators

The increment **++** and decrement operators **--** are among those that can be overloaded in C++. Recall that each operator comes in a "pre" and "post" form:

```
int x = 6;
++x; // preincrement
x++; // postincrement
```

Accordingly, we can overload the preincrement, postincrement, predecrement, and post-decrement operators.

The declaration

```
operator++();
```

with no parameters overloads the preincrement operator, and the declaration

```
operator++( int );
```

with a single **int** parameter overloads the postincrement operator. (Similar comments apply to the decrement operator.) The **int** parameter in the postincrement form serves to distinguish it from the preincrement form. The parameter itself may be, but need not be, used.

EXAMPLE 8.6.3. Class **Clock**, shown in Figure 8.6.5, overloads both the prein-crement and postincrement operators so that they act on **Clock**s just as the built-in preincrement and postincrement operators act on numeric types such as **int**s. If **c** is a **Clock**, **c++** advances the time one minute. The value of the *expression* **c++** is the *original* **Clock**. Executing **++c** also advances the time one minute, but the value of the expression **++c** is the *updated* **Clock**.

```
class Clock {
public:
   Clock( int = 12, int = 0, int = 0 );
   Clock tick();
   friend ostream& operator<<( ostream&, Clock& );
   Clock operator++();        // ++c
   Clock operator++( int ); // c++
private:
   int hour;
   int min;
   int ap; // 0 is AM, 1 is PM
};
Clock::Clock( int h, int m, int ap_flag ) {
   hour = h;
   min = m;
   ap = ap_flag;
}
Clock Clock::tick() {
   ++min;
   if ( min == 60 ) {
      hour++;
      min = 0;
   }
   if ( hour == 13 )
      hour = 1;
   if ( hour == 12 && min == 0 )
      ap = !ap;
   return *this;
}
Clock Clock::operator++() {
   return tick();
}
Clock Clock::operator++( int n ) {
   Clock c = *this;
   tick();
   return c;
}
ostream& operator<<( ostream& out, Clock& c ) {
   out << setfill( '0' ) << setw( 2 ) << c.hour
       << ':' << setw( 2 ) << c.min
       << setfill( ' ' );
   if ( c.ap )
      out << " PM";
   else
      out << " AM";
   return out;
}
```

FIGURE 8.6.5 A `Clock` class with overloaded preincrement and postincrement operators.

The default constructor, which results from using the default values specified for all the parameters, sets the clock to 12:00 AM. Method **tick** adds one minute to the **Clock** and then returns it. Method **operator++()** overloads the preincrement operator. It advances the time one minute by invoking **tick** and returns the updated **Clock**.

Method **operator++(int)** overloads the postincrement operator. It saves the current **Clock**, referenced as ***this**, in **c**. The pointer **this** is available to each method. Its value is the address of the object whose method is invoked. Thus ***this** *is* the object on which the method is invoked. Further details are given in Section 9.5.

After saving the current **Clock** in **c**, **operator++(int)** then advances the time one minute by invoking **tick** and returns **c**, the (unchanged) original **Clock**. The parameter **n** is not used; it serves only to distinguish the postincrement operator from the preincrement operator.

The left-shift operator is overloaded to output a **Clock**. It prints the time in the form

xx:xx XX

where **XX** is either **AM** or **PM**.

The output of the code

```
int main() {
  Clock c, d;
  c = d++;
  cout << "Clock c: " << c << endl;
  cout << "Clock d: " << d << endl;
  ...
}
```

is

```
Clock c: 12:00 AM
Clock d: 12:01 AM
```

The output of the code

```
int main() {
  Clock c, d;
  c = ++d;
  cout << "Clock c: " << c << endl;
  cout << "Clock d: " << d << endl;
  ...
}
```

is

```
Clock c: 12:01 AM
Clock d: 12:01 AM
```

∎

Type Conversions

Recall that a convert constructor for class **C** is a one-parameter constructor (not of type **C&**). If the parameter is of type *paramtype*, the convert constructor converts type *paramtype* to type **C**.

> **EXAMPLE 8.6.4.** In the code segment
>
> ```
> class C {
>    ...
>    C( int ); // convert constructor
>    ...
> };
> ...
> int main() {
>    int i = 8;
>    C c;
>    c = i;
>    ...
> }
> ```
>
> in the statement
>
> ```
> c = i;
> ```
>
> the convert constructor converts **i**, which is of type **int**, to type **C**, after which the converted result is assigned to **c**. ∎

The convert constructor converts some other type to a class type. To convert a class type to some other type, the programmer can overload the type conversion operator. To convert class type **C** to *othertype*, the programmer writes a method whose declaration is

operator *othertype***();**

Note that the declaration does *not* include a return type, not even **void**. Nevertheless, the body of the method *must* contain a **return** statement to return the converted value.

> **EXAMPLE 8.6.5.** We amend the **Clock** class (see Figure 8.6.5) by adding a conversion operator to convert the time of the clock to an integer
>
> ```
> class Clock {
> public:
>    operator int();
>    ...
> };
> ```

```
Clock::operator int() {
   int time = hour;
   if ( time == 12 )
      time = 0;
   if ( ap == 1 )
      time += 12;
   time *= 100;
   time += min;
   return time;
}
```

The integer time is "military time," in which 1:00 PM becomes 1300, 2:00 PM becomes 1400, 12:00 AM becomes 0, and so on. For example, if the time is 8:34 AM, the integer value is 834. If the time is 4:08 PM, the integer value is 1608. As an example of the use of the conversion operator, the output of the code segment

```
Clock c( 8, 55, 1 );
int i;
i = c;
cout << i << endl;
```

is

```
2055
```
∎

EXAMPLE 8.6.6.   The code segment

```
char next;
while ( cin >> next )
   cout << next;
```

copies the standard input to the standard output until end-of-file is reached (assuming that the flag is set for not skipping white space). The **while** condition must evaluate to an integer or pointer value. However, the input expression

```
cin >> next
```

evaluates to an object. A type conversion operator handles the conversion to **void***. If **void*** is zero, the condition is false; otherwise, the condition is true. ∎

Despite their convenience, type conversion operators should be used with caution because the compiler, not the programmer, typically invokes a type conversion operator. The normal call to a type conversion operator is thus *hidden* from the programmer, who may not have anticipated all the situations in which such an operator would be invoked.

EXERCISES

1. If we overload the index operator, how many parameters does `operator[ ]` have?

2. If we overload the function call operator, how many parameters does `operator()` have?

3. Overload `>>` for input for the `intArray` class of Example 8.6.1. (The overload should input `get_size` values.)

4. Overload `<<` for output for the `intArray` class of Example 8.6.1. (The overload should output `get_size` values.)

5. Overload `>>` for input for the `intTwoArray` class of Example 8.6.2. (The overload should input `get_size1 * get_size2` values.)

6. Overload `<<` for output for the `intTwoArray` class of Example 8.6.2. (The overload should output `get_size1 * get_size2` values.)

7. Overload the index operator for the `String` class of Example 8.1.2 so that, if `s` is a `String` object and `i` is a legal index, `s[ i ]` is the character at index `i` in the array `str`. If `i` is not a legal index, output an error message and return zero.

8. Rewrite the class `intArray` of Example 8.6.1; replace the overloaded index operator with an overloaded function call operator.

9. Overload the preincrement operator for the `intArray` class of Example 8.6.1 so that 1 is added to each entry in the array. Return the updated `intArray` object.

10. Overload the postincrement operator for the `intArray` class of Example 8.6.1 so that 1 is added to each entry in the array. Return the original `intArray` object.

11. Overload the predecrement operator for the `intTwoArray` class of Example 8.6.2 so that 1 is subtracted from each entry in the array. Return the updated `intTwoArray` object.

12. Overload the postdecrement operator for the `intTwoArray` class of Example 8.6.2 so that 1 is subtracted from each entry in the array. Return the original `intTwoArray` object.

13. Explain the error:

```
class String {
   ...
   char* operator char* ();
   ...
};
```

14. Write a type conversion operator for the `String` class of Example 8.1.2 that converts `String` to `bool`. The conversion returns `false`, if the `String` is the null string, and `true`, otherwise.

15. Write a type conversion operator for the `String` class of Example 8.1.2 that converts `String` to `char*`. The conversion returns the address of the first cell of a null-terminated array of `char` that represents the string.

8.7 SAMPLE APPLICATION: AN ASSOCIATIVE ARRAY

Problem

Create a dictionary class **Dict** that supports *word-definition* pairs, together with appropriate methods. In particular, the index operator should be overloaded so that if **d** is a **Dict** object, the following should be valid:

```
d[ "pixel" ] = "picture element";
```

Here **pixel** is defined as a **picture element**. An array that takes noninteger indexes is called an **associative array**. A statement such as

```
cout << d[ "pixel" ];
```

should print the definition of **pixel**, provided that **pixel** is in the dictionary. If it is not in the dictionary, a failure message should be printed.

Sample Input/Output

The output from the **main** function of Figure 8.7.1 is

```
dump
residual fm defined as: incidental fm
pixel defined as: in a daffy state

dump
residual fm defined as: incidental fm
pixel defined as: picture element

lookup
residual fm defined as: incidental fm
pixie defined as: *** not in dictionary
pixel defined as: picture element
```

Solution

We begin by implementing an auxiliary class **Entry** that holds a word, its definition, and a flag to show whether a word and its definition are stored. In addition, **Entry** has a default constructor to initialize its word and definition to the null string; methods to add a word and its definition, test for a word match, and to get and set the flag; an overload of **<<** to print the word and its definition; and an overload of the assignment operator to copy a string, regarded as a definition, into an **Entry** object.

The **Dict** class has a single data member—an array of **Entry** to store word-definition pairs. In addition, **Dict** has an overload of **<<** to print all the entries in the dictionary, and the overload of the index operator.

The major challenge is to design the overload of the index operator. In an expression such as

```
d[ "pixel" ]
```

```
int main() {
   // Create a dictionary of word-definition pairs
   Dict d;
   // Add some pairs
   d[ "residual fm" ] = "incidental fm";
   d[ "pixel" ] = "in a daffy state";
   // Print all pairs in the dictionary.
   cout << "\n\ndump\n" << d;
   // Change definition of pixel
   d[ "pixel" ] = "picture element";
   // Print all pairs in the dictionary.
   cout << "\n\ndump\n" << d;
   // Look up some words
   cout << "\n\nlookup\n\n";
   cout << d[ "residual fm" ] << endl;
   cout << d[ "pixie" ] << endl;
   cout << d[ "pixel" ] << endl;
   return 0;
}
```

FIGURE 8.7.1 A test driver for the Dict class.

the overload must search the array of **Entry** for **pixel**. If it finds **pixel**, it returns the **Entry** cell in the array that contains **pixel**. Since class **Entry** contains an overload of the output operator **<<**, we can use **<<** to output the entry:

```
cout << d[ "pixel" ];
```

If **pixel** is not found, the overload of the index operator must return a dummy **Entry** cell whose word is **pixel** and whose definition is

```
*** not in dictionary
```

Thus if **pixel** is not found, the output is

```
pixel defined as: *** not in dictionary
```

We use the first **Entry** cell that does not contain an actual definition for this purpose. We *always* reserve at least one extra cell for just this purpose.

Consider the situation when we enter a definition:

```
d[ "pixel" ] = "picture element";
```

Again the overload searches for the word **pixel**. Assuming that it is not found, it again returns the first unused **Entry** cell. Notice that this is exactly the right cell in which to add the new word-definition pair! Again the overload stores the word **pixel** and the definition

```
*** not in dictionary
```

in this cell. This time we want the assignment operator to replace

```
*** not in dictionary
```

by **picture element**. Since the left side of the assignment operator is of type **Entry**, we overload the assignment operator in class **Entry** to copy the definition **picture element** into the **Entry** cell and set the flag to indicate that a valid entry is now stored.

C++ Implementation

```cpp
const int MaxWord = 100;
const int MaxEntries = 100;

class Entry {
public:
   Entry();
   void add( const char*, const char* );
   bool match( const char* ) const;
   void operator=( const char* );
   friend ostream& operator<<( ostream&, const Entry& );
   bool& valid() { return flag; }
private:
   char word[ MaxWord + 1 ];
   char def[ MaxWord + 1 ];
   bool flag;
};

void Entry::operator=( const char* str ) {
   strcpy( def, str );
   flag = true;
}

Entry::Entry() {
   word[ 0 ] = '\0';
   def[ 0 ] = '\0';
   flag = false;
}

ostream& operator<<( ostream& out, const Entry& e ) {
   out << e.word << " defined as: "
       << e.def;
   return out;
}

void Entry::add( const char* w, const char* d ) {
   strcpy( word, w );
   strcpy( def, d );
}

bool Entry::match( const char* key ) const {
   return strcmp( key, word ) == 0;
}
```

```
class Dict {
public:
    friend ostream& operator<<( ostream&, Dict& );
    Entry& operator[ ]( const char* );
private:
    Entry entries[ MaxEntries + 1 ];
};

ostream& operator<<( ostream& out, Dict& d ) {
    for ( int i = 0; i < MaxEntries; i++ )
        if ( d.entries[ i ].valid() )
            out << d.entries[ i ] << endl;
    return out;
}

Entry& Dict::operator[ ]( const char* k ) {
    for ( int i = 0; i < MaxEntries && entries[ i ].valid(); i++ )
        if ( entries[ i ].match( k ) )
            return entries[ i ];
    entries[ i ].add( k , "*** not in dictionary" );
    return entries[ i ];
}
```

Discussion

Class **Entry** has **char** arrays to hold a word and its definition, and a **bool** member that is either **true**, to indicate that a word-definition pair is stored, or **false**, to indicate that a word-definition pair is not stored.

Class **Entry**'s default constructor sets **word** and **def** to the null string, and **flag** to **false**.

Method **add** uses **strcpy** to copy a word and its definition into **word** and **def**.

Method **match** uses **strcmp** to check whether the string passed matches **word** and returns **true** or **false** to signal the result.

Method **valid** returns **flag** by reference so that it can be read

```
Entry e;
if ( e.valid() )
    ...
```

or written

```
Entry e;
e.valid() = true;
```

Operator **<<** is overloaded for output as a **friend**, using the technique explained in Section 8.5.

The overloaded assignment operator copies the definition passed and sets **flag** to **true** to indicate that a valid entry has been stored.

Class **Dict** contains the data member **entries**, an array of **Entry** objects. The array is of size **MaxEntries + 1**, so it can hold up to **MaxEntries** actual entries; one cell is always reserved for a dummy cell to hold "not found" information as described in the preceding Solution subsection. The **Entry** default constructor initializes **word** and **def** in each cell of the array to the null string, and **flag** in each cell of the array to **false**.

Operator **<<** is also overloaded for output for the class **Dict**. It loops through all the cells in the array **Entry**. Each cell that holds an actual word-definition pair is output using the overloaded **<<** operator in class **Entry**.

The overloaded index operator checks each valid entry for a match of the word **k** that is passed

```
for ( int i = 0; i < MaxEntries && entries[ i ].valid(); i++ )
   if ( entries[ i ].match( k ) )
      return entries[ i ];
```

If a match is found, it returns the matching **Entry** cell. The **Entry** cell is returned by reference, because it may be modified. For example if **pixel** is already in the dictionary, the statement

```
d[ "pixel" ] = "picture element";
```

modifies **pixel**'s definition.

If a match is not found, the overload stores the word that was passed and

```
*** not in dictionary
```

for use in a "not found" message and returns the **Entry** cell

```
entries[ i ].add( k , "*** not in dictionary" );
return entries[ i ];
```

If a word-definition pair is being added to the dictionary

```
d[ "pixel" ] = "picture element";
```

execution of the statement is completed by the overload of the assignment operator in class **Entry**, which replaces

```
*** not in dictionary
```

by the actual definition (**picture element** in this case).

EXERCISES

1. Could **operator=** be implemented so that its declaration is

```
void operator=( const char* ) const;
```

Explain.

2. Implement

```
void Dict::remove( char* w )
```

which removes word **w** from the dictionary if **w** occurs there.

3. Could **operator[ ]** be implemented so that its declaration is

```
Entry& operator[ ]( const char* ) const;
```

Explain.

friend Classes

A method in one class may be a **friend** in another class.

EXAMPLE.   Class **c**

```
class F {
public:
    int f();
private:
    int adm;
};

class C {
public:
    int m();
    // F's method f is a friend of class C
    friend int F::f();
private:
    int adm;
};
```

declares the **friend** function **f**, which is a method in class **F**; thus, **f** can access **c**'s **private** data member **adm**.   ∎

If *every* method in a class **F** is to be a **friend** of another class **c**, instead of individually declaring each method in **F**, we can declare **F** to be a **friend** class of **c**.

EXAMPLE.   The code

```
class F {
    ...
};

class C {
    friend F;
    ...
};
```

makes **F** a **friend** of class **c**. As a result, any method in **F** has full access to all members of **c**, even **private** and **protected** ones.   ∎

COMMON PROGRAMMING ERRORS

1. It is an error to overload these five operators:

Operator	Purpose
.	Class member operator
.*	Class member dereference operator
::	Scope resolution operator
? :	Conditional operator
sizeof	Size in bytes operator

2. It is an error to assume that the assignment operator is inherited in a derived class. It is the *single* operator *not* inherited.

3. Except for the memory management operators, **new**, **new[ ]**, **delete**, and **delete[ ]**, an operator must either be overloaded as a method or have at least one class object among its arguments. For example,

```
// ***** ERROR: neither a method nor a
// function that takes a class argument
int operator+( int num1, int num2 )  {
   ...
}
```

has an error because the overloaded operator is not a method and does not have a class object among its arguments.

4. It is an error to overload the index operator **[ ]** except as a method.

5. It is an error to overload the function call operator **()** except as a method.

6. It is an error to overload the assignment operator **=** except as a method.

7. It is an error to overload the indirect selection operator **->** except as a method.

8. If a binary operator is overloaded as a method, it has *one* parameter. For example,

```
// ***** ERROR: + is binary
Complex Complex::operator+( const Complex& c1,
                            const Complex& c2 ) const {
   ...
}
```

contains an error because **+** is a binary operator. An expression such as

```
c1 + c2  // c1 and c2 are Complex
```

is shorthand for

```
c1.operator+( c2 )
```

Method **operator+** therefore should take one argument:

```
// ok
Complex Complex::operator+( const Complex& c ) const {
   ...
}
```

9. If a unary operator is overloaded as a method, except for the postincrement and post-decrement overloads, it has *no* parameters. For example,

```
// ***** ERROR: ! is binary
String String::operator!( String& s ) {
   ...
}
```

contains an error because **!** is a unary operator. An expression such as

```
!ss // ss is String object
```

is shorthand for

```
ss.operator!()
```

Method **operator!** therefore should take no arguments:

```
// ok
String String::operator!() {
   ...
}
```

10. If a binary operator is overloaded as a top-level function, it has *two* parameters. For example,

```
// ***** ERROR: + is binary
Complex operator+( const Complex& c ) {
   ...
}
```

contains an error because **+** is a binary operator. An expression such as

```
c1 + c2  // c1 and c2 are Complex
```

is shorthand for

```
operator+( c1, c2 )
```

The function **operator+** therefore should take two arguments:

```
// ok
Complex operator+( const Complex& c1,
                   const Complex& c2 ) {
   ...
}
```

11. If a unary operator is overloaded as a top-level function, it has *one* parameter. For example,

```
// ***** ERROR: ! is unary
String operator!() {
   ...
}
```

contains an error because `!` is a unary operator. An expression such as

```
!ss // ss is a String
```

is shorthand for

```
operator!( ss )
```

The function **operator!** therefore should take one argument:

```
// ok
String operator!( String& s ) {
   ...
}
```

12. A top-level function that overloads an operator for class **C** does not have access to **C**'s **private** or **protected** members, unless it is a **friend** of **C**.

13. A top-level function—even a **friend**—is *not* a method. Thus it is an error to connect it to a class with the scope resolution operator:

```
class C {
   ...
   friend C operator+( C&, C& );
   ...
};
// ***** ERROR: operator+ not a method in class C
C C::operator+( C& c1, C& c2 ) {
   ...
}
```

The top-level function **operator+** is properly written as

```
// Correct
C operator+( C& c1, C& c2 ) {
   ...
}
```

14. When `>>` is overloaded for input, the class object *must* be passed by reference, because the data input are to be written into the object and *not* into a *copy* of the object. For this reason, the following is an error:

```
istream& operator>>( istream& in, Complex c ) {
   return in >> c.read >> c.imag;
}
```

The error is corrected by writing

```
istream& operator>>( istream& in, Complex& c ) {
   return in >> c.read >> c.imag;
}
```

15. The method declaration

```
operator++();
```

overloads the *preincrement* operator, not the postincrement operator. The method declaration

```
operator++( int );
```

overloads the *postincrement* operator. The **int** parameter serves to distinguish the two overloads. The parameter itself may be, but need not be, used. Similar statements apply to the predecrement and postdecrement operators.

16. It is an error to specify, in either a declaration or a definition, the return data type—even **void**—for a type conversion operator despite the fact that such an operator contains a **return** statement. For example,

```
// ***** ERROR: can't give return data type
char* String::operator char*() {
   ...
   return str;
}
```

PROGRAMMING EXERCISES

8.1. Overload the equals (==), not equal (!=), unary minus (-), and right shift operator (>>) for the **Complex** class. Complex numbers $z_1 = a + bi$ and $z_2 = c + di$ are equal if and only if a equals c and b equals d. If $z = a + bi$ is a complex number, $-z$ equals $-a - b$. Overload the right shift operator for input.

8.2. For the **string** class of Example 8.1.2, overload ! and write a type conversion operator to convert **String** to **void***. Each returns a suitable value if the **String** is null.

8.3. Overload the function call operator to set the time for the **Clock** class of Example 8.6.3. The overload should behave similarly to the constructor. Also overload == and != so that two **Clock**s can be compared. Two **Clock**s are equal if and only if they have the same time.

8.4. Overload the operator ~ for the **Deck** class of Programming Exercise 5.6 so that if **d** is a **Deck**, ~**d** (pronounced "twiddle dee") shuffles **d**. Also overload the << operator for output of a **Deck**.

8.5. Overload + (union), - (difference), * (intersection), << (output), >> (input), and the function call operator (to add an element) for the **Set** class of Programming Exercise 5.12.

8.6. Overload **+** (union), **<<** (output), **>>** (input), and the function call operator (to add an element) for the **Bag** class of Programming Exercise 5.13.

8.7. Overload the preincrement and postincrement **++** operators for the **Spaceship** class of Programming Exercise 5.14. The preincrement operator advances the time one unit, updates the **Spaceship**'s position, and returns the updated **Spaceship**. The postincrement operator advances the time one unit, updates the **Spaceship**'s position, and returns the original **Spaceship**.

8.8. Overload the operator **+** for the **LAN** (local area network) class of Programming Exercise 5.17. The code segment

```
LAN lan1, lan2, lan3;
...
lan3 = lan1 + lan2;
```

makes **lan3** a **LAN** that includes **lan1** and **lan2** as sub**LAN**s. A combined **LAN** includes all the nodes from the **LAN**s that it combines. However, its topology may differ from theirs because, for example, we might combine a *star* and a *bus* **LAN** into a new **LAN** with a hybrid topology.

8.9. Suppose that a class hierarchy has a **virtual** method **print**

```
class C {
    ...
    virtual void print( ostream& );
    ...
};
```

that outputs **C**'s members to the stream **ostream**. Write *one* overload of **<<** so that the statement

```
out << p;
```

outputs **p**'s members to the stream **out**, where **p** is *any* object that belongs to a class in the hierarchy.

8.10. Suppose that **Matrix2** is a two-dimensional matrix class. Overload the index operator **[ ]** so that if **m** is a **Matrix2** object,

```
m[ i ][ j ]
```

references the cell in the **i**th row and **j**th column.

CHAPTER
9

STORAGE

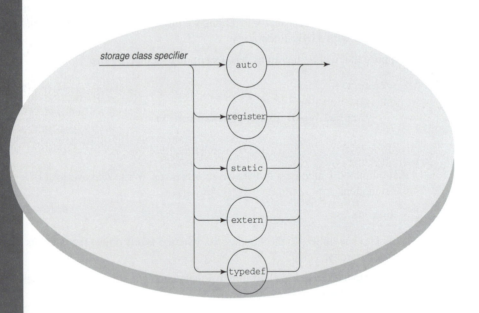

storage class specifier

auto

register

static

extern

typedef

T his chapter examines different ways for a program to meet its storage requirements. We look at **storage classes**, which determine the scope and lifetime of variables. We also look at how storage needs may be determined dynamically, that is, at run time rather than at compile time. Because dynamic storage requires pointer variables (see Sections 4.3 and 9.3), we review pointers. We also consider issues that arise when a class has pointers as data members and, in particular, when a class dynamically allocates storage whose address is stored in a pointer data member. We begin with a section on basic concepts.

9.1 COMPILE-TIME AND RUN-TIME STORAGE

A program's storage requirements can be determined at either compile time or run time. When the compiler translates the program

```
int main() { //*** Program 1: compile-time storage
    float ar[ 100 ];
    // no more variables defined
    return 0;
}
```

the compiler determines that the program requires storage for 100 `float` cells because **ar**'s size is given in its definition as 100. (We assume that Program 1 uses only 100 `float` variables.) We therefore characterize the storage for Program 1 as **compile-time storage**. By contrast, when the compiler translates the program

```
#include <iostream>
using namespace std;
int main() { //*** Program 2: run-time storage
    unsigned n;
    float* p;
    cout << "How many floats do you need? ";
    cin >> n;
    p = new float[ n ];   // dynamic storage
    // no more variables defined
    return 0;
}
```

the compiler cannot determine how much storage is required. The program first prompts the user for an integer, which is stored in **n**. The program then uses the **new[ ]** operator (see Section 9.3) to allocate **n** contiguous `float` cells. The address of the first `float` cell is stored in the pointer variable **p** (see Figure 9.1.1). The amount of storage to which **p** points is determined at run time rather than at compile time. We say that **p** points to **run-time** or **dynamic storage**.

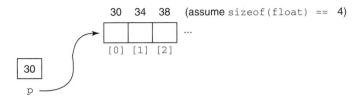

FIGURE 9.1.1 Pointer **p** pointing to **float** cells allocated dynamically.

Storage	Run-Time or Compile-Time?
For variable **n**	Compile-time
For variable **p**	Compile-time
For cells to which **p** points	Run-time

FIGURE 9.1.2 Mix of storage in Program 2.

A program may have a mix of compile-time and run-time storage. For example, Program 2 uses *compile-time* storage for variables **n** and **p**, but it uses *run-time* storage for the **float** cells to which **p** points. Figure 9.1.2 summarizes the storage used in Program 2.

To refine the distinction between compile-time and run-time storage, we consider how a computer's storage system looks to the C++ programmer.

The Program Area, the Stack, and the Heap

From a programmer's perspective, a modern computer's memory system has three sections (see Figure 9.1.3):

- The **program area**, which holds the code for function bodies and the cells for **extern** and **static** variables (see Section 9.2).
- The **stack**, which holds cells for parameters and non**static** local variables.
- The **heap**, which holds cells that are allocated dynamically. The heap is also called the **free store**.

Memory

Program area	Stack
Heap	

FIGURE 9.1.3 The program area, the stack, and the heap.

The Program Area

The program in Figure 9.1.4 has a global **int** variable named **n** and function **main**, which prompts the user for **n**'s value and then prints **n** to the standard output. The executable code (see Section 0.4) in **main**'s body consists of a **cin** statement, two **cout** statements, and a **return** statement. Storage for the global variable and the four executable statements comes from the memory system's *program area*.

```
#include <iostream>
using namespace std;
int n;
int main() {
   cout << "Please enter an integer: "
   cin >> n;
   cout << "You entered: " << n << endl;
   return 0;
}
```

FIGURE 9.1.4 A program to illustrate program area storage.

The Stack

The program in Figure 9.1.5 has two functions, **main** and **f**. Function **main** has two local **int** variables, **x** and **y**; and function **f** has one **int** parameter **p** and a local **int** variable **d**. When **main** starts executing, the system allocates, on the stack, storage for the two **int** variables (see Figure 9.1.6). When **main** invokes **f**, the system allocates, on the stack, storage for **f**'s parameter **p** and for **f**'s local variable **d** (see Figure 9.1.7).

```
#include <iostream>
using namespace std;
int f( int );
int main() {
   int x = 7, y = 9; // local variables
   cout << f( x + y ) << endl;
   return 0;
}
int f( int p ) { // parameter p
   int d; // local variable d
   cout << "Input an integer multiplier: " << endl;
   cin >> d;
   return p * d;
}
```

FIGURE 9.1.5 A program to illustrate stack storage.

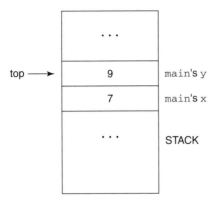

FIGURE 9.1.6 Stack storage for **main**'s local variables.

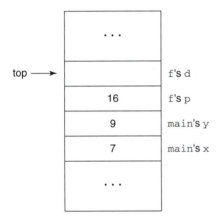

FIGURE 9.1.7 Stack storage for **f**'s parameter and local variable.

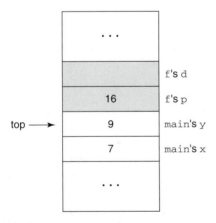

FIGURE 9.1.8 Freeing the stack storage used by **f**.

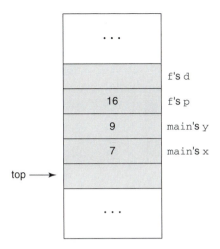

FIGURE 9.1.9 Freeing the stack storage used by `main`.

When `f` returns to `main`, the system frees the stack storage used by `f` (see Figure 9.1.8). When `main` returns, the system frees the stack storage used by `main` (see Figure 9.1.9). Of course, when `main` returns, the program itself terminates. The point is that stack storage is *automatically allocated and deallocated* to meet storage requirements for a function's local variables and parameters. When control enters a function, the system allocates stack storage for the function's parameters, if any, and for the function's (non`static`) local variables, if any. (Section 9.2 explains the keyword `static`). We say that the stack *grows* and *shrinks* to meet the different storage requirements that functions have for parameters and local variables. Stack storage is efficient in that it is *reusable*.

EXAMPLE 9.1.1. Figure 9.1.10 shows an amended version of the the program in Figure 9.1.5. In the amended program, `main` calls function `g` after function `f` returns to `main`. Function `g` requires storage for two parameters. The storage that the system releases when `f` returns to `main` can be reused to meet `g`'s requirements. ∎

CPU Registers and the Stack

Modern compilers try to use CPU registers (see Section 0.2) in place of the stack because access time to CPU registers is faster than access time to the stack, which is part of the memory system. CPU registers typically have a capacity in the *thousands* of bits, whereas the main memory system typically has a capacity in the *millions* of bits. In any case, the local variables and parameters that would otherwise use stack storage may in fact use CPU registers if these are available. At the conceptual level, parameters and local variables go on the stack; at the implementation level, parameters and local variables may go into registers, which then are used instead of the stack.

```
#include <iostream>
using namespace std;
int f( int );
void g( int, int );
int main() {
    int x = 7, y = 9; // local variables
    cout << f( x + y ) << endl;
    g( x * x, y );
    return 0;
}
int f( int p ) { // parameter p
    int d; // local variable d
    cout << "Input an integer multiplier: " << endl;
    cin >> d;
    return p * d;
}
void g( int a, int b ) {
    cout << a * b << endl;
}
```

FIGURE 9.1.10 An amended version of the program in Figure 9.1.5.

The Heap

The program in Figure 9.1.11 dynamically allocates 298 **double** cells by using the operator **new[ ]** and later deallocates the same 298 **double** cells by using the operator **delete[ ]** (see Section 9.3). Storage for these **double** cells comes from the heap. Heap storage, unlike stack storage, is neither allocated automatically nor deallocated automatically. To allocate heap storage, the *programmer* uses the **new** or **new[ ]** operator. To deallocate heap storage, the *programmer* uses the **delete** or the **delete[ ]** operator.

```
using namespace std;
int main() {
    double* p;
    p = new double[ 298 ]; // allocate heap storage
    // process the storage
    delete[ ] p; // free the allocated heap storage
    return 0;
}
```

FIGURE 9.1.11 A program to illustrate heap storage.

Heap storage is *not* initialized when allocated. In particular, heap storage does *not* contain some special value such as 0.

EXAMPLE 9.1.2. In the program

```
#include <iostream>
using namespace std;
int main() {
   int* p = new int[ 10 ];
   for ( int i = 0; i < 10; i++ )
     cout << p[ i ] << endl; // arbitrary values
   return 0;
}
```

we allocate 10 **int** cells on the heap. These cells are *uninitialized*. Therefore, the output consists of arbitrary values. ■

Problems with Heap Storage

Heap storage poses a challenge to the programmer.

EXAMPLE 9.1.3. In the code segment

```
void f();
int main() {
   f();
   // can't get at the storage that f allocates
   ...
}
void f() {
   float* p = new float[ 1000000 ]; // 1,000,000 floats
   // process floats but fail to deallocate them
} //***** Caution: 1,000,000 inaccessible floats left behind
```

f allocates 1,000,000 **float** cells from the heap but fails to deallocate or free them before returning to **main**. The only access to these cells is through pointer **p**, which is *local* to **f**. Therefore, **main** cannot access the 1,000,000 cells that **f** allocates. Because **f** does not free the allocated cells, they remain allocated until the program itself terminates. Therefore, **f** generates **inaccessible storage**, that is, storage that remains allocated after **f** exits even though this storage cannot be accessed after **f** exits.

The example illustrates the difference between stack and heap storage. Pointer **p** goes on the stack because it is a local variable in **f**. Once **f** returns to **main**, the system automatically recovers this storage for other use. So once **f** returns to **main**, the stack storage for **p** is inaccessible—yet **p** is the program's *only access* to the heap storage that **f** allocates. The programmer is thus remiss in not freeing the heap storage *before* **f** returns to **main**. ■

EXERCISES

1. Does **f** use compile-time or run-time storage?

```
void f() {
   float a[ 200 ];
   int   i;
   ... // no other variables defined
}
```

2. In **g**, explain which storage is compile time and which is run time.

```
void g() {
   double d1, d2;
   float* ptr;
   ptr = new float[ 100 ];
   ... // no other variables defined
}
```

3. Are a program's executable instructions stored in the program area, on the stack, or on the heap?

4. Are a function's parameters stored in the program area, on the stack, or on the heap?

5. Are a function's local variables stored in the program area, on the stack, or on the heap?

6. Are a program's global variables stored in the program area, on the stack, or on the heap?

7. In the following program, indicate for each variable and parameter whether its corresponding cell comes from the program area, the stack, or the heap.

```
int x;
float y;
void g( double );
int main() {
   double d = 3.14;
   g( d );
   int* p;
   p = new int[ 100 ];
   // no other variables defined
   ...
}
void g( double a ) {
   int x;
   // no other variables defined
}
```

8. Why does the stack represent an efficient use of storage?

9. What is *inaccessible storage*?

10. Can stack storage become *inaccessible storage*?

11. Can heap storage become *inaccessible storage*?

12. How much inaccessible storage is produced each time **f** is called?

```
void f( char s[ ], unsigned len ) {
   char* p = new char[ len + 1 ];
   strncpy( p, s, len );
   p[ len ] = '\0';
   cout << p << endl;
}
```

13. Why does the compiler try to use CPU registers instead of the stack whenever possible?

9.2 STORAGE CLASSES FOR VARIABLES

C++ has four storage classes for variables: **auto**, **static**, **extern**, and **register**. The first three are commonly used; the last, **register**, is used rarely (see C++ Postscript). This section clarifies the three common storage classes for variables. A variable's storage class determines its *scope* (that is, where in the program the variable can be accessed) and its *lifetime* (that is, how long the underlying storage cell exists). A top-level function also has a storage class, which we clarify in the C++ Postscript. This section considers storage classes only for variables.

The Storage Class auto

Any variable defined *inside a block* has **auto** as its default storage class. An **auto** variable *must* be defined inside a block.

EXAMPLE 9.2.1.   In the code segment

```
int main() {
   int x;
   ...
}
```

variable **x**'s storage class is **auto**, the default for any variable defined inside a block such as **main**'s body. The keyword **auto**

```
int main() {
   auto int x; // using the keyword auto
   ...
}
```

is rarely, if ever, used. If used, the keyword **auto** is placed to the left of the data type, in this example **int**.   ∎

EXAMPLE 9.2.2.   The code segment

```
class C {
public:
  C();
  void m();
private:
  ...
};
C::C() {
  int x;    // auto
  ...
}
void C::m() {
  int arr[ 100 ]; // auto
  ...
}
```

illustrates that local variables in class methods likewise default to **auto**. Variable **x** in the constructor and array **arr** in **m** default to **auto** because each is defined inside a block, in this example a method's body. ∎

EXAMPLE 9.2.3.   The code segment

```
auto int x; //***** ERROR: must be defined in a block
int main() {
  ...
}
```

contains an error because an **auto** variable cannot be defined outside all blocks. ∎

Scope and Lifetime of **auto** Variables

An **auto** variable can be visible from the point of its definition to the end of the block that contains its definition. (Recall that this block is called the variable's **containing block**.) An **auto** variable is never visible outside its containing block. An **auto** variable's lifetime begins when control enters its containing block and ends when control leaves its containing block. Storage for an **auto** variable comes from the *stack*. The name **auto** signals that storage for a variable is allocated and deallocated **auto**matically as control enters and leaves the variable's containing block.

EXAMPLE 9.2.4.   The code segment

```
#include <iostream>
using namespace std;
int main() {
   unsigned x;
   cout << "Enter a positive integer: ";
```

```
  cin >> x;
  if ( x % 2 ) {  // is x odd?
    int y;
    cout << "Enter another: ";
    cin >> y;
    ...
  } //*** y's scope and lifetime end
  ...
} // *** x's scope and lifetime end
```

contains two variable definitions, both inside blocks. Variable **x**'s containing block is **main**'s body, whereas **y**'s containing block is an **if** block inside **main**'s body. Both variables default to **auto** because each is defined inside a block. Storage for **x** and **y** comes from the stack. Variable **x** is visible inside **main**'s body, from the point of its definition until the right brace that ends **main**'s body. Storage for variable **x** exists until control exits **main**. Variable **y** is defined inside an **if** statement's block. The variable is therefore visible only inside this block, and storage for it exists until control exits the **if** block.   ■

EXAMPLE 9.2.5.   The code segment

```
#include <iostream>
using namespace std;
int main() {
   unsigned x;
   cout << "Enter a positive integer: ";
   cin >> x;
   if ( x % 2 ) {  // is x odd?
     int y;
     cout << "Enter another: ";
     cin >> y;
     ...
   } //*** y's scope and lifetime end
   cout << y << endl; //***** ERROR: y out of scope
   ...
}
```

contains an error because **y** is accessed outside its containing block. We say that **y** *goes out of scope* once control leaves its containing block, thereby underscoring that **y** is not accessible outside its containing block. In general, it is an error to access a variable that has gone out of scope.   ■

An **auto** variable has **block scope**; that is, an **auto** variable is visible only in its containing block. An **auto** variable *goes out of existence* when it goes out scope. In other words, an **auto** variable's containing block limits both its scope and its existence. Recall that stack storage is *reusable*. Therefore, once an **auto** variable goes out of scope, the system is free to reuse that variable's stack storage. If a programmer tries to access an **auto** variable that has gone out of scope, the system may have already allocated that variable's stack storage to some other **auto** variable or to a parameter.

If an **auto** variable is *initialized* in its definition, the initialization occurs anew *each time* control enters its containing block.

EXAMPLE 9.2.6.   In the code segment

```
void f();
int main() {
   for ( int i = 0; i < 10; i++ )
      f();
   ...
}
void f() {
   int count = 0;
   cout << "In f " << ++count // prints 1 every time
        << "times." << endl;
}
```

main calls **f** 10 times. Each time **f** is called, its **auto** variable **count** is initialized to 0. The variable is then preincremented to **1** and this value is printed. When control exits **f**, **count** goes out of scope and out of existence. When control enters **f** again, **count** comes into scope and into existence—and it is initialized again to 0.   ∎

Initializing auto Variables

The compiler does *not* initialize **auto** variables. An uninitialized **auto** variable therefore contains garbage, that is, an arbitrary value presumably of no use to the program.

EXAMPLE 9.2.7.   In the code segment

```
#include <iostream>
using namespace std;
int main() {
   int x;
   int y = -999;
   cout << x          // value unknown
        << y          // -999
        << endl;
   ...
}
```

auto variable **x** is not initialized in its definition. Therefore, **x** contains some arbitrary value, which is output in the **cout** statement. It would be an error to assume that **x** has some particular value such as zero. By contrast, **auto** variable **y** is initialized in its definition to −999, and so −999 is output as its value.   ∎

Because storage for **auto** variables comes from the stack, use of such variables represents efficient use of storage. Further, because an **auto** variable's scope is limited to its containing block, use of **auto** variables is a straightforward way to avoid *name conflicts*.

EXAMPLE 9.2.8. The code segment

```
void f();
int main() {
   int i;  // main's i
   for ( i = 0; i < 100; i++ )
     f();
   ...
}
void f() {
   int i = 0;  // f's i--no relation to main's i
   while ( i < 1000 )
      ...
}
```

contains two **auto** variables named **i**. Because the two have distinct containing blocks, they are altogether distinct variables.   ∎

It is illegal for two variables with the same scope to have the same name.

EXAMPLE 9.2.9. The code segment

```
int main() {
   int i;
   int i; //***** ERROR: i already defined
   ...
}
```

contains an error because it tries to define two variables with the same name and the same scope.   ∎

EXAMPLE 9.2.10. The code segment

```
#include <iostream>
using namespace std;
int main() {
   int i = 9;
   {
      int i = -888;  // OK, different scope
      cout << i << endl;  // outputs -888
   }
   cout << i << endl; // outputs 9
   ...
}
```

is legal but it also represents bad programming. There are two **auto** variables named **i**. Nonetheless, the two do *not* have the same scope and so the definitions are legal. The **i** initialized to −888 occurs in a block nested inside **main**'s body; its scope is this nested block. The **i** initialized to 9 occurs in the block that is **main**'s body; it thus has broader scope than the other **i**.

The code segment represents bad programming because it creates a name conflict, which is confusing and serves no useful purpose. In general, a name conflict is resolved in favor of the variable *with the narrower scope*, which explains why the first output is −888. ■

The Storage Class **static**

The keyword **static** is used in two contexts in C++. One context is inside classes. When used in this context, the keyword **static** specifies *class* as opposed to *object* members (see Section 5.7). The other context is outside classes. This subsection deals with **static** variables outside classes.

The keyword **static** must be used to define a **static** variable. A **static** variable may be defined inside a block or outside all blocks.

EXAMPLE 9.2.11. The code segment

```
static int x;
void f() {
   static int y;
   ...
}
```

defines two **static** variables. Variable **x** is defined outside all blocks, whereas variable **y** is defined inside the block that is **f**'s body. ■

Storage for a **static** variable comes from the program area, and a **static** variable's lifetime is the program's lifetime, regardless of whether a **static** variable is defined inside a block or outside all blocks.

EXAMPLE 9.2.12. The function

```
void f() {
   static int count = 0; // initialized once only
   cout << "In f " << ++count << " times." << endl;
   ...
}
```

has a **static** variable defined inside its body. This variable counts how many times **f** is invoked. The initialization occurs *once only*. Storage for **count** remains in existence even when control exits **f**. Because **count** has the *same storage cell* throughout the program's lifetime, **count** can be used to count how many times **f** is invoked. ■

The compiler initializes **static** variables to zero in the absence of programmer initialization. Even if we amend Example 9.2.12 to

```
void f() {
    static int count; // compiler initializes to 0
    cout << "In f " << ++count << " times." << endl;
    ...
}
```

count still has zero as its initial value.

Scope of **static** Variables

A **static** variable's scope depends on where it is defined. A **static** variable defined *inside a block* has block scope. A **static** variable defined *outside all blocks* can be visible from the point of its definition to the end of the file in which the definition occurs. A **static** variable cannot be visible outside its containing file.

EXAMPLE 9.2.13. The code segment

```
//*** start of file
static int x = -999; // file scope
void f();
int main() {
    static int z;
    f();
    x += 1; // OK, x has file scope
    y = 23; //***** ERROR: y not visible in main
    ...
}
void f() {
    static int y = 888;   // block scope
    z = 777; //***** ERROR: z not visible in f
    ...
}
//*** end of file
```

has three **static** variables. Variable **x** is defined outside all blocks at the top of the file that contains the code segment. Therefore, **x** is visible from the point of its definition until the end of file, which occurs at the end of **f**'s body. In particular, **x** is visible in **main** and **f**. By contrast, **z** and **y** are defined inside blocks; hence, each has block scope. The two errors result from illegal attempts to access **static** variables outside their scopes: **z** cannot be accessed outside **main**'s body, and **y** cannot be accessed outside **f**'s body. ∎

There are two common uses for **static** variables outside of classes (see Section 5.7). First, **static** variables can be used to save values between invocations of a function. Example 9.2.12 illustrates this use by having **count** count how many times top-level function **f** is invoked. A **static** variable used in this way typically has block scope. Second, **static** variables can be used as *global* variables in a file, that is, as variables that are visible in a file from their point of definition until the end of the file but are not visible in any other file.

EXAMPLE 9.2.14.   The code segment

```
static const int n = 100;
static float nums[ n ];
int main() {
   for ( int i = 0; i < n; i++ )
     nums[ i ] = i + 1;
   ...
}
```

illustrates the use of **static** variables as global variables in a file. Variable **n** is **static** and **const**. It is used to specify an array's size in its definition and to control a loop in **main**. Note that the storage class **static** is to the left of **const** in the case of **n**. Array **nums** is also **static**. Both **n** and **nums** have file scope because they are defined outside all blocks at the top of the file. Neither **n** nor **nums** is visible in any other file. ∎

The Storage Class **extern**

Any variable defined *outside all blocks* has **extern** as its default storage class. An **extern** variable *must* be defined outside all blocks.

EXAMPLE 9.2.15.   The code segment

```
int x;  // defaults to extern
int main() {
   ...
}
```

defines a variable **x** outside all blocks. Its default storage class is therefore **extern**. ∎

An **extern** variable may be initialized in its definition. If the programmer does not initialize an **extern** variable, the compiler initializes it to zero.

EXAMPLE 9.2.16.   In the code segment

```
int x = -999;
int y; // initialized to 0
int main() {
   ...
}
```

the compiler initializes the **extern** variable **y** to zero. ∎

Storage for an **extern** variable comes from the program area. An **extern** variable's lifetime is the program's lifetime. In these two respects, an **extern** variable is like a **static** variable. We now examine how **extern** and **static** variables differ, beginning with the distinction between a variable's definition and its declaration.

Definition versus Declaration of an **extern** Variable

In C++, every variable has a *declaration* that specifies its name and data type, and a *definition* that creates the underlying storage cell. Except for **extern** variables, the declaration and the definition coincide. For convenience, we therefore say that the code segment

```
void f() {
   int x;   // auto: definition and declaration coincide
   ...
}
```

defines an **auto** variable **x** instead of saying that the code segment *declares and defines* the variable. However, it is critical to distinguish between the definition and the declaration of an **extern** variable. The two points to remember are these:

- An **extern** variable has exactly *one definition*, which must occur *outside all blocks*. The keyword **extern** is typically omitted in the definition.

- An **extern** variable may have *many declarations*, which can occur either inside a block or outside all blocks. The keyword **extern** *must* occur in a declaration.

EXAMPLE 9.2.17.   In the code segment

```
int main() {
   extern int x; // declare x to make it visible in main
   ...
}
int x;  // define x
void f() {
   ...  // x is visible in f
}
```

x is defined outside all blocks and therefore defaults to **extern**. Its definition occurs *below* **main**, which means that **x** is not visible in **main** by virtue of its *definition*. Because **x**'s definition occurs *above* **f**, **x**'s definition makes it visible in **f**. To make **x** visible in **main**, we can *declare* it inside **main** by using the keyword **extern**.   ■

EXAMPLE 9.2.18. We amend Example 9.2.17

```
extern int x; // declaration
int main() {
    ... // x is visible in main
}

int x;  // definition
void f() {
    ...  // x is visible in f
}
```

by placing a *declaration* of **x** above **main**. Of course, it would have been easier simply to place **x**'s *definition* above **main**, in which case no declaration would be needed. ■

If the keyword **extern** occurs in an **extern** variable's *definition*, the programmer must supply an initial value in order to distinguish the definition from a declaration.

EXAMPLE 9.2.19. The code segment

```
extern int x;            // declaration
int main() {
    ...
}
extern int x = -999;  // definition
```

uses the keyword **extern** in **x**'s definition. The initialization distinguishes **x**'s definition from a declaration, which occurs above **main** in the example. If we omitted the initialization, we would have *two declarations* but *no* definition of **x**. ■

It is illegal to initialize an **extern** variable in a declaration.

EXAMPLE 9.2.20. The code segment

```
int main() {
    extern int x = 0;  //***** ERROR: declaration
    ...
}
int x = -999;  // definition and initialization
```

contains an error because it tries to initialize **extern** variable **x** in a declaration. The error would remain if the declaration were outside all blocks because an **extern** variable cannot be initialized in any declaration. ■

Because the keyword **extern** is optional in an **extern** variable's *definition* but required in any *declaration*, we recommend that the keyword *not* be used in defining an **extern** variable. Besides, the programmer must remember to initialize the variable if the keyword **extern** occurs in the definition. If the keyword is not used, the programmer can either initialize the variable or let the compiler initialize it to zero.

Scope of **extern** Variables

An **extern** variable is visible from the point of its definition until the end of the file in which the definition occurs. So an **extern** variable, like a **static** variable defined outside all blocks, is visible in its containing file.

EXAMPLE 9.2.21.   In the code segment

```
//*** start of file
static int x;
int y;
int main() {
   ...
}
void f() {
   ...
}
//*** end of file
```

the **static** variable **x** and the **extern** variable **y** are visible in their containing file. In particular, both variables are visible in **main** and **f**, as these functions occur *after* the variable definitions. ■

An **extern** variable is also visible wherever a *declaration* of it occurs. In Example 9.2.17, the **extern** variable **x** is defined *after* **main** so that its definition does not make it visible in **main**. However, **x** is *declared* in **main** and, for this reason, is visible in **main**. Declarations can make an **extern** variable visible in files other than the file that contains its definition.

EXAMPLE 9.2.22.   The program in Figure 9.2.1 occupies two files. Function **main** resides in *F1.cpp*, whereas function **f** resides in *F2.cpp*. The **extern** variable **x** is *defined* in file *F1.cpp* above **main** so that its definition makes it visible in **main**. Because **x** is **extern**, the compiler initializes it to zero in the absence of a programmer initialization. Note that the keyword **extern** is not used in the definition, as we recommended earlier. The variable **x** is *declared* in *F2.cpp*. Recall that the keyword **extern** must occur in all declarations. After **main** prints **x**, **main** invokes **f**, which assigns −999 to **x**. When **main** prints **x** after the call to **f**, the output is thus −999. Although the program's functions reside in two different files, these functions have access to the *same* variable named **x**. ■

```
//*** start of file F1.cpp: contains main
#include <iostream>
using namespace std;
void f(); // declared here, defined in F2.cpp
int x;     // initialized to 0
int main() {
   cout << x << endl; // outputs 0
   f();
   cout << x << endl; // outputs -999
   return 0;
}
//*** end of file F1.cpp

//*** start of file F2.cpp
extern int x; // declaration
void f() {
   x = -999;
}
//*** end of file F2.cpp
```

FIGURE 9.2.1 Making an **extern** variable visible across files.

Separate Compilation and **extern** Variables

All C++ systems allow the programmer to distribute a program's source code among different files, which then can be compiled separately. During the *link* stage of the compilation process, these separately compiled files are linked together to create the executable program (see Section 0.4). Suppose that program *P*'s source code is distributed among the files *F1*, *F2*,...,*Fn* and that we want variable **x** to be visible throughout *P*. We cannot make **x** a **static** variable because a **static** variable cannot be made visible outside its containing file. The solution is to make **x** an **extern** variable. We *define* **x** in any one of the source files and *declare* it in all the others. This makes **x** visible throughout *P*. (It is common practice to put **extern** variable *declarations* in a header file and then **#include** this header file wherever needed.) Because an **extern** variable can be made visible throughout a program, we say that it can have **program scope**.

Figure 9.2.2 summarizes the storage classes with respect to scope, lifetime, and storage source.

Storage Class	Maximum Scope	Lifetime	Storage Source
auto	Block	Block	Stack
static	File	Program	Program area
extern	Program	Program	Program area

FIGURE 9.2.2 Summary of storage classes for variables.

EXERCISES

1. What is **x**'s storage class?

```
int main() {
   int x;
   ...
}
```

2. What is the error?

```
int main() {
   int auto x;
   ...
}
```

3. What is the error?

```
#include <iostream>
using namespace std;
int main() {
   int x, y;
   cin >> x >> y;
   if ( x > y ) {
     int z = x + y;
   }
   else
     z = x - y;
   ...
}
```

4. Does the system initialize **auto** variables to zero if the programmer does not provide initial values?

5. What is the error?

```
auto unsigned z = 999;
int main() {
  ...
}
```

6. What is the output?

```
#include <iostream>
using namespace std;
void f();
int main() {
   for ( unsigned i = 0; i < 3; i++ )
     f();
   return 0;
}
```

```
void f() {
    int count = 0;
    cout << ++count << endl;
}
```

7. What is an **auto** variable's scope?

8. What is an **auto** variable's lifetime?

9. Are cells for **auto** variables in the program area, on the stack, or on the heap?

10. What is the output?

```
#include <iostream>
using namespace std;
int main() {
    int x = 10, y = 2 * x;
    if ( x > 0 ) {
        int y = -999;
        cout << y << endl;
    }
    cout << y << endl;
    return 0;
}
```

11. What is the output?

```
#include <iostream>
using namespace std;
void f();
int main() {
    for ( unsigned i = 0; i < 3; i++ )
        f();
    return 0;
}
void f() {
    static int count = 0;
    cout << ++count << endl;
}
```

12. What is the scope of a **static** variable defined inside a block?

13. What is the scope of a **static** variable defined outside all blocks?

14. What is the lifetime of a **static** variable?

15. Can the same **static** variable be visible in more than one file?

16. Are cells for **static** variables in the program area, on the stack, or on the heap?

17. Does the system initialize **static** variables to zero if the programmer does not provide an initial value?

18. If a **static** variable is defined inside a class method, is there one copy of the variable for the entire class or one copy per class object?

19. What is **x**'s storage class?

```
int x;
int main() {
   ...
}
```

20. What is the error?

```
extern int x; // x's declaration
int main() {
   ...
}
extern int x; // x's definition
```

21. Does the system initialize an **extern** variable to zero if the programmer does not provide an initial value?

22. May an **extern** variable have more than one definition?

23. May an **extern** variable have more than one declaration?

24. In the code segment

```
extern int z;
int main() {
   ...
}
extern int z = -999;
```

indicate which is the definition and which is the declaration of **x**.

25. Must the keyword **extern** be present in an **extern** variable's definition?

26. Must the keyword **extern** be present in an **extern** variable's declaration?

27. Are cells for **extern** variables in the program area, on the stack, or on the heap?

28. What is the scope of an **extern** variable?

29. What is the lifetime of an **extern** variable?

30. List two differences between **static** and **extern** variables.

9.3 POINTERS AND DYNAMIC STORAGE

A program can dynamically allocate storage with the operators **new** and **new[ ]**, which return the address of a cell from the memory system's heap if the storage can be allocated. If the requested storage cannot be allocated, **new** and **new[ ]** throw a **bad_alloc** exception (see C++ Postscript, Chapter 7). The address that **new** or **new[ ]** returns is typically stored in a *pointer variable*.

EXAMPLE 9.3.1.   The code segment

```
int main() {
   int* pInt;       // pointer to int
   pInt = new int;  // request one int cell from heap
   ...
}
```

defines a pointer variable **pInt**. The data type **int*** is "pointer to **int**." The code segment then uses the **new** operator to request one **int** cell from the heap. If the request succeeds, **new** returns the requested cell's address, which is then assigned to **pInt** (see Figure 9.3.1). ∎

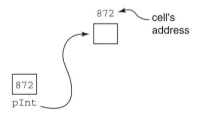

FIGURE 9.3.1 Dynamically allocating storage with **new**.

EXAMPLE 9.3.2.   The code segment

```
int main() {
   float* pFlt;                 // pointer to float
   pFlt = new float[ 1000 ]; // request 1,000 float cells
   ...
}
```

defines a pointer variable **pFlt** and then uses **new[ ]** to request 1,000 contiguous **float** cells from the heap. If the request succeeds, **new[ ]** returns the address of the *first* of these cells. ∎

The operator **new** is used to request storage for *one* cell (see Example 9.3.1). The operator **new[ ]** is used to request storage for more than one cell (see Example 9.3.2). When **new[ ]** is invoked, the square brackets **[ ]** are used to specify how many cells are requested (see Example 9.3.2). This syntax deliberately resembles the syntax for specifying an array's size.

The operators **new** and **new[ ]** may be used to allocate storage for built-in and user-defined data types. In particular, these operators can be used to allocate storage for class objects.

EXAMPLE 9.3.3. The code segment

```
class C {
public:
   C() {...}    // default constructor
   ...          // rest of interface
private:
   ...          // implementation
};
int main() {
   C* p;
   C* q;
   C* v;
   p = new C;        // allocate one C object
   q = new C();      // alternative syntax
   v = new C[ 1000 ]; // allocate 1,000 C objects
   ...
}
```

reviews the use of **new** and **new[ ]** to allocate class objects. The syntax

```
q = new C();
```

explicitly invokes the default constructor to underscore that a new **C** object is being constructed. Many C++ programmers like this style of explicitly invoking the default constructor, which is equivalent to

```
q = new C;
```

The default constructor is likewise invoked for each of the 1,000 **C** objects allocated with **new[ ]**. ■

Constructors other than the default constructor may be invoked explicitly with the operator **new**.

EXAMPLE 9.3.4.   We amend Example 9.3.3

```
class C {
public:
   C() { ... } // default constructor
   C( char s[ ] ) { ... } // convert constructor
   ...            // rest of interface
private:
   ...            // implementation
};
int main() {
   C* p;
   p = new C( "A bang, not a whimper" );
   ...
}
```

to illustrate how a convert constructor may be invoked with the **new** operator.   ■

If the programmer allocates storage with **new** or **new[ ]**, the programmer should deallocate the same storage with either **delete** or **delete[ ]**, respectively, to prevent the creation of inaccessible storage.

EXAMPLE 9.3.5.   In the code segment

```
void f() {
   int* p = new int;        // allocate 1 int
   int* v = new int[ 100 ]; // allocate 100 ints
   ... // process the ints
   delete p;         // deallocate 1 int
   delete[ ] v;      // deallocate 100 ints
}
```

f dynamically allocates one **int** cell to which **p** points and 100 **int** cells to which **v** points. The operator **new** is used to allocate the *one* cell to which **p** points, whereas the operator **new[ ]** is used to allocate the *multiple* cells to which **v** points. To free storage for *one* dynamically allocated cell, the operator **delete** is used. To free storage for *multiple* dynamically allocated cells, the operator **delete[ ]** is used. If **new[ ]** is used, then **delete[ ]** should be used to free the dynamically allocated storage. Both **delete** and **delete[ ]** expect a pointer to the cell(s) to be freed. By the way, the initialization

```
int* p = new int; // allocate in initialization
```

is equivalent to the pair of statements

```
int* p;
p = new int;
```
■

Forgetting to deallocate a single dynamically allocated **int** cell is not good practice, but it is also not a major disaster. The real problem arises when the programmer dynamically allocates a vector of cells but forgets to deallocate the vector. A vector is the heap counterpart of an array; that is, a **vector** is an aggregate of dynamically allocated cells.

EXAMPLE 9.3.6. The code segment

```
void f() {
   int* pInt = new int[ 1000000 ]; // 1,000,000 ints
   ... // process the vector
} //***** Caution: vector not deallocated, now inaccessible
```

produces inaccessible storage. In **f**, the programmer dynamically allocates 1,000,000 **int**s but forgets to free them before exiting **f**. The sole access to the **int** vector is the **auto** variable **pInt**, which goes out of scope once **f** exits. Storage for the vector remains until the program terminates, but the program cannot access the vector once **f** exits. In short, **f** generates 1,000,000 **int**s of inaccessible storage each time it is invoked. ∎

Pointers as Function Arguments and Return Values

The program in Figure 9.3.2 has three functions:

- **main**, which prompts the user for a vector size, stores the input in integer variable **n**, invokes **getVector** and **fillVector**, and deallocates the storage for the vector.
- **getVector**, which tries to allocate an integer vector of size **n** and returns a pointer to the vector's first cell if the allocation succeeds.
- **fillVector**, which fills the vector with randomly generated integers.

The header for **fillVector** could be written

```
// Style 1: array style
fillVector( unsigned v[ ], unsigned n )
```

This is the style used throughout Chapter 4. The style

```
// Style 2: pointer style
void fillVector( unsigned* v, unsigned n )
```

is probably more common because it is easier to type.

In the **for** loop of **fillVector**'s body

```
for ( unsigned i = 0; i < n; i++ )
   v[ i ] = rand();
```

we use **v** as a base address from which to take an offset, given by the index **i**. The result is to populate the vector **v** with randomly generated integers. The parameter **n** specifies the vector's size.

```
#include <cstdlib>
#include <iostream>
using namespace std;
unsigned* getVector( unsigned n );
void fillVector( unsigned* v, unsigned n );
int main() {
   int n;
   // Prompt for and read a positive integer
   do {
     cout << "Vector size? " << endl;
     cin >> n;
   } while ( n <= 0 );
   // Request storage for vector.
   unsigned* pInt = getVector( n );
   // Fill vector with random integers
   fillVector( pInt, n );
   // do some processing
   delete[ ] pInt; // deallocate
   return 0;
}
unsigned* getVector( unsigned n ) {
   return new unsigned[ n ];
}
void fillVector( unsigned* v, unsigned n ) {
   for ( unsigned i = 0; i < n; i++ )
     v[ i ] = rand();
}
```

FIGURE 9.3.2 A program to illustrate pointers as arguments and return values.

Function `getVector`

```
unsigned* getVector( unsigned n ) {
   return new unsigned[ n ];
}
```

returns the value of the expression

```
new unsigned[ n ]
```

This expression evaluates to the address of the vector's first **unsigned** cell, if the dynamic storage allocation succeeds. The return type reads "pointer to **unsigned**."

The Dereference Operator *

In C++, the asterisk * is the **dereference** operator. The dereference operator is applied to a pointer in order to *reference* the cell to which the pointer points.

EXAMPLE 9.3.7.   The code segment

```
int main() {
  int x = 1;      // store 1 in x
  int* ptr;
  ptr = &x;
  *ptr = -999;  // store -999 in x
  ...
}
```

first defines an **int** cell **x** initialized to 1 and then defines an **int*** cell and assigns it **x**'s address (see Figure 9.3.3). Assuming that **x**'s cell is at address 32 on the stack, here is a summary of relevant expressions and their values after **x** has been initialized to 1 and **p** has been initialized to **&x**:

Expression	Value	Description
x	1	**x**'s contents
&x	32	**x**'s address
ptr	32	**ptr**'s contents equals **x**'s address
*ptr	1	**ptr** dereferenced equals **x**'s contents

The definition of **ptr**

```
int* ptr;
```

provides a hint about the relationship between **ptr** and an **int**. As noted earlier, the data type **int*** reads "pointer to **int**." Because **ptr** points to **x**, we can access **x** through **ptr** by dereferencing **ptr**. So the assignment

```
*ptr = -999;  // store -999 in x
```

stores −999 in **x** by using the dereferenced **ptr**, that is, ***ptr**. ■

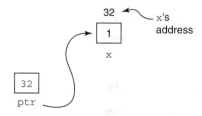

FIGURE 9.3.3 **ptr** pointing to **x**.

EXAMPLE 9.3.8.   The code segment

```
int main() {
   int x = -7;      // x at address 32
   int* p1 = &x;    // p1 at address 28
   int** p2 = &p1;
   ...
}
```

defines an **int** variable **x** initialized to −7, a pointer variable **p1** that points to **x**, and a pointer variable **p2** that points to **p1** (see Figure 9.3.4). There is one level of indirection between **p1** and **x**, and two levels of indirection between **p2** and **x**. In a pointer definition, each asterisk ***** is read "pointer to"; hence, **p2** is a *pointer to a pointer to* an **int**. In Figure 9.3.4, the number of arrows that we must follow from **p2** to the **int** cell **x** equals the number of asterisks that we must attach to **p2** to get an **int**, that is, to reference **x**. Accordingly, the statement

```
cout << **p2 << endl; // x's contents
```

prints −7, which is **x**'s contents. We must dereference **p2** twice because there are two levels of indirection between **p2** and **x**. The statement

```
cout << *p1 << endl; // print x's contents
```

prints **x**'s contents as well. Pointer **p1** is dereferenced only once because there is a single arrow from it to **x** (see Figure 9.3.4). Finally, the statement

```
cout << x << endl; // print x's contents
```

requires *no* dereferencing because **x** itself is an **int**, not a pointer of any kind.   ■

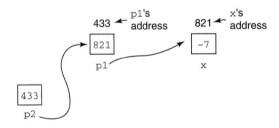

FIGURE 9.3.4 A pointer to a pointer to an **int**.

EXAMPLE 9.3.9.   The code segment

```
#include <cstdlib>
int main() {
   int a1[ 5 ], a2[ 5 ];
   for ( int i = 0; i < 10; i++ ) {
      a1[ i ] = rand();
      *( a2 + i ) = rand();
   }
   ...
}
```

populates two arrays of size five with random integers. For **a1**, we use the index operator **[ ]** with loop counter **i** as the index and the array's name **a1** as a base address. For **a2**, we again use the array's name as a base address but we explicitly add **i** to this base address. The expression **a2 + i** is thus a pointer to one of **a2**'s cells. Figure 9.3.5 illustrates for the case in which **i** equals 3. We dereference the pointer expression **a2 + i** to access the appropriate array cell so that we can store a random integer in this cell. Of course, the syntax

```
a1[ i ] = ...
```

is simpler and clearer than the syntax

```
*( a2 + i ) = ...
```

Nonetheless, either syntax could be used to access array elements. ■

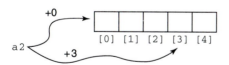

FIGURE 9.3.5 The expression `*(a2 + i)`.

Call by Value with Pointers

Chapter 3 explains the relative merits of call by value (see Section 3.3) and call by reference (see Section 3.5). Call by reference can be *simulated* by passing *pointers* as values.

EXAMPLE 9.3.10. The code segment

```
#include <iostream>
using namespace std;
void f( int& );   // call by reference
void g( int* );   // simulated call by reference
int main() {
   int x = 777;
   f( x );      // call by reference
   cout << x << endl; //*** prints 787
   g( &x );  // simulated call by reference
   cout << x << endl; //*** prints 797
   ...
}
void f( int& a ) { // reference as an argument
   a += 10;
}
void g( int* a ) { // pointer as an argument
  *a += 10;
}
```

illustrates how **g** uses a pointer argument to simulate **f**'s call by reference. Because **g**'s argument is a pointer with one level of indirection, we must dereference this pointer once to access the **int** cell to which it points.

The example shows that there is no advantage to simulating call by reference by passing a pointer. Indeed, passing a pointer is more complicated on the invoking side (in this example, we must apply the address operator **&** to **x**) and on the invoked side (in this example, we must dereference the pointer argument to increment **x**). Call by reference is thus preferable to call by pointer when either could be used. ∎

EXAMPLE 9.3.11. The code segment

```
#include <cstdlib>
#include <iostream>
using namespace std;
void fill( int* v, unsigned n );
int main() {
   unsigned n;
   int* v;
   // Prompt for and read an integer.
   cout << "Vector size? " << endl;
   cin >> n;
   v = new int[ n ];
   fill( v, n ); // fill array
   ...
}
```

```
void fill( int* p, unsigned n ) {
   for ( unsigned i = 0; i < n; i++ )
      p[ i ] = rand();
}
```

defines a pointer variable **v** as the target of a **new** operation. If **new** succeeds in allocating the requested storage, **main** invokes **fill** with pointer **v** as one of the arguments. We thus have call by value with a pointer as the value: a *copy* of **v** is passed to **fill** because call by value—not call by reference—is in effect. Assuming that **v**'s value is 459, Figure 9.3.6 illustrates that **fill**'s parameter **p** is a copy of **main**'s local variable **v**. In the case of a pointer, a copy is as good as the original because either can be dereferenced to access the same cell, in this case the first **int** cell in the vector to which local variable **v** and parameter **p** point. In **fill**'s header, we use pointer syntax

```
void fill( int* p, unsigned n )
```

instead of array syntax

```
void fill( int p[ ], unsigned n )
```

for the first parameter only to underscore that **p** is indeed a pointer. In general, we prefer array syntax for parameters that represent array or vector names; but pointer syntax is probably more common among C++ programmers. ∎

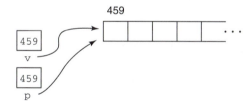

FIGURE 9.3.6 Pointer parameter **p** as a copy of pointer **v**.

The Pointer Data Type **void***

A C++ pointer is defined to point to a specific data type such as **char** or **double**. The pointer's own data type reflects the type to which it points. For example, a pointer to a **char** is type **char***, whereas a pointer to a **double** is type **double***. A pointer to **char** is a data type distinct from a pointer to **double**.

EXAMPLE 9.3.12.   When compiling the code segment

```
char c;     // char variable
double* p; // pointer to double, not char
p = &c;     //***** ERROR: wrong type!
```

our compiler issues the error message

```
cannot convert from 'char*' to 'double*'
```

because the source expression **&c** is of type **char***, whereas the target expression **p** is of type **double***. The code segment illustrates again the danger of mixing data types. A cast

```
p = static_cast<double*>(&c); //**** dubious
```

is needed to eliminate the error. The cast changes the source expression's type to **double***. Yet this cast represents bad programming. If the programmer needs to store **c**'s address in a pointer variable, the programmer should define a variable of type **char*** to match the data type of **&c**. ∎

Because **void** is also a C++ data type, pointers to **void**—that is, variables of type **void***—are supported. Any pointer type converts to **void*** without requiring explicit casting.

> **EXAMPLE 9.3.13.**   We amend Example 9.3.12
>
> ```
> char c;     // char variable
> void* p;    // generic pointer
> p = &c;     // ok, no cast needed
> ```
>
> by changing **p**'s data type from **double*** to **void***. In effect, this makes **p** a generic pointer that can be assigned any address expression, regardless of its type. ∎

Pointers to **void** have various uses in C++. In Section 9.4, we introduce the library functions **qsort** (quicksort) and **bsearch** (binary search), which can be used to sort and search arrays of *any data type*. The first argument to **qsort** is an array or vector address:

```
qsort( void* p,   // address where sorting begins
       ...         // other arguments
```

The array or vector may be of *any data type*: an array of a built-in type such as **int**s, an array of user-defined type such as **Employee**s, and so on. Accordingly, **qsort**'s first argument is of type **void*** to accommodate any type of pointer argument.

EXERCISES

1. What is the error?

```
int p = new int;
```

2. What is the error?

```
int* p = new int 25;
```

3. When should **delete[ ]** be used instead of **delete**?

4. If a class has a default constructor, does it execute when class objects are dynamically allocated?

5. Express in words the data type **int*****.

6. What is the output?

```
int x = -999;
int* p = &x;
int** pp = &p;
**p = *p + 100;
cout << x << endl;
```

7. Given the array definition

```
int a[ 100 ]; // array definition
```

do the assignments

```
a[ 72 ] = 1;
```

and

```
*( a + 72 ) = 1;
```

have the same result?

8. What is the output?

```
#include <iostream>
using namespace std;
void f( int* );
int main() {
   int x = 100;
   cout << x << endl;
   f( &x );
   cout << x << endl;
   return 0;
}
void f( int* p ) {
    *p += 100;
}
```

9. If either call by reference or call by value with a pointer as the value could be used, which is preferable and why?

10. Explain the error.

```
char c = 'A';
double* p = &c;
```

11. Does the code segment

```
char c = 'A';
char* p = &c;
char* q;
q = p;
```

contain any errors?

9.4 SAMPLE APPLICATION: SORTING AND SEARCHING

Problem

Fill a vector with randomly generated integers and then sort the vector in ascending order. The user should specify the vector's size. The user also should help determine the range of the randomly generated integers. Once the vector is sorted, generate more random integers to serve as **search keys** (**keys** for short), that is, values to be searched for in the sorted array. If a key is *not* found in the sorted vector, save it in a separate vector, keeping track of how many search keys must be generated in order to fill the vector of search keys not found. The user should specify how many search keys are to be generated. Output both the sorted vector of integers and the sorted vector of search keys not found in it. For sorting, use the library function **qsort**; for searching, use the library function **bsearch**.

Sample Input/Output

After prompting for and reading the vector and the keys-not-found sizes, the output consists of *n* randomly generated integers, where *n* is the user-specified size of a vector **nums** in which the integers are stored, followed by *m* randomly generated search keys not found in **nums**, where *m* is the user-specified number.

```
Vector size? 100
Multiplier for range (>= 2)? 4
Keys-not-found size? 10

Sorted random integers:
7
10
11
14
14
17
19
21
...
366
367
370
374
375
379
394
397
```

```
**** 11 tries to find 10 keys not in the array.
58
123
129
184
204
244
294
386
387
390
```

Solution

We use the library function **rand** to generate random integers to populate the initial array and to generate search keys. We use the library function **srand** to seed the random number generator so that different sequences of random integers are generated each time the application is run. For sorting and searching, we use the library functions **qsort** and **bsearch**, respectively. Our C++ implementation is modular in that it divides the labor among various functions. We have five user-defined functions:

- **promptAndRead** prompts the user for a positive integer (e.g., a vector's size), reads integers from the standard input until a positive integer is read, and returns the positive integer as an **unsigned**.

- **allocate** uses **new** to allocate a vector of **unsigned** integers, returning a pointer to the vector's first cell, if successful.

- **fillVector** populates a vector with randomly generated integers.

- **comp** is a **callback function**, or **callback** for short, invoked by **qsort** and **bsearch** when these library functions need to do comparisons (see Discussion). A *callback* is a function that the programmer does not *explicitly* invoke; instead, a callback is invoked by another function such as **qsort** or **bsearch**.

- **main** controls the invocation of the other functions and prints results to the standard output.

C++ Implementation

```cpp
#include <iostream>
#include <cstdlib>
using namespace std;
// callback for qsort and bsearch
int comp( const void*, const void* );
unsigned promptAndRead( char prompt[ ] );
unsigned* allocate( unsigned );
void fillVector( unsigned*, unsigned, unsigned );
```

```cpp
int main() {
    unsigned* nums;  // vector of random integers
    int n;           // its size
    unsigned* keysNotFound; // vector of keys not in nums
    int m;                  // its size
    unsigned range; // of integers in vectors
    int i, j;

    // Prompt for vector size.
    n = promptAndRead( "Vector size? " );
    // Prompt user for range of random numbers as
    // an integer multiple of array size (e.g., if array
    // size is 100, range could be 100 * 2, 100 * 3,
    // 100 * 4, etc.).
    range = promptAndRead( "Multiplier for range (>= 2)? " );
    range *= n;
    range++;
    // Prompt for size of vector of keys not found in nums.
    m = promptAndRead( "Keys-not-found size? " );

    // Allocate heap storage for the vector.
    nums = allocate( n );
    keysNotFound = allocate( m );

    // Fill array with random numbers.
    fillVector( nums, n, range );

    // Sort it using library function qsort.
    qsort( nums,                 // vector to sort
           n,                    // its size
           sizeof( nums[ 0 ] ),  // element size in bytes
           comp );               // comparison function
    // Print sorted array.
    for ( i = 0; i < n; i++ )
        cout << nums[ i ] << endl;

    // Generate random numbers as keys to be
    // searched for in the array, halting when
    // m such keys are not in the array. Save
    // these keys into an array of their own for
    // later printing. Library function bsearch used
    // for searching.
    unsigned key, count = 0;
    j = 0; // index into keysNotFound
    do {
        key = rand() % range; // generate random key
        count++;              // count it
```

```cpp
            // if key not in vector, add it to keysNotFound
            if ( !bsearch( &key,                    // key's address
                           nums,                    // search vector
                           n,                       // its size
                           sizeof( nums[ 0 ] ),     // element size
                           comp ) )                 // callback
               keysNotFound[ j++ ] = key; // add it to vector
         } while ( j < m );

         // Print keys not found in array, after sorting.
         qsort( keysNotFound, m, sizeof( *keysNotFound ), comp );
         cout << "\n**** " << count
              << " tries to find " << m
              << " keys not in the array." << endl;
         for ( j = 0; j < m; j++ )
            cout << keysNotFound[ j ] << endl;
         return 0;
   }

   // qsort and bsearch callback:
   // returns one of three integer values:
   //     < 0 means that *p1 < *p2
   //     > 0 means that *p1 > *p2
   //       0 means that *p1 == *p2
   int comp( const void* p1, const void* p2 ) {
      return *static_cast<const unsigned*>(p1) -
             *static_cast<const unsigned*>(p2);
   }

   // Prompts user for size of arrays and for range.
   unsigned promptAndRead( char prompt[ ] ) {
      int temp;
      // Prompt user for vector size.
      do {
         cout << prompt;
         cin >> temp;
      } while ( temp <= 0 );
      return temp;
   }

   unsigned* allocate( unsigned n ) {
      return new unsigned[ n ];
   }

   void fillVector( unsigned* v, unsigned n, unsigned r ) {
      for ( unsigned i = 0; i < n; i++ )
         v[ i ] = rand() % r;
   }
```

Discussion

We prompt the user for the sizes of two vectors: one to hold random integers to be searched and the other to hold the random search keys. We also prompt the user for a multiplier to be used in determining the range of random integers. Suppose that the user enters 100 as the search vector's size and 4 as the multiplier. The code segment

```
range *= n;
range++;
```

sets **range** to 401. The expression

```
rand() % range
```

then evaluates to an integer 0, 1, ..., 400. We use this modulus expression to generate both the integers that populate the search vector and the search keys. We have the user specify the range for these integers to promote experimentation. Suppose, for example, that the search array's size is 100 and search key array's size is 10. A multiplier of 100 makes the range of integers in the search array and the range of sort keys 0 to 10,000. With such a relatively large range, it is likely that only 10 or so tries will be required to generate 10 keys *not* in the sorted array. By contrast, if the range is set to 200—the smallest range allowed when the search array's size is set to 100—then more than 10 tries will likely be required to generate 10 search keys not in the sorted array. (The minimum range is twice the size of the search vector.)

After prompting the user for vector sizes, we invoke **allocate** with one argument, the number of **unsigned** cells to allocate:

```
unsigned* allocate( unsigned n ) {
   return new unsigned[ n ];
}
```

If the allocation succeeds, a pointer to the vector's first cell is returned. The return type is **unsigned*** because the allocated cells are **unsigned**.

The function **fillVector**

```
void fillVector( unsigned* v, unsigned n, unsigned r ) {
   for ( unsigned i = 0; i < n; i++ )
      v[ i ] = rand() % r;
}
```

is then invoked to populate the vector with randomly generated integers. We use pointer syntax

```
unsigned* v
```

for the vector's parameter declaration, but then use array syntax

```
v[ i ] = rand() % r;
```

when populating the vector in the **for** loop. We mix syntax only to illustrate that it can be done. In general, we recommend array syntax wherever possible. We could have used

```
*( v + i ) = rand() % r;
```

as the **for** loop's body: **v** provides the base address and **i** the offset from it. The dereference operator is used to access the cell at specified address **v + i**. We prefer the array syntax **v[i]** because it is easier.

We use the library function **qsort** to sort the vector:

```
// Sort it using library function qsort.
qsort( nums,                  // vector to sort
       n,                     // its size
       sizeof( nums[ 0 ] ),   // element size in bytes
       comp );                // comparison function
```

Function **qsort** expects four arguments:

- The address at which to begin sorting. This is typically an array or vector name, as we usually want to sort from the first through the last element. We thus invoke **qsort** with **nums** as its first argument.

- The number of elements in the array or vector. We thus provide **n** as the second argument.

- The size in bytes of each element. In a vector, as in an array, elements are of the same type and so of the same size in bytes. We thus use the expression **sizeof(v[0])** as the third argument.

- The address of a function that does pairwise comparisons on array or vector elements. A comparison determines whether two elements are equal, the first is greater than the second, or the second is greater than the first. A function's *name*, like an array's name, is a *pointer constant*. A function's name points to the address in the program area at which the function's body begins. Recall that this address is known as the function's *entry point* (see Section 7.1).

As its first argument, **qsort** expects an expression of type **void***. We pass it **nums**, whose type is **unsigned***. Recall that *any* pointer converts automatically (that is, with no explicit casting) to **void***. Because **qsort** can sort an array or vector of *any* type, it is known as a **generic function**. That its first argument is of type **void*** signals that **qsort** is a generic function.

The challenge in using **qsort** is to write the comparison function, the callback for **qsort** to use when comparing vector elements in the course of putting them in sorted order. Elements are compared pairwise, and we call the two elements being compared the *sort cells*. When **qsort** invokes the callback, it passes a *pointer to each sort cell*. Because **qsort** is generic, the sort cells could be of any data type. Therefore, the two arguments to the callback are of type **void***. The parameters are marked as **const** because the callback merely compares the sort cells; the callback does not change them.

Our callback for **qsort** is named **comp** for **comp**arison, though any function name is legal. The callback must return an **int**. In particular, the callback must return

- A positive **int** if the first sort cell is greater than the second sort cell.
- A negative **int** if the second sort cell is greater than the first sort cell.
- Zero if the two sort cells are equal.

Of course, *we* define "the first sort cell is greater than the second sort cell," "the second sort cell is greater than the first sort cell," and "the two sort cells are equal." In **comp**, we return the result of subtracting the second sort cell from the first:

```
int comp( const void* p1, const void* p2 ) {
   return *static_cast<const unsigned*>(p1) -
          *static_cast<const unsigned*>(p2);
}
```

We know that **nums** is a vector of **unsigned** integers. Therefore, the two parameters **p1** and **p2** actually point to **unsigned** cells in **nums** (see Figure 9.4.1). We use a **static_cast** to cast each parameter to its actual type, namely, a pointer to **unsigned**:

```
static_cast<const unsigned*>(p1)
```

However, we want to compare the *integers*, not their *addresses*. So we dereference each cast pointer

```
*static_cast<const unsigned*>(p1)
```

to access the integer to which it points. In Figure 9.4.1, **p1** points to a cell with 7 as its contents, and **p2** points to a cell with 2 as its contents. Our callback thus returns $7 - 2$, a positive **int** that signals that 7 is greater than 2.

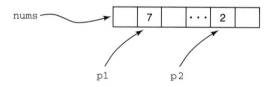

FIGURE 9.4.1 The parameters to **qsort**'s callback function.

To search **nums** for randomly generated keys, we use the library function **bsearch** (**binary search**):

```
if ( !bsearch( &key,               // key's address
               nums,               // search vector
               n,                  // its size
               sizeof( nums[ 0 ] ), // element size
               comp ) )            // callback
    keysNotFound[ j++ ] = key; // add it to vector
```

The last four arguments passed to **bsearch** are the same as the four arguments passed to **qsort**. Note that **bsearch** uses the same callback as **qsort**, which is typical. The first argument to **bsearch** is the *address* of the search key. In this invocation, **bsearch** searches **nums** for **key**. If the search succeeds, **bsearch** returns a pointer to the vector element that matches the key; if the search fails, **bsearch** returns **NULL**. Recall that **NULL** is defined as 0, which is **false**. So our **if** condition tests whether a randomly generated **key** occurs in **nums**. If not, we add the key to the vector **keysNotFound**. After filling **keysNotFound**, we sort it

```
qsort( keysNotFound, m, sizeof( *keysNotFound ), comp );
```

In this call, **qsort**'s third argument is

```
sizeof( *keysNotFound )
```

instead of

```
sizeof( keysNotFound[ 0 ] )
```

Either syntax works. Since **keysNotFound** is a *pointer* to the vector's first element, dereferencing this pointer gives us the first element as the operand for the **sizeof** operator.

EXERCISES

1. Why is the first argument to **qsort** of type **void***?

2. Library functions such as **qsort** and **bsearch** are known as *generic functions*. Explain what this means.

3. In our application, the comparison function **comp** is a *callback function*. Explain what this means.

9.5 CLASSES WITH POINTERS AS DATA MEMBERS

Class design poses special challenges if the class contains a data member that points to dynamically allocated storage. We focus on two such challenges. The first involves a class's copy constructor and assignment operator. We explain when and why the class author should define these rather than accept the compiler's versions. The second challenge involves a class destructor. We explain when and why a destructor should be made **virtual**.

Defining a Class's Copy Constructor and Assignment Operator

The C++ compiler provides a class with a *copy constructor* and an *assignment operator* if the class author does not provide a copy constructor or overload the assignment operator.

EXAMPLE 9.5.1. In the code segment

```
class C {
public:
   C() { x = -999; }
   void dump() { cout << x << endl; }
private:
   int x;
};
int main() {
   C c1;        // default constructor
   c1.dump();   // -999 is printed
   C c2( c1 ); // compiler-supplied copy constructor
   c2.dump();   // -999 is printed
   C c3;
   c3 = c2;     // compiler-supplied assignment operator
   c3.dump();   // -999 is printed
   ...
}
```

we do not define a copy constructor or overload the assignment operator for **C**. As the code segment in **main** shows, operations involving the copy constructor and assignment operator are still legal because the *compiler* furnishes them. The compiler's versions do a byte-by-byte copy of data members from the target to the source. For example, in **c2**'s definition

```
 C c2( c1 );  // c2 is the target, c1 the source
```

the compiler's version of the copy constructor copies the value of **c1**'s data member **x** into **c2**'s data member **x**. In the assignment

```
c3 = c2; // c3 is the target, c2 the source
```

the compiler's version of the assignment operator copies the value of **c2**'s data member **x** into **c3**'s data member **x**. As a result of these operations, all three **C** objects have −999 as data member **x**'s value. ∎

A class author typically defines a copy constructor and overloads an assignment operator for a class *whose data members include a pointer to dynamically allocated storage.* We illustrate the reason with an example.

EXAMPLE 9.5.2. The program in Figure 9.5.1 defines two objects of type **C**, **c1** and **c2**. Each has a data member **p** that points to dynamically allocated storage, in this example to **MaxString + 1 char** cells. We assume that the cells are allocated as requested. Class **C** does *not* have a user-defined copy constructor, which means that the compiler-supplied version is used in **c2**'s definition:

```
 C c2( c1 );  // compiler-supplied copy constructor
```

```
#include <iostream>
#include <cstring>
using namespace std;
const unsigned MaxString = 10;
class C {
public:
    C() { p = new char[ MaxString + 1 ]; }
    void set( char s[ ] ) { strcpy( p, s ); }
    const char* get() { return p; }
    void dump() { cout << p << endl; }
private:
    char* p;
};
int main() {
  C c1;
  c1.set( "foo" );
  c1.dump();          // foo is printed
  C c2( c1 );         // compiler-supplied copy constructor
  c2.dump();          // foo is printed
  c2.set( "bar" );
  c2.dump();          // bar is printed
  c1.dump();          //**** Caution: bar is printed
  return 0;
}
```

FIGURE 9.5.1 Using the compiler versions of the copy constructor and assignment operator.

Because **c2** is defined as a copy of **c1**, the first call to **c2.dump()** prints **foo**, the string to which **c1.p** and **c2.p** both point (see Figure 9.5.2). In Figure 9.5.2, the numbers above the cells represent their addresses for reference. The call

```
c2.set( "bar" );
```

changes the string to which **c2.p** points from **foo** to **bar**. However, **c1.p** points to the very same cell as does **c2.p**, namely, the cell at address 549 (see Figure 9.5.2). Therefore, the second call to **c1.dump()** prints **bar**—despite the fact that **c1** never invoked its **set** method! This is a subtle error. We presumably want the definition

```
C c2( c1 );
```

to result in **c2**'s having its *own copy* of **foo**, not sharing a copy with **c1**. But the compiler's copy constructor simply copies **c1.p** into **c2.p** so that both data members point to the cell at address 549.

If we replace the line

```
C c2( c1 );
```

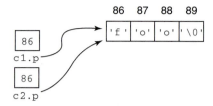

FIGURE 9.5.2 `c1.p` and `c2.p` point to the same string.

with the lines

```
C c2;
c2 = c1;   // assignment operation
```

the output is the same. Because we do not overload the assignment operator for **C**, the compiler provides an overload that copies **c1**'s data members into **c2**'s corresponding data members. In this case, **c1.p** is copied into **c2.p** so that, once again, the two pointers point to the same cell, the cell at address 549. Also, the storage to which **c2.p** pointed *before* the assignment operation is no longer accessible. The assignment operation thus results in inaccessible storage. ■

The program in Figure 9.5.1 illustrates the danger of using the compiler's versions of the copy constructor and assignment operator. We will show shortly how to write our own versions to avoid the danger. First, though, it should be emphasized that the assignment operator must be overloaded *as a method*. It is an error to overload the assignment operator as a top-level function.

EXAMPLE 9.5.3. The code segment

```
class C {
   ...
};
//***** ERROR: must be overloaded as a method
C& operator=( C& target, C& source ) {
   ...
}
```

contains an error because it tries to overload **=** as a top-level function rather than as a method. ■

EXAMPLE 9.5.4. The program in Figure 9.5.3 amends the program in Figure 9.5.1 by providing a programmer-written copy constructor and overloading the assignment operator. In the revision, the definition

```
C c2( c1 );
```

```
#include <iostream>
#include <cstring>
using namespace std;
const unsigned MaxString = 10;
class C {
public:
   C() { p = new char[ MaxString + 1 ]; }
   C( C& c ) : p( 0 ) { copyIntoP( c.get() ); }
   C& operator=( C& c ) {
     if ( this != &c )  // assigning an object to itself?
       copyIntoP( c.get() ); // if not, proceed
     return *this; // return the object
   }
   void set( char s[ ] ) { strcpy( p, s ); }
   const char* get() { return p; }
   void dump() { cout << p << endl; }
private:
   char* p;
   void copyIntoP( const char* s ) {
     if ( !p ) {    // if p is NULL, allocate storage for s
       p = new char[ strlen( s ) + 1 ]; // +1 for '\0'
       strcpy( p, s );
     }
     // copy s into p if two have same length
     else if ( strlen( s ) == strlen( p ) )
       strcpy( p, s );
     // else free p, allocate new storage, and copy s into p
     else {
       delete[ ] p; // free current storage
       p = new char[ strlen( s ) + 1 ]; // +1 for '\0'
       strcpy( p, s ); // copy string into it
     }
   }
};
int main() {
   C c1;
   c1.set( "foo" );
   c1.dump();        // foo is printed
   C c2( c1 );
   c2.set( "bar" );
   c2.dump();        // bar is printed
   c1.dump();        // foo is printed
   return 0;
}
```

FIGURE 9.5.3 Writing our versions of the copy constructor and assignment operator.

uses *our* version of the copy constructor, which does *not* simply copy **c1.p** into **c2.p**. Instead, our version ensures that **c1.p** and **c2.p** point to *different* cells, although these different cells hold the same string, **foo** (see Figure 9.5.4). An assignment such as

```
C c1();
c1.set( "foo" );
C c2;
c2 = c1; // our version of =
```

also results in **c2**'s getting its *own copy* of the string to which **c1.p** points. We now look at the details of our revision, starting with the overloaded assignment operator.

The revised program's assignment operator

```
C& operator=( C& c ) {
  if ( this != &c )   // assigning an object to itself?
    copyIntoP( c.get() ); // if not proceed
  return *this; // return the object
}
```

takes a single argument, a reference to a **C** object. An assignment such as

```
c2 = c1; // c1 and c2 are C objects
```

is equivalent to

```
c2.operator=( c1 );
```

In our overload of the assignment operator, we first check whether an object is being assigned to itself, for example:

```
c2 = c2; // assigning an object to itself
```

The pointer **this** points to the object whose method is being invoked. Therefore, in the assignment

```
c2 = c1;
```

this points to **c2**. So we check whether **this** points to the parameter

```
if ( this != &c ) // assigning an object to itself?
  copyIntoP( c ); // if not, proceed
```

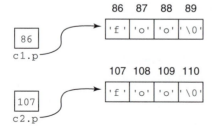

FIGURE 9.5.4 **c1.p** and **c2.p** point to different copies of the same string.

before proceeding. If the object and the parameter differ, then we invoke the **private** method **copyIntoP** to do the work:

```
void copyIntoP( const char* s ) {
   if ( !p ) {    // if p is NULL, allocate storage for s
     p = new char[ strlen( s ) + 1]; // +1 for '\0'
     strcpy( p, s );
   }
   // copy s into p if two have same length
   else if ( strlen( s ) == strlen( p ) )
     strcpy( p, s );

   // else free p, allocate new storage, and copy s into p
   else {
     delete[ ] p; // free current storage
     p = new char[ strlen( s ) + 1]; // +1 for '\0'
     strcpy( p, s ); // copy string into it
   }
}
```

There are three cases for **copyIntoP** to handle:

1. **p** is **NULL**. In this case, we dynamically allocate enough storage to hold the parameter string and then copy the parameter into the storage. This case holds when the copy constructor invokes **copyIntoP**.

2. **strlen(p)** equals **strlen(s)**. In this case, we copy parameter **s** into the cells to which **p** points. This is one of two cases that may hold when the assignment operator invokes **copyIntoP**.

3. **strlen(p)** does not equal **strlen(s)**. In this case, we free the storage to which **p** currently points, allocate new storage sufficient to hold the parameter string, and copy the parameter into the new storage. This is one of two cases that may hold when the assignment operator invokes **copyIntoP**.

Our overload of the assignment operator, unlike the compiler-supplied version, thus ensures that the target object and the source object have *their own copies* of the same string (see Figure 9.5.4).

Our overload of the assignment operator returns a **C** reference. The expression returned is ***this**. Because **this** points to an object, we get the object itself by dereferencing **this**. For example, in the assignment

```
c2 = c1;
```

operator= returns a reference to **c2**. It is common for an overloaded assignment operator to return a reference to the object that invoked the operator. This practice allows assignments to be cascaded. For instance, the cascaded assignment

```
c3 = c2 = c1; // all C objects
```

is equivalent to

```
c3.operator=( c2.operator=( c1 ) );
```

The call **c2.operator=(c1)** returns a reference to **c2**, which then is the argument for the call **c3.operator=(...)**.

Our version of the copy constructor is similar to our overload of the assignment operator. Indeed, it is common in C++ to define *both* or *neither*. In other words, if our class design requires that we overload the assignment operator, the class design likely requires that we overload the copy constructor as well. Here is our version of the copy constructor:

```
C( C& c ) : p( 0 ) { copyIntoP( c.get() ); }
```

We initialize **p** to **NULL** (that is, 0) in the constructor's header so that the **if** condition evaluates to **true** in **copyIntoP**:

```
if ( !p ) { // if p is NULL, allocate storage for s
  p = new char[ strlen( s ) + 1 ]; // +1 for '\0'
  strcpy( p, s );
}
```

Because the underlying functionality of the copy constructor and the assignment operator is so similar, we have **private** method **copyIntoP** provide the shared functionality. This is yet another example of code reuse.   ∎

virtual Destructors

We illustrate the need for **virtual** destructors with an example.

EXAMPLE 9.5.5. The program in Figure 9.5.5 has a base class **A** whose constructor dynamically allocates five bytes and whose destructor frees this storage so that it does not become inaccessible. Derived class **Z** has a constructor that dynamically allocates 5,000 bytes and a destructor that frees this storage so that it does not become inaccessible. We have **main** invoke **f** three times:

```
void f() {
   A* ptr;         // pointer to base class
   ptr = new Z(); // points to derived class object
   delete ptr; // ~A() fires but not ~Z()
} //***** Caution: 5,000 bytes of inaccessible storage
```

The constructors and destructors in **A** and **Z** print trace messages. The output is

```
A() firing
Z() firing
~A() firing

A() firing
Z() firing
~A() firing
```

```
#include <iostream>
using namespace std;
class A { // base case
public:
   A() {
      cout << endl << "A() firing" << endl;
      p = new char[ 5 ];   // allocate 5 bytes
   }
   ~A() {
      cout << "~A() firing" << endl;
      delete[ ] p;         // free 5 bytes
   }
private:
   char* p;
};
class Z : public A {
public:
   Z() {
      cout << "Z() firing" << endl;
      q = new char[ 5000 ];   // allocate 5,000 bytes
   }
   ~Z() {
      cout << "~Z() firing" << endl;
      delete[ ] q;            // free 5,000 bytes
   }
private:
   char* q;
};
void f();
int main() {
   for ( unsigned i = 0; i < 5; i++ )
      f();
   return 0;
}
void f() {
   A* ptr;          // pointer to base class
   ptr = new Z(); // points to derived class object
   delete ptr; // ~A() fires but not ~Z()
} //***** Caution: 5,000 bytes of inaccessible storage
```

FIGURE 9.5.5 Program to show the need for **virtual** destructors.

```
   A() firing
   Z() firing
   ~A() firing
```

Note that only **A**'s destructor fires when **f** is invoked. Pointer **ptr** is of type **A*** ("pointer to **A**"), although we have it point to a derived class object:

```
ptr = new Z(); // points to derived class object
```

The call to **new** causes the constructors **A()** and **Z()** to fire in that order. (Because **z**'s default constructor does not explicitly invoke an **A** constructor, the compiler ensures that **A**'s *default* constructor is invoked.) When we invoke **delete** on **ptr**, however, only ~**A()** fires—despite the fact that **ptr** points to a **z** object. Because the destructors are *not* **virtual**, compile-time binding is in effect (see Section 7.1). The compiler uses **ptr**'s data type **A*** to determine which destructor to call. Therefore, only ~**A()** is called. Because ~**Z()** is not called, the 5,000 bytes allocated by **Z()** are *not* freed. So 5,000 bytes of inaccessible storage are generated each time that **f** is called. ■

EXAMPLE 9.5.6.   The problem with the program in Figure 9.5.5 can be fixed by making the destructors **virtual**:

```
class A { // base case
public:
   ...
   virtual ~A() { //***** virtual destructor
     cout << "~A() firing" << endl;
     delete[ ] p;          // free 5 bytes
   }
   ...
};
```

By making the base class destructor ~**A()** **virtual**, we thereby make derived class destructor ~**Z()** **virtual** as well. For code clarity, we should put the keyword **virtual** in ~**Z()**'s declaration, but ~**Z()** is still **virtual** even if we fail to do so. With this change, the output becomes

```
A() firing
Z() firing
~Z() firing
~A() firing

A() firing
Z() firing
~Z() firing
~A() firing

A() firing
Z() firing
~Z() firing
~A() firing
```

Because the destructors are **virtual**, *run-time* binding is in effect when the object to which **ptr** points is destroyed. Because **ptr** points to a **z** object, ~**Z()** is called. Recall that destructors fire *bottom to top*, which explains why ~**A()** is then called as well. By making the destructors **virtual**, we thus prevent **f** from creating inaccessible storage. ■

If a base class has a data member that points to dynamically allocated storage and a destructor to free such storage, the destructor should be made **virtual** to ensure that polymorphism is at work as derived classes are added. In commercial libraries such as the Microsoft Foundation Classes, destructors are typically **virtual** to prevent the kind of storage leakage illustrated by the program in Figure 9.5.5.

EXERCISES

1. If the class author does not provide a copy constructor, does the compiler provide one?

2. If the class author does not provide an overload of the assignment operator, does the compiler provide one?

3. What is the output?

```
#include <iostream>
using namespace std;
class C {
public:
    C() { p = new int; }
    void set( int a ) { *p = a; }
    int get() { return *p; }
private:
    int* p;
};
int main() {
  C c1, c2;
  c1.set( 1 );
  cout << c1.get() << endl;
  c2 = c1;
  c2.set( -999 );
  cout << c1.get() << endl;
  return 0;
}
```

4. What is the output?

```
#include <iostream>
using namespace std;
class C {
public:
    C() { p = new int; }
    void set( int a ) { *p = a; }
    int get() { return *p; }
private:
    int* p;
};
```

```
int main() {
  C c1;
  c1.set( 1 );
  cout << c1.get() << endl;
  C c2( c1 );
  c2.set( -999 );
  cout << c1.get() << endl;
  return 0;
}
```

5. When should a class author define a copy constructor and overload the assignment operator for the class?

6. What is the output?

```
#include <iostream>
using namespace std;
class C {
public:
   C() { p = new int; }
   C( C& c ) {
     p = new int;
     *p = c.get();
   }
   void set( int a ) { *p = a; }
   int get() { return *p; }
private:
   int* p;
};
int main() {
  C c1;
  c1.set( 1 );
  cout << c1.get() << endl;
  C c2( c1 );
  c2.set( -999 );
  cout << c1.get() << endl;
  return 0;
}
```

7. An overload of the assignment operator

```
C& C::operator=( C& c ) {
  // code to implement the overload
  return *this;
}
```

typically returns the object—*this—by reference. Explain the reason for returning the object by reference.

8. What is the output for this program?

```cpp
#include <iostream>
using namespace std;
class A { // base class
public:
    A() { cout << "A()" << endl; }
    ~A() { cout << "~A()" << endl; }
};
class Z : public A { // derived class
public:
    Z() { cout << "Z()" << endl; }
    ~Z() { cout << "~Z()" << endl; }
};
int main() {
  A* p = new Z();
  delete p;
  return 0;
}
```

9. What is the output for this program?

```cpp
#include <iostream>
using namespace std;
class A { // base class
public:
    A() { cout << "A()" << endl; }
    virtual ~A() { cout << "~A()" << endl; }
};
class Z : public A { // derived class
public:
    Z() { cout << "Z()" << endl; }
    ~Z() { cout << "~Z()" << endl; }
};
int main() {
  A* p = new Z();
  delete p;
  return 0;
}
```

10. When is it prudent to make a base class destructor **virtual**?

11. What problems might arise if an overload of the assignment operator were written as in Exercise 7 except that we **return** the parameter **c** instead of ***this**?

12. Overload the +=, -=, *=, and /= operators as methods for the **Complex** class of Section 8.2 and show code segments that use the overloaded operators.

13. Overload the +=, -=, *=, and /= operators using top-level functions for the **Complex** class of Section 8.3 and show code segments that use the overloaded operators.

The Storage Class `register`

Parameters and local variables may have **register** as their storage class.

EXAMPLE. In the code segment

```
void f( register int x ) {
  register int y = x;
  ...
}
```

parameter **x** and local variable **y** have **register** as their storage class. By using **register** as a storage class, the programmer *recommends* that the compiler use a CPU register rather than the stack for the storage cell. However, the compiler is free to ignore the recommendation; and modern compilers typically do so. If the compiler ignores the recommendation, the parameter or local variable has **auto** as its storage class. ∎

It is an error to apply the address operator **&** to a **register** parameter or variable:

```
void g() {
  register int q;
  int* ptr = &q; //***** ERROR: q is register
  ...
}
```

Storage Classes for Top-Level Functions

Top-level functions have either **extern** or **static** as their storage class. The default is **extern**.

EXAMPLE. In the code segment

```
//*** start of file S1.cpp
void f() { // defaults to extern
  ...
}
extern void g() { // extern explicit
  ...
}
static void h() { // static storage class
  ...
}
//*** end of file S1.cpp
```

f and **g** have **extern** as their storage class, whereas **h** has **static** as its storage class. An **extern** function has *program scope*; that is, any other function in the same program can invoke it. Functions **f** and **g** thus can be invoked by any other functions in the same program, regardless of whether the invoking functions are defined in source file *S1.cpp*. A **static** function has *file scope*; that is, only functions in the same source file can invoke it. For example, **h** can be invoked only by functions in source file *S1.cpp*, that is, only by **f** and **g**. ■

COMMON PROGRAMMING ERRORS

1. It is an error not to free dynamically allocated storage before it becomes inaccessible:

```
void f() {
   double* p = new double[ 10000 ]; // 10,000 doubles
   // process the vector p
} //***** ERROR: 10,000 doubles of inaccessible storage
```

Dynamically allocated storage should be released before it becomes inaccessible by calling the **delete** or **delete[ ]** operator:

```
void f() {
   double* p = new double[ 10000 ]; // 10,000 doubles
   // process the vector p
   delete[ ] p; // free before it becomes inaccessible
}
```

2. When **new[ ]** is used to allocate a vector, then **delete[ ]** should be used to free the storage. When **new** is used to allocate a single cell, then **delete** should be used to free the storage:

```
class C {
   ...
};
C* pOne = new;              // one C cell
C* pMany = new C[ 100 ]; // a vector of C cells
delete pOne;   // ok
delete pMany; //***** ERROR: should be delete[ ] pMany
```

3. A variable's storage class, if present, occurs to the *left* of its data type:

```
int main() {
   auto int x; // correct
   int auto y; //***** ERROR
   ...
}
```

4. It is an error to assume that **auto** variables are initialized by the compiler. If the programmer does not initialize an **auto** variable, it contains an arbitrary value presumably of no use to the programmer:

```
#include <iostream>
using namespace std;
int main() {
   int x; // uninitialized auto variable
   int y = 0; // initialized auto variable
   cout << x << endl; // an arbitrary value is printed
   ...
}
```

5. It is an error to define an **auto** variable outside all blocks:

```
auto int x; //***** ERROR: auto must be in a block
int main() {
   ...
}
```

6. It is an error to reference a variable that is not in scope. The code segment

```
int main() {
   int x = 0;
   if ( x >= 0 ) {
     int y = -999;
     ...
   } // y goes out of scope
   int z = x + y; //***** ERROR: y is not in scope
   g = z * z;      //***** ERROR: g is not in scope
   ...
}
int g; // g is not visible in main
```

contains two scope errors. Because **y** is defined inside the **if** block, it is not visible outside the **if** block. The **extern** variable **g** is not visible in **main** because it is defined below **main** and is not declared either in or above **main**.

7. It is an error to initialize an **extern** variable in a declaration. The code segment

```
int main() {
   extern int x = -9; //***** ERROR: declaration
   ...
}
int x; // definition
```

contains an error because it initializes **x** in a declaration rather than a definition. The correction is

```
int main() {
   extern int x; // declaration
   ...
}
int x = -9; // ok, definition
```

8. If the keyword **extern** is used in an **extern** variable's *definition*, then the variable must be initialized:

```
// definition of x
extern int x;   //***** ERROR: x must be initialized
int main() {
   ...
}
```

There are two possible corrections. The first is to *omit* the keyword **extern** from the **extern** variable's definition. The second is to initialize the **extern** variable in its definition. The code segment

```
extern int x = 0; // ok, initialized in definition
int y;            // ok, keyword extern not used
int main() {
   ...
}
```

illustrates the corrections. It is easiest *not* to include the keyword **extern** in an **extern** variable's *definition*. The keyword *must* be used in an **extern** variable's *declaration*.

9. It is an error to store operator **new**'s return value in a nonpointer:

```
int p;  // not a pointer
p = new int[ 100 ]; //***** ERROR: new returns a pointer
int* q; // a pointer
q = new int[ 100 ]; // ok
```

10. It is an error to assign an address expression of one data type (e.g., **char***) to a pointer variable of a different type other than **void*** (e.g., **double***):

```
char* p;  // pointer to char
double d; // double variable
p = &d;   //***** ERROR: mismatched data types
```

Although a cast operation may be used to suppress the error, the best correction is not to mismatch the data types in the first place:

```
double* p;  // pointer to double
double d;   // double variable
p = &d;     // preferred correction
char* q;
q = static_cast<char*>(&d); // legal but bad practice
```

However, any pointer expression can be assigned to a **void*** pointer without casting:

```
void* p;
double d;
p = &d; // ok, no cast needed
```

11. It is an error to overload the assignment operator as a top-level function rather than as a method:

```
class C {
  ...
};
//***** ERROR: not a method!
C& operator=( C& target, C& source ) {
  ...
}
// ok, a C method
C& C::operator=( C& source ) {
  ...
}
```

∎

PROGRAMMING EXERCISES

9.1. Software engineers often profile an application to determine how modules consume resources such as storage or CPU cycles. Profile the Sample Application of Section 9.4 by tracking

- How many times each of the application's functions is invoked. For example, **main** is invoked just once, but **comp** is invoked multiple times.

- How much overall time is spent in each function.

The library functions **time** and **difftime**, which require the header file *time.h*, are useful in gathering temporal data. The code segment

```
#include <ctime>
using namespace std;
void f() {
  static time_t howLong = 0; // initialized once only
  time_t start = time( 0 ); // current time
  ...
  time_t stop = time( 0 );  // current time
  howLong += difftime( stop, start );
}
```

illustrates how **time** and **difftime** might be used.

9.2. A **list** is a finite sequence of elements with order taken into account. A list can be implemented in C++ by using linked objects known as **nodes**, which are the list's elements. A node can be represented as a C++ class

```
class Node {
public:
   Node* getNext(); // successor's address or NULL
   ...
private:
   Node* nextNode; // successor's address or NULL
   ...
};
```

with several data members and methods, including a data member to store the node's content, for example, a character string. Of particular interest are the **Node** members that store, access, and manipulate a successor **Node**'s address. **Node**s can be used to implement a **(singly) linked list**, which consists of ordered **Node**s

$$N_1, N_2, \ldots, N_n$$

together with the address of N_1. For $i = 1, \ldots, n - 1$, N_i contains the address of the following **Node**. (N_n has no successor because it is the last node.) For generality, we admit the **empty linked list**, which consists of no **Node**s. Create a **LinkedList** class to represent a singly linked list of **Node**s. The class should have methods to add and delete **Node**s at a user-specified position; to traverse the **List** and print each **Node**'s content; and to count how many **Node**s are in the list. Write a test client for the **LinkedList** class.

9.3. Expand Programming Exercise 9.2 by adding two methods to the **LinkedList** class. First, add a method to find a **Node**, if any, with a specified content. The code segment

```
LinkedList list;
Node* next;
// add Nodes to list
// test if any Node has content "foo"
if ( ( next = list.find( "foo" ) ) != NULL )
   next->printContents(); // if so, print contents
```

illustrates how **find** might be used. Second, add a method to **append** two **Linked-Lists**. If **list1** is

$$N_1, N_2, N_3$$

and **list2** is

$$N_A, N_B$$

then the code segment

```
list1.append( list2 );
```

changes **list1** to

$$N_1, N_2, N_3, N_A, N_B$$

and leaves **list2** unchanged. Once **append** is written, you might overload **+** for **LinkedList**s so that user can write

```
list1 + list2; // append list2 to list1
```

Write a client to test whether the new methods behave as expected.

9.4. Write a copy constructor and overload the assignment operator for the `LinkedList` class (see Programming Exercises 9.2 and 9.3). Write a client that then tests a code segment such as

```
LinkedList list1;
// add Nodes to list1
LinkedList list2( list1 ); // clone list1 through copy
// add or remove some Nodes from list2
LinkedList list3;
list3 = list2; // clone list2 through assignment
```

9.5. Overload `<<` for the `LinkedList` and the `Node` classes (see Programming Exercise 9.2). The overloads should support a code segment such as

```
LinkedList list1;     // create a list
Node node1( "foo" ), // create some nodes
     node2( "bar" ),
     node3( "baz" );
list1.addNodeB( node1 ); // add to beginning
list1.addNodeB( node2 ); // ditto
list1.addNodeB( node3 ); // ditto
cout << node3 << endl; // prints "baz"
cout << list1 << endl; // print all Nodes
```

9.6. A **doubly linked list** is like a singly linked list (see Programming Exercise 9.2) except that each node has a pointer to its predecessor as well as to its successor. Create a `DblLinkedList` class with methods to add and delete `Node`s at a user-specified position; to traverse the list from either front to back or back to front, printing each `Node`'s contents; to append two `DblLinkedList`s; and to find a `Node`, if any, with a specified content.

9.7. Write a copy constructor and overload the assignment operator for the `DblLinked-List` class (see Programming Exercise 9.6). Write a client to test these additions.

9.8. The following figure depicts a binary tree that represents the algebraic formula $(A + B) \times (E - F)$:

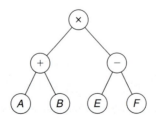

A **binary tree** is a finite set of nodes and edges that satisfies these conditions:

- There is a node with no parent designated as the tree's **root**. In the preceding figure, the node labeled $\times$ is the root. (Hereafter, for convenience, we refer to "$\times$" rather than "the node labeled $\times$.")

- Every node except the root has a single parent. In the preceding figure, for instance, A has $+$ as its parent, and $-$ has $\times$ as its parent.

- Every node has zero, one, or two children. A child is either a **left child** or a **right child** depending on whether it is connected to its parent by a left or a right edge. In the preceding figure, for example, $+$ has A as its left child and B as its right child. A has no children.

- If N_1 and N_2 are nodes in binary tree BT, there is a unique simple path from N_1 to N_2. In the preceding figure, for instance, the unique simple path from node A to node E goes from A to $+$ to $\times$ to $-$ to E.

A binary tree can be represented similarly to a linked list (see Programming Exercise 9.2):

```
class Node {
public:
// methods to manipulate implementation
private:
  Node* lchild; // pointer to left child or NULL
  Node* rchild; // pointer to right child or NULL
  Node* parent; // pointer to parent or NULL
};
```

Complete the **Node** class by providing methods to get and set the data members. Also, add an **id** member (e.g., a **char**) that uniquely identifies a **Node** and serves as its content. Next, create a **BinaryTree** class with methods to add a **Node** as either the root, the left child of a **Node** already in the tree, or the right child of a **Node** already in the tree. The **add** method can be parameterized

```
void add( Node* node, Node* parent, char where );
```

to ease the task of adding a **Node** to the tree. Sample calls would be

```
BinaryTree bt;
Node root, n1, n2, n3;
bt.add( &root, NULL, ' ' ); // add as root
bt.add( &n1, &root, 'L' );  // root's left child
bt.add( &n2, &root, 'R' );  // root's right child
bt.add( &n3, &n2, 'R' );    // n2's right child
```

9.9. To **traverse** a tree such as a binary tree (see Programming Exercise 9.8) is to visit each node in the tree, perhaps to print the node's contents. There are three standard algorithms for traversing a binary tree. All traversals begin with the binary tree's root. The **preorder traversal** algorithm may be described as follows, with *Node* initialized to the tree's root:

1. Visit *Node*.
2. Traverse *Node*'s left subtree. In the figure for Programming Exercise 9.8, for example, the root's left subtree is the binary tree rooted in node $+$.
3. Traverse *Node*'s right subtree. In the figure for Programming Exercise 9.8, for example, the root's right subtree is the binary tree rooted in node $-$.

The **inorder traversal** algorithm may be described as follows, with *Node* initialized to the tree's root:

1. Traverse *Node*'s left subtree.
2. Visit *Node*.
3. Traverse *Node*'s right subtree.

The **postorder traversal** algorithm may be described as follows, with *Node* initialized to the tree's root:

1. Traverse *Node*'s left subtree.
2. Traverse *Node*'s right subtree.
3. Visit *Node*.

Expand Programming Exercise 9.8 by adding methods to **BinaryTree** to do preorder, inorder, and postorder traversals. *Hint*: Recursion is an ideal programming technique for implementing the traversals. The base condition occurs when the binary tree's left and right children are both **NULL**, which means that the left and right subtrees are both empty. Recursion thus occurs only on a nonempty subtree.

9.10. Overload **<<** so that it can be used to print the contents of all **Node**s in a **Binary-Tree** (see Programming Exercises 9.8 and 9.9). The overload should support a code segment such as

```
BinaryTree bt;
// add Nodes to bt
cout << bt << endl; // print all Nodes in bt
```

Hint: Have the overloaded **<<** perform one of the standard traversals (see Programming Exercise 9.9).

9.11. Write a program that reads an algebraic expression from the standard input in infix notation and then prints the expression to the standard output in prefix notation and postfix notation. In **infix notation**, an operator occurs between its operands. In **prefix notation**, an operator occurs before its operands. In **postfix notation**, an operator occurs after its operands. To simplify the problem, assume only binary operators, that is, operators that have two operands. Here are some examples:

Infix	Prefix	Postfix
$A + B$	$+AB$	$AB+$
$A + (B \times C)$	$+A \times BC$	$ABC \times +$
$(A + B) \times C$	$\times +ABC$	$AB+C \times$
$(A + B) \times (C - D)$	$\times +AB-CD$	$AB+CD- \times$

Prefix and postfix notations have the advantage of not requiring parentheses. *Hint:* If an infix expression is represented as a binary tree (see Programming Exercises 9.8 and 9.9), then the tree's preorder traversal generates the expression in prefix notation, and the tree's postorder traversal generates the expression in postfix notation.

TEMPLATES AND THE STANDARD TEMPLATE LIBRARY

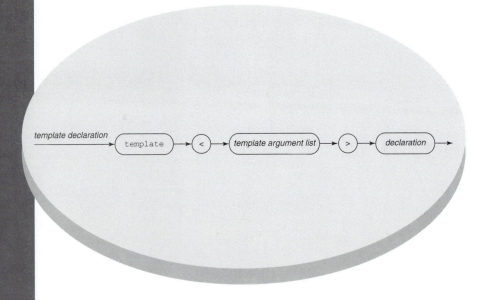

C++ supports code reuse in different ways. For example, through inheritance a derived class is able to reuse a base class's members, in particular the inherited methods. This chapter examines template classes, another C++ mechanism for code reuse, and also introduces the Standard Template Library (STL), a powerful C++ library of template classes and functions. Programming with STL requires familiarity with C++ namespaces, which can be used to avoid name conflicts. Accordingly, we devote a section to namespaces as well.

10.1 TEMPLATE BASICS

Figure 10.1.1 creates an **intArray** class, which is a variant of the one in Section 8.6. We could build a separate **charArray** class, a separate **doubleArray** class, and other separate classes modeled after **intArray**. C++ has a better way, however. We can write all the code for an **Array** class *only once* and then use this code to create **Array**s of *any data type*, built-in or user-defined. We do so by making **Array** a **template class**, that is, a class that is *not* data-type specific. A template class is created with at least one **class parameter**, a symbol that serves as a placeholder for a specific data type.

```
class intArray {
public:
    int& operator[ ]( int );
    intArray( int );
    int get_size() { return size; }
private:
    int* a;
    int size;
    intArray();
};

int& intArray::operator[ ]( int i ) {
    if ( i < 0 || i >= size ) {
        cerr << "index " << i << " out of bounds: ";
        return a[ 0 ];
    }
    return a[ i ];
}

intArray::intArray( int s ) {
    a = new int[ size = s ];
}
```

FIGURE 10.1.1 The class **intArray**.

EXAMPLE 10.1.1. The code in Figure 10.1.2 creates a template class `Array`. The declaration begins

```
template< class T >
class Array {
  ...
};
```

`T` is the class parameter, which follows the keyword `class` or the keyword `typename` inside angle brackets; `class` and `typename` have the same meaning. (`template` is also a C++ keyword.) Any legal C++ identifier can serve as a class parameter, but `T` has become a common choice. In our class declaration, we place the **template header**

```
template< class T >
```

on a separate line only for readability. The declaration

```
template< class T > class Array {
  ...
};
```

is legal and equivalent to our original.

In the template header, white space can occur between `template` and the left angle bracket `<`. The style

```
template < class T > // legal
```

is legal but uncommon. Inside the angle brackets, the only required white space is between `class` and the class parameter. So

```
template<class T>
```

is also legal.

Our parameterized `Array` constructor and the overloaded index operator are defined *outside* the class declaration, which requires that we repeat the template header

```
template< class T >
```

in each definition. Further, there is new syntax for specifying the class to which the methods belong. For example, the definition of the convert constructor is

```
template< class T >
Array< T >::Array( int s ) {
    a = new T[ size = s ];
}
```

Because `Array` is a template class, the class name is `Array< T >`, where `T` is the class parameter in the template header. Therefore, `Array< T >` occurs to the left of

```
template< class T >
class Array {
public:
    T& operator[ ]( int );
    Array( int );
    int get_size() { return size; }
private:
    T* a;
    int size;
    Array();
};
template< class T >
T& Array< T >::operator[ ]( int i ) {
    if ( i < 0 || i >= size ) {
        cerr << "index " << i << " out of bounds: ";
        return a[ 0 ];
    }
    return a[ i ];
}
template< class T >
Array< T >::Array( int s ) {
    a = new T[ size = s ];
}
// top-level overload of operator<<
template< class T >
ostream& operator<<( ostream& os, Array< T >& a ) {
    for ( int i = 0; i < a.get_size(); i++ )
        os << a[ i ] << endl;
    return os;
}
```

FIGURE 10.1.2 The template class `Array`.

the scope resolution operator `::` in the definition of the constructor and the overloaded index operator. The syntax is simpler if a method is defined *inside* the class declaration. Here, for instance, is how we would define the convert constructor inline:

```
template< class T >
class Array {
public:
    T& operator[ ]( int );
    Array( int s ) {
        a = new T[ size = s ];
    }
    ...
};
```

A template class may have more than one class parameter, in which case the class parameters are separated by commas. The keyword **class** or **typename** must occur to the left of each class parameter.

EXAMPLE 10.1.2. The declaration

```
template< class T1, class T2, class T3 >
class Sample {
public:
  T2 m( T3 p ) {...} // expects a T3 arg, returns a T2
private:
  T1 x;  // var of type T1
};
```

illustrates the syntax for a template class with multiple class parameters. ■

The syntax for creating a template class is somewhat tricky. By contrast, the syntax for using a template class is relatively straightforward. The programmer uses a template class by specifying data types in angle brackets.

EXAMPLE 10.1.3. Given the template class declaration in Figure 10.1.2, the code segment

```
Array< double > a1( 100 ); // Array of 100 doubles
```

defines **a1** as an **Array** of 100 **double**s. Object **a1**'s data type is

```
Array< double >
```

The syntax indicates that the data type **double** replaces the class parameter **T** in **Array**'s declaration. The compiler replaces occurrences of the class parameter **T** in **Array**'s declaration with **double**. For example, the compiler changes the overloaded assignment operator's declaration from

```
T& operator[ ]( int ); // template version
```

to

```
double& operator[ ]( int ); // Array< double > version
```

The compiler likewise changes data member **a**'s declaration from

```
T* a; // template version
```

to

```
double* a; // Array< double > version
```

If we define object **a2** as

```
Array< char > a2( 50 );
```

then **a2**'s data type is

```
Array< char >
```

and the compiler replaces occurrences of the class parameter **T** in **Array**'s declaration with **char**. ∎

Template Classes in a Parameter List

A template class may occur as a data type in a parameter list. For example, the code in Figure 10.1.2 overloads the output operator at the top level:

```
template< class T >
ostream& operator<<( ostream& os, Array< T >& a ) {
    for ( int i = 0; i < a.get_size(); i++ )
      os << a[ i ] << endl;
    return os;
}
```

The operator's second argument is a reference to an **Array< T >**, where **T** is the class type in the template header.

> **EXAMPLE 10.1.4.** Given the code in Figure 10.1.2, the program
>
> ```
> #include <iostream>
> using namespace std;
> // Code from Figure 10.1.2 is here
> int main() {
>     Array< int > a( 3 );
>     a[ 0 ] = 0; a[ 1 ] = 1; a[ 2 ] = 2;
>     cout << a; // overloaded <<
>     return 0;
> }
> ```

prints

```
0
1
2
```

to the standard output. The **cout** statement uses an overload of the output operator whose second argument is an **Array< T >** reference. In this example, the compiler replaces occurrences of the class type **T** with **int** because **a**'s type is **Array< int >**. ∎

Template Instantiations

We refer to **Array< double >** and **Array< char >** as **template instantiations** or simply **instantiations** of the template class **Array< T >**, where **T** is the class parameter in the template header. The syntax for using a template instantiation is the same as the syntax for using an ordinary, nontemplate class.

EXAMPLE 10.1.5. The code segment

```
#include <iostream>
using namespace std;
// declaration of template class Array
int main() {
    Array< double > a1( 100 ); // array of 100 doubles
    a1[ 6 ] = 3.14;
    cout << a1[ 6 ] << endl;
    // etc.
    ...
}
```

creates a **double** instantiation of the template class **Array**. Once **a1** has been defined as an object of type **Array< double >**, we access its elements in the usual way. ∎

A template instantiation can be created with either a built-in or a user-defined data type.

EXAMPLE 10.1.6. Given the class declaration

```
class Task { // user-defined data type
   ...
};
```

we can create the **Array** instantiation

```
Array< Task > tasks( 500 ); // Task instantiation
```

and access **tasks**'s elements in the usual way. ∎

An object cannot belong to a template class but only to a template class instantiation. For example, given the template class declaration

```
template< class T >
class Array {
   ...
};
```

there cannot be an object whose type is **Array** or **Array< T >**, but there can be an object whose type is **Array< int >**. An object does not belong to a template class such as **Array** but rather to a template class instantiation such as **Array< char >**.

EXAMPLE 10.1.7. The code segment

```
template< class T >
class Array {
  ...
};
Array a0( 50 );        //***** ERROR: not an instantiation
Array< T > a1( 50 );   //***** ERROR: not an instantiation
template< class T >
Array< T > a2( 50 );   //***** ERROR: not an instantiation
Array< int > a3( 50 ); // ok, int instantiation
```

illustrates three illegal object definitions involving a template class and one legal object definition involving a template class **int** instantiation. ∎

Function-Style Parameters

A template class must have at least one class parameter, and it may have multiple class parameters. A template class also may have parameters that are not class parameters. These are called **function-style parameters** because they resemble the parameters passed to a function. A template class may have any number of function-style parameters whose data types can be either built-in or user-defined. The class parameters always come first; the function-style parameters follow. All parameters are separated by commas in the template header.

EXAMPLE 10.1.8. The declaration

```
template< class T, int X, float Y >
class Sample {
  ...
};
```

illustrates function-style parameters. Class parameter **T** comes first, followed by two function-style parameters separated by a comma: **int** parameter **X** and **float** parameter **Y**. ∎

EXAMPLE 10.1.9. The declaration

```
//***** ERROR: class params first!
template< class T, int X, class Z >
class C {
  ...
};
```

contains an error because the function-style parameter **X** occurs to the left of the class parameter **Z** in the template header. ∎

```
template< class T, int S >
class Array {
public:
   T& operator[ ]( int );
   Array();
   int get_size() { return size; }
private:
   T* a;
   int size;
};
template< class T, int S >
T& Array< T, S >::operator[ ]( int i ) {
   if ( i < 0 || i >= size ) {
      cerr << "index " << i << " out of bounds: ";
      return a[ 0 ];
   }
   return a[ i ];
}
template< class T, int S >
Array< T, S >::Array() {
   a = new T[ size = S ];
}
```

FIGURE 10.1.3 Template class **Array** with a function-style parameter.

EXAMPLE 10.1.10. The code in Figure 10.1.3 amends the declaration for the template class **Array** by adding an **int** function-style parameter, which we name **S** for size. In the original code, we use a convert constructor to specify the size of an **Array**:

```
Array< double > a1( 10 ); // Array of 10 doubles
Array< char > a2( 50 );   // Array of 50 chars
```

In the amended code, we use the function-style parameter to do so:

```
Array< double, 10 > a1; // Array of 10 doubles
Array< char, 50 > a2;   // Array of 50 chars
```

The amended code therefore can use the default constructor instead of a convert constructor to allocate storage for the **Array**:

```
template< class T, int S >
Array< T, S >::Array() {
   a = new T[ size = S ];
}
```

Note that the template class's name is now

```
Array< T, S >
```

where **T** is the class parameter and **S** is a function-style parameter, both specified in the template header

```
template< class T, int S >                                    ■
```

EXAMPLE 10.1.11. The code segment

```
template< class T, int S >
class Array {
  ...
};
Array< float > a1; //***** ERROR: no function-style param
```

contains an error because an **Array** instantiation requires

- A class parameter such as **float**, which is given.
- An **int** function-style parameter, which is missing.

A correct object definition is

```
Array< float, 100 > a2; // ok, both parameters given          ■
```

A template class is instantiated by replacing each class parameter in the template header with a data type and each function-style parameter in the template header with a value. For this reason, a template class is sometimes called a **parameterized class**. The **Array** class in Figure 10.1.3 is thus instantiated by replacing class parameter **T** with a data type such as **float** and function-style parameter **S** with a value such as 100.

Restrictions on Template Classes with Function-Style Parameters

In Figure 10.1.2, we overload the output operator at the top level:

```
template< class T >
ostream& operator<<( ostream& os, Array< T >& a ) {
   for ( int i = 0; i < a.get_size(); i++ )
     os << a[ i ] << endl;
   return os;
}
```

The operator's second argument is a reference to an **Array< T >**, where **T** is the class parameter specified in the template header. Note that the template **Array** class in Figure 10.1.2 has *no function-style parameters*.

Suppose that we try to adapt the overloaded output operator to the code in Figure 10.1.3, a template **Array** class with a function-style parameter:

```
//***** ERROR: top-level overload has a template class
// with a function-style parameter as an argument type
template< class T, int S >
ostream& operator<<( ostream& os, Array< T, S >& a ) {
   for ( int i = 0; i < a.get_size(); i++ )
     os << a[ i ] << endl;
   return os;
}
```

The code generates a fatal compile-time error, although the specific error message may differ from one compiler to another. The problem is that if **f** is a top-level template function

```
template< tparams >
returntype f( fparams ) {
   ...
}
```

each parameter in *tparams* (the template parameters) must be a class parameter; function-style parameters are not allowed. Furthermore, each class parameter in *tparams* must be used in *fparams* (the function's parameters). These restrictions diminish the usefulness of template classes with function-style parameters because binary operators in general, and the input and output operators in particular, are typically overloaded at the top level. We thus recommend that template classes generally be built *without* function-style parameters.

EXERCISES

1. What is a class parameter in a template class?

2. Explain the error:

```
template< T > class Queue {
   ...
};
```

3. May a template header have more than one class parameter?

4. Explain the error:

```
template< class T > class Queue {
public:
   Queue();
};
template< class T >
Queue::Queue() {...}
```

5. Can a method in a template class be defined inline?

6. Explain the error:

```
template< class T > Queue {
   ...
};
Queue< T > q1;
```

7. In a template class, what is a function-style parameter?

8. What is the difference between a template class and a template class instantiation?

9. Explain the error:

```
template< class T >
class Queue {
   ...
};
Queue< double > q1;
Queue< T > q2;
```

10. Explain the error:

```
template< class T >
class Queue {
   ...
};
Queue q1;
```

11. Explain the error:

```
template< class T, int Size >
class Queue {
   ...
};
Queue< double > q1;
```

10.2 SAMPLE APPLICATION: A TEMPLATE STACK CLASS

Problem

Create a template **stack** class to represent a **stack**, that is, a list of zero or more elements in which insertions and deletions occur at the same end (see Section 5.1). Implement methods to push elements onto a **Stack**, to pop them off a **Stack**, to inspect a **Stack's** top element, to print a **Stack**'s contents, to determine whether a **Stack** is empty, and to determine whether a **Stack** is full. Make the **Stack** implementation robust so that standard stack operations do not lead to run-time errors.

Sample Output

The output for the test client in Figure 10.2.1 is

```
*** Stack contents: ***
pushing A, B
*** Stack contents: ***
B
A
popping
*** Stack contents: ***
A
pushing 1, 2, 3
*** Stack contents: ***
3
2
1
A
Top of stack == 3
popping
*** Stack contents: ***
2
1
A
popping
*** Stack contents: ***
1
A
pushing Y, Z
*** Stack contents: ***
Z
Y
1
A
```

Solution

Our template **stack** class has the required class parameter but no function-style parameters. The class has a default constructor that sets the **Stack**'s size to **DefaultStack**, currently set at 10, and a convert constructor that sets the **Stack**'s size to a user-specified value. Storage for **Stack** elements is dynamically allocated. The **Stack** destructor deallocates the dynamically allocated storage. A **Stack**'s interface also includes methods to push and pop **Stack** elements, to inspect the **Stack**'s top element without popping it, to check for a full or an empty **Stack**, and to print the **Stack**'s contents. We also use assertions (see Program Development section) to promote the systematic testing of applications that use the **Stack** class.

```
// #includes and Stack declaration
int main() {
   Stack< char > cStack( 20 );
   cout << cStack << endl;  // empty stack
   cout << "pushing A, B" << endl;
   cStack.push( 'A' );
   cStack.push( 'B' );
   cout << cStack << endl;  // BA (top at left)
   cout << "popping" << endl;
   if ( !cStack.empty() ) // test empty method
     cStack.pop();
   cout << cStack << endl; // A
   cout << "pushing 1, 2, 3" << endl;
   cStack.push( '1' );
   cStack.push( '2' );
   cStack.push( '3' );
   cout << cStack << endl;  // 321A (top at left)
   cout << "Top of stack == "
        << cStack.topNoPop() << endl; // 3
   cout << "popping" << endl;
   cStack.pop();
   cout << cStack << endl;  // 21A (top at left)
   cout << "popping" << endl;
   cStack.pop();
   cout << cStack << endl;  // 1A (top at left)
   cout << "pushing Y, Z" << endl;
   if ( !cStack.full() ) { // test full method
     cStack.push( 'Y' );
     cStack.push( 'Z' );
   }
   cout << cStack << endl; // ZY1A (top at left)
   return 0;
}
```

FIGURE 10.2.1 Test client for `Stack< char >`.

C++ Implementation

```
#include <iostream>
#include <cstdlib>
//#define NDEBUG //**** enable/disable assertions
#include <cassert>
using namespace std;
template< class T >
```

```
class Stack {
public:
   enum { DefaultStack = 10, EmptyStack = -1 };
   Stack();
   Stack( int );
   ~Stack();
   void push( const T& );
   T pop();
   T topNoPop() const;
   bool empty() const;
   bool full() const;
private:
   T* elements;
   int top;
   int size;
   void allocate() {
     elements = new T[ size ];
     top = EmptyStack;
   }
   void msg( char m[ ] ) const {
     cout << "*** " << m << " ***" << endl;
   }
   friend ostream& operator<<( ostream&, const Stack< T >& );
};

template< class T >
Stack< T >::Stack() {
   size = DefaultStack;
   allocate();
}

template< class T >
Stack< T >::Stack( int s ) {
   if ( s < 0 )         // negative size?
     s *= -1;
   else if ( 0 == s ) // zero size?
     s = DefaultStack;
   size = s;
   allocate();
}

template< class T >
Stack< T >::~Stack() {
   delete[ ] elements;
}
```

```cpp
template< class T >
void Stack< T >::push( const T& e ) {
   assert( !full() );
   if ( !full() )
     elements[ ++top ] = e;
   else
     msg( "Stack full!" );
}

template< class T >
T Stack< T >::pop() {
   assert( !empty() );
   if ( !empty() )
     return elements[ top-- ];
   else {
     msg( "Stack empty!" );
     T dummy_value;
     return dummy_value; // return arbitrary value
   }
}

template< class T >
T Stack< T >::topNoPop() const {
   assert( top > EmptyStack );
   if ( !empty() )
     return elements[ top ];
   else {
     msg( "Stack empty!" );
     T dummy_value;
     return dummy_value;
   }
}

template< class T >
bool Stack< T >::empty() const {
   return top <= EmptyStack;
}

template< class T >
bool Stack< T >::full() const {
   return top + 1 >= size;
}

template< class T >
ostream& operator<<( ostream& os, const Stack< T >& s ) {
   s.msg( "Stack contents:" );
   int t = s.top;
   while ( t > s.EmptyStack )
     cout << s.elements[ t-- ] << endl;
   return os;
}
```

Discussion

The template **Stack** class has two constructors so that **Stack** objects can be created in one of two ways. A definition such as

```
Stack< float > s1; // default constructor
```

invokes the default constructor, which sets the **Stack**'s size to **DefaultStack**, currently set at 10. A definition such as

```
Stack< unsigned > s2( 500 );
```

invokes the convert constructor, which sets the **Stack**'s size to 500. The **private** data member **size**, which stores the **Stack**'s size, serves as an argument to operator **new[ ]** to request storage for the **Stack**. The **private** method **allocate** does the work:

```
void allocate() {
  elements = new T[ size ];
  top = EmptyStack;
}
```

In the call to **new[ ]**

```
elements = new T[ size ]
```

T is the class parameter from the template header

```
template< class T >
```

When the user creates a **Stack** instantiation such as

```
Stack< double > s1;
```

the data type, in this case **double**, is substituted for **T**.

Data member **top** is used as an index into the vector **elements**. The index is initialized to **EmptyStack**, the constant −1. Whenever an element is pushed onto the **Stack**, the preincremented **top** serves as the index in the vector **elements** at which the new element is inserted:

```
template< class T >
void Stack< T >::push( const T& e ) {
  assert( !full() );
  if ( !full() )
    elements[ ++top ] = e;
  else
    msg( "Stack full!" );
}
```

When the first element is pushed onto the **Stack**, **top** is incremented from −1 to 0 and the element is inserted into **elements[0]**; the second element pushed onto the **Stack** is inserted into **elements[1]**; and so on. The **Stack** thus grows by incrementing the index **top**: from −1 to 0 to 1 to ... **size** − 1. The Program Development section explains the **assert**, which is the first statement in **push**'s body.

When elements are popped off the **Stack**, **top** is decremented if the **Stack** is not empty:

```
template< class T >
T Stack< T >::pop() {
   assert( !empty() );
   if ( !empty() )
     return elements[ top-- ];
   else {
     msg( "Stack empty!" );
     T dummy_value;
     return dummy_value; // return arbitrary value
   }
}
```

Because **top** is the index of the element currently at the top of the **Stack**, we return

```
elements[ top-- ]
```

Recall that the value of the expression **top--** is **top**'s *current* value. Once the expression is evaluated, **top** is decremented. The **Stack** shrinks by decrementing **top**, whose maximum value is **size** − 1 because this is the largest legal index into a vector of **size** elements. If **top** is ever decremented to −1, the **Stack** is again empty.

Data member **size** also is used to test whether the **Stack** is full. The **public** method **full**

```
template< class T >
bool Stack< T >::full() const {
   return top + 1 >= size;
}
```

returns **true**, if the **Stack** is full, and **false**, if the **Stack** is not full. The method does so by doing a bounds check. Suppose that the **Stack**'s vector, **elements**, has a **size** of 10. Legal indexes would then be 0, 1, ..., 9. The maximum value for index **top** therefore would be 9. Method **full** thus checks whether **top + 1** is greater than or equal to the vector's **size**. If so, the **Stack** is full and no more elements should be pushed onto it. Index **top** is used to test whether the **Stack** is empty:

```
template< class T >
bool Stack< T >::empty() const {
   return top <= EmptyStack;
}
```

EmptyStack is −1, which is an illegal index into the vector **elements**. So the checks for a full and an empty **Stack** are, in effect, bounds checks on the vector **elements**. We supply two methods for accessing the **Stack**'s top element. Method **pop** returns the top element, if the **Stack** is not empty, and *changes* the **Stack** in the process: after the pop, the next element, if any, is in the top position. Our second method for accessing the **Stack**'s top element is **topNoPop**, which returns the **Stack**'s top element but leaves the **Stack** unchanged. This allows the user to inspect the **Stack**'s top element without removing it from the **Stack**. We say that **pop** is *destructive* because it changes the **Stack**, whereas **topNoPop** is *nondestructive* because it does not change the **Stack**.

Finally, as a convenience, we overload the output operator as a top-level **friend**

```
template< class T >
ostream& operator<<( ostream& os, const Stack< T >& s ) {
   s.msg( "Stack contents:" );
   int t = s.top;
   while ( t > s.EmptyStack )
     cout << s.elements[ t-- ] << endl;
   return os;
}
```

so that a **Stack** can be printed to an output stream such as **cout**.

Program Development

The **Stack** class is designed to be robust. For example, method **push** first tests whether the **Stack** has room before inserting an element into the **Stack**:

```
if ( !full() )                // enough room?
   elements[ top++ ] = e; // if so, insert element
```

Method **pop** tests whether the **Stack** has any elements before deleting the top one. These checks guard against vector overflow and underflow, respectively, because the **Stack**'s implementation is a vector of **size** elements. Further, the **empty** and **full** methods do checks beyond what may seem to be required. For example, **empty** checks whether index **top** is *less than* or equal to **EmptyStack**, the constant −1:

```
template< class T >
bool Stack< T >::empty() const {
   return top <= EmptyStack;
}
```

The **Stack** code as a whole ensures that **top** cannot be less than −1 because only **pop** decrements **top**, and **pop** always invokes **empty** before such a decrement. Nonetheless, as a precaution, **empty** checks whether **top**'s value is either less than or equal to −1. In similar fashion, **full** checks whether **top** + 1 is either greater than or equal to the vector's **size**.

Some other small measures guard against run-time errors. For example, the convert constructor checks whether the user-specified **Stack** size is either zero or a negative number. If the user specifies zero as the **Stack** size, the constructor uses **DefaultStack** as the size. If the user specifies a negative **Stack** size, the constructor converts the negative number to a positive one. These measures are well worth the small amount of code required.

Assertions

An **assertion** is a condition that must be true at a specified point in a program's execution. If an assertion fails, the system halts the program's execution and reports the failure. Assertions can be used to ensure that, during execution, a program conforms to specification at selected points. Assertions are commonly used during application development. They are a powerful and convenient means of testing and debugging software.

C++ supports assertions with the **assert** macro, which requires that the header file *cassert* be **#include**d. Method **push** has an assertion:

```
template< class T >
void Stack< T >::push( const T& e ) {
   assert( !full() ); //**** line 59 in source file
   ...
```

The statement

```
assert( !full() );
```

asserts that the **Stack** must be not full. On our system, an attempt to **push** an element onto a full **Stack** halts the program's execution and generates the error report

```
Assertion failed: !full(), file stack.cpp, line 59
```

The message is useful for debugging, as it indicates the line in the source file at which the assertion failed. Methods **pop** and **topNoPop** have similar **assert**s, but ones that check whether the **Stack** is empty.

As these examples show, an **assert** expects an expression that evaluates to **true** or **false**. Relational expressions, logical expressions, and functions that return a **bool** are commonly used as **assert** expressions.

C++ assertions can be easily disabled. Our C++ implementation contains the lines

```
//#define NDEBUG //**** enable/disable assertions
#include <cassert>
```

The **#define** of **NDEBUG** (No DEBUG) has been commented out. To disable our assertions, we place a **#define** of **NDEBUG** *above* the **#include** of *cassert*. So this change

```
#define NDEBUG //**** enable/disable assertions
#include <cassert>
```

disables the **assert**s in our code. We do not have to remove the **assert** statements themselves, which might be many in a large application.

Even with disabled assertions, the **Stack** class still performs checks to prevent run-time errors. For example, **pop**

```
template< class T >
T Stack< T >::pop() {
  assert( !empty() );
  if ( !empty() )                    // anything to pop?
    return elements[ top-- ]; // if so, pop element
  else {
    msg( "Stack empty!" );
    T dummy_value;
    return dummy_value; // return arbitrary value
  }
}
```

first checks whether the **Stack** is empty before removing an element from it. If the **Stack** is empty, **pop** returns **dummy_value**, an arbitrary value that satisfies the requirement that **pop** return an expression of the **Stack** instantiation's type (e.g., **int**). This is not as powerful a safeguard as an **assert**, but it does prevent our attempting to remove an element from an empty **Stack** if the **assert**s have been disabled.

EXERCISES

1. What is the effect of changing the line

   ```
   //#define NDEBUG
   ```

   to

   ```
   #define NDEBUG
   ```

   in the application?

2. Write a sample client that pushes too many items onto a **Stack** under two conditions: first, with the assertions enabled; second, with the assertions disabled.

3. Explain why the method **pop** returns a dummy value if the **Stack** is empty.

4. What is the difference in behavior between **pop** and **topNoPop**?

10.3 NAMESPACES

Suppose that each of two class libraries has a **String** class. If an application tried to use both libraries, a name conflict would result. Such name conflicts are also a potential problem in large applications involving several programmers, who must be careful to find unique names for classes, global variables, and top-level functions. C++ provides **namespaces** to prevent name conflicts.

EXAMPLE 10.3.1.   Suppose that two class libraries have a class named `String`. If each class's vendor enclosed the class within a namespace, an application could use both libraries at once. The syntax for enclosing a class in a namespace is

```
namespace mfc { // vendor 1's namespace
   class String { //*** vendor 1's String class
     ...
   };
} //*** no closing semicolon required

namespace owl { // vendor 2's namespace
   class String { //*** vendor 2's String class
     ...
   };
} //*** no closing semicolon required
```

A namespace begins with the keyword `namespace` and generally is followed by a name such as `mfc` or `owl` that identifies the namespace. This name must be a legal C++ identifier. (The C++ Postscript explains unnamed namespaces.) An opening and a closing brace mark where the namespace begins and ends. ■

A namespace resembles a class with respect to syntax, except that a namespace does not have separate `public`, `protected`, and `private` sections as does a class. Also, a namespace does not require a semicolon after its closing right brace. Whatever can be declared or defined outside a namespace can be declared or defined inside one as well; hence, class declarations, function declarations and definitions, variable and object definitions, `typedef`s, and the like all may occur inside a namespace.

EXAMPLE 10.3.2.   We amend Example 10.3.1 by adding a function definition to `mfc`'s namespace:

```
namespace mfc { // vendor 1's namespace
   class String { //*** vendor 1's String class
     ...
   };
   void g() { cout << "g" << endl; }
}
```

The `mfc` namespace now includes the top-level function `g` along with the class `String`. ■

A namespace can be used to disambiguate a name that otherwise would cause a conflict.

EXAMPLE 10.3.3.   Given the namespaces of Example 10.3.1, the code segment

```
mfc::String s1; // mfc String object
owl::String s2; // owl String object
```

defines two `String` objects, one from each namespace. The scope resolution operator `::` occurs between the namespace name such as `owl` and the class name `String`. ■

EXAMPLE 10.3.4. We simplify Example 10.3.3 with a **using declaration** that lets us use **String** as shorthand for **mfc::String**. The code segment

```
using mfc::String; // using declaration for mfc::String
String s1;         // mfc::String
owl::String s2;    // namespace name needed
```

illustrates a using declaration. After this declaration, we can drop the **mfc::** part and simply use **String** to reference **mfc::String**. Therefore, **s1**'s definition mentions only **String**. However, **s2**'s definition requires the full name **owl::String** because the using declaration makes **String** shorthand for **mfc::String**.

A using declaration applies to a *single* item in the namespace. For example, the **mfc** namespace includes not only class **String** but also top-level function **g** (see Example 10.3.2). The using declaration for **mfc::String** does *not* cover **mfc::g**. To invoke **g**, we need to use the full name

```
mfc::g();  // ok, full name
```

or introduce a using declaration that covers **g** in particular

```
using mfc::g; // using declaration for g
g();          // ok
```
■

EXAMPLE 10.3.5. The code segment

```
using namespace mfc; // using directive
String s1;           // mfc::String
g();                 // mfc::g()
owl::String s2;      // full name needed
```

illustrates a **using directive**, which is equivalent to a using declaration for each item in a namespace. Note that the keyword **namespace** occurs in a using *directive*, which covers *all* items in a namespace. This keyword does not occur in a using *declaration*, which covers *one* item in a namespace. Our programs and code segments typically include the using directive

```
using namespace std;
```

This using directive covers all the items in C++'s **std** namespace.
■

EXAMPLE 10.3.6. The code segment

```
using mfc; //***** ERROR: missing "namespace"
```

contains an error. The syntax for using an entire namespace (using directive) is

```
using namespace mfc;
```

The syntax for using a particular item in a namespace (using declaration) is

```
using mfc::String;
```
■

EXERCISES

1. What purpose does a namespace serve?

2. Does a namespace require a semicolon after its closing brace?

3. Explain the error:

```
namespace baz {
public:
   ...
private:
   ...
}
```

4. Can a top-level function's declaration belong to a namespace?

5. Can a top-level function's definition belong to a namespace?

6. Can a class be declared inside a namespace?

7. Explain the error:

```
namespace foo {
  class Date {
  public:
    void showDate() {...}
  };
}
namespace bar {
  class Date {
    void showDate( bool fullDate ) {...}
  };
}
using foo::Date;
Date d1;
d1.showDate( true );
```

8. Given the namespace and class declaration

```
namespace myLib {
  class Baz {
    ...
  };
}
using myLib::Baz;
using namespace myLib;
```

indicate which is the using declaration and which is the using directive.

9. Explain the error:

```
namespace myLib {
  class Baz {
    ...
  };
}
using namespace Baz;
```

10. Explain the error:

```
namespace myLib {
  ...
}
using myLib;
```

10.4 THE STANDARD TEMPLATE LIBRARY

The Standard Template Library (hereafter, STL) is part of the standard C++ library. STL has very powerful features in its own right, and it also promises to have significant impact on the organization of future C++ libraries. STL's template classes provide C++ with **data structures**, that is, high-level data types, such as stacks (see Section 10.2), together with appropriate operations on these high-level data types, such as *push*es and *pop*s.

Containers, Algorithms, and Iterators

STL's three basic components are **containers**, **algorithms**, and **iterators**. An STL container is a collection of objects. Examples are vectors, stacks, queues, deques, lists, sets, and maps. In more formal language, an STL container is a data structure. An STL algorithm is a function for processing a container. Examples are functions that copy, sort, search, merge, and permute containers. In more formal terms, an STL algorithm is a recipe or procedure (see Section 0.1) for processing a data structure. An STL iterator is a mechanism for accessing the objects in a container. Suppose that we have a list of elements

$$L, A, Z, K, D, F$$

and need to search for element K. We could use an iterator to move through the list, element by element, so that K could be compared one by one against the elements in the list. STL provides iterators to move through containers from front to back, from back to front, in either direction, and randomly. STL also has special iterators for input and output operations. STL algorithms use iterators to process STL containers.

Reasons for Using STL

STL containers, unlike C++ arrays or dynamically allocated vectors, grow and shrink in size *automatically*. Suppose, for example, that an application needs to aggregate floating-point numbers but cannot anticipate beforehand exactly how many will need to be aggregated. The programmer might define an array with a presumably large enough size and then constantly check to ensure that the array does not overflow. This approach requires tedious, low-level programming that is prone to error. Instead, the programmer might dynamically allocate a **float** or **double** vector; and, if the vector fills, free it after copying the current entries and a candidate entry to a newly allocated vector of larger size. This approach, too, is tedious and prone to error. Such problems are eliminated with STL containers, which grow automatically as elements are inserted and shrink automatically as elements are removed. STL thus contributes to programming ease, program robustness, and storage efficiency. Further, STL offers an assortment of containers (e.g., vectors, associative arrays, sets, stacks, queues) to meet application needs. STL also publicizes the time and storage complexity of its containers, which allows the programmer to make reasoned decisions about which type of container to use. We return to this topic shortly.

In addition to containers, STL provides built-in algorithms for processing them. Algorithms for sorting, searching, replacing, reversing, partitioning, and testing containers are provided. STL also supports powerful numeric algorithms. The algorithms are designed to be intuitive and easy to apply. Further, STL algorithms work on any appropriate container. For example, the **sort** algorithm can be used to sort a **vector**, a **deque**, or a **set**, which are three STL containers. Of particular interest are STL algorithms such as **for_each** and **copy**, which provide built-in iteration. Suppose, for example, that we want to double the value of each element in an aggregate. If the numbers are stored in, say, an STL **vector** of **int**s, and we have a function called **sq** that expects an **int** and returns its square, we can process the vector without any loops:

```
vector< int > v;
... // fill it up
for_each( v.begin(), v.end(), sq ); // square each element
```

This code is easier to write and to understand than a C++ **while** loop that does the same work. The **copy** algorithm can be used to copy an aggregate—not only to another aggregate but also to a disk file. Similarly, the **copy** algorithm can be used to copy from an input file to an aggregate, such as a **vector**, or from an input file to an output file. Such flexibility is a hallmark of STL algorithms. Because STL algorithms such as **for_each** and **copy** are high level and have intuitive names, their use contributes to overall code clarity and correctness.

STL containers and algorithms are flexible and efficient because they use iterators. Under the hood, an STL iterator is a pointer, which means that STL algorithms exploit the inherent efficiency of C++ pointers. Yet STL iterators are, at the same time, high-level constructs that allow the STL programmer to work with them as if they were *not* pointers. For example, it is rarely necessary to dereference an STL iterator.

EXAMPLE 10.4.1. The code segment

```
#include <vector>
#include <deque>
#include <algorithm>
using namespace std;
int main() {
  vector< int > v;
  deque< double > d;
  // fill v with integers, d with floating-points
  sort( v.begin(), v.end() );
  sort( d.begin(), d.end() );
  ...
}
```

illustrates the flexibility of an STL algorithm such as **sort**, which can be used to sort STL containers such as **deque**s and **vector**s. The **sort** algorithm does not need to know the type of container to be sorted but only where to start sorting, where to end, and how to sort (e.g., in ascending or descending order). The **deque** and **vector** methods **begin** and **end** return *iterators*, which mark the container's beginning and end. The **sort** algorithm uses such iterators in the process of moving elements into sorted order. By the way, ascending order is the default sort order; hence, the **deque** and the **vector** will be sorted in ascending order in this example. ∎

Finally, STL is **extensible**, which means that users can add new containers and new algorithms. STL algorithms can be used on built-in or user-defined containers. User-defined algorithms can be applied to built-in or user-defined containers. STL's efficiency, flexibility, ease of use, and extensibility should make it increasingly popular among C++ programmers.

Container Basics

STL has seven basic containers divided into two groups, sequential and associative (see Figure 10.4.1). Sequential containers resemble ordinary C++ arrays in that their elements can be accessed by position, for example, by using an index. For instance, if **v** is an STL **vector** of **int**s, then the statement

```
int x = v[ 2 ];
```

initializes **x** to the value of **v**'s third element. Sequential containers also provide methods such as **begin** and **end** that can be used to access elements. STL sequential containers are the list, the vector, and the deque. For now we emphasize the similarities among them, although shortly we clarify how they differ. Elements in an associative container can be accessed by *key*, that is, by specifying a unique value of arbitrary data type such as a string. For example, if **m** is an STL map that stores a nation's gross national product as a floating-point number and uses the nation's name as a key, then the statement

```
float gnp = m[ "china" ];
```

Container	Type	Description
`list`	Sequential	Collection of zero or more elements
`vector`	Sequential	Array that grows and shrinks as needed
`deque`	Sequential	Array with efficient insertions/deletions at either end
`set`	Associative	Collection of nonduplicate keys
`multiset`	Associative	A `set` with duplicates allowed
`map`	Associative	Collection of nonduplicate elements with access by key
`multimap`	Associative	A `map` with duplicates allowed

FIGURE 10.4.1 Basic STL Containers.

initializes **gnp** to the floating-point value in **m** associated with the key **china**, which is a string. An associative array (see Section 8.7) is thus an example of an associative container. STL associative containers are the **map**, the **multimap**, the **set**, and the **multiset**. For now, we emphasize the similarities among associative containers, although shortly we clarify how they differ. We introduce sequential and associative containers with a series of examples.

Basic Sequential Containers: `vector`, `deque`, and `list`

EXAMPLE 10.4.2. The program in Figure 10.4.2 shows the basic syntax and functionality of STL's template **vector** class. The program's output is

```
14
-999
57

57
```

The program first defines an **int** instantiation of the **vector** class. Note that no size is specified. A **vector** grows and shrinks automatically to meet its own storage needs, thus relieving the programmer of this obligation. This feature alone makes **vector**s superior to ordinary C++ arrays. It is common *not* to specify a **vector**'s initial size in its definition; however, this can be done. The definition

```
vector< double > d( 1000 );
```

defines a vector with an initial size of 1,000. The size still increases automatically if required. If a **vector** is created with an initial size, all the cells are initialized to zero. A **vector** supports insertions at either end and provides the methods **begin** and **end** to access its beginning and its end, respectively. The **erase** method, like the **insert** method, can access either end of the **vector**. The **erase** method removes an element from the **vector**. The **size** method returns the **vector**'s current size. We are able to use the index operator **[ ]** with the object **nums**

```
cout << nums[ i ] << endl;
```

```
#include <iostream>
#include <vector>
using namespace std;
int main() {
  int i;
  vector< int > nums;
  nums.insert( nums.begin(), -999 ); // -999
  nums.insert( nums.begin(), 14 ) ;  // 14 -999
  nums.insert( nums.end(), 57 );     // 14 -999 57
  for ( i = 0; i < nums.size(); i++ )
    cout << nums[ i ] << endl; // 14 -999 57
  cout << endl;
  nums.erase( nums.begin() ); // -999 57
  nums.erase( nums.begin() ); // 57
  for ( i = 0; i < nums.size(); i++ )
    cout << nums[ i ] << endl; // 57
  return 0;
}
```

FIGURE 10.4.2 The STL **vector** container.

because **vector** overloads **[ ]** so that it behaves the same for **vector**s as for ordinary C++ arrays.

The header file *vector* contains the declaration for the template **vector** class. We also have the using directive

```
using namespace std;
```

because **vector**, together with the other STL components, is in the **std** namespace. ∎

At first glance, a **deque** seems almost indistinguishable from a **vector**. For the program in Figure 10.4.2, if we replace

```
#include <vector>
```

with

```
#include <deque>
```

and

```
vector< int > nums;
```

with

```
deque< int > nums;
```

the output is exactly the same. A **vector** and a **deque** differ in their underlying implementation, in particular with respect to insertions and deletions. For a **vector**, insertions at the *beginning* are less efficient than insertions at the *end*. Insertions at the end take about the same amount of time whether the **vector**'s size is 0, 100, or 100,000. Insertions at the beginning take an amount of time directly proportional to the **vector**'s size. For example, inserting at the beginning of a **vector** with 1,000 elements takes about 100 times longer than inserting into the beginning of a **vector** with 10 elements. The same rule holds for deletions in a **vector**. For this reason, **vector**s should be used only when insertions and deletions are typically done at the end. A **deque** is equally efficient whether insertions and deletions are done at the beginning or at the end. For example, insertions or deletions at the beginning of a **deque** take about the same amount of time whether the **deque**'s size is 0, 100, or 100,000. For this reason, a **deque** is to be preferred over a **vector** if insertions and deletions typically need to be done at the beginning. After an example of a **list**, we summarize efficiency considerations for **vector**s, **deque**s, and **list**s.

EXAMPLE 10.4.3. The program in Figure 10.4.3 creates a list of C++ strings

```
list< cstring > names;
```

where **cstring** is a **typedef** for **const char***, that is, for string constants such as **"fooey."** After **insert**ing three strings at the **list**'s beginning and one at its end, we pass the list by reference to **dump**, which prints its contents to the standard output. Function **dump** provides a first look at iterators. All the STL containers have an associated iterator data type. For example, a container such as

```
list< int >
```

has the associated iterator type

```
list< int >::iterator
```

The container

```
vector< double >
```

has the associated iterator type

```
vector< double >::iterator
```

So in **dump** we define an iterator **it**, which is used to traverse the **list**. After initializing **it** to the **list**'s beginning

```
it = l.begin(); // initialize iterator
```

we loop until reaching the **list**'s end

```
while ( it != l.end() )
```

A container's **begin** and **end** methods return iterator values that mark the container's beginning and end, respectively. This allows us to loop safely without knowing how many elements happen to be in the **list**.

In each loop iteration, we print a **list** element to the standard output and increment the iterator **it** to access the next **list** element:

```
cout << *it << endl;
it++; // increment iterator
```

```
#include <iostream>
#include <list>
using namespace std;
typedef const char* cstring;
void dump( list< cstring >& );
int main() {
  list< cstring > names;
  // insert four names into a list
  names.insert( names.begin(), "Kamiko" );
  names.insert( names.end(), "Andre" );
  names.insert( names.begin(), "Chengwen" );
  names.insert( names.begin(), "Maria" );
  dump( names ); // Maria Chengwen Kamiko Andre
  names.reverse(); // reverse the list
  cout << endl;
  dump( names ); // Andre Kamiko Chengwen Maria
  return 0;
}
void dump( list< cstring >& l ) {
  list< cstring >::iterator it; // list iterator
  // print list to standard output
  it = l.begin(); // initialize iterator
  while ( it != l.end() ) { // is iterator at the end?
    cout << *it << endl;
    it++; // increment iterator
  }
}
```

FIGURE 10.4.3 The STL `list` container.

In the **cout** statement, we dereference the iterator—the expression is ***it**. This suggests that an iterator is very much like a pointer. Indeed, an STL iterator can be viewed as a high-level pointer. The expression **it++** increments the iterator because the postincrement operator is overloaded for iterators. In **main** we then reverse the **list**

```
names.reverse();
```

and again **dump** it. ∎

Efficiency of vectors, deques, and lists

The **vector**, **deque**, and **list** are STL's three basic *sequential* containers. The three are alike in some respects. For example, each has an **insert** method for adding elements and an **erase** method for deleting them. They differ among themselves in other methods. For example, [ ] is overloaded for **vector**s and **deque**s, but not for **list**s. Another important difference among the three is the *efficiency*, in time and storage, associated with their common operations. Recall that inserting into the beginning of a **deque** requires about the same amount of time, regardless of whether the **deque** has, for example, 10 or 100 elements. By contrast, inserting at the beginning of a **vector** with 100 elements takes about 10 times longer than inserting at the beginning of a **vector** with 10 elements. We say that the time required to insert a **vector**'s beginning is **linear**, that is, directly proportional to the number of elements. For a **deque**, the time required to insert into the beginning is **constant**: it takes the same time to insert at the beginning of a **deque** with 100 elements as it does to insert at the beginning of a **deque** with 10 elements.

By publicizing the efficiency of standard operations on its containers, STL supports intelligent decisions about which containers to use. For example, if our application requires insertions at the beginning and at the end, we might pick a **deque** over a **vector** for reasons of efficiency. Figure 10.4.4 summarizes the efficiency of standard operations on the three sequential containers.

Operation	vector	deque	list
Insert/erase at beginning	Linear	Constant	Constant
Insert/erase at end	Constant	Constant	Constant
Insert/erase in middle	Linear	Linear	Constant
Access first element	Constant	Constant	Constant
Access last element	Constant	Constant	Constant
Access middle element	Constant	Constant	Linear

FIGURE 10.4.4 Time complexity of basic sequential container operations.

Basic Associative Containers: **set**, **multiset**, **map**, and **multimap**

The four associative containers fall into two groups: sets and maps. A **set** is a collection of zero or more nonduplicate, unordered elements called *keys*. For example, the set

$$\{jobs, gates, ellison\}$$

contains three keys, which are last names of three computer moguls. A **map** is a collection of zero or more unordered pairs; in each pair, one element is a nonduplicate *key* and the other is a *value* associated with the key. For example, the map

$$\{(jobs, apple), (gates, microsoft), (ellison, oracle)\}$$

contains three pairs. In each pair, the first element such as *gates* is the key associated with a value such as *microsoft*. A **multiset** is a **set** that allows duplicate keys, and a **multimap** is a **map** that allows duplicate keys. To clarify basic functionality, we focus on **set** and **map**.

```
#include <iostream>
#include <set>
using namespace std;
int main() {
   set< int > s;
   s.insert( -999 );
   s.insert( 18 );
   s.insert( 321 );
   s.insert( -999 ); // not inserted -- duplicates not allowed
   set< int >::iterator it;
   it = s.begin();
   while ( it != s.end() )
     cout << *it++ << endl; // -999 18 321 in some order
   // prompt user for an integer
   int key;
   cout << "Enter an integer: ";
   cin >> key;
   it = s.find( key );
   if ( it == s.end() ) // not found
     cout << key << " is not in set." << endl;
   else
     cout << key << " is in set." << endl;
   return 0;
}
```

FIGURE 10.4.5 The STL **set** container.

EXAMPLE 10.4.4. The program in Figure 10.4.5 illustrates the **set** container. The definition

```
set< int > s;
```

creates an **int** instantiation of the template **set** class. The **set** class overloads the **insert** method so that it can be invoked in similar fashion to a **vector**'s version

```
s.insert( s.begin(), 66 ); // insert at beginning
s.insert( s.end(), 99 );   // insert at end
```

or with no specified position

```
s.insert( 123 ); // insert somewhere
```

Whatever the overloaded version, **set**'s **insert** ensures that the set does not contain duplicates. Among other methods, **set** has **find**, which checks whether a **set** contains a specified key: if so, **find** returns an iterator that marks the key's occurrence in the **set**; if not, **find** returns the value of the **set**'s **end** method. The code segment

```
int key;
cout << "Enter an integer: ";
```

```
cin >> key;
it = s.find( key );
if ( it == s.end() ) // not found
   cout << key << " is not in set." << endl;
else
   cout << key << " is in set." << endl;
```

compares the value of **s.find(key)** against the value of **s.end()** to determine whether **s** contains a user-specified key. ∎

An STL **map** is an **association list**, that is, a list that associates a key with a value. (For an array implementation of an association list, see Section 8.7.)

```
#include <iostream>
#include <string>
#include <map>
using namespace std;
int main() {
  map< string, int > m;
  m[ "zero" ]  = 0; m[ "one" ]   = 1;
  m[ "two" ]   = 2; m[ "three" ] = 3;
  m[ "four" ]  = 4; m[ "five" ]  = 5;
  m[ "six" ]   = 6; m[ "seven" ] = 7;
  m[ "eight" ] = 8; m[ "nine" ]  = 9;
  cout << m[ "three" ] << endl   // 3
       << m[ "five" ]  << endl   // 5
       << m[ "seven" ] << endl;  // 7
  return 0;
}
```

FIGURE 10.4.6 The STL **map** container.

EXAMPLE 10.4.5. The program in Figure 10.4.6 illustrates the **map** container. In **m**'s definition

```
map< string, int > m;
```

string and **int** are the data types of the key and the value, respectively. For example, the string **"two"** is the key that can be used to store and then to look up the **int** value 2. The **map** container, like all the basic STL containers, has an **insert** method; but **map** also overloads **[ ]** so that it can be used both to insert new key/value pairs into the association list

```
m[ "zero" ] = 0;
```

and to search for elements in the association list

```
cout << m[ "zero" ] << endl; // prints 0
```

Because **map**s cannot contain duplicates, the effect of

```
m[ "one" ] = 1;
m[ "one" ] = -1; // cancels any previous association
```

is to associate the value **-1** with the key **one**.   ■

Container Adaptors

A container **adaptor** adapts a container to behave in a particular way. The three container adaptors are the **stack**, the **queue**, and the **priority_queue**. The **stack** adaptor creates a LIFO list (see Section 10.2). The **queue** adaptor creates a **FIFO** (**First In, First Out**) list. The **priority_queue** adaptor creates a queue whose elements are removed in some priority order. We illustrate container adaptors with two examples.

EXAMPLE 10.4.6.   The program in Figure 10.4.7 illustrates the **stack** adaptor. The definition

```
stack< int > s;
```

is shorthand for

```
stack< int, deque< int > > s;
```

because, by default, a **stack** adapts a **deque**. We could force a **stack** to adapt a **vector** with the definition

```
stack< int, vector< int > > s;
```

The **push** method inserts an element into the **stack**, and the **pop** method removes an element from the **stack**. The STL **pop** returns **void** in contrast to the **pop** in the Sample Application of Section 10.2, which returns the top element. The **top** method does return the top element, which explains why we use **top** for the printing:

```
cout << s.top() << endl;
```
■

```
#include <iostream>
#include <stack>
using namespace std;
int main() {
   stack< int > s; // == stack< int, deque< int > >
   s.push( 1 ); s.push( 3 ); s.push( 5 );
   s.push( 7 ); s.push( 11 ); s.push( 13 );
   // pop and print until stack is empty
   // output is 13 11 7 5 3 1
   while ( !s.empty() ) {
     cout << s.top() << endl; // returns integer
      s.pop(); // returns void
   }
   return 0;
}
```

FIGURE 10.4.7 The STL **stack** adaptor.

EXAMPLE 10.4.7.   The program in Figure 10.4.8 illustrates the **queue** adaptor. Like the **stack**, the **queue** adapts a **deque** by default. The **queue** also has **push** and **pop** methods for inserting and removing elements. The method **front** accesses the element at the front of the **queue**, which is why we use it for printing.   ■

```
#include <iostream>
#include <queue>
using namespace std;
int main() {
   queue< int > q; // == queue< int, deque< int > >
   q.push( 1 ); q.push( 3 ); q.push( 5 );
   q.push( 7 ); q.push( 11 ); q.push( 13 );
   // pop and print until queue is empty
   // output is 1 3 5 7 11 13
   while ( !q.empty() ) {
     cout << q.front() << endl; // returns integer
     q.pop(); // returns void
   }
   return 0;
}
```

FIGURE 10.4.8 The STL **queue** adaptor.

Algorithms

STL has a rich assortment of algorithms for processing containers. The algorithms fall into standard categories: sorting and searching, numerical processing, set operations, copying, and so forth. Just as STL containers are implemented as template *classes*, so STL algorithms are implemented as template *functions*. Here, for example, is the prototype for STL's **reverse** algorithm:

```
template< class BidirectionalIterator > // template header
void reverse( BidirectionalIterator it1,   // iterator 1
              BidirectionalIterator it2 ); // iterator 2
```

Note that **reverse**'s two arguments are *iterators*, that is, **BidirectionalIterators**, which can traverse a container from either beginning to end or end to beginning. STL algorithms process a container by using iterators to traverse the container. This greatly simplifies the algorithm implementation, for the algorithm does not require any container-specific information to process a container. Instead, the algorithm requires only the appropriate iterators. In different terms, an algorithm such as **reverse** cannot distinguish between, say, a **vector** and a **deque**. The algorithm works the same way on both: it uses iterators to access the container's elements so that these can be put in reverse order. We illustrate various STL algorithms with short examples. The goal is to highlight the processing power that these algorithms bring to STL containers.

EXAMPLE 10.4.8.   The program in Figure 10.4.9 illustrates four STL algorithms: `generate`, `replace_if`, `sort`, and `for_each`. After defining an `int` vector with 10 elements

```
vector< int > v( 10 ); // vector of 10 elements
```

the program uses the **generate** algorithm to populate **v** with random integers:

```
generate( v.begin(), v.end(), rand );
```

The first two arguments are the iterators returned by the vector's **begin** and **end** methods, for we want to generate a random integer for each of **v**'s 10 elements. Because **v** is an **int** vector, **generate**'s third argument is an **int** value to be generated for each vector element. In this case, it is the value of a call to the library function **rand**, which returns a random integer.

```
#include <cstdlib>
#include <iostream>
#include <vector>
#include <algorithm> //*** for STL algorithms
using namespace std;

void dump( int i ) { cout << i << endl; }
bool odd( int i ) { return i % 2 != 0; }
bool comp( const int& i1, const int& i2 ) { return i1 > i2; }
int main() {
   vector< int > v( 10 ); // vector of 10 integers
   generate( v.begin(), v.end(), rand ); // fill with random ints
   replace_if( v.begin(), v.end(), odd, 0 ); // replace odds with 0
   sort( v.begin(), v.end(), comp ); // sort in descending order
   for_each( v.begin(), v.end(), dump ); // print
   return 0;
}
```

FIGURE 10.4.9 The STL algorithms `generate`, `replace_if`, `sort`, and `for_each`.

After populating a **vector** with random integers, the program uses **replace_if** to replace odd integers with 0:

```
replace_if( v.begin(), v.end(), odd, 0 );
```

The first two arguments are again the two iterators returned by the vector's **begin** and **end** methods, for we want the replacements to occur from **v**'s beginning to its end. The third argument is a function's name, **odd**. This function tests whether its integer argument is odd. Because **v** is an **int** vector, the function **odd** expects an **int** parameter. The last argument 0 is the replace value to use if the test succeeds. This argument is also an **int** value precisely because **v** is an **int** vector. So **replace_if** invokes **odd** on each integer in **v**. If **odd** returns **true**, the integer is replaced by 0.

The program then sorts the vector in descending order:

```
sort( v.begin(), v.end(), comp ); // sort the vector
```

The first two arguments to **sort** are also the iterators returned by the vector's **begin** and **end** methods. The third argument is optional. If omitted, the vector would be sorted in *ascending* order, that is, in the order determined by the appropriate overload of **operator<**. Because **v** is an **int** vector, and **operator<** is defined for **int**s, we could sort **v** in ascending order simply by invoking **sort** with two arguments:

```
sort( v.begin(), v.end() ); // order by operator<
```

Because we want to sort **v** in descending order, we provide **sort** with a third argument, in this case the function **comp**'s name. This function takes two **int** references as arguments because **v** is an **int** vector, and it returns a **bool**. We return **true** if the first argument is greater than the second and **false** otherwise. This causes the **sort** algorithm to sort the vector in *descending* order.

To print the integers, the program uses **for_each** instead of a loop:

```
for_each( v.begin(), v.end(), dump ); // print it
```

The first two arguments are again the iterators returned by the vector's **begin** and **end** methods, for we again want to traverse the entire vector. The third argument is the name of a function, **dump**, to invoke on each of the vector's elements. Because **v** is an **int** vector, **dump** expects an **int** argument. Function **dump** prints its argument to the standard output.

The program has no loops. Algorithms such as **generate**, **for_each**, and **replace_if** have built-in iteration through their use of iterators. The iterators themselves are intuitive:

```
v.begin() // start at beginning
v.end()   // go to the end
```

The STL **sort** is easier to understand than **qsort**. For one thing, **sort** requires only two arguments to sort in ascending order. If a function's name is provided as the optional third argument, the function takes references rather than pointers to **void** as arguments.

Finally, we **#include** the header file *algorithm*, which contains prototypes and supporting constructs for the STL algorithms. Other header files (e.g., *queue*) may have an **#include** for *algorithm*.   ■

EXAMPLE 10.4.9.   The program in Figure 10.4.10 shows that STL algorithms work on ordinary C++ arrays. After defining the array **alph** and initializing it to a string consisting of the 26 lowercase letters, the program partitions the array into two sets using the algorithm **nth_element**. This algorithm expects three arguments, which specify

- Where to start, in this case at address **alph**.
- Which element to use as the **pivot**, that is, as the element used to partition the other elements. Elements less than the pivot are moved to its left, and elements greater than or equal to the pivot are moved to its right. We use the 14th character, **n**, as a pivot.
- Where to end, in this case at address **alph + 26**.

```
#include <iostream>
#include <algorithm>
using namespace std;
int main() {
   char alph[ ] = "abcdefghijklmnopqrstuvwxyz";
   nth_element( alph, alph + 12, alph + 26 ); // partition
   random_shuffle( alph, alph + 13 ); // shuffle 1st set
   random_shuffle( alph + 13, alph + 26 ); // shuffle 2nd set
   copy( alph, alph + 13, // lower partition
         ostream_iterator< char >( cout, " " ) );
   cout << endl;
   copy( alph + 13, alph + 26, // upper partition
         ostream_iterator< char >( cout, " " ) );
   cout << endl;
   return 0;
}
```

FIGURE 10.4.10 The STL algorithms `nth_element`, `random_shuffle`, and `copy`.

After partitioning **alph**, the program does a **random_shuffle** of the lower partition, which contains the letters **a** through **m**, and a **random_shuffle** of the upper partition, which contains the letters **n** through **z**. The algorithm expects arguments that specify where the shuffle is to begin and where it is to end. Because **alph** is a C++ array rather than an STL container such as a **vector**, we use pointer expressions. For the lower partition, **alph** marks its beginning and **alph + 13** marks its end. For the upper partition, **alph + 13** marks its beginning and **alph + 26** marks its end.

Finally, the program uses the **copy** algorithm to print each partition to the standard output:

```
copy( alph + 13, alph + 26, // upper partition
      ostream_iterator< char >( cout, " " ) );
```

The algorithm's first two arguments, as usual, mark where the **copy** is to begin and to end. The last argument is an **output iterator**, that is, a special STL iterator used to do output. Because **alph** consists of **char**acters, we use a **char** instantiation

```
ostream_iterator< char >
```

of **ostream_iterator**. The expression

```
ostream_iterator< char >( cout, " " )   // constructor call
```

invokes a parameterized constructor to create the iterator. The constructor's first argument is an output stream, in this case **cout**. The second argument is optional. If provided, it acts as a separator for the items written to the output stream. So we specify a blank as the separator for the characters written to the standard output. On a sample run, the program's output was

```
e d a c k m i l f b g j h
w q t r x o n p y z v u s
```

```
#include <iostream>
#include <fstream>
#include <vector>
#include <algorithm>
using namespace std;
int main() {
   // populate vector with first 32 Fibonacci numbers
   vector< int > fibs( 32 );
   fibs[ 0 ] = fibs[ 1 ] = 1; // base cases
   for ( int i = 2; i < 32; i++ )
      fibs[ i ] = fibs[ i - 1 ] + fibs[ i - 2 ];
   // create output stream and iterator
   ofstream outfile( "output.dat" );
   ostream_iterator< int > outFileIt( outfile, " " );
   ostream_iterator< int > stdOutIt( cout, "\n" );
   // copy to output file and to standard output
   copy( fibs.begin(), fibs.end(), outFileIt );
   copy( fibs.begin(), fibs.end(), stdOutIt );
   return 0;
}
```

FIGURE 10.4.11 The STL output iterator.

EXAMPLE 10.4.10.   The program in Figure 10.4.11 populates a **vector** with the first 32 Fibonacci numbers and then copies the **vector** to a disk file and to the standard output. In the disk file, the numbers are separated by blanks; in the standard output, the numbers are separated by new lines. The program uses two **ostream_iterator**s:

```
ostream_iterator< int > outFileIt( outfile, " " );
ostream_iterator< int > stdOutIt( cout, "\n" );
```

We use one iterator associated with the standard output (see Figure 10.4.11) and a second iterator associated with a disk file. The iterator associated with the disk file uses blanks to separate the output, whereas the iterator associated with the standard input uses blanks. The iterators **outFileIt** and **stdOutIt** are **int** instantiations of the template class **ostream_iterator** because **fibs** is an **int** vector. We again use the **copy** algorithm with an output iterator as the third argument:

```
copy( fibs.begin(), fibs.end(), outFileIt );
copy( fibs.begin(), fibs.end(), stdOutIt );
```

This allows us to dispense with loops.

   Out application writes the Fibonacci numbers in ascending order because this is the order in which they are added to the **vector**. It is straightforward to reverse this order. A **vector** has methods **rbegin** and **rend** (**r** stands for **r**everse) that could be used to print the **vector** in descending (that is, reverse) order:

```
copy( fibs.rbegin(), fibs.rend(), stdOutIt );
```

STL also provides input iterators for **copy**ing from input streams into containers such as **vector**s and **deque**s. ∎

Other STL Constructs

Containers and algorithms are the core parts of STL, and iterators are the means by which algorithms manipulate containers. STL has other constructs as well, which we describe briefly in this subsection.

A **function object** is a template class in which the function call operator is overloaded as a **public** method. An STL function object may be used instead of a function's name in algorithms that require one or the other.

EXAMPLE 10.4.11. The program in Figure 10.4.9 has a **dump** function

```
void dump( int i ) { cout << i << endl; }
```

whose name is used as the third argument to the **for_each** algorithm

```
for_each( v.begin(), v.end(), dump );
```

Instead of this approach, we could create a function object

```
template< class T >
struct dumpIt {
   void operator()( T arg ) { cout << arg << endl; }
};
```

and then invoke the overloaded function call operator of an **int** instantiation:

```
for_each( v.begin(), v.end(), dumpIt< int >() ); // print
```

By the way, most STL programmers would create the **dumpIt** class with the keyword **struct** because the class's members then default to **public** (see C++ Postscript, Chapter 5); and the overloaded function call operator must be **public** for a function object to be used outside the class. ∎

A **function adaptor** is a construct for building new function objects from already existing ones. A function adaptor is thus analogous to a container adaptor. There are function adaptors to negate a function object, to bind a constant to an argument in a function object's overloaded function call operator, to convert a function pointer to a function object, and to compose a new function object out of already existing ones.

```
#include <iostream>
#include <functional>
#include <algorithm>
using namespace std;
struct even : public unary_function< unsigned, bool > {
    bool operator()( unsigned n ) const { return n % 2 == 0; }
};
int main() {
    int a[ ] = { 1, 2, 3, 4, 5 };
    int n;
    n = count_if( a, a + 5, even() );
    cout << "a has " << n << " even integers." << endl;
    n = count_if( a, a + 5, not1( even() ) );
    cout << "a has " << n << " odd integers." << endl;
    return 0;
}
```

FIGURE 10.4.12 The STL function adaptor **not1**.

EXAMPLE 10.4.12. The program in Figure 10.4.12 creates a function object **even** to test whether an integer is even. Function adaptors apply only to function objects that subclass one of two built-in STL function object types: **unary_function** and **binary_function**. Because **even** is a unary function, it subclasses **unary_function**. The first template parameter in **unary_function** is the argument type that the overloaded function call operator expects, in this case **unsigned**. The second template parameter is the operator's return type, in this case **bool**.

In the first call to the algorithm **count_if**, we pass **even** as the third argument. The algorithm uses this function object to test whether integers in array **a** are even, keeping count of the ones that are:

```
n = count_if( a, a + 5, even() );
```

The algorithm's return value is stored in **n**, which we then print to the standard output. In the second call to **count_if**, we invert **even** with the function adaptor **not1** (1 stands for *unary*):

```
n = count_if( a, a + 5, not1( even() ) );
```

The return value is now the count of *odd* integers in **a**. To use function adaptors, the header file *functional* must be **#include**d. ∎

An STL **allocator** is a template class that supports memory management. For example, a programmer working in a PC environment could use STL allocators to adapt an application to one of the four standard PC memory models: small, compact, medium, and large. Programmers working in a UNIX, OS2, Apple, or Win32 environment typically can avoid allocators.

EXERCISES

1. What is the difference between an STL container and an STL algorithm?

2. Explain the relationships among containers, algorithms, and iterators in STL.

3. What is the difference between a sequential and an associative container?

4. Suppose that you need a sequential container in which assertions and deletions must occur at either end. Would a **deque** or a **vector** be the more efficient container?

5. Are a **deque** and a **vector** equally efficient in inserting at the end?

6. Are a **deque** and a **vector** equally efficient in inserting at the beginning?

7. What is the difference between a **set** and a **multiset**?

8. What is the difference between a **set** and a **map**?

9. Remove the line

   ```
   using namespace std;
   ```

   from the program in Figure 10.4.2 and try to compile the program.

10. Is [ ] overloaded for the **vector** class?

11. Is [ ] overloaded for the **list** class?

12. For a **list** container, are insertions at the beginning, in the middle, and at the end equally efficient?

13. Explain what a container adaptor does and give an example.

14. Why do the two basic container adaptors adapt the **deque** rather than the **vector** by default?

15. Run the program in Figure 10.4.9. Then change the line

   ```
   sort( v.begin(), v.end(), comp )
   ```

   to

   ```
   sort( v.begin(), v.end() );
   ```

   Recompile and run. How does the output differ between the two runs?

16. What is an STL function object?

17. Explain what a function adaptor does and give an example.

18. Can STL algorithms be used on ordinary C++ arrays?

19. What advantage does an STL **vector** have over a C++ array?

20. STL provides algorithms such as **for_each** and **copy** that *discourage* the use of loops. What advantage does an algorithm such as **for_each** have over an ordinary C++ loop?

10.5 SAMPLE APPLICATION: STOCK PERFORMANCE REPORTS

Problem

Generate three reports on the daily performance of stocks for an exchange such as NASDAQ. The data come from a file of records in the format

$$< \; symbol \; > \quad < \; opening \; price \; > \quad < \; closing \; price \; > \quad < \; volume \; >$$

For example, the record

MSFT 135.87 137.98 8301700

represents information about Microsoft's stock, whose NASDAQ symbol is **MSFT**. For the day in question, Microsoft opened at $135.87 per share and closed at $137.98 per share; and 8,301,700 Microsoft shares were traded. The data file is correctly formatted, but it contains an arbitrary number of unsorted records. After reading data from the file, generate three reports to the standard output. Each report lists the stock's symbol, its opening and closing price, its percentage of gain or loss during the day, and the volume of shares traded. The first report prints the stocks in *descending order by percentage of gain*. The second report prints the stocks in *ascending order by percentage of loss*. The third report prints the stocks in *descending order by volume*.

Sample Input/Output

For the input file

```
BUTI    8.75    7.54   159000
ZTEC   39.54   39.23   100300
COHU   48.90   51.43   134900
TMXI    3.41    2.87   255000
ALCD   60.42   61.91   230000
EPEX   15.98   13.21    54000
MSFT  135.87  137.98  8301700
GMGC    2.76    2.81   129400
```

the output is

```
******* Gainers in descending order:
*** COHU
  % Changed:      5.17382
  Opening Price: 48.9
  Closing Price: 51.43
  Volume:         134900
*** ALCD
  % Changed:      2.46607
  Opening Price: 60.42
  Closing Price: 61.91
  Volume:         230000
```

```
*** GMGC
 % Changed:      1.81159
 Opening Price: 2.76
 Closing Price: 2.81
 Volume:        129400
*** MSFT
 % Changed:      1.55296
 Opening Price: 135.87
 Closing Price: 137.98
 Volume:        8301700
*** ZTEC
 % Changed:      -0.784016
 Opening Price: 39.54
 Closing Price: 39.23
 Volume:        100300
*** BUTI
 % Changed:      -13.8286
 Opening Price: 8.75
 Closing Price: 7.54
 Volume:        159000
*** TMXI
 % Changed:      -15.8358
 Opening Price: 3.41
 Closing Price: 2.87
 Volume:        255000
*** EPEX
 % Changed:      -17.3342
 Opening Price: 15.98
 Closing Price: 13.21
 Volume:        54000

******* Losers in ascending order:
*** EPEX
 % Changed:      -17.3342
 Opening Price: 15.98
 Closing Price: 13.21
 Volume:        54000
*** TMXI
 % Changed:      -15.8358
 Opening Price: 3.41
 Closing Price: 2.87
 Volume:        255000
*** BUTI
 % Changed:      -13.8286
 Opening Price: 8.75
 Closing Price: 7.54
 Volume:        159000
```

```
*** ZTEC
 % Changed:     -0.784016
 Opening Price: 39.54
 Closing Price: 39.23
 Volume:        100300
*** MSFT
 % Changed:     1.55296
 Opening Price: 135.87
 Closing Price: 137.98
 Volume:        8301700
*** GMGC
 % Changed:     1.81159
 Opening Price: 2.76
 Closing Price: 2.81
 Volume:        129400
*** ALCD
 % Changed:     2.46607
 Opening Price: 60.42
 Closing Price: 61.91
 Volume:        230000
*** COHU
 % Changed:     5.17382
 Opening Price: 48.9
 Closing Price: 51.43
 Volume:        134900

******* Volume in descending order:
*** MSFT
 Volume:        8301700
 % Changed:     1.55296
 Opening Price: 135.87
 Closing Price: 137.98
*** TMXI
 Volume:        255000
 % Changed:     -15.8358
 Opening Price: 3.41
 Closing Price: 2.87
*** ALCD
 Volume:        230000
 % Changed:     2.46607
 Opening Price: 60.42
 Closing Price: 61.91
*** BUTI
 Volume:        159000
 % Changed:     -13.8286
 Opening Price: 8.75
 Closing Price: 7.54
```

```
*** COHU
  Volume:           134900
  % Changed:        5.17382
  Opening Price: 48.9
  Closing Price: 51.43
*** GMGC
  Volume:           129400
  % Changed:        1.81159
  Opening Price: 2.76
  Closing Price: 2.81
*** ZTEC
  Volume:           100300
  % Changed:        -0.784016
  Opening Price: 39.54
  Closing Price: 39.23
*** EPEX
  Volume:           54000
  % Changed:        -17.3342
  Opening Price: 15.98
  Closing Price: 13.21
```

Solution

We create a class **Stock** to represent stocks as objects. The class has data members for the stock's symbol, its opening and closing price, the percentage of gain or loss during the day's trading, and the volume of stocks traded. The class interface consists of constructors to create **Stock** objects and other **public** methods to access data members. We use an STL **deque** container to hold the **Stock**s created from data in the input file. We use the STL **sort** algorithm to sort the **deque** twice:

- In descending order by percentage of gain.
- In descending order by volume.

After the first sort, we use the STL **for_each** algorithm to print the **deque**'s contents (that is, **Stock** objects) to the standard output. By printing the **deque** in regular order, we get the stocks in descending order by percentage of gain. By printing the **deque** in reverse order, we get the stocks in ascending order by percentage of loss. We then sort the **deque** in descending order by volume and print it again. We provide the appropriate STL function objects to handle comparisons used by the **sort** algorithm and to provide output functionality for the **for_each** algorithm.

C++ Implementation

```cpp
#include <iostream>
#include <fstream>
#include <deque>
#include <algorithm>
#include <cstring>
using namespace std;
```

```
//*** file names and miscellaneous globals
const char inFile[ ] = "stockData.dat";
const unsigned MaxSymbol = 4;
const char Unknown[ ] = "????";

//*** objects generated from input records
class Stock {
public:
   Stock() {
      strcpy( symbol, Unknown );
      open = close = gainLoss = volume = 0;
   }
   Stock( const char s[ ],       // symbol
          double o,               // opening price
          double c,               // closing price
          unsigned long v ) {   // volume traded
      strncpy( symbol, s, MaxSymbol );
      symbol[ MaxSymbol ] = '\0';
      open = o;
      close = c;
      volume = v;
      gainLoss = ( close - open ) / open;
   }
   const char* getSymbol() const {
      return symbol;
   }
   double getOpen() const {
      return open;
   }
   double getClose() const {
      return close;
   }
   unsigned long getVolume() const {
      return volume;
   }
   double getGainLoss() const {
      return gainLoss;
   }
private:
   char          symbol[ MaxSymbol + 1 ];
   double        open;     // opening price
   double        close;    // closing price
   double        gainLoss; // gain or loss fraction
   unsigned long volume;   // shares traded
};
```

```
//*** Sort comparison: gains in descending order
template< class T >
struct winCmp {
   bool operator()( T& t1, T& t2 ) const  {
      return t1.getGainLoss() > t2.getGainLoss();
   }
};

//*** Sort comparison: volume in descending order
template< class T >
struct volCmp {
   bool operator()( T& t1, T& t2 ) const {
      return t1.getVolume() > t2.getVolume();
   }
};

//*** invoked by function objects to do output
void output( bool volFlag,
             const char name[ ],
             const char openLabel[ ],  double open,
             const char closeLabel[ ], double close,
             const char gainLabel[ ],  double gain,
             const char volLabel[ ],   unsigned long vol ) {
   cout << "*** " << name << endl;
   if ( volFlag ) // if true, volume comes first
     cout << '\t' << volLabel << vol << endl;
   cout << '\t' << gainLabel  << gain  << endl
        << '\t' << openLabel  << open  << endl
        << '\t' << closeLabel << close << endl;
   if ( !volFlag ) // if false, volume comes last
     cout << '\t' << volLabel << vol << endl;
}

//*** Write Stocks sorted by gain-loss to standard output.
template< class T >
struct winPr {
   void operator()( Stock& s ) {
      output( false,
              s.getSymbol(),
              "Opening Price: ", s.getOpen(),
              "Closing Price: ", s.getClose(),
              "% Changed:     ", s.getGainLoss() * 100,
              "Volume:        ", s.getVolume() );
   }
};

//*** Write Stocks sorted by volume to standard output.
template< class T >
```

```cpp
struct volPr {
   void operator()( Stock& s ) {
      output( true,
              s.getSymbol(),
              "Opening Price: ", s.getOpen(),
              "Closing Price: ", s.getClose(),
              "% Changed:       ", s.getGainLoss() * 100,
              "Volume:          ", s.getVolume() );
   }
};

void herald( const char[ ] );
void input( deque< Stock >& );
int main() {
   deque< Stock > stocks;
   //*** Input stocks and separate into vectors for
   //    winners, losers, and break-evens.
   input( stocks );
   //*** Sort winners in descending order and output.
   herald( "Gainers in descending order: " );
   sort( stocks.begin(), stocks.end(), winCmp< Stock >() );
   for_each( stocks.begin(), stocks.end(), winPr< Stock >() );
   //*** Output losers in ascending order.
   herald( "Losers in ascending order: " );
   for_each( stocks.rbegin(), stocks.rend(), winPr< Stock >() );
   //*** Sort volume in descending order and output
   herald( "Volume in descending order: " );
   sort( stocks.begin(), stocks.end(), volCmp< Stock >() );
   for_each( stocks.begin(), stocks.end(), volPr< Stock >() );
   return 0;
}

void input( deque< Stock >& d ) {
   char s[ MaxSymbol + 1 ];
   double o, c, v;
   ifstream input( inFile );
   //*** Read data until end-of-file,
   // creating a Stock object per input record
   while ( input >> s >> o >> c >> v )
      d.insert( d.end(), Stock( s, o, c, v ) );
   input.close();
}

void herald( const char s[ ] ) {
   cout << endl << "******* " << s << endl;
}
```

Discussion

By using an STL **deque** container and STL algorithms to process it, we are able to make the application's control structure relatively straightforward. After defining a **deque** to hold **Stock**s in **main**

```
deque< Stock > stocks;
```

we pass the **deque** to **input**, which reads data from an input file:

```
input( stocks );
```

The **deque** is passed *by reference* rather than by value because it is critical that the **deque** defined in **main**, and not a copy of this **deque**, hold the **Stock**s created from the input data. If the **deque** were passed by value, the **Stock**s would be entered into a *copy* of the **deque**; and **main** would be left with an empty **deque** to sort and output.

The function **input**

```
void input( deque< Stock >& d ) {
   char s[ MaxSymbol + 1 ];
   double o, c, v;
   ifstream input( inFile );
   //*** Read data until end-of-file,
   // creating a Stock object per input record
   while ( input >> s >> o >> c >> v )
     d.insert( d.end(), Stock( s, o, c, v ) );
   input.close();
}
```

opens an **ifstream** and then uses a **while** loop to read data until end-of-file. The **deque** grows automatically to meet our storage requirements. We happen to insert at the **deque**'s end

```
d.insert( d.end(), Stock( s, o, c, v ) );
```

but it would be equally efficient to insert at the **deque**'s beginning. Recall that a **deque** does insertions at *either* end in constant time, whereas a **vector** does insertions at the end in constant time, but insertions at the beginning in *linear* time. A **deque** thus gives us flexibility for insertions without any penalty in efficiency, which is a major reason for our choosing it over a **vector** in this application. We insert a **Stock** by invoking the parameterized **Stock** constructor as the second argument to the **deque**'s **insert** method. By the way, the **while** loop in **input** is the only explicit loop in the application. All other looping is done implicitly by STL algorithms. This accounts for the application's relatively simple control structure.

When **input** returns, **main** invokes **sort** twice to sort the **Stock**s by percentage of gain and by volume. After the first sort, we use **for_each** to output the **deque** twice: first in regular order and then in reverse order. The code for the first sort is

```
sort( stocks.begin(), stocks.end(), winCmp< Stock >() );
```

The first two arguments to **sort** specify where the sort is to begin and end, respectively. We use calls to the **deque** methods **begin** and **end** as these arguments. The third argument is the overloaded function call operator in the function object **winCmp< Stock >**. Recall that a function object is a templated STL class in which the function call operator is overloaded as a **public** method. Our definition

```
template< class T >
struct winCmp {
    bool operator()( T& t1, T&t2 ) const  {
        return t1.getGainLoss() > t2.getGainLoss();
    }
};
```

uses the keyword **struct** rather than **class** because all members default to **public** when **struct** is used. This style is common in STL for defining function objects. In any case, the overloaded function call operator expects two references, in this case references to **Stock** objects. The **sort** algorithm is responsible for invoking the overloaded function call operator with the appropriate arguments, in this case two **Stock** objects that **sort** needs to compare in the course of sorting the **deque**. Because **winCmp** is used to sort the **Stock**s in *descending* order by their percentage of gain, we return the **bool**ean expression

```
t1.getGainLoss() > t2.getGainLoss()
```

So if **t1** has a greater gain than **t2**, we return **true**; otherwise, we return **false**. The **sort** algorithm uses the return value to order **Stock** objects as its sorts the **deque**.

After the first sort, we use **for_each**

```
for_each( stocks.begin(), stocks.end(), winPr< Stock >() );
```

to print the **Stock**s to the standard output. Because the **deque** is now sorted in descending order by percentage of gain, the output is in this order. The first two arguments are the same as in the call to **sort**. The third argument is again a call to the overloaded function call operator in a function object, in this case **winPr< Stock >**. The actual printing is handled by the top-level function **output**. After sorting by volume, we output a **Stock**'s volume first. After sorting by gain and loss, we output a **Stock**'s percentage of gain or loss first.

The second **for_each** statement

```
for_each( stocks.rbegin(), stocks.rend(), winPr< Stock >() );
```

prints the **deque** in ascending order by percentage of loss. Because the **deque** is already sorted in descending order by percentage of gain, we simply print the **deque** in *reverse* order with calls to the methods **rbegin** and **rend** as the first two arguments to **for_each**. (The **r** stands for **r**everse.) This is simpler and more efficient than sorting the **deque** again.

We use two separate function objects to handle the comparisons in the **sort**. This modular approach means that each function object's overloaded function call operator can consist of a single **return** statement. For output, we also have two function objects. The outputs for winners and losers share an overloaded function call operator in **winPr**, whereas the output for volume has its own overloaded function call operator in **volPr**.

Using STL for the application has two obvious benefits. First, the STL **deque** container grows dynamically to meet our storage requirements without forcing us to keep track of how many elements are inserted. Our input file is of an arbitrary size; hence, we cannot anticipate before reading the input data how many **Stock** objects the application requires. STL allows us to grow the **deque** as needed. Second, the STL **for_each** algorithm eliminates the need for output loops. Instead of using a **while** or a **for** loop to output the **Stock** objects, we use **for_each** to iterate through the **deque**, applying the appropriate overloaded output operator to each **Stock** object. The **deque** methods **begin**, **end**, **rbegin**, and **rend** allow us straightforwardly to output in either regular or reverse order. STL thus contributes to the application's overall simplicity, clarity, and robustness.

C++ POSTSCRIPT

Unnamed Namespaces

One way to prevent a top-level function from being visible outside its containing file is to make it **static** (see C++ Postscript, Chapter 9). This method comes to C++ from C. The preferred C++ way is to place such a function in an *unnamed namespace*.

> **EXAMPLE.** The unnamed namespace
>
> ```
> // Occurs in file F1.cpp
> namespace { // unnamed namespace
>    void g() { cout << "g" << endl; }
> }
> ```
>
> contains a definition for **g**. Only functions defined in the same file as **g**, *F1.cpp*, are able to invoke **g**. ∎

Template Classes and Inheritance

A template class can be derived from a base class that is template or nontemplate. A template class or an instantiation of a template class can be a base class for a derived class that is template or nontemplate.

> **EXAMPLE.** The code segment
>
> ```
> class B { // nontemplate base class
>    ...
> };
> template< class T >
> class TD : public B { // template derived class
>    ...
> };
> ```

illustrates the case in which the template class **TD** is derived from the nontemplate base class **B**. The code segment

```
template< class T >
class TB { // template base class
  ...
};
class D : public TB< int > { // derived class
  ...
};
```

illustrates the case in which nontemplate class **D** is derived from an **int** instantiation of the template class **TB**. The code segment

```
template< class T >
class TB { // template base class
  ...
};
template< class T >
class D : public TB< T > {
  ...
};
```

illustrates the case in which template class **D** is derived from template class **TB**. The template header must be included as part of **D**'s declaration because the class type **T** occurs in **D**'s declaration. ∎

Inheritance from STL template classes is also supported. For an example, see Figure 10.4.12.

COMMON PROGRAMMING ERRORS

1. The template header uses *angle* brackets:

```
template{ class T } //***** ERROR: should be < class T >
class A {
  ...
};
template[ class T ] //***** ERROR: should be < class T >
class Z {
  ...
};
```

2. It is an error to omit the keyword **class** when specifying a class parameter in a template's header:

```
template< T > //****** ERROR: keyword class missing
class C {
  ...
};
```

The correct syntax is

```
template< class T >
class C {
  ...
};
```

3. It is an error to omit the template header from a method definition that occurs *outside* the class declaration:

```
template< class T > class Array {
public:
  void m();   // declaration
  ...
};
//***** ERROR: template header missing
Array< T >::m() {...} // definition
```

The correct syntax is

```
template< class T >
class Array {
public:
  void m();   // declaration
  ...
};
template< class T >
Array< T >::m() {...} // definition
```

4. If a template class method is defined *outside* the class declaration, the class's name must occur, in template form, to the left of the scope resolution operator:

```
template< class T > class Array {
public:
  void m();   // declaration
  ...
};
template< class T >
Array::m() {...} //***** ERROR: should be Array< T >::m()
```

5. It is an error for a template class not to have at least one class parameter:

```
template< int x > //***** ERROR: no class parameter
class C {
  ...
};
```

6. It is an error for a function-style parameter to occur to the left of a class parameter in a template header:

```
//***** ERROR: x is left of T2
template< class T1, int x, class T2 >
class C {
   ...
};
```

7. It is an error for a top-level template function, including a top-level overload of an operator, to have function-style parameters:

```
//***** ERROR: function-style parameter in top-level
// template function
template< class T, int S >
ostream& operator<<( ostream& os, Array< T, S >& a ) {
   for ( int i = 0; i < a.get_size(); i++ )
     os << a[ i ] << endl;
   return os;
}
```

Further, each class parameter in the template header must occur in the function's parameter list.

8. If a template header has multiple parameters, they must be separated by commas:

```
template< class T int x > //***** ERROR: no comma
class C {
  ...
};
```

9. Every function-style parameter's data type, built-in or user-defined, must be specified in the template header:

```
template< class T, x > //***** ERROR: no data type for x
class C {
  ...
};
```

10. It is an error to define objects that belong to a template class rather than a template class *instantiation*:

```
template< class T >
class Array {
  ...
};
Array a1;          //***** ERROR: not an instantiation
Array< T > a2;     //***** ERROR: not an instantiation
template< class T >
Array< T > a3;     //***** ERROR: not an instantiation
Array< int > a4;   // ok
```

11. It is an error to use **assert**ions without an **#include** of the header file *cassert* or *assert.h*.

12. It is an error to use the keyword **namespace** in a *using declaration*, which applies to a *single* item in a namespace:

```
namespace gar {
   void f() {...}
   int x;
}
using namespace gar::f(); //***** ERROR: "namespace" used
```

The correct syntax is

```
namespace gar {
   void f() {...}
   int x;
}
using gar::f();
```

13. It is an error to omit the keyword **namespace** from a *using directive*, which applies to *all* items in a namespace:

```
namespace gar {
   void f() {...}
   int x;
}
using gar; //***** ERROR: "namespace" missing
```

The correct syntax is

```
namespace gar {
   void f() {...}
   int x;
}
using namespace gar;
```

14. In the absence of a using declaration or a using directive, it is an error to reference an item in a namespace without the namespace's name:

```
namespace gar {
   void f() {...}
   int x;
}
int main() {
   f(); //***** ERROR: should be gar::f()
   ...
}
```

A using declaration for **f** or a using directive for **gar** would obviate the need for the full name **gar::f()**:

```
namespace gar {
   void f() {...}
   int x;
}
int main() {
   using gar::f(); // using declaration for f
   f(); // ok
   ...
}
```

15. STL containers and functions must be referenced by their full names

```
vector< float > f; //***** ERROR: full name needed
std::vector< int > v; // ok, full name
```

in the absence of a using declaration or directive. It is easiest to include a using directive:

```
using namespace std; // std namespace includes all of STL
vector< int > v; // ok
```

16. It is an error to reference STL components without the appropriate **#include** directive, which uses the *new* C++ style. For example, to use a **vector**, we must **#include** the header file *vector* (new style), not the header file *vector.h* (old style).

PROGRAMMING EXERCISES

10.1. Implement a template **Pair** class

```
template< class T1, class T2 >
class Pair {
public:
   // appropriate methods
private:
   T1 first;
   T2 second;
};
```

The class interface should include methods to create **Pair**s, to set and to get each element in the **Pair**, and to swap the elements so that, after the swap, the first element becomes the second and the second becomes the first.

10.2. Implement a template **Set** class (see Programming Exercise 5.12). Overload **+** (union), **-** (difference), **<<** (output), and **>>** (input).

10.3. Implement a template **Bag** class. A **bag** is like a set (see Programming Exercise 10.2) except that duplicates are allowed.

10.4. Implement a template **Queue** class, where a **queue** is a **F**irst **I**n, **F**irst **O**ut list of zero or more elements. Provide methods to insert and delete elements from a **Queue**, to check for full and empty **Queue**s, and to inspect a **Queue**'s front element without removing it. Name the insertion method **push** and the deletion method **pop** so that a **Queue**'s interface resembles a **Stack**'s interface (see Section 10.2). Use **assert**ions to promote systematic testing of **Queue** clients. Storage for **Queue** elements should be dynamically allocated.

10.5. Implement a template **Deque** class, where a **deque** is a list of zero or more elements that supports insertions and deletions at either end. Provide methods to insert and delete elements at either end (e.g., **push_front** and **push_back**), to check for full and empty **Deque**s, and to inspect a **Deque**'s front and rear elements without removing them. Use **assert**ions to promote systematic testing of **Deque** clients. Storage for **Deque** elements should be dynamically allocated.

10.6. Implement a template **ForwardIterator** class that supports iteration through the template **Array** class (see Figure 10.1.2). If the **Array**'s sequence of elements is $E_1, E_2, \ldots, E_n$, a **forward iterator** first selects E_1, then E_2, and so on. The iterator's interface consists of methods to associate it with a sequence, to **reset** it to the sequence's first element, to test whether it is at the end of the sequence, and to return the sequence's next element. The code segment

```
Array< float > f;           // Array instance
ForwardIterator< float> fi( f ); // ForwardIterator for f
// fill f with floating-point numbers
while ( fi.hasMoreElements() ) // iterate through f
   cout << fi.nextElement(); // return next f element
// fi is now at the end of the sequence
fi.reset(); // reset to f's first element
```

illustrates how a **ForwardIterator** might be initialized and used.

10.7. Implement a template **BackwardIterator** class that supports iteration through the template **Array** class (see Figure 10.1.2). If the **Array**'s sequence of elements is $E_1, E_2, \ldots, E_{n-1}, E_n$, a **backward iterator** first selects E_n, then E_{n-1}, and so on. This iterator shares an interface with the **ForwardIterator** (see Programming Exercise 10.6) with appropriate changes in behavior (e.g., a **BackwardIterator**'s **reset** method sets it to the sequence's last element rather than its first element).

10.8. Implement a template **RandomIterator** class for iteration through the template **Array** class (see Figure 10.1.2). A **random iterator** randomly selects an element from a sequence. A random iterator is guaranteed to select every element once before selecting any element twice. A **RandomIterator** shares an interface with the **ForwardIterator** (see Programming Exercise 10.6) with appropriate changes in behavior (e.g., a **RandomIterator**'s **reset** method resets it to a random element in the sequence).

10.9. Rewrite Sample Application 9.4 (Sorting and Searching) using STL containers and algorithms for storing, sorting, and searching the randomly generated integers.

10.10. Write a program that tests the time complexity (see Figure 10.4.4) of STL **vector**s and **deque**s. In particular, test whether insertions and deletions at the beginning are more efficient for a **deque** than for a **queue**, and whether insertions and deletions at the end are equally efficient for a **deque** and **queue**. The library functions **time** and **difftime** are useful for collecting timing data. The program

```
#include <ctime> //*** for time functions
#include <iostream>
#include <vector>
#include <algorithm>
using namespace std;
int main() {
   time_t start, finish;
   vector< int > v;
   // fill v with random integers
   start = time( 0 );   // set start time
   sort( v.begin(), v.end() ); // sort v
   finish = time( 0 );  // set finish time
   cout << difftime( finish, start ) << endl;
   return 0;
}
```

illustrates how **time** and **difftime** can be used to collect timing data.

10.11. Rewrite Sample Application 4.8 (Merging Files) using STL input and output iterators together with the **merge** algorithm, whose prototype is

```
template< class InputIter1,
          class InputIter2,
          class OutputIter >
OutputIter merge( InputIter1 b1, // beginning of file 1
                  InputIter1 e1, // end of file 1
                  InputIter2 b2, // beginning of file 2
                  InputIter2 e2, // end of file 2
                  OutputIter o ); // output file
```

10.12. A World Wide Web site maintains a file of **hits**, that is, of visits to its site. The file has the format

```
<Visitor's IP Address> <day of year> <year>
```

where **IP** stands for **I**ternet **P**rotocol. Sample records are

```
140.192.16.8 34 1998
129.78.55.6 3 1999
140.192.34.6 35 1998
```

The file may hold duplicate records, which indicate multiple visits from the same visitor on the same day in the same year. A **visitor** is identified by an IP address. The file supports an interactive application that allows the user to

- List all visitors on a given day in any year.
- List all visitors on a given day in a given year.
- Count how many times a particular visitor has visited on a given day or in a given year.
- List the n most frequent visitors on a given day or in a given year, where n is a user-specified value.
- Print the file to the standard output sorted by either IP address, or day of year, or by year.

Write the application using whatever STL containers and algorithms seem appropriate. In particular, attempt to eliminate all C++-style loops (e.g., **for** or **while** loops) from the application.

10.13. Write a program that simulates shuffling a deck of cards and dealing a bridge hand. A bridge deal divides a 52-card deck into four hands of 13 cards each. The hands are labeled North, East, South, and West. A bridge deck has four suits: Clubs, Diamonds, Hearts, and Spades. In each suit, the cards are labeled Ace, King, Queen, Jack, 10, 9, ..., 2. Major bridge tournaments play with computer-generated hands. *Hint*: See Figure 10.4.10.

10.14. Write a program that assigns faculty to courses for a given term. Each faculty member has a **teaching load**, which is the number of courses that the faculty member must teach in a given term. A faculty member expresses **preferences** for courses, which are numeric values that signal the faculty member's desire to teach a course. The preferences are integers $1, 2, \ldots, n$, with 1 as the highest preference. Courses have **priorities**, which are numeric values that determine the order in which the courses are assigned to faculty. Courses with a priority of 1 are scheduled first, those with a priority of 2 are scheduled second, and so on. Assume that faculty members and courses have unique identifiers (e.g., unique employee numbers for the faculty and unique course numbers for the courses). The course assignment application should use randomness to promote fairness. For example, if 10 courses have a priority of 1, the program should assign these courses to faculty in random order. If 20 faculty have a preference of 1 for a given course, the program should randomly select candidates from this pool in trying to assign the course. The program should reflect commonsensical constraints. For example, a faculty member cannot teach two courses at the same time. If conflicts prevent a course from being assigned, it should be marked as *NotAssigned*. If a faculty member cannot be assigned courses up to his or her teaching load, the faculty member should be marked as *Underworked*.

10.15. Two statements in a computer program could be executed concurrently if the order of their serial execution is irrelevant. For example, consider the C++ statements

```
p = x + y; // statement 1
q = x * y; // statement 2
r = q - p; // statement 3
```

Statements 1 and 2 can be executed in either order—1 first and then 2, or 2 first and then 1—with the same result. However, statement 1 must be executed *before* statement 3 because statement 3 uses the value of **p** computed in statement 1.

Conditions known as *Bernstein's conditions* can be used to determine whether two statements can be executed concurrently. Before stating Bernstein's conditions, we define two sets of variables. A statement's **write set** consists of variables whose values are changed when the statement executes, and its **read set** consists of variables whose values are unchanged when the statement executes. In a simple assignment statement such as

```
x = y;
```

the write set consists of the assignment's target **x** and the read set consists of its source **y**. In our earlier example, statement 1's write set consists of **p** and its read set of **x** and **y**.

We now can state Bernstein's conditions for concurrent execution. Statements S_1 and S_2 can be executed concurrently if and only if they satisfy these conditions:

- The intersection of S_1's read set and S_2's write set is empty.
- The intersection of S_2's read set and S_1's write set is empty.
- The intersection of S_1's write set and S_2's write set is empty.

In our example, statement 1's write set is {**p**} and statement 3's read set is {**q, p**}. Their intersection is thus {**p**}, which is not empty. Therefore, statements 1 and 2 cannot be executed concurrently. Using either the **set** class of Programming Exercise 10.2 or the STL **set** container, write a program that prompts the user for two assignment statements that are read as character strings. After building the read and write sets for each statement, the program prints

1. The read and write sets of each statement.
2. The intersection sets specified in Bernstein's conditions.
3. A message about whether the statements can be executed concurrently.

APPENDIX A

ASCII TABLE

Table A.1 ASCII Codes

Decimal	Hexadecimal	Octal	Standard Function
0	00	000	NUL (Null)
1	01	001	SOH (Start of heading)
2	02	002	STX (Start of text)
3	03	003	ETX (End of text)
4	04	004	EOT (End of transmission)
5	05	005	ENQ (Enquiry)
6	06	006	ACK (Acknowledge)
7	07	007	BEL (Ring bell)
8	08	010	BS (Backspace)
9	09	011	HT (Horizontal tab)
10	0A	012	LF (Line feed)
11	0B	013	VT (Vertical tab)
12	0C	014	FF (Form feed)
13	0D	015	CR (Carriage return)
14	0E	016	SO (Shift out)
15	0F	017	SI (Shift in)
16	10	020	DLE (Data link escape)
17	11	021	DC1 (Device control 1)
18	12	022	DC2 (Device control 2)
19	13	023	DC3 (Device control 3)
20	14	024	DC4 (Device control 4)
21	15	025	NAK (Negative acknowledge)
22	16	026	SYN (Synchronous idle)
23	17	027	ETB (End of transmission block)
24	18	030	CAN (Cancel)
25	19	031	EM (End of medium)

Table A.1 ASCII Codes (Continued)

Decimal	Hexadecimal	Octal	Standard Function
26	1A	032	SUB (Substitute)
27	1B	033	ESC (Escape)
28	1C	034	FS (File separator)
29	1D	035	GS (Group separator)
30	1E	036	RS (Record separator)
31	1F	037	US (Unit separator)
32	20	040	SP (Space)
33	21	041	!
34	22	042	"
35	23	043	#
36	24	044	$
37	25	045	%
38	26	046	&
39	27	047	'(Single quote)
40	28	050	(
41	29	051	)
42	2A	052	*
43	2B	053	+
44	2C	054	, (Comma)
45	2D	055	- (Hyphen)
46	2E	056	.
47	2F	057	/
48	30	060	0
49	31	061	1
50	32	062	2
51	33	063	3
52	34	064	4
53	35	065	5
54	36	066	6
55	37	067	7
56	38	070	8
57	39	071	9
58	3A	072	:
59	3B	073	;
60	3C	074	<
61	3D	075	=
62	3E	076	>
63	3F	077	?
64	40	100	@
65	41	101	A
66	42	102	B

Table A.1 ASCII Codes (Continued)

Decimal	Hexadecimal	Octal	Standard Function
67	43	103	C
68	44	104	D
69	45	105	E
70	46	106	F
71	47	107	G
72	48	110	H
73	49	111	I
74	4A	112	J
75	4B	113	K
76	4C	114	L
77	4D	115	M
78	4E	116	N
79	4F	117	O
80	50	120	P
81	51	121	Q
82	52	122	R
83	53	123	S
84	54	124	T
85	55	125	U
86	56	126	V
87	57	127	W
88	58	130	X
89	59	131	Y
90	5A	132	Z
91	5B	133	[
92	5C	134	\
93	5D	135	]
94	5E	136	^
95	5F	137	_ (Underscore)
96	60	140	` (Grave accent)
97	61	141	a
98	62	142	b
99	63	143	c
100	64	144	d
101	65	145	e
102	66	146	f
103	67	147	g
104	68	150	h
105	69	151	i
106	6A	152	j
107	6B	153	k

Table A.1 ASCII Codes (Continued)

Decimal	Hexadecimal	Octal	Standard Function
108	6C	154	l
109	6D	155	m
110	6E	156	n
111	6F	157	o
112	70	160	p
113	71	161	q
114	72	162	r
115	73	163	s
116	74	164	t
117	75	165	u
118	76	166	v
119	77	167	w
120	78	170	x
121	79	171	y
122	7A	172	z
123	7B	173	{
124	7C	174	|
125	7D	175	}
126	7E	176	~
127	7F	177	DEL (Delete)

APPENDIX

B

THE PREPROCESSOR

The C++ preprocessor processes a C++ source file before the compiler translates the program into object code:

$$\text{C++ Source Code} \rightarrow \text{Preprocessor} \rightarrow \text{Compiler}$$

The preprocessor follows the programmer's directives, which are commands that start with the character **#**. An example is the **#include** directive

```
#include <iostream>
```

which provides a proper interface to the standard input/output libraries. Figure B.1 lists all the directives with brief explanations.

Preprocessor directives may start in any column, although they traditionally start in column 1. Directives may occur on any line inside or outside blocks, but they typically occur at the beginning of a file so that they take effect in all succeeding lines. Although directives can be quite elaborate, our examples are straightforward. The programmer must keep in mind that the preprocessor follows directives literally. It knows nothing about C++'s syntax or semantics, much less about the programmer's intentions!

File Inclusions

The **#include** directive

```
#include <iostream>
```

instructs the preprocessor to include the contents of the file *iostream*. The angle brackets indicate that this file is to be found in a directory already known to the operating system. The brackets typically are used to **#include** any standard header files as well as any other header files provided by the local implementation. The preprocessor searches the directory for the file; and when it finds the file, it replaces the **#include** line by the specified file.

The **#include** directive

```
#include "mydefs.h"
```

Directive	*Meaning*
`#include`	Include the contents of a text file.
`#define`	Define a macro.
`#undef`	Cancel a previous `#define`.
`#if`	If a test succeeds, take specified actions.
`#ifdef`	If a macro is defined, take specified actions.
`#ifndef`	Opposite of `#ifdef`—if a macro is not defined, take specified actions.
`#else`	If the previous `#if`, `#ifdef`, or `#ifndef` fails, take specified actions.
`#endif`	Mark the end of an `#if`, `#ifdef`, or `#ifndef` body.
`#elif`	"Else if"—a way around nested `#if`-`#else` constructs.
`#line`	Set line number for the compiler to use when issuing warning or error messages.
`#error`	Specify a compile-time error and accompanying message.
`#pragma`	Provide implementation-specific information to the compiler.
`#`	Ignore this line.

FIGURE B.1 Preprocessor directives.

with the file name in double quotation marks, directs the preprocessor to include the contents of a file to be found in the default (generally the current) directory.

A file may contain any number of `#include` directives. Further, the directives may be nested: One file may include another, which includes another, and so on. At least eight levels of nesting are guaranteed. A good way to manage `#include` directives is to consolidate them in one file and then include this file wherever needed.

Care must be taken when recompiling programs whose component functions have `#include` directives. Suppose that *defs.h* is included in six different files, each holding one or more functions. If we later change the contents of *defs.h*, we must be sure to recompile all the functions that the `#include` directive affects. If we forget to recompile all the affected functions, some functions may work with the old contents of *defs.h*, whereas others may work only with the new version. This is almost sure to cause a run-time error that may be very hard to track down.

Macros

Constants can be defined using the `#define` directive. For example, the constant `EOF` might be defined as

```
#define EOF  (-1)
```

This `#define` directs the preprocessor to replace subsequent occurrences of `EOF` with `(-1)`, an expression that evaluates to the negative integer -1. The technical name for the `#define`d `EOF` is **macro**, and it is common to say that the macro `EOF` expands into `(-1)`, which is its value. The use of parentheses in the `#define` for `EOF` is a habitual precaution to ensure that the preprocessor correctly expands `EOF`.

EXAMPLE.   Consider this series of #defines

```
#define NormalMeetings   3   // with Boss1, Boss2, Boss3
#define SpecialMeetings  2   // morning nap and afternoon
                             // cocktail
#define TimePerMeeting  20   // in minutes
// ***** Caution!
#define TotalMeetings  NormalMeetings + SpecialMeetings
#define TotalTime      TotalMeetings * TimePerMeeting
```

which shows how a macro, once #defined, can be used in the #define of a subsequent macro.

The value of TotalTime is 43, not the expected 100. The macro TotalMeetings expands into

```
NormalMeetings + SpecialMeetings
```

and these macros expand into

```
3 + 2
```

TotalTime expands into TotalMeetings multiplied by TimePerMeeting, or

```
3 + 2 * 20
```

Since multiplication occurs before the addition, TotalTime expands into

```
3 + ( 2 * 20 )
```

which evaluates to 43. The problem can be avoided by parenthesizing the #define for TotalMeetings:

```
#define TotalMeetings ( NormalMeetings + SpecialMeetings )
```

TotalTime now expands into the expression

```
( 3 + 2 ) * 20
```

which has 100 as its value. Of course, it would be prudent to use parentheses in the #define for TotalTime as well:

```
#define TotalTime  ( TotalMeetings * TimePerMeeting )          ■
```

While it is illegal to change the definition of a macro by using a second #define statement (unless the macro is first undefined using the #undef directive), it is legal to *repeat* a #define statement.

A #define may occur on more than one line if the backslash is used. For example,

```
#define TotalMeetings  \          // carry over to next line
         ( NormalMeetings + \     // ditto
           SpecialMeetings )
```

allows the #define to occur on three lines in all.

In C++, const variables have largely replaced #defined constants. The advantage of a const variable over the #define directive is that the variable becomes a bona fide part of the program and, as such, can be referenced by name by the debugger, has storage allocated for it, has a type, and so on. On the other hand, a #define directive is handled by the preprocessor prior to compilation; consequently, the macro name cannot be referenced by the debugger, has no storage allocated for it, and has no type.

Parameterized Macros

Macros may be #**define**d with parameters, which act as placeholders for actual arguments. A parameterized macro begins with #**define**. Next comes the name of the macro and then parentheses containing the parameters. The parameters are separated by commas. No white space is allowed between the macro name and the left parenthesis. (When white space follows the macro name, the macro is assumed to be an unparenthesized macro like those in the preceding subsection.) The macro name and parentheses are followed by the macro's definition. In the code that follows a macro definition, the preprocessor substitutes each occurrence of the macro by its definition.

For example, suppose that our program repeatedly needs to print three values on a new line, separated by tabs. We can write a macro to do this printing, as follows:

```
#define PRINT3( e1, e2, e3 ) \
        cout << endl << (e1) << '\t' << (e2) << '\t' << (e3)
```

We show how the preprocessor handles the code:

```
#include <iostream>
using namespace std;
#define PRINT3( e1, e2, e3 ) \
        cout << endl << (e1) << '\t' << (e2) << '\t' << (e3)
int main() {
   char char1 = 'A';
   char char2 = 'Z';
   int  num = 999;
   PRINT3( char1, char2, num + 1 );
   return 0;
}
```

The macro **PRINT3** expects three arguments, as indicated by the three parameters **e1**, **e2**, and **e3** in its definition. We use **PRINT3** in the function's body with **char1**, **char2**, and **num + 1** as the actual arguments:

```
PRINT3( char1, char2, num + 1 );
```

Notice that we supply the semicolon, as it is not included in **PRINT3**'s definition. Substituting the three actual arguments **char1**, **char2**, and **num + 1** in **PRINT3**'s definition gives

```
cout << endl << (char1) << '\t' << (char2) << '\t'
     << (num + 1)
```

for the expansion. The output is

```
A    Z    1000
```

In the **cout** expression, we enclosed each of **PRINT3**'s parameters in parentheses because, as noted previously, in certain contexts omitting the parentheses may cause problems.

Parameterized Macros Versus Functions

The similarity in syntax between parameterized macros and functions should not obscure important differences between them.

EXAMPLE.   The code

```
#include <iostream>
using namespace std;
#define min( x, y )  ( ( (x) < (y) ) ? (x) : (y) )
int max( int x, int y );
int main() {
    int num1, num2;
    cout << "Enter two integers: ";
    cin >> num1 >> num2;
    // Macro
    cout << "Min: " << min( num1, num2 ) << endl;
    // Function
    cout << "Max: " << max( num1, num2 ) << endl;
    return 0;
}
int max( int x, int y ) {
    return ( x > y ) ? x : y;
}
```

implements **min** as a parameterized macro and **max** as a function. Although it is common to say that a parameterized macro such as **min** is invoked (within the **cout** statement), this is technically wrong. No arguments are passed to **min** and **min** returns no value. Instead, the preprocessor merely replaces

```
min( num1, num2 )
```

with

```
( ( (num1), (num2) ) ? (num1) : (num2) )
```

before the code is even compiled, let alone run. By contrast, **max** is implemented as a function. Ordinary function calls have an associated overhead when a program is executed because the system must make copies of any arguments passed to the function, keep track of where to resume program execution when the function returns, and so on. Macros and *inline* functions do not incur such run-time overhead and, in this sense, are more efficient than functions. ∎

Just as **const** variables have largely replaced **#define**d constants in C++, for similar reasons inline functions have largely replaced parameterized macros.

Other Directives

The **#undef** directive

```
#undef SFlag
```

instructs the preprocessor to cancel any definition of **SFlag**. An **#undef** can be used to guard against conflicts between two macros or between a macro and a variable.

The **#ifdef** directive

```
#ifdef      BIG_TABLE
#define     ROWS        10000
#define     COLUMNS     10000
#define     TAB_SIZE    ( ROWS * COLUMNS )
#endif
```

instructs the preprocessor to define macros **ROWS**, **COLUMNS**, and **TAB_SIZE** if the macro **BIG_TABLE** is already defined. So if the preprocessor first encounters

```
#define   BIG_TABLE
```

it then **#define**s **ROWS**, **COLUMNS**, and **TAB_SIZE**. Note that the **#endif** directive marks the end of the conditional directive. In this example, the **#define** does not specify a value for **BIG_TABLE**. The **#ifdef** test does not check whether a macro has a particular value but, rather, whether it has been **#define**d at all.

The **#ifndef** directive is the opposite of **#ifdef**. The **#ifndef** directive

```
#ifndef     INTEGER
#define     INTEGER       short int
#endif
```

instructs the preprocessor to define **INTEGER** as **short int** if **INTEGER** has not been defined already. The directive says, in effect: Use this definition of **INTEGER** if you do not have one already.

The **#ifndef** directive

```
#ifndef     BIG_TABLE
#define     ROWS        10000
#define     COLUMNS     10000
#define     TAB_SIZE    ( ROWS * COLUMNS )
#endif
```

directs the preprocessor to define **ROWS**, **COLUMNS**, and **TAB_SIZE** if **BIG_TABLE** has not been defined already.

The **#ifndef** directive can be used to assure that a header file is, in effect, included only once per file. For example, suppose that we write header files *pers.h*

```
// pers.h
#ifndef PERS
#define PERS
#define persBuffSize 512
    ...
#endif
```

and *payroll.h*

```
// payroll.h
#include "pers.h"
   ...
```

Suppose that in source file *pay.cpp* we include both *pers.h* and *payroll.h*

```
// pay.cpp
#include "pers.h"
#include "payroll.h"
   ...
```

When the directive

```
#include "pers.h"
```

in *pay.cpp* is processed, the code

```
#define PERS
#define persBuffSize 512
   ...
```

is inserted in *pay.cpp* since **PERS** is not defined. Next, the directive

```
#include "payroll.h"
```

in *pay.cpp* is processed, which, in turn, inserts the directive

```
#include "pers.h"
```

(from file *payroll.h*) in *pay.cpp*. When the second occurrence of

```
#include "pers.h"
```

is processed in *pay.cpp*, the code

```
#define PERS
#define persBuffSize 512
   ...
```

is *not* inserted in *pay.cpp* since **PERS** is now defined. In effect, *pers.h* is not included in *pay.cpp* a second time. Repeating some C++ statements can cause errors (e.g., it is illegal to repeat a class declaration.) Using flags (e.g., **PERS**) guards against inadvertently repeating statements.

The preprocessor also recognizes the term **defined**. The code

```
#if defined( BIG_TABLE )  &&   !defined( SMALL_TABLE )
#define   ROWS      10000
#define   COLUMNS   10000
#define   TAB_SIZE  ( ROWS * COLUMNS )
#endif
```

shows how the **#if** directive, together with the **defined** construct, accomplishes what otherwise would require an **#ifndef** nested in an **#ifdef**:

```
#ifdef      BIG_TABLE
#ifndef     SMALL_TABLE
#define     ROWS         10000
#define     COLUMNS      10000
#define     TAB_SIZE     ( ROWS * COLUMNS )
#endif
#endif
```

The two examples have the same effect, but the first is more concise. Both **#ifdef** and **#ifndef** are restricted to a *single* expression as a test, but the **#if** combined with **defined** allows compound expressions.

The following code

```
#define  TRACE  1
int main()
{
   int      current_count;
   float    percentage;
   ...
   #if TRACE
   cout << "Current count == " << current_count << endl;
   cout << "Percentage == " << percentage << endl;
   #endif
   ...
}
```

illustrates *conditional compilation*. We use the **#if** directive to implement a tracer. The tracer is turned on by defining **TRACE** as any nonzero value and turned off by defining **TRACE** as 0. If **TRACE** is nonzero, the compiler compiles the lines

```
cout << "Current count == " << current_count << endl;
cout << "Percentage == " << percentage << endl;
```

If **TRACE** is 0, these lines are not compiled. If we no longer need the tracer, we simply **#define TRACE** as zero instead of deleting the **cout** statements.

The **#else** directive has the expected meaning. Suppose that we know that a program will be run either on a SUN, which implements a **short int** as a 16-bit cell, or on an IBM PC, which implements an **int** as a 16-bit cell. If we want our integer variables to be implemented as 16-bit cells on either machine, we can declare them as **INTEGER** data types; for example,

```
INTEGER count;
```

and include the following directives at the beginning of the program:

```
#ifdef     SUN_COMPUTER
#define    INTEGER    short int
#else
#define    INTEGER    int
#endif
```

If the program is to run on a SUN, we **#define** the macro **SUN_COMPUTER**; otherwise, we leave it undefined.

The **#elif** directive is short for "else if" and gives an alternative to nested **#if** directives. In the code

```
#if         defined( SUN )
#define     GREETING  cout << "Welcome to SUN C++!" << endl
#elif       defined( IBM )
#define     GREETING  cout << "Welcome to IBM C++!" << endl
#elif       defined( ATT )
#define     GREETING  cout << "Welcome to ATT C++!" << endl
#else
#define     GREETING  cout << "Welcome C++, PERIOD!" << endl
#endif
```

the preprocessor checks whether **SUN** is **#define**d; and, if so, it **#define**s **GREETING** with a SUN message. If not, it checks whether **IBM** is **#define**d; and, if so, it **#define**s **GREETING** with an IBM message, and so on. Note that we terminate with **#endif** and use **#else** to complete the construct.

Suppose that the file *prog1.cpp* is

```
#include "mydefs.h"
int main() {
   ...
}
```

If *mydefs.h* contains 24 lines of text and the 13th line of *prog1.cpp* contains a syntax error, the typical C++ compiler issues a message that an error has occurred at line 37, not line 13, because the preprocessor includes the 24 lines from *mydefs.h* before passing the *prog1.cpp* file along to the compiler. The experience can be very frustrating, especially if you look at line 37 in *prog1.cpp*. Indeed, there may be no line 37 in *prog1.cpp*! The **#line** directive directs the compiler how to number lines and, optionally, which file name to use in reporting an error.

If we change *prog1.cpp* to

```
#include "mydefs.h"
#line 1
int main() {
   ...
}
```

the **#line** directive instructs the compiler to treat the following line as number 1, the next as number 2, and so on. Now, when the compiler detects the syntax error at line 13 of *prog1.cpp*, it reports the error as occurring at line 13 of *prog1.cpp*.

The **#line** directive has an optional second argument, a character string, that should be the name of a file. For example, the directive

```
#line   25    "oldprog1.cpp"
```

instructs the compiler to treat the following line as number 25 and to report any errors as originating in the file *oldprog1.cpp*.

The **#error** directive

```
#if  defined( ATT )  &&  defined( IBM )
#error "You can't be on two computers at once!!!"
#endif
```

instructs the compiler to generate an error and to display a corresponding message. The directive lets the programmer extend the compiler's own error-detection and error-message capabilities.

The **#pragma** directive gives the compiler implementation-specific instructions. One simply writes **#pragma** and then the name of the instruction. For example, we might write

```
#pragma  InLine
```

to tell the compiler that the file contains in-line assembly code. If the compiler does not understand the instruction in a **#pragma** line, it simply ignores it.

A line containing only **#** is called a *null directive* and is simply ignored by the compiler.

SELECTED C++ FUNCTIONS AND METHODS

Before summarizing in detail several useful library functions and class methods, we shall briefly describe each. The following lists group the functions by type:

Math Functions			
abs	Absolute value	**floor**	Floor
acos	Arccosine	**log**	$\log_e x$
asin	Arcsine	**log10**	$\log_{10} x$
atan	Arctangent	**pow**	x^y
atof	Convert string to **double**	**rand**	Generate a random integer
atoi	Convert string to **int**	**sin**	Sine
atol	Convert string to **long**	**sinh**	Hyperbolic sine
ceil	Ceiling	**sqrt**	Square root
cos	Cosine	**srand**	Seed the random number generator
cosh	Hyperbolic cosine	**tan**	Tangent
exp	e^x	**tanh**	Hyperbolic tangent

Input/Output Class Methods			
clear	Replace or clear stream state	**open**	Open a file
close	Close a file	**put**	Write character
eof	Signal end-of-file	**putback**	Return character to stream
get	Read characters and strings	**read**	Read binary data
getline	Read a line	**write**	Write binary data

Type and Conversion Functions

`atof`	Convert string to `double`	`islower`	Lowercase character?
`atoi`	Convert string to `int`	`isprint`	Printable character?
`atol`	Convert string to `long`	`ispunct`	Punctuation character?
`isalnum`	Alphanumeric?	`isspace`	Space character?
`isalpha`	Alphabetic character?	`isupper`	Uppercase character?
`iscntrl`	Control character?	`isxdigit`	Hexadecimal character?
`isdigit`	Decimal digit?	`tolower`	Convert from uppercase to lowercase
`isgraph`	Nonblank, printable character?	`toupper`	Convert from lowercase to uppercase

String Functions

`memchr`	Find leftmost character in object	`strlen`	Length of string
`memcmp`	Compare objects	`strncat`	Concatenate strings
`memcpy`	Copy object	`strncmp`	Compare strings
`memmove`	Copy object	`strncpy`	Copy string
`memset`	Copy character	`strpbrk`	First break character
`strcat`	Concatenate strings	`strrchr`	Find rightmost character in string
`strchr`	Find leftmost character in string	`strspn`	Span
`strcmp`	Compare strings	`strstr`	Find substring
`strcpy`	Copy string	`strtok`	String tokenizer
`strcspn`	Complement of span		

Miscellaneous Functions

`abort`	Cause abnormal program termination
`bsearch`	Binary search
`difftime`	Compute difference between times
`exit`	Terminate program
`qsort`	Quicksort
`set_terminate`	Specify function for `terminate` to call
`set_unexpected`	Specify function for `unexpected` to call
`signal`	Invoke a function to handle a signal
`system`	Execute a command
`terminate`	End because of exception handling error
`time`	Find time
`unexpected`	Called when illegal `throw` specification

We now list the functions and class methods alphabetically. Class methods are designated as such and the class to which each belongs is specified. Each description consists of the file to include, the function's declaration, and a few sentences that describe what the function does. All character codes are given in ASCII. When we write **string**, it is the address of (pointer to) a sequence of null-terminated, contiguous **char**s.

abort

```
#include <cstdlib>
void abort();
```

Causes abnormal program termination. The status "unsuccessful termination" is returned to the invoking process.

abs

```
#include <cstdlib>
int abs( int x );
long abs( long x );
float abs( float x );
double abs( double x );
long double abs( long double x );
```

Returns the absolute value of **x**.

acos

```
#include <cmath>
float acos( float real );
double acos( double real );
long double acos( long double real );
```

Returns the arccosine (in radians) of **real**. The value returned is between 0 and π.

asin

```
#include <cmath>
float asin( float real );
double asin( double real );
long double asin( long double real );
```

Returns the arcsine (in radians) of **real**. The value returned is between $-\frac{\pi}{2}$ and $\frac{\pi}{2}$.

atan

```
#include <cmath>
float atan( float real );
double atan( double real );
long double atan( long double real );
```

Returns the arctangent (in radians) of **real**. The value returned is between $-\frac{\pi}{2}$ and $\frac{\pi}{2}$.

atof

```
#include <cstdlib>
double atof( const char* string );
```

Converts a real number, represented as **string**, to **double**. Returns the converted number; **string** consists of optional tabs and spaces followed by an optional sign followed by digits followed by an optional decimal point followed by an optional exponent. The optional exponent is **e** or **E** followed by an integer. See also **atoi** and **atol**.

atoi

```
#include <cstdlib>
int atoi( const char* string );
```

Converts an integer, represented as **string**, to **int**. Returns the converted number; **string** consists of optional tabs and spaces followed by an optional sign followed by digits. See also **atof** and **atol**.

atol

```
#include <cstdlib>
long atol( const char* string );
```

Converts an integer, represented as **string**, to **long**. Returns the converted number; **string** consists of optional tabs and spaces followed by an optional sign followed by digits. See also **atof** and **atoi**.

bsearch

```
#include <cstdlib>
void* bsearch( const void* key,
               void* start,
               size_t no_elts,
               size_t size_elt,
               int ( *cmp ) ( const void*, const void* ) );
```

Searches for ***key** in a sorted array of size **no_elts** whose initial cell is at address **start**. The parameter **size_elt** is the size in bytes of one cell of the array. The parameter **cmp** is a pointer to a function that compares ***key** and an element in the array and returns an integer to signal the result of the comparison. The first argument to the comparison function ***cmp** is **key** and the second is a pointer to an item in the array. The value of the expression ***cmp(*first, *second)** is negative if ***first** precedes ***second** in the sorted order; ***cmp(*first, *second)** is zero if ***first** is equal to ***second**; and ***cmp(*first, *second)** is positive if ***first** follows ***second** in the sorted order. If ***key** is in the array, **bsearch** returns a pointer to a cell containing ***key**; if ***key** is not in the array, **bsearch** returns **NULL**.

ceil

```
#include <cmath>
float ceil( float real );
double ceil( double real );
long double ceil( long double real );
```

Returns the least integer (as a **double**) greater than or equal to **real**.

clear

```
#include <iostream>
void basic_ios::clear( iostate st = goodbit );
```

Changes stream state to **st**.

close

```
#include <fstream>
void basic_ifstream::close();
void basic_ofstream::close();
void basic_fstream::close();
```

Closes the file, if any, attached to the object.

cos

```
#include <cmath>
float cos( float real );
double cos( double real );
long double cos( long double real );
```

Returns the cosine of **real**; **real** must be in radians.

cosh

```
#include <cmath>
float cosh( float real );
double cosh( double real );
long double cosh( long double real );
```

Returns the hyperbolic cosine of **real**.

difftime

```
#include <ctime>
double difftime( time_t end, time_t begin );
```

Returns the difference (**end** − **begin**), in seconds, between the times **end** and **begin**. See also **time**.

eof

```
#include <iostream>
bool basic_ios::eof() const;
```

Returns **true** if a read was attempted past the end of the stream; otherwise, returns **false**.

exit

```
#include <cstdlib>
void exit( int status_value );
```

Terminates the program and sends the value **status_value** to the invoking process (operating system, another program, etc.). The constants **EXIT_SUCCESS** and **EXIT_FAILURE**, defined in *cstdlib*, may be used as arguments to **exit** to indicate successful or unsuccessful termination. The function **exit** flushes all buffers and closes all open files.

exp

```
#include <cmath>
float exp( float real );
double exp( double real );
long double exp( long double real );
```

Returns e^{real}, where e (2.71828...) is the base of the natural logarithm. See also **pow**.

floor

```
#include <cmath>
float floor( float real );
double floor( double real );
long double floor( long double real );
```

Returns the greatest integer (as a **double**) less than or equal to **real**.

get

```
#include <iostream>
basic_istream<charT,traits>&
    basic_istream::get( char_type* buff,
                        streamsize n );
basic_istream<charT,traits>&
    basic_istream::get( char_type* buff,
                        streamsize n,
                        char_type stop );
basic_istream<charT,traits>&
    basic_istream::get( char_type& c );
```

In the first version, characters are read from the stream into the array **buff** until a newline is encountered, until end-of-stream, or until **n - 1** characters have been read into **buff**, whichever happens first. The newline character is *not* placed in the array **buff**, nor is it removed from the stream. The method **get** adds a null terminator **'\0'**. The second version is like the first, except that newline is replaced by **stop**. In the third version, the next character, white space or not, is read into **c**. In all versions, **get** returns the updated stream.

getline

```
#include <iostream>
basic_istream<charT,traits>&
    basic_istream::getline( char_type* buff,
                            int n );
basic_istream<charT,traits>&
    basic_istream::getline( char_type* buff,
                            int n,
                            char stop );
```

In the first version, characters are read from the stream into the array **buff** until end-of-stream, until a newline is encountered, or until **n - 1** characters have been read into **buff**, whichever happens first. The newline character is *not* placed in the array **buff**, but it is removed from the stream. The method **getline** always adds a null terminator **'\0'**, even if it read no characters. The second version is like the first except that newline is replaced by **stop**.

isalnum

```
#include <cctype>
int isalnum( int character );
```

Returns a nonzero integer if **character** is an alphanumeric character (`'a'` through `'z'`, `'A'` through `'Z'`, or `'0'` through `'9'`); otherwise, it returns 0.

isalpha

```
#include <cctype>
int isalpha( int character );
```

Returns a nonzero integer if **character** is an alphabetic character (`'a'` through `'z'` or `'A'` through `'Z'`); otherwise, it returns 0.

iscntrl

```
#include <cctype>
int iscntrl( int character );
```

Returns a nonzero integer if **character** is a control character (integer value decimal 127 or less than decimal 32); otherwise, it returns 0.

isdigit

```
#include <cctype>
int isdigit( int character );
```

Returns a nonzero integer if **character** is a decimal digit (`'0'` through `'9'`); otherwise, it returns 0.

isgraph

```
#include <cctype>
int isgraph( int character );
```

Returns a nonzero integer if **character** is a nonblank printing character (integer value greater than or equal to decimal 33 and less than or equal to decimal 126); otherwise, it returns 0.

islower

```
#include <cctype>
int islower( int character );
```

Returns a nonzero integer if **character** is a lowercase character (**'a'** through **'z'**); otherwise, it returns 0.

isprint

```
#include <cctype>
int isprint( int character );
```

Returns a nonzero integer if **character** is a printable character (integer value greater than or equal to decimal 32 and less than or equal to decimal 126); otherwise, it returns 0.

ispunct

```
#include <cctype>
int ispunct( int character );
```

Returns a nonzero integer if **character** is a punctuation character (integer value decimal 127 or integer value less than decimal 33); otherwise, it returns 0.

isspace

```
#include <cctype>
int isspace( int character );
```

Returns a nonzero integer if **character** is a space character (space, tab, carriage return, form feed, vertical tab, or newline—decimal 32 or greater than decimal 8 and less than decimal 14); otherwise, it returns 0.

isupper

```
#include <cctype>
int isupper( int character );
```

Returns a nonzero integer if **character** is an uppercase character (**'A'** through **'Z'**); otherwise, it returns 0.

isxdigit

```
#include <cctype>
int isxdigit( int character );
```

Returns a nonzero integer if **character** is a hexadecimal digit (**'0'** through **'9'**, **'a'** through **'f'**, or **'A'** through **'F'**); otherwise, it returns 0.

log

```
#include <cmath>
float log( float real );
double log( double real );
long double log( long double real );
```

Returns the natural logarithm (log to the base e) of **real**.

log10

```
#include <cmath>
float log10( float real );
double log10( double real );
long double log10( long double real );
```

Returns the logarithm to the base 10 of **real**.

memchr

```
#include <cstring>
const void* memchr( const void* block,
                    int character,
                    size_t numb );
void* memchr( void* block,
              int character,
              size_t numb );
```

Returns the address of the first occurrence of **character** in the first **numb** bytes of the object at address **block**, or if **character** does not appear in the first **numb** bytes of the object, it returns **NULL**. On some systems, **memchr** may execute faster than **strchr**. See also **strchr** and **strrchr**.

memcmp

```
#include <cstring>
int memcmp( const void* block1,
            const void* block2,
            size_t numb );
```

Compares the first **numb** bytes of the object at address **block1** with the first **numb** bytes of the object at address **block2**. Returns a negative integer if the item at **block1** is less than the item at **block2**. Returns zero if the item at **block1** is equal to the item at **block2**. Returns a positive integer if the item at **block1** is greater than the item at **block2**. On some systems, **memcmp** may execute faster than **strncmp**. See also **strcmp** and **strncmp**.

memcpy

```
#include <cstring>
void* memcpy( void* block1, const void* block2, size_t numb );
```

Copies the first **numb** bytes of the object at address **block2** into the object at address **block1** and returns **block1**. The copy may not work if the objects overlap. On some systems, **memcpy** may execute faster than **memmove** and **strncpy**. See also **memmove**, **strcpy**, and **strncpy**.

memmove

```
#include <cstring>
void* memmove( void* block1, const void* block2, size_t numb );
```

Copies the first **numb** bytes of the object at address **block2** into the object at address **block1** and returns **block1**. The objects are allowed to overlap. On some systems, **memmove** may execute faster than **strncpy**. See also **memcpy**, **strcpy**, and **strncpy**.

memset

```
#include <cstring>
void* memset( void* block, int c, size_t numb );
```

Copies **c** into the first **numb** bytes of the object at address **block** and returns **block**.

open

```
#include <fstream>
void basic_ofstream::open( const char* filename,
        ios_base::openmode mode
        = ios_base::out | ios_base::trunc );
void basic_ifstream::open( const char* filename,
        ios_base::openmode mode
        = ios_base::in );
void basic_fstream::open( const char* filename,
        ios_base::openmode mode
        = ios_base::in | ios_base::out );
```

Opens the file **filename** in mode **mode** and associates it with an already existing object.

pow

```
#include <cmath>
float pow( float real1, float real2 );
float pow( float real1, int real2 );
double pow( double real1, double real2 );
double pow( double real1, int real2 );
long double pow( long double real1, long double real2 );
long double pow( long double real1, int real2 );
```

Returns $real1^{real2}$. An error occurs if **real1** is negative and **real2** is not an integer. See also **exp**.

put

```
#include <iostream>
basic_ostream<charT,traits>& basic_ostream::put( char_type c );
```

Writes **c** to the output stream and returns the updated stream.

putback

```
#include <iostream>
basic_istream<charT,traits>&
    basic_istream::putback( char_type c );
```

Puts the character **c** back into the stream and returns the updated stream.

qsort

```
#include <cstdlib>
void qsort( void* start, size_t no_elts, size_t size_elt,
            int ( *cmp ) ( const void*, const void* ) );
```

Sorts an array of size **no_elts** whose initial cell is at address **start**. The parameter **size_elt** is the size of one cell of the array in bytes. The parameter **cmp** is a pointer to a function that compares two elements whose data type is the same as that of the array and returns an integer to signal the result of the comparison. The arguments to the comparison function ***cmp** are pointers to the two items to be compared. The value of the expression ***cmp(*first, *second)** is negative if ***first** precedes ***second** in the sorted order; ***cmp(*first, *second)** is zero if ***first** is equal to ***second**; and ***cmp(*first, *second)** is positive if ***first** follows ***second** in the sorted order.

rand

```
#include <cstdlib>
int rand();
```

Returns a pseudorandom integer in the range 0 to **RAND_MAX** (a constant defined in *cstdlib*). See also **srand**.

read

```
#include <iostream>
basic_istream<charT,traits>&
    basic_istream::read( char_type* buff, streamsize n );
```

Reads **n** characters into **buff** and returns the updated stream.

set_terminate

```
#include <exception>
terminate_handler set_terminate( terminate_handler h ) throw();
```

Sets **h** as the handler function for terminating exception processing. Returns the function previously specified.

set_unexpected

```
#include <exception>
unexpected_handler
    set_unexpected( unexpected_handler u ) throw();
```

Sets **u** as the unexpected handler. Returns the function previously specified.

signal

```
#include <csignal>
void ( *signal( int sig, void ( *handler ) ( int ) ) )( int );
```

Catches a signal and invokes a function to handle the signal. If the request can be handled, **signal** returns the value of **handler** for the previous call to **signal** for the given **sig**; otherwise, it returns **SIG_ERR**.

sin

```
#include <cmath>
float sin( float real );
double sin( double real );
long double sin( long double real );
```

Returns the sine of **real**, which must be in radians.

sinh

```
#include <cmath>
float sinh( float real );
double sinh( double real );
long double sinh( long double real );
```

Returns the hyperbolic sine of **real**.

sqrt

```
#include <cmath>
float sqrt( float real );
double sqrt( double real );
long double sqrt( long double real );
```

Returns the square root of **real**.

srand

```
#include <cstdlib>
void srand( unsigned int seed );
```

Seeds the random number generator. Calling **srand** with **seed** equal to 1 is equivalent to calling the random number function **rand** without first invoking **srand**. See also **rand**.

strcat

```
#include <cstring>
char* strcat( char* string1, const char* string2 );
```

Copies **string2** to the end of **string1**. Returns **string1** (the address of the first string). See also **strncat**.

strchr

```
#include <cstring>
const char* strchr( const char* string, int character );
char* strchr( char* string, int character );
```

Returns the address of the first occurrence of **character** in **string**, or if **character** does not occur in **string**, it returns **NULL**. See also **strrchr**, **strstr**, and **memchr**.

strcmp

```
#include <cstring>
int strcmp( const char* string1, const char* string2 );
```

Returns a negative integer if **string1** is (lexicographically) less than **string2**. Returns 0 if **string1** is equal to **string2**. Returns a positive integer if **string1** is greater than **string2**. See also **strncmp** and **memcmp**.

strcpy

```
#include <cstring>
char* strcpy( char* string1, const char* string2 );
```

Copies **string2** to **string1**. Returns **string1** (the address of the first string). See also **strncpy**, **memcpy**, and **memmove**.

strcspn

```
#include <cstring>
size_t strcspn( const char* string1, const char* string2 );
```

Returns the number of consecutive characters in **string1**, beginning with the first, that do not occur anywhere in **string2**. See also **strspn**.

strlen

```
#include <cstring>
size_t strlen( const char* string );
```

Returns the length of **string** (not counting the null terminator).

strncat

```
#include <cstring>
char* strncat( char* string1, const char* string2,
               size_t max_len );
```

Copies **string2** or **max_len** characters from **string2**, whichever is shorter, to the end of **string1**. In either case, a terminating null is placed at the end. Returns **string1** (the address of the first string). See also **strcat**.

strncmp

```
#include <cstring>
int strncmp( const char* string1,
             const char* string2, size_t max_len );
```

Let **s** denote the string obtained by choosing **string2** or **max_len** characters from **string2**, whichever is shorter. Returns a negative integer if **string1** is (lexicographically) less than **s**. Returns 0 if **string1** is equal to **s**. Returns a positive integer if **string1** is greater than **s**. See also **strcmp** and **memcmp**.

strncpy

```
#include <cstring>
char* strncpy( char* string1, const char* string2,
               size_t max_len );
```

Copies exactly **max_len** characters (counting the null terminator '**\0**') from **string2** to **string1**. If the length of **string2** is less than **max_len**, null terminators are used to fill **string1**. The resulting string is *not* null terminated if the length of **string2** is greater than or equal to **max_len**. Returns **string1** (the address of the first string). See also **strcpy**, **memcpy**, and **memmove**.

strpbrk

```
#include <cstring>
const char* strpbrk( const char* string1,
                     const char* string2 );
char* strpbrk( char* string1,
               const char* string2 );
```

Returns the address of the first character in **string1** that occurs anywhere in **string2**, or if no character in **string1** is also in **string2**, it returns **NULL**.

strrchr

```
#include <cstring>
const char* strrchr( const char* string, int character );
char* strrchr( char* string, int character );
```

Returns the address of the last occurrence of **character** in **string**, or if **character** does not occur in **string**, it returns **NULL**. See also **strchr**, **strstr**, and **memchr**.

strspn

```
#include <cstring>
size_t strspn( const char* string1, const char* string2 );
```

Returns the number of consecutive characters in **string1**, beginning with the first, that occur somewhere in **string2**. See also **strcspn**.

strstr

```
#include <cstring>
const char* strstr( const char* string1, const char* string2 );
char* strstr( char* string1, const char* string2 );
```

Returns the address of the first occurrence in **string1** of **string2**, or **NULL** if **string2** is not a substring of **string1**. See also **strchr** and **strrchr**.

strtok

```
#include <cstring>
char* strtok( char* string1, const char* string2 );
```

Tokenizes a string. If **string1** is not **NULL**, it tells **strtok** where to begin searching for tokens. The second argument, **string2**, is a string of delimiters. When it finds a delimiter, **strtok** stops searching and substitutes a null terminator for the delimiter. In subsequent calls to **strtok**, **string1** is **NULL** to signal **strtok** that it should continue from its current position in its search for tokens. Since we normally use the same delimiters throughout, **string2** typically remains unchanged. The function **strtok** returns the address of the next token or **NULL** if it encounters the null terminator.

system

```
#include <cstdlib>
int system( const char* string );
```

Executes the command **string**. The value returned is implementation dependent. (The value returned usually indicates the exit status of the command executed.)

tan

```
#include <cmath>
float tan( float real );
double tan( double real );
long double tan( long double real );
```

Returns the tangent of **real**, which must be in radians.

tanh

```
#include <cmath>
float tanh( float real );
double tanh( double real );
long double tanh( long double real );
```

Returns the hyperbolic tangent of **real**.

terminate

```
#include <exception>
void terminate();
```

The function **terminate** is called when there is an error in the exception handling mechanism (e.g., a handler is missing for a thrown exception). The function **terminate**, in turn, calls the function most recently specified by **set_terminate**.

time

```
#include <ctime>
time_t time( time_t* storage );
```

Returns the time (typically measured in seconds elapsed since midnight, January 1, 1970 GMT). If **storage** is not equal to **NULL**, **time** stores the current time at address **storage**. See also **difftime**.

tolower

```
#include <cctype>
int tolower( int character );
```

Converts **character** from uppercase to lowercase and returns the converted value. If **character** is not **'A'** through **'Z'**, **tolower** returns **character**.

toupper

```
#include <cctype>
int toupper( int character );
```

Converts **character** from lowercase to uppercase and returns the converted value. If **character** is not **'a'** through **'z'**, **toupper** returns **character**.

unexpected

```
#include <exception>
void unexpected();
```

When a function throws an exception not specified in its **throw** specification, **unexpected** is called. The function **unexpected**, in turn, calls the function most recently specified by **set_unexpected**.

write

```
#include <iostream>
basic_ostream<charT,traits>&
    basic_ostream::write( const char_type* buff, streamsize n );
```

Writes **n** characters from the array **buff** to the output stream. Returns the updated stream.

RUN-TIME TYPE IDENTIFICATION

Run-time type identification provides mechanisms to permit type conversions that are checked at run time, to determine the type of an object at run time, and to allow the user to extend the run-time type identification provided by C++.

The `dynamic_cast` Operator

C++ provides the `dynamic_cast` operator to perform safe type conversions at run time for classes with virtual methods. The operator is invoked as

```
dynamic_cast< T* >( p )
```

where `p` is a pointer and `T` is a type. If `p` points to an object of type `T` or to an object in a class derived from `T`, the value of the expression is `p` and the type is `T*`. If `p` does not point to an object of type `T` or to an object in a class derived from `T`, the value of the expression is zero. The action of the dynamic cast operator is twofold: it determines if the conversion of `p` to `T*` is valid and, if it is valid, it performs the conversion. Thus the dynamic cast operator is a safe method of performing casts. Its principal use is to perform a safe cast from a base class to a derived class.

> **EXAMPLE.** Given the declarations
>
> ```
> class Book {
> public:
>    virtual void print_title();
> };
>
> class Textbook : public Book {
> public:
>    void print_title();
>    virtual void print_level();
> };
> ```

```
class Paperback : public Book {
public:
   void print_title();
};
```

the dynamic cast operator can be used to print appropriate information about an arbitrary book:

```
void print_book_info( Book* book_ptr ) {
   Textbook* ptr = dynamic_cast< Textbook* >( book_ptr );

   if ( ptr ) { // used if book_ptr points to Textbook
      ptr -> print_title();
      ptr -> print_level();
   }
   else // used if book_ptr does not point to a Textbook
      book_ptr -> print_title();
}
```

In the function **print_book_info**, if at run time the pointer **book_ptr** points to a **Textbook** object, the dynamic cast operation

```
Textbook* ptr = dynamic_cast< Textbook* >( book_ptr );
```

succeeds, and the address of the **Textbook** object is stored in **ptr**. In this case, the methods of class **Textbook** are used to print information about the **Textbook**:

```
ptr -> print_title();
ptr -> print_level();
```

If, on the other hand, at run time the pointer **book_ptr** does not point to a **Textbook** object, the dynamic cast operation fails, and zero is stored in **ptr**. In this case, the **virtual** method **print_level** is used:

```
book_ptr -> print_title();
```
■

EXAMPLE.   A dynamic cast expression can also be used as a condition. For example, the function **print_book_info** can be rewritten as

```
void print_book_info( Book* book_ptr ) {
   if ( Textbook* ptr
           = dynamic_cast< Textbook* >( book_ptr ) ) {
      ptr -> print_title();
      ptr -> print_level();
   }
   else
      book_ptr -> print_title();
}
```
■

An alternative to the technique of the first example is to change the declarations of the classes and simply use polymorphism.

EXAMPLE. We revise the code of the first example to use polymorphism to achieve the same effect:

```
class Book {
public:
   virtual void print_title();
   virtual void print_level();
};

class Textbook : public Book {
public:
   void print_title();
   void print_level();
};

class Paperback : public Book {
public:
   void print_title();
   void print_level();
};

void print_book_info( Book* book_ptr ) {
   book_ptr -> print_title();
   book_ptr -> print_level();
}
```
■

The code of the preceding example is much cleaner than that of the first example and is preferable. In the last example, the use of **virtual** functions automatically takes care of the details of determining which version of **print_title** and **print_level** to use. If, however, the programmer cannot modify the classes, the technique of the first example may be the only safe way to obtain the desired result.

The **typeid** Operator

The **typeid** operator returns a reference to an object in the system class **type_info** that describes the run-time type of an object. When using the **typeid** operator, the header file *typeinfo* must be included.

The **typeid** operator is invoked as

```
typeid( typename )
```

or

```
typeid( expression )
```

If the operand of the **typeid** operator is the type *typename*, **typeid** returns a reference to a **type_info** object that represents *typename*. If the operand of the **typeid** operator is the expression *expression*, **typeid** returns a reference to a **type_info** object that represents the *expression*'s type. The programmer need not know the details of the return type to use the **typeid** operator to compare types, as the following examples illustrate.

EXAMPLE. The **typeid** operator can be used with built-in types and operators. Figure D.1, which assumes the definitions

```
float x;
long val;
```

shows the values of several expressions that use the **typeid** operator. ■

Expression	Value
typeid(x) == typeid(float)	true
typeid(x) == typeid(double)	false
typeid(x) == typeid(float*)	false
typeid(val) == typeid(long)	true
typeid(val) == typeid(short)	false
typeid(5280) == typeid(int)	true
typeid(9.218836E-9L) == typeid(long double)	true

FIGURE D.1 Using the **typeid** operator to test run-time built-in types.

EXAMPLE. Figure D.2, which assumes the declarations of the first example and the definition

```
Book* book_ptr = new Textbook;
```

shows the values of several expressions that use the **typeid** operator.

Expression	Value
typeid(book_ptr) == typeid(Book*)	true
typeid(book_ptr) == typeid(Book)	false
typeid(*book_ptr) == typeid(Book)	false
typeid(book_ptr) == typeid(Textbook*)	false
typeid(book_ptr) == typeid(Textbook)	false
typeid(*book_ptr) == typeid(Textbook)	true

FIGURE D.2 Using the **typeid** operator to test run-time class types.

The value of the expression

```
typeid( book_ptr )
```

represents the type (**Book***) *declared* for **book_ptr**, *not* the type of object (**Textbook**) to which **book_ptr** points. For this reason, the first expression is true, but the second, fourth, and fifth expressions are false.

The value of the expression

```
typeid( *book_ptr )
```

represents the type of object (**Textbook**) to which **book_ptr** points. For this reason, the third expression is false, but the last expression is true.　　■

The programmer can extend the run-time type identification provided by the system by deriving classes from the system class **type_info**.

E

EXCEPTION HANDLING

An **exception** is a run-time error caused by some abnormal condition, for example, an out-of-bounds array index. In C++, a function **f** can define conditions that identify exceptions. Another function **g** that calls **f** can test whether the exceptions defined by **f** occur while the program executes. Further, **g** can provide its own **exception handlers**, that is, code to deal with these exceptions when they occur. We illustrate with an example.

EXAMPLE. The program in Figure E.1 illustrates exceptions. Function **f**, called by **main**, checks whether its parameter **i** either underflows or overflows the array parameter **a**. In either case, **f** uses the keyword **throw** to **throw an exception**, that is, to signal that an abnormal condition has occurred. If the index underflows the array, **f** throws an exception of type **Underflow*** by using the **new** operator to create an **Underflow** object; and if the index overflows the array, **f** throws an exception of type **Overflow***. **Underflow** and **Overflow** happen to be user-defined types (i.e., classes), but in principle **f** could throw an exception of a built-in type

```
throw "Oh, darn!" // throwing a string
```

or simply throw an exception with no type (i.e., a **void** exception)

```
throw; // typeless throw
```

The latter example illustrates what we call a *typeless throw*.

Once *thrown*, an exception can be *caught* or handled by a **catch** block. (**catch** is a keyword.) A **catch** block is an exception handler that occurs after a **try** block, which is used to indicate interest in exceptions. (**try** is a keyword.) The general form is

```
//*** signal willingness to handle exceptions
//    that may occur when this block executes
try {
  ... // code that may throw exceptions
}
```

```
#include <iostream>
#include <cstdlib>
#include <ctime>
using namespace std;
class OutOfBoundsEx { // index out of bounds exception
public:
    OutOfBoundsEx( long index ) {
      badIndex = index;
    }
    void warn( const char* msg ) {
       cerr << "Index is " << badIndex << ": "
             << msg << endl;
    }
protected:
   long badIndex;
private:
   OutOfBoundsEx(); //*** disable: must supply offending index
};
class Underflow : public OutOfBoundsEx {
public:
   Underflow( long index ) : OutOfBoundsEx( index ) { }
private:
   Underflow(); //*** disable: must supply offending index
};
class Overflow : public OutOfBoundsEx {
public:
   Overflow( long index ) : OutOfBoundsEx( index ) { }
private:
   Overflow(); //*** disable: must supply offending index
};
void f( int a[ ], unsigned s, int i ); // array, size, index
int main() { //*** test driver for exception classes
   srand( time( 0 ) ); // seed the random number generator
   const unsigned size = 100; // array's size
   int array[ size ];   // legal indexes are 0,1,...,n - 1
   int ind = rand();   // generate a random index
   if ( ind % 2 )      // if it's odd
     ind *= -1;        // then make it a negative number
   //*** Be prepared to catch an exception that f may throw
   try {
     f( array, size, ind );
   }
   catch( Underflow* ePtr ) { // exception handler for array underflow
     ePtr->warn( "Array underflow!" );
   }
   catch( Overflow* ePtr ) { // exception handler for array overflow
     ePtr->warn( "Array overflow!" );
   }
   cout << "Goodbye, main!" << endl;
   return 0;
}
void f( int a[ ], unsigned s, int i ) {
   if ( i < 0 ) // underflow?
     throw new Underflow( i );
   else if ( i >= s )
     throw new Overflow( i );
   //*** otherwise, process the array...
}
```

FIGURE E.1 Throwing and catching exceptions.

```
//**** exception handlers
catch( int x ) {
   // code to handle a thrown int
}
catch( char* s ) {
   // code to handle a thrown char*
}
catch( void ) {
   // code to handle a typeless throw
}
//*** other catch blocks
```

The **catch** blocks may occur in any order. The critical requirement is that the **catch**ers come *after* the **try** block from which the exceptions are to be thrown.

A function that invokes **f**, such as **main**, indicates its willingness to handle any exceptions that **f** may throw by

1. Placing the call to **f** in a **try** block.
2. Providing one or more **catch** blocks after the **try** block to handle exceptions actually thrown by **f**.

When a **try** block is executed without throwing any exceptions, execution continues with the code that follows the **catch** blocks that come after the **try** block. In our example, execution would resume at the **cout** statement in **main**. Our example has two **catch** blocks: one to handle exceptions of type **Overflow*** and the other to handle exceptions of type **Underflow***. Our **catch**ers simply print a warning to the standard error. Our program then continues to the **cout** statement before exiting. In general, a **catch** block can execute any legal C++ statement, including a **throw** of its own. However, we recommend against elaborate **throw** and **catch** constructs because they tend to obscure a program's flow of control. A **catch** block typically issues a warning and, if the underlying exception is serious enough, aborts the program.

If **f** were to throw an exception of, say, type **char***, neither of **main**'s two **catch** blocks would handle the exception because neither expects a thrown **char***. In general, if a program throws an exception but has no **catch**er to handle it, the system handles the exception by invoking the function **unexpected**. In effect, **unexpected** is the default handler for exceptions not caught by user-supplied **catch** blocks. Function **unexpected** typically prints an error message before aborting the program. ■

Assertions, discussed in Section 10.2, provide another means of dealing with exceptions. Conditions are introduced that *must* be satisfied in order for the code to be correct. If a condition fails, the code is incorrect and so the program terminates with a message. One problem with assertions is that they do not permit the program to attempt to recover from the violation and continue executing.

C++ through the header file *csignal* provides yet another method of dealing with certain kinds of exceptions [see, e.g., R. Johnsonbaugh and M. Kalin: *Applications Programming in ANSI C*, 3rd ed., (New York: Prentice Hall, 1996), Section 11.2]. Signals can be used to handle exceptions such as keyboard interrupts that are external to the program (such exceptions are called *asynchronous exceptions*). Throwing and catching exceptions handles only exceptions that result from executing the C++ code itself (such exceptions are called *synchronous exceptions*).

HINTS AND SOLUTIONS TO ODD-NUMBERED EXERCISES

Section 0.1

1. Input: n
   Output: $\frac{1}{2^2} + \frac{1}{3^2} + \cdots + \frac{1}{(n+1)^2}$

   1. $sum = 0$
   2. $i = 0$
   3. $i = i + 1$
   4. $sum = sum + 1/(i+1)^2$
   5. Repeat lines 3 and 4 until $i == n$.

3. Input: $s_1, s_2, \ldots, s_n, n$
   Output: min_index, where $s_{min\_index} = \min\{s_1, s_2, \ldots, s_n\}$

   1. $min\_index = 1$
   2. $i = 2$
   3. While $i \leq n$, repeat lines 4 and 5.
   4. If $s_i < s_{min\_index}$, execute $min\_index = i$.
   5. $i = i + 1$

Section 0.2

1. Hardware refers to physical devices, such as the CPU, whereas software refers to computer programs.
3. Tapes are generally more portable than disks and can hold larger amounts of data.
5. Among the responsibilities of an operating system on a multiuser mainframe are controlling user access to hardware and scheduling peripheral devices.

Section 0.3

1. 210, D2
3. 10100011, 163
5. 0010100010001000, 2888
7. 10111000
9. -46
11. -23566
13. 1111101110011001
15. 00001110
17. -1.78125×2^{100}, -2.258003×10^{30}
19. $-236{,}716{,}032$
21. NUL, space
23. 0 01110101 1 $\underbrace{00000000000000000000000}_{\text{22 zeros}}$

25. 16,777,216, which is represented as 0 10010111 $\underbrace{00000000000000000000000}_{\text{23 zeros}}$

27. Register 000 contains 52 and register 111 contains 10.

Section 0.4

1. Assembler directives allow the programmer to use symbolic names rather than addresses. Symbolic names are less error-prone than hexadecimal addresses, and they make the program easier to read and to understand.

3. Assembly language, by definition, is targeted at a specific processor; thus, IBM assembler runs only on IBM or IBM-compatible computers. A high-level language is independent of a particular processor. The compiler translates a high-level language into a program that can be run on a particular processor. C++, for example, can be run on any computer for which a C++ compiler has been written.

5. High-level languages are typically targeted at particular uses. The syntax and meaning are created for the convenience of particular kinds of applications. For example, FORTRAN was created to solve mathematical problems. The name is short for FORmula TRANslation. The meaning of FORTRAN expressions is derived from the meaning of the corresponding mathematical expressions. C was developed as a system language, although today, its descendent, C++, is used for a wide variety of applications.

Section 0.5

1. The program may not handle certain instances of the problem at all. The program may not solve certain instances of the problem as desired.

3. Input: $r_1, r_2, \ldots, r_n, n$ (r_i is the ith reference)
Output: $r_1, r_2, \ldots, r_n$
1. $i = 1$
2. While $i \leq n$, repeat lines 3 and 4.
3. Print r_i.
4. $i = i + 1$

5. The construction of a complex object (e.g., a car) is divided into the construction of many smaller objects (e.g., the engine, the doors), after which the smaller objects are combined to construct the complex object.

7. The input is a hand of five cards. The output is the number of combinations in the hand that sum to 15. We use a straightforward approach, also referred to as a brute-force approach, in which we check the sum of every combination that might equal 15. (A single card has value at most 10, so we need not consider one-card combinations.) The execution time can be shortened in many cases if we terminate a while loop when the sum of a combination exceeds 15. (In this case, adding more cards cannot result in a sum equal to 15.) Input to test this algorithm might include hands with no combinations of 15, sorted and unsorted hands, hands with many combinations of 15, hands with small denominations, and hands with large denominations.

Input: c_1, c_2, c_3, c_4, c_5 (c_i is the ith card)
Output: *comb*, the number of combinations that sum to 15

We assume that $val(c_i)$ gives the value of card c_i

1. $comb = 0$
2. $i1 = 1$
3. While $i1 \leq 4$, repeat lines 4 through 20.
4. $i2 = i1 + 1$
5.   While $i2 \leq 5$, repeat lines 6 through 19.
6.   If $val(c_{i1}) + val(c_{i2}) == 15$, then $comb = comb + 1$.
7. $i3 = i2 + 1$
8.   While $i3 \leq 5$, repeat lines 9 through 18.
9.   If $val(c_{i1}) + val(c_{i2}) + val(c_{i3}) == 15$, then $comb = comb + 1$.
10. $i4 = i3 + 1$
11.   While $i4 \leq 5$, repeat lines 12 through 17.
12.   If $val(c_{i1}) + val(c_{i2}) + val(c_{i3}) + val(c_{i4}) == 15$, then
                $comb = comb + 1$.
13. $i5 = i4 + 1$
14.   While $i5 \leq 5$, repeat lines 15 and 16.
15.   If $val(c_{i1}) + val(c_{i2}) + val(c_{i3}) + val(c_{i4}) + val(c_{i5}) == 15$,
                then $comb = comb + 1$.
16. $i5 = i5 + 1$
17. $i4 = i4 + 1$
18. $i3 = i3 + 1$
19. $i2 = i2 + 1$
20. $i1 = i1 + 1$

Section 1.1

3. The first (**#include**) line should be followed by

```
using namespace std;
```

The alternate, older form is

```
#include <iostream.h>
```

The **cout** line should be

```
cout << "There you go again" << endl;
```

The **return** line should end with a semicolon.

Section 1.2

1. The definition tells us that the cell named **x** can store one item of type **int** (i.e., one integer).

3. **a**'s value is -7, **b**'s value is 28, and **c**'s value is -35.

5.
```
#include <iostream>
using namespace std;

main() {
    cout << "int occupies " << sizeof( int )
         << " bytes" << endl;
    return 0;
}
```

Section 1.3

1. The identifiers are different because C++ distinguishes between uppercase and lowercase characters.

3. Legal

5. Illegal; `namespace` is a keyword.

7. Illegal; the hyphen, `-`, is not a legal character in an identifier.

9. Illegal; space is not a legal character in an identifier.

Section 1.5

1. `unsigned char c1 = 66, c2 = '\n', c3 = 87;`

3. An `int` cell is typically larger than a `char` cell. (An `int` cell is typically two or four bytes, whereas a `char` cell is always one byte.) When the value of an `int` cell is output, for example using `cout`, the integer value is output. But when the value of a `char` cell is output, the character corresponding to the integer value stored is output. Type `int` is *always* signed. Type `char` may be signed or unsigned.

5. Yes

7. `z`

9. `z`

11. `7` followed by a space followed by ringing the bell

13. `int x = 01554;`

15. Yes

Section 1.6

1. `double`

3. `3.14f`

5. `double` includes all the values of `float`.

Section 1.7

1. `3.99481772e5`

3. `2.2815e-10`

5. The code segment is illegal because the modulus operator `%` can only be applied to operands of integer type.

Section 1.9

1. `1`
   `1`
   `0`
   `1`
   `1`

3. `0`. The expression is equivalent to

   `( 'z' >= 'f' ) >= 'a'`

   because `>=` is evaluated from left to right. The value of the expression

   `'z' >= 'f'`

is 1 (**true**) because the code for **z** follows the code for **f** in the ASCII table. Thus the original expression becomes

```
1 >= 'a'
```

This latter expression is 0 (**false**) because 1 is not greater than or equal to the ASCII code for **a** (97).

5. At least one

7. All disjuncts need to be **false** for the disjunction to be **false**.

Section 2.1

1. 5

3. 3
   5

5. `Public Relations Representative`

7. 6

9. `Code red`

11. `Code red`

13. `Code undefined`

15. `Code red`

17. `Code undefined`

Section 2.3

1. 7
   5
   3
   1

3. −1

5. 0

Section 2.5

1.
```cpp
#include <fstream>
using namespace std;
main() {
    ifstream in;
    ofstream out;
    int yard;
    in.open( "yard.in" );
    out.open( "length.out" );
    in >> yard;
    while ( yard >= 0 ) {
        out << yard << " yards" << endl;
        out << "    = " << yard * 3 << " feet" << endl;
        out << "    = " << yard * 36 << " inches" << endl;
        in >> yard;
    }
    in.close();
    out.close();
    return 0;
}
```

3. For Exercise 1.

```
#include <fstream>
#include <cstdlib>
using namespace std;

main() {
    ifstream in;
    ofstream out;
    int yard;
    in.open( "yard.in" );
    if ( !in ) {
        cout << "Unable to open yard.in" << endl;
        exit( 0 );
    }
    out.open( "length.out" );
    if ( !out ) {
        cout << "Unable to open length.out" << endl;
        exit( 0 );
    }
    while ( in >> yard ) {
        out << yard << " yards" << endl;
        out << "    = " << yard * 3 << " feet" << endl;
        out << "    = " << yard * 36 << " inches" << endl;
    }
    in.close();
    out.close();
    return 0;
}
```

Section 2.6

1. x = 2
   x = 0

Section 2.7

1. 2
   3
   4
   5
   6
3. 5

Section 2.8

1. 9
   22
   22
3. -44
   -90
   -90

5. 4
   5
   6
   5
   5
   4

Section 2.9

1. No, because the lines

```
if ( next > max )
    max = next;
else
    min = next;
```

assign **next** to **min** if **next** is less than or equal to the current value of **max**, and we want to assign **next** to **min** only if **next** is less than the current value of **min**.

Section 2.10

1. 2
   bottom of loop
   4
   bottom of loop
   6
   bottom of loop

3. Diamondbacks
   *** End of baseball team listing

5. Devil Rays
   *** End of baseball team listing
   Rockies
   *** End of baseball team listing
   No team
   *** End of baseball team listing
   Strike 3

Section 2.11

1. If i is prime, *no* integer greater than 1 and less than i divides i, so, in particular, no integer k, $2 \le k \le \sqrt{i}$, divides i.

Suppose that no integer k, $2 \le k \le \sqrt{i}$, divides i. We must show that i is prime. We argue by contradiction and assume that i is not prime. Then $i = ab$ where a and b are integers greater than $\sqrt{i}$. Now $i = ab > \sqrt{i}\sqrt{i} = i$, which is a contradiction. Therefore i is prime.

3. Except for 2 itself, no prime has 2 as a divisor. So, once beyond 2, we generate only odd numbers as both possible primes and possible divisors.

Section 2.12

1. 90

3. **y** is promoted to **float**.

5. 30.2

7. 0

9. The rule is that **signed char** and **unsigned short** are promoted to **int**, if **int** can represent all values of the original type; otherwise, the promotion is to **unsigned int**. On any machine, **int** can represent all values of **signed char**, so the **signed char** will be promoted to **int**. However, whether **int** can represent all values of **unsigned short** is machine dependent. For example, **int** *cannot* represent all values of **unsigned short** if **unsigned short** is the same as **unsigned int**. If, on the other hand, **unsigned short** uses a smaller cell size than does **unsigned int**, **int** can represent all values of **unsigned short**.

If both **c** and **s** are promoted to **int**, the expression **c + s** will be of type **int**. If **c** is promoted to **int** and **s** is promoted to **unsigned int**, the expression **c + s** will be of type **unsigned int**.

Section 2.13

1. `cout << setw( 12 );`

3. `cout << setprecision( 0 );`

5. `cout << right << showpos;`

7. The output is the program itself.

9.
```
cout << "Sun   Mon   Tue   Wed   Thu   Fri   Sat\n";
// advance to correct position for first day
// 5 = size of month name + 2 spaces
for ( count = 1; count <= day * 5; count++ )
    cout << " ";
for ( count = 1; count <= stop; count++ ) {
    // field width is 3 because day names
    // are 3 characters.
    cout << setw( 3 ) << day;
    if ( ( count + day ) % 7 > 0 ) // before Sat?
        // move 2 spaces to next day in same week.
        // (2 spaces separate the day names.)
        cout << "  ";
    else  // skip to next line to start with Sun
        cout << endl;
}
```

Section 3.1

1. False

3. False

5. False

7. True

9. The function's name is **type**. It expects one **float** argument and returns an **int**.

11. The function returns the **double** value **3.14**, although it is supposed to return no value (i.e., **void**).

13.
```
double power( double base, int exponent ) {
    // function's body
}
```

15.
```
#include <iostream>
using namespace std;
unsigned echo_chars(); // declaration
int main() {
    unsigned n;
    n = echo_chars();
    cout << n << " characters echoed." << endl;
    return 0;
}
```

17.
```
#include <iostream>
using namespace std;
unsigned echo_some_chars( unsigned max_echo );
int main() {
    unsigned arg = 2, n;
    while ( ( n = echo_some_chars( arg ) ) > 0 ) {
      cout << n << " chars echoed." << endl;
      arg *= 2;
    }
    return 0;
}
```

19. Yes. In C++, the comma is an operator. The comma expression

```
val1, val2
```

has **val2** (i.e., the *last* term) as its value. So the **return** statement has the same effect as

```
return val2;
```

21. `void print_char( char c = '*', int how_many = 60 );`

23. Parameter **err_flag** must be given a default value if any parameter to its left is given a default value, which is the case.

25. Either **void** or the type returned must be specified.

Section 3.2

1. Variable **stop** is visible from the point of its definition until the end of the source file; hence, **stop** is visible in **main** and **f**. Variable **i** is visible only inside **main**, from the point of its definition until the end of **main**. Variable **j** is visible only in the **for** loop's body. Parameter **k** is visible only in **f**.

Section 3.3

1. c = 8
   d = -2

Section 3.4

1. 33%, i.e., a winning ratio of 1/3

3. 50%, i.e., a winning ratio of $(1/3 \times 1/2) + (2/3 \times 1/2)$

5.
```
char get_each_game_flag() {
    char each_game_flag;
    do {
       cout << "Display results of each game [Y]es, [N]o? ";
       cin >> each_game_flag;
    } while ( each_game_flag != 'N' && each_game_flag != 'Y' );
    return each_game_flag;
}
```

Section 3.5

1.
```
// akin to library function toupper
void upper( char& c ) {
   const char a = 'a';
   const char A = 'A';
   const char z = 'z';
   const int  d = a - A; // in ASCII, 32
   if ( c < a || c > z ) // lower-case char?
      return;             // if not, no change
   c -= d; // otherwise, convert to upper
}
```

3. Presumably the function's purpose is to read data into the parameters so that an *invoking* function, such as **main**, can then use the values. A sample call might be

```
int main() {
   ifstream in;
   in.open( "myData.dat" );
   short x;
   int   y;
   read_data( in, x, y );
   // now use the data read into x and y
   cout << x << endl << y << endl;
   ...
}
```

For this to work, the parameters must not be passed by value. Instead, we could pass them by reference:

```
void read_data( ifstream& in, short& a, int& n ) {
   in >> a >> n;
}
```

Section 3.7

1.
```
void print( char c ) { // prints ASCII value
   cout << static_cast< int >( c ) << endl;
}
```

Section 3.8

1.
```
unsigned fact( unsigned n ) {
   unsigned retval = 1;
   while ( n > 1 )
      retval *= n--;
   return retval;
}
```

3.
```
unsigned s( unsigned n ) {
   if ( n < 2 )     // base case
      return 2 * n;
   return s( n - 1 ) + 2 * n;
}
```

```
5. unsigned walkRecur3( unsigned dist ) {
     // base cases: 1 meter:  1 way  (1)
     //             2 meters: 2 ways (1,1 or 2)
     //             3 meters: 4 ways (1,1,1 or 1,2 or 2,1 or 3)
     switch ( dist ) {
     case 1:
     case 2:
       return dist;
     case 3:
       return 4;
     default: // recursive case
       return walkRecur3( dist - 1 ) +
              walkRecur3( dist - 2 ) +
              walkRecur3( dist - 3 );
     }
   }
```

7. The base cases ($n = 5, 6$) can be verified directly. For the inductive step, assume that $n > 6$. Then

$$\text{walk}(n) = \text{walk}(n - 1) + \text{walk}(n - 2)$$

$$> \left(\frac{3}{2}\right)^{n-1} + \left(\frac{3}{2}\right)^{n-2}$$

$$= \left(\frac{3}{2}\right)^{n-2} \left(1 + \frac{3}{2}\right)$$

$$> \left(\frac{3}{2}\right)^{n-2} \left(\frac{3}{2}\right)^{2} = \left(\frac{3}{2}\right)^{n}$$

Section 4.1

1. 25

3. 5,000

5. `double bigNums[ 100 ];`

Section 4.2

1. Third

3. Array overflow occurs. Because the array's *size* is 10, the legal indexes are $0, 1, \ldots, 9$.

5. Array underflow occurs when an index is negative.

7. *Bounds checking* is checking whether an index underflows or overflows an array.

9. The array's size is three, but four initial values are provided.

11. 40 bytes and 10 elements

Section 4.3

1. An array's name, as a pointer *constant*, cannot be the target of an assignment.

3. Value of **x**: 7. Value of **&x**: 42.

5. `letters[ 0 ]`

7. Yes

9. No, a pointer constant

11. `char*` (pointer to `char`)

Section 4.4

```
3. #include <iostream>
   #include <fstream>
   using namespace std;

   int main() {
       ifstream infile;         // data file
       const unsigned n = 50; // number of precincts
       unsigned pigeon[ n ] = { 0 }; // pigeon votes
       unsigned dove[ n ] = { 0 };   // dove votes
       unsigned falcon[ n ] = { 0 }; // falcon votes
       unsigned robin[ n ] = { 0 };  // robin votes
       unsigned precinct, bird, votes, j;
       // Read counts from input file and update totals
       infile.open( "votes.dat" );

       while ( infile >> precinct >> bird >> votes ) {
         switch ( bird ) {
         case 0: // pigeon
           pigeon[ precinct - 1 ] += votes; break;
         case 1: // mourning dove
           dove[ precinct - 1 ] += votes; break;
         case 2: // falcon
           falcon[ precinct - 1 ] += votes; break;
         case 3: // robin
           robin[ precinct - 1 ] += votes; break;
         }
       }

       infile.close();
       // Print vote totals to the standard output
       cout << "Vote totals are:" << endl;
       cout << "Pigeons by precinct:" << endl;

       for ( j = 0; j < n; j++ )
         cout << "Precinct: " << j + 1
              << " Votes: " << pigeon[ j ] << endl;
       cout << "Mourning doves by precinct:" << endl;
       for ( j = 0; j < n; j++ )
         cout << "Precinct: " << j + 1
              << " Votes: " << dove[ j ] << endl;
       cout << "Falcons by precinct:" << endl;
       for ( j = 0; j < n; j++ )
         cout << "Precinct: " << j + 1
              << " Votes: " << falcon[ j ] << endl;
       cout << "Robins by precinct:" << endl;
       for ( j = 0; j < n; j++ )
         cout << "Precinct: " << j + 1
              << " Votes: " << robin[ j ] << endl;
       return 0;
   }
```

Section 4.5

1. No

3. Three

5. 15

7. The array's size is 10, but the initializing string requires 14 `char` cells: 13 for `War and Peace` and 1 for the null terminator.

9. One

11. The first character is `A`. `name` is a string.

13. `s` is not null-terminated yet the output operation starts at address `s` and continues until a null-terminator is encountered.

Section 4.6

1. `f1` is passed the *address* of the array's first element, whereas `f2` is passed a copy of the array's third element.

3.
```
2
4
6
8
10
16
```

5.
```
bool find( const char s[ ], char c ) {
    int i = 0;
    while ( s[ i ] != '\0' )
      if ( c == s[ i++ ] )
         return true;
    return false;
}
```

Section 4.7

1. 3

3. 1. Yes, the empty string.

5. An access violation likely occurs.

7.
```
Six
Six Easy Pieces
```

9.
```
Mite
Mighty Mi
```

11. A positive integer

13.
```cpp
#include <iostream>
using namespace std;
int main() {
    char s[ ] = "Destry Rides Again";
    char c = 'A';
    int i = 0;
    while ( s[ i ] != '\0' )
        if ( c == s[ i++ ] ) {
            cout << c << " is in " << s << endl;
            break;
        }
    return 0;
}
```

15.
```
foo baz
foo baz
baz
foo baz
```

Section 4.8

1. Let n be the number of records to be merged into the output file. Recall that the two input files are already sorted. In this case, merging the input files requires about n record comparisons in the worst case. The time-complexity is thus linear in the number of records to be merged.

3.
```
1
2
3
3
```

Section 4.9

1. Four

3. 10

5. No, unless all sizes beyond the first dimension are equal to one

7. Index 1 designates the array's *second* element, and index 4 designates the *fifth* cell in the second element.

9.
```cpp
for ( unsigned i = 0; i < 12; i++ )
    cout << months[ i ] << endl;
```

11.
```cpp
int a[ 3 ][ 2 ] = { { 1, 2 }, { -3, -4 }, { 5, 6 } };
```

13.
```cpp
void store( char n[ ][ 81 ] );
```

Section 5.1

1. Modules are program parts that can be written and tested separately before being assembled into a program.

3. A class

5. A class is a collection of objects, all of which share the class's attributes and operations.

7. A class implementation consists of members—variables and functions—that are private, that is, hidden from the outside. The implementation supports the class public interface, which is open to the outside.

9. A data type is abstract if it exposes in its public interface only high-level operations and hides in its implementation the low-level details in support of these operations.

11. Under this model, a class and its objects provide services to clients, which are applications that request such services by invoking the methods that belong to the class's public interface.

13. The class *Human* inherits from the class *Mammal*, which makes *Human* a subclass of *Mammal*, and *Mammal* a superclass of *Human*.

Section 5.2

1. A class declaration must end with a semicolon.

3. `private`

5. `private`

7. Yes

9. If a method is defined outside the class declaration, the class name must be included. The correct definition is

```
float Circus::getHeadCount() {
   // function body
}
```

11.
```
class Person {
public:
    inline unsigned getAge();
    // other members
};
```

Section 5.3

1.
```
class Clock {
public:
    void set( unsigned long t = 0 ) { ticks = t; }
    unsigned long get() { return ticks; }
    void tick() { ticks++; }
    void print() { cout << ticks << endl; }
private:
    unsigned long ticks;
};
```

3. *Clock.h* is presumably in the same directory as the file that has the `#include`, rather than in some system directory.

Section 5.4

1. A *thin wrapper* is a class that packages, in an object-oriented style, functionality already available in a procedural library.

3. The `TimeStamp`'s public interface consists exclusively of high-level functions such as `getMonth`, `getYear`, and the like. Implementation details, such as the `private` method `extract` and the two `private` data members, are hidden from the user.

5. If the user invokes the `set` method with no arguments, the `TimeStamp` is set to the current time. If the user invokes the method with a positive integer as an argument, the `TimeStamp` is set to the time that this integer represents.

```
7. int main() {
      void dumpTS( TimeStamp& );
      const int n = 5;
      int i;
      TimeStamp ts[ n ];
      time_t now = time( 0 );
      time_t increment = 6000;
      // Set to now or now + an increment
      for ( i = 0; i < n; i++ ) {
         if ( i % 2 ) { // i is odd
            ts[ i ].set( now );
            now += increment;
         }
         else // i is even
            ts[ i ].set();
      }
      // Print each TimeStamp.
      for ( i = 0; i < n; i++ )
         dumpTS( ts[ i ] );
      // try a bogus argument
      ts[ 0 ].set( -987654 );
      dumpTS( ts[ 0 ] );
      return 0;
   }
   void dumpTS( TimeStamp& ts )
   {
      cout << endl << "Testing methods: " << endl;
      cout << '\t' << ts.get() << endl;
      cout << '\t' << ts.getAsString();
      cout << '\t' << ts.getYear() << endl;
      cout << '\t' << ts.getMonth() << endl;
      cout << '\t' << ts.getDay() << endl;
      cout << '\t' << ts.getHour() << endl;
      cout << '\t' << ts.getMinute() << endl;
      cout << '\t' << ts.getSecond() << endl;
   }
```

Section 5.5

1. The class name is **C** (uppercase), not **c** (lowercase). So the default constructor is **C()**, not **c()**. The technical error is that **c()** must return a value because it is not a constructor or destructor.

3. Yes, and this is common.

5. No

7. Because the default constructor is **private**, it cannot be invoked in a nonmethod such as **main**. In **main**, the statement

```
   K k1;
```

therefore causes an error by trying to invoke the default constructor.

9. The copy constructor expects a *reference* to an object of the class type. The correct declaration is

```
   class R {
```

```
    public:
        R( R& arg ); // ok, a reference to R
    };
```

11. ```
class Person {
public:
    Person(Person& p) {
      // method body
    }
    // other members
};
Person foo;
Person fooTwin(foo); // clone foo
```

13. A convert constructor is a one-parameter constructor other than the copy constructor. The name indicates that the convert constructor converts an argument of some type into an object of the class type. For example, we could provide the **TimeStamp** class with a constructor **TimeStamp( time_t )** that converts a **time_t** value into a **TimeStamp** object.

15. No. The convert constructor converts the **int** 999 into a **c** object that is passed to **g**.

17. A **const** variable, including a data member, cannot be the target of an assignment operation. The **const**ant **c** must be initialized in the constructor's header; it cannot be assigned a value in the constructor's body.

19. Header initialization is legal only in constructors. Therefore, **f** cannot initialize **c** in its header.

21. ```
1 created
2 created
3 created
3 destroyed
2 destroyed
1 destroyed
```

Section 5.6

1. If an **ofstream** is opened in **out** mode for an already existing file, the file's contents are first deleted and writing then begins at the beginning of the file. In our sample application, each invocation of **logToFile** would first delete the records written during all previous invocations. Therefore, the log file at any time would contain records about one object at most.

Section 5.7

1. For an *object data member* of, for example, type **int**, there is one **int** cell per object. So each object has its own **int** cell. For a *class data member* of the same type, there is *one* cell shared by all objects.

3. The **static** data member **x** is declared but not defined. It must be defined outside all blocks:

```
    int C::x; // define static data member
```

5. ```
1
2
3
```
```

Section 5.9

1. Because a pointer rather than a reference to a **c** object is passed to **g**, the indirect selection operator—not the member operator—must be used in **g**. The correct syntax is

```
p->m();
```

3. The member operator is used exclusively with objects and object references.

Section 6.1

1.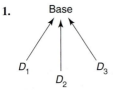

3. Data members that might be added are **boss**, **dept**, and **salary**. Methods to get and set the added data members might be added.

Section 6.2

1. Two: **y** is local to **B** and **x** is inherited from **A**.

3.
```
R
↑
Q
↑
P
```

Section 6.4

1. We explain with an example. In the hierarchy

```
class Base {
public:
    void m() {...}
protected:
    int pro;
private:
    int pri;
};
class Derived : public Base {
    // Derived's local members
};
```

Derived inherits **pro** and **pri** from **Base**. Because **pri** is **private** in **Base**, it cannot be accessed by any of **Derived**'s local methods. (However, the **m** that **Derived** inherits from **Base** can access **pri**.) Because **pro** is **protected** in **Base**, it can be accessed by any of **Derived**'s local methods.

3. A **protected** member is visible only within an inheritance hierarchy and, in this sense, represents information hiding. By contrast, a **public** member is visible outside the hierarchy and, in this sense, compromises information hiding.

5. Because **A**'s members **f1** and **f2** are **protected**, they are visible only within **A** and classes derived from **A**. In particular, these **protected** members are not visible in **main**.

7.
```
void D::init( int n1, int n2, int n3 ) {
    num1 = n1; num2 = n2; num3 = n3;
}
```

Section 6.5

1. Base class **B** has a convert constructor, but no *default* constructor. Therefore, derived class **D**'s constructor must invoke **B**'s convert constructor in its header. A better solution would be to provide **B** with a default constructor, in which case **D**'s constructor would not be forced to invoke explicitly a **B** constructor.

3.
```
B constructor
B constructor
D1 constructor
B constructor
D1 constructor
D2 constructor
D2 destructor
D1 destructor
B destructor
D1 destructor
B destructor
B destructor
```

5. No

7. No

9. No

11.
```
class Singer : public Human {
public:
    Singer() : Human() { }
    Singer( int c ) : Human( c ) { }
    void set_range( int i ) { range = i; }
    int get_range() { return range; }
protected:
    int range; // 0 = soprano, 1 = alto, etc.
};

class PopSinger : public Singer {
public:
    PopSinger() : Singer() { }
    PopSinger( int c ) : Singer( c ) { }
    void set_loudness( long double i ) { loudness = i; }
    int get_loudness() { return loudness; }
protected:
    long double loudness;
};
```

Section 7.1

1. A function's entry point is the starting memory address at which the executable code in its body begins.

3. (1) An inheritance hierarchy. (2) A pointer or reference to a base class that points to an object in the hierarchy. (3) Use of the pointer or reference to invoke an overridden **virtual** method.

5. Only a method can be **virtual**, and **hi** is not a method.

7. Yes

9. If a derived class redefines a **virtual** method in a base class, the derived class is said to *override* the method.

11. The storage penalty is the size of the vtable. The time penalty is the time required to do vtable lookups when **virtual** methods are invoked.

13. Yes

15. A constructor cannot be **virtual**.

Section 7.2

1. Because the invocation of **input** is no longer polymorphic, **Film::input** is called each time the statement

```
films[ next++ ]->input( fin );
```

executes in **readInput**'s loop. Similarly, each time the statement

```
films[ i ]->output();
```

executes in **main, Film::output** is called. This is all right only if the data file contains only **Film** records.

Section 7.3

1. Here is an overloading at the top level of a **print** function:

```
void print( unsigned n ) {...}
void print( char c ) {...}
void print( double n1, double n2 ) {...}
```

3. Compile-time binding

5. Compile-time binding

7. Run-time binding

9. **A::m**

11. The statement

```
a1.m(); //****** ERROR: missing argument
```

is in error because **A::m** expects a **double** argument.

13. **baz**
    26

Section 7.4

1. It must contain a pure **virtual** method, that is, a **virtual** method initialized to zero in its declaration.

3. Only a **virtual** method can be initialized to zero in its declaration, and **m** is not **virtual**.

5. Class **z** is abstract because it does not override **m2**. It is thus an error to define a **z** object such as **z1**.

7. Yes

Section 8.1

1. The overload definition's header is missing the keyword **operator**. The header should be

```
bool String::operator>( const String& s ) const
```

3. The declaration

```
bool operator>( const String& ) const;
```

does not match the definition header

```
bool String::operator>( const String& s )
```

because the latter is missing the **const** after the parameter list.

5.
```
class String {
public:
    bool operator!();
    ...
};
```

7.
```
class String {
    ...
    bool operator<=( const String& ) const;
    ...
};
bool String::operator<=( const String& s ) const {
    int i, minlen;
    if ( len < s.len )
        minlen = len;
    else
        minlen = s.len;
    for ( i = 0; i < minlen; i++ )
        if ( str[ i ] < s.str[ i ] )
            return true;
        else if ( str[ i ] > s.str[ i ] )
            return false;
    return len <= s.len;
}
```

9.
```
class String {
    ...
    bool operator>=( const String& ) const;
    ...
};
bool String::operator>=( const String& s ) const {
    int i, minlen;
    if ( len < s.len )
        minlen = len;
    else
        minlen = s.len;
    for ( i = 0; i < minlen; i++ )
        if ( str[ i ] > s.str[ i ] )
            return true;
        else if ( str[ i ] < s.str[ i ] )
            return false;
    return len >= s.len;
}
```

```
11. class String {
       ...
       String operator+( const String& ) const;
       ...
    };
    String String::operator+( const String& s ) const {
       int i;
       String t;
       for ( t.len = 0; t.len < len; t.len++ )
          t.str[ t.len ] = str[ t.len ];
       for ( i = 0; i < s.len && t.len < 100; t.len++, i++ )
          t.str[ t.len ] = s.str[ i ];
       return t;
    }
```

Section 8.2

1. Yes. When the object is passed by value, the copied object's data members are not changed.

3.
```
Complex Complex::operator~() const {
   return Complex( real, -imag );
}
```

Section 8.3

1. This attempted top-level overload of || takes two **bool** arguments and, therefore, is indistinguishable from the built-in binary operator. At least one of the arguments must be of a class type.

3. The operator () must be overloaded as a class *method*; it cannot be overloaded as a top-level function.

5.
```
#include <cmath> // for sqrt
double operator!( const Complex& c ) {
   return sqrt( c.get_real() * c.get_real() +
                c.get_imag() * c.get_imag() );
}
```

Section 8.4

1. c data member **stored** is **private** and, therefore, inaccessible to the top-level overload of the operator !, which is not a **friend** of c.

3. The operator ! is declared as a **friend** of c but then defined as if it were a c method. The correct definition is

```
void operator!( C& c ) {
   c.stored = !c.stored;
}
```

5.
```
#include <cmath> // for sqrt
double operator!( const Complex& c ) {
   return sqrt( c.real() * c.real() +
                c.imag() * c.imag() );
}
```

7.
```cpp
class String {
    ...
    friend bool operator<=( const String&, const String& );
};
bool operator<=( const String& s1, const String& s2 ) {
    int i, minlen;
    if ( s1.len < s2.len )
        minlen = s1.len;
    else
        minlen = s2.len;
    for ( i = 0; i < minlen; i++ )
        if ( s1.str[ i ] < s2.str[ i ] )
            return true;
        else if ( s1.str[ i ] > s2.str[ i ] )
            return false;
    return s1.len <= s2.len;
}
```

9.
```cpp
class String {
    ...
    friend bool operator>=( const String&, const String& );
};
bool operator>=( const String& s1, const String& s2 ) {
    int i, minlen;
    if ( s1.len < s2.len )
        minlen = s1.len;
    else
        minlen = s2.len;
    for ( i = 0; i < minlen; i++ )
        if ( s1.str[ i ] > s2.str[ i ] )
            return true;
        else if ( s1.str[ i ] < s2.str[ i ] )
            return false;
    return s1.len >= s2.len;
}
```

11.
```cpp
class String {
    ...
    friend bool operator!=( const String&, const String& );
};
bool operator!=( const String& s1, const String& s2 ) {
    if ( s1.len != s2.len )
        return true;
    for ( int i = 0; i < s1.len; i++ )
        if ( s1.str[ i ] != s2.str[ i ] )
            return true;
    return false;
}
```

Section 8.5

1. The overloaded input operator >> is going to change its second argument, a `Complex` object. Therefore, the `Complex` object should not be passed by value, but rather by reference.

```
3. class Complex {
      ...
      friend ostream& operator<<( ostream&, const Complex& );
   };
5. class String {
      ...
      friend ostream& operator<<( ostream&, const String& );
   };
   ostream& operator<<( ostream& os, const String& s ) {
      for ( int i = 0; i < s.len; i++ )
         os << s.str[ i ];
      return os;
   }
```

Section 8.6

1. One

```
3. istream& operator>>( istream& is, intArray& a ) {
      for ( int i = 0; i < a.get_size(); i++ )
         is >> a[ i ];
      return is;
   }
5. istream& operator>>( istream& is, intTwoArray& a ) {
      for ( int i = 0; i < a.get_size1(); i++ )
        for ( int j = 0; j < a.get_size2(); j++ )
          is >> a( i, j );
      return is;
   }
7. // outOfBounds is a private char data member returned
   // if the index i is out of bounds
   char& String::operator[ ]( int i ) {
      if ( i < 0 || i >= len ) { // out of bounds?
        cerr << i << " is a bad index." << endl;
        return outOfBounds;
      }
      return str[ i ];
   }
9. intArray& intArray::operator++() {
      for ( int i = 0; i < size; i++ )
         ++a[ i ];
      return *this;
   }
11. intTwoArray& intTwoArray::operator--() {
      for ( int i = 0; i < size1; i++ )
        for ( int j = 0; j < size2; j++ )
            --a[ i * size2 + j ];
      return *this;
   }
```

13. No return type may be specified in overloading a type conversion operator. The correct declaration is

```
operator char*();
```

```
15. class String {
    public:
       operator char*() {
          // null terminate
          if ( len < 100 )
             str[ len ] = '\0';
          else
             str[ 99 ] = '\0';
          return str;
       }
       ...
    private:
       char str[ 100 ];
       int len;
    };
```

Section 8.7

1. No, because the overloaded assignment operator changes an **Entry**'s definition.

3. No. The overloaded index operator invokes a non**const Entry** method (**valid**) on its data member **entries**, and it may use method **add** to change the **entries** array.

Section 9.1

1. Compile-time storage

3. Program area

5. Stack

7.
```
int x;          //** program area
float y;        //** program area
void g( double );
int main() {
   double d = 3.14;      //** stack
   g( d );
   int* p;               //** stack
   p = new int[ 100 ];   //** 100 ints: heap
   // no other variables defined
   ...
}
void g( double a ) {   //** stack
   int x;              //** stack
   // no other variables defined
}
```

9. Inaccessible storage is storage that a program dynamically allocates but can no longer access, even to release.

11. Yes

13. Access time to CPU registers can be significantly faster than to the stack, which is in main memory.

Section 9.2

1. **auto**

3. The `auto` variable `z` is defined inside the `if` block and, therefore, cannot be accessed outside this block. So the error is the reference to `z` in the statement

```
z = x - y; //***** ERROR: z not visible here
```

5. An `auto` variable must be defined inside a block.

7. The block in which it is defined

9. Stack

11. 1
   2
   3

13. A `static` variable defined outside all blocks is visible from the point of its definition until the end of the file in which this definition occurs.

15. No

17. Yes

19. `extern`

21. Yes

23. Yes

25. No

27. Program area

29. The program's lifetime

Section 9.3

1. `p` must be a pointer. The correct code is

```
int* p = new int;
```

3. If `new[ ]` is used to allocate storage, `delete[ ]` should be used to free it.

5. Pointer to a pointer to a pointer to an `int`

7. Yes

9. Call by reference is preferable because its syntax is easier.

11. No

Section 9.4

1. `qsort` can then sort an array of any data type, as any pointer (variable or constant) converts to `void*` without explicit casting.

3. A callback function is written by the programmer but typically not called explicitly by other functions that the programmer writes. Instead, a callback is usually invoked by some library function such as `qsort`.

Section 9.5

1. Yes

3. 1
   -999

5. In general, whenever the class has any pointers as data members

7. Returning a reference to an already existing object is more efficient than returning a *copy* of an object.

9. `A()`
   `Z()`
   `~Z()`
   `~A()`

11. The object **c**, being the right operand of the assignment operator, could be a temporary object. For example, in the assignment

    ```
    c1 = c2 + c3;
    ```

    the system creates an unnamed temporary object to hold the result of the operation **c2 + c3**. This temporary object is then passed to the overloaded assignment operator. The problem is that when the assignment operator overload finishes executing and returns a reference to the temporary object, the temporary object no longer exists.

13.
    ```
    Complex& operator+=( Complex& c1, const Complex& c2 ) {
        return c1 = c1 + c2;
    }
    int main() {
        Complex c1( 8.8, 4.4 ), c2( 7.7, -3.3 );
        c1 += c2;
        c1.write();
        ...
    }
    ```

Section 10.1

1. A class parameter is a user-selected symbol introduced in the template header by the keyword **class**. The parameter represents a generic type for which the compiler substitutes an actual data type, built-in or user-defined, when a template class instantiation is created. In the code segment

   ```
   template< class T >
   class C {
     ...
   };
   ```

   T is a class parameter.

3. Yes

5. Yes

7. A function style parameter is a user-selected symbol introduced in the template header by a data type, built-in or user-defined, rather than by the keyword **class**. In the code segment

   ```
   template< class T, double d >
   class Z {
     ...
   };
   ```

   d is a function-style parameter of type **double**.

9. Objects can be created only for *instantiations* of a template class. The definition

   ```
   Queue< T > q2; //***** ERROR: not a template instantiation
   ```

   is therefore an error.

11. If a template class has function-style parameters, values for these must be provided in a template instantiation. The statement

    ```
    Queue< double > q1; //***** ERROR: no function-style argument
    ```

    can be corrected as

    ```
    Queue< double, 100 > q1; // OK, function-style argument given
    ```

Section 10.2

1. All the **assert**s are disabled.

3. **pop** returns a **Stack** element. If the **Stack** is empty, **pop** returns a dummy value—not on the **Stack** but of the same type as a **Stack** element—to satisfy this requirement.

Section 10.3

1. Namespaces can be used to avoid name conflicts.

3. Unlike a class, a namespace does not have **private**, **protected**, and **public** regions.

5. Yes

7. Because of the using directive, **Date** defaults to **foo::Date**; but the **showDate** method in **foo::Date** expects no arguments. The error can be avoided by changing the code to either

```
bar::Date d1; // bar::Date's showDate expects an argument
```

or

```
d1.showDate(); // no argument to showDate
```

9. The namespace is named **myLib**, not **Baz**.

Section 10.4

1. An STL container is a templated data structure, whereas an STL algorithm is a templated function that processes an STL container by, for example, sorting it.

3. A sequential container such as a **vector** resembles a C++ array in that its elements are typically accessed by position. In an associative container such as a **map**, the elements are typically accessed through keys, that is, identifying values.

5. Yes

7. A **multiset** can contain duplicate key values, whereas a **set** cannot.

9. The program should not compile.

11. No

13. A container adapter adapts a basic container such as a **deque** so that the basic container behaves in some special way. For example, the **stack** adapter can be used to adapt a **deque** so that it behaves like a stack, with **push**es, **pop**s, and other stack-appropriate methods.

15. If **comp** is provided as the third argument, the elements are sorted in *descending* order; otherwise, they are sorted in *ascending* order.

17. A function adaptor adapts an STL function object so that the STL function behaves in a special way. For example, the program in Figure 10.4.12 uses the function adaptor **not1** to invert our function object **even** so that

```
not1( even( n ) ); // n is an unsigned int
```

returns **false**, if **n** is even, and **true**, if **n** is odd.

19. The user need not specify the size of an STL **vector**, whose size grows and shrinks automatically to meet storage needs. Also, a **vector** has built-in methods such as **begin**, **end**, **rbegin**, and **rend** to reference its beginning and end. This safeguards against underflow and overflow.

INDEX